International Marketing

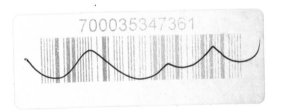

International Marketing

Ogenyi Omar

First published 2009 by
PALGRAVE MACMILLAN
Houndmills, Basingstoke, Hampshire RG21 6XS and
175 Fifth Avenue, New York, N.Y. 10010
Companies and representatives throughout the world

PALGRAVE MACMILLAN is the global academic imprint of the Palgrave Macmillan division of St. Martin's Press, LLC and of Palgrave Macmillan Ltd. Macmillan® is a registered trademark in the United States, United Kingdom and other countries. Palgrave is a registered trademark in the European Union and other countries.

ISBN-13: 978-1-4039-0068-5 paperback
ISBN-10: 1-4039-0068-X   paperback

This book is printed on paper suitable for recycling and made from fully managed and sustained forest sources. Logging, pulping and manufacturing processes are expected to conform to the environmental regulations of the country of origin.

A catalogue record for this book is available from the British Library.

A catalog record for this book is available from the Library of Congress.

10 9 8 7 6 5 4 3 2 1
18 17 16 15 14 13 12 11 10 09

Printed and bound in China

Contents overview

Contents

Figures

Tables

Mini case studies

Acknowledgements

A textbook such as this draws on a number of previous publications by many authors, and we are grateful to the following for permission to reproduce material from the following copyright publications:

D. Aaker, *Managing the Brand Equity*, Free Press, 1991; I. Ajzen and M. Fishbein, *Understanding Attitudes and Predicting Social Behaviour*, Prentice Hall, 1980; Gerald Albaum, Jesper Strandskov and Edwin Duerr, *International Marketing and Export Management*, Financial Times/Prentice-Hall, 2003; Frank Bradley, *International Marketing Strategy*, Financial Times/Prentice Hall, 2002; A. B. Carroll, *The Four Faces of Corporate Citizenship*, Dushkin/McGraw-Hill, 2000; Harold Chee and Rod Harris, *Global Marketing Strategy*, Financial Times, 1998; A. Crane and D. Matten, *Business Ethics*, Oxford University Press, 2004; M. Czinkota and I. A. Ronkainen, *International Marketing*, Dryden, 1993 and 1996; J. D. Daniels, L. H. Radebaugh and D. P. Sullivan, *International Business: Environments and Operations*, Pearson/Prentice Hall; Sean de Burca, Richard Fletcher and Linden Brown, *International Marketing: An SME Perspective*, FT/Prentice Hall, 2004; Isobel Doole and Robin Lowe, *International Marketing Strategy*, Thomson Learning, 2004; S. Douglas and C. Craig, *Global Marketing Strategy*, McGraw-Hill, 1995; T. Duncan, *IMC: Using Advertising and Promotion to Build Brands*, McGraw-Hill/Irwin, 2002; J. Dunning, *The Globalisation of Business*, Routledge, 1993; J. H. Ellsworth and M. V. Ellsworth, *Marketing on the Internet: Multimedia Strategies for the World Wide Web*, Wiley, 1996; D. Ford, P. Berthon, S. Brown, L. E. Gadde, P. Naude, T. Ritter, I. Snehota and H. Hakansson, *The Business Marketing Course*, Wiley, 2003; Forrester Research, *Worldwide Ecommerce Growth*, 2004; *The Fortune Global 500*, July 2002; J. K. Galbraith, *Economics of the Public Purpose*, Penguin, 1975; V. Govindarajan and A. Gupta, *The Quest for Global Dominance*, Jossey-Bass, 2002; C. Gronroos, *Service Management and Marketing*, Wiley, 2002; E. Gummesson, *Total Relationship Marketing*, Butterworth-Heinemann, 2002; Svend Hollensen, *Global Marketing: A Decision-Oriented Approach*, FT/Prentice-Hall, 2004; Jean-Pierre Jeannet and David Hennessey, *Global Marketing Strategies*, Houghton Mifflin, 1998; J. K. Johansson, *Global Marketing: Foreign Entry, Local Marketing and Global Management*, McGraw-Hill/Irwin, 2003; G. Johnson and K. Scholes, *Exploring Corporate Strategy*, Prentice-Hall, 2002; Warren J. Keegan, *Multinational Marketing Management*, Prentice Hall, 1984; Masaaki Kotabe and Kristiaan Helsen, *Global Marketing Management*, Wiley International Edition, 2004; P. Kotler, *Marketing Management*, Prentice Hall, (various editions); S. London, *Less Hunger for Space*, Financial Times, 1995; A. McAuley, *International Marketing*, Wiley, 2001; J. McCarthy, *Basic Marketing*, Irwin, 1960; Peter McGoldrick, *Retail Marketing*, McGraw-Hill, 2003; Peter McGoldrick and Gary Davies, *International Retailing: Trends and Strategies*, Pitman, 1995; H. McRae, *The World in 2020*, Harvard Business School Press, 1994; H. Mintzberg, 'Crafting strategy', in H. Mintzberg, B. Quinn and S. Ghoshal, *The Strategy Process*, Prentice-Hall, 1995; Hans Muhlbacher, Helmuth Leihs and Lee Dahringer, *International Marketing: A Global Perspective*, Thomson Learning, 1999; F. Newell, *loyalty.com*, Free Press, 2000; J. Nielsen, *Designing Web Usability*, New Riders,

2000; A. Rugman, *The End of Globalisation*, Random House, 2000; A. Rugman and J. Cruz, *Multinational as Flagship Firms: Regional Business Networks*, Oxford University Press, 2002; D. E. Schultz and P. J. Kitchen, *Global Communications: An Integrated Approach*, NTC Business, 2000; O. Shenkar and Y. Luo, *International Business*, Wiley, 2004; W. Stanton, M. Etzel and B. Walker, *Fundamentals of Marketing*, McGraw-Hill, 1991; M. Stone and J. McCall, *International Strategic Marketing*, Routledge, 2004; V. Terpstra and R. Sarathi, *International Marketing*, South Western College Publishing, 2000; G. S. Yip, *Total Global Strategy: Managing for Worldwide Competitive Advantage*, Prentice-Hall, 1992

I also thank Emerald Publishing for material from its numerous journals including *International Marketing Review, Journal of International Consumer Marketing* and *European Journal of Marketing.*

Table 7.2, The 'eight Os', is adapted from Czinkota and Ronkainen (1993). Table 9.2, The marketing mix modified for services, is adapted from B. Booms and M. Bitner, *Marketing of Services*, American Marketing Association, 1981. Table 14.1, Push and pull factors, is adapted from McGoldrick and Davies (1995); Table 16.1, International fair trade sales, is from EFTA (2006); Figure 10.1, Distribution channel for a grocery product manufacturer, is from Douglas Lambert and James Stock, *Strategic Logistics Management*, Irwin, 1993. Figure 15.1, Tripartitioned approach to optimizing communications, is from F. Heldal, E Sjovold and A. F. Heldal, 'Success on the Internet: optimizing relationships through the corporate site', *International Journal of Information Management,* Vol. 24, Issue 2, pp. 115–29. Figure 15.3, Base model of consumer acceptance of websites, is from L. Chen and J. Tan, 'Technology adaptation in e-commerce: key determinants of virtual stores acceptance', *European Management Journal*, Vol. 22, No. 1, pp. 74–86. Figure 16.1, Retailer engagement with fair trade, is from W. Low and E. Davenport, 'Has the medium (roast) become the message? The ethics of marketing fair trade in the mainstream', *International Marketing Review,* Vol. 22, No. 5, pp.494–511.

The seminar case study, 'The entry of the Silver Streak Restaurant Corporation into Mexico', was adapted and abstracted from John Hadjimarcou and John Barnes, *Journal of Consumer Marketing,* MCB UP Ltd. 1998. The seminar case study, 'The Valamo Monastery', is taken from I. Bjorkman and S. Kock, *International Journal of Service Industry Management,* 1997. The seminar case study, 'International account management', is from D. M. Sanford and L. Maddox, *International Marketing Review,* 1999. The seminar case study, 'Louis Vuitton Moet Hennessy: global retailer', draws on information from http://www.ivmh.com, 2006. Mini case 16.2, 'Organic meat – accusation of hypocrisy in buying local organic food products', is from the *Financial Times,* 2007. The seminar case study, 'The global revolution in ethical business', is modified from McRae (1994). Mini case 6.1, 'Export of ideas in industrial gases', is from the *Financial Times,* 1998. Mini case 7.1, 'Retailers pushing for positions in the global markets', is from the *Economist,* 1999; Mini case 8.1, 'Universal Feeder Ltd', is from K. Pawar and S. Sharif, *Integrated Manufacturing System* (2002). Mini case 10.1, 'Organisational neglect of natural channels', is from N. Tsukamoto, *Nikkei Weekly,* 1994; Mini case 10.2, 'Retailers' alteration of the international competitive environment', is from the *Economist,* 1999. Mini case 10.3, 'Relative channel differences in Europe', is from B. Benoit, *Financial Times,* 2000. Mini case 11.2, 'Examples of brand and/or product piracy', is from L. Jacobs, A. C. Samli and T. Jedlik, *Industrial Marketing Management,* 2001. Mini case 13.1, Disintermediation in the Japanese distribution system, is from A. Nusbaum,

Financial Times, 2000. Mini case 16.3, 'The ecological market in Romania', is from *Food Industry News,* 2004. Mini case 16.4, 'Produce of Britain', is from *The Times,* 2007.

Every effort has been made to contact all the copyright holders, but if any have been omitted the publisher will be very happy to make the necessary arrangements at the earliest opportunity.

1
Introduction to International Marketing

Contents

LEARNING OBJECTIVES

After reading this chapter you should be able to:

- understand the nature of, and changes in, the international marketing process
- know the differences between international trade and international marketing
- evaluate the various reasons that companies pursue international marketing strategies
- examine the nature of foreign direct investment, the advantages and implications
- discuss the cultural factors in international marketing development
- assess managerial issues in international marketing operations.

Introduction

Dramatic world economic changes in the new millennium, such as the new euro currency, the Asian economic downturn, instantaneous flows of capital, new international conglomerates, and the growth of the Internet, are resulting in new ways of managing international marketing operations. These changes are having profound impacts on international marketing management, including increasing risk and uncertainty, real-time information management, and rapid response to international developments. Cross-impact analysis has become a more important tool for dealing with uncertain interactions among complex forces. The managerial mindset will have to discount the present to create the future, and move far beyond benchmarking. This will lead to changes in decision-making orientations, including a shift from relatively stable environments and mechanistic management approaches to more turbulent environments and systemic management approaches. It will also lead to a shift from hard facts for solving problems to virtual facts for problem prevention.

In his viewpoint assessment, Paliwoda (1999) observed that the confluence of several important external developments has challenged international marketing managers with situations unlike those encountered previously. Sheth and Parvatiyar (2001) noted that many changes in macromarketing forces are reshaping international marketing management thought and practice. As macromarketing forces have carried over into the new millennium they:

- continue to establish critical parameters for international marketing plans and strategies
- raise questions regarding widely held beliefs about multinational marketing operations
- result in rethinking many of the accepted assumptions and paradigms
- lead to different approaches to and perspectives on international marketing decision making.

This chapter charts recent macromarketing developments and the impact that they are having on international marketing management operations. The ideas presented are based on a comprehensive review of the current international marketing literature and the work of academic thinkers around the world The chapter starts by considering the nature and the definition of international marketing. This is followed by a review of the theoretical framework relevant to international marketing, looking at trade theories, foreign direct investment and the cultural factors impacting on international marketing development.

The nature of international marketing

International marketing is about the application of marketing concepts, philosophy, skills and techniques to markets across the world. The marketing concept and philosophy are universal but the ways in which marketing skills and techniques are applied vary between markets to take account of the environmental differences. The discipline of international marketing provides an understanding of marketing practices in different countries (comparative descriptions); its structural determinants anchored to national differences (comparative explanations); and the deployment of country-specific marketing strategies and operations by multidomestic firms (comparative prescriptions). Its primary focus is on description, explanation, and managerial control of marketing practices across national boundaries. Compared with international trade and export marketing, international marketing is a more recent phenomenon (Sheth and Parvatiyar 2001). It has grown since the Second World War, and presumably was a consequence of the demise of colonialism and the re-creation of numerous independent nations.

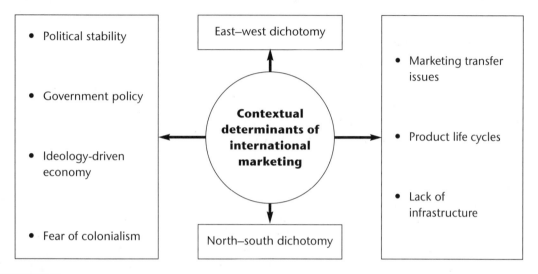

Figure 1.1 Contextual determinants of international marketing

This origin of the rise of international marketing resulted in a number of contextual determinants for its practice, and became the focus of academic research and thinking.

Contextual determinants of international marketing

Figure 1.1 shows the contextual determinants of international marketing. The first four determinants (political stability, government policy, ideology-driven economy, and fear of colonialism) are the most responsible for the prescription of multi-domestic marketing practices. This includes such managerial decisions as selection of countries with which to do business and specific entry strategies. As Sheth and Parvatiyar (2001), noted most of this has required the understanding and use of what has been recently referred to as the fifth 'P' of marketing (politics and public relations). Unfortunately, there is very little theoretical foundation underlying these determinants, partly because international marketing has not borrowed constructs and theories from the social sciences, including political science. Instead it has relied on the framework provided in international business literature, wherein barriers to conducting international business have received considerable attention (Keegan and Schlegelmilch 2001). However, much of it is based simply on the environmental and policy differences across countries, and their impact on the choice of market entry modes and operating strategies.

The next three determinants (marketing transfer issues, lack of infrastructure, and north–south dichotomy) need a little more description. Marketing transfer issues relate to the operational challenges of product, price, distribution, and promotion adjustments across national boundaries as a result of divergence in support and core value chain activities, including materials, people, processes and facilities. The purpose is to understand what market factors, including consumer differences and the unavailability of marketing institutions, would pose difficulties to the multinational firm in transferring its successful international marketing programmes to other countries.

The lack of infrastructure refers to inadequate availability of transportation, communications, physical, financial, natural and human resources, especially in the emerging markets of Africa and South America. This lack of infrastructure impacts the adjustment process for the marketing mix as well as the implementation of the marketing programme in foreign countries. The north–south dichotomy refers to the 'have' and 'have-not' countries of the world, and is a direct reflection of traditional economic development theories and their importance to international marketing practices.

Of the remaining determinants, east–west dichotomy refers to the cultural differences between nations at both the macro and micro levels of understanding and explanation. Product life cycles refer to the birth and death theories of product life as they move across national boundaries. Again, the product life cycle concept has benefited from its basis in population ecology and biological theories, and to that extent it seems to have face validity and empirical support.

This analysis clearly suggests why international marketing has remained a predominantly contextual practice, and why it has been difficult to develop a theory of international marketing even based upon contingency propositions. Most determinants of international marketing are ad hoc, dynamic and unstable, and therefore do provide theory-building opportunities. For example, who could have forecast the demise of the Soviet Union (political stability), the development of regional integration (as in the European Union), the privatization of public sector industries (for example, in Japan and the United Kingdom) and pro-Western links by Muslim states (such as Indonesia and Egypt)?

Historical development

Early international marketing work was a practical extension of the international trade field. Books dealing with an international theme focused mainly on the 'how-to' aspects, covering issues such as export and import mechanics, financing and documentation. Over time, the field tends to have developed a comparative marketing approach, examining similarities and differences among consumers, institutions and environments in different markets. During the mid-1960s an approach to international marketing that explicitly recognized the importance of the policy dimension was in place in the marketing literature. This approach highlighted the variations among countries that arise from differences in basic systems of society, and the distortions of international trade patterns by nationalist government policies. Since then, authors such as Philip Kotler, writing about marketing on a domestic level, have reiterated the essential role of policy within the marketing framework. Thus marketing managers need to acquire skills and understandings of political forces and public opinion in order to manage efficiently.

Definition of international marketing

The basic definition of international marketing is simple. It is the marketing of goods, services and information across political boundaries. Thus it includes the same elements as domestic marketing: planning, promoting, distributing, pricing, and support of the goods, services and information to be provided to the ultimate consumers. The process of international marketing, however, is typically much more complex than domestic marketing. The international marketer must deal with a number of key differences in foreign environments from the characteristics of domestic environments. These may include, for example, differences in consumer tastes and needs, economic levels, market structures, ways of doing business, laws and regulations. Any one of these factors can make a company's international approach to marketing ineffective, counterproductive, and/or violate local law in the foreign market. Together, these differences require a careful and well-planned approach to entering and expanding in the international marketplace. There are facilitating organizations that can provide assistance in the process, but the marketing manager has the responsibility for developing an effective and efficient approach to marketing in other nations. This requires an understanding of all of the differences that must be accommodated.

The business activities that must be carried out in marketing, and adjusted to accommodate differences in the international market (Van Mesdag 2000), include:

- the analysis of markets and potential markets
- the planning and development of products and services that consumers want, clearly identified in a suitable package
- the distribution of products through channels that provide the services or conveniences demanded by purchasers
- the promotion of products and services, including advertising and personal selling to inform and educate consumers about those products and services, or persuade consumers to try new, improved or different ways of satisfying their wants and needs
- the setting of prices that reflect both a reasonable value (or utility) of products or services to the consumers, and a satisfactory profit or return on investment
- the technical and non-technical support given to customers, both before and after a sale is made, to ensure their satisfaction, and thus pave the way for possible future sales that are necessary for company survival and growth.

An international dimension has to signify more than just being non-domestic. It ought also to incorporate one or more dimensions of a social, legal, economic, political or technological nature (see Chapter 2), so as to enable fuller comparisons to be drawn, and delineate clearly for marketers the points to which particular attention has to be paid.

Relationship with other business fields

International marketing is related to other business fields of study such as international business and international trade. In general terms, international marketing is a subset of international business, which could be defined as the performance of all business functions across national boundaries. International business includes all functional areas such as international production, international financial management, international human resources management and international marketing (see also Jeannet and Hennessey 2001). International trade theory explains why nations trade with each other (see the discussion below). The trade theory is aimed at understanding product flows between countries in the form of exports or imports.

Like every other term used in marketing, 'international' and 'global' do not have a sharp dividing line. For example, 'multinational' merely refers to a corporate entity that owns operations in a number of countries. The term gives no indication of the marketing strategy followed in those countries. They can be totally diverse and unconnected. 'International marketing' simply refers to a company operating in more than one country, whose marketing strategy in each country is chosen deliberately – from being very diverse to being rigidly standardised between countries.

Figure 1.2 Subsets of international business

Global marketing is a particular form of international marketing, and in its purest form does not exist. Its essence is that it covers a broad spread of the world's countries, and strives consciously to standardize the marketing strategy between those countries (see Van Mesdag 2000). The majority of international marketing approaches today are still based predominantly on culture-sensitive adaptation as each new foreign market is entered. As Kapferer (1992) stated, 'it is time to realize that the majority of the brands operating across Europe are neither global nor local, but "glocal"'. International marketing still has to differentiate itself clearly from international business, which touches everything but nothing in depth, and international management, which may include other disciplines such as human resource management and operations management.

A theoretical framework for international marketing

As noted earlier, international marketing discipline, despite its history of several decades, has been relatively unsuccessful in developing well-accepted theories. International marketing is a discipline containing a number of paradigms which draw on a number of theories. Theories are operated through the decisions taken by managers in dealing with the international environment in which they operate. As Ghauri and Cateora (2006) explained, it is important to be able to identify paradigms that indicate what international marketing should be concerned with, what questions it should ask, and what rules should be followed. International marketing is not a single theory but a discipline containing a number of theories which, when applied, become the operating technologies of practitioners engaged in the international marketing process (Van Mesdag 2000).

The purpose of a theory of international marketing is to explain marketing behaviour as it crosses national boundaries. The objective of a good theory in this field should include the following:

- the behaviour of consumer and industrial buyers in different countries
- the reaction of companies to changes in cultural differences
- the flow of imports and exports throughout the world
- the arrangements of joint ventures, strategic alliances and licensing activities
- the location and direction of foreign investment
- the impact of different value systems in various cultures.

While some progress has been made, one problem of international marketing as a discipline, and hence its inability to develop well-grounded theories, is that it is anchored in the contextual differences between nations. Also the variables are so contextual that generalization and theory development becomes very difficult (Doole and Lowe 2001). As a result of the contextual variability it seems that a differentiated approach to international marketing is required and should be preferred.

It is also becoming increasingly evident that we can build on well-accepted concepts of economic and social sciences to develop a theory of integrated international marketing. Furthermore, these theories, if well grounded, might in time contribute to the development of a more general theory of marketing. Such an approach must take into consideration that international marketing is a subset of international business and is linked to other fields of study such as international trade.

Approaches to internationalization

Over the past 30 years, one of the most frequently researched topics in international marketing has been the internationalization of the firm. For the most part, studies of the internationalization of firms have been devoted to the factors that cause internationalization, or to the processes by which firms become increasingly involved in international marketing activities (Fletcher 2001). One conclusion that emerges from such studies is that internationalization is a complex and multidimensional process. There are many definitions of internationalization: Fletcher (2001) describes it as 'a process by which firms increase their involvement in international business activities'.

Factors causing internationalization

The factors causing internationalization can be grouped into management characteristics, organization characteristics, external impediments and external incentives to engage in business overseas.

Management characteristic factors

These may include the following factor groupings:

- demographic, such as age and education
- international exposure, such as country of birth, time spent living overseas, and frequency of business trips overseas
- knowledge of international business, such as familiarity with culture and international business practices, and international transactions experience
- structured approach to management, such as planning orientation, and having a strategic or proactive approach.

(Fletcher 2001)

Organizational characteristic factors

The most important organizational characteristics are willingness to:

- develop products for overseas markets
- gain technological advantage
- fund international marketing activities
- gain market size as measured by employment
- research overseas markets
- have a focus on research and development (R&D)
- appraise the nature of the product and/or service.

(Evangelista 1994)

External impediments

The most important external impediments are:

- marketing activities by competitors in overseas markets
- perception of higher risk in overseas markets, including lack of continuity in overseas orders, tariff and non-tariff barriers, and exchange rate movements
- knowledge of the market and how it operates
- issues relating to agents and control, including attitudes of foreign governments, cost elements, lack of export training and government assistance.

External incentives

The most important external incentives are:

- availability of export incentives from government
- overseas demand factors such as competitiveness
- inquiries via industry bodies or government representatives overseas

- fall in domestic demand or excess capacity
- reduction in costs of production.

(Ogunmokun and Ng 1998)

These factors causing internationalization categorize the degree of international operation according to the nature of involvement in exporting, or progression from one stage of outward-driven international behaviour, for instance exporting, to another, such as foreign direct investment (FDI). In all cases, the focus is on international operation as an outward-driven activity (Fletcher 2001).

The process of firms' internationalization

There are four main approaches to internationalization: the stages approach, learning approach, contingency approach and network approach (see Table 1.1).

There have been some challenges to the above approaches on the grounds that they do not reflect how firms actually behave, especially in hi-tech and service industries (see Bell 1995). Such challenges have not gone beyond questioning the relevance of these approaches to outward forms of internationalization, but raise the question of how relevant the more traditional approaches to internationalization of firms are in the current international marketing environment. There are two main reasons for the change in the environment for international marketing (see further discussion in Chapter 2):

Table 1.1   Firms' internationalization process

	Approach	Firms' internationalization process
1	The 'stages' approach	Views internationalization as involving changes in the firm as it increases its commitment to foreign markets. Firms start with the entry mode, which requires the least commitment of resources, and gradually increase their level of commitment.
2	The 'learning' approach	Attempts to explain rather than describe patterns of internationalization behaviour. With this approach, the process is treated as an evolutionary, sequential build-up of foreign commitments over time, due to the interaction between knowledge of foreign markets, on the one hand, and increasing commitment of resources to their development, on the other.
3	The 'contingency' approach	Based on the premise that firms' international evolution is contingent upon a wide range of market-specific and firm-specific characteristics. External situations or opportunities may cause firms to leapfrog stages or to enter markets that are psychically distant from the home country (O'Farrell and Wood 1994).
4	The 'network' approach	Attributes internationalization to the development of networks of relationships over time as international buyers and sellers build up knowledge about each other. At a point in time, the firm has a position in an overseas network that characterizes its relations with other firms. The network approach concentrates on the market and the relationship of the firm to that market as opposed to internal development of a firm's knowledge and resources (see Leonidou and Kaleka 1998).

- National borders are becoming increasingly irrelevant. This is evidenced by the expansion of regional trade groupings, developments in the international trade environment such as the World Trade Order and the difficulties faced by governments in enforcing national sovereignty. This aspect is illustrated by the rise in incidence of transfer pricing, promotion activity via the Internet and the expanded focus of global policies on issues such as the environment and human rights.
- Firms are forming strategic alliances across national boundaries (see Chapter 5). These are driven by the information revolution, rising fixed costs, the need for increasing R&D expenditures, rapid dispersion of technology, shorter product life cycle, converging consumer tastes, and increasing value placed on brand equity. All these factors encourage firms to enter into cooperative arrangements with organizations in other countries.

These issues require firms to adopt a more dynamic approach as opposed to an incremental approach, and switch between forms of international involvement as changing market circumstances require.

A holistic approach

In response to the developments in the international marketing environment, more complex forms of international behaviour have evolved.

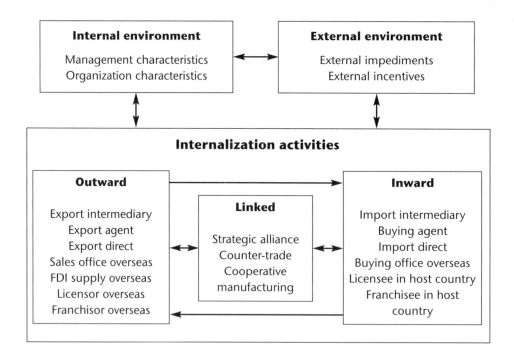

Figure 1.3   A holistic approach to internationalization

These forms of behaviour have been influenced by the increasing need to:

- serve customers in the international environment
- bring products to market more quickly
- introduce products into several countries simultaneously
- lower costs by firms in each country focusing on their core competencies
- reduce promotion costs by marketing world-wide under one brand.

Underlying these needs is a realization by firms that in order to be internationally competitive, they also need to be internationally cooperative. Whilst the early approaches to internationalization such as the 'stages', 'learning' and 'contingency' approaches were developed on the basis of empirical surveys of export practices in the United States and Europe in the 1970s and 1980s, changes in the international business environment mean that such approaches may no longer be relevant. These changes in the environment call for a new approach which embraces a more holistic view of international operation (see Figure 1.3). This new approach needs to recognize the following factors:

- Firms can also become internationalized by inward-driven activities such as indirect importing, direct importing, becoming the licensee for a foreign firm, and being the joint venture partner with an overseas firm in their domestic market, or by manufacturing overseas to supply the home market.
- Outward internationalization can lead to inward internationalization and vice versa, as when the franchisee or licensee in one country becomes the franchisor or licensor in another.
- Internationalization often requires more complex forms of international behaviour in which there is a linking of both inward and outward international activities, as happens with strategic alliances, counter-trade and cooperative manufacture.
- Internationalization should be viewed as a world-wide activity rather than as an activity with respect to a firm's involvement in a specific overseas country. This means that internationalization should focus not only on expansion of international involvement in a particular country but also on contraction. This is because a firm might involuntarily or deliberately reduces its involvement in one country so as to devote resources to more beneficial activities in other countries. This relates to the concept of de-internationalization as proposed by Welch and Benito (1996).

Figure 1.3 is a conceptual framework of a holistic approach to internationalization. It shows that factors previously found to apply to outward-driven internationalization also impact on inward and linked forms of internationalization. It also shows that outward forms can lead to inward forms and vice versa. In addition, it illustrates that linked forms of internationalization can be driven by outward forms (for example, a desire to export) or by inward forms (for example, a desire to tie up a long-term supply from overseas of a difficult-to-obtain product). Within each of the above forms, various types of international marketing activity are shown such as exporting, licensing, production overseas, strategic alliances and counter-trade.

The motivation for firms to go international

International marketing becomes a vital issue for companies that are considering inter-nationalization. They need to take a broad view of the issues that inevitably make the overseas market more complex and unfamiliar than marketing within a national market. The first consideration for firms going international must be their motivation for devel-oping outside their own national markets. Where the opportunity in the domestic market is limited it is reasonable to expect that firms will seek expansion opportunities in inter-national markets. This reasonable expectation underlies 'push and pull' analysis of the motivations for international marketing processes. Such an assumption is fundamental to an interpretation that sees international marketing as a reactive response to the competitive environment.

Push factors may be described as those issues that encourage international marketing, or make it imperative, as a result of environmental or company-specific conditions in the domestic market. They are therefore characterized by unattractive trading conditions. Environmental factors such as poor economic conditions, negative demographic trends and regulatory constraints are commonly referred to in this context. Company-specific issues, such as the stage of the company's development, are also commonly seen as instrumental in prompting international marketing action. Where, for example, there are limited growth opportunities in the domestic market, they will be interpreted as pushing the company out of this market and into international markets.

The pull factors are essentially attractive conditions that draw companies into new markets overseas. The push and pull factors should be viewed as relative rather than absolute. For example, push factors within the European environment during the 1970s encouraged international marketing activities, while pull factors from the United States encouraged investment in that market. The US market, with relatively attractive social, economic and regulatory conditions, pulled European companies into North America, while unhealthy operating conditions and limited commercial opportunities at home prompted expansion outside the domestic market.

Trade theories and economic development

According to the marketing principle, whenever a seller and buyer come together, each expects to gain something from the other. The same expectation applies to nations that trade with each other. It is virtually impossible for a country to be completely self-suffi-cient without incurring undue costs. Trade therefore becomes a necessary activity. Thus, the importance of international trade to a nation's economic welfare and development has been heavily documented in the economics literature since Adam Smith's (1776) pioneering *Inquiry into the Nature and Causes of the Wealth of Nations*. The rationale underlying this relationship suggests that economies need to export goods and services in order to generate revenue to finance imported goods and services, which cannot be produced indigenously.

One of the broad indicators of a nation's economic strength can be gauged from its gross domestic product (GDP), as this measure is an estimate of the value of goods and services produced by an economy in a given period. The notion that international trade can influence GDP has been explored by several economic theorists (Marin 1992), and

MINI CASE 1.1

Example of retail internationalization (push and pull factors)

Table 1.2 distinguishes between the 'push' and 'pull' factors that help to shape retailers' motives for international expansion.

Table 1.2 Push and pull factors in retail internationalization

Push factors	Pull factors
Unstable political structure	Stable political structure
Unstable economy	Stable economy
Matured domestic market	Underdeveloped retail structure
Retail format saturation	Larger market
Small domestic market	Relaxed regulatory environment
Restrictive regulatory environment	Good economic conditions
Hostile competitive environment	Positive social environment
Poor economic conditions	Favourable operating environment
Negative social environment	Favourable exchange rate
Unfavourable operating environment	Low share prices
High operating costs	Niche opportunities
Consumer credit restrictions	Attractive socio-cultural fabric
Lack of government support	Company-owned facilities
Poor infrastructure	Innovative retail culture

Other push factors not mentioned in Table 1.2 are:

- intense competitive pressures within the domestic marketplace
- the prospect of saturation in the domestic marketplace, leaving little room for business development
- sluggish performance in the domestic economy, resulting in flat sales in the domestic market
- restrictive legislation on new business developments.

To a large extent, many companies opt for international market expansion by being reactive to these push factors. By contrast, other companies take an active approach through being attracted by opportunities in other countries. Here, there are a number of pull factors at work, including:

- the identification of fragmented, underdeveloped or niche marketing opportunities in other countries
- the opportunity to establish a bridgehead for further expansion
- the presence of attractive acquisition targets.

There are some other important facilitating factors that come into play, including improved data communications, the international mobility of managers, and the accumulation of company experience in international trading.

culminated in the export-led growth thesis. The tenet underlying this volume of research is that as export sales increase, other things being equal, the GDP of a nation will rise and provide a stimulus to improved economic well-being and societal prosperity. The way in which this relationship can be interpreted suggests that export performance has a stimulating effect throughout a country's economy in the form of technological transfer and other related favourable externalities (Marin 1992). Export activities may exert these influences because exposure to international markets demands improved efficiency, and supports product and process innovation activities, while increases in specialization encourage profitable exploitation of economies of scale. Thus, the export-led growth thesis predicts that export growth will cause economy-wide productivity gains in the form of enhanced levels of GDP.

Another mechanism through which exports are connected with sustainable rates of economic growth is the balance of payments. The balance of payments constraint can be expressed as follows. In general, economic growth creates a variety of demands, which cannot be satisfied solely by domestic output. Beyond a certain level, the faster the rate of domestic demand, the more accelerated the growth of imports. However, any excess of imports over and above exports requires the trade deficit to be financed by either government borrowing from overseas or drawing on the economy's stock of assets. If this situation is sustained, it becomes vital for the home government to address the issue of such a trade imbalance (de Jonquieres 1994). The method of addressing the issue of trade imbalance is the consideration of national economic advantage (absolute and comparative).

Absolute advantage

Over 200 years ago, the great classical economist Adam Smith first explained how, within a single production unit, output could be increased if workers specialized in different tasks in the manufacturing process. Smith had established one of the most fundamental of all economic principles: the benefits of specialization or the division of labour.

The benefits of the division of labour suggest that if each of the world's countries, with its own endowment of both natural resources and 'man-made' resources, specializes in 'what it does best', total world output or production can be increased over that possible in a situation without specialization. In economic terms, being 'better at' producing a good or service means that a country can produce a defined amount of the good at the lowest cost in terms of resources used (factors of production or inputs). The country is technically and productively efficient in producing the good. That is, if a country is 'best at' producing a good or service, it possesses an absolute advantage in the good's production, whereas if it is not the best at producing it, the country has an absolute disadvantage. According to this principle, a country should export a commodity that it can produce at a lower cost than can other nations. Conversely, it should import a commodity that it can only produce at a higher cost than can other nations.

Comparative advantage

Absolute advantage must not be confused with the rather more subtle comparative advantage. To introduce and illustrate this most important economic principle, we can construct a highly simplified model of the 'world' economy, by assuming just two countries – say, the United States and China – each with just two units of resource (for example man-years of labour) that can produce either of two commodities – say, guns or rice. Each unit of resource, or indeed a fraction of each unit, can be switched from one industry to the other if so desired in each country. Suppose the production possibilities are that one unit of resource can produce four guns or two tons of rice in the United States, and one gun or one ton of rice in China.

Quite clearly, the United States is best at, or has an absolute advantage in, producing both guns and rice, but it only possesses a comparative advantage in gun production. This is because comparative advantage is measured in terms of opportunity cost, or of what a country gives up when it increases output of one industry by one unit. The country that gives up least when increasing output of a commodity by one unit possesses the comparative advantage in that good. The United States has to stop producing or give up two guns in order to increase its rice output by one ton, but China would only have to give up one gun to produce an extra ton of rice. Thus China possesses a comparative advantage in rice production although it has an absolute disadvantage in both products. When one country possesses an absolute advantage in both industries, as in the example above, its comparative advantage will always lie in producing the good in which its absolute advantage is greatest. Similarly, the country that is worst at both activities will possess a comparative advantage in the industry in which its absolute disadvantage is least.

MINI CASE 1.2

Example of specialized production

The United States and China example above could be used to show that total world production will be greater if each country specializes in the activity in which it has a comparative advantage, than when each country devotes exactly half its resources to each industry. Of cause it is necessary to specify carefully the degree of specialization undertaken in each country. Suppose for example that no specialization occurs and each country (the United States and China) devotes one unit of resource to each industry. The total world production will be five guns and three tons of rice. But now suppose that each country completely specializes in producing the good in which it possesses a comparative advantage. In this case, world production becomes eight guns and two tons of rice.

It is important to note that while production of one good (guns) has risen, production of the other (rice) has fallen. Since we are not comparing like for like, this does not necessarily represent a net gain in output. Let us suppose finally that China completely specializes, but that the United States – the country with the absolute advantage in both goods – devotes just enough resource (half a unit) to 'top up' world production of rice to three tons. This would allow the United States to partially specialize, directing one and half units of resource into gun production and producing six guns. The total world production will now be six guns and three tons of rice. Since at least as much rice and more guns are now produced than in the earlier 'self-sufficient' situation, quite clearly specialization in accordance with the principle of comparative advantage has led to an increased output.

The assumptions underlying the principles of comparative advantage

To show that definite benefits are likely to result from specialization and trade in accordance with the principle of comparative advantage, a number of rather strong assumptions have to be made. The case for trade – and hence the case against import controls and other forms of protectionism – is thus heavily dependent upon the realism of these assumptions. Equally, the case against trade and the case in favour of import controls is be based on questioning the realism of the assumptions underlying the principle of comparative advantage. The assumptions include:

- Each country's endowment of factors of production, including capital and labour, is assumed to be fixed. Capital and labour are treated as being immobile between countries, though they are capable of being switched between industries within a country. Finished goods, but not factors of production or inputs, are assumed to be mobile between countries.
- The principle of comparative advantage assumes constant returns to scale. One unit of resource is assumed to produce four guns or two tons of rice in the United States whether it is the first unit of resource employed or the hundredth unit. But in the real world, increasing returns to scale and decreasing returns to scale are both possible. In a world of increasing returns, the more a country specializes in a particular industry, the more efficient it becomes, thereby increasing its comparative advantage. But if decreasing returns to scale occur, specialization erodes efficiency and destroys the initial comparative advantage. In agriculture, over-specialization can result in monoculture, in which the growing of a single cash crop for export may lead to soil erosion, vulnerability to pests and falling agricultural yields in the future.
- Over-specialization may also cause a country to become particularly vulnerable to sudden changes in demand, or to changes in the cost and availability of imported raw materials or energy. Changes in costs and new inventions and technical progress can eliminate a country's comparative advantage. The principle of comparative advantage implicitly assumes relatively stable demand and cost conditions. The greater the uncertainty about the future, the weaker the case for complete specialization. Indeed, if a country is self-sufficient in all important respects, it is effectively neutralized against the danger of importing recession and unemployment from the rest of the world if international demand collapses.

International trade theories

Economists usually identify three categories of international trade issues (Morgan and Katsikeas 1997):

- explanations for trade flows between at least two nations
- the nature and extent of gains or losses to the national economy
- the effects of trade policies on the national economy.

Most theories of international trade are dedicated to the explanation of trade flows between nations, and economists generally turn their attention to the theoretical response in the form of classical trade theory, factor proportion theory and product life cycle theory.

Table 1.3	Selected theories of international trade

	Type of theory	Theoretical emphasis	Credited writers
1	Classical trade theory	Countries gain if each devotes resources to the production of goods and services in which it has an advantage	Ricardo (1817) Smith (1776)
2	Factor proportion theory	Countries will tend to specialize in the production of goods and services that use their most abundant resources	Hecksher and Ohlin (1933)
3	Product life cycle theory (for international trade)	The cycle follows that: a country's export strength builds; foreign production starts; foreign production becomes competitive in export markets; and import competition emerges in the country's home market.	Vernon (1966, 1971) Wells (1969).

Classical trade theory

This trade theory dictates that the extent to which a country exports and imports relates to its trading pattern with other nations. That is, countries are able to gain if each devotes resources to the generation of goods and services in which it has an economic advantage (Ricardo 1817, Smith 1776). Classical trade theory therefore effectively describes the scenario where a country generates goods and services in which it has an advantage, for consumption indigenously, and subsequently exports the surplus. Conversely, it is sensible for countries to import those goods and services in which they have an economic disadvantage. Economic advantages/disadvantages may arise from country differences in factors such as resource endowments, labour, capital, technology or entrepreneurship. Thus, classical trade theory contends that the basis for international trade can be sourced to differences in production characteristics and resource endowments which are founded on domestic differences in natural and acquired economic advantages. However, over and above such a general insight into international trade, classical trade theory is unable to offer any explanation of what causes differences in relative advantages.

The factor of proportion theory

In contrast to classical trade theory, proportion theory is able to provide an explanation for the differences in advantage exhibited by trading countries. According to this theory, countries will tend to generate and export goods and services that harness large amounts of production factors they possess in abundance, while they will import goods and services that require large amounts of production factors that are relatively scarce (Hecksher and Ohlin 1933). This theory therefore extends the concept of economic advantage by considering the endowment and costs of factors of production.

The product life cycle theory

Both the classical and the factor of proportion theories have been shown to be deficient in explaining more recent patterns of international trade. For example, the 1960s witnessed significant technological progress and the rise of the multinational enterprise, which resulted in a call for new theories of international trade to reflect changing commercial realities (Leontief 1966). At that time, the product life cycle theory of international trade was found to be a useful framework for explaining and predicting international trade patterns as well as multinational enterprise expansion. The product life cycle theory explains the pattern of world production, specialization and trade in manufactured goods in terms of the nature of technical progress. Early in its life cycle and immediately following its successful innovation, a product is likely to be strongly differentiated from competing products. By creating a highly profitable relative monopoly position for the innovative firm, such product differentiation provides an important motive for technical development (Porter 1990).

At this stage of the product's life cycle, manufacture is usually located in the country of origin of the innovative company, where its research and development facilities are concentrated. But at a later stage when the company loses its monopoly over the existing technology, when the product becomes more standardised with agreed international specifications, and when mass production combines economies of scale with the application of routine relatively unskilled labour, the advanced economies lose their comparative advantage and production shifts to the new industrialized countries (NICs). Meanwhile, the innovative firms in the advanced industrial countries attempt to maintain their lead by further technical progress and product development, while at the same time owning subsidiaries in the NICs in which they manufacture for export back to the developed world the 'older' products which are now well into their life cycles (Wells 1969).

This theory suggested therefore that a trade cycle emerges where a product is produced by a parent firm, then by its foreign subsidiaries and finally anywhere in the world where costs are at their lowest possible (Vernon 1971, Wells 1969). Furthermore, it explains how a product may emerge as a country's export and work through the life cycle to ultimately become an import (see Table 1.3). The essence of the international product life cycle is that technological innovation and market expansion are critical issues in explaining patterns of international trade. That is, technology is a key factor in creating and developing new products, while market size and structure are influential in determining the extent and type of international trade.

While the theories outlined in Table 1.3 are insightful, a number of modern international trade theories have also emerged which take account of other important considerations such as government involvement and regulation. However, it remains that these theories make several assumptions that detract from their potential significance and contribution to international trade. For instance, they assume that factors of production are immobile between countries, perfect information for international trade opportunities exists, and traditional importing and exporting are the only mechanisms for transferring goods and services across national boundaries.

Foreign direct investment (FDI)

Over the past two decades direct investments by multinational firms have grown significantly faster than trade flows, particularly among the world's most developed economies. International economic activities increasingly involve foreign production and intra-firm trade by multinational firms, and it is now estimated that about 30 per cent of world trade is intra-firm.

Foreign direct investment (FDI) refers to the establishment, management and control of a new venture overseas. The establishment of such venture usually involves a heavy financial and managerial commitment on the part of the investing company. The investing company transmits equity capital, entrepreneurship, technology or other productive knowledge in the context of an industry-specific package.

One of the major implications of neoclassical growth theory is that all countries will eventually converge to the same level of productivity. The lack of evidence that this is happening prompted the development of 'new growth theories'. One of the major characteristics of these new theories is the endogenization of technology. In the evolutionary approach technology is considered as an endogenous factor. Furthermore, in a microeconomic context, technology has important private good characteristics as well as public good characteristics. This implies that the benefits of innovation can be partly appropriated. Technological differences between countries remain, to a certain extent, persistent under the assumption that diffusion occurs more easily within a country than between countries. In other words, it is likely that no country can rely fully on imitation to obtain the technological frontier. This also suggests that technology gaps stem from an accumulation process, rather than resulting from different 'natural' endowments. In the neoclassical growth models, long-run growth stems from technological progress and labour force growth, which are both assumed to be exogenous (see Dunning 1998).

The eclectic paradigm

Dunning (1980) developed the eclectic paradigm, which synthesizes previous theories under a single conceptual scheme, which was subsequently reformulated (see Dunning 1998). His developments, along with the complementary works of Buckley and Casson (1998), constitute the eclectic conceptual framework. The eclectic paradigm proposes that the undertaking of FDI is determined by the realization of three groups of advantages:

- Ownership advantages are specific to the company and are related to the accumulation of intangible assets, technological capacities or product innovations.
- Internalization advantages stem from the capacity of the firm to manage and coordinate activities internally in the value added chain. They are related to the integration of transactions into multinational hierarchies through FDI.
- Location advantages refer to the institutional and productive factors that are present in a particular geographic area. They arise when it is better to combine products manufactured in the home country with irremovable factors and intermediate products of another location.

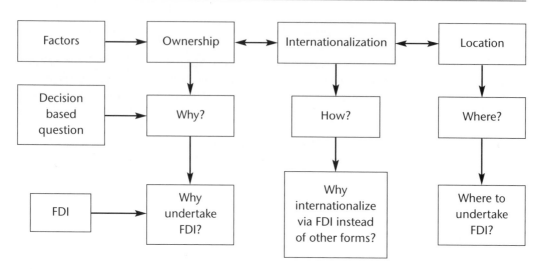

Figure 1.4   Key decisions in the FDI process

FDI will take place when these three kinds of advantage come together. According to the reasoning of Buckley and Casson (1998), all the advantages are interconnected and affect indistinctly the likewise interconnected decisions of 'why', 'how' and 'where' to internationalize (see Figure 1.4).

It is apparent from Figure 1.4 that ownership advantages mostly determine the 'why' decision, internalization advantages mostly determine the 'how' decision and location advantages mostly determine the 'where' decision. The eclectic paradigm is dynamic. The continuous incorporation of new companies to the internationalization process and the changing and more and more receptive policies in developing countries are giving rise to new trends in the way of carrying out FDI (Dunning 1997).

The impact of FDI on national economies

FDI should have only a short-run effect on output growth, but the adoption of endogenous growth theory has encouraged research into channels through which FDI can be expected to promote economic growth in the long run (Borensztein, de Gregorio and Lee 1998). The view of FDI is therefore optimistic, suggesting that multinational firms have important complementarities with local industry, and stimulate development and welfare in the host economy. The impact of FDI on growth runs through the following channels:

1   By capital accumulation in the recipient country, FDI increases economic growth by encouraging the incorporation of new inputs and foreign technologies in the production function of the recipient economy (Borensztein et al. 1998). Thus, a catch-up process in the level of technology explains growth rates in host countries.
2   By knowledge transfers, FDI is expected to boost levels of knowledge in the recipient economy through labour training/skill acquisition (de Mello 1997).
3   FDI may also change the structure of imperfectly competitive industries by intensifying

competition, and this in turn may create demands for local output and strengthen the local supply industries.

4 FDI promotes technological upgrading, in the case of start-up, marketing and licensing agreements. It may also lead to the establishment of local industrial sectors, and these sectors may grow to the point where local production overtakes and forces out FDI plants (Markusen and Venables 1999).

FDI can therefore be seen as a catalyst for industrial development and technological upgrading. As a result, foreign investors may increase productivity and technological progress in the recipient economy and therefore have a large impact on economic growth and welfare.

The determinant factors of FDI

Figure 1.5 depicts some of the factors that multinational firms consider in making FDI decisions. The state of the economic environment may affect the volume and type of FDI inflows in the recipient economy (see also Galan and Gonzalez-Benito 2001). Similarly, the technological capability of the recipient economy is likely to correlate significantly with the extent of FDI. If foreign multinational enterprises are exactly identical to domestic firms, they will not find it profitable to enter the domestic market. In other words, technological advantages, lower factors costs, factor endowments, and higher productivity of the recipient country should increase the attractiveness of FDI (see Bradley 2002). These are quite consistent with international investment theory, as proposed by Dunning (1998), who suggested that three conditions (ownership, location and internalization) all need to be present for a firm to have a strong motive to undertake direct investment.

Additional factors that may have strong association with FDI inflows are the degree of macroeconomic stability and the trade policy of the host country. The host economy becomes more attractive once it has implemented monetary and fiscal discipline to control inflation, liberalization reforms, and has promoted trade and provided the necessary institutional framework for property rights and cross-border legal and financial settlements. All these factors can be deemed to foster growth, and the ensuing higher growth rate may then attract larger FDI inflows. The effectiveness of macroeconomic policies is important in making the economic environment attractive to foreign investors. Furthermore, FDI influences growth through the 'catch-up' process in technology and through knowledge transfer. By promoting growth in the recipient economy, inflows of FDI will increase and this in turn will have additional effect on growth and welfare.

The advantage of endogenous growth models is that the long-run growth is affected not only by technological changes but also by institutional and country-specific factors. For example, government policy can induce a permanent increase in the rate of output growth by making the state of the economic environment in the recipient economy more appealing to foreign investors. Thus, the following factors are likely to have significant impact on FDI inflows (see de Mello 1997): the recipient economy's trade policy, productivity growth, legislation, political stability, balance of payment constraints, and the size of the domestic market. These factors are mostly related to the moderating role of the environmental risk elements in the recipient economy and the uncertainty involved, which the investor needs to consider.

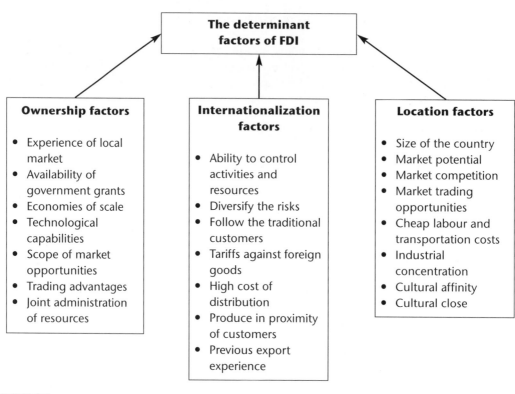

Figure 1.5 Factors favouring FDI decisions

FDI and risks consideration

The strength of the relationship between uncertainty and the firm's decision to engage in FDI is moderated by factors such as capital intensity and firm size. Many multinational firms are known to serve foreign markets through FDI in preference to exporting and licensing. Many determinants of FDI – spanning host country, product, industry and firm characteristics – are known to contribute to firms' decisions to use FDI. Of these, environmental uncertainty occupies a position of pre-eminence. In the international marketing literature, uncertainty is categorized as:

- Internal uncertainty, caused primarily by the firm's lack of knowledge of host markets because of a dearth of international experience or entry into culturally unfamiliar host markets. A firm perceives internal uncertainty when it lacks market-related knowledge in a particular entry situation. Internal uncertainty can arise from the firm's lack of experience in international markets, or from the cultural distance between the firm's home country and host country: that is, the differences between the countries' cultures, languages and business practices. The more culturally dissimilar two countries are, the greater the internal uncertainty perceived by the firm. Internal uncertainty causes managers to discount investment opportunities and refrain from ownership. It also makes managers unsure of their ability to manage foreign operations and impedes transfer of home-country management expertise to host-country operations.

- External uncertainty, resulting from volatility in the host markets. External uncertainty arises out of the volatility or the unpredictability of the host country. Political instability, economic fluctuations, currency changes, labour disputes and infrastructural difficulties all contribute to unpredictability in overseas markets and represent major sources of external uncertainty. High country risk, a variable used to represent external uncertainty, discourages commitment of resources to foreign markets.

This internal–external dichotomy is consistent with the broader strategic management perspective put forth by Miller (1993), that uncertainty can arise from inadequacy of information on certain variables or from the unpredictability of the environment. Miller has found that firms reduce resource commitments in the face of growing uncertainty. In turn, reduction in resource commitments would favour non-FDI modes over FDI modes. But, it is not clear whether the strength of the relationship between uncertainty and choice of FDI remains constant in all situations. Miller also observed that firms do not respond to uncertainty with equal intensity in all situations. Cultural factors are usually one of the major considerations when FDI decisions are made.

Culture and international marketing development

Belk (1996) argues that internationalization does not necessarily entail homogenization of markets, especially the assimilation of other cultures to the Euro-American models. Cultures transform international marketing meanings into unique local market meanings, which are interpreted very differently. Thus, cultures are resilient and enduring, and so is the concept of international multiculturalism. Although internationalization might not adequately homogenize cultures, it might polarize them on the basis of both material and abstract cultural differences (Manrai and Manrai, 1996).

East and west cultures

At the primary level of analysis, we could dichotomize the world into two cultures:

- Eastern cultures – these are characterized by high power distance, collectivism, femininity and long-term orientation. For example, Japan in comparison with Western Europe is a high power distance, collectivist, long-term-oriented society. It is also a very strong uncertainty avoider, which is reflected in tight, stable and long-lasting relationships (Van Den Bosch and Van Prooijen 1992).
- Western cultures – these are characterized by low power distance, individualism, masculinity and short-term orientation (see Hofstede 1991).

Another important distinction is that eastern countries are 'high-context' cultures in comparison with western countries, which are 'low-context' cultures. This means that the social context of transactions is given high importance in eastern cultures. For example, Hall and Hall (1987) observed that eastern cultures have a polychronic view of time (multiple activities at a time) whereas western cultures have a monochromic view of time (single activity at a time).

At the secondary level of analysis, we can also see differences within each major grouping. Within the western culture, Anglo (for example Canada, Ireland, the United Kingdom and the United States) and Germanic countries (for example Austria, Germany, Switzerland) are high on masculinity, whereas the Nordic countries (for instance, Denmark, Norway, Sweden) are high on femininity. Similarly, within the western cultures, North America (the United States and Canada) can be considered relatively higher in the cultural context than Western Europe (Manrai and Manrai 1996). Hence, in the continuum of time concept, East Asian countries are polychronic, Western European countries are monochromic, and North American countries lie in-between the two although closer to the Western European countries.

Cultural influences

Culture to many people is a 'dustbin word' (Holden 1998). If cultural differences are assumed to have an influence, culture is seen as 'a convenient catchall for the many differences in market structure and behaviour that cannot readily be explained in terms of more tangible factors' (Buzzell 1968). If we take Europe as an example, international marketers would like us to believe that in the 'new Europe' with a single currency, people will become more similar, will increasingly eat the same food, wear jeans and sports shoes and watch the same television programmes. The reality is of course different. Few people watch international (English language) television programmes regularly (see de Mooij 2000). Understanding of the English language still varies widely and few Europeans, apart from the British and the Irish, regularly watch English language television without translation (EMS 1999). There also remain large differences between the value systems of the peoples of Europe. These differences were expected to disappear with the single European market in 1992 but they did not. They have not disappeared with the introduction of the euro either. Values are strongly rooted in history and appear to be stable over time.

Cultural values

Although there is evidence of convergence of economic systems (see Paliwoda 1999), there is no evidence of convergence of people's value systems. On the contrary, there is evidence that with converging incomes, people's habits diverge (de Mooij 2000). More discretionary income gives people more freedom to express themselves, and they normally do that according to their own specific value patterns. According to de Mooij, there are basically four reasons that international marketers are reluctant to accept this viewpoint:

- What unites marketers worldwide is the wish for change. Change and trends are what the marketing environment thrives on. New trends mean new business. This preoccupation with change makes it so difficult to understand the stability of cultural values.
- The origin of most multinational companies is America and/or Britain, or Anglo-

American management dominates them so they are very individualistic. Individualism implies universalism, thinking that the rest of the world is like oneself, or will become like oneself. For individualists, it is difficult to understand that others may be different, and will remain so in the foreseeable future. Their focus (Holden 1998) is on global markets, on similarities, not on the differences.

- Those who preach the importance of cultural differences in the international marketplace do not have much empirical evidence to refer to. The few results of cross-cultural academic research trickle down too slowly.
- The problem of cultural values is that they are difficult to vocalize. Cross-cultural studies that can be applied to international marketing are few.

Thus, a model that distinguishes values of national culture, developed by Geert Hofstede (1991) for the purpose of intercultural management, can also be used to understand differences in consumption and consumer behaviour.

National culture and consumption patterns

Many of the differences in product usage and buying motives across Europe for example, are correlated with Hofstede's dimensions. Values of national cultures influence, for example, the volume of mineral water and soft drinks consumed, ownership of pets, of cars, the choice of car type, ownership of insurance, possession of private gardens, readership of newspapers and books, television viewing, ownership of consumer electronics and computers, use of the Internet, sales of video cassettes, use of cosmetics, toiletries, deodorants and hair care products, consumption of fresh fruit, ice cream and frozen foods, use of toothpaste and numerous other products and services, fast-moving consumer goods and durables. These differences are stable or becoming stronger over time.

This stability of cultural values is in contrast to what economists expect: that with converging incomes, cultural values and habits will also converge. The opposite is true. Cultural values are stable and with converging incomes they will become more manifest. When people possess more or less enough of everything, they will spend their incremental income on what most fits their value pattern. Americans will for example buy more cars, the Dutch will buy more luxurious caravans and the Spanish will eat out even more than they do now.

Many of the current marketing theories have been developed and validated only in western cultures, particularly the United States. The further advancement of international marketing as an academic discipline requires that the validity of marketing theories and models be examined in other cultural settings as well, to identify their degree of generality and to uncover boundary conditions. This will assist international marketers to select foreign markets that are culturally compatible.

For international marketing, the future is predictable, but in a different way than is generally expected. Disappearing income differences will not cause homogenization of needs. On the contrary, along with converging incomes, the manifestation of value differences will become stronger. This phenomenon makes it increasingly important to understand values of national culture and their impact on consumer behaviour. This knowledge can be a powerful tool for international marketing. If it is accepted that the core values of national cultures are stable and will influence both existing and future consumer behaviour, the future use of innovations can be predicted. Thus international marketing can be more efficient.

Management issues in international marketing

International marketing management is faced with three basic decisions. The first is whether to engage in international marketing activities at all. Second, if a company decides that it wants to do business in international markets, then a decision has to be made concerning what specific individual markets are to be served. Finally, the company must determine how it is going to serve these markets: that is, what method should be used to get product(s) to the consumers in foreign markets. This last decision is the basic marketing mix decision, and includes planning and strategy with regard to market entry, products, promotion, channels of distribution and price.

International marketing management includes the management of marketing activities for products that cross the political boundaries of sovereign states. It also includes marketing activities of firms that produce and sell within a given foreign nation, if the firm is a part of an organization that operates in other countries, and there is some degree of control of such marketing activities from outside the country in which the firm produces and sells the product. International marketing management involves the management of marketing not only to but also in foreign countries. From an overall perspective these dimensions relate to the broad area of foreign market entry strategy. The planned and coordinated combination of marketing tools employed to achieve a predetermined goal is called a marketing programme. A central feature of marketing is consumer orientation. The marketing programme should be formulated with the interests and needs of consumers in mind. It must be structured in such a way as to integrate the customer into the company and to lead to creating and maintaining a solid relationship between the company and the customer. A firm operating in this manner is said to be market driven, and is concerned with what the consumer will buy that can be made profitably.

Modern international marketing thought means having a customer focus identifying values desired by customers, providing them in the same way, communicating these values to customer groups and delivering the values. Values mean benefits focused on solving customer problems and not merely on the products and services that serve as the vehicle of the solution. The focus is on the customer and on solving problems faced by the customer. The fundamental management issue is to understand the international customers' perception of value, to determine a superior value position from this perspective, and to ensure that, by developing a consensus throughout the company, value is provided and communicated to the customer group in the world markets. The role of marketing management is to:

- understand customers' perception of value – identify the value the firm expects to provide
- determine a superior value position for the company – provide the value expected
- determine the appropriate positioning and brand strategy – communicate the value
- distribute and price the product/service – deliver the value to the customer.

It is misleading to think, however, that only the marketing function in the company affects marketing outcomes. Value emanates from the business system in which the company operates, and the company may leverage other firms and individuals in the system (customers, suppliers and particularly others that complement the firm in what it provides) in creating that value. A long-term marketing orientation draws together suppliers, customers, competitors and partners to create value in the entire organization. It is the international marketing system as a whole that creates value within a set of dynamic relationships (Brandenburger and Nalebuff 1996) among customers, suppliers, competitors, partners and the company itself. The international marketing system thus consists of customers, competitors, partners, suppliers and the company itself. In this system the company is the focus of attention, as it establishes relationships with all the other participants located in the domestic market and abroad. In establishing relationships in this international marketing system the company must also consider the environment of international marketing, which reflects the influence of culture, economics and politics on the system (see Chapter 2). Developing an appropriate international marketing strategy in the firm involves coping with the specified relationships within this international marketing system.

In the international marketing system the company can offer its customers a different way of perceiving its business. This is particularly true in an Internet world. The customer in the foreign market can see upstream into the company's organization and processes, directly to its capabilities and skills. This mechanism also extends beyond the company to its suppliers, which are also part of its proximate environment. In a process that goes beyond 'customization', the customer is able to design unique mixes of skills and capabilities to match its requirements. In this view of the international marketing system the company is not only placing its capabilities at its customer's disposal, it is also aligning its own upstream supply chain for the customer.

In this framework, rather than place discrete orders for goods and services with the company, the foreign-based customer can link its production process seamlessly, and perhaps electronically, back up the value chain through the company's manufacturing, account management and procurement processes. Increasingly, international customers, especially those in high technology and industrial products markets, work with the company's capabilities as if they owned them. Single sourcing is facilitated in such a regime, whereby the relationship marketing paradigm dominates the exchange paradigm.

Summary

This chapter charted recent macromarketing developments and the impact that they are having on international marketing management. The chapter started by discussing the nature and definition of international marketing, then reviewed the trade theories from where international marketing originated. The chapter placed emphasis on the following factors:

- The discipline of international marketing provides an understanding of marketing practices indifferent countries, its structural determinants anchored to national differences, and the deployment of country-specific marketing strategies.
- International marketing is related to other fields of study such as international business and international trade.
- The purpose of a theory in international marketing is to explain marketing behaviour as it crosses national boundaries.
- Firms internationalize to overcome domestic saturation and to exploit their competitive marketing advantage in new markets.

- Trade will be advantageous if each of two countries specializes in the production of those commodities in which it has a comparative advantage.
- Both multinationals and the recipient nations benefit from foreign direct investments but firms must consider carefully the risk involved in making FDI decisions.
- Cultures transform international marketing meanings into unique local market meanings which are interpreted differently, and values of national cultures influence products and/or services consumption.
- International marketing management is concerned with the understanding of international consumer perception of value and how this is taken into consideration in the preparation of international marketing plans.

Revision questions

1 Explain what you understand by international marketing.
2 International marketing is about the application of marketing concept and philosophy but has predominantly remained a contextual practice. Discuss this statement and explain why it has been difficult to develop theories of international marketing.
3 What do you consider to be the factors causing firms' internationalization?
4 The theory of comparative advantage states that trade will be advantageous if each of two countries specializes in the production of those commodities in which it has a comparative advantage. Explain this theory with the aid of suitable examples.
5 Briefly describe classical trade theory, factor proportion theory, and the product life cycle theory for international trade.
6 Describe the key decision processes for a firm embarking on foreign direct investment
7 What are the factors that are likely to be considered by multinational firms when making foreign direct investment decisions?
8 Cultures transform international marketing meanings into unique local market meanings that are interpreted very differently. Evaluate this statement using suitable examples.
9 The fundamental management issue for international marketers is to understand the international consumers' perception of value. Discuss the role of international marketing management with regard to this issue.

SEMINAR CASE STUDY

Market opportunities and barriers in the Chinese emerging market

During the last two decades, the Chinese emerging market has undergone a dramatic transformation, with a tendency to privatization, liberal trade policies and free market forces. While FDI has become a major force driving economic growth in developing countries, foreign-funded projects have not always led to profitable enterprises. Similarly, while many multinational corporations (MNCs) have engaged in infrastructure projects, a significant number of them have invested in local manufacturing to explore the untapped market potential, ranging from family cars, appliances and consumer electronics to food and beverage products in China. While some MNCs have enjoyed rapid growth and increasing revenues in China, they have also encountered a whole array of problems, the solution of which has eluded even some of the biggest global companies. Some companies have taken heavy losses from their operations in China, and these reached their climax in the aftermath of the recent Asian financial crisis.

Many MNCs have not given enough attention to understanding of the Chinese market structure and local consumers. Despite the preponderant reporting of the surge in consumer power in China, they have stayed at the level of descriptive information such as rapid urbanization and other macroeconomic statistics, and sometimes led to a distorted view of the marketplace and misreading of consumer demand. While the ongoing economic transformations in the Chinese market are revolutionary in nature, international marketing strategists have yet to translate such information into actionable strategies for MNCs. The lack of valid and reliable data, compounded by rapid changes in these societies, has contributed to the paucity of in-depth analysis which MNCs desperately need to make informed decisions.

Attracted by the concept of a 'global consumer', including those in the emerging markets, MNCs foresaw incremental sales and soaring profit. The assumption was that consumers regardless of their country of residence migrate towards the same aspiration: high-quality goods to enhance their quality of life. However, market evolution in China is less likely to replicate the development process that happened in developed nations. To compete effectively, MNCs need to define the consumers of emerging markets − which are significantly different from those in the west − and to develop an approach to serving their needs. Assessing effective market size and consumer purchasing power, and understanding people's attitudes to new and western products, are among the critical issues that remain significant challenges for multinationals.

One of the delusions that impaired many MNCs was the assumption that China is a huge and single market. In reality, geographic diversity and economic disparity are prevalent in China. While the metropolitan area of Shanghai has become the hotly contested market, vast areas of China show quite a different picture. In fact, the Chinese market includes a number of smaller sub-markets which are distinct from one another in many ways, including language, culture and economic development. Regional disparities in economic infrastructure, consumer purchasing power and distribution channels often pose significant barriers for MNCs trying to adopt uniform strategies in China. Thus, understanding of regional diversity within the Chinese market can help firms assess the opportunities and risks there and enact effective marketing strategies.

China is attractive to MNCs for two reasons: its substantial size and the high growth rate of its consumer market. With a geographic area comparable to that of the United States, China has 1.3 billion people, who represent one-fifth of the world population. Most Chinese reside in the eastern provinces, making it a highly concentrated market. With a birth rate higher than those of western nations, the country has a relatively young population. Their common language and cultural heritage, reinforced by decades of Communist rule, give the appearance of a homogeneous market. With a growing economy, an enormous and presumably homogeneous population, China promises many opportunities for rapid growth and expansion with efficient marketing operations.

In the last two decades, the Chinese government has reformed its economy, introduced market forces, and opened one industry after another to foreign investors. As part of its campaign to join the World Trade Organization (WTO), China has reduced tariffs and the number of products requiring import licences, revised customs laws, and strengthened intellectual property protection. At the macroeconomic level, its GDP reached $954 billion in 1998, making it the sixth largest economy in the world (US-China Business Council 1999). Since 1992, China has welcomed broad-based foreign participation in the retail sector. Rapid increases in consumer purchasing power and changing spending patterns have driven up sales of many consumer goods. The retail market of China grew from $200 billion in 1996 to $351 billion in 1998.

Attracted by these quickly multiplying figures, many MNCs have dreamed of turning every Chinese into a customer. Today, China is the second largest recipient of FDI, with more than 320,000 foreign investment projects operating in the country. Global companies such as Coca-Cola and Kodak have established a significant presence in China, with multiple production sites and distribution networks that can reach even the remote parts of the country. Meanwhile, many MNCs in China have encountered daunting challenges and found the market elusive. They have overestimated the demand for their products while underestimating the level of competition in China. As some MNCs expand aggressively into inland regions, incremental sales from these new markets have not kept up with the escalating costs, resulting in lacklustre performance. As at June 2001, significant numbers of foreign firms operating in China were not profitable.

In spite of the well-publicized emerging 'middle class' consumers with increasing income and a craze for foreign goods, focusing on sheer size of the population and rising income alone as an indication of market readiness creates an inaccurate perception of the opportunities and risks there. The profile of a 'super consumer' found in some coastal areas hardly reflects the diversity among the majority of Chinese. Such misconception has led many MNCs to engage in rapid capacity building and in deferrable projects, which would help them take pre-emptive positions or keep competitive parity but only led to overshooting the local demand. For instance, competing with its arch-rival to expand in China, Pepsi-Cola established three bottling plants there, yet they are reportedly running below capacity and bottling for local producers.

Contrary to the popular belief, China is largely a developing country and consists of multiple markets segmented by regional economic development and local culture. While residents in China's coastal areas and major cities are increasingly better off, most people in rural areas are still living from hand to mouth. Following the 'open door' policy, the coastal areas of China were the first to attract outside investment and have benefited the most from economic reforms. The vast interior provinces are lagging behind in economic development. Furthermore, the Chinese also have diverse cultural patterns exhibited by variations in dialects, values, lifestyles, traditions and customs. Regional differences in consumer purchasing power, distribution channels and transportation logistics can erect major barriers for MNCs trying to exercise a uniform approach to the local markets.

For MNCs seeking entry and expansion in China, it is important to recognize that China is actually a conglomeration of markets divided by such factors as level of economic development, industrial priorities and local cultures. Although many companies have focused on specific groups of Chinese consumers, including women and young people, these are usually urban consumers based in a few big cities. As MNCs continue to increase their stake in the country, understanding of regional differences in consumer purchasing power and lifestyles is critical for them to assess local market demand accurately and to enact effective marketing strategies.

The importance of regional disparities for marketing operations in China is vivid. Lately, several companies including Pepsi-Cola have embarked upon a geographic segmentation of China based on location, economic development and local culture. The geographic segmentation is intended for the understanding of the Chinese consumers and for improving marketing strategies.

Finally, it is important for MNCs to understand the overall market potential of China as well as regional differences. Each regional market has its unique geographic typography, economic base and cultural heritage. Consumers in various regions are also known to differ in income, values, lifestyles and extent of contact with the outside world. These differences may in turn affect people's perception of foreign goods and their purchase readiness, and present tremendous hidden barriers between the markets, making it difficult for MNCs to exercise a national marketing and distribution strategy. Thus, for MNCs striving for a nation-wide presence, understanding the impact of regional variations can improve planning and marketing strategies. Since sales of foreign goods are limited to the cities, it may be necessary for MNCs to have this knowledge for successful international marketing strategy implementation in China.

Case study seminar questions

1 In the light of the information contained in the case study, discuss what you consider to be the opportunities and barriers to international marketing operation in China.
2 In spite of the implications and the likelihood of failure, China is one of the largest recipients of FDI. Why do you think this is happening?
3 According to the case study, to compete effectively, MNCs need to define consumers in China – who are significantly different from those in the West – and to develop an approach to serving their needs. Expand and discuss how this could be done.

Managerial assignment task

You have recently been employed by ABF, an UK-based international foods, ingredients and discount clothing retailer, as a marketing manager in charge of discount clothing. The company has operations in North America, Australia, New Zealand, Poland and China. The marketing director has now decided that you will be representing the company in China. During the initiation seminar, you were reminded of the following international marketing functions:

International marketing means identifying needs and wants of customers, providing products and services to give the firm a differential marketing advantage, communicating information about these products and services, and distributing and exchanging them internationally through one or a combination of foreign market entry modes.

In preparation for your official duties, you were asked to write a report on how you would carry out these international marketing functions on behalf of ABF in China to give it a competitive marketing advantage. Your report should be presented to the board of ABF in London, and a copy should be submitted to the marketing director for evaluation.

References

Aulakh, P. S. and Kotabe, M. (1993) 'An assessment of theoretical and methodological development in international marketing: 1980–1990', *Journal of International Marketing*, Vol. 1, No. 2, pp. 5–28.

Belk, R. W. (1996) 'Hyperreality and globalization: culture in the age of Ronald McDonald', *Journal of International Consumer Marketing*, Vol. 8, No. 3/4, pp. 23–37.

Bell, J. (1995) 'The internationalization of small computer software firms', *European Journal of Marketing*, Vol. 29, No. 8, pp. 60–74.

Borensztein, E., De Gregorio, J. and Lee, J-W. (1998) 'How does foreign direct investment affect economic growth?' *Journal of International Economics*, Vol. 45, pp. 115–35.

Bradley, F. (2002) *International Marketing Strategy*, 4th edn, London: Financial Times/Prentice Hall.

Brandenburger, A. M. and Nalebuff, B. J. (1996) *Co-Opetition*, New York: Doubleday.

Buckley, P. J. and Casson, M. C. (1998) 'Analysing foreign market entry strategies: extending the internationalization approach', *Journal of International Business Studies*, Vol. 29, No. 3, pp. 539–62.

Buzzell, R. D. (1968) 'Can you standardize multinational marketing?' *Harvard Business Review*, Vol. 46, No. 6, pp. 102–13.

De Jonquieres, C. (1994), 'ECGD to step up support for UK exporters', *Financial Times*, 30 June, p. 3.

De Mello, L. R. (1997) 'Foreign direct investment in developing countries and growth: a selective survey', *Journal of Development Studies*, Vol. 34, No. 1, pp. 1–34.

De Mooij, M. (2000) 'Viewpoint: the future is predictable for international marketers: converging incomes lead to diverging consumer behaviour', *International Marketing Review*, Vol. 17, No. 2, pp. 103–13.

Doole, I. and Lowe, R. (2001) *International Marketing Strategy: Analysis, Development and Implementation*, 3rd edn, London: Thomson Learning.

Dunning, J. H. (1980). 'Toward an eclectic theory of international production: Empirical tests', *Journal of International Business Studies*, Vol. 11, No. 1, pp. 9–31.

Dunning, J. H. (1998) 'Location and multinational enterprise: a neglected factor?' *Journal of International Business Studies*, Vol. 29, No. 1, pp. 45–66.

EMS (1999) *European Media and Marketing Survey*, a research survey of print media readership and TV audience levels within the upscale consumer group in Europe (EU, Switzerland and Norway), Inter/View International.

Evangelista, F. U. (1994) 'Export performance and its determinants: some empirical evidence from Australian manufacturing firms', pp. 207–29 in S. T. Cavusgil and C. T. Axmin (eds), *Advances in International Marketing*, Vol. 6, Greenwich, Conn.: JAI Press.

Fletcher, R. (2001) 'A holistic approach to internationalization', *International Business Review*, Vol. 10, pp. 25–49.

Galan, J. I. and Gonzalez-Benito, J. (2001) 'Determinant factors of foreign direct investment: some empirical evidence', *European Business Review*, Vol. 13, No. 5, pp. 269–78.

Ghauri, P. and Cateora, P. R. (2006) *International Marketing*, 2nd edn, Berkshire: McGraw-Hill.

Hall, E. T. and Hall, M. R. (1987) *Hidden Differences: Doing Business with the Japanese*, 1st edn, New York: Anchor/Doubleday.

Hecksher, E. and Ohlin, B. (1933) *Interregional and International Trade*, Cambridge, Mass.: Harvard University Press.

Hofstede, G. H. (1991) *Cultures and Organizations, Software of the Mind*, Maidenhead: McGraw Hill.

Holden, N. (1998) 'Viewpoint: international marketing studies – time to break the English language strangle-hold?', *International Marketing Review*, Vol. 15 No. 2, pp. 86–100.

Hornby, D. (1994) 'BOTB – building a UK edge in exporting', *INSTEP*, April, p. 12.

Jeannet, J.-P. and Hennessey, H. D. (2001) *Global Marketing Strategies*, 5th edn, New York: Houghton Mifflin.

Kapferer, J. N. (1992) 'How global are global brands?', ESCOMA Seminar: The Challenge of Branding Today and in the Future.

Keegan, W. J. and Schlegelmilch, B. B. (2001) *Global Marketing Management: A European Perspective*, London: Financial Times/Prentice Hall.

Kotler, P. (1988) 'Competitor analysis practices of British Charities', reproduced in *Financial Times* special supplement, Mastering Marketing, 14 September.

Leonidou, C. L. and Kaleka, A. A. (1998) 'Behavioural aspects of international buyer–seller relationships: their association with export involvement', *International Marketing Review*, Vol. 15, No. 5, pp. 373–97.

Leontief, W. (1966) *Input–Output Economics*, Oxford: Oxford University Press.

Manrai, L. A. and Manrai, A. K. (1996) 'Current issues in cross-cultural and cross-national consumer research', *Journal of International Consumer Marketing*, Vol. 8, No. 3/4, pp. 9–22.

Marin, D. (1992) 'Is the export led growth hypothesis valid for industrialized countries?', *Review of Economics and Statistics*, Vol. 74, pp. 678–88.

Markusen, J. R. and Venables, A. J. (1999) 'Foreign direct investment as a catalyst for industrial development', *European Economic Review*, Vol. 43, pp. 335–56.

Meier, G. M. (1984) *Leading Issues in Economic Development*, Oxford: Oxford University Press.

Miller, K. D. (1993) 'Industry and country effects on managers' perceptions of environmental uncertainties', *Journal of International Business Studies*, Vol. 24, No. 4, pp. 693–714.

Morgan, R. E. and Katsikeas, C. S. (1997) 'Theories of international trade, foreign direct investment and firm internationalization: a critique', *Management Decision*, Vol. 35, No. 1, pp. 68–78.

O'Farrell, P. N. and Wood, P. A. (1994) 'International market selection by service firms: key conceptual issues and methodological issues', *International Business Review*, Vol. 3 No. 3, pp. 243–61.

Ogunmokun, G. and Ng, S. (1998) 'An investigation of the problems encountered by exporter in international marketing and factors influencing exporting: a study of Australian exporters', *Journal of International Marketing and Exporting*, Vol. 3, No. 2, pp.123–33.

Paliwoda, S. J. (1999) 'Viewpoint: international marketing – an assessment', *International Marketing Review*, Vol. 16, No. 1, pp. 8–17.

Porter, M. E. (1990) *The Competitive Advantage of Nations*, New York: Free Press.

Ricardo, D. (1817) 'Principles of political economy', in P. Saffra (ed.) (1951), *The Works and Correspondence of David Ricardo*, Vol. 1, Cambridge: Cambridge University Press.

Sheth, J. N. and Parvatiyar, A. (2001) 'The antecedent and consequences of integrated global marketing', *International Marketing Review*, Vol. 18, No. 1, pp. 16–29.

Smith, A. (1776/1961) *An Inquiry into the Nature and Causes of the Wealth of Nations*, ed. E. Cannan (London: Methuen).

US-China Business Council (1999) *US–China Trade Statistics and China's World Trade Statistics*, US-China Business Council (USCBC).

Van Den Bosch, F. A .J. and Van Prooijen, A. A. (1992) 'The competitive advantage of European nations: the impact of national culture – a missing element in Porter's analysis?', *European Management Journal*, Vol. 10, No. 2, pp. 173–7.

Van Mesdag, M. (2000) 'Culture-sensitive adaptation or global standardization – the duration-of-usage hypothesis', *International Marketing Review*, Vol. 17, Issue 1, pp. 74–84.

Vernon, R. (1966) 'International investment and international trade in the product cycle', *Quarterly Journal of Economics*, Vol. 80, No. 2, pp.190–207.

Vernon, R. (1971) *Sovereignty at Bay: The Multinational Spread of US Enterprises*, New York: Basic Books.

Welch, L. and Benito, G. R. G. (1996) 'De-internationalization', Working paper 5/1996, Department of Marketing, University of Western Sydney, Nepean.

Wells, L. T. Jr. (1969), 'A product life cycle for international trade', *Journal of Marketing*, Vol. 32, July, pp. 1–6.

2

The International Marketing Environment

Contents

LEARNING OBJECTIVES

After reading this chapter you should be able to:

- understand the nature of the international marketing environment in which firms operate
- review the influences of macroenvironmental factors for firms operating in international markets
- establish the effects and implications of legal developments in the use of the Internet for international marketing operations
- outline the need for environmental scanning for firms engaged in international marketing
- understand the methods and various ways in which international markets can be classified.

Introduction

The key difference between domestic marketing and international marketing is the multi-dimensionality and complexity of the many foreign markets in which a company may wish to operate. These complexities may come as a result of political, economic, social, legal and technological factors (see Figure 2.1). It is important for an international manager to have a good knowledge and awareness of these complexities and the implications they have for international marketing management.

There are many models that could be used for analysing the international marketing environment ,but the most popular is SLEPT (social, legal, economic, political and technological). This chapter therefore examines the various aspects of the international marketing environment through these variables (see also Figure 2.1) in the light of the complexity of the international environment.

As the international environment becomes more turbulent, firms have had to increase their ability to scan the environment to gather information that can be used to anticipate or respond to environmental changes. Unpredictable changes or discontinuities in international environment are a major threat, which must be anticipated by international marketers. A good example of an unanticipated discontinuity is the Iraq war and its impact on international economic performance. Another example of unanticipated discontinuity

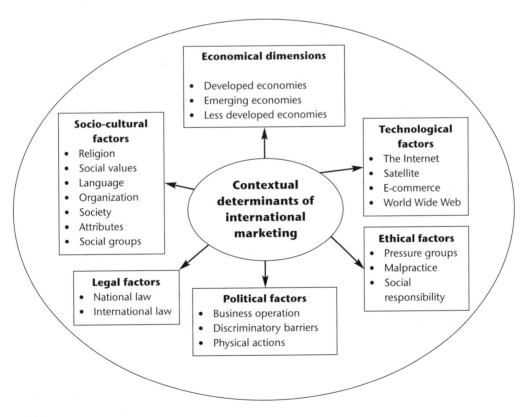

Figure 2.1 The international marketing environment

can be seen in the technology arena with deployment of advanced telecommunications infrastructures, and the increasing business transactions via the Internet.

The firm in international markets operates in an environment of opportunities and threats in which it is necessary to develop appropriate international marketing strategies configured to compete with other firms while providing value to customers. In such circumstances the firm responds by developing new products or by adapting existing products to the needs of consumers in international markets. International marketing also means deciding which markets to enter, and developing the sequence and timing of entry. One of the most important issues is the firm's decision on how to enter international markets. The nature and significance of international marketing for the firm are described in this chapter. The performance and growth of the firm as it diversifies into new international markets are also examined in the context of defined international marketing strategies.

The international marketing environment

The international marketing environment is a set of forces that either directly or indirectly influence the firm's acquisitions of inputs or generation of outputs. Kotler (2006) defines the marketing environment as 'the actors and forces that affect the company's ability to develop and maintain successful transactions and relationships with its target customers. It comprises non-controllable actors and forces that impact on the company's market and marketing practice.' Whenever the international marketing environment changes, companies are likely to face uncertainty, threats and opportunities in their business environment. Companies wishing to capitalize on such opportunities must be ready to predict likely outcomes and react quickly. Marketing managers who fail to recognize changes in environmental forces leave their firms unprepared to capitalize on marketing opportunities or to cope with threats created by changes in the environment (see Dibb 1996). As Keegan (2002) noted, fast moving consumer goods (FMCG) manufacturers, for example, need to be particularly vigilant as consumer goods are particularly sensitive to environmental factors.

The international marketing environment consists of a number of elements that lie outside the control of the firm (refer to Figure 2.1). This marketing environment (see also Keegan and Green 2000) is sometimes broken down into components including the micro and macroenvironment.

- The microenvironment concerns aspects that are close to the individual company and over which the company has some control.
- The macroenvironment, sometimes called the wider marketing environment, consists of those elements that are external to the company and have a broader effect on it. These include economic, demographic, political, legal, technological, social and cultural factors.

These macroenvironmental factors are discussed individually in the latter part of this chapter.

The international marketing environment is therefore a complex constellation of demands and constraints that multinational companies face as they attempt to

The International Marketing Environment ○ 37

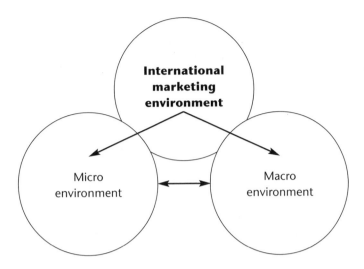

Figure 2.2   The micro and macro marketing environment

compete and grow. International market fragmentation is caused by low market entry costs and high exit costs, no experience curve effects, a typical cost structure and government interference in the market. Persistent differences in consumer tastes, differences in culture and language, and variation in technical standards also contribute (see Figure 2.2). In addition, tariffs and non-tariff barriers force manufacturers to think locally. At the same time, retailers for example are still very much national organizations focused on one country only, although this is changing. Tariff and non-tariff barriers dictate, to a large extent, the nature of the consumer products market in many parts of the world.

In the regime of international markets characterized by tariffs and non-tariff barriers, large firms are deprived of one of their favourite weapons, cost leadership stemming from manufacturing scale effect, while smaller firms proliferate and compete by serving speciality niches. Additional causes of market fragmentation in international markets are low industry entry costs and high exit costs. The absence of experience curve effects in some industries ensures that the industry remains fragmented. The strong determination of national governments to support the development of industries believed to be of strategic importance can also contribute to market fragmentation, which is especially true, but waning, in telecommunications and airlines, and was true in consumer electronics in Europe.

In traditional consumer mass markets, as are found for example in the United States, population age structures, the increase in the number of women working away from the home and the recognition of a multilingual and multicultural society have forced many companies to cope with fragmented markets by developing niche strategies. Many of the same influences have always existed in Europe. At the same time, the media are saturated with claims for standardized products, while consumers seek variety and supermarkets for instance seek higher margins. Multinational companies seek higher margins and control of marketing activities so they rarely allow decisions in the international marketing area to be made without care.

These are among the more important factors that have influenced trends toward increased fragmentation in markets. They are more influential in some markets than others, and the ability of firms to cope with them varies correspondingly. Highly culture-bound items such as food, clothing and medicine are more likely to be sold in fragmented markets, whereas consumer electronics and music, especially music aimed at the youth market, will probably continue to serve a standardized consolidated market. The reasons for international market fragmentation include:

• Differences in tastes, languages, cultures and technical standards represent obstacles to market consolidation, which force managers to 'think local'.
• Recognition of multilingual and multicultural societies forces many companies to develop niche strategies in coping with fragmentation.
• Retailers are still nationally focused.
• Large firms are deprived of a favourite competitive weapon, cost leadership, arising from scale effects in manufacturing and marketing.
• There are regulated markets, low industry entry costs and high industry exit costs.
• New information technologies may be used effectively to serve fragmented markets.

Markets are continually fragmenting and companies face the task of consolidating them. It is difficult to deal with markets that are highly fragmented but the nature of the innovation and expansion processes of firms necessarily involves fragmentation. The development of new product markets introduces fragmentation into existing stable markets. When the firm first expands abroad into new international markets it usually discovers that the markets for its products and services are fragmented. At the other end of the product life cycle, when markets have reached maturity, innovation is again necessary. Mature markets are typified by numerous product extensions and a disintegration of traditional product markets. Faced with such circumstances firms attempt to develop new product-market strategies, new business strategies and new market entry strategies to consolidate markets again, and so the process continues.

Consolidation of markets is achieved when low-cost standardized products are provided, marketing expenditures are systematically raised, a spate of acquisitions occurs and large capital investments raise the minimum scale to be efficient. Other factors that promote the consolidation of markets are attempts by companies to rationalize production capacity across a number of markets, and increases in investment in knowledge to raise labour productivity. These are the kinds of strategies pursued by the large well-known multinational companies. In general, international markets may be consolidated when:

• successful international firms introduce low-cost standardized products covering most market needs – this replaces many specialized products
• large marketing expenditures force less well-funded competitors to leave the market – this is a common strategy in packaged consumer goods markets
• companies pursue policies of acquiring competitors and rationalizing production capacity – a strategy often followed by alcoholic beverage and electrical products companies.

The continuous process of market fragmentation followed by consolidation presents firms with growth and development opportunities for international product-market development.

The international economic environment

A generally accepted measure of the economic attractiveness of an overseas market is the level of gross domestic product (GDP) per capita. The demand for most products increases as this figure increases. However, organizations seeking to sell goods and services overseas should also consider the distribution of income within a country. This may enable them to identify valuable niche markets. For example, the relatively low GDP per head of South Korea still allows a small and relatively affluent group to create a market for high-value overseas holidays.

An organization assessing an overseas market should place great emphasis on future economic performance and the stage that a country has reached in its economic development. While many western developed economies face saturated markets for a number of products, less developed economies may be just moving on to that part of their growth curve where a product begins to appeal to large groups of people. In order to assess an international market, companies need to identify the type of economic system in which the national market is classified.

Economic systems

There are generally three types of economic system: capitalist, socialist and mixed economies. This grouping is based on the type of resource allocation: market allocation, central plan allocation or mixed allocation of resources (see Figure 2.3). The role of the state also varies with the type of economic system.

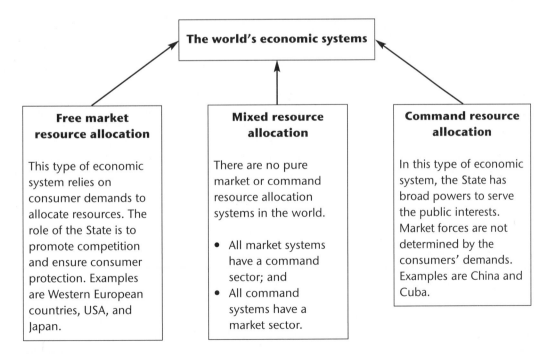

Figure 2.3 The world's economic systems

For example, in a mixed economy (see Figure 2.3), all systems have a combination of a command sector and a market sector. In a market economy, the command allocation sector is the proportion of GDP that is taxed and spent by the government. According to the *Economist* (April 2000), this proportion varies among the 24 member countries of the Organization for Economic Cooperation and Development (OECD) from 32 per cent of GDP in the United States to 64 per cent in Sweden. Thus, in Sweden, where the government controls 64 per cent of all expenditures, the economic system is more 'command' than 'market'. The reverse is true for the United Kingdom.

Stages of market and economic development

Countries in international markets are at different stages of development. Gross national product (GNP) per capita provides a very useful way of grouping these countries. On this basis markets are usually grouped into four categories: high-income countries, upper-middle-income countries, lower-middle-income countries and lower-income countries. Although the income definition for each of the stages is arbitrary, countries in each of the four categories have similar characteristics. As a result, the stages provide a useful basis for international market segmentation and targeting.

The stages of market development based on GNP per capita are usually in line with the stages of economic development. Thus, low and lower-middle-income countries are referred to as less developed countries (LDCs). The upper-middle-income countries are also called industrializing countries, and high-income countries are referred to as advanced, industrialized or post-industrial nations. It is important to remember that the shares of world GNP and the GNP per capita data are based on income in national currency translated into US dollars at year-end exchange rates. They do not reflect the actual purchasing power and standard of living in the different countries.

In practice, some countries are moving up the economic ladder while other countries are stagnating in their economic development. In terms of the country income category movement, the OECD review (*Economist*, 2000) showed that Estonia, Peru and South Africa were moving from the lower-middle to the upper income category.

Another way of looking at changes in economic development is by considering emerging markets. These are markets that have an annual GNP greater than $100 billion, are growing at rates faster than the world average, and are well positioned to move into the next higher income category. International marketers should be aware of the tremendous growth potential that exists in these countries, and develop plans accordingly.

Competitive analysis

A crucial part of the analysis of an overseas market focuses on the level of competition within that market. This can be related to the level of economic development achieved within a country. In general, as an economy develops, its markets become more saturated. This is true, for example, of the market for household insurance which is mature and highly competitive in North America and most Western European countries, but is relatively new and less competitive in many developing economies of the Pacific Rim, allowing better margins to be achieved.

Multinational organizations need to be aware of the economic policies of countries and the direction in which a particular market is developing economically, in order to make an assessment whether they can profitably satisfy market demand and compete with other organizations already in the market. One of the key challenges facing companies trying to develop an integrated marketing strategy across a number of international markets is the divergent level of economic development they have to deal with, making it often very difficult to have a cohesive strategy. For instance, Doole and Lowe (2001, p.15) cited the *Economist* 'Big Mac' Index as a useful illustration of the impact this has on firms. This index, they noted, gives a guide to comparative purchasing power by examining how many minutes somebody needs to work to buy a McDonald's 'Big Mac'.

The level of competitive pressure within a market is also a reflection of government policy on the regulation of monopolies and the ease with which it allows new entrants to enter a market. The government of a country can significantly affect the competitive pressure within a market by legislation aimed at reducing anticompetitive practices. In general, a range of economic factors, which may have an impact on spending power and market behaviour, affect economic conditions. For instance, the Asia Pacific region has enjoyed considerable growth and has remained relatively unaffected by the 1990s worldwide recession (see Dibb 1996). The countries of Asia are expanding trade, investment and technology links among themselves, rather than depending on Europe or the United States as is the case with many African countries.

The cultural environment

An understanding of cultural differences between markets is very important for international marketers. Individuals from different cultures not only buy different products but may also respond in different ways to similar products. Examples of differing cultural attitudes and their effects on international marketing of goods and services include the following:

- Buying processes vary between different cultures. For example, the role of women in selecting a product may differ from market to market, and these differences might call for a different approach to product design and promotion.
- Some categories of goods and services may be rendered obsolete by certain types of social structure. For example, where there is an extended family structure unit, including caring for children and elderly members, there will be less need for care services than when nuclear families are the focus.
- A product that is taken for granted in the domestic market may be seen as socially unacceptable in an overseas market. Frequently encountered examples include pork products in Muslim countries and beef in Hindu countries.
- Attitudes towards promotional programmes differ between cultures. The choice of colours in advertising or sales outlets needs to be made with care because of symbolic associations (for example, the colour associated with bereavement varies between cultures).
- What is deemed to be acceptable activity in procuring sales varies between cultures. In Middle Eastern markets, for example, a bribe to a public official may be considered essential, whereas it is unacceptable in most western countries.

MINI CASE 2.1

Rapid economic growth in Asia

As Chinese reforms take shape, China is experiencing a rapid increase in its economy, with predictions that double-figure growth rates will continue. Since the run-up to the handover of power in Hong Kong, a three-way economic relationship between China, Hong Kong and Taiwan has been emerging. The size of the combined populations of these countries means that this relationship is bound to impact significantly on other trading conditions in the region.

Meanwhile, the Japanese economy has suffered as a result of world recession. Since 1991, Japan has seen a decline in private investment accompanied by a fall in consumption and profits. However, despite these setbacks, Japan remains the second biggest global economy. Here again, the diversity of economic outlook is starkly illustrated.

The economic characteristics of different countries in the region will inevitably affect the business prospects and marketing approach of multinationals operating there. To take an extreme case, consumers in Hong Kong and Singapore have relatively higher spending power than those in Indonesia and China. Not surprisingly, given the economic conditions in these countries, marketing is more sophisticated in Hong Kong and Singapore, where individuals spend a high proportion of their incomes on consumer items. This, in turn, affects the business attractiveness of these countries for international marketers. For example, Hong Kong is attractive because it is highly urbanized and has a relatively large local and tourist population who spend large amounts of income on consumer items. However, the high level of competition that the market attracts usually mediates these positive features. China, on the other hand, has a much less well-developed marketing system and the number of competing firms is relatively low. Despite low incomes and less urbanization, improving economic conditions make this an attractive market too.

The contrasting economic characteristics of China and Hong Kong are self-evident. However, despite striking differences between the two markets, each has a number of positive and negative features that affect how multinational firms develop their marketing effort. Investment in the vibrant Hong Kong has allowed businesses to build turnover and develop strong brands. Similarly, the combination of strong brand image and the firms' financial security is allowing multinational corporations to explore quite different options in China. However, the difference in consumer prosperity in each country means that companies have to modify their location strategy in China to ensure that the most affluent Chinese are reached.

The interaction of culture and consumer behaviour

Figure 2.4 is a model of the mutual influence of culture and consumer behaviour. An individual's behaviour is a result of that individual's cultural value system in a particular context. Individuals' cultural value systems are developed over time as they are socialized into a particular group. Societal culture, regional subculture and familial values all influence the formation of an individual's cultural value system. Thus, the cultural value system includes cultural elements that individuals have in common with the groups(s) to which they belong, as well as idiosyncratic values unique to the individual.

As the model suggests, culture affects consumer behaviour, which itself may reinforce

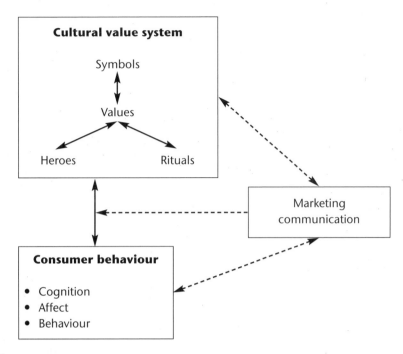

Figure 2.4 A model of the interaction of culture and consumer behaviour
Source: Luna and Gupta (2001).

the manifestations of culture (Peter and Olson 1998). An individual's consumption behaviour may be viewed and imitated or rejected by others. It can then become the group's norm of behaviour and be identified as part of the culture of a given population. International marketers' actions serve as a vehicle to transfer meanings or values from the culturally constituted world to consumer goods, so marketing communications are represented in the model as a moderator of the effect of culture on consumer behaviour. At the same time, marketing communications may also affect a culture's manifestations through advertising (for example, Calvin Klein's ads have reinforced the 'thinness' value in American society).

Of course, as Figure 2.4 shows, marketing communications can affect consumer behaviour independent of culture. When considering this model, it is worth noting that culture may not be seen as a construct apart from and causing behaviour. Luna and Gupta (2001) view culture as inseparable from the individual, as an inherent quality. They depicted culture as causing consumer behaviour in order to develop a framework that managers can easily implement to compare the behaviour of consumers from different cultures and isolate the cultural causes of consumer behaviour differences. Similarly, there are many dimensions to culture, as summarized in Figure 2.5. Some of the great religions of the world, for example, transcend national boundaries and thus contribute to cultural homogeneity among certain nations.

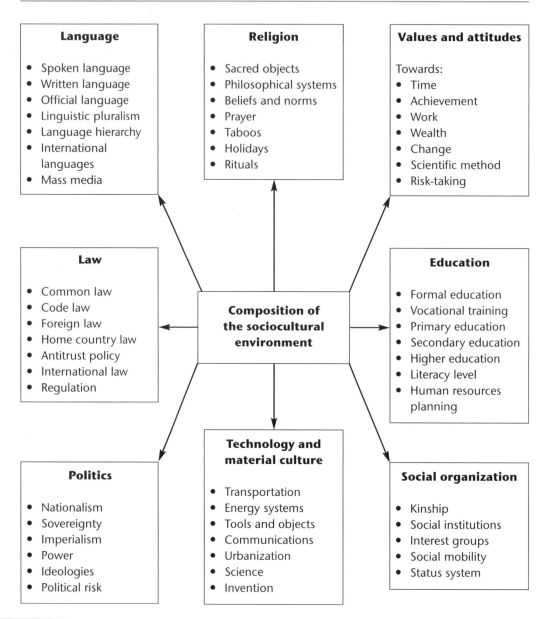

Language

- Spoken language
- Written language
- Official language
- Linguistic pluralism
- Language hierarchy
- International languages
- Mass media

Religion

- Sacred objects
- Philosophical systems
- Beliefs and norms
- Prayer
- Taboos
- Holidays
- Rituals

Values and attitudes

Towards:
- Time
- Achievement
- Work
- Wealth
- Change
- Scientific method
- Risk-taking

Law

- Common law
- Code law
- Foreign law
- Home country law
- Antitrust policy
- International law
- Regulation

Composition of the sociocultural environment

Education

- Formal education
- Vocational training
- Primary education
- Secondary education
- Higher education
- Literacy level
- Human resources planning

Politics

- Nationalism
- Sovereignty
- Imperialism
- Power
- Ideologies
- Political risk

Technology and material culture

- Transportation
- Energy systems
- Tools and objects
- Communications
- Urbanization
- Science
- Invention

Social organization

- Kinship
- Social institutions
- Interest groups
- Social mobility
- Status system

Figure 2.5   Composition of the sociocultural environment
Source: adapted and modified from Albaum, Strandskov and Duerr (2002), p.97.

The impact of religion and language

The impact that cultural factors have on purchasing behaviour is well established (Luna and Gupta 2001). Culture is a complex concept, and international marketers generally agree that culture has an important impact on behaviour. For example, it plays an important role in determining buying patterns (see Peter and Olson 1998). Thus in exploring culture, there are various areas to consider, including religion and language.

Although religion may be a less significant factor in some countries than in others, its role in determining personal values and morals, and the effect it has on consumers' attitudes towards particular products and services, are important. For example, Muslims reject the consumption of alcohol, an important consideration for those trading in Muslim countries such as Saudi Arabia, Indonesia and Malaysia. Other religious groups have particular eating restrictions or may have codes of conduct relating to the purchase and consumption of other types of goods.

Language is often regarded as the biggest potential barrier to the marketing of goods and services in Nigeria. International marketers must take into consideration the wide range of adopted languages and dialects for each national market. For example, it is estimated that there are more than 80 different dialects spoken in Nigeria. But fortunately for organizations operating in Nigeria, many consumers are multilingual, and the acceptance of English as a commercial language is widespread. However in reaching out to consumers, it is important for international marketers to understand that the use of English by itself as a communication medium is not sufficient and may not be appealing. Even in countries such as Nigeria and Ghana where English is used in commerce, dialects including 'pidgin English' are mainly spoken outside working hours. There are also a great number of people (especially the older generations) who do not communicate in English at all. As a result, companies must take care to reflect the language requirements of locals in the application of international marketing mix elements including branding, advertising, promotion and packaging.

Culture does not begin and end with the family, religion and language. In addition to these significant considerations, multinational companies must be aware of many other cultural variations and nuances. For example, for Malaysians the colour green is associated with illness, while the Chinese, Koreans and Japanese avoid everyday clothing that is entirely white or black, as these colours are reserved for mourning and/or weddings. The complex cultural factors at play must be carefully monitored and considered by all businesses involved in international marketing.

The international political environment

At a national level, individual governments may influence market attractiveness in a number of ways:

- At the most general level, the stability of the political system affects the attractiveness of a particular national market. While radical change rarely results from political upheaval in most western countries, the instability of many Eastern European governments leads to uncertainty about the economic and legislative framework in which goods and services will be traded.
- Governments may apply licensing systems in an attempt to protect domestic producers. Licences can be used to restrict individuals from practising a particular profession (for example, the licensing requirements for accountants or solicitors may not recognize experience and licences obtained overseas) or they can be used to restrict foreign owners setting up an overseas operation (for example, the UK government does not allow overseas investors to own more than 25 per cent of the shares in UK scheduled airlines).

- Regulations governing product standards may require an organization to expensively reconfigure its products to meet local regulations, or may prohibit their sale completely.
- Controls can be used to restrict the import of manufactured goods, requiring a company to create a local source of supply, leading to possible problems in maintaining consistent quality standards and also possibly the loss of economies of scale.
- Production possibilities can be influenced by government policies. Minimum wage levels and conditions of service can be important in determining the viability of an overseas operation. For example, many countries restrict the manner in which temporary or seasonal staff can be employed. This could make the operation of a seasonal holiday hotel inflexible and uneconomic.
- Restrictions on currency movements may make it difficult to repatriate profits earned from an overseas operation.
- Governments are major procurers of goods and services, and may formally or informally give preference in awarding contracts to locally owned organizations.
- Legislation protecting trademarks varies between companies. In some countries, such as Greece and Thailand, the owner may find it relatively hard to legally protect itself from imitators.

Companies increasingly look towards free trading agreements between specific countries as a means of gaining access to the largest possible market. Many companies have invested in manufacturing capacity in the United Kingdom not just because of the attractiveness of the UK market, but also because of the access that it will offer to the wider EU market.

Firms recognize that international success is predicated on gaining the right to operate in their chosen markets. Unfortunately, their ability to do so is often hampered by political barriers erected by the host government. While political agreements and arrangements (for example, the World Trade Organization (WTO)) signal increased economic cooperation around the globe, the problems posed by political threats promise to remain a key issue for firms engaged in international operations. In the past, a firm would usually take political issues into consideration in its conventional strategic thinking. However, there is increasing evidence that the firm, through political behaviour, can manipulate this component of the international market environment to its own advantage.

Political behaviours can be defined as the acquisition and application of power to either overcome the resistance of other entities or create a cooperative partnership with those entities. Thus, firm-level political behaviour comprises the core strategy, and specific implementation tactics, employed by the firm for interacting with the various players in the political environment. In such circumstances, political behaviours can be both in response to, or in anticipation of, political threats. The intensity and form of political behaviours engaged in by firms are the result of the threats faced, outside influences, and other conflicting strategic issues.

Political imperatives (barriers to operation)

Political imperatives represent formal political barriers to international trade, which are the result of governments attempting to achieve policy objectives through formal trade impediments. The existence of political imperatives is the result of restrictions placed by governmental decision makers on firms in an attempt to further national policy objectives. Political imperatives in the international market environment generally fall into one of two categories:

- Restrictions on transfers, which might be either foreign or domestic in origin. Such transfer restrictions involve trade barriers, which impede the ability of firms to conduct cross-national marketing activities.
- Ownership and/or control restrictions. These restrictions involve trade barriers that affect an industry or individual firm's decision making and/or revenue distribution.

The existence of political imperatives can affect a firm's international marketing effort in several ways:

- Trade impediments serve as direct barriers to international marketing by inhibiting the ability of firms to conduct trade through mechanisms, such as tariffs, which do not exist in the domestic market environment.
- Another means by which political imperatives can impact marketing strategy is in their influence on the marketing mix. For example, price can be affected by tariffs and other import taxes, product strategy by product content restrictions, distribution by import restrictions, and promotion by sales promotion and advertising regulations.
- A further argument for political imperatives being directly related to international marketing strategy is the effect these barriers have on market segmentation. They determine to a large extent which foreign markets are the most viable, and may represent an effective means by which the international marketplace can be segmented.

The political behaviour of international firms

Firm-level political behaviours are the tactics available to individual firms for managing political imperatives. They take the form of lobbying, public and government relations, public and industry alliances and associations, and a variety of political incentives. These issues are briefly explored to argue out the case for international marketing management implications.

Lobbying

Typically lobbying is considered to be contact targeted at government policy makers and initiated by a firm using a third-party contact. It is the most personal of the tactics, and because of the high levels of specificity it allows, lobbying can also be very precise. One common lobbying technique is to offer assistance to elected officials in their preparation of legislation and policy statements. Frequently, politicians are overwhelmed by the volume of their job responsibilities and the knowledge they require. Individual firms and industry associations have specialized knowledge which is often invaluable to politicians, and it is common for lobbyists to broker contacts between these two groups. Lobbying can also take the form of constituency programmes, where various groups are organized in an attempt to influence policy makers. Lobbying is generally distinguished by its focus on achieving specific political objectives, such as the introduction or withdrawal of proposed legislation, the modification of existing legislation, or the rewriting of legislation in favour of industry, or individual firm, interests.

Public and government relations

Public and government relations differ from lobbying by providing a formal internal mechanism in which the firm can interact with the player in the non-market environment. Where lobbying tends to focus on the accomplishment of a single objective, public and government relations tend to be directed at relational goals. Both of these activities are designed to develop ongoing relationships with various public entities and government decision makers in an effort to increase the likelihood of a favourable market environment in the future.

The focus of public relations is an attempt to ensure that the public at large has an ongoing favourable impression of the firm and its offerings. Government relations activities in contrast are concerned with developing relationships with political decision makers over an extended period of time. Unlike lobbying, these activities are frequently targeted at professional, rather than elected, political decision makers. It is not uncommon for such relational activities to take the form of personal interactions between individuals. The development of such 'friendships' with officials not only has the potential to influence policy making, it also allows the firm to have a wider understanding of the political environment as it relates to firm operations. Along the same lines, association with government-operated intelligence services provides an additional valuable political contact point regarding various issues in the international market environment.

Public and industry alliances

Politically based public and industry alliances or associations are unique in that they represent an effort on the part of the firm to increase its influence by banding together with other organizations that have the same goals. Conceivably, an individual firm may determine that its ability to influence a foreign government is not sufficient to achieve the desired result of reducing, or eliminating, trade barrier(s). However, if it forms an alliance with other firms in the same industry that influence is greatly increased. Such combinations enable individual firms to draw on a wider range of resources, but may reduce firm-specific advantages. Therefore, in the case of gaining market access through reduced trade impediments, alliances and associations are more likely to focus on reducing political imperatives, which are defined as market imperfections resulting from government policies. The elimination of these imperfections may result in a market environment that takes on the characteristics of a 'free' market. Thus, if a firm chooses to engage in political behaviour through an alliance with other parties, whether public or industry, it may achieve a reduction in trade impediments at the expense of any firm-specific strategic advantages.

Political incentives

The final form of firm-level political behaviour is the offering of incentives. These may take the form of overt bribes or other 'gifts' to an individual. Offering these incentives may be an attempt on the part of the firm to actively promote advantages to the targeted political entity by providing increased market access to the firm. In the United States bribery and other forms of gifts in exchange for specific political favours is clearly illegal. At the same time, in many other nations such activities are normal and expected, particularly in the case of a foreign firm desirous of gaining access to a particular market. However, it is equally possible for a firm in a foreign market to offer an incentive that benefits society at large and not just an individual. One of the primary attractions of FDI to many nations is the possibility of obtaining hard currency. An individual firm through direct investment can often achieve a reduction in trade impediments. Individual decision makers can successfully be targeted through a societal incentive approach if the firm can convince these decision makers that their own position will be enhanced when they are identified with obtaining benefits for the society at large.

Political targets

In the international marketplace, political targets are frequently part of the strategic objectives of the firm and related to obtaining legitimacy or market access. Legitimate market access may result in a firm's having the right to operate in a foreign market in the same way as an indigenous firm. This right to operate may be restricted through the application of trade barriers, or more subtly controlled through structural impediments. It has been argued that the key to success for firms engaged in international marketing operations is to gain the same operational rights and privileges as local firms. At the same time, it has been argued that only a very small proportion of international marketing is without some form of impediment being placed on foreign firms (see Keillor, Pettijohn and Bashaw 2000). Its own national laws do not protect the foreign firm in overseas markets, nor is it automatically entitled to the same rights and privileges as local firms under host country laws. Gaining the same operational rights as domestic firms, through the use of political behaviours, becomes a key component in the strategic mix of overall global operations. It is the degree of legitimacy, or market access, enjoyed by a firm that dictates its efficiency and market power and ultimately the firm's level of success in its international marketing operations.

The international legal environment

Legal systems vary in both content and interpretation. A company is not just bound by the laws of its home country but also by those of its host country and the growing body of international law. Firms operating in the European Union are facing an increasing number of directives that affect their markets across Europe. This can affect many aspects of a marketing strategy, for instance advertising in the form of media restrictions and the acceptability of particular creative appeals. Product acceptability in a county can be affected by minor regulations on such things as packaging and by more major changes in legislation. In the United States, for instance, the MG sports car was withdrawn when the increasing difficulty of complying with safety legislation changes made exporting to that market unprofitable.

It is important, therefore, for the firm to know the legal environment in each of its markets. These laws constitute the 'rules of the game' for business activity. The legal environment in international marketing is more complicated than domestic since it has two major dimensions:

- Domestic laws in the home country. The organization's domestic (home market) legal system is important for two reasons. First, there are often export controls which limit the free export of certain goods and services to particular marketplaces, and second, there is the duty of the organization to act and abide by its national laws in all its activities, whether domestic or international.

- International law. The only way to find a route through the legal system in any international market is to use experts on the legal systems and laws pertaining to it. There are a number of international regulations that can affect the organization's activity. Some are international laws covering piracy and hijacking; others are international conventions and agreements. These include International Monetary Fund (IMF) and WTO treaties, patents and trademarks legislation, and harmonization of legal systems within regional economic groupings such as the European Union.

It will be readily understandable how domestic, international and local legal systems can have a major impact upon the organization's ability to market into particular overseas countries. Laws will affect the marketing mix quite dramatically in terms of products, price, distribution and promotional activities. For many firms, the legal challenges they face in international markets, including antitrust issues, are usually barriers preventing the operation of international marketing. Many multinational corporations face ethical challenges in deciding how to deal with differing cultural perceptions of legal practices (see Mini case 2.2).

MINI CASE 2.2

Antitrust and bribery regulations hinder international marketing operations

Antitrust issues relate to potential monopolies and unfair competition in the international market. Thus some international marketers believe that the US antitrust laws, for example, put non-US firms at a disadvantage in the global marketplace. Similarly, bribery is one of the most troublesome issues affecting international marketing because it is freely practised in many countries. Bribes, kickbacks and sometimes even extortion payments are facts of life in many international distribution systems. Bribery has existed to varying degrees in buying and selling worlds. It has various names such as 'mordida', 'dash', 'baksheesh', 'backhander', 'pot de vin' and 'la bustarella' in different parts of the world. Since bribery is still a commonly accepted business practice in many parts of the world, many American and European companies believe that their domestic anti-corruption legislation puts countries at a competitive disadvantage, because companies from other foreign countries without similar legislation are better able to influence decision makers.

Although there is no enforceable body of international law, certain treaties and agreements respected by a number of countries influence international marketing operations. These include the General Agreement on Tariffs and Trade (GATT) and the Friendship, Commerce, and Navigation (FCN) treaty. An FCN agreement defines the rights of firms doing business in the host country. For example, favourable trade relationships exist between Indonesia and the Philippines. Imports of Indonesian products by Philippine companies are well regulated, although there is trade barriers imposed to deter the expansion of trade to an excessive level.

Source: based partly on information produced by Philippine Department of Trade & Industry, 1999.

In many mature markets companies face quite specific, and sometimes burdensome, regulations. In Germany as in all other EU countries, for instance, environmental laws mean a firm is responsible for the retrieval and disposal of the packaging waste it creates and must produce packaging which is recyclable, whereas in many emerging markets there may be limited patent and trademark protection, still evolving judicial systems, non-tariff barriers and instability through an ever-evolving reform programme.

McDonald's sued to try to win the right to use its brand name in South Africa, but the case was dismissed on the grounds that it was already used by several indigenous firms in the fast-food market (Johnson 1996). Some governments are reluctant to develop and enforce laws protecting intellectual property partly because they believe such actions favour large rich multinationals.

Piracy in markets with limited trademark and patent protection is another challenge. Bootlegged software has been estimated to constitute 87 per cent of all personal computer software in use in India, 92 per cent in Thailand and 98 per cent in China, resulting in a loss of US$8 billion for software markers a year.

India has been seen by many firms to be an attractive emerging market beset with many legal difficulties, bureaucratic delay and lots of red tape. Companies such as Mercedes-Benz, Coca-Cola and Kellogg's have found that in spite of the apparent vast potential, India's market is somewhat hard to break into. Its demanding consumers can be difficult to read and local rivals can be surprisingly tough. Political squabbles, bureaucratic delays, infrastructure headaches and unprofessional business practices create one obstacle after another. Foreign companies are often viewed with suspicion, especially with the arrival and increased used of the Internet as a tool for international marketing operations.

International law and the Internet

Internationally, businesses operate within a complex web of national and regional legal systems, further complicated by bilateral and multilateral agreements between countries, such as tax treaties and regional trade agreements (for example, the North American Free Trade Agreement (NAFTA) and the European Union). Businesses may also be subject to regulations promulgated by supranational agencies and treaties, such as the WTO, the World Intellectual Property Organization (WIPO) and the Berne Convention on copyright law. Firms domiciled in the Anglo-Saxon world (mainly the United Kingdom, the United States, Canada, Australia and New Zealand) operate within a familiar, well-established legal framework, based on the precepts of Roman law, English common law, statutes and well-documented judicial interpretation. Elsewhere, however, the legal system can be very different. It might be based on a codified system of law (for example, France, Mexico, Argentina), religious principles (for example, Saudi Arabia, Iran), or the writ of the prevailing political party (for example, China, Vietnam, Cuba). Furthermore, many countries in emerging markets and transitional economies are currently implementing far-reaching reforms of their political and legal systems, creating a legal minefield for the unwary international business person in which even local businesses and legal experts may be unsure about the application and scope of the law.

E-commerce adds a greater level of complexity to the matrix of international business law, raising issues such as what constitutes a contract in cyberspace, international tax harmonization and tax collection for online transactions, intellectual property protection, disparagement and defamation, and consumer protection for international e-commerce clients – including unfair trading practices and the consumer's right to privacy. Then there is the overriding issue of jurisdiction: in the case of a dispute in international e-commerce, is legal jurisdiction in the domicile of the buyer, the seller, neither or both? While these are legitimate issues for governments to resolve, there seems to be a consensus, in the United States at least, that it is too early yet for the government to get involved in regulating e-commerce and that intervention at this stage would be likely to stifle the growth of online transactions (Merrill Lynch 1999).

With the Internet representing the frontier of international marketing, the lack of a unitary regulatory system means that, for the present, international e-commerce faces a somewhat chaotic situation in which multiple and contradictory national laws may apply to the same transaction, leaving the Internet marketer open to the possibility of unintentionally violating the law of a foreign country and being subjected to a lawsuit brought in a foreign jurisdiction. The law governing the dissemination of information, advertising, contracting and intellectual property ownership remains largely nationally based at present, with very little international case law to serve as precedent. However, several universal legal issues associated with operating websites have begun to emerge, including issues of consumer protection and intellectual property violations.

Consumer protection

The laws and regulations that address unfair and deceptive trade practices, such as unsubstantiated advertising claims, false endorsements and omitted information, apply to Internet advertising. There is still no international treaty providing a world-wide law governing advertising and the prevention of unfair and deceptive trade practices. Due to the reach of the Internet, information and advertising claims fall under the scrutiny of the law of many nations. In the United States, for example, the Federal Trade Commission (FTC), which takes offensive action against misleading and deceptive online practices that occur in the country, has largely regulated interstate advertising. But US law certainly does not determine what constitutes unfair Internet practice on a global basis.

Consumer privacy

Most consumers do not realize that when they go browsing on the Internet, they leave behind digital footprints: the operators of website can collect data about the user's identity, address, age, income, interests and online purchases. Some online marketing firms also collect information from census databases, telephone companies, motor vehicle databases, health and education records and credit reports. These online marketing firms sell this detailed information about individual consumers, which it would have been prohibitively expensive to gather by traditional means (*Business Week* 1999).

E-commerce marketers find it essential to gather as much personal information as possible in order to better tailor their marketing to individual consumers and to provide a high quality of service. As international e-commerce grows, the opportunities for gathering data about international customers multiply, but using online technology to gather, exchange and sell personal information about consumers is illegal in many countries.

The European Union gives European consumers the right to check on data that is held about them and to prevent its use (*Economist* 1999). There is also an EU requirement that EU companies do business online only with firms in countries whose governments have introduced regulations to protect data privacy. European privacy laws are generally much stricter than those in the United States, and there are fears that this directive could slow the growth in transatlantic e-commerce (Jacobson 1999). Potentially, this could prevent US marketers from compiling and maintaining any information about European consumers, since the United States has a self-regulatory system of data privacy rather than the government-regulated system that the EU directive requires. In addition, the European Union could insist that US marketers maintain a higher standard of privacy protection than is currently in effect, thus preventing them from collecting or selling personal data without an individual's consent. If other countries adopt regulations similar to those of the European Union, it could make it difficult for US-based marketers to gather and maintain the necessary information to optimize the technological capabilities of the Internet.

Defamation and disparagement

The publication of an untrue statement that damages the reputation of a person, a business, or its products or services may be considered defamation or disparagement (Zugelder, Flacherty and Johnson 2000). Since web marketers are considered 'publishers', such 'online libel' will be judged in the same way as any other mass media advertising medium. Indeed, because of a web page's vast reach, such claims can be more numerous, potentially more dangerous, and lead to a lawsuit in a foreign country.

In many countries throughout the world libel laws tend to favour the plaintiff. Until the UK Defamation Act (1996), London was regarded as the libel capital of the world because of the number of libel cases heard by the High Court. For example, in 1997 McDonald's won a celebrated lawsuit against two self-proclaimed anarchists who had published leaflets defaming the fast-food chain, a case estimated to have cost McDonald's over $15 million to pursue (Vidal 1997; Wikipedia 2008).

While comparative advertising is permitted and even encouraged by US law, in many countries comparative advertising is seen as a form of product disparagement, so that even the mention of a rival firm's product or brand name is unlawful. As web-based international advertising evolves, Internet marketers must be aware that what passes for fair comment and free expression at home might be regarded as illegal elsewhere.

Intellectual property violations

Like any other mass medium, the Internet, and particularly a website, can infringe on the intellectual property rights of others. Since the Internet is worldwide, infringements can occur on a global basis, greatly increasing the likelihood of injury and subsequent suits. There is a plethora of intellectual property violation issues associated with copyright and trademark infringement.

Copyright infringement

Copyright law generally protects the owners of creative works of authorship from the unauthorized copying, reproduction, distribution, dissemination, transmission or other use of any significant part of the work. Any such use without the owner's permission may constitute a copyright infringement. Like the laws governing unfair and deceptive trade practices and disparagement, there is no single international copyright law to comply with. Approximately 80 countries have ratified the Berne Convention on copyright law, which requires all member countries to open their courts for enforcement of all members' copyrights, so that a copyright that is established in one member country can be enforced in another. Berne also aims to raise the level of copyright protection in each member's jurisdiction to that adopted by the convention.

However, half the nations in the world do not belong to or recognize the Berne Convention, and thus may not recognize the validity of the web marketer's copyright. Among the most notorious offenders are China, India, Brazil and Taiwan, where copyright protection ranges from weak to almost nonexistent. This presents a potential problem for the future development of international e-commerce, since these countries represent a potentially huge online market in the next decade. A new treaty promulgated by WIPO, a UN agency based in Geneva, Switzerland, is expected to improve copyright protection in the signatory countries, but although over 160 states are members of WIPO, it is unlikely they will all ratify the treaty. If copyright protection in the non-signatory countries continues to be as haphazard as it is at present, a global treaty on e-commerce copyright is unlikely to be achieved for many years.

Although there is still no universal copyright law or copyright protection, international marketers can rely on one basic legal principle in all countries where copyright is recognized: the use of copyrighted material without permission, whether it be from non-Internet sources (books, dramatic performances, music recordings etc.) or Internet-based sources (website design, text, graphics etc.), constitutes infringement, triggering potential copyright liability somewhere in the world. The fact that websites have received copyright protection surprises many marketers. There is a common presumption that information taken from a website is in the 'public domain', so no infringement can occur. This is clearly not the case. Scanning in and posting text, images, or graphics of another's website, without permission, can certainly constitute copyright infringement. Additional copyright violations can also occur through the common practices of linking and framing.

A central feature of the Internet is its ability to access information linked together through 'hypertext links', whereby the user is transported from one website to another. Most legal commentators have opined that simply linking to another website should not constitute copyright infringement or lead to liability. This is based on the notion that web operators' placement of websites on the Internet gives an 'implied licence' for others wishing to link to their sites. The relative absence of litigation so far suggests that this view is correct. But the practice of 'deep linking' – that is, bypassing a website's home-page and linking directly to its interior pages – is unlawful. As the use of international linking becomes more widespread, firms must be careful about the implications of linking to sites that are not their own.

Framing

Framing occurs when a user links to a second site, and then views the second site's contents framed by the logo and advertising of the first site. Marketers are encouraged to obtain permission, by way of agreements from the owner of the target site, before framing another's website since framing is unlawful. Legal commentators agree that framing is a very dangerous and invasive practice that can support a variety of legal theories of liability, including copyright infringement (Abel 1998; Sovie 1999). For example, it would probably be considered copyright infringement for a US firm to frame a rival's website in order to provide a comparison between its own products and those of the rival. Furthermore, it is likely that the rival could successfully sue for copyright infringement in its home country, increasing the legal and associated costs of the US firm.

Trademark infringement

In the initial creation of websites, an important issue involves the acquisition of a domain name so a company can uniquely identify itself on the Internet. The domain name is a firm's unique identity on the World Wide Web and it also identifies the location of the firm's server (Hartnick 1997). Acquiring a domain name involves registering a primary-level (or 'top-level') domain (a suffix such as .net, .com, .org) along with a secondary-level name (a prefix such as Acme Inc) to yield 'acmeinc.com'. Once domain name registration occurs, no one else can use that name on the Internet. Network Solutions, Inc. (NSI) (http://www.networksolutions.com/) exclusively provided registration services in the .com, .net, and .org domains on a first-come, first-served basis under a 1993 Cooperative Agreement with the US government (ICANN Homepage). However, on 21 April 1999, the Internet Corporation for Assigned Names and Numbers (ICANN) announced five entities selected to participate in the first testing phase of a competitive Shared Registry System for the .com, .net, and .org domains. The five new registrars were America Online, CORE (Internet Council of Registrars), France Telecom, Melbourne IT and register.com.

Since the Internet has grown at such an unprecedented rate, additional second-level and country-level domain names (e.g. '.uk' for United Kingdom) have been added. This was done in order to accommodate the growth in the more than 180 countries that register domain names. Over one-third of these, such as Britain, Mexico, Russia and Venezuela, operate like NSI, whereby a national agency registers a domain name on a first-come, first-served basis. This implies that company names, brand names and product images may be put at risk if a company does not register them as domain names in each country in which it wants to be recognized.

Technological developments

An analysis of the technological environment of an overseas market is important for organizations that require the use of a well-developed technical infrastructure and a work force that is able to use technology. Communications are an important element of the technological infrastructure; poorly developed telephone and postal communications may inhibit attempts to make credit cards widely available, for instance.

One of the powerful forces in the international marketing environment that requires organizations to rethink their marketing models is technology. The velocity of change in the technology world is tremendous. Changes in communications, manufacturing, retailing, material sciences and telecommunications technologies are allowing multinational organizations to question some very basic assumptions about their international business operations.

As Prabhaker (1997) observed, technologies develop in response to the pressure to lower manufacturing and distribution costs, typically enable companies to achieve lower costs and the same levels of customer satisfaction. The competitive advantage enabled by such technologies usually results in improved corporate performance and possible increased market share if prices are reduced. The limits of this sort of improvement are the scale–scope trade-offs dictated by the market and the diminishing marginal returns to both scale and traditional production technology (see Prabhaker, Sheehan and Coppett 1997).

Information technology

Information-based technologies, such as flexible manufacturing, retailing and distribution, developed in response to the pressure to meet the needs of customers, enabling companies to achieve higher levels of customer satisfaction by lessening the relevance of scale–scope trade-offs. Thus the improvement in international marketing performance enabled by these newer technologies is not subject to diminishing marginal returns.

There is significant evidence in the marketing literature that technological capabilities developed in response to market needs have far superior effects on a firm's market performance to those developed as a result of improved engineering capabilities. A good example here is the Panasonic Bicycle custom ordering system. The technology that makes this one-at-a-time, fit-to-your-body, reasonably priced product is not especially complex. It resulted in a near monopoly on custom-fit bikes for Panasonic. The profitability of Panasonic's custom bike business, although small in volume, is far superior to the high-volume standard bike operations at the same factory.

Technology advances

Technology advances, especially in digital electronics and electronic commerce, have revolutionized business processes and practices (Sheth and Parvatiyar 2001). The computerization of people, machinery and physical facilities has literally reshaped the traditional economic concepts of scale, scope and structure. Similarly, the use of telecommunications and information technologies has reduced the time and place barriers of doing business. It is no exaggeration to suggest that the traditional marketing theories based on location (for example, the law of retail gravitation, wheel of retailing, inventory management, logistics and physical distribution) may need to be redefined when customers and suppliers could do business at anytime and anywhere. For example, the emergence of the Internet has revolutionized the way we provide information, communication and transactions. It is resulting in disintermediation and reintermediation on a global basis (Sheth and Sisodia 1998). The Internet is fostering global marketing by allowing businesses to connect on a real time basis from anywhere and everywhere in the world. Time zone differences do not matter when connectivity is universal and continuously available.

The era of digital electronics is also fundamentally changing global market expansion strategies. In the digital world, product life cycles get considerably shortened, and research and development (R&D) costs mount. Marketers must therefore recover their development costs as soon as possible. They do not have the same luxury provided by electro-mechanical technology, wherein new products and technology could be introduced one country at a time, saturating the most developed markets first, then entering the next most developed market, and so on. Today marketers have no choice but to intro-duce products almost concurrently all over the world to ensure that they reach as large a market as soon as possible, before their product and technology become obsolete. Market penetration, and not market skimming, has become the prevailing strategy in global marketing of technological products.

Scanning for international marketing opportunities

The rise of international marketing as a viable strategic option requires a synthesis of what we know about international marketing and strategy. The role and importance of external environments and marketing research in formulating international marketing decisions and strategies are very specific in marketing management. In addition, a review of the strategy literature reveals that strategy formulation is influenced by the external environment, industry, and internal organizational variables. These variables need to be monitored and forecasted so that strategies can be developed that are appropriate given a set of environmental conditions.

As more firms continue to market across national boundaries, a key area of interest is environmental scanning. Scanning is critically important since it provides informa-tional inputs for the development of strategies and specific market-based decisions. This is particularly true for those firms increasingly operating in more diverse business environments such as international markets.

The purpose of this section is therefore to evaluate the importance of competitive envi-ronmental scanning activities for international marketing decision making. It identifies various dimensions of competitive environmental scanning, and then examines the status of these scanning activities for firms with different levels of international marketing involvement. Environmental scanning can be defined as the process of collecting infor-mation about the events and relationships in a company's outside environment, the knowledge of which will assist top management in its task of charting the company's future course of action. The increase in strategic uncertainty means that both the general environment and the task environment must be scanned.

Environmental analysis is a key step in the strategy formulation process. Environmental analysis has become even more critical as the environment has become more turbulent and as the rate of environmental change has accelerated. Successful firms are those that are sensitive to changes in international events and forces. As the environ-ment becomes more turbulent, firms have had to increase their ability to scan the environment to gather information that can be used to anticipate or respond to environmental changes.

Competitive environmental scanning

There seems to be a positive relationship between scanning and performance. Success-ful firms also differ from unsuccessful firms in that successful firms tended to do more scanning and have a broader pattern of scanning. For firms operating in numerous international markets, the need for superior environmental scanning capabilities is becoming critically important for success, as the level of uncertainty and complexity in their multiple and geographically dispersed operating environments rises. Despite the increasing uncertainty, many MNCs have formal in-house scanning capabilities. Moreover, the pattern and categories of environmental scanning may vary widely among firms operating in international markets.

Several macroenvironmental sectors need to be monitored, including the economic, technological, governmental, social, competitor and customer area. These areas may create different levels of strategic uncertainty for managers, with the customer, competitor and economic sectors having the highest levels of uncertainty. An important consideration for firms that are early in the international marketing process is monitoring government programmes at the national, state and local level that support international marketing efforts. Government programmes are usually important in developing awareness of opportunities, planning and organizational capabilities, and can provide cost-sharing opportunities. More specifically, firms may need assistance with logistics-related problems, legal procedures, and in developing foreign market intelligence. Various types of promotion programmes have been developed to meet these needs, and are available through public organizations to the business community. In spite of the availability, most small firms do not seem to use government programmes. There are many explanations for this, including the fact that small firms tend to have generally underdeveloped environmental scanning capabilities.

Three categories of environmental scanning systems can be identified:

- Irregular – systems respond to a crisis in the environment and tend to be short-term oriented.
- Regular –models periodically assess the environment.
- Continuous – models constantly assess the environment and gather data that will be used as an input for strategic decisions.

As firms evolve in size and complexity there tends to be an increased need for information and more sophisticated scanning systems. Similarly, managerial intuition may play an important role in scanning and subsequent decision-making processes, and simple data-gathering techniques, such as consultation with outsiders, may be appropriate for managers.

International marketing involvement

There is an important relationship between a firm's international market involvement and its international marketing behaviour and strategy. International market involvement is the extent to which a company is dependent on international marketing activities for its business. The ability and resource commitment to scan the environment may be important in the decisions regarding international marketing involvement. As companies expand and grow they are more likely to have a systematic scanning process and become increasingly aware of international opportunities.

The classification of international markets

One natural method of thinking of the markets of the world is in terms of their geographical location and groupings. Thus, some of the main market groups of the world could be distinguished as Western Europe, Eastern Europe, North America, Central America, South America, Africa, the Middle East, the Far East and Australasia. This geographical classification is useful because markets which have similar climatic conditions may be potential markets for goods related to those conditions, such as surfboards, fur-lined boots and air-conditioning equipment.

In most cases, geographical characteristics often continue across political boundaries and thus form natural market groups in certain parts of the world. For example, air-conditioning equipment sold in West Africa could also be sold in the Middle East. Skiing equipment in North America would be sold in the markets defined by the Rocky Mountains, which run north and south in the west of the United States and Canada, rather than in any political defined area.

Economic classification

It is necessary to realize that classifying markets by size of population does not show the value of that population as a potential market for the international marketer. It is therefore necessary to classify markets by spending power. The spending power of a market is largely related to the stage of economic development of the market, and to how much business and industrial activity there is in that market. Using economic development criteria, countries of the world can be classified in five groups according to their stages of economic development:

- subsistence economies
- less developed economies (LDCs)
- emerging economies
- industrialized economies
- high-technology economies.

These variations in the stage of economic development and industrial structure have a large effect on national income. These factors also affect the types of goods and services that the market is likely to need, and also the ability to buy. As a result of varying economic conditions, levels of economic development and GNP per capita, it is important that the international marketer has an understanding of economic developments and how they impinge on marketing strategy. This understanding is important at both international and national levels for better international marketing management.

Subsistence economies

These are probably the poorest countries of the world, and are those that can barely feed themselves, or at least barely feed the majority of the population. These are the countries without any oil or exportable raw materials, and without any significant industry. This group includes the countries with GNP per capita of less than $200 a year. This group includes many of the smaller African and Central American countries. The composition of the group will always change as the standard of living rises in some countries and falls in others. These countries therefore represent very poor market opportunities. However, the market potential must be watched, as these countries are frequently recipients of aid from the richer countries. The aid often creates marketing opportunities for capital goods, infrastructure projects and agricultural machinery.

LDCs

This group includes underdeveloped countries and developing countries. The main features are a low GDP per capita, a limited amount of manufacturing activity and a very poor and fragmented infrastructure. Typical infrastructure weaknesses are in transport, communications, education and healthcare. In addition, the public sector is often slow-moving and bureaucratic.

It is common to find that LDCs are heavily reliant on one product and often on one trading partner. Of 28 LDCs seven receive over half and nine receive between 25 per cent of their export earnings from their main export commodity. In addition, three-quarters of LDCs depend on their main trading partner for more than one-quarter of their export revenue. The risks posed to the LDC by changing patterns of supply and demand are great. Falling commodity prices can result in large decreases in earnings for the whole country. The resultant economic and political adjustments may affect exporters to that country through possible changes in tariff and non-tariff barriers, changes in the level of company taxation and restrictions on the convertibility of currency and the repatriation of profits. In addition, substantial decreases in market size within the country are probable.

The typical pattern for single-product dependence is reliance on one agricultural crop or on mining. Colombia (coffee), Cuba (sugar), Ghana (cocoa), Mali (cotton), Rwanda (coffee) and Somalia (live animals) are examples of extreme dependence upon agriculture. Gabon (oil), Jamaica (base metal ores), Mauritania (iron ore), Niger (uranium and thorium ores) and Nigeria (oil) are examples of reliance on the extraction of minerals.

A wide range of economic circumstances influence the development of LDCs. Some countries are small with few natural resources. For these countries it is difficult to start the process of substantial economic growth. Poor health and education standards need money on a large scale, yet the pay-off in terms of a healthier, better-educated population takes time to achieve. At the same time, there are demands for public expenditure on transport systems, communication systems and water control systems. Without real prospects for rapid economic development, private sources of capital are reluctant to invest in such countries. This is particularly the case for long-term infrastructure projects, and as a result, important capital spending projects rely heavily on world aid programmes.

The emerging economies

In countries such as China, Brazil, Vietnam and India there is a huge and growing demand for everything from automobiles to cellphones. Many of these countries, which were seen only a few years ago as LDCs, have shown considerable economic advancement. For example, Indonesia, China, Mexico, Brazil, Chile, Hungary, Poland, Turkey, the Czech Republic and South Africa are all viewed as key growth markets.

In these emerging markets, there is an evolving pattern of government-directed economic reforms, lowering of restrictions on foreign investment and increasing privatization of state-owned monopolies. These factors tend to be an indication of significant opportunities for international marketing firms. Such markets often have what is termed as a 'dual economy'. Usually there tends to be a wealthy urban professional class alongside a poorer rural population. From negligible numbers a few years ago, China now has a middle class of 82 million, which is forecast to grow to 500 million in the next century. Brazil and Indonesia have middle classes of 15 million each. High economic growth is often accompanied by high inflation. Countries such as Poland, Brazil, Mexico and China have all recently suffered from high rates of inflation. Tied to an inflationary environment are generally high levels of external debt. The total external debt of LDCs exceeds US$1 trillion. As countries have to prioritize the servicing of external debt, it invariably leaves little availability of hard currency to buy imported products.

Industrialized economies

These are the countries that have been industrialized for some time and have developed a wide range of industries, and are consequently exporters and importers of manufactured goods. The industrialized countries have highly developed industries, which are interrelated and develop their own specialities. These countries represent great market opportunities for international marketing (see also Fahey 2002).

Many manufacturers from these countries that develop special skills can find markets all over the world where those skills are appreciated and wanted. So the industrialized countries trade more with other industrialized countries, and as the technology and skill content of their products gets higher, so the proportion of the product represented by the cost of raw materials get lower. The volume of raw materials required from the countries of origin does not rise in proportion to the increased value of the end product. The consequence of this is that, although the volume of trade between the industrialized countries continues to rise, the trade of the less well-developed countries does not benefit to the same extent.

High-technology economies

The economic classification of markets has traditionally recognized those groups from the subsistence economies to the industrialized economies, but now at the developed end of the scale a new type of economy is beginning to emerge – the high-technology economy. The most successful industrialized economies have always enjoyed a standard of living ahead of most other countries. Two of the symbols of success have been the creation of capital and the development of educational and research organizations. This has resulted in the concentration of high technology in the countries with the most successful economies, and one of the aspects of high-technology industry is that it requires very high capital expenditure to develop it.

The manufacture of for example computers, microprocessors, space vehicles, medical electronics and sophisticated armaments is tending to be concentrated in those countries that have achieved considerable success with their industrial marketing and have generated large amounts of capital and high-technology expertise necessary to develop these new high-technology industries. These countries are the few high-technology economies that are moving ahead of the main body of industrialized economies.

Finally and in conclusion, the triad economies of NAFTA countries, the European Union and Japan account for 80 per cent of world trade. For many firms this constitutes much of what is termed the international (global) market. It is from this triangle that global consumers with similar lifestyles, needs and desires emanate. However emerging markets are now becoming more economically powerful and moving up the ranks so that in the near future China, South Korea and Taiwan will be among the top tier of national economies.

Summary

International marketing involves operation across a number of countries between which the influences of macroenvironmental forces differ significantly. Similarly, controllable factors such as cost elements, marketing overheads and price structure vary significantly between markets. Opportunities for integrated communications, distributive infrastructure and product presentation format are also likely to differ significantly. It is these differences and variations in both macro and microenvironmental forces that create complexities in international marketing operation.

The key to successful international marketing is the marketer's ability to understand and identify the complexities of each element and reconcile them for better marketing, planning and management. Although there are several environmental analysis models that could be used in evaluating international market, this chapter used the social, legal, economic, political and technological (SLEPT) approach. It then examined the various aspects of these macroenvironmental factors in relation to their effects on international marketing operations. In order to operate efficiently, markets are also classified by regional location and economic development to enable the assessment of various factors in each market.

The overall observation of the chapter is that changes in macroenvironments are taking place as the political structures are also changing. Major trading blocs and strategic alliances between nations are being formed, taking advantage of rapid development in technological innovations. Similarly, many countries are undergoing changes and consumers are becoming more demanding throughout the world. The implications of these changes are significant for international marketing management, but it is this challenge that international marketers must learn to face and tackle.

Revision questions

1 Discuss why it is important for an international marketing manager to have a good knowledge and awareness of the complexities of the international marketing environment.
2 International markets are continually fragmenting and companies are facing the task of consolidating them. Explain when in your opinion international markets may be consolidated.
3 The general accepted measure of the economic attractiveness of an overseas market is the level of GDP per capita. Thus the demand for most products increases as this figure increases. Discuss.
4 Evaluate why in your opinion an understanding of cultural differences between markets is very important for international marketers.
5 Discuss how at a national level individual governments can influence market attractiveness.
6 Why is it necessary for the firm to know the legal environment in each international market?
7 The arrival of e-commerce adds a greater level of complexity to the matrix of international law. Explain.

8   Environmental scanning is a necessary requirement for the assessment of international market opportunities. Explain why this process is important.

9   What do you understand by a 'single-product dependent' country?

10 Describe how international markets can be classified on an economic basis. Explain how the manufacturer of air-conditioning equipment could benefit from such economic classification.

SEMINAR CASE STUDY

The international marketing environment: a focus on brands in the grey market

Parallel importation – the selling of branded products through unauthorized distribution channels – can erode brand image, strain channel relationships and disrupt international marketing planning efforts. The selling of genuine brands through unauthorized international distribution channels, leads to the development of grey markets. Grey markets typically develop when the trademarked item (a brand) is being sold for substantial price differences between markets or market shortages arise.

Grey market goods are neither copies nor counterfeit goods; rather, they are genuine trademarked items, imported legally into the country (see Clarke and Owens 2000). Since brand (trademark) assignments typically give the assignee distribution rights in a particular market, problems arise, as the grey market good is a foreign-manufactured good, with a valid brand name, that is imported without the consent of the domestic brand owner. Trying to prevent grey market items from appearing by legal means is problematic since the goods are genuine. The domestic brand owner must therefore compete against an unofficial distributor of the foreign produced brand inside its own domestic market. The issue is therefore not one of product legality, but one of the legality of the means of distribution.

In the United Kingdom and elsewhere in Europe competition is rife. This is nowhere more so than in the field of branded goods, where companies continually look for bigger slices of corporate profit. Companies with highly visible brands have the opportunity for those bigger shares to become a reality. But success comes at a high price, with continual threats from competitors. Some of the latest dangers to the corporate brand owners come from those retailers developing their own branded ranges of products. Some such retailers have packaged and presented these goods in similar sounding and looking fashion to the prevailing market leaders. This 'piggyback' approach has been much to the annoyance of the brand proprietors. It has tended to encourage bitter spurts of litigation to restore the status of the brand ownership rights. In addition, other threats are posed from the grey market, where parallel brand imports are sold at discount prices, further antagonizing the original trademark owners. Coincidentally, much of this activity seems to take place in the highly successful UK supermarkets, where controversy has arisen as a result. For example in 2001 Tesco, the UK leading grocery retailer, vowed to continue its grey market campaign despite losing a battle in the European Court of Justice for the right to sell cut-price Levi's jeans. Other UK supermarkets followed Tesco's example in selling cut-price grey market goods. Rival chain Safeway at one point had 120,000 pairs of Levi's jeans in its stores, while Asda was selling £25 million worth of grey market goods (see *Retail Week*, November 23, 2001, p. 3 and 11).

According to Clarke and Owens (2000), 'trade in the "discounted brand market" has been more traditionally associated with archetypal "Del Boy" characters who wheel and deal, but make a run for it at the first sight of trouble, often leaving customers to their own devices'.

Such behaviour was often linked with counterfeit goods and could never be classified as in the public interest. In contrast, the modernized grey market deals predominantly with genuine branded goods from the manufacturer, often from outside the United Kingdom or the European Community, and often at reduced cost. These reduced costs are passed on to the consumer, who enjoys the benefits from increased competition, which is the backbone of the barrier-free EU Single Market. Such activity clearly has an appeal for the public as a whole. Nowadays the grey market is big business, and the major brand owners have started to flex their corporate muscle in an attempt to preserve the exclusivity of their brands.

Essentially the emergence of the grey market was a response to these big boys' antics, with 'entrepreneurs' realizing that an exploitable market existed for discounted brands sold other than at the recognized outlets. But no longer was it the individual market trader or odd retail outlet. Instead powerful retailers such as Tesco, Asda and other leading supermarkets had cottoned on to the positive benefits associated with stocking price-discounted 'right-on brands' such as Levi's, Calvin Klein and Nike. The reason that such supermarket chains used the grey market route was often the unwillingness of the brand manufacturer to supply directly to the supermarket shelves. Understandably, the likes of Calvin Klein did not wish their exclusive and expensive designer clothing to be sold next to the Tesco own brand of baked beans.

Such reluctance was reflected in the frustration of supermarkets, which argued that customers wanted a range of branded goods, but because of selective distribution and the spurious criteria brand manufacturers laid down, they were unable to get supplies. As a result, all the supermarket giants, despite their bargaining power, found it easier to engage the sources of the grey market, and in turn managed to pass on savings direct to the consumer. But this behaviour did not go unnoticed and bitter disputes arose. On the one side, there were the brand owners, who alleged the grey market served to dilute the profitability and exclusivity of their property. The brand owners' argument for higher prices was that they needed to charge more to support retail advertising, research and build the brand mystique. On the other side were the brand importers and discount retailers who argued for greater customer choice and satisfaction.

While all these are going on, the European Commission and European Parliament sat on the fence. Meanwhile, as a result of the decision by the European Court of Justice in the Tesco vs Levi's case, retailers will need to live in a prohibitive world for the foreseeable future. High-profile cases concerning the grey market activities did not just occur in supermarkets, they also extended to sportswear outlets and motorcycle showrooms.

One associated development of the grey market boom was brand holders publicizing various accusations and writs aimed at the supermarkets. The complaints all concerned the merchandising of pirated goods – goods that illegally bore the marks of famous brands. In 1998 the Tommy Hilfiger Corporation issued proceedings against Tesco Stores Ltd on the basis of alleged counterfeit goods discovered amongst Tesco's Tommy Hilfiger products (see *Financial Times*, 29 May 1998). Of course, both sides claimed that the other was using underhand tactics for corporate gain, but in the end the claims often proved unfounded. However, these events may represent a shift for the future. It is unlikely that over the longer term outlets such as Tesco will continue to actively undercut the prices of these designer goods. Already these companies have been developing their own clothing labels to take over from the alternative niches that have developed through the use of the high-profile brands. For instance, Asda hoped that its 'George' label would become synonymous with value clothing.

In the meantime retailers are likely to continue attracting right-on consumers for the right-on brands, at least until the effects of changes in the law filter through to the practical operations of the marketplace. However, the situation is far from straightforward, with the supermarkets facing a number of obstacles. One particular problem concerns the relatively restrictive regulations with regard to planning permission. Certainly in comparison to their EU counterparts, retailers such as Asda and Tesco may face difficult battles to extend existing floor space. In Europe, the more spacious hypermarkets are able to stock a wider variety and range of their own and others' branded goods. However, the ongoing advancements of various information technologies may ensure that restricted floor space can be used more efficiently. Consequently stock can be more accurately ordered and turned over, allowing opportunities for other goods to be on display, such as designer perfumes and clothing.

In general, the brand owners are far from happy. But despite their outrage, they have found themselves walking on thin ice, with the grey market turning white in the wash following support from consumer associations and the various national governments. Various consumer affairs ministers have voiced their support for reductions in prices for the consumer, and one way of achieving this has been to undermine the selective strategies of the premium brands.

Finally, the grey market constitutes a large portion of consumer and industrial sales throughout the world. Grey markets are significant as they now exceed $10 billion per year in North America and affect almost every major branded product. In Europe, grey markets have grown at more than 22 per cent annually and further growth is expected as export operations increase. The loss of control associated with grey markets can only be regained through an aggressive deterrent strategy. The international marketer must develop methods for protecting against this ever-increasing, most direct form of competition.

Sources: Clarke and Owens (2000), Elsmore (2000), *Guardian* (1998).

Case study seminar questions

1 In the light of what your have read from this seminar case study and your knowledge of the international marketing environment, if you were employed as a marketing manager by one of the brand owners facing grey market threats, discuss what action you would recommend in order to eliminate grey market threats.
2 From the standpoint of consumers, the argument that brand owners need to charge high prices to support their advertising, research and other distribution overheads is nonsense. What do you think European Parliament could do to reduce the prices charged by brand owners for the 380 million consumers across Europe?
3 Most major UK retailers have vowed to continue grey market campaigns in spite of the decision by the European Court of Justice to support Levi's in lawsuit against Tesco. What options would you recommend British retailers to now follow?

Managerial assignment task

You have been employed by one of the UK's leading food retailers as an environmental scanning officer, responsible for evaluating and analysing international market opportunities and threats for the organization. Your organization currently operates stores in many countries of Europe, North America and Asia but has never considered African countries as variable international retail markets for its products. This is despite the reported shortage of food products in many parts of Africa year after year. However, during the last board meeting, one of the directors suggested that the organization should try out South Africa as an initial attempt to expand to Africa. Your organization now wishes to expand its food retail operations to South Africa in the next two years to beat other European competitors thinking along similar lines.

Write a report to your Board of Directors explaining some of the numerous factors you think your organization should consider in making the decision whether to expand to South Africa. Your report should identify clearly those factors that represent opportunities and those that pose threats, and should not be longer than 2,500 words.

References

Abel, S. M. (1998) 'Trademarks issues in cyberspace: the brave new frontier' [online] http://www.fenwick.com/pub/trademark-issues-in-cyberspace.htm (accessed 20 October 1998).

Albaum, G., Strandskov, J. and Duerr, E. (2002) *International Marketing and Export Management*, 4th edn, London: Financial Times/Prentice Hall.

Babbar, S. and Rai, A. (1993), 'Competitive intelligence for international business', *Long Range Planning*, Vol. 26, No. 3, pp. 103–13.

Boddewyn, J. J. and Brewer, T. L. (1994) 'International business political behaviour: new theoretical directions', *Academy of Management Review*, Vol. 19, pp. 119–43.

Business Week (1999) 'Privacy', Special Report, 15 April, pp. 84–90.

Clarke, I. and Owens, M. (2000) 'Trademark rights in grey markets', *International Marketing Review*, Vol. 17, No. 3, pp. 272–86.

Dibb, S. (1996) 'The impact of the changing marketing environment in the Pacific Rim: four case studies', *International Journal of Retail and Distribution Management*, Vol. 24, No. 11, pp. 16–29.

Doole, I. and Lowe, R. (2001) *International Marketing Strategy: Analysis, Development and Implementation*, 3rd edn, London: Thomas Learning.

Economist (1999) 'Direct hit', 9 January [online] http://www.economist.com/archive (accessed 29 October 2004).

Economist (2000) 'OECD Review: predicting the evolution and effects of the Asia crisis from the OECD perspective', *Economist*, 6 April [online] http://www.oecd.org/eco/eco (accessed on 20 June 2003).

Elsmore, M. J. (2000) 'The implication of intellectual property law for the auditing and protection of national and international brands: part 2, brands in the grey market', *Managerial Auditing Journal*, Vol. 15, No. 4, pp. 169–81.

Fahey, J. (2002) 'A resource-based analysis of sustainable competitive advantage in a global environment', *International Business Review*, Vol. 11, pp. 57–78.

Guardian (1998) 'Sainsbury withdraws "fake" Nike sportswear', 28 August.

Hartnick, A. J. (1997) 'Copyright and trademark on the Internet – and where to sue', *New York Law Journal*, 21 February [online] http://www.ljx.com/internet/0221intip3.html (accessed 29 October 2004).

Jacobson, L. (1999) 'The transatlantic tiff over privacy', *National Journal*, Vol. 31, No. 6, p. 348.

Johnson Publishing (1996) 'McDonald's wins trademark battle in South Africa' [online] http://www.mcspotlight.org/media/press/jet_23sep96.html (accessed 10 July 2008).

Keegan, W. J. (2002) *Global Marketing Management*, 7th edn, Upper Saddle River, N.J.: Prentice Hall International.

Keegan, W. J. and Green, M. S. (2000) *Global Marketing*, 2nd edn, Upper Saddle River, N.J.: Prentice-Hall.

Keillor, B. D., Pettijohn, C. E. and Bashaw, R. E. (2000) 'Political activities in the global industrial marketplace', *Industrial Marketing Management*, Vol. 29, pp. 613–22.

Kotler, P. (2006) *Marketing Management: Analysis, Planning, Implementation and Control*, 12th edn, New Jersey: Prentice-Hall/ Pearson.

Luna, D. and Gupta, S. F. (2001) 'An integrative framework for cross-cultural consumer behaviour',

International Marketing Review, Vol. 18, No. 1, pp. 45–69.

Merrill Lynch (1999) 'E-commerce: virtually here' [online] http://e-commerce.research.ml.com), 23 April.

Peter, J. P. and Olson, J. C. (1998) *Consumer Behaviour and Marketing Strategy*, Boston, Mass.: McGraw-Hill.

Prabhaker, P. (1997) 'Integrated marketing-manufacturing strategies', *Marketing Intelligence and Planning*, Vol. 15, No. 2, pp. 54–9.

Prabhaker, P., Sheehan, M. and Coppett, J. (1997) 'The power of technology in business selling', *Journal of Business and Industrial Marketing*, Vol. 12, Nos 3/4, pp. 220–31.

Sheth, J. N. and Parvatiyar, A. (2001) 'The antecedents and consequences of integrated global marketing', *International Marketing Review*, Vol. 18, No. 1, pp. 16–29.

Sheth, J. N. and Sisodia, R. S. (1998) 'Revisiting marketing's law-like generalizations', *Journal of the Academy of Marketing Science*, Vol. 29, Fall.

Sovie, D. (1999) 'Copyright entanglements on the Net', *IP Magazine* [online] http://www.iipmag.com/monthly/99-feb/sovie.html (accessed 29 October 2004).

Vidal, J. (1997) *McLibel: Burger Culture on Trial*, Basingstoke: Macmillan.

Wikipedia (2008) 'McDonald's Restaurants v Morris & Steel' [online] http://en.wikipedia.org/wiki/McLibel_case (accessed 10 July 2008).

Zugelder, M. T., Flacherty, T. B. and Johnson, J. P. (2000) 'Legal issues associated with international Internet marketing', *International Marketing Review*, Vol. 17, No. 3, pp. 253–71.

3

The International Marketing Information and Research Process

Contents

Introduction

The first section of this chapter looks at the role of information technology (IT). It shows that there is widespread acceptance that IT is a central component of international marketing operations. Aligned to this is the belief that international marketing is experiencing radical and dynamic changes, many of which are IT driven. International marketing is therefore heavily influenced by IT, and marketers who do not adapt to this new technological era will not survive. The benefits of IT to international marketing must centre on successful IT management, changes in processes, the use of unfamiliar and challenging IT, and creative innovative strategies to cope with this different and dynamic market. However it should be noted that there are limits to what IT can do without the benefit of good international marketing management. IT-based systems cannot work miracles. They will not offset a poorly conceived or poorly executed international marketing strategy, compensate for an inferior sales force, sell inferior products or deliver benefits in these circumstances. What is needed is a transformation in international marketing activities to harness the opportunities from IT. Ultimately with IT the wisdom of its use depends on the wisdom of the user.

The second part of the chapter deals with international marketing research, and observes that the conduct of international marketing research is much more complex than domestic marketing research. This section reviews the viability of international marketing programmes, noting that the research design appropriate for one country may not be suitable in another because of environmental differences. The suggestion in the chapter is that researchers must isolate and examine the impact of the self-reference criterion (SRC), or the unconscious reference to their own cultural values. before defining the problem.

International marketing information systems

The collection of primary and secondary information is not just a marketing issue, it is also an organizational one. The function of the marketing information system (MIS) is to systematically provide information resources to the company to evaluate the markets it wishes to enter. In other words, it must provide information for effective decision making. It should be a cost-effective resource base. The MIS should contain detailed information, provide a solid platform for the company to assess the degree of its competitive advantage in the global marketplace, and enable cross-country comparisons and the identification of threats and opportunities so that the firm can design appropriate marketing strategies. In addition, an MIS should keep management abreast on a daily basis of international markets, competition, countries and products. In sum, the MIS should provide the company with cost-effective, timely and relevant information.

One of the implications of the information explosion in the global marketplace is that knowledge and information are being perceived as assets in their own right. With respect to the marketing process, the role of information is changing from a support tool to a strategic asset that can generate wealth. One effect of this reconstituted role of information is that some organizations have restructured so that they have 'flatter', less hierarchical and less centralized decision-making structures. Such organizational structures are supposed to facilitate the flow and exchange of information between different departments. The more information-intensive the company, the greater marketing's role will be in other functional areas of the company.

The basis for competitive advantage will therefore lie no longer in the product itself, but in the relationships that the company cultivates with its consumers, markets and suppliers. The implication of this assumption is that market intelligence has a key role to play in these relationships, and is thus an important strategic asset for the company. Information is a crucial strategic resource. Information and its management are even more important in the international setting, where entirely new parameters and environments are encountered.

The marketing literature continues to highlight the links between international information, competitiveness and corporate success. For example, a lack of information is probably the major deterrent to international market participation by small and medium-sized firms. Some see management's willingness to gather information as crucial for international marketing success (Czinkota 2000). Multinational companies can expect to remain competitive in the international marketplace only if they are aware of crucial macro and micro information from around the world. International market learning may be the only source of sustainable competitive advantage.

It is likely that most international marketing errors could have been avoided if the firm and its managers had obtained adequate market information first. Thus, for a company to be a world-class organization it needs world-class information. On the overall point of the importance of information, Bill Gates, chairman of Microsoft, raises the stakes even higher when he argues, 'How you gather, manage and use information will determine whether you win or lose' (1999: 3).

Managers understand that international marketing information gathering is crucial to the success of their enterprise. The rapid growth of international activities by the leading business research organizations provides clear evidence of the corporate awareness of and desire for information on an international basis. Three key dimensions of international marketing information and knowledge can be identified:

- Information and knowledge are useful for learning and progress.
- Information and knowledge can emanate from multiple worldwide sources.
- Information and knowledge, when shared, become more valuable.

Overall knowledge is precious, and it becomes even more precious when shared internationally. Multinational organizations in particular should feel an obligation to encourage international cross-fertilization of marketing information through their international activities.

International marketing information needs

Knowledge of existing and potential markets, business trends, competitors, and the effectiveness of marketing programmes is critical to the success of any international marketing effort. In carrying out international marketing analysis, planning, implementation and control, marketing managers need information at almost every turn. Thus, the generation and dissemination of marketing information is a critical element of a marketing orientation.

Many complex and diverse types of information are needed by multinational organizations. Complexity is the result of the number of variables involved, and the degree to which these variables can be controlled or predicted. The limits of human information processing capacity mean that increasing diversity leads to increasing uncertainty, while the reduced life span of information in volatile environments similarly increases uncertainty. On the other hand, experience in a particular industry might be expected to have a moderating effect, reducing the impact of volatility and diversity on uncertainty. Thus the scope of consequences (that is, the possible outcome of good or bad decisions) helps to prioritize information needs and can be expressed as the cost of error. Based on the cost of error idea, if for example the wrong decision has no cost implications, or there is no uncertainty in the marketer's mind, then clearly there is no need for marketing information. If however the cost of error is very high, or the uncertainty is very great, the need for marketing information will increase correspondingly.

An information-gathering approach

International marketing information gathering appears to require a combination of the following elements: a purpose or goal, typically specific information needs to be met, a source of information that meets the purpose, and a communication mechanism for the information. In addition, ongoing techniques of international marketing information gathering require an adaptation mechanism to provide negative feedback. This will help the technique continue to achieve its purpose in a changing international marketing environment. The components of the approach in Figure 3.1 match variations in information gathering to variations in information needs, by using information need to guide selection of the information gathering method. Specifically, as the cost of error increases, information gathering should become more formal or exactly specified; as volatility increases, there should be more frequent information gathering; as diversity increases, information should be increasingly analysed or summarized before it reaches the user. For example, if the wrong act or decision will put the company out of business (a very high cost), the information-gathering method should be exactly specified to minimize the chance of error. However, if the wrong act or decision merely results in a deadline being missed by two days, detailed specification is neither required nor appropriate.

Similarly, if there is a stable market (with predictable, often controllable, variables), a

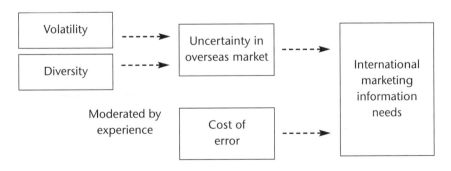

Figure 3.1   A model of marketing information need

single investigation should be sufficient to establish relative pricing levels and product offerings. However, if volatility is high (say with lots of unpredictable, uncontrollable action by competitors), information may rapidly become out of date, and frequent reports will be required. If diversity is high, with many markets, customers and suppliers (that is, with many sources of uncertainty), one person would find it difficult to gather and understand the detailed information needed about all these areas. Reliance must therefore be placed on third parties (such as market research houses, other staff, or an information-processing infrastructure such as a computer system) to gather the information, analyse and/or summarize it, and communicate it via an appropriate medium. The method for analysing or summarizing the information should still be appropriate to the volatility and cost of error of the problem.

This allows a matrix to be constructed (Figure 3.2), that matches methods of information gathering to different combinations of volatility and cost of error. For each major information need, the matrix allows the user to select a method matched to predictability, or volatility, and the cost of getting the information wrong. The second source of uncertainty, diversity, is not explicitly included in the matrix, as it does not affect the choice of a general method of information gathering. Rather, diversity affects the implementation of this general method. This could be seen as a third dimension of the matrix, which expands each general method into a set of specific techniques with varying degrees of analysis and summary of information to match the varying degrees of diversity.

This view of the marketing information system also recognizes that there is a continuous interaction with other systems inside and outside the organization, and that information is constantly being received, analysed or summarized, and passed between these different systems. In addition to linking horizontally with other systems, the marketing information function integrates vertically; it analyses information and passes it up and down between different levels of recursion. Higher levels of recursion are likely to cover

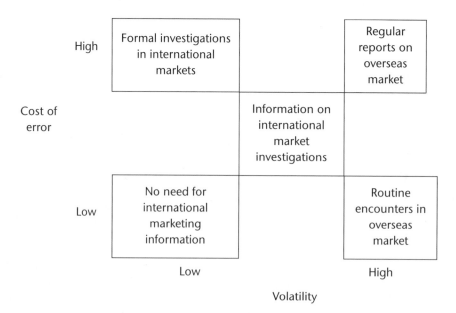

Figure 3.2   International marketing information-gathering matrix

more diverse areas with a greater cost of error, leading to more formal systems, and greater reliance on analysis or summary of information by others.

The complexity of these interactions may make it virtually impossible to develop a complete model of an organization's international marketing information system. However, such a complete model is not required. The matrix approach can easily be applied to sub-sections of the organization, at varying levels of aggregation, without any need to develop a complete model of the organization's marketing information flows. Given the need for modification and redefinition of marketing information, Figure 3.2 provides an improved theoretical basis for researching international marketing information needs, and displays strong explanatory power. On one hand it addresses a broader range of insights while on the other hand it remains narrow enough to offer more immediate practical application. A particular advantage of this approach is that it is accessible to managers who lack the resources of large organizations, sophisticated computer systems or formal market research. All that is required are the following steps:

1   Identify each information need, and the associated cost of error, volatility and diversity.
2   Identify the method used to meet each information need, and the method's degree of specification, frequency of application, and degree of analysis or summary of results.
3   Determine whether there is a match between cost of error and specification, volatility and frequency of application, and degree of analysis or summary of results before use.

Managers can then use the new approach to identify and correct hidden information mismatches before they have a serious effect on the business. Alternatively, they can use the new approach to diagnose failures to meet information needs, and to identify the type of solution required. When an information need is recognized for the first time, IT can be used to identify the type of information-gathering technique that is appropriate to that need.

IT and marketing planning

IT is conceptualized as a catalyst for a period of seminal change within the global economy (Leverick et al. 1997). The advances in IT and its influence on the reordering of organizations, have encouraged a variety of intellectual debates relating to the societal development defined as 'globalization'. IT tends to have an epochal impact on the development process, as it continues to punctuate the shift from traditional development to an emerging social totality with its own distinct organizing principle. This shift is exemplified by networked organizations, de-differentiation and an increased demand for symbolic goods (that is, ones that can be consumed symbolically – gazed at, dreamed about, talked about, photographed and handled, such as information goods, education, arts; culture and leisure pursuits). IT has been credited with bringing into being the 'globalization' option (an advanced and complex form of internationalization that implies a degree of functional integration between internationally dispersed economic activities, which has combined and uneven effects across social space and time) in the way that industrialization brought about the capitalist-industrial state. Like industrialization, it seems to imply a progressive economic and administrative realization and differentiation of the social world.

IT marketing

The pace of implementation of IT within multinational organizations is relentless and its scope pervasive. Its benefits to international marketing organizations, such as increased efficiency and higher levels of customer service, are highly exaggerated. In particular, much literature has focused on the power of IT to facilitate and accentuate dramatic changes in international marketing structures. Management practices associated with the increased use of IT, such as business reprocessing, downsizing, the 'boundaryless organization' and the 'knowledge based enterprise', have become a significant part of organizational language. IT has also been said to facilitate the way in which information is processed, with the potential to change the way in which decision making is undertaken, and even to effect a shift in the nature and scope of activities undertaken by the business. For example, IT at least promises dramatic repercussions for:

- the form and content of inter-organizational relationships as well as intra-organizational communication
- the bases on which organizations compete
- the means of production
- the process of distribution
- customer service support
- every aspect of accepted organizational activity.

In reality, whether radical organizational changes have truly occurred alongside the implementation of IT systems is not clear. Few would disagree, however, that IT, because of the speed with which it can process, analyse and transmit huge amounts of data and present these in palatable, convenient and specific ways, offers at least the potential to facilitate significant change in the way in which international marketing organizations are structured and undertake activities. The extent to which these changes are realized and the form they take are likely to flow from a continuing process in which a number of parties, including of course IT suppliers and end users, play a role.

Marketing expenditure on IT

As the adoption of IT for marketing applications has received much contemporary consideration, there has been significant investment in IT for marketing purposes. For example, in 1997 the UK expenditure on IT to support sales and marketing totalled an estimated £4.5 billion, which accounted for around 15 per cent of total IT expenditure by organizations, and was one of the fastest growing areas of IT investment (Leverick et al., 1997). Various explanations have been forwarded (by Leverick et al. 1997) for such substantial expenditure on IT in marketing. It may be driven by:

- environmental imperatives
- the technology itself, which excites interest by its very availability
- the promises it offers
- the constant search to increase efficiency because of the impact of lower-cost competition

- the apparently increasingly rapidly changing marketing environment
- the corresponding growth in marketing information available to organizations
- consumer demand for higher quality products and services
- pressure on organizations to improve customer service.

It may equally be the case that IT has come simply to be regarded as a prerequisite for competitiveness, and this belief has itself fuelled developments in IT. Almost inevitably, suppliers will generate much hype in order to create a climate conducive to the greater acceptance of IT in marketing.

Whatever the reasons for the heralded IT 'revolution' in marketing, the apparently radical benefits flowing from its application have understandably captured the attention of practitioners. The benefits of IT to international marketer may be noted to include:

- enhancing personal productivity
- supporting decision-making systems
- developing relationship marketing
- improving the effectiveness of sales and promotion
- a means to improve product development
- a source of product and service innovation
- improving the efficiency of marketing tasks and decision-making processes
- the ability to manage large volumes of data at greater speed.

The introduction of an IT system in any part of the marketing organization is a complex process. It is introduced by and affected itself by individuals within and outside the organization: numerous stakeholder groups which themselves impinge on and shape the direction and content of the IT system and the resulting process of organizational change through a continuing process of negotiation and renegotiation. Concerns might also be raised over the direction of causation. It may be just as valid to suggest that organizational change itself impacts upon the nature and scope of IT systems as it is to conceptualize IT as 'causing' organizational change.

Changes in the employment of marketing mix variables

The areas in which IT systems can be applied to marketing are considerable and varied. The applications of IT can be listed, and include customer profile analysis, sales forecasting, budgeting, inventory control, order processing, pricing decisions, competitive analysis, price quotes, sales force analysis and statistical analysis, although some of these are clearly not applications unique to marketing. There is a difference between sales-related applications, such as sales reporting, sales forecasting, sales order processing, product databases, lead tracking, telemarketing and sales route planning, and marketing-related applications, such as customer databases, market research, competitor analysis and promotion campaign management/tracking.

It is possible to distinguish between four broad areas of IT application to marketing activities, although the categories do not appear to be entirely clear-cut:

- IT to enhance operating efficiency – the application of IT to marketing activities already carried out in the organization, such as the maintenance of customer records, budgeting, preparing and making presentations or analysing sales statistics.

- IT and changed methods – the application of IT to enable the marketing department to carry out internal functions which were not possible before – often extending the applications noted in the first point. This involves using databases for segmentation and positioning studies, more sophisticated forecasting and modelling, and better and faster communication with a field sales force.
- IT for enhancing customer service – the use of IT to provide better and faster communication with customers, and using customer data to reach conclusions on changing market 'needs' and preferences.
- IT and marketing innovation, including the use of online databases, direct mail services, external segmentation packages such as MOSAIC and ACORN, and the provision of electronic banking services.

Far from the radical transformation of marketing promised by IT, the use of IT for marketing has thus far focused primarily on routine and tactical: activities such as database management systems, providing facilities including sales lead tracking and order taking. Indeed, it has recently been argued that the utilization of IT by the marketing function is still a relatively recent phenomenon and is by no means as widespread as is sometimes claimed.

Managerial use of IT for making decisions

Through the appropriate use of customer information, IT can facilitate goal satisfaction and compatibility between the firm and its customers, and provide ways in which to recognize and enhance the long-term value of customers. IT has significantly impacted decision making by facilitating information availability and customer/firm dialogues. It is likely that this in turn will allow decision makers to link decisions with outcomes more quickly and directly. Skill and effectiveness in the use of information is seen as critical to becoming market-oriented and gaining success in an intensely competitive international marketing environment. In the context of competitive strategy, firms have typically made a trade-off between two types of information value:

- product experience/knowledge (typically underpinning a high volume/low cost strategy and focusing on the extrinsic potency component of value creation)
- market experience/knowledge (typically underpinning a differentiation strategy and focusing on the intrinsic potency component of value creation).

One of the most profound implications of using IT for strategic thinking is the realization that this traditional strategic trade-off may be obsolete. If managers must now integrate both these types of knowledge, information processing and the resultant decision-making activities of firms take on a new dimension. This change in managerial decision making is also reflected in the need for 'dynamically stable' organizations which are capable of serving the widest range of customers and changing product demands while building long-term process capabilities and the collective knowledge of the organization, or what might be termed an 'enterprise model' of the firm which maps key processes, how information is interpreted, and who is accountable for what.

Speed and flexibility of decision making is of increasing importance in the IT-enabled international marketing environment, requiring both rational and intuitive abilities in formulating insight on the part of decision makers. This need for speed and flexibility may be both helped and hindered by the use of IT. Fast decision makers review more information than their slower counterparts. The important difference is in the type of information they use. Rather than turning to predictive or planning information, fast decision makers seek 'real-time' information, focused on the present (and thus rely more heavily on 'horizontal' systems). In addition, fast decision makers tend to increase the number of alternatives as a result of their information. These skills will become increasingly important to international marketing decision makers, as the possibility of two-way dialogues between firms and their customers becomes a reality. Marketing in real time will enable firms to spot problems and opportunities – and develop strategic responses – with increasing planning skill and speed. Marketing information available in 'real time' will help focus managerial efforts to refine marketing tactics, in addition to its more traditional role of supporting longer-term strategic planning.

Sources of marketing information

Business executives in the new millennium are forced to deal in the international marketplace. The enormous growth and potential profits in overseas markets motivate this, as does the desire to survive the onslaught of international competition. However, when considering overseas markets, managers face relatively complex strategic planning assignments given today's rapidly shifting alternatives in terms of risk, stability and potential returns inherent in the myriad markets around the world.

Selecting among alternative international markets, whether for exporting, licensing, joint ventures, strategic alliances or direct investment, requires information. Likewise, the assessment of information across different types of markets determines, in large part, the degree of success (or failure) achieved in the international arena. In theory, decision makers' perceptions of the importance of different types of foreign market information may be driven by a combination of things, including the industry they represent, the specific markets they are considering, and the type of transactions they would favour when entering specific markets.

While the political climate in one country or region may be perceived as a key dimension to an international venture's success (or failure), the level of economic development may be the key in another. Likewise, while an advanced infrastructure may place one foreign market ahead of another in favourability for one industry, the existence of a stable and transparent legal system might do the same for another industry. Similarly, the importance of information concerning the legal structure in different markets may be related to the type of international transaction being considered (exporting, joint venture, direct investment, etc.). In theory, international business decision makers, representing different industries, evaluating different markets, and favouring different means of transacting their foreign ventures, should value certain types of information differently depending on the specific perceived impact of such information on their firm's success (and/or failure).

Classification and sources of information

International marketing information can be classified according to the internal and external sources:

- Internal sources include company documentation and records, and the knowledge gained by company individuals who in the course of their work obtain data from their contacts with customers, suppliers, government personnel and even competitors.
- External sources include primary and secondary sources.

Secondary sources of information

Secondary sources refer to published information from home government publications, commercial banks, foreign embassies and consulates, trade papers, magazines, business and trade association publications, books and other published research studies. International institutions such as the World Bank, International Monetary Fund (IMF), European Union and United Nations, provide statistical data, with a wide coverage of topics on many countries. A major development in secondary information has been the development and availability of online and CD-ROM databases. Specialist information can now be accessed with this new technology at a competitive cost even to the small firm that is trading internationally. The type and volume of information available through online data has expanded spectacularly; the Internet has only added to this information base, and the danger is now of information saturation, Finding the *right* information has become crucial for researchers.

In a rapidly changing environment, these sources of information are critical to companies wishing to build market databases on potential markets. Relevant information is a strategic asset and can contribute to a firm's competitive advantage. There are advantages, disadvantages and problems when using secondary data for research purposes. Table 3.1 shows the criteria for selecting and evaluating international information sources.

Table 3.1   Criteria for selecting and evaluating sources of information

	Factor	Executive analysis
1	Accuracy	The quality of the information depends on its accuracy. It may be the case that different sources may report different values for variables such as demographic data, GNP, household incomes, etc. of a particular country market. This difference may be attributed to a number of factors including, problem definition, the time frame used, data collection method, the purpose of data collection.
2	Reliability	The reliability of information is affected by the objectivity of the information base. If the interested party (supplier or government) wishes to encourage consumers or investors to behave in a particular way, the information is unlikely to be accurate. Tourist organizations may not report epidemics or political instability, for example, for fear of hurting the tourist industry. Food retailers and the government may not report food poisoning incidents because it may be harmful to the retail industry. In the United Kingdom, the government has been accused of providing incomplete and even inaccurate information concerning the spread of 'mad cow disease' or BSE.

	Factor	Executive analysis
3	Timeliness	This refers to being up to date and is a defining quality of good data. Data that is too old may be irrelevant for the current problem. An indicator of timeliness is when the data was last published. Some data variables change rather slowly (such as per capita income, income distribution, population density); other data change rapidly (such as political opinion polls, where data from a week ago is considered old information).
4	Availability	Data is not always available in equal quantity, aggregation and detail from all country markets. Developed economies with the necessary resources tend to have much more detailed data than emerging markets. The scarcity of data, especially in undeveloped and developing economies, is a very serious problem for international marketers. For example, the Asia Pacific markets are considered key markets for growth in this millennium, and detailed information is required in this region. Yet there is a consensus that countries such as China, Vietnam and Taiwan do not have reliable data for various reasons, from government influence to lack of information infrastructure.
5	Compar-ability	This is another measure of data quality. Comparable data may not be available to make cross-national comparisons. Some countries may not use the same categories when displaying the distribution of income, or data may be available only in some of the markets. For researchers to make a judgement about the value of the data, they need to assess who collected the data, how was it collected and for what purpose.
6	Relevance	Sometimes good-quality information may be worthless to the decision makers in the company if the contents are irrelevant. The data must assist management to formulate their strategic marketing plans and to make decisions. This relevant criterion is an important variable in evaluating the type of information.
7	Costs	The firm needs to assess the costs of acquiring data against the value it derives from improved decision making resulting from better information flow. Some types of information come at a nominal price or even free, but the firm needs to guard against processing costs: it still has to gather, analyse, store and discard unwanted data. The firm needs to evaluate the costs of gaining information that is cheap but not relevant to its needs: it may even be worthwhile for the firm to undertake primary research to gain specific data for its strategic marketing needs.

Primary sources of information

Primary sources are information obtained by experiments, observation, surveys and other techniques. Here the company involved specifically commissions the research. Conducting primary research is complicated by different environmental factors and market conditions (refer to the section on the international marketing research environment, page 85). In many instances, primary research is essential for the formulation of a marketing plan. For example, for international marketing segmentation strategies, the firm will need data on how segmentation variables such as lifestyle and income can be applied to different country markets. In these instances, primary research is necessary.

Usually, primary data collection is undertaken only when the sources for secondary data are inadequate. There are a number of problems faced in primary research, especially in the undeveloped world, such as inaccurate sampling leading to errors, respondent biases in the interview stage of the process and researcher bias. The latter two are usually the major cause for non-comparability of results from different country markets. Table 3.2 highlights some of the basic problems of primary research in international markets.

Table 3.2 Primary research problems

	Factor	Executive analysis
1	Respondent bias	Different cultural markets will inevitably produce different responses to interviews or surveys. There are three types of respondent bias: • Social bias may include courtesy, social desirability, and topic bias. Courtesy bias relates to respondents in some cultures (e.g. Middle Eastern and Asia) who give researchers answers they feel are desired by the interviewers. Japanese culture, for example, is deeply imbued with the concept of not offending another person. • Social desirability bias refers to the response of some people in giving answers that reflect their social standing. • Topic bias deals with the sensitivity of particular topics or areas in different cultures: certain subjects like sex, women's role in society are taboo in some African and Middle Eastern cultures and in countries like China and India; therefore, in some of these cultures women may not be able to respond to interview or surveys personally. Under these circumstances a mailed questionnaire for researching the female market would be more appropriate.
2	Non-response bias	There are cultural patterns of non-response at both country and individual levels. There is also variation in individual item non-response and this varies according to different countries. For example, US respondents are more likely to answer personal questions than UK respondents. Also Africans and Indian respondents are probably more reluctant to answer questions related to sexuality or which have sexual connotation.
3	Researcher–respondent interaction bias	Most primary research requires researcher-respondent interaction. There are two aspects to this problem: • The location in which the interaction takes place. In some cultures it is virtually impossible to interview a respondent alone, either at home or in some neutral place, because the respondent is always accompanied. In such a situation the presence of 'others' can affect the response outcome for there may be an inclination to give 'appropriate' answers. • The social status of the researcher and respondent could affect the outcome. For example, a researcher from the upper strata interviewing a lower-strata respondent may find the response biased and misinterpretation of the objective of the study can occur.

	Factor	Executive analysis
4	Researcher biases	One of the main problems concerning the researcher is the self-reference criterion problem, particularly in interview situations using open-ended questions. This can lead to misinterpretation of data and ineffective communication between the researcher and respondent. The researcher will tend to perceive behaviour in other cultures in terms of their own culture and this can lead to systematic bias in reporting the findings. An attempt to overcome this problem is to build into the research design the perspectives of the researcher in order to minimize the bias, or hire a local research agency.
5	Literacy and sampling problems	The low level of literacy in many emerging markets means that to some extent the marketing research techniques used in many industrialized economies cannot be utilized in these markets and pictorial response charts may have to be used. There is also a problem in obtaining valid and reliable sampling frames in international markets, partly because of the lack of secondary data and marketing infrastructure and partly because data is collected in a more informal manner. Consequently, the construction of the sample will rely heavily on experience and judgement that could inevitably lead to distorted results.

Other problems concern the translation of the questionnaire, which could be grammatically correct but does not incorporate local nuances or convey the appropriate message. Similarly, the researcher needs to make a decision about which language to use for the questionnaire or interview. In Nigeria for example, there are at least four official languages: Hausa, Yoruba, Ibo and English. In Singapore, there are two main official languages, Chinese and English. Apart from which language to use in the market concerned, the researchers need to be fluent in the language of the targeted market to avoid mistakes and misunderstandings.

Data and research for the international marketing process

Given the time and expense associated with the collection of primary data, the use of secondary data in international marketing research will continue to grow. Evaluation of secondary data is even more critical for international than for domestic projects. Different sources report different values for a given statistic, such as GDP, because of differences in the way the unit is defined. Measurement units may not be equivalent across countries. In France, for example, workers are paid a 13th-monthly salary each year as an automatic bonus, resulting in a measurement construct that is different from other countries. The accuracy of secondary data may also vary from country to country. Data from highly industrialized countries like the United States and the United Kingdom are likely to be more accurate than those from developing countries. The taxation structure and the extent of tax evasion affect business and income statistics. Population censuses may vary in frequency and the year in which the data were collected. With the proliferation of the Internet, international secondary data has become more available and accessible. The need to systematically evaluate these data before using them will become even more crucial.

Qualitative research

Since the researcher is often not familiar with the foreign product market to be examined, qualitative research is crucial in international marketing research. In the initial stages of cross-national research, qualitative research can provide insights into the problem and help in developing an approach by generating relevant research questions and hypotheses, models, and characteristics that influence the research design. Thus, qualitative research may reveal the differences between the foreign and domestic markets.

Focus groups can be used in many settings, particularly in industrialized countries. The moderator should not only be trained in focus group methodology, but should also be familiar with the language, culture and patterns of social interaction prevailing in that country. The focus group findings should be derived not only from the verbal contents but also from nonverbal cues like voice intonations, inflections, expressions and gestures. The size of the focus group could also vary. For example, in Asia seven respondents produce the highest level of interaction among group members. In some countries, such as in the Middle or Far East, people are hesitant to discuss their feelings in a group setting. In other countries such as Japan, people think it is impolite to disagree with others publicly (Malhotra and Peterson 2001). In these cases, depth interviews should be used. Moreover, qualitative data that are generated should be interpreted in the context of the culture.

Survey methods

The feasibility and popularity of the different survey methods vary widely from country to country. In the United States and Canada, the telephone has achieved almost total penetration of households. As a result, telephone interviewing is the dominant mode of questionnaire administration. The same situation exists in some European countries such as Sweden. However, in many other European countries telephone penetration is still not complete. In developing countries few households have telephones (Huang 1998). In-home personal interviews are the dominant mode of collecting survey data in many European countries such as Switzerland, newly industrialized countries (NICs) and developing countries. While shopping centre intercepts are conducted in some European countries, such as Sweden, they are not popular in Europe or developing countries. In less developed countries this is usually the only possible method of data collection. In contrast, street interviews constitute the dominant method of collecting survey data in European countries such as France and the Netherlands.

As a result of low cost, mail interviews continue to be used in most developed countries where literacy is high and the postal system is well developed: the United States, Canada, Denmark, Finland, Iceland, Norway, Sweden and the Netherlands, for example. In Africa, Asia and South America, however, the use of mail surveys and mail panels is low because of illiteracy and the large proportion of the population living in rural areas. Mail panels are used extensively in only a few countries outside the United States, such as Canada, the United Kingdom, France, Germany and the Netherlands. However, the use of panels may increase with the advent of new technology. Likewise, although a website can be accessed from anywhere in the world, access to the web or email is limited in many countries, particularly developing countries. Hence the use of electronic surveys is not currently feasible, especially for interviewing households, although this is expected to change in the next decade.

Videotaping of consumers in purchase or consumption situations can provide a rich source of information relating to the impact of contextual and situational factors on consumer behaviour and response patterns in different cultures and contexts. Videotaping of consumers in an in-store environment provides a wealth of information about visual cues and their role in product evaluation, which is not easily obtained from other forms of data collection. In some cases, in-store videotaping can be used to prompt or elicit responses from consumers. In emerging markets, videotaping of consumer usage and consumption behaviour often provides deeper understanding of how consumers use products and how these are embedded in the cultural fabric of society, as well as perceptions of and associations with foreign products and brands.

Projective and elicitation techniques such as collages, picture completion, analogies and metaphors, psycho drawing and personalization can be used to encourage respondents to project their private and unconscious beliefs, and personal and subjective associations. Collages were, for example, used in a study of teenagers worldwide to explore their feelings about the future (Thiesse, 1996). This revealed significant differences between countries especially in terms of the degree of pessimism and hedonism. Equally, brand perceptions can be explored through personalization; association techniques or analogies, to probe culturally embedded images and associations that vary across cultures.

Focus groups and extended creativity groups can also be used to explore underlying motivations, feelings and points of view. These techniques can be used to screen new product ideas and concepts, develop ideas for a new positioning or advertising theme, or to examine future trends. The use of such techniques is likely to become increasingly critical in the twenty-first century, as managers seek to identify new products or ideas that will appeal to cross-national segments or consumers worldwide. Their unstructured character facilitates identification of ideas, concepts and trends that are truly universal, rather than reflecting the influence of any specific culture or country.

Incorporating technological advances into research design and methodology

At the same time, international marketing researchers will need to incorporate the latest technological developments in data collection and dissemination into the research design. These enable researchers to dramatically reduce the time required to collect data across geographic distances, as well as substantially enhancing and enriching the type of stimuli that can be used in collecting data from international markets. It is, however, important to recognize that the use of sophisticated technological techniques is subject to certain limitations in international markets, because of the degree of either development of the technological infrastructure, or technological sophistication of respondents.

Advances in computer technology such as scanners, computer-assisted telephone interviewing (CATI) and computer-assisted personal interviewing (CAPI), are well established in the developed countries and are beginning to be used elsewhere. They provide faster, more accurate methods of data collection, providing direct input of response and facilitating steering of data collection based on response. Techniques such as CATI and CAPI can also be used to centrally administer and organize data collection from international samples, subject to telephone and computer penetration in different countries as well as use of a common language or availability of software to automatically translate questionnaires.

As these technologies evolve and advance, they also provide innovative ways to present stimuli and collect data particularly suited to international research issues. Multimedia CAPI makes possible the presentation of highly complex stimuli, and facilitates obtaining consumer reactions to video and audio stimuli. Developments in virtual reality CAPI will heighten the realism in stimulus portrayal and expand the range of topics on which marketing research can meaningfully be conducted.

Equally, as the Internet evolves, it offers the potential to dramatically change the way in which much international marketing research is conducted, in providing both ready access to secondary data and a new means of collecting primary data. Rather than visiting a traditional research library, the marketer can have virtually instant access to data from traditional sources as well as sources that are only available on the Internet. The Internet can also be used to collect primary data, either by tracking visitors to a website, or through administering electronic questionnaires over the Internet. To the extent that websites are increasingly likely to be accessed by users world-wide, information on an international sample can be gathered. Behaviour at the site can be tracked, revealing interest in the products and services or information offered, as well as responses to promotional material or offers.

The Internet can also be used to collect data in a more systematic fashion, which is closer in character to more traditional marketing research practice. Subject to the availability of suitable Internet sampling frames, questionnaires can be administered directly over the Internet. Questionnaires are sent via email to respondents and the responses are also returned via email. This represents a very quick and totally automated means to conduct a survey with a broad geographic scope. The results are available almost instantaneously, as the responses can be checked and analysed in real time as they are received. Questionnaires administered via the World Wide Web also have the advantage that product details, pictures of products, brands and the shopping environment can be portrayed with integrated graphics and sound.

This approach is most suited to surveys among respondent populations that are technology literate, and at present for certain types of products such as computers, computer software or business-to-business research. However, as use of the Internet becomes more commonplace, email surveys will begin to replace mail and phone surveys. Progress will occur most rapidly in the United States and Europe, and will spread more slowly in other parts of the world (Worldwide Internet Conference 1999).

An important limiting factor is the extent to which Internet sampling frames correspond to respondent populations that are of interest to marketers. Versions of web software available in different countries may not be compatible. Technical issues may daunt respondents, resulting in non-response bias. Factors such as overall response rate and item non-response will also continue to be important. Consequently, a large number of surveys need to be sent out to obtain a large enough sample to analyse. However, the fact that results are obtained rapidly allows additional sampling, with enhanced incentives, to compensate for shortfalls. While lower costs and rapidity of response make this mode attractive for international research, potential bias problems suggest that, at least in the short run, and particularly where part of the target market is likely to be in countries with low Internet access, this approach will need to be used with some caution.

Finally, no one questionnaire administration method is superior in all situations. The use of computer-assisted methods and mail panels depends heavily on the state of technological development in the country. Likewise, the use of shopping centre intercept interviewing is contingent on the dominance of shopping centres in the retailing environment. The same is true for email and Internet surveys, which rely on access to computers and the Internet. Another very important consideration in selecting the methods of administering questionnaires is to ensure equivalence and comparability across countries. Different methods may have different reliabilities in different countries. In collecting data from different countries, it is desirable to use survey methods with equivalent levels of reliability, rather than the same method.

The international marketing research environment

As businesses expand further and further in international markets, the role of timely and accurate marketing research to guide decision making becomes increasingly critical. Research to support international marketing decisions has evolved over the past four decades and must change even more to support firms in the twenty-first century. There are four key areas where progress must be made.

- International marketing research efforts need to be more closely aligned with market growth opportunities outside the industrialized nations.
- Researchers must develop the capability to conduct and coordinate research that spans diverse research environments.
- International marketing researchers need to develop new creative approaches to probe the cultural underpinnings of behaviour.
- Technological advances need to be incorporated into the research process in order to facilitate and expedite research conducted across the globe.

Multinational firms preparing to compete in the twenty-first century are increasingly confronted with the task of crafting strategies that anticipate and respond to the rapid pace of change in global markets. As a result, their information needs are changing and becoming ever more complex and diverse. Timely, relevant information is essential to provide an adequate basis for day-to-day decision making as well as to chart the firm's path in an increasingly fast-paced, turbulent and competitive environment.

Information needs are changing in both developed and developing countries. Established markets in industrialized countries are becoming more geographically integrated, as direct vertical links and information flows are established between customers, retailers and suppliers. As a result, there is a growing need to conduct research spanning country boundaries, in order to identify regional or global market segments, or to examine opportunities for integrating and better coordinating strategies across national boundaries. At the same time, speed in collection and interpretation of results from multiple and geographically diverse sources becomes imperative in order to anticipate market changes and devise an effective response strategy.

As firms push the geographic frontiers of their operations to take advantage of growing opportunities, they need to collect information from a broader and more diverse range of markets. Increasingly, this entails conducting research in unfamiliar and distant markets in the Far East, the Middle East, Latin America and Africa. This in turn poses a number of challenges, not only in collecting accurate and reliable information on exist-ing behaviour patterns in an expeditious and cost-effective fashion, but also in predict-ing response to new and unfamiliar stimuli, and interpreting the implications for marketing strategy.

Advances in technology both facilitate and at the same time render more complex the collection of data on a global basis. The growth and increasing technological sophistica-tion of the communication infrastructure enable data collection on a much broader and diverse geographic scale. Yet at the same time, marketing management has to master these tools and understand their inherent limitations and implicit biases.

The purpose of this section is to explore these changes in information needs and tech-nology, and suggest the implications for conducting marketing research in the interna-tional marketing environment. Specifically, the section examines the capabilities and skills international researchers will need to acquire in order to conduct research in the increasingly diverse and rapidly changing international marketplace of the twenty-first century.

The changing international marketing environment

To understand the research needs of the twenty-first century it is important to consider how they have changed over the past four decades. In the 1960s and 1970s, many US firms, faced by slackening rates of growth in their domestic markets, began to venture into international markets. Japanese and European firms with smaller domestic markets also expanded internationally, in order to broaden the geographic scope of their opera-tions and take advantage of potential economies of scale, or to respond to foreign competition entering their domestic markets. In this initial phase of international market entry, firms were mostly concerned with collecting information to identify and assess market opportunities in other countries, to determine which markets to enter, how to position products in these markets and how far to adapt different elements of the marketing mix to local market conditions.

At this phase of the firm's expansion, the country was typically used as the unit of analysis for the research design, for developing the sampling frame and for data collec-tion. Owing to economic, political, linguistic and cultural barriers, the country was the focal point of entry decisions. Equally, the firm's international operations were often organized on a country-by-country basis. Marketing research agencies were also typically national organizations, with relatively few having the capability to conduct research on a multi-country basis. Most secondary data as well as sampling lists were available on a national basis.

However, as firms have expanded internationally and product markets are becoming increasingly integrated world-wide, the key decision issues facing the firm in the 1990s changed dramatically. As a result, research and information needs changed and broadened. In industrialized nations such as North America, Europe and Japan, regional market inte-gration and the removal of barriers between countries, the growth of a regional and global market infrastructure and the increased mobility of consumers created pressures to consol-idate and integrate marketing strategy across countries. Consequently, increased attention is focused on conducting studies that cover multiple countries, examining differences and similarities in behaviour and response patterns across countries.

At the same time, as growth in these markets slows, future market potential lies in emerging market economies, with countries such as China and India accounting for over one-third of the world's population. The explosive population growth in these countries, together with the opening up of markets in the former Soviet Union, makes entry into these markets mandatory for firms aspiring to be global leaders in the future. In entering these markets, as in initially entering international markets, firms need to collect information to assess potential opportunities, to determine how to position, price, promote and distribute their products and brands, whether to develop local variants and so on.

The heterogeneity of research contexts

Currently, the vast majority of research, both commercial and academic, is conducted within the nations of the Industrial Triad. In 1995, the world market for commercial research was estimated at approximately $10.2 billion. This figure increased to $23.5 billion in 2007 representing an annual increase of almost 10 per cent. Of this, approximately 45 per cent was conducted in Europe (42 per cent within the European Union), 34 per cent in the United States and 10 per cent in Japan. These three geographic areas accounted for all but 11 per cent of total spending on marketing research (ESOMAR 1996; US Department of Commerce 2008). This imbalance is likely to change in the future, as an increased amount of research is conducted in emerging market economies.

In emerging markets, conditions are not only changing very rapidly, but are also substantially different from those in industrialized countries. Not only are consumers' standards of living and purchasing power much lower, but also attitudes towards foreign products are often extremely complex, sometimes ambivalent and difficult to predict. Coupled with the lack of a research or technological infrastructure to facilitate the collection and analysis of data, this poses a considerable challenge not only in designing research, but also in developing and implementing the collection of data.

In the less developed countries of the world, notably Africa and parts of Asia, technological advances focus on development of the basic infrastructure – roads, electricity, running water, and rudimentary transportation and distribution systems. Such developments are essential in building the marketing infrastructure. Electricity not only powers television sets which carry commercials, but also is essential for the application of computer technology and the development of more technologically advanced communications. Further, a dependable electrical supply makes possible retail stores with refrigeration for staples and hence the distribution of consumer packaged goods. The developments open up new markets and dramatically change the ways in which people live and consume. This in turn adds to the complexity of conducting marketing research, as the range and nature of research contexts become increasingly heterogeneous.

International marketing research implications

The dramatic changes in the international marketing environment, coupled with technological advances in data collection, analysis and dissemination, imply that researchers will need to broaden their capabilities in order to design, implement and interpret

---

MINI CASE 3.1

Retail influence on international marketing research

Developments in mass communications technology, international and regional media such as CNN, BBC 24, and SKY TV create an environment where certain segments of the population world-wide:

- are developing a common set of expectations
- have familiarity with a common set of symbols
- have similar preferences for products and services
- have an overall desire to improve their standard of living.

Market segments such as teenagers share common interests in clothing fashions, music, films and sports, as new trends and related products are rapidly diffused by retailers world-wide through global media. Increasing discretionary expenditures in industrialized markets also expand the range of choice and the role of services in consumer choice decisions. This, coupled with the multiplicity of shopping modes available to the consumer, results in increased emphasis on examining the role of the shopping environment. Information needs to be collected relating not only to customer preferences and the choice process, but also to situational and contextual variables, including the interaction of choice with the shopping context: for example, the impact of store ambience on shopping mood.

The expansion of retailers world-wide also facilitates marketing research. As chains expand, they incorporate their 'best practices' in the new stores. They incorporate new retail technology, modern merchandising practices and product mixes that both respond to local tastes and reflect the firm's desire for economies of scale in buying from suppliers. The development of shopping centres, where there were none, makes possible shopping centre intercept interviews. Another consequence of the development of the marketing infrastructure is the greater need for marketing research. As retailers expand in new markets, changing and integrating the marketing infrastructure, more marketing research is needed to track these changes and guide decision making.

---

research in the twenty-first century. As research efforts are aligned to match markets with the highest market potential, researchers will need to develop the capabilities and skills to conduct and design research in these environments. New tools incorporating the latest technology will need to be mastered, and creative approaches to understanding behaviour in differing cultural contexts developed. The ability to interpret and integrate complex data from diverse sources and environments will also be critical in order to provide meaningful recommendations for the firm's global marketing strategy.

The organization of international research

In addition to developing the capabilities to conduct research spanning diverse environments, international marketing researchers also need to create and make imaginative and thoughtful use of new approaches to understand the changing marketplace. As qualitative research techniques advance and mature, they offer increasing promise as a means of understanding and interpreting trends in diverse cultural contexts. Qualitative research provides insights and understanding of the consumption and purchase context and the underlying determinants of behaviour, as well as a means of interpreting the results of quantitative research and predicting future trends.

Qualitative research techniques offer a number of advantages in international marketing research, insofar as they are unstructured and do not entail the imposition of the researcher's prespecified conceptual model or terminology on the respondent. As a consequence, qualitative techniques are especially helpful in probing the contextual embedding of attitudes and behaviour, providing deep understanding of situational and contextual factors, and providing inputs into interpreting observed differences between countries and cultures. In addition, as qualitative techniques are often observational or unstructured, they require minimal cognitive skills, and are particularly suited to research in emerging markets. They can also provide insights into underlying or hidden motivations as well as probing future trends and scenarios.

Measurement and sampling

Attitude scales will become more widely used in cross-national research as consumers become more educated and experienced in responding to marketing research questions (Kumar 2000: 391). From the viewpoint of the respondents, nominal scales are the simplest to use, whereas ratio scales are the most complex. Respondents in many developed countries, with higher education and more consumer sophistication levels, are quite used to providing responses on interval and ratio scales. However, opinion formation may not be well crystallized in some developing countries. Hence, these respondents may experience difficulty in expressing the gradation required by interval and ratio scales. Preferences can therefore best be measured by using ordinal scales. In particular, the use of binary scales (such as preferred/not preferred), the simplest type of ordinal scale, is recommended. This trend toward using simple but reliable measures that can be translated easily into multiple languages and cultural contexts will continue to gain momentum, as determining cross-cultural equivalence of scales poses special challenges.

Sampling methods used in cross-national studies will increase in sophistication. Implementing the sampling design process in international marketing research is seldom an easy task. Several factors should be considered in defining the target population. For example:

- The relevant element (respondent) may differ from country to country. In the United Kingdom for example, children play an important role in the purchase of children's cereals. However, in countries with authoritarian child-rearing practices, the mother may be the relevant element.
- Women play a key role in the purchase of cars and other durable goods in the United Kingdom. But in male-dominated societies, such as in the Middle East, men make such decisions.
- Accessibility varies across countries. In Mexico, because of boundary walls and servants, strangers cannot enter houses.
- In some countries, dwelling units may be unnumbered and streets unidentified, making it difficult to locate designated households.

Given the lack of suitable sampling frames, the inaccessibility of certain respondents, such as women in some cultures, and the dominance of personal interviewing, probability-sampling techniques are uncommon in international marketing research. Quota sampling has been used widely in developed and developing countries in both consumer and industrial surveys. Snowball sampling is also appealing when the characteristic of interest is rare in the target population or when respondents are hard to reach. For example, in Saudi Arabia and many other relatively undeveloped countries, graduate students are employed to hand-deliver questionnaires to relatives and friends. These initial respondents can be asked for referrals to other potential respondents, and so on. This approach results in a large sample size and a high response rate.

Sampling techniques and procedures vary in accuracy, reliability and cost from country to country. If the same sampling procedures are used in each country, the results may not be comparable. In order to achieve comparability in sample composition and representatives, it may be desirable to use different sampling techniques in different countries. When conducting marketing research in foreign countries, statistical estimation of sample size may be difficult, as estimates of the population variance may be unavailable. If statistical estimation of sample size is attempted at all, it should be realized that the estimates of the population variance might vary from country to country. Thus, the sample size may vary across countries. In the past, it has been difficult to implement probability-sampling techniques but this will change, as the development of required infrastructure will allow greater use of probability sampling. Also, the greater use of telephone and Internet survey methods will facilitate the use of probability techniques in international sampling contexts.

Analysis of the findings

Given the complexity of cross-national fieldwork, project management for multi-country studies will become more of a distinctive skill area for research agencies. The selection, training, supervision and evaluation of field workers is critical in international marketing research. Local fieldwork agencies are unavailable in many countries, so it may be necessary to recruit and train local field workers or import trained foreign workers. The use of local field workers is desirable, as they are familiar with the local language and culture. They can thus create an appropriate climate for the interview and be sensitive to the concerns of the respondents. Extensive training may be required and close supervision may be necessary.

It has been observed in many countries that interviewers tend to help respondents with the answers and select household or sampling units based on personal considerations rather than the sampling plan. Interviewer cheating may be more of a problem in many developing countries than in the developed nations. Validation of fieldwork is critical. As we look to the future, the decrease in the cost of international calls and the availability of ethnic field workers locally will make it feasible to conduct multi-country telephone surveys from a single location. This, along with the use of Internet surveys, will greatly facilitate international fieldwork.

The researcher should ensure that the units of measurement are comparable across countries or cultural units analysing the data. For example, the data may have to be adjusted to establish currency equivalents or metric equivalents. Furthermore, standardization or normalization of the data may be necessary to make meaningful comparisons and achieve consistent results. The data analysis could be conducted at individual levels: within countries or cultural units, and across countries or cultural units.

The similarities as well as the differences between countries should be investigated. When examining differences, not only differences in means but also differences in variance and distribution should be assessed. All the commonly used statistical techniques can be applied to within-country or across-country analysis and, subject to the amount of data available, to individual-level analysis as well. Data analysis procedures and techniques will become increasingly standardized in international marketing research (Peterson and Malhotra 1997).

Report preparation may be complicated by the need to prepare reports for management in different countries and in different languages. In such a case, the researcher should prepare different versions of the report, each geared to specific readers. The different reports should be comparable, although the formats may differ. Most marketing decisions are made from facts and figures arising out of marketing research. But, these figures have to pass the test and limits of logic, subjective experience and gut feelings of decision makers. The subjective experience and gut feelings of managers could vary widely across countries, making it necessary to give different recommendations for implementing the research findings in different countries (Mitevska and Meyer 1997). The Internet is likely to become a common medium for distributing marketing research findings and reports internationally.

Reporting the findings

Marketing research reports will be routinely published or posted directly to the Web, on locations that are protected by passwords or on corporate intranets. These reports will incorporate all kinds of multimedia presentations, including graphs, pictures, animation, audio and full motion video. It will be easy to integrate these reports, and for findings to become a part of the decision support system.

The benefits of intranets include not only increased organizational learning, but also enhanced productivity for the corporate marketing researcher. Once reports are posted to an intranet, the corporate marketing researcher no longer has to directly field queries from managers throughout the organization who become interested in the results of specific studies. Time on the phone, briefing such managers, declines precipitously. In this way, the marketing researcher is freed to be more forward-focused, instead of repeatedly disseminating the same information to different managers.

Research problems in developing countries

A first priority is to focus research effort and capabilities on markets with future growth potential. As indicated earlier, marketing research expenditures are heavily concentrated in the industrialized countries of North America, Europe and Japan. This reflects the current size and attractiveness of these markets. However, the countries with the highest growth potential are the emerging market economies in Asia, Latin America, Eastern Europe and the countries of the former Soviet Union. Firms that wish to succeed in the international markets of the twenty-first century will need to pay greater attention to examining markets in these regions of the world, and developing or acquiring the capabilities to conduct research in these markets.

The stark differences between the developed and developing world are reflected in information taken from the Human Development Report (UNDP 1999). The United Nations categorized 45 countries as having a high level of human development (HHD), 94 as medium (MHD) and 35 as low (LHD). The data dramatically illustrate the gulf that exists between the richest countries and the poorest. The per capita GNP in HHD countries was more than 18 times that of MHD countries, and 87 times that of LHD countries. Over 80 per cent of the world's population live in countries that are categorized as either MHD or LHD. Equally critical for conducting marketing research are differences in illiteracy – less than 5 per cent in HHD countries compared with over 50 per cent of the population in LHD countries (UNDP 1999).

Conducting research successfully in these regions requires both understanding and sensitivity to differences in the market environment, as well as an ability to deal with the lack of a well-developed market research infrastructure. The accuracy of results hinges in part on the respondents' ability to understand the questions being posed. Low levels of literacy in emerging markets, as well as lack of familiarity with stimuli or response formats from industrialized markets, create challenges. In designing research instruments, caution needs to be exercised in directly transposing stimuli or research formats commonly adopted in industrialized countries. Rather, researchers need to think creatively in designing instruments that are readily understood and unambiguously interpreted, and as far as possible devoid of cultural bias. In particular, it is more effective to design instruments that employ visual as well as verbal stimuli, and occur in a familiar and realistic setting, rather than requiring abstract cognitive skills.

The absence of a well-developed market research infrastructure is also a major hindrance to the conduct of marketing research in emerging markets. The quality of the research infrastructure is reflected in statistics on telephone lines and Internet hosts per 1,000 people. In the HHD countries there were ten times as many telephone lines as in MHD countries and over 125 times those in LHD countries. Internet connections, which are becoming a critical element of research in many of the HHD countries, were directly available to less than one person in 1000 in the MHD and LHD countries.

Interpretation of results from emerging market countries may also pose some challenges, especially for researchers from other sociocultural backgrounds. Researchers need to be wary of interpreting results in terms of their own culture and experience, and in particular, of generalizing from experience in industrialized markets to emerging markets. Indigenous researchers, on the other hand, trained in a different research paradigm, may interpret results in terms of the local context, and focus on the uniqueness of these patterns. Consequently teams of researchers from different backgrounds will be needed to provide a broad and balanced interpretation.

Conducting research in diverse environments

The increasing diversity of the sociocultural and economic environment in which research is being conducted implies that international marketing researchers will need to develop the capability to conduct and coordinate research spanning a broad range of environmental contexts and research questions. In essence, researchers will need to be able to tailor research questions, and adapt research instruments and administration procedures, to different environments, as well as to interpret results at global level. This goes beyond geographic coordination of multi-country studies, translation and development of multilingual questionnaires or research instruments, and requires skills in designing multi-site studies that include a common core and purpose, and at the same time address country-specific issues (Douglas and Craig 1997).

At a first level, skills in designing multi-site studies in diverse environments will increasingly be required. Here, although the key research questions are clearly identified and common across sites, attention needs to be paid to how constructs are operated, research instruments designed, and sampling and data collection conducted at each site. The definition of product categories may differ, for example, as well as brand availability, the nature of the retail environment, or more insidiously, the sociocultural context of consumption. Constructs or definitions used in one context are not necessarily appropriate in another. Research instruments, data collection or sampling procedures may incorporate bias, requiring reformulation or adaptation to ensure meaningful results (Craig and Douglas 2000).

Use of a team incorporating members from different cultural backgrounds and sites helps to strike a balance between the needs for local input and adaptation to local site conditions, and for comparability and equivalence across sites. Researchers from each site should participate in the early stages of research design and in the interpretation of data and results, rather than merely acting as local implementers of a centrally designed study. They can then provide input in the formulation of research questions and the design of the research instrument, as well as in sampling and data collection procedures. Equally, local researchers are best placed to interpret findings from their sites in terms of local contextual factors, and to explain local anomalies or differences.

At a higher or 'supra-country' level, skills and capabilities in designing and managing a research programme that spans multiple, diverse environments are likely to become increasingly critical. A research programme might, for example, cover a product business or industry world-wide. If the business is at different stages of the product life cycle in different regions, or market conditions differ substantially, (as for example with detergents), different types of research or information will need to be collected. The abilities to define relevant research issues in each context, and to coordinate and manage the different studies, will be critical to provide meaningful input for the development of the firm's long-run strategy in world markets.

Ethical issues in international marketing research

International marketing research has often been described (see Malhotra and Miller 1999) as having four stakeholders:

- the marketing researcher
- the client
- the respondent
- the public.

These stakeholders have certain responsibilities to each other and to the research project. Ethical issues arise when the interests of these stakeholders are in conflict, and when one or more of the stakeholders are lacking in their responsibilities (Malhotra and Miller 1999). Stakeholders behaving honourably will best resolve ethical issues. Codes of conduct, such as the Chartered Institute of Marketing code of ethics, are available to guide behaviour and help resolve ethical dilemmas. Some of the common ethical dilemmas encountered at the various stages of the marketing research process are discussed in this section.

The researchers must ensure that the research design utilized will provide the information needed to address the marketing research problem that has been identified. The client should have the integrity not to misrepresent the project, and should describe the constraints under which the researcher must operate and not make unreasonable demands. Longitudinal research takes time. Descriptive research might require interviewing customers. If time is an issue, or if customer contact has to be restricted, the client should make these constraints known at the start of the project. The client should not take undue advantage of the research firm to solicit unfair concessions for the current project by making false promises of future research contracts. Partnering relationships between clients and researchers will become the norm in the future, helping to resolve such ethical issues.

Given the limitations of secondary data, it is often necessary to collect primary data in order to obtain the information needed to address the management decision problem. The use of secondary data alone when the research problem requires primary data collection could raise ethical concerns. Such concerns are heightened when the client is being billed a fixed fee for the project and the proposal submitted for the project did not adequately specify the data collection methodology. On the other hand, in some cases it may be possible to obtain the information needed from secondary sources alone, making it unnecessary to collect primary data. The unnecessary collection of expensive primary data, when the research problem can be addressed based on secondary data alone, may be unethical. These ethical issues become more salient if the research firm's billings go up, but at the expense of the client. Given the extensive nature of secondary data that will be abundantly available, these issues will become even more relevant in the future.

Ethical issues relating to qualitative research

When conducting qualitative research, ethical issues related to the respondents and the general public will be of primary concern. These issues include:

- disguising the purpose of the research
- disguising the use of deceptive procedures
- videotaping and recording the proceedings
- the comfort level of the respondents
- misusing the findings of qualitative research.

All indirect procedures require researchers to disguise the purpose of the research, at least to some extent. Often, a cover story is used to camouflage the true purpose. This can not only violate the respondents' right to know but also result in psychological harm. To minimize such negative effects, the respondents should be informed up-front that the true purpose of the research is being disguised so as not to bias the responses. After completing the research tasks, debriefing sessions should be held in which the respondents are informed about the true purpose and given opportunities to make comments or ask questions. We expect that greater attention will be paid in the future to avoiding deceptive procedures that violate respondents' right to privacy and informed consent: for example, allowing clients to observe focus groups or in-depth interviews by introducing them as colleagues helping with the project (Malhotra and Miller 1998).

One ethical dilemma involves videotaping or recording a focus group or depth interview without the prior knowledge or consent of the participants. Ethical guidelines suggest that respondents should be informed and their consent obtained prior to the start of the proceedings, preferably at the time of recruitment. Furthermore, at the end of the meeting, participants should be asked to sign a written statement conveying their permission to use the recording. This statement should disclose the true purpose of the research, and all people who will have access to the recording. Participants should be given an opportunity to refuse to sign. The tapes should be edited to completely omit the identity and comments of the respondents who have refused. We expect that in the future codes of ethical conduct will stipulate such practices.

Another concern that will receive more attention is the comfort level of the respondents. During qualitative research, particularly in in-depth interviews, respondents should not be pushed beyond the point where they become uncomfortable. Respect for the respondent's welfare should warrant restraint on the part of the moderator or interviewer. If a respondent feels uncomfortable and does not wish to answer more questions on a particular topic, the interviewer should not aggressively probe further.

Ethical issues relating to quantitative research

The marketing research industry will become more proactive and aggressive in positioning its undertaking as distinct from selling. Branding techniques will be incorporated more frequently, such as announcing to respondents that the research project is 'CASRO-approved', or 'meets the standards of the European Society for Opinion and Market Research (ESOMAR)'. The use of survey research as a guise for selling or fundraising is clearly unethical. Another ethical issue that is salient in survey and observation research is respondents' anonymity. Researchers have an obligation to not disclose respondents' names to outside parties, including the client. This is more critical if the respondents were promised anonymity in order to obtain their participation. The client is not entitled to the names of respondents. Only when respondents are notified in advance, and their consent is obtained prior to administering the survey, can their names be disclosed to the client. Even in such situations, the researcher should have the assurance that the client will not use respondents' names in a sales effort or misuse them in other ways. Researchers should not place respondents in stressful situations. Disclaimers such as 'There are no right or wrong answers, we are only interested in your opinion' can relieve much of the stress inherent in a survey.

Ethical issues related to observing and recording the behaviour of respondents will gain in importance. Often the behaviour of people is observed without their knowledge because informing the respondents may alter their behaviour. However, this can violate the respondents' privacy. One guideline is that people should not be observed for research in situations where they would not expect to be observed by the public. However, even observing people in public places like a mall or a grocery store is only appropriate if certain procedures are followed. Notices should be posted in these areas stating that they are under observation for marketing research purposes. After the data have been collected, the researcher should obtain the necessary permission from the respondents. If any of the respondents refuse to grant permission, the observation records pertaining to them should be destroyed. These guidelines should also be applied when using cookies on the Internet. Cookies are small bits of information about a user's previous access to a single website. These cookies are usually created by the website programs and stored in a user's browser.

Several ethical issues related to the researcher–respondent relationship and the researcher–client relationship need to be addressed in questionnaire design. Of particular concern are the use of overly long questionnaires, asking sensitive questions and deliberately biasing the questionnaire. Respondents are volunteering their time and should not be overburdened by soliciting too much information. The researcher should avoid overly long questionnaires. Sensitive questions deserve special attention. On one hand, candid and honest responses are needed to generate meaningful findings. On the other hand, the researcher should not invade respondents' privacy or cause them undue stress. Finally, the researcher has the ethical responsibility of designing the questionnaire so as to obtain the required information in an unbiased manner. Deliberately biasing the questionnaire in a desired direction – for example, by asking leading questions – cannot be condoned. Also, the questionnaire should be thoroughly pre-tested before fieldwork begins, or an ethical breach will have occurred.

The researcher has several ethical responsibilities to both the client and the respondents in the sampling process, and these will become increasingly important in the future. Pertaining to the client, the researcher must develop a sampling design that is appropriate for controlling sampling and non-sampling errors. When appropriate, probability sampling should be used. When non-probability sampling is used, effort should be made to obtain a representative sample. It is unethical and misleading to treat non-probability samples as probability samples and to project the results onto a target population.

Researchers must be sensitive to preserving the anonymity of the respondents when conducting business-to-business research, employee research, and other projects in which the population size is small. When the population size is small, it is easier to discern the identities of the respondents than when the samples are drawn from a large population. Sampling details that are too revealing or verbatim quotations in reports to the client can compromise the anonymity of the respondents. In such situations, the researcher has the ethical obligation to protect the identities of the respondents, even if it means limiting the level of sampling detail that is reported to the client and other parties.

Future directions in ethics

As clients become more sophisticated, they will increasingly participate in marketing research decisions along with the researchers. This will occur as researchers participate more in marketing decision making, as discussed earlier. This blending of the roles will lead to more openness, communication and understanding, minimizing the ethical conflicts related to the researcher and the clients.

Greater attention will be paid to preserving the rights of the respondents. The invasion of respondents' privacy has already become a burning issue (Nowak and Phelps 1997). For example, the use of telephone surveys is being threatened by legislation. About half of the states in the United States have introduced bills to regulate unsolicited telephone calls, and the remainder are considering similar legislation. A California law, designed to limit eavesdropping, makes it illegal to listen in on an extension, and this might limit supervisory monitoring of telephone interviewers.

In the network era, the individual consumer's power position among the stakeholders will improve so that marketers will increasingly rely on consumers' permission to offer them goods and services online (Godin 1999). This development will heighten consumers' concerns about privacy in the world of online transactions. Such concern will become a critical issue in the future of online business. Consumer advocates believe that consumers will ultimately own and control their own historical profile of activity with businesses (Clemons and Bradley 1998). In this setting, consumers would have the ability to bring their profile to any online exchange opportunity. In this way, the consumer's first visit to a virtual store will be as satisfying as a repeat visit. However, the control over consumer information will confer such significant influence over consumer activities that the struggle over who captures, controls, owns and uses consumer information will be a titanic one. If the issue of privacy for individual consumers cannot be resolved satisfactorily for consumers, government regulatory intervention could be likely.

One way in which this dilemma will be resolved is by the marketing research industry voluntarily adopting practices and codes of conduct that show a greater respect for the rights of the respondents and general public. We expect to see codes of conduct receive more emphasis and significance. While several national marketing and marketing research associations have ethical guidelines, a truly international code of marketing research ethics seems to be lacking. However, such a code should emerge in the near future. For example, ESOMAR (www.esomar.nl), has a detailed and comprehensive code of ethical research behaviour that could be used as a starting point for formulating a more global marketing research code of ethics.

Using the Internet for international marketing research

The World Wide Web (WWW) is the dominant component of the Internet, and many use the terms 'web' and 'Internet' synonymously. The Internet is transforming the way marketing research is being conducted. As James (2000) remarked, 'fuelled by the Internet, the network era is exploding bringing about more sweeping change than the advent of the personal computer'. The technological infrastructure being created will enable rich, individual telecommunication between marketers and individual consumers (Struse 2000). As the network era ushers in ultimate customization or 'one-to-one' marketing, marketing research is adapting to these new technologies.

Exploratory and qualitative research

Bulletin boards (newsgroups), web-moderated interviewing consisting of Internet forums, and chat rooms are increasingly being used for exploratory research. They are used to communicate with experts or individuals representing the target audience in order to obtain background information and develop an understanding of the research context. Bulletin boards are conducted by inviting respondents to a specific website where a discussion topic is posted. As responses are made to the question, others can read what has been submitted. Like a 'slow-motion focus group', bulletin boards could be useful when a researcher needs to discuss issues with a panel of experts or participants in a beta test.

The importance of the Internet as a source of external secondary data will continue to grow. The Internet – or Net – will be increasingly used for identifying marketing research information on companies. This includes information on firms that supply specific services and client organizations, as well as competitors, collaborators and affiliates. Some data that would previously have been otherwise difficult to obtain is now accessible easily and quickly through the Net. The Internet gives information on new and current subjects that is not published yet. Information on the web is of good quality if it comes from original sources and it is current. The utility of the Internet for the market researcher is further enhanced due to the easy accessibility and retrieval of information and easy cross-validation of the information available from several sources.

The current benefits of online secondary research to the competitive intelligence efforts of companies have been overshadowed by the potential benefits of online primary research to customer research efforts. The excitement of receiving more rapid feedback from customers has been fanned by research agencies bringing automation to the previously slow and laborious data collection efforts they have offered. The gains of integrating information technologies with survey research practices have been trumpeted many times in recent years (Taylor 2000). Meanwhile, the undeniable benefits gained from using the World Wide Web to keep abreast of competitor actions by collecting and analysing secondary data have arrived with much less fanfare (Dutka 1999). The competitive intelligence capabilities offered by the Internet will become more pronounced in the international arena as penetration for the Internet increases in more countries.

An often-heard claim is that 90 per cent of the information an organization needs is in the public domain. If this was true, much time and expense needed to be invested to actually come into possession of such information ten years ago. Five years ago, exhaustive searches of the World Wide Web might not have returned much of that mythical 90 per cent. Now, more complete information is available on the Web and the researcher now has the power of search agents (also called 'bots' or 'spiders'), which can theoretically compare prices and features across every available retailer on the Internet (Dolan and Moon 2000). The 90 per cent' is now more accessible than ever to the web-savvy researcher, and the availability and accessibility of this information will increase even further.

An example of the new sophistication in search agents is the third-party price comparison site MySimon.com (see also Pricescan.com, Compare.Net and DealTime.com). Visitors to this site indicate the item of interest, and the search agent scans product and pricing information from a list of hundreds of online sellers stocking the item. Full-colour visual images of products can be included. A recent competitive intelligence project done by an international marketer of fashion watches returned rich information about 12 competitors' image and price positioning in cyberspace. This project not only suggested strategic image positioning for the fashion watch marketer, but also tactical moves in pricing.

The freewheeling atmosphere prevalent in cyberspace currently encourages use of such search agents, as these sites are seeking notoriety. However, these search agents were not developed specifically for researchers. (The sites featuring these agents typically earn a commission every time a buyer accesses a merchant site and ultimately buys an item through the search.) In time, researchers will likely develop their own search agents in order to avoid ethical dilemmas as use of the web matures. The desire for more customized versions of these search agents will also spur researchers to develop their own search tools.

For those researchers with access to fee-based databases of periodicals, journals, and company-based information, such as ABI/Inform, Dow Jones Interactive and Lexis/Nexis, background research can be accomplished with new power. For those without access to such fee-based databases, free-access sites remain extremely useful. The implications of the recent advances in Internet research to managers are plain. They must either develop a team that has become well versed in using the tools and resources of the Internet, or make decisions with lower-quality information than competitors. Firms failing to do this will have their business models changed from providing valued goods and services to providing commodities – if they survive, at all. The good news for small businesses in all this is that the Internet brings them closer to having the rich information formerly available only to major corporations with multi-million dollar research budgets. Managers adept as Internet researchers are likely to lead firms who capitalize on this opportunity.

Organizations will increasingly use intranets that greatly facilitate the search for access to internal secondary data. The Coca-Cola Company, for example, has developed powerful intranet applications that enable its managers worldwide to search for past and current research studies and a wide variety of marketing-related information on the basis of key words. Once located, the information can be accessed online. More and more qualitative research will be conducted on the Internet. Online focus groups will become commonplace, and even be preferred to traditional focus groups for a wide range of scenarios. The Internet enables the researcher to reach segments that are usually hard to access: doctors, lawyers, professional people, working mothers, and others who lead busy lives and are not interested in taking part in traditional focus groups. They offer several advantages, including less time and low costs, and can bridge the time and distance gap in recruiting respondents. Even individual depth interviews (IDIs) and projective techniques will gain popularity on the Net. The traditional disadvantages of the Internet in responses being less spontaneous, lack of interactivity between/with respondents, and limited group dynamics will be substantially overcome as the Internet becomes a way of life (Edmondson 1997).

Descriptive and quantitative research

Internet surveys will increase in popularity. One reason is that the cost in most cases is less than for phone and mail surveys or personal interviews, three of the most common types of survey. The Internet survey is also not as inconvenient as the phone call in the middle of dinner. The online survey can be completed in people's own time and place. Quick response time and the ability to target specific populations are also advantages worth noting. As Internet usage becomes more widespread, the disadvantages of this method in terms of sampling limitations and representativeness will be substantially reduced.

Surveys on the Internet can be conducted by way of email, websites, or downloading from websites. The survey can be included in the email or attached. Click buttons and boxes and fill-in text boxes are features used in these surveys. Additional programming using CGI (a scripting language that reads the data into a database when it is received) or HTML can automate the data entry process for such a web survey. A multiple-page web survey using fixed-form interactive authoring tools will present questions individually as in a CATI. A more graphically elaborate version of the multiple-page web survey can be created using customized interactive programming. Downloadable surveys that shift the computing tasks to the respondent's PC have also been used successfully. Once the respondent downloads software provided by the researcher, a smaller file containing the survey is run on the respondent's computer. The resulting data file from this survey can then be uploaded the next time the Internet is accessed. The additional costs of programming and time required by respondents for downloadable surveys (20 minutes to two hours) make downloadable surveys more demanding to field. However, with advances in technology and increasing use of broadband, this situation is likely to change, making downloadable surveys more attractive.

The Internet will be used increasingly for observation. The primary observations are the number of times a webpage is visited and the time spent on the page. Further, various other links can be provided by the researcher on the webpage and it can be observed which links are accessed more often. This provides the researcher with important information about the information needs of the individuals and also of the interests of the target segment. Analysis of the links from which a company site is approached by the individuals provides market researchers with important information regarding consumers' related interests, and an in-depth analysis of the link sites provides information on advertising, image, competitors, consumers, target market demographics and psychographics.

The Internet will become a useful vehicle for conducting causal research. Different experimental treatments can be displayed at different websites. Respondents can then be recruited to visit these sites and respond to a questionnaire that obtains information on the dependent variable. Thus, the Internet will provide a mechanism for controlled experimentation, in a laboratory type of environment. Sampling potential respondents who are surfing the Internet will become more meaningful as such samples will increasingly approximate populations of interest as the penetration of the Internet increases. More and more industries will meet this criterion. In software, computers, networking, technical publishing, semiconductors and graduate education, it is rapidly becoming feasible to use the Internet for sampling respondents for quantitative research, such as surveys. Sampling on the Internet will also become practical for many non-computer-oriented consumer products. Extensive pre-recruited pools of respondents will be more frequently used to approximate probability sampling. Such panels will be recruited via mail and personal contact, not via the Internet. Panels such as these already exist and have millions of potential respondents from just about every country in the world (Decision Analyst 2000). Such techniques will further enhance the Internet research findings.

Summary

In the new millennium, the field of international marketing research holds great promise. In this chapter an attempt has been made to combine theoretical and practical

perspectives to identify the issues and trends pertinent in the future. It is highly important to blend these two perspectives. For the potential of international marketing
research to be realized, it is crucial that the gap between academic and commercial
marketing research be bridged. This can occur by academic researchers examining
substantive issues that are managerially relevant. Simultaneously, applied marketing
researchers must realize that marketing research should be grounded in theory. Theory
enables a meaningfully interpretation and integration of the findings with previous
research. Thus, a cross-fertilization of academic and applied research is needed.

Change is occurring in virtually all aspects of business and personal life. These
changes are being played out at different rates in different parts of the world. Against this
backdrop, marketing researchers are being challenged to conduct research that is of the
highest possible quality, as quickly as possible, in multiple diverse settings. The issues
marketing researchers face are multifaceted, and relate to where and how research will
be conducted, who the respondents will be, and the tools and techniques that will be
used.

Marketing researchers must find creative ways to harness new technologies to facilitate the conduct of research and enhance its value to clients. At the same time,
research organizations must begin to develop the capability to conduct marketing
research simultaneously in the developed and the developing world. Increasingly,
multinational marketers are designing and selling global brands and need research to
guide their decision making across an increasingly diverse and disparate world. Sound
and timely marketing research becomes even more critical for firms as they compete in
the twenty-first century.

Revision questions

1   What do you consider to be the importance of information in decision-making process
    relating to international marketing?
2   Discuss the use of IT for international marketing planning.
3   What are the benefits of secondary data collection for evaluating international
    markets?
4   Discuss the major sources of information available to the international marketing
    researcher.
5   What are the main advantages of qualitative research?
6   Rapid changes in the international marketing environment have affected the way
    international marketing research is conducted. Discuss.
7   Implementing the sample design process in international markets is a complex
    process. Suggest the factors that should be taken into consideration in defining the
    target population.
8   Explain how the Internet has affected the international marketing information
    systems and its implications for international market researchers.
9   Describe some of the survey techniques used by the international market researchers
    for obtaining field information.
10 What do you consider to be the main problems of researching in less developed
    countries, and how could these problems be resolved?

Managerial assignment task

You are a researcher for a UK manufacturer of biscuits who is considering selling these products to the Nigerian market. You are required to write a research proposal for entering this market, which should include:

- a design of a market research project for your company, giving a detailed evaluation of the Nigerian market to enable the production of a marketing plan
- an explanation of how market research information can assist the company to decide on the marketing mixes for the Nigerian market
- an outline of the problems the company is likely to encounter in planning market research in an underdeveloped country such as Nigeria.

References

Clemons, E. K. and Bradley, S. P. (1998) 'Strategic uncertainty and the future of online consumer interaction', pp. 85–106 in S. P. Bradley, and R. L. Nolan (eds), *Sense and Respond*, Boston, Mass.: Harvard Business School Press.

Craig, C. S. and Douglas, S. P. (2000) *International Marketing Research*, 2nd edn, Chichester: Wiley.

Czinkota, M. R. (2000) 'International information cross-fertilization in marketing: an empirical assessment', *European Journal of Marketing*, Vol. 34, Nos 11/12, pp. 1305–14.

Decision Analyst Economic Index (2000) 'No Y2K hangover' [online] http:// www.decisionanalyst. com/publ_data/2000/economy.dai (accessed 10 July 2008).

Dolan, R. and Moon, Y. (2000) 'Pricing and market making on the Internet', *Journal of Interactive Marketing*, Vol. 14, No. 2, pp. 56–73.

Douglas, S. P. and Craig, C. S. (1997) 'The changing dynamic of consumer behaviour: implications for cross-cultural research', *International Journal of Research in Marketing*, Vol. 14, pp. 379–95.

Dutka, A. (1999) *Competitive Intelligence for the Competitive Edge*, Lincolnwood, Illl.: NTC Business Books.

Edmondson, B. (1997) 'The wired bunch', *American Demographics,* June, pp. 10–15.

ESOMAR (1996) *ESOMAR 1995 Pricing Study*, Amsterdam.

Gates, B. (1999) *Business @ The Speed of Thought*, New York: Warner,

Godin, S. (1999) *Permission Marketing*, New York: Simon & Schuster.

Honomichl, J. (2000) 'Research revenues on the rise in '99', *Marketing News*, 2 June, p. 6.

Huang, C. L. (1998) 'Canadian business pursuits in the PRC, Hong Kong and Taiwan, and Chinese perception of Canadians as business partners', *Multinational Business Review*, Vol. 6, No. 1, pp. 73–82.

James, D. (2000) 'The future on online research', *Marketing News*, January, pp. 1, 11.

Kumar, V. (2000) *International Marketing Research*, Upper Saddle River, N.J.: Prentice-Hall.

Leverick, F., Littler, D., Wilson, D. and Bruce, M. (1997) 'The role of IT in the reshaping of marketing', *Journal of Marketing Practice*, Vol. 3, No. 2, pp. 87–106.

MacElroy, B. (1999) 'Comparing seven forms of on-line surveying', *Quirk's Marketing Research Review*, July, pp. 40–5.

Malhotra, N. K. and Miller, G. (1998) 'An integrated model for ethical decisions in marketing research', *Journal of Business Ethics*, Vol. 17, No. 2, pp. 63–80.

Malhotra, N. K. and Miller, G. (1999) 'Social responsibility and the marketing educator: a focus on stakeholders, ethical theories, and related codes of ethics, *Journal of Business Ethics*, Vol. 19, No. 2, pp. 11–24.

Malhotra, N. K. and Peterson, M. (2001) 'Marketing research in the new millennium: emerging issues and trends', *Marketing Intelligence and Planning*, Vol. 19, No. 4, pp. 216–35.

Mitevska, N. G. and Meyer, M. (1997) 'The role of marketing research in Bulgaria: activities, scope, and importance', *Journal of Euromarketing*, Vol. 6, No. 2, pp. 57–73.

Nowak, G. J. and Phelps, J. (1997) 'Direct marketing and the use of individual-level consumer information: determining how and when privacy matters', *Journal of Direct Marketing,* Vol. 11, No. 4, pp. 94–108.

Peterson, M. and Malhotra, N. K. (1997) 'Comparative marketing measures of societal quality of life: substantive dimensions in 186 countries', *Journal of Macromarketing*, Vol. 17, No. 1, pp. 25–38.

Struse, D. (2000) 'Marketing research's top 25 influences', *Marketing Research*, Winter/Spring, pp. 5–9.

Taylor, H. (2000) 'The power of on-line research', *Quirk's Marketing Research Review*, Vol 46 (April), pp. 48–9.

Thiesse, M. (1996) 'The latest developments in qualitative research', unpublished document, Research International Qualititif, Paris.

United Nations Development Programme (1999) *Human Development Report*, New York: Oxford University Press.

US Dept of Commerce (2008) *Commercial Research*, Annual Report of the Committee on Commercial Research, US Department of Commerce.

Worldwide Internet Conference (1999) *Net Effects*, Amsterdam: ESOMAR.

4

International Competitive Marketing Strategies

Contents

LEARNING OBJECTIVES

After reading this chapter you should:

- understand many of the theories that explain why one country is more competitive than another
- know the structural analysis of a firm and the five forces that determine the long-term profitability of a given industry
- understand the rationale for combining corporate and marketing strategies for international competitiveness

- be able to evaluate the role of psychic distance in the corporate marketing performance in the international marketplace
- know the factors that influence strategic marketing planning for multinational firms
- be able to evaluate the generic strategic options in world markets.

Introduction

The movement towards an international consumer market has increased the competitive environment of multinational organizations. As a result of the increase in competition, organizations have attempted to implement a variety of strategy programmes. In international marketing, managers have focused on the debate between standard, regional and local-based strategies. However, the implementation of marketing strategy is not a question of regional, local or standardization, but is rather an issue of knowing when to use each strategic alternative. Effective marketing strategy adoption can be determined by examining the foundation (that is, the core competences) on which the firm operates. By adopting a marketing strategy that is compatible with the multinational's corporate strategy, the firm can achieve a strategic competitive advantage in the international marketplace.

This chapter provides a concept of successful corporate marketing and behaviour segmentation strategy – combinations that will allow multinational corporations to achieve dominance. Cost, customer and innovation-based corporate strategies provide the impetus for defining both international marketing (standard, local and regional) and target market behaviour segmentation. The concepts are combined to provide a new unified concept for determining the most effective marketing strategy to implement, based on the firm's corporate strategy.

International market competitive theories

Many theories have tried to explain why one country is more competitive than another. For some, national competitiveness comes from macroeconomic phenomena (see Chapter 2) directed by change rates, interest rates and the national balance of payments. For others, it depends on the abundance of cheap labour or raw materials (see Passemard and Kleiner 2000). Some have shown the importance of the political support. However, none of these explanations is *sufficient* to explain the commercial success of a country.

Michael Porter developed an alternative to these rather macroeconomic explanations. Porter's work consists in studying specific industrial sectors and segments of a nation instead of the overall economy. He studied what specific element conditions the international success of a firm in a certain segment, and found that the firms in a country must have competitive advantage in the form of lower costs or a differentiated product if they are to achieve worldwide success. Porter (1991) further observed that the advantage is situated in the products rather than in the external elements of a country. Thus, it is interesting to consider what is the fundamental basis of competitive advantage, and how firms improve their competitive advantage through the internationalization of economic factors.

The origin and nature of competitive advantage

The evolution of competitive advantage is a function of the way the firm organizes and manages its activities. The functioning of a firm can be divided into various activities, including solicitation of customers, conception and realization of new products by the research and development (R&D) department, and maintenance activities. Each of these activities creates value for customers (see Porter 1985), and the final value created is determined by the price the customers agree to pay for the product or service. The firm is profitable if this value is greater than the internal cost elements. In order to achieve a competitive advantage against its competitors, the firm should supply its customers with the same value as competitors and be more efficient in its production (a cost domination strategy), or elaborate specific activities that generate a greatest final value and authorize higher purchase prices (a differentiation strategy). These activities can be classified in what Porter called the 'value chain' (see Figure 4.1).

All the activities in the value chain contribute to create value for the customers. These activities are of two types: primary activities involved in the continuity of production, and support activities. Whatever the activity, the firm requires an infrastructure (including the board of directors) and finance. The firm's strategy will define the way the value chain is organized. When the firm conceives a new way to manage its activities, uses new technologies or different means of production, it may acquire a competitive advantage. However, a firm is more than a simple addition of these activities. The value chain is a real network of interdependent activities whose costs are linked (see Passemard and Kleiner 2000). For example, the firm can reduce the cost of services by investing more in the conception of the product, or by integrating more expensive but better-quality components. The good management of this system of interdependence is a real source of competitive advantage, which can be decisive. The advantageous exploitation of these interdependencies requires the company to succeed in both organizational coordination and making compromises between the different departments.

The value system

Besides the value chain, which is the basis of the competitiveness of a firm, there is a larger flow of activities called the 'value system'. This value system includes the value chains of the firm's suppliers, the firm itself, its distributors and its customers. The product goes from one value chain to another, becoming each time a means of production. Competitive advantage can then be seen as more a function of the firm's know-how in

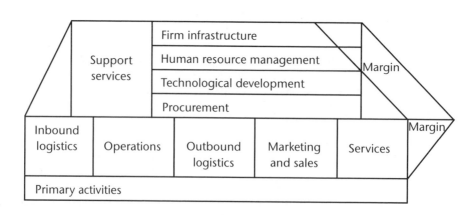

Figure 4.1   The value chain
Source: adapted and modified from Porter (1985).

managing the international value system, so it is up to the firm to create competitive advantage by optimizing and coordinating its existing external relationships. The value chain appears to be a useful evaluator of cost advantage since to be sure to get this kind of advantage, the firm has to ensure the optimization and the coordination of its functional activities. It also highlights the factors of differentiation, since differentiation results from the way products and/or services affect the customers' activity. Thus, the ideas of the value chain and value system allow us not only to analyse more deeply the different types of competitive advantage, but also to understand the role of competitive scope in the acquisition of a competitive advantage.

Competitive scope is very important since it is controls the nature of all the activities within the firm, and the configuration of the value chain. The firm that chooses a narrow target is able to adjust precisely its performance to the needs of the segment. It has a superior potential to reduce its costs, and to practise product differentiation, over firms which choose a large target. However, a larger target can allow a firm to reduce its cost through economies of scale. To ensure a competitive advantage the firm may choose a different competitive scope or a different segment from its competitors.

The competitive strategy

The appropriate unit of analysis in setting competitive strategy is the industry (which is a group of firms in direct competition). Strategically, one industry may be distinguished from another by the fact that its products have similar sources of competitive advantage. In other words, the industry is the environment within which firms win or lose competitive advantage. The firm, with its competitive advantage, must define and elaborate a profitable approach to its industry. There is no universal strategy, but to be successful, a strategy must be specific to the firm and the industry under consideration. The strategy must be based on the firm's scope of competence and capabilities.

In every competitive strategy, there are two components to distinguish. The first is the structure of the industry in which the firm evolves. For instance, levels of profitability vary considerably from one industry to another (for example, the pharmaceutical industry is much more profitable than the iron and steel industry). Second, one positioning of the firm within the industry may be more advantageous than another whatever the profitability level.

A competitive strategy should therefore be based on a deep analysis of the structure of the industry and its evolution. As Michael Porter observed, in every industry (taken nationally or world-wide), the competitive strategy can be described through five forces (see Figure 4.2):

- the threat of incoming enterprises
- the threat of replacement products
- the suppliers' power of bargaining
- the customers' power of bargaining
- the rivalry inside between the firms in the same sector.

The action of these five forces determines the long-run profitability of a given industry. When the five forces act favourably, a great number of firms will see a good return on investment. On the contrary, when one or several forces are more active than the others

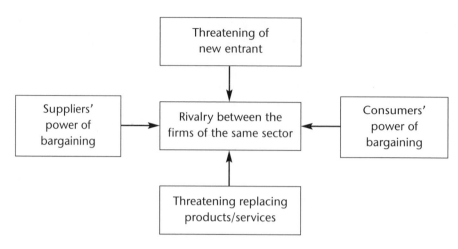

Figure 4.2   The five competitive forces
Source: adapted from Porter (1990).

(such as in the iron and steel industry or the computer industry) the number of profitable firms will be smaller. The intensity of these five forces depends on the structure of the industry: that is, its main economic and technical characteristics. For instance, how difficult it is for a new firm to come into the industry depends on the height of the barriers to entry, such as customers' fidelity and economy of scale. Each industry has its specific structure. However, this structure may evolve with the sector. Indeed, firms can have an influence on the forces. For example, they can reduce the pressure from incoming firms by increasing the barriers to entry (for example, raising the level of fixed costs).

It is not enough for a firm to consider the structure of the industry; it also has to take an appropriate position within the industry. The positioning of a firm has to match the option it had taken with regard to the market. For example, in the confectionery industry, the US company M&M/MARS preferred mass production of average-quality confectionery products, while Swiss companies such as Lindt chose to market high-quality chocolate through a more limited distribution network.

The fundamental component of the positioning is competitive advantage, which as noted above must be based on either low costs or differentiation. Advantage by low costs means that the company is more efficient than its competitors in the conception, production and marketing of a product. Thus, for a given price, the firm will be more profitable than others (see Figure 4.3). Differentiation is the ability of the firm to supply its customers with the same type of product, but of a better quality. In both cases, the competitive advantage translates into a higher profit for the firm.

It is very difficult for a firm to obtain both cost and differentiation advantages simultaneously. A firm can improve its technology and method of production to reduce its cost and differentiate itself, but in the long-run competitors will imitate its behaviour, and the firm will be required to choose which type of advantage to pursue.

Another criterion for positioning is competitive scope: that is, the extent of the target within an industry. The firm must determine the range of products it will produce, the type of customers it will attract, the geographical area it will invest in, and so on. This criterion is very important since all industries can be segmented (that is, the same types of products are aimed at different markets). For example, a T-shirt from Primark and a T-shirt from Lacoste are both clothing items, but they are considered by customers as different because they target different sectors of the clothes market. Supplying different segments requires the firm to have the necessary capacities and the specific strategies. Thus, it is possible to find various types of competitive scope within the same industry.

The concept of strategic platform has been developed to categorize the types of strategy a firm should adopt in order to get the best performance in any given industry. Figure 4.3 shows the four archetypes of strategic platform. This concept explains why there is no universal strategy. Many profitable strategies could coexist and result in competitive advantage. Then to ensure its leadership, the firm should define sharply the type of advantage it is seeking, and the scope over which the advantage is to be reached. The worst strategy for the firm is not to choose a particular strategy. This will drive the company to a bad strategy position that will bring low profitability.

Competitive advantage in an international market

The pattern of international competition differs markedly from industry to industry. Industries can be classified along a spectrum from multidomestic to global in their competitive scope.

In *multidomestic industries* (banking, insurance, caustic chemicals), competition in each country is independent from competition in other countries. Thus, competition occurs on a country-by-country basis. The competitive advantage of enterprises evolving in such industries is largely specific to the country.

An *international industry* is a collection of domestic industries. The international firm's strategy should be country-centred and its subsidiaries should enjoy great autonomy.

At the other end of the spectrum are *global industries* (typically producing electrical goods such as televisions, semi-conductors, motor cars), which can be defined as industries in which a firm's competitive position in one country may be significantly affected by its position in other countries.

An *international market* is a series of linked domestic industries in which the rivals compete against each other on a world-wide basis. All competitors in an international market compete with increasingly coordinated strategies. The firms must integrate their activities on a world-wide basis to capture the linkage between countries.

		Competitive advantage	
		Lower cost	Lower cost
Competitive scope	Large target	Domination by lower costs	Differentiation
	Narrow target	Global cost strategy	Specialized strategy

Figure 4.3   Four archetypes of strategic platform

International competitive strategy

There is no single ideal international strategy (see Passemard and Kleiner 2000). There are several ways to get involved in international competition, each of which demands choices about geographical scope and the coordination of activities. Table 4.1 lists some potential international strategies. The simplest international strategy is to concentrate as many activities as possible in one country, serve the world from this home base, and tightly coordinate through standardization those activities that must inherently be performed near the purchaser. This was the strategy used by Japanese car firms such as Toyota during the 1960s and 1970s.

Table 4.1 International marketing strategies

		Configuration of activities	
		Geographically dispersed	Geographically concentrated
Coordination of activities	High	High foreign investment with extensive coordination among subsidiaries	Simple international strategy
	Low	Country-centred strategy by multinational or domestic firms operating in only one country	Export-based strategy with decentralized marketing

There are many different kinds of international strategy, depending on firms' choices about configuration and coordination throughout the value chain (see page 108). Competitors with country-centred strategies can coexist in an industry, but international strategies by some competitors frequently force other firms to follow. Thus, an international strategy can be defined as one in which a firm seeks to gain competitive advantage from its international presence through a concentrated configuration, dispersed and coordinated activities, or both. The degree of internationalization will also depend on the position upstream or downstream of activities. For example, in the aluminium industry, the upstream stages (alumna, ingot) are international, and the downstream stage of semi-fabrication is a group of multiple domestic businesses because product needs vary by country, transport costs are high, and intensive local customer service is required.

Sustainable competitive advantage

Competitive advantage is born as soon as a firm discovers and implements a new or a more efficient way to operate within an industry: that is, when it innovates. However, the word 'innovation' should be understood in its widest meaning. Defining the source of innovation is equivalent to describing the ways to create competitive advantage. It is in fact possible to distinguish five main sources of innovation:

- new technologies
- modification of demand or a new demand
- the occurrence of a new segment
- changes in the costs or the availability of means of production
- changes in regulations.

The creation of competitive advantage may be a tough task, but preserving it is much harder (Porter 1985). The preservation of competitive advantage depends on three conditions. The first concerns the sources of the advantage. There is a hierarchy among advantages, which can be minor (say, a small reduction in workforce costs), or major (exclusive possession of a special technology). The second determining factor is the number of sources of competitive advantage (the more, the better). The third factor of preservation is related to the continuous effort of modernizing and perfecting: virtually every advantage is susceptible to being copied. So the preservation of competitive advantage requires the firm to adopt an unnatural behaviour consisting of continuous changes in its strategies. But no one would naturally change a winning team.

Corporate and marketing strategy

As noted earlier, corporate strategy is what position multinationals in the international marketplace ,and it is guided by the firm's core competences. For a firm to compete in the competitive international marketplace, it must select and implement a marketing strategy that is compatible with – indeed has a synergistic bond with – its corporate strategy. Through the correct strategy combination, a multinational can maximize its own competitive advantage(s), thus allowing it to compete effectively and efficiently throughout the world.

The schema for combining marketing and corporate strategy is illustrated in Figure 4.4. By analysing traditional corporate strategies under behavioural characteristics, multinationals may be able to flexibly implement the appropriate marketing strategy (whether standardization, regional or local), while targeting in an effective way specific consumer segments throughout the world. The rationale for combining corporate and marketing strategy for international competitiveness is twofold:

- Each strategy combination either does or does not make sense conceptually when real-world considerations are weighed. For example, the control and centralization that is required for a low-cost approach supports a one-size-fits-all standardization strategy and is appropriate for a target market of international sophisticates (see page 123), whereas low-cost production and standardization targeted for acceptance in a provincial customer market are contradictory.
- The international strategic marketing decision tree is compelling from a strictly practical position.

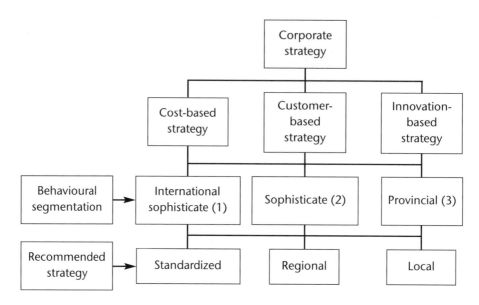

Figure 4.4 International strategic marketing decisions

Operating strategies

There are three core types of operating strategy: low cost, customer-based and innovation-based. These strategy options are briefly discussed below.

Low-cost strategy

Firms using a low-cost strategy are likely to provide customers with quality products and services at competitive prices. These companies follow an organizational philosophy of leading the industry in price and convenience. Relying on economies of scale and competitive pricing, organizations position themselves in the market as a cost leader.

It is important to differentiate the concept of cost-based corporate strategy from pricing strategy. Whereas the latter seeks to position the product in consumers' minds using price as a cue, the former focuses on becoming the most cost-efficient producer of the product.

Multinationals using this strategy – McDonald's, United Parcel Service and Coca-Cola, for example – target customers who are interested in getting quality products at the lowest possible price with the least possible hassle, rather than in the specific product features or attributes they are buying.

Customer-based strategy

Multinationals refining their products and services to meet specific customer needs are said to be following a customer-based corporate strategy. By redefining their products according to specific market needs, these multinationals are able to establish strong customer relationships. Employing a corporate strategy aimed at understanding their customers, these firms are able to provide a higher level of service and re-establish the level of value expected by their customers.

Firms using this strategy target customers who are concerned more with getting exactly what they need than with the price that they pay. Through the redefinition of value in the segment of the marketplace, firms such as Procter & Gamble, Volvo and Philips have been able to achieve strategic competitive advantages in their respective industries.

Innovative strategy

Multinationals competing on the basis of innovation may strive to produce top-of-the-range, cutting-edge products. These organizations believe that by fostering an entrepreneurial environment their employees will continually challenge themselves to produce innovative products. The production of innovative products will allow the multinational to establish itself as an innovative organization. The use of this philosophy means targeting customers who are willing to pay premium prices in order to obtain state-of-the-art products.

Firms such as Michelin, Ciba-Geigy and Sony use this strategy to position themselves as innovators throughout the world.

The different corporate strategies highlight the core competence the organization is using to differentiate itself from its competitors. Not only does the corporate strategy identify how the organization positions itself in the marketplace, it also identifies consumer choice criteria. For example, customers who value innovative products, or low-cost products, can be found throughout the world. Whether the organization is targeting customers in New York, London, Paris, Madrid or Brussels, those using similar choice criteria are known to exist. However, it is crucial to develop and implement the appropriate marketing strategy within the framework of the firm's product, core competences and the international competitive environment. This raises the question of which strategic approach multinationals should adopt.

Strategic options (regional, local or standardization)

Standardization proponents have argued from the beginning that consumers are becoming more homogeneous in terms of their wants and needs (Levitt 1983), due most notably to an increase in international television broadcasting and international travel. By standardizing marketing strategy, managers seek to achieve economies of scale and brand-image consistency.

Champions of localization argue that the use of international marketing strategy is based on a flawed assumption (the world population is becoming homogeneous). The localization advocates argue that standardization authors ignore the importance of culture. Cultural differences, a fatal omission in the homogenization argument, cannot be ignored and may have a significant impact on consumer behaviour. Since cultural differences between individuals and societies are the barriers to standardization, marketers need to identify specific target markets and then service them effectively. Accordingly, firms are customizing their marketing strategies to compete effectively in individual markets.

The advocates of regional segmentation strategy contend that the practice of market segmentation in domestic markets is a clear indicator of the ineffectiveness of treating the whole world as a homogeneous market. Regional market segmentation usually examines homogeneous segments (that is, those with similar demand functions, across

MINI CASE 4.1

The cost-effectiveness of standardization

The cost-based strategy indicates not only the corporate focus, but also the type of customer the multinational is targeting. Since the organization is striving for price competitiveness, products produced under this philosophy need to be standardized and made inherently less culturally sensitive. McDonald's, United Parcel Service and Coca-Cola have implemented a standardized marketing strategy effectively when targeting the international sophisticate segment (see page 123). McDonald's' march across continents provides evidence that cost advantages coupled with a unified global marketing strategy produce outstanding results. UPS and Coca-Cola's adherence to an international marketing strategy designed to capitalize on cost efficiencies, as demonstrated in their sponsorship of the 1996 centennial Olympics and the commercials aired during the period, enabled them to achieve competitive advantages in their respective industries.

Since these organizations compete on the basis of price and convenience, while targeting the international sophisticate customer type, standardization has been effective. Through standardization, these international organizations have been able to achieve significant cost savings in comparison with their competitors, thereby leading to a competitive advantage.

This strategy combination is in stark contrast to one capable of satisfying the provincial segment (see page 123). A local strategy is contrary to the principles of cost-based efficiencies and therefore cannot be combined effectively with them. Cost-based organizations targeting provincial markets find profits lacking. If Coca-Cola began by adapting its product and advertising for each local market, would it be as successful as it is today?

world markets). By assessing the similarities and differences between consumers across markets, this strategy may achieve the advantages of both standardization and localization. This notion, however, ignores the cultural factors that can prevent firms from learning about foreign market environments: that is, the concept of psychic distance, which we now explore.

Psychic distance and corporate marketing performance

The definition of psychic distance has changed substantially since its first use in Beckerman's (1956) study on the distribution of international trade. Hallen and Wiedersheim-Paul (1984) defined psychic distance as 'factors preventing or disturbing the flow of information between potential and actual suppliers and customers'. They subsequently redefined it as 'factors preventing or disturbing firm's learning about and understanding a foreign environment'. This refinement was justified on the basis that learning and understanding, rather than the mere access to information, are essential in the development of appropriate operating strategies in foreign markets.

O'Grady and Lane (1996) further refined the definition by incorporating the consequence of such learning and by specifying the factors that impede learning. Thus, psychic distance is defined as 'a firm's degree of uncertainty about a foreign market resulting from cultural differences and other business difficulties that present barriers to learning about the market and operating there'.

While the continuous redefinition of psychic distance has resulted in a deeper under-standing of the concept, current definitions still fail to articulate adequately the two most important elements: that is, 'psychic' and 'distance'. 'Psychic' is derived from the term psyche, which refers to the mind or soul. Thus, it does not involve the simple presence of external environmental factors, as the definitions imply. Rather, it is the mind's process-ing, in terms of perception and understanding, of cultural and business differences, that forms the basis of psychic distance.

Cultural distance is defined as 'international marketer's perceived sociocultural distance between the home and target country in terms of language, business practices, legal and political systems and marketing infrastructure' (Lee 1998: 9). The distinction between cultural distance and psychic distance can be made on the basis of the way in which the two concepts are operated. Cultural distance is most commonly measured using Hofstede's (1983, 1991) dimensions of national culture. In contrast, psychic distance operates in terms of differences in language, business practices, political and legal systems, education, economic development, marketing infrastructure, industry structure and culture.

It is apparent that there is little consensus within the international marketing literature over the precise definition and operation of psychic distance. On the basis of this review of existing definitions, I would propose that psychic distance be defined as the distance between the home market and a foreign market resulting from the perception and under-standing of cultural and business differences. Such business differences may include the legal and political environment, economic environment, business practices, language, and industry or market sector structure.

Psychic distance and organizational performance

The psychic distance concept provides a helpful theoretical framework to explain varia-tions in the performance of international marketing operations. However, other factors must be included if the performance of international firms is to be fully explained. International marketing literature identifies a number of factors that influence the performance of firms operating in foreign markets, including:

- the strategic decision-making process
- entry strategy
- degree of adaptation of the company's products
- organizational characteristics
- business structure
- size and ownership of the firm
- the firm's level of international experience
- management's country of origin
- experience in the foreign market.

All these factors and probably more are likely to influence international marketing oper-ations. It can be argued that these factors intervene in the relationship between psychic distance and organizational performance, and contribute to a holistic framework that explains variations in the performance of international marketing operations. Figure 4.5 depicts these relationships.

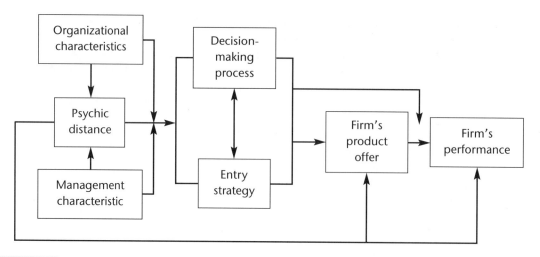

Figure 4.5 A theoretical framework of psychic distance and organizational performance

It is more likely that psychic distance alone cannot explain variations in the perform-ance of international marketing operations. It is the inclusion of the intervening influence of the strategic decision-making process, entry strategy, and the degree of adaptation of the company's product offering and the moderating role of organizational and manage-rial characteristics that provides an holistic framework. This framework suggests that the perception of cultural and business differences, such as the legal and political environ-ment, economic environment, business practices and industry structure, between the home market and a foreign market will lead to a sense of uncertainty. As a means of reducing this uncertainty a firm will characteristically undertake an extensive programme of planning and research in order to reach a deeper understanding of the foreign market. This can then be used to determine the appropriate entry strategy and product/service offering, thereby enhancing the profitability prospects of the operation.

Moderating the relationships between these variables are the firm's international experience, its nature, size, ownership and structure of decision making. The country of origin and international experience of the firm's management are also important, as are management's perception and understanding of the foreign market and the firm's abilities, which will ultimately determine both the entry and operating strategies. Oper-ating in a psychically close country may not necessarily lead to superior performance, as the assumption of similarity prevents executives from noticing subtle, but critical, differences in the foreign market. For example, the assumptions held by Canadian retailers about the similarity of the US market were directly linked to problems in performance (O'Grady and Lane, 1996). Thus, it could be argued that a psychic distance paradox exists, where psychic closeness is negatively related to organizational performance.

The paradoxical nature of psychic distance was evidenced by the fact that psychic distance is not the only factor to explain variations in the performance of international marketing operations. O'Grady and Lane (1996) identified the strategic decision-making process and certain managerial characteristics as key intervening variables in the rela-tionship between psychic distance and organizational performance. It can be argued that the perception of cultural and business differences will lead to a sense of uncertainty about the foreign market, which will result in a more extensive strategic decision-making process. This, in turn, will provide management with a greater understanding of the foreign market, which will lead to the appropriate entry strategy and degree of adaptation of the product offering.

International marketing and strategic planning

Planning is at the heart of the strategic management process, and global strategic marketing planning is the culmination of managerial efforts to reconcile environmental change within the resource constraints of the corporation (Keegan 2002). While some companies can get by using informal planning efforts (for example, small companies or firms operating in rapidly changing market environments), for most companies, growth brings with it increasing pressures to formalize the planning process.

Growth pains multiply as companies expand into international markets and their planning procedures are stretched across national boundaries. Efforts to plan on an international basis have seemingly always been met with obstacles. Impediments to international marketing planning efforts have always been severe. Head offices seeking to formalize their international planning have been challenged not only to produce explicit planning procedures that thoroughly analyse and take account of foreign market environments (see Chae and Hill 2000), but also to implement the planning effort in such a way as to gain the involvement and commitment of the principal stakeholders. Yet while international competition mounts, the planning processes underlying strategy formulation have come under increasing attack. Campbell and Alexander (1997) noted various planning deficiencies, with managers:

- being confounded by process and producing directionless strategies
- underestimating or overestimating environmental uncertainty
- not being strategic
- not being sufficiently democratic in tapping the creative juices of grassroots organizations.

As corporations expand into international markets, so the task of coordinating far-flung commercial empires becomes more complex.

Factors influencing strategic marketing planning

According to Chae and Hill (2000), the catalysts to international strategic marketing planning formality come from both inside and outside of organizations. Internal factors include the chief executive officer's (CEO's) involvement, organizational climate and firm size. External environmental factors include environmental complexity and environmental uncertainty.

The chief executive officer's involvement

Top management support and involvement is a crucial factor in upgrading planning formality. The success of strategic planning could depend almost wholly on the

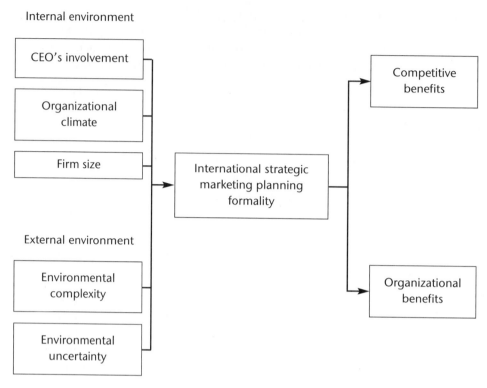

Internal environment

Figure 4.6 A model of strategic formal planning

willingness and ability of senior managers to conceptualize strategy and make appropriate strategic decisions. Unless chief executives see the need for formal international marketing planning systems and make efforts to understand and participate in them, it may be virtually impossible for lower-level executives to fill this void in top management orientation. A major function of CEOs is to influence the setting of organizational values, and to develop suitable management styles. In the small business context, CEO characteristics usually impact the interaction between planning formality and product/service innovation.

Organizational climate

Formalizing the planning process does not necessarily lead to better strategies. A supportive organizational climate is also an essential ingredient. For example, if line managers are not part of the planning process, strategies can encounter roadblocks further down the organization. It is necessary for every organization to have a positive organizational climate. Hostility, lack of skills, lack of data, lack of resources and unsuitable organizational structures are likely to be associated with adverse organizational climates. MNCs with new strategic business planning systems should reassess the amount of resistance to the new system from entrenched interest groups, and the corporate culture as it relates to entrepreneurial and risk-taking activities in long-term planning. Short-term employment and functional heterogeneity may have a positive effect on strategic planning formality.

The size of the firm

Corporate size is a primary determinant of the type of international marketing planning system used. As companies grow and diversify, it becomes progressively more difficult for top management to maintain their intimate knowledge of industry and business conditions and to exercise control through informal written procedures. Hence more structured decision-making frameworks become necessary. This enables management to react rationally to a greater variety of day-to-day pressures. Marketing planning in small firms may differ from that of large firms because of limited resources, insufficient specialist expertise and limited impacts on the marketplace. In general therefore, the larger the company, the greater is the likelihood of standardized, formalized marketing planning processes.

External factors

International marketers must often function in highly diverse markets, many of which have variable sets of customers, suppliers, competitors, sociopolitical and technological environments. Organizational environments can be broken down into their internal and external components. External factors included customers, suppliers, competitors, sociopolitical and technological environments. These can be further subdivided into environmental complexity factors (how simple or complex the industry environment is) and environmental uncertainty (how static or dynamic the industry environment is).

Environmental complexity

Chae and Hill (2000) observed that firms in more complex environments were more likely to use formal planning. Similarly, complex production, financial and marketing processes also increase the need for formal planning. Environmental complexity may be evaluated with respect to:

- relationships with suppliers, customers and distributors
- predictability of changes in demand
- degree of technological innovation
- frequency of new product introductions
- competitiveness
- market heterogeneity (the diversity of markets served).

It is likely that greater levels of environmental complexity are associated with more extensive planning, shorter planning horizons and more frequent plan reviews. It is also likely therefore that environmental complexity is positively related to strategic formal planning.

Environmental uncertainty

International marketing management who see the impact of turbulent market conditions on formal planning might come to widely differing conclusions:

- Organizational structures with lower centralization and formalization characteristics are likely to be better suited to more dynamic environments.
- Uncertainty may not impact strategic planning.
- Comprehensive planning in uncertain and complex environments may cause more problems than it solves.
- Formal planning procedures can suppress the creativity and spontaneity so essential in responding to fast-changing marketplaces.

By way of contrast, there is evidence in the marketing literature (Chae and Hill 2000) supporting a positive relationship between formal planning and marketplace turbulence:

- Large firms in fast-changing environments are more likely than small firms to use formal planning.
- Large firms, regardless of industry type, are more likely to make efforts to tailor their long-range planning processes to their perceived environmental conditions.
- Planning comprehensiveness is likely to be positively related to performance in stable market environments.
- Formal planning systems work well in industries characterized by high rates of technological innovation and new product introductions.
- New competitors, technological innovation and market structure changes all increase the need for comprehensive planning.
- Firms with vulnerable core technologies (such as those in high-tech industries) need more specialist planners and more sophisticated forecasting and evaluative techniques than companies in stable technology industries.

Planning formality

The concept of formal planning has evolved over time, and also along two separate (but related) dimensions: planning completeness (what elements are included in the plan) and commitment (how rigorously planning guidelines are followed). As planning becomes more process-oriented, marketing managers are less inclined to view planning holistically and more inclined to divide it up into its component parts. For example, they may identify objectives, strategy generation, strategic evaluation and results monitoring as four steps of the strategic planning process. Monitoring will thus include the analysis of environmental changes, corporate and competitor activities. This type of approach formalises the link between corporate planning systems and the processes prescribed by most strategic management theorists (see for example Ansoff 1965).

A second element of formal planning is commitment to the planning process. Planning formality effectiveness is a function of both content and commitment, and measurements of planning formality should endeavour to capture both dimensions including:

- formulation of goals/objectives
- external environmental analysis
- internal environmental analysis
- generation of global marketing strategies
- marketing strategy selection
- implementation and control.

Generic strategic options in world markets

Let us now turn our attention to some of the generic international strategies that firms can adopt. 'Generic strategies' are so called because they can be applied across markets and across different industry and product sectors. There exist different major and sub-strategies that companies can purse to compete effectively in the international markets. Firms will tend to pursue several types of strategies from different categories rather than just selecting from one category. In fact, many firms have so many strategic options available to them that they are spoilt for choice.

International market segmentation

The formulation of an international marketing strategy is derived from the development of corporate strategy. The initial step is to choose the markets the firm wishes to enter. Once the target market is selected, the firm needs to segment its markets and target them to provide benefits to itself and its customers. It will also need to establish the type of entry and competitive strategies it will pursue in these markets through positioning. These processes are discussed in the following sections.

International market segmentation is the process of identifying potential consumers at the national or sub-national level who are likely to exhibit similar buying behaviour patterns or respond to the same marketing mix stimuli (see Keegan 2002). If segmentation is used effectively, it allows the firm to exploit the benefits of marketing standardization, while at the same time enabling it to meet the particular needs and expectations of a specific target group. Firms segment markets is because it enables them to (Chee and Harris 1998):

- allocate resources appropriately and efficiently
- evaluate the competition and opportunities
- focus marketing strategies and positioning
- fine tune the marketing mix programme.

International marketers have usually used environmental factors such as geographical, economic, political and cultural variables for segmenting international markets (see Chapter 2). Other factors used include psychographics (attitudes, values and lifestyles), demographics (age, gender, income, occupation, education and so on), and behaviour (usage rates, user status and so on). There are many bases for segmenting the international market, and the major challenge for the multinational firm is to choose the most appropriate.

In general, a combination of factors is used in order to produce significant results. For instance, using economic variables alone would not generate sufficient information on which to base a firm's targeting decisions. However, the suitability of some of these approaches has been questioned, and new segmenting criteria have emerged. Markets that exhibit a high degree of homogeneity with respect to the marketing variables, for example, could be perceived as a segment. In addition, such a grouping could respond to a standardized marketing approach.

One of the effects of globalization on the distribution system is the converging of channel structures, so that regional and international chains are emerging (Chee and Harris 1998). Outlet types for defining groupings can therefore be used to segment markets. For example, producers of toys can segment their market not only by the number of children but also how international chains such as Toys 'R' Us reach their markets. If we look at the product variables (attitudes towards product attributes, stages of the product life cycle and so on) we also find international segments emerging regardless of the economic constraints. Producers of durable electronic consumer products such as cassette recorders and microwaves have found sales of their products were buoyant in low-income markets (Chee and Harris, 1998). This may be the result of buying behaviour being based upon status or emotional needs.

The implications of such buyer behaviour for international marketing are that product modifications will be minimal, and that international segments are emerging across markets of contrasting economic and cultural factors. It is not surprising given that a global segment has existed for teenage groups for some time. It has been said that the teenage segment is converging even more now because of common tastes in music and sports, and the process has been helped by global communications and increased travel by that market segment.

According to Keegan (2002), there are three major criteria for assessing opportunities in the targeted markets:

- Current market size and growth potential: the key question is whether the current market segment is large enough to sustain long-term profitability. A small segment in one market may not be a profitable proposition, but a small segment in a several international markets would be more attractive in the intermediate to long term.
- Potential competition: if there is intense rivalry in the market segment, an avoidance strategy may be the best policy. However, there are many cases whereby firms have made a competitive offensive and gained market share. In the colour film market, the classic rivalry between Kodak and Japan's Fuji company saw the latter entering the US market and managing to gain market share, albeit a small one, in spite of Kodak's well-entrenched position.
- Compatibility and feasibility: once the company has established that the market segment is viable and there are limited barriers to entry, it needs to decide whether the option is feasible. That is, does the company have the resources to reach the segment, and is the targeted segment compatible with the company's objectives and consistent with its distinctive competencies?

Composition of a target market

Behavioural characteristics may be effective for segmenting the consumer market. According to Keegan (2002), international markets can be classified into international sophisticates, sophisticates and provincials. This segmentation can be based on behavioural characteristics, rather than any set of demographic characteristics, and can include a wide range of ages, incomes and educational levels within each segment. This could be achieved by segmenting on the basis of the behavioural characteristic of 'degree of cultural sensitivity', which is then used to select the appropriate advertising strategy, whether regional, local or standardization.

- **International sophisticates** are a small group of consumers who might be termed 'world citizens'. These consumers have an appreciation of other cultures. They are open and receptive to cultural differences and international products. Since these consumers are interested in other cultures and have a great deal of cross-cultural exposure, brand-image consistency is increasingly important to a multinational that is targeting this market segment. The international philosophy of these consumers plus the heightened sensitivity to brand-image consistency are the cornerstones of standardization.
- **The sophisticated consumer** segment, although intrigued by other cultures, still perceives those other cultures to be socially distant. Overall, these consumers fall somewhere between the international and the ethnocentric in their consumption philosophy.
- **Provincial consumers** are defined as individuals who lack an interest in, or an appreciation of, other cultures, and consequently are hesitant about purchasing 'foreign' products. They have an overall ethnocentric consumer philosophy. Hesitant about the unfamiliar in terms of products, this segment may be receptive to a locally based strategy.

Many multinationals that study their market closely find that they are concentrating on one behavioural type, or they may find that individual customer types can be associated with different products in their portfolio. As a result, the effective use of behavioural segmentation strategy can provide a multinational with a strategic competitive advantage, and enable it to apply a suitable market targeting strategy.

International targeting strategy

After the identification of the segments, the international marketer needs to target the international markets, which means selecting appropriate segments as a focus for marketing effort. Targeting is an important step, as it reflects the fact that the company should identify only consumers who have the potential to respond and whom they can reach most effectively. In order to reach their chosen target markets, firms need to establish the positioning for their product offering: that is, the position the product occupies in the consumer's mind along a criteria spectrum. Three types of targeting strategies can be identified for international marketing:

- **Undifferentiated marketing** is really mass marketing to multiple countries, and the firm uses a standardized marketing mix. This approach involves a standardized product and communications strategy as well as an extensive distribution system. For example Nike has adopted an undifferentiated approach to its world markets, promoting shoes and T-shirts with a universal theme of 'Just do it'.
- **Concentrated marketing** involves creating a marketing mix to reach a single segment of the international market. Many clothing and cosmetics companies use this approach. For example Giorgio Armani, Valentino, Boss and other fashion houses have successfully targeted the luxury and prestige segment of the market in the United Kingdom and United States.
- **Differentiated marketing** involves targeting two or more distinct market segments with varied marketing mixes in order to capture a wider market. For instance, Ford

Motor Corporation targets the upper end of the market with its Mondeo model while the Fiesta and Escort are mass-market brands.

Having segmented the market and targeted one or more segments, the company needs to reach the target groups. This is achieved by a positioning strategy whereby the firm creates an image of its product offerings relative to the competitors in the minds of the consumer. For example, Sony is synonymous with quality and BMW is associated with high-quality German engineering and sophistication. There are many different positioning strategies that a firm can employ for its international marketing operations.

International market positioning

Positioning is the act of locating a product in a market, in the channels of distribution, in relationship to other products, and ultimately in the minds of prospective or target customers (see Figure 4.7 showing the market positions of international retailers). As a good example, the marketing specialists Foote, Cone and Belding that have positioned their client, Bermuda, in the island vacation market as the place to go for unhurried and civilized fun. The copy and appeals have not changed for almost a decade. The competition, on the other hand, changes every year. The result has been an increasing share of market for Bermuda because it is consistent. The basic rule of positioning is consistency, and firms need to be consistent at all times.

MINI CASE 4.2

Positioning international retailers

Figure 4.7 shows the positioning of some international retailers. In developing a positioning strategy the retailer takes a position relative to its competitors, and explains why its merchandise is better than or distinct from others, so creating its distinctive advantage (Alexander 1990). The early market leaders in international retailing, such as IKEA, C&A, Benetton, Habitat and The Gap, are mostly in quadrant A. Retailers in this quadrant continue to expand. Others taking this strategy include Body Shop, Hennes & Mauritz, Tie Rack and Zara.

These retailers tend to have an own-label focus, and as a result they are often able to supply stock from their own production units. For example, Zara, which has an estimated 600 stores of which 150 are outside its home country, Spain, supplies 60 per cent of its outlets from its own production units in Spain with the rest coming from Asia.

Given the dual emphasis on retailing and manufacturing, these retailers can break even in a country with as few as one or two stores. However, to succeed they have to:

- support their brands with extensive advertising
- develop products that constitute innovations in the international market environment
- develop and provide attractive product package which appeals to the majority of the international customers
- avoid the supply of 'me-too' products that are likely to damage the reputation of the retailer in the world marketplace
- develop a distinctive brand image and customer franchise internationally
- achieve international marketing management capability which enables the retailer to anticipate and coordinate international retail marketing activities successfully.

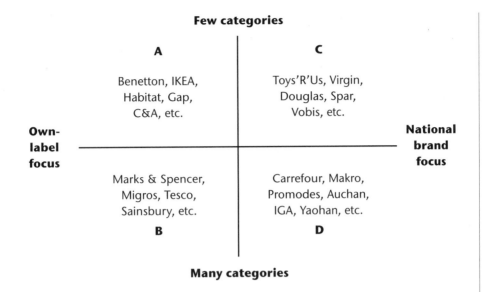

Figure 4.7 International retailers and their market position

For retailers in quadrant B of Figure 4.7, it may be significantly more difficult to succeed internationally because they stock many merchandise categories and mainly own-label brands, but those retailers that have targeted a small segment of the population in foreign markets may find it easier. For example, Marks & Spencer sells its St Michael brand of clothing, food and home furnishings through 286 stores in the United Kingdom and another 172 stores and franchises worldwide. But more traditional mass-market supermarkets that focus on own-label brands in their home country, such as Sainsbury (UK) and Migros (Switzerland), are finding international expansion difficult. These retailers have to convince customers in the new country to switch both store and brand, which requires a significant change in every-day consumption patterns.

In contrast to the own-label focus of early international retailers, we are now seeing 'true' retailers going international. Quadrant C retailers in Figure 4.7 are primarily 'category killers' such as Blockbuster Video, Toys' R' Us and Virgin Stores. To succeed these retailers must outperform the local competition and overwhelm customers with the depth of their product range while offering competitive prices.

The most exciting area of international marketing is probably to be found in quadrant D in Figure 4.7, with retailers such as Carrefour (France), Dairy Farm (Hong Kong), 7-Eleven convenience stores (Japan, part of Ito-Yokado), Makro (Netherlands) and Wal-Mart (USA) marketing globally. Since the merchandise they offer is often already available, one of the main distinctive competencies they bring is excellence in distribution.

In the car distribution sector in the US market for example, Mercedes-Benz is positioned as a prestige, well-engineered car representing a high status symbol. Hyundai, on the other hand, is positioned as a cheap but dependable means of transport. These companies employ positioning strategy as a bundle of benefits (Kotler 2006) that is attractive to customers in their target market and distinguishes their companies from their competitors. Positioning therefore serves to establish a reason to buy from a particular firm.

Firms can use positioning analysis to determine whether the desired position has been established in the minds of customers and whether the store is achieving this goal more successfully than its competitors. A major challenge for multinational firms is to identify and adopt the most appropriate positioning within foreign national markets. This requires careful appraisal of existing competition, possible gaps and customer needs within the target market. It is not difficult to find examples of retail formats, excellently positioned within their home markets, that have been unsuccessful outside them. Most require at least some adaptation to local expectations, purchasing habits, customs and competition.

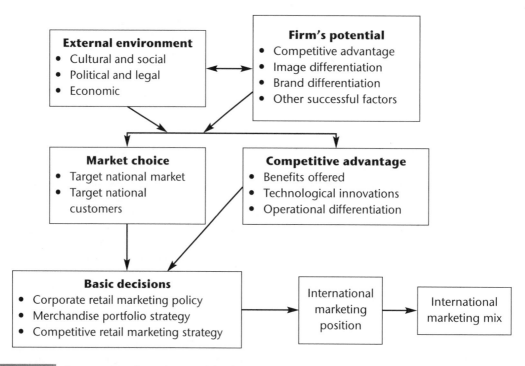

Figure 4.8 International market positioning

Alternative positioning strategies

There are many different ways firms can position themselves or their products in international markets, but there are only four basic positioning strategy alternatives (Chee and Harris 1998): market leadership, market challenger, market follower and market niche (see Table 4.2).

There are several other positioning strategies that a firm can employ, (Akehurst and Alexander 1995) including:

- Positioning by benefits – many products and services offer solutions to specific consumer problems. For instance, DHL positions its worldwide parcel delivery service

| Table 4.2 | Basic positioning strategy alternatives |

Positioning alternative	Relative performance
Market leader	The market leader is usually the brand or firm that established a leading position at the beginning of the product life cycle and that has successfully defended its position of leadership. A typical market leader has twice the share of market of the number two brand and twice again as much as the number three firm. A leader might have 40 per cent of the market, with the number two firm holding 20 per cent, number three 10 per cent and all others 30 per cent. Once a fragmented industry has been integrated, market leaders will appear. Usually, market leadership is based on successfully integrating the threads of what was a fragmented industry. The market leader is always in a paradoxical position. In the short run, a market leader really has very little to worry about. There is tremendous momentum in the dominant position. In the longer run, however, the market leader must maintain constant vigilance or risk being displaced by an aggressive challenger.
Market challenger	In some markets, there is a strong challenger who is seeking to displace the market leader. The challenger announces publicly its avowed intention of overtaking number one. There are a number of strategies available to the challenger including price advantage, product innovation and promotion. (These issues are discussed in detail elsewhere in this book.)
Market follower	A market follower is a runner-up in an industry, that consciously or unconsciously seeks to emulate the strategy of the market leader. This strategy works under one condition, and that is when either consciously or unconsciously the leader seeks to maintain equilibrium in the industry. Maintaining a price umbrella over the industry and not seeking to maximize market share can accomplish this. There are many reasons a market leader would hold an umbrella over market followers, not the least of which is that the government may insist on multiple suppliers or a number of competitors. In any event, the market follower's strategy is potentially dangerous because if the leader decides to eliminate a follower, it is within its power to do so. This, of course, is assuming that the leader is a well-managed organization and has been able to take advantage of its leadership position.
Market niche	This is the strategy for a firm that is neither the leader nor the strong number two. A niche is a segment or a cluster of customers whose particular needs can be met better than anybody else by a firm that is focused on this market segment. The key to the market niche strategy is to identify the segment basis for defining the niche.

as completely reliable, and American Express cards are positioned as being widely accepted.

- Positioning against the competitor's product – this strategy involves comparative promotion against other leading brands, and mainly concerns consumer products such as air travel and car hire. For example, British Airways is positioned as the 'world's favourite airline'.
- Positioning by user category – an emphasis on the type of consumers who use the product or service. For example, some holiday tour packages are obviously aimed at a younger and less affluent segment, whereas Caribbean holiday cruises are aimed at older and more well-off segments of the population.
- Positioning by usage – this relates the product to specific occasions or usage situations. For example, British Airways emphasizes that it caters globally for individual as well as business travellers' needs.

Chee and Harris (1998) suggest that global product positioning can be more effective if either end of the 'high-touch–high-tech' continuum is applied. 'High-tech products' are usually purchased on the basis of concrete features, and so consumers tend to seek more technical information about them. Examples of products in this category are cars, electronic goods and computers. 'High-touch' products on the other hand require more emphasis on image and less specialized information, and the consumers for such products are highly involved. See Table 4.3.

Finally, it must be emphasized here that regardless of which positioning strategy a firm wishes to pursue, it is necessary to assess internal competencies and obtain a suitable product offering before selecting an international market entry strategy (see Chapter 5). This approach will enable the firm to evaluate and forecast what it is possible to achieve within the international environment.

Market-based options (MBO)

MBOs are those alternatives that arise from exploiting marketing opportunities, and build on the analysis of customers and competitors. MBO strategies do not preclude an analysis of the firm's internal resources and the value chain, but the primary emphasis is on external industry-market factors. The firm's strategy is developed as a response to the industry-market imperatives, and the market-based option model makes the following assumptions:

- Firms within the industry are identical in terms of the strategic resources they have or control.
- The major drivers of the firm's international competitive strategies are industry-market factors rather than organizational resources or characteristics.
- The firm's goal is to attain above-normal returns.

Under the MBO model, a firm's sustained competitive advantage is obtained by implementing strategies which differentiate products or offer them at low prices, erect barriers to entry, benefit from scale economies, or exploit experience curve effects. Thus exploiting the firm's internal strengths through responding to environmental opportunities

Table 4.3	High-touch and high-tech positioning strategies

High-touch positioning

Products that solve common problems	The benefits in this product category are understood world-wide and solve everyday problems, such as soap powder to wash clothes or Coca-Cola to quench a thirst.
Global village products	These products have a global positioning based on the cosmopolitan lower-priced items such as mineral water. They can also have global appeal by virtue of their country of origin labels. For instance, Toyota is associated with Japanese quality while Levi's, Calvin Klein and Coca-Cola are associated with America.
Products using universal themes	Some products have global appeal but they have other additional themes, which can be transferred to the international arena such as heroism (images of romance and courtship).

High-tech positioning

Technical products	Most consumers buying these products require a great deal of product information and share a common language such as bond, sky digital, Pentium microprocessor. The marketing implications are that promotion should emphasize product features and be very informative. Financial services, chemicals and computers are in this category.
Special-interest products	These are characterized by a shared experience and high involvement among the buyers. These products are less technical and more leisure oriented. There is a common language with users, and items such as Nikon cameras and Nike sports products are typical.
Products that demonstrate well	The product features and benefits of goods in this category are self-evident; the Polaroid instant camera, which was a very successful global product, is an example.

attains competitive advantage, neutralizing external threats and avoiding internal weaknesses.

Market-based options can be divided into three groups as shown in Figure 4.9:

- generic strategies (already discussed)
- market-based options (the Ansoff matrix)
- expansion strategies (for example, joint ventures, strategic alliances, licensing (discussed in Chapter 5).

Resource-based alternatives

Empirical evidence repeatedly suggests that industry structure is not the sole determinant of competitive strategy and performance. The search for other factors led a group identified as the 'resource-based theorists' to conclude that differential endowment of

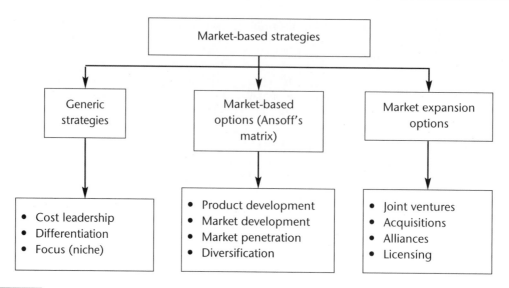

Figure 4.9 Market-based strategic options

strategic resources among firms is the ultimate determinant of strategy and performance. The notion of differentiated internal resource portfolios is gaining rapid acceptance in academic circles, and this is likely to be the richest theory of competitive advantage and strategy, especially in the context of international strategy.

When the term 'resource' is used in a broad sense, internal organizational resources may be defined as all assets, capabilities, organizational processes, business attributes, information, knowledge and so forth, controlled by a firm and enabling it to conceive of and implement strategies which improve its efficiency and effectiveness. Internal organizational resources can be classified into physical capital, human capital and organizational capital. Not all of these are strategically relevant. Some may prevent a business from conceiving of and implementing valuable strategies, others may lead to strategies that reduce its performance, and yet others may have no effect on a firm's strategic choice. The most critical resources are those that are superior in use, hard to imitate, difficult to substitute for, and more valuable within the business than outside.

According to Porter (1991), such resources can arise either from performing activities over time which create internal skills and routines, or from acquiring them outside the firm for less than their intrinsic value because of factor market imperfection, or a combination of the two. The most appropriate types of resources to examine in strategy research are the skills and organizational routines that drive business activities. These underlie the firm's ability to link activities or share them across units.

The resource-based theory is grounded on two fundamental assumptions in analysing sources of competitive advantage and business strategy:

- Firms within an industry or a strategic group may be heterogeneous with respect to the strategic resources they control.
- Since these resources may not be perfectly mobile across firms, heterogeneity can be long-lasting.

In the resource-based theory, competitive advantage is said to reside in the inherent heterogeneity of the immobile strategic resources the business controls. Thus, strategy may be viewed as a firm's conscious move to capitalize on its idiosyncratic endowment of strategic resources. Following this logic, the principal drivers of competitive strategy and performance are internal to the business. While the resource-based theory recognizes firms' physical resources as the important drivers of strategy and performance, it places particular emphasis on the intangible skills and resources of the business as the main driver of competitive choice.

The performance objective of resource-based theory

The resource-based theory sees above-normal returns as the firm's ultimate goal. Obtaining such returns requires either that the firm's product be distinctive in the eyes of buyers in comparison to competing products or that the firm sell a product identical to that of competitors at a lower cost (Porter 1985). Thus, the critical problem is how to maintain product distinctiveness or low cost without making excessive investment. The resource-based theory contends that product distinctiveness or low cost are tied directly to distinctiveness in the inputs (resources) used to make the product. In fact, it is hard-to-copy resources rather than monopoly power or market position that bring persistent, above-normal earnings to the firm. Moreover, the distinctiveness of those resources results from the firm's acumen or luck in acquiring, combining and deploying them, not from the forces related to industry structure, such as the number of sellers, barriers to entry, product differentiation or market growth.

Application of resource-based theory

In applying the resource-based theory, two hypotheses about international competition can be identified:

- The historical evolution of a firm constrains its global strategic choice and so will affect global market outcomes.
- Complex social phenomena, or 'invisible' assets, can be a source of sustained competitive advantage and will affect organization structure independently of global strategic choice.

Apart from these two factors, more attention should be paid to understanding how managers assemble unique portfolios of resources and how they develop distinctive capabilities, which provide sustainable competitive advantage in international markets. The resource-based strategy is one of the most promising ways to address the longitudinal nature of competitive strategy and performance. It is likely that the resource-based view will become very significant in future research, and any purported theory of global strategy must incorporate internal organizational characteristics.

International market expansion strategies

Any firm attempting to expand international operations must decide on the number of countries and market segments it will attempt to penetrate in any given period (see

Chapter 5). Given a fixed marketing budget the firm must also decide how to allocate its efforts among the different markets. There are two major and opposing strategies for making these decisions:

- A **market diversification strategy** implies a fast penetration into a large number of markets and diffusion of efforts among them.
- A **market concentration strategy** is based on concentration of resources in a few markets and gradual expansion into new markets.

Both strategies may lead the firm to export into (or operate in) the same number of markets after a number of years in operation. The alternative expansion routes may, however, generate totally different consequences in terms of sales, market shares and profits over time. In this section these two strategies are compared and the factors impinging on the choice between them are analysed. Within the framework of the two major strategies, a number of more detailed strategic choices are identified, and alternative measurements of market expansion are discussed.

The major strategic alternatives

A market concentration strategy has been described as a slow and gradual rate of growth in the number of markets served by a company. In contrast, a strategy of market spreading is characterized by a fast rate of growth in the number of markets served at the early stages of expansion.

These two strategies represent extremes on a continuum of different expansion alternatives. Pellegrini (1994) presents an important distinction in explaining paths for growth. He relates the search for growth to extension of the firm's proprietary know-how to extract the implied rents, and optimization of the scale of operations (economies of scale) or the mix of operations (economies of scope) to reduce costs and increase efficiency.

He acknowledges that these actions can be proactive or reactive. Firms will begin their international expansion in countries that are culturally or geographically similar to the home country. As they gain experience in each country or region, they move into another area. The concept of risk is normally considered as an explanation why firms expand internationally. The choice of a market expansion policy is a key decision in international marketing:

- Different patterns are likely to cause development of different competitive conditions in different markets over time. For example, a fast rate of growth into new markets characterized by short product life cycles can create entry barriers for competitors and give rise to higher profitability.
- The two market expansion policies lead to different levels of marketing effort and marketing mixes in each market. Thus, with the same levels of financial and organizational resources, the allocation of resources to each market will be higher in the case of market concentration strategy than with the strategy of spreading.

In order to develop such a policy, a firm has to make decisions in the following three areas:

- identification of potential markets and determination of some order of priorities for entry into them
- the overall level of marketing effort the firm is able and willing to commit
- rate of market expansion over time, and the allocation of effort among different markets.

This section concentrates on the third area, assuming that decisions in the first two areas have already been made. In practice, the process will frequently be iterative; analysis of the third area will be helpful in clarifying and reviewing the first two areas.

A strategy of market concentration is characterized by a slow and gradual rate of growth in the number of markets served. On the other hand, a strategy of market diversification is characterized by a fast rate of growth in the number of markets served at the early stages of expansion. It is, therefore, expected that a strategy of concentration will result in a smaller number of markets served, at each point in time, relative to a strategy of diversification.

In the long run, a strategy of diversification will frequently lead to a reduction in the number of markets, as a result of consolidation and abandonment of less profitable markets. A fast rate of market expansion is usually accomplished by devoting only limited resources and time to a careful study of each market prior to entry. The firm is therefore bound to make a few mistakes, and is more likely to enter unprofitable markets and drop them later.

The different patterns of market expansion are likely to cause development of different competitive conditions in different markets over time. The profitability of a late entry into new markets is affected by these competitive conditions and the length of the product life cycle. As a result, the optimal number of markets served in the long run is not necessarily the same for both strategies.

The two strategies of concentration versus diversification lead to the selection of different levels of marketing effort and different marketing mixes in each market. Given fixed financial and managerial resources, the level of resources allocated to each market in a strategy of diversification will be lower than with concentration. The size of the budget gives an indication about possible selection of means or marketing mix. Specifically, a lower level of marketing effort implies less promotional expenditure, more reliance on commission agents and a stronger tendency for a skimming approach to pricing. A strategy of concentration, on the other hand, involves investment in market share. This implies heavy promotional outlays, a stronger control of the distribution channel, and in some cases penetration pricing.

Summary

In order to create a competitive advantage, the enterprise is required to progress, to innovate, and to discover the best competitive opportunities and exploit them. The firm should not stop improving the quality of its products and its methods. Its main role is to take risks and to invest.

A country succeeds in a sector when the national frame creates a favourable environment to this continuous effort, and when the capacity is given to the enterprise to be strategically aggressive and to react quickly. The preservation of a competitive advantage, in the long run, requires this advantage to be continuously improved thanks to a policy of sustained investments. In order to keep this advantage, the firm has to evolve continuously, which is not comfortable from an organizational point of view. Internationally, to succeed it is required to transform a domestic position into a global one.

Revision questions

1 Explain how a firm may achieve a competitive advantage.
2 Define the terms 'value system' and 'value chain' and differentiate between them.
3 Identify the five sources of innovation for an international firm and briefly explain each of them.
4 Discuss the suggestion that 'a multinational corporation operating in a competitive international marketplace must develop a synergistic bond between marketing and corporate strategies'.
5 When a firm conceives a new way to manage its activities, uses new technologies, and/or different means of production, it may acquire a competitive advantage. Discuss the importance of marketing in monitoring such acquired competitive advantage.
6 Although there is little consensus within the international business literature over the precise definition and operation of psychic distance, how would you define psychic distance in the context of international marketing operation?
7 Identify and explain some of the key factors that may influence international strategic marketing planning.
8 What difficulties would you encounter in applying generic strategies?

SEMINAR CASE STUDY

McDonald's – a global retailer

From its headquarters in Oak Brook, near Chicago, Illinois, USA, McDonald's straddles the world. In just over 46 years since Roy Kroc became Mac and Dick McDonald's first franchisee and later bought the chain, the restaurants have spread to over 98 countries on six continents, and is widening its coverage every year. McDonald's is perhaps the world's largest single retailer of food. It estimates that 28 million people enter its 16,000 restaurants to consume food and drink everyday. That is why McDonald's is the second most recognized brand in the world, after Coca-Cola.

The company's world-wide strategy has three strands: adding restaurants, maximizing sales and profits at existing restaurants, and improving international profitability. McDonald's had nearly 1,000 outlets in America (its domestic market) before it first ventured abroad, to Canada and Puerto Rico in 1967. The arrival and growth of McDonald's in the United Kingdom, for example, was one of the biggest British success stories of the past three decades. Whether they love it or hate it – the company is only too aware of its detractors – people now take McDonald's for granted on the high street. It was not always like that. Over 30 years ago, if a family with young children wanted a quiet Sunday lunch in London, with no queuing and no problem about finding a table, the place to go was McDonald's very first British outlet in Woolwich. It was unusual for children to be allowed into restaurants in those days, and when and where they were allowed in, it was waiter service with knives, forks and tablecloths.

McDonald's team, arrived from America, realized that they had to change a nation's eating habits. After an agonizingly slow start, there are now about 800 UK outlets and this figure is growing by at least 50 outlets a year. This represents an investment of approximately £998 million, and jobs for 42,000 people in Britain. In addition there are those who work in the 6,000 businesses that supply and service the group, from window cleaners to architects. Many McDonald's customers cannot remember a time when it was not a regular part of their lives. Ironically, this means it is also suffering the brickbats that go with being identified as a big, impersonal corporation steamrolling its way down the high street.

The 6,900 non-American branches account for more than 50 per cent of total sales and more than 55 per cent of the group's £750 million annual profits. It is that, together with the belief that American coverage is near to saturation point, is encouraging the drive to spread to more and more countries.

Global scale has also given McDonald's the opportunity for global buying. The group used to have 30 suppliers of cups, but saved £2 million when it brought that down to three. Similarly, almost all the sesame seeds for the hamburger buns come from one supplier in Mexico. Conversely, when McDonald's arrives in a new country it can introduce new standards of food and hygiene. In order to guarantee the right quality of supplies in Moscow, for example, the company set up its own farms, produced its own beef, and processed the result into the form in which it crosses the counter.

Equally important for the group is the need to conform to a country's religious and social customs. Sabbath opening times or the sale of beef can be prohibited, and this must be taken into account when business plans are drawn up. One tangible and worthwhile way to win hearts and minds of customers is McDonald's community efforts. Ronald McDonald's Children Charities was founded 16 years ago to further child welfare. Rather than make blanket contributions to charities, McDonald's prefers to meet specific needs, such as children's hospitals. A cornerstone of this campaign is the Ronald McDonald House, where families of children in hospital can stay to comfort the sick child. There are over 150 of these houses spread around the world, creating a global presence for McDonald's.

Case study review questions

1 McDonald's now operates its fast food retailing in over 98 countries throughout the world. What key elements of its global fast food retail marketing strategy do you think make McDonald's a global success story?
2 In the United Kingdom, McDonald's succeeded in changing the eating habit of its British consumers. Evaluate the relevance and the implications of adopting a similar policy in other countries.

Classroom discussion question

After reading the case study, you might wonder whether a common global retail marketing policy could be adopted in every national market. On the other hand the case study emphasizes variations in retail marketing policy and the need for international retailers to consider aspects of religion, social customs and cultural values in their retail marketing operation. Discuss what you think differentiates McDonald's fast food retail marketing operations in the United Kingdom from the US market.

Managerial assignment task

Michael Porter recognizes the interdependency among various country markets, and contends that a global strategy has two basic dimensions: configuration of value-adding activities and coordination of the activities across markets. He maintains that the strategic imperative in global markets is to concentrate value-added activities to exploit factor cost differentials and extend competitive advantages by coordinating interdependencies among markets. Thus, success demands achieving integration of the firm's competitive position across markets (see Porter 1986).

As a senior manager within your firm responsible for international marketing development, explain fully Porter's statement to other members of staff.

References

Akehurst, G. and Alexander, N. (1995) 'Developing a framework for the study of the internationalization of retailing', pp. 204–9 in G. Akehurst and N. Alexander (eds), *The Internationalization of Retailing,* London: Frank Cass.

Alexander, N. (1990) 'Retailers and international markets: motives for expansion', *International Marketing Review,* Vol. 7, No .4, pp.75–85.

Ansoff, I. H. (1965) *Corporate Strategy,* New York: McGraw-Hill.

Barney, J. (1991) 'Firm resources and sustained competitive advantage', *Journal of Management,* Vol. 17, March, pp. 99–120.

Beckerman, W. (1956) 'Distance and the pattern of intra-European trade', *Review of Economics and Statistics,* Vol. 28, pp. 31–40.

Campbell, A. and Alexander, M. (1997) 'What's wrong with strategy?', *Harvard Business Review,* Vol. 75, No. 6, pp. 42–51.

Chae, M. S. and Hill, J. S. (2000) 'Determinants and benefits of global strategic marketing planning formality', *International Marketing Review,* Vol. 17, No. 6, pp. 538–62.

Chee, H. and Harris, R. (1998) *Global Marketing Strategy,* London: Financial Times/Pitman.

Hallen, L. and Wiedersheim-Paul, F. (1984) 'The evolution of psychic distance in international business relationships', pp. 15–27 in I. Hagg and F. Widersheim-Paul (eds), *Between Markets and Hierarchy,* Department of Business Administration, University of Uppsala, Sweden.

Hofstede, G. (1983) 'National cultures in four dimensions: a research-based theory of cultural differences among nations', *International Studies of Management and Organization,* Vol. 13, Nos 1–2, pp. 46–74.

Hofstede, G. (1991) *Cultures and Organizations: Software of the Mind,* Maidenhead: McGraw-Hill.

Keegan, W. J. (2002) *Global Marketing Management,* New York: Prentice Hall.

Kotler, P. (1997) *Marketing Management: Analysis, Planning, Implementation, and Control,* 9th edn, New Jersey: Prentice Hall,

Kotler, P. (2006) *Marketing Management: Analysis, Planning, Implementation and Control,* 12th edn, New Jersey: Prentice-Hall/ Pearson.

Lee, D. J. (1998) 'The effect of cultural distance on the relational exchange between exporters and importers: the case of Australian exporters', *Journal of Global Marketing,* Vol. 11, No. 4, pp. 7–22.

Levitt, T. (1983) 'The globalization of markets', *Harvard Business Review,* Vol. 61, No. 3, pp. 92–102.

Morden, T. (1991) 'Thinking globally and managing locally', *Management Decision,* Vol. 29, No. 2, pp. 32–9.

O'Grady, S. and Lane, H. (1996) 'The psychic distance paradox', *Journal of International Business Studies,* Vol. 27, No. 2, pp. 309–33.

Passemard, D. and Kleiner, B. H. (2000) 'Competitive advantage in global industries', *Management Research News,* Vol. 23, No. 7/8, pp. 111–17.

Pellegrini, L. (1994) 'Alternatives for growth and internationalization in retailing', *International Review of Retail, Distribution and Consumer Research*, Vol. 4, No. 2, pp. 121–48.

Porter, M. E. (1985) *Competitive Advantage: Creating and Sustaining Superior Performance,* New York: Free Press.

Porter, M. E. (1986) 'Competition in global industries; a conceptual framework', pp. 15–60 in M. E. Porter (ed.), *Competition in Global Industries*, New York: Free Press.

Porter, M.E. (1990) *The Competitive Advantage of Nations*, New York: Free Press.

Porter, M. E. (1991) 'Towards a dynamic theory of strategy', *Strategic Management Journal,* Vol. 12, pp. 95–117.

5

Market Selection Decisions and Entry Strategies

Contents

LEARNING OBJECTIVES

After reading this chapter you should be able to:

- understand the process of eliminating unsuitable markets from the list of contemplated international markets
- describe the market selection and market entry mode selection processes
- make market entry decisions that are likely to achieve the company's international marketing objectives

- evaluate the role and influence of national culture on international market entry decisions
- assess the company's motives for joining strategic alliances (co-marketing) as a suitable market entry alternative
- discuss the current trends in corporate partnerships in emerging markets.

Introduction

Companies intending to pursue an international marketing strategy must determine the types of market entry that are appropriate for achieving corporate objectives. The methods of entry and market selection process are major choice issues with which every company must concern itself. These initial decisions on market entry tend to be of medium to long-term importance, and may leave very little room for manoeuvre once a commitment has been made. It is therefore important to treat these decisions with the utmost care because of the financial implications and the future competitive strategies the company may wish to follow.

This chapter concentrates on some of the major entry strategy alternatives. It explains each strategy in detail and cites relevant company examples. Each entry strategy is treated from an integrated point of view, and there is guidance on how to select a specific strategy to suit the company's international marketing objectives. Combinations of theory and practical application have been reconciled in discussing issues relating to each entry strategy.

The holistic model of the market entry mode selection process (MEMS), introduced in this chapter, has been designed to accommodate international marketing contexts and practices. The chapter examines the great variety of influences on the MEMS process outcomes. References made throughout the chapter to the organization's context are designed to help better explicate the character of influences. They also make it possible for readers to compare the suggestions in this chapter with their own prior understanding of these influences, and facilitate further refinement of that understanding. The scope of the MEMS model evaluation process is presented in this chapter from two angles: market selection and market entry mode selection. However, the evaluation of MEMS model comes after a discussion on unsuitable markets.

Understanding international markets

When a company decides to go into international marketing, it is likely to face a host of decisions ranging from the choice of countries to financial and/or investment decisions. In order to make these decisions, a good understanding of international markets is required. This understanding will usually come from international market research information (see Chapter 3). In general however, whichever country or method of entry has been selected, the most important factor is that the corporate objectives must be achieved. Companies must address issues of marketing, distribution and logistics before deciding to enter the market. This approach is necessary because of the differences that exist between nations (O'Donnell and Jeong 2000).

A range of methods for gaining entry into international markets also complement different geographical approaches. There is apparently no consensus on the most appropriate method for a particular market. Different kinds of companies have their own preferences, and what works for one company will probably not work so well for another. On the whole, companies with limited international marketing experience appear to choose high-control entry strategies, often involving acquisition. By contrast, many small-scale organizations appear to have a preference for organic growth, particularly through franchising, which represents a low-cost, but low-control, method of entry into international markets.

The elimination of unsuitable markets

One approach to targeting international markets is to select for consideration just those countries where experience or research has suggested there may be worthwhile business. This approach starts with a cluster of countries that have characteristics similar to those the company is familiar with. Another approach sometimes described as 'contractible', which might be worth pursuing, even if in parallel with the first one, is to start with all countries and then eliminate those that are proved to be unsuitable (Keegan 1999). The effect may ultimately be the same, but this approach has the virtue of not unnecessarily eliminating potential markets that are less than obvious.

A number of methods can be used to filter out unsuitable markets. Chee and Harris (1998) listed a many of them (see Table 5.1).

In general terms, having made the various decisions, the company will then need to consider how its portfolio of country operations is balanced, and how their different strengths and weaknesses complement the overall marketing operation.

Foreign market selection

This section describes the foreign market selection process. It covers both the internal and external factors influencing the selection. These factors fall into three broad categories:

- internal factors
- external factors
- mixed internal and external factors.

The internal factors are shown in Figure 5.1.

Figure 5.1   Internal factors influencing market selection

Table 5.1   The process of eliminating unsuitable markets

Factor used	Unsuitability considerations
Common sense	Some groups of countries that are clearly unlikely to buy significant quantities of some products or services. For example, strict Islamic countries are poor markets for alcoholic drinks, and the poorest of the less-developed countries are unlikely to be large-scale purchasers of mainframe computers.
Size of population	Some countries (for example, Belize) are smaller than some English or American counties, and their markets for foreign goods may be smaller than some towns in the developed world. Only products with very large sales world-wide will justify the 'infrastructure' that is needed to export to them.
State of development	Even the larger less-developed countries such as Ethiopia or Bangladesh may be so underdeveloped that a population the size of a European country will, once more, generate a market that is scarcely larger than a French or American town.
Regulatory considerations	A number of countries have regulations or laws that can constrain the marketing of certain products, or the activities of certain organizations (particularly foreign companies).
Economic considerations.	GDP in total, its growth rate, and in particular GDP per capita, say a lot about the potential spending power and patterns of a country's population. These figures are available in reference books, such as OECD economic surveys and United Nations Yearbooks, which are usually found in larger reference libraries. However, care should be exercised in using any such data on a comparative basis, since the bases for the different sets of data may not be strictly comparable.
Social and business structures	Regulatory issues have already been mentioned. However, the culture itself can play a decisive role in deciding whether a product is accepted. As well as the special issues in Islamic countries, there are many other cultural barriers. Business cultures also have their idiosyncrasies. In certain countries, it is a business way of life for 'access' to be 'purchased'. In US and European eyes this may be seen as bribery, but locally it is often seen simply as part of the normal costs of trading. Equally, in certain countries the structure of business may be very informal, so that it takes a deal of accumulated expertise to understand exactly what a deal that is struck actually means. The state of development of the society can be gauged by the degree of literacy, and the employment levels as well as employment by sector service versus manufacturing versus primary agriculture, for example. The level of education may become a deciding factor in the use of any product that requires a degree of skill, or the following of written instructions.
Living standards	Individual living standards may often be estimated by reference to a few simple measures, such as ownership of television sets, telephones or cars. Indications of the infrastructure may be obtained from data such as the percentage of houses with mains drainage. Certain infrastructure elements may be very important to specific products or services. General Foods failed to make a success of selling packaged cake mixes in Japan, despite heavy promotion, because very few Japanese households own ovens in which to bake cakes. The 'skew' of living standards can be estimated from the distribution of income in general, or the presence or otherwise of 'luxury' industries.
Market accessibility	The final issue is the ease of access to a market. The potential it offers must be balanced against the costs of providing the necessary infrastructure.

Source: Chee and Harris (1998).

Internal factors influencing the selection

The key internal factors that can be assumed to exercise a moderate to strong degree of influence on the market selection process include (Koch 2001a):

- company strategic orientation
- stages of internationalization
- company strategic objectives
- overseas market selection experience
- company international competitiveness.

Company strategic orientation

This reflects the experience, values and attitudes of the company's employees. It may also include changes in the company's marketing environment and its strategic objectives. Strategic orientation may predispose companies to more, or less, collaboration with their competitors. It is also likely to strongly influence the company's international marketing process.

Stage of internationalization

Classifications of international marketing stages refer to either international marketing in general or export involvement in particular (Johansson 1997). The nexus between these classifications and the ethnocentric, regiocentric, polycentric and geocentric types of strategies pursued in international marketing is well worth examining, for both theory-building and practical purposes. The stages of company internationalization are strongly influenced by the company's strategic orientation (which might increase, reduce or eliminate interest in progress) and its international competitiveness (which will expedite or delay international involvement depending on its level). The increasing availability of international market information on the Internet calls for a revision of the traditional view of the stages and dynamics (Hamill, Jevons and Poon 1997).

Company strategic objectives

The choice of strategic objectives is dependent on company tradition, industry specificity, and the personal preferences/interests of those in charge of formulating them. They might be formulated in terms of international/local market shares, growth of international/local market sales revenue, export/total sales revenue ratio or profit. They might concern establishing/reinforcing perception of the company as a market leader, or reducing strategic risks associated with company survival or growth, and so on.

The strategic planning horizon is an important factor. Johansson (1997) proposed that the longer the time horizon in its strategic plans, the more likely the company is to prefer countries that show greater long-term prospects over those where only the immediate market prospects appear comparatively favourable. This implies that companies with a relatively short planning horizon will in most instances deny themselves most chances to enhance the firm's competencies, capabilities and skills through international market participation. Johansson also suggests that, when the company seeks highest sales and market share prospects, markets believed to be most likely to accept the product quickly are preferred.

Overseas market selection experience

Evaluation of the company's international business experience involves examining its intensity, relevance and character (positive or negative). Experience is a major factor shaping strategic directions, company corporate culture and collective knowledge, or common wisdom. Without sufficient relevant experience and knowledge, there tends to be a stronger sense of risk and uncertainty involved in international marketing decisions, which in turn constrains at least the subjective, if not the objective, freedom of choice of market servicing modes.

Company international competitiveness

Success in the contemporary international marketing environment is contingent on companies being able to access certain capabilities and skills that are considered to be of critical importance for a wide array of industries and business situations. Competitive performance tends to be ultimately assessed against specific criteria, or targets, and benchmarked against both general and specific key success factors. The specific depend more on deductive processes for definition, the general on inductive.

International competitiveness is often examined in an opportunistic manner, for example by using easily accessible information on international market shares held by individual companies. Although this may prove a legitimate method for some purposes, it does not answer one of the fundamentally important questions: which competencies, capabilities and skills explain the company performance? It might also fail to answer another crucial strategic management question: how has the company developed, or obtained access to, its current set of critically important competencies, capabilities and skills?

Among the major relevant distinctions are those that contrast risk assessment with benefit evaluation, and cost logic with degree of marketing control (Porter 1980). The relevant marketing practice depends on the industry's tradition, which in turn is correlated with availability of information, legislation and the general infrastructure. The individual preferences of those in a position to determine the choice of methods used should not be underestimated.

Mixed factors influencing the selection

The factors resulting from the combined influences of internal and external forces include the company's own resources, its networking capacity, the similarity and/or proximity of the overseas market, market portfolio congruity and expansion sequence optimization. They are depicted in Figure 5.2.

Accessible resources

Companies with more of their own resources, and/or better access to the resources of other companies through various forms of alliances, are less restricted in their international market selection (Koch 2001b). In larger, multidivisional companies with many product categories, multiple perspectives may need to be adopted to cater to the different strategy requirements of each individual product and /or service line. The strategic options of various forms of strategic alliances or the more temporary measure of piggybacking are increasing in popularity as markets become more international, competition becomes more intense and the response time to market continues to decrease.

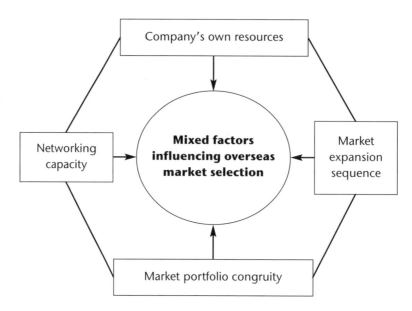

Figure 5.2 Mixed factors influencing market selection

The company's networking capacity

Companies can develop their networks and increase their international marketing practice through measures such as:

- participation in international trade fairs
- participation in exhibitions
- sharing the same suppliers and buyers
- joining strategic alliances
- forming joint ventures
- forming ad hoc consortia (for a tendering process).

For example, the Chinese are more likely than many nationals to develop their business networks on the basis of shared ethnicity. Contemporary requirements of internationalization, and in particular the implications of the rapid growth of electronic commerce, may affect these tendencies.

Similarity and/or proximity of the overseas market

Psychic distance can influence overseas market selection. In this regard, several factors are known to exercise a considerable influence on the choice of markets and on the order in which they are selected:

- the strength of the culture
- business links between the home country and a foreign country
- stereotypes or dominant perceptions
- employees' familiarity with different countries
- individual perceptions of decision makers or influencers.

The role of relevant experience, including that of expatriates, in forming perceptions of foreign markets is difficult to underestimate in this respect.

Market portfolio congruity

A company's market portfolio will be a result of incremental changes brought about by decisions taken in pursuing various international market expansion objectives. Over a long period of time, not only the market environment, but also the company logic of market selection may change. Thus, the market portfolio often appears incompatible with the current environment and strategy. The company may need to modify its market portfolio to ensure its congruity and a better match with current objectives and the external environment. This is an opportunity to look for synergies that reduce risk or costs. More specifically, such an analysis should take into consideration:

- similarity of customer requirements between selected countries
- customer expectations in selected countries
- similarity of product uses and circumstances
- similarity of standards between countries.

It is also useful to estimate the costs of supplying different products and/or services to different countries, and their impact on customer demand and on brand loyalty.

Expansion sequence optimization

If future international market expansion objectives become the frame of reference, another market selection problem emerges: what would be the most suitable new foreign markets, and the sequence of entering them, given the anticipation of the international market environment and company's future resources, competencies and capabilities? Initial stages of this analysis may draw on an available clustering of countries based on their general socioeconomic characteristics. A good and proper conceptual evaluation of such clustering needs to be undertaken on most occasions, with reference to the appropriate industry, and prediction of its changes.

Many companies expand in a cascade manner into overseas markets. One option is to start with markets that are considered the least demanding, then enter more and more challenging markets as experience, competencies, capabilities and skills grow. Another is to enter markets where demand for some new product has already reached a level that makes an entry a commercially viable proposition, then move on to markets that follow the pioneers. The best sequence of market expansion should be sought for the company to use its resources efficiently and sustain its international market growth.

External factors influencing the selection

These are the factors that are usually outside the control of the company. Companies simply operate in their context. They include:

- market potential
- market competitive significance

Figure 5.3 External factors influencing market selection

- market risk anticipation
- market opportunities.

See Figure 5.3 above.

Country market potential

Country market potential is a common criterion used in market selection, but the role of judgment, and the potential for political contamination of product statistics or country rankings, are often underestimated. Both information and the methods used in obtaining it are usually evaluated by managers before making decisions. The appears to be a need for further examination of product market specific variables to be used in estimating market potential in many industries (Johansson 1997). This would assist educators as well as enhance communication of theory with concrete business contexts.

Competitive significance of the market

Another traditional point of interest concerns the importance of lead markets as cues used in assessing a company's current performance and predicting changes. Leading (or lead) markets (which are usually large, strong, at the high end of the product line, free from government regulation and protective measures, with strong competitors and demanding customers) are of considerable strategic significance in international market-ing. Managing to get into these markets and staying there provides the company with an excellent opportunity to bring its capabilities and skills up to the highest levels required in international markets. Its presence in them can also be used as a positive promotional factor when the company is introduced to other markets.

There are gaps in both product performance and customer expectations between lead markets and other countries. These might be used as a basis to compare the competencies, capabilities and skills of competing companies. Ongoing study of the relevant trends helps reduce the danger of developing rankings based on outdated market information. Attacking a competitor's profit base (usually its domestic market) is an increasingly popular strategy amongst those pursuing an international marketing strategy. Pre-empting a competitor's move into a new, important market is another one (see Porter 1980).

Anticipated overseas market risks

Another market selection aspect that has received major attention is foreign market risk assessment. This has been driven by the interest of export credit guarantee organizations, banks and companies involved in international business. Czinkota and Ronkainen (1996) identified two major categories of international business risks. One involves the risks of business ownership – covering expropriation, confiscation and domestication – and the risks of marketing operation, including exchange risks, over-investment, price controls related risks and transfer risks. An equally important area is managerial perception of risks, and information reliability, which managers need to consider while making market selection decisions. The role of risk perception by managers is growing as an aspect for consideration in selecting international marketing operations.

Decision criteria for choice of market entry mode

The basic categories for the choice of market entry mode (see Figure 5.4) under the MEMS model put forward here are the same as for market selection. The factors to consider are also grouped under the headings of internal, external and mixed. (Some category names used in this model do not strictly correspond with those used in other classifications, but it should not be difficult for interested readers to map them onto the categories used elsewhere.) A mixed category is necessary because some of the factors, such as company international competitiveness, involve data from both inside and outside the company.

Internal factors

Companies vary in sizes and in the resources available to them. Smaller companies usually have fewer market servicing options (Benito and Welch 1994), as their limited resources will preclude some choices. For example, establishing a fully owned subsidiary often involves very substantial investment and correspondingly high risk levels. Similarly, small companies may not have sufficient management potential and specialist skills to establish fully owned foreign-based subsidiaries or international joint ventures. The influence of company size also depends, of course, on the nature of the industry. Koch (2001a) noted that in the chemical industry, for example, relationships are much stronger than in the computer software industry.

The significance of management locus of control in these choices is often underestimated, if not overlooked altogether. Yet strong internal, or external, loci of control are likely to considerably affect manager perception. The way managers' intuition works may play a large part in determining their market entry mode decisions, particularly in less experienced companies.

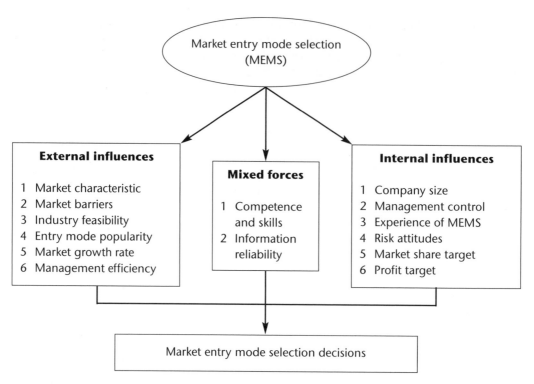

Figure 5.4 Factors influencing market entry mode selection

Experience in using a market entry mode

How many times, how recently and in what circumstances (similar enough or dissimilar) the company (or its competitors) have used any particular market entry mode, and with what success, obviously influences both the market entry selection process and the choices themselves (Paliwoda and Thomas 1998). Companies that have gathered a considerable knowledge of a region might prefer to invest resources in business ventures in that region rather than seek contractual modes there (Root 1994: 324).

Managerial succession often explains changes in the preferred market servicing modes. The market entry selection process is more likely to be subject to scrutiny and ongoing improvement, if shared reflection-in-action becomes commonplace. Increased accessibility of information on the Internet can be anticipated to speed up experience acquisition.

Management risk attitudes

The level to which the company will accept various international marketing risks depends on, among other factors:

- its financial situation
- its strategic options
- the competitiveness of its environment
- its relevant experience.

Risks can be estimated by using appropriate formulae. It should, however, be borne in mind that the *perception* of risks associated with individual market entry modes or countries may also influence companies' decisions considerably. The less risk-averse the management, the more likely the company is to select countries that show greater long-term prospects and promise to enhance the company's capabilities (Johansson 1997).

Market share and profit targets

When the criterion used in mode selection is sales or market share maximization, modes that are believed to be most likely to deliver the desired results within established planning periods will be preferred. For instance, if maximization of market share appears to be contingent on the development of the company's own distribution and after-sales network, it might decide to opt for a fully owned/majority marketing subsidiary. If the aim is to maximize export sales revenue growth over the next two or three years, indirect exporting might be the choice. More details on export as a mode of entry strategy are in Chapter 6, which discusses export and import management.

The dynamics of profit generation for various modes (take, for example, indirect export and investment in a new manufacturing and marketing overseas operation) are very dissimilar. The former venture will show some profits almost immediately, but they might soon level off. The latter might mean there are no profits for three or four years (during the construction cycle, the time needed to establish all necessary market contacts, acquire/build all necessary assets, train the sales force as required, develop customer base and so on). Those with a long decision horizon might prefer the latter; those with a short one will prefer the former. The suitability of the method used in estimating and comparing anticipated profits between various entry modes, and the reliability of inputs, are two other important concerns. Johansson (1997) suggested that the lower the target rates of return, the more likely it is for the company to select countries that show greater long-term prospects and promise to enhance the firm's capabilities.

Mixed factors

Owing to the transformation of the international marketing environment (see Chapter 2), reappraisal of the mechanisms through which international competitiveness can be established and furthered is a necessity for international market participants (Jagodka 1997). The importance of individual competencies, capabilities and skills depends on the context components: product category, area of (contemplated) presence, form of business and company strategic objectives. It is important that human resource policy should lead, rather than follow, company overall international strategy. There are some important implications for international market participants.

The lack of availability of information needed to make comparisons between various entry modes, different definitions and methods used in gathering data in different foreign countries, and inaccuracies in and obsolescence of data, as well as various forms of bias, may make it difficult, or impossible, to compare competing market entry modes properly.

External factors

While it is usually very easy these days to obtain information about the general characteristics of an overseas marketing environment , industry and company-specific information is usually more difficult to acquire. Information is not always free from bias, complete and up-to-date, and the marketing environment is quite sensitive. Among the characteristics that normally attract the attention of potential market entrants are the similarity and volatility of general business regulation/practices, business infrastructure and supporting industries, levels of development, forms, scope and intensity of competition, customer sophistication and customer protection legislation.

Market barriers

Of the barriers that can make access to foreign markets more difficult, the following are considered of major importance (Johansson 1997):

- tariff barriers
- governmental regulations
- distribution access
- natural barriers (market success and customer allegiances)
- differences between advanced and developing countries
- exit barriers.

The law in some countries excludes some entry modes, such as fully owned foreign subsidiaries and international joint ventures. Some of these exclusions only apply to selected industries considered to be of strategic significance for the state. Some entry modes (licensing) may involve excessive know-how dissemination risk, particularly if the country is not a signatory to the appropriate international conventions. Other hindrances (such as restrictive labour regulation and practices, cost of labour, insufficient level of skill) may discourage the company from establishing a subsidiary or a joint venture operation in a foreign market. Investing in a foreign subsidiary may secure favourable taxation treatment and save the company a lot of money on custom duties. Because of the specific risks and costs involved in individual entry modes, and the varying sales potentials over a period of time, some modes may turn out less viable than others in a given situation.

Popularity of individual modes in the overseas market

In some country markets and industries, particular modes of market entry are especially popular (Seabright 1996). The selection of entry mode will be influenced by the experience of the proposed entrant, the degree of success of former entrants and the anticipated product market situation. In most instances, if a particular entry mode has proved successful in the past, and there are expectations of growing demand and a stable business environment, a newcomer is likely to follow the popular choice. On the other hand, if it has had positive experience with a different entry mode in another market, it might be tempted to stick with that if it would improve the strategy match.

Market growth rate

The market growth rate is normally an issue of considerable significance. If a market is growing fast, and this rate of growth does not seem sustainable over several years, the company will be well advised to tap into the opportunity without delay and use indirect or direct exporting. If demand in a foreign market is anticipated to be very large, establishing the company's own manufacturing or marketing subsidiary may be the best answer.

Critical success factors and companies' core capabilities must be examined to find the optimal organizational structure and strategy to follow. It is good advice for most international marketers to avoiding excessive diversity in the international market entry portfolio. All possible economies of scale (and scope) that may flow from such a portfolio must be investigated, and organization structures and strategies of all competitors considered. Companies' management cultures are likely to influence the decision-making process regarding the choice of market entry modes, and must therefore be considered, along the lines discussed in the next section.

The role of culture in entry decisions

Culture can be regarded as giving a sense of belonging, forming a reference towards life. Hofstede (1984) equates culture with value systems, and views values as the 'building blocks of culture'. Culture affects people, and affects or even dictates the way they live their lives. It influences many day-to-day decisions. However, the different components of culture have varying degrees of importance for both individuals and societies, and this variation could be expressed in terms of the 'immediacy' or 'closeness' to the individual in the society.

A country's culture has long been identified as a key environmental characteristic underlying systematic differences in behaviour. Cultural norms and beliefs are powerful forces shaping consumers' perceptions, dispositions and behaviours. Culture is reflected in general tendencies for people to persistently prefer particular states of affairs over others, specific social processes over others, and general rules for selective attention, interpretation of environmental cues and responses. National culture (which is obviously different in different nations) (Steenkamp 2001) must be considered in making international marketing entry decisions. This will ensure that the company's presence and its products and/or services will be culturally acceptable to the consumers.

Culturally close or distant

Cultural distance (psychic distance) is the extent to which the norms and values of two individuals or companies differ because of their different nationalities. It is an outcome of the differing cultural backgrounds of individuals involved in the process of international marketing interaction.

The more different the other person's culture seems, the greater the degree of cultural distance. Cultural distance is therefore a potentially powerful determinant of the way international marketing relationships can develop. Indeed, there is the possibility that what are intended to be universal prescriptions for international relationship marketing will fail in a firm's foreign markets, where a buyer–seller relationship means something quite different from its meaning in the same firm's domestic markets. For example, the

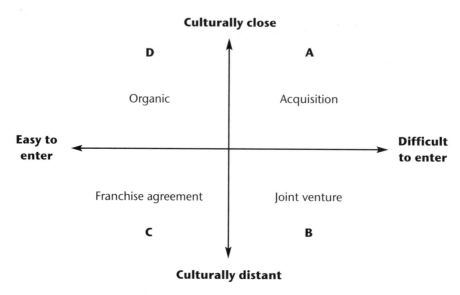

Figure 5.5 A cultural framework for an international market entry strategy

overall approach to relational exchange might be a 'win–win' situation, but in cultures where there is the presumption that there is only one winner – the seller – this may be inappropriate.

Figure 5.5 summarizes a culturally based framework for international market entry strategies. In quadrants A and D, the culture of the foreign country the company is entering is relatively close to its domestic market in both consumer behaviour and the structure of the market. In quadrants B and C, the foreign country differs significantly from the home country in either or both of consumer behaviour and the structure of the market. The differences in structure could arise from the degree of market concentration, the nature of marketing, or the structure and patterns of consumer demands. The type of international marketing operation will determine whether consumer behaviour or market structure is more important in deciding whether a country is considered culturally close or distant.

Countries in quadrants A and B in Figure 5.5 are difficult to enter. Barriers to entry may include:

- strong competitors
- unavailability of skilled workers
- strict licence requirements
- strict and preventive advertising regulations
- business and/or office location restrictions
- financial barriers
- unfavourable insurance systems.

As a result of the importance of national culture in international marketing, the failure to take cultural differences between countries into account when making market selection decisions will result in international marketing failure. For countries in quadrants C and D, the barriers discussed above are either non-existent or relatively easy to overcome. When taken together, the two axes of Figure 5.5 help to distinguish four types of entry strategy: self-start (organic), franchise, acquisition and joint venture. (These are discussed below.)

Entry as an international marketing strategy

The choice of a method of market entry has significant implications for international marketing strategy. At one level, the choice could be seen in terms of the degree of freedom that the company has in choosing the target market, and in the ways in which the company subsequently goes about the process of matching market demand. At a deeper level, the choice of method of entry has direct consequences for the company's ability to develop an international image (Melewar and Saunders 1998) and reap the benefits of the economies of large scale and standardized international marketing programmes. In this section attention is given to the way in which the choice of market entry either enhances or inhibits the company's freedom to operate in the international market. The strategies discussed include organic growth, franchises, joint ventures, acquisitions, licensing and alliances.

Self-start entry (organic growth) strategy

With this strategy, the company is built up by organic growth from a very modest initial investment (Akehurst and Alexander 1995). Woolworth's early development in the United Kingdom and Laura Ashley in the United States are commonly cited examples of self-start entry. Before embarking on this entry strategy, companies need to assess the degree of cultural distance of the target market and the severity of any entry barriers. Once international marketing objectives have been set, companies are faced with problems of market adaptation and relations with local competitors.

International marketing expansion via self-start entry is usually restricted by the company's capacity to finance any initial losses and withstand pressure from shareholders. It is important that the main domestic company continue subsidizing the new overseas company until specific sales targets are met. For example, Yaohan, a Japanese company with 21,000 employees in Japan, decided to move its headquarters to Hong Kong as an entry point to China. It then started to invest heavily in supermarkets on the Chinese coast around Shanghai and opened a ten-floor department store in Shanghai. However, it failed to assess correctly the amount of time it would take to succeed in China, and was forced into receivership with a high level of debt (Vanhonacker 1997). Issues to be considered include the amount of adaptation that will be necessary and the accuracy of information about local market environment.

Franchising arrangements

International business format franchising is a contract-based organizational structure for entering new markets. It involves a franchisor firm that undertakes to transfer a business concept it has developed, with corresponding operational guidelines, to non-domestic parties for a fee. This business concept tends to pertain most to service-based industries such as fast-food restaurants and car repair and rental, and to professional services such as hotel management and real estate services. Once the potential franchisor has estab-lished a reputation for its business concept, this develops demand as a 'leasable' commodity. The franchisor packages the business concept, operating guidelines and access to its trade and brand marks, and offers this business format to firms that purchase the rights to exploit commercially the concept and trade names for a given period of time (typically between 5 and 15 years) in a given geographical territory. Typical franchise contracts require an up-front payment to the franchisor as well as royalty payments based upon sales in the stipulated territory.

At the outset, it is important to note that the transfer of rights surrounding the franchise format to an independent foreign firm can be achieved in several ways (Burton and Cross 1997).

- **Direct franchising** – the franchisor negotiates and transacts with each owner-oper-ator of the franchise outlet, the franchisee, on a one-to-one basis in the host market.
- **Area development franchising** – the area developer is granted the right by the franchisor to establish a network of internal outlets run by its employee-managers in a specified territory. However, the area developer is not permitted to sub-franchise; that is, sell the franchise on to other local concerns.
- **Master franchising** –a master sub-franchiser is granted by the franchisor the right to sell, or sub-franchise, the format to individual owner-operators of outlets. In effect, it becomes the direct franchisor to sub-franchisees in the market.

Benefits to the franchisee

- It is clear that most franchisors offer a proven business concept and established brand equity to franchise buyers.
- Franchisors usually support and enhance this brand equity through an advertising cooperative financed by specific fees levied on franchise buyers, or by apportioning a component of the royalty payments received from them.
- When a large system of outlets operating the franchise format is created, repeat expo-sures to consumers further help to consolidate brand awareness. In the process entry barriers are erected, limiting the ability of new entrants to succeed in the market area.
- Franchisors may provide practical support to buyers of the franchise in terms of site selection, outlet design and bank loan negotiation.
- Franchisors may also assist in training the local workforce, with respect, for example, to operational procedures, management practices and accounting methods, according to the operational guidelines that serve as the backbone to the franchise agreement.
- Franchisors may also coordinate centrally the bulk purchase of requisite inputs for the franchise system. This provides opportunities for scale economies to be leveraged, allowing system members to reduce input costs in a manner that would probably be otherwise unavailable to them. In some circumstances, these purchases may provide a means for franchisors to earn revenue on mark-ups on the products and services sourced centrally, although in some jurisdictions competition legislation may limit the opportunities for generating profit from tied purchases and other similar activities.

On balance, the support provided by franchisors to buyers of their franchise is widely believed to heighten the probability of success for the new business compared with an independent start-up operation.

Advantages to the franchisor

In turn, buyers of the franchise also provide valuable resources to the franchisor. The franchisee may:

- provide the working capital for new outlets (either directly or via sub-franchisees in the case of master franchising)
- help the franchisor to expand through avoiding the need to raise capital internally
- provide a significant amount of capital. made immediately available to the franchisor in the form of up-front payments by the franchisee
- establish a revenue stream with little downside risk to the franchisor, as royalties are typically paid to the franchisor based on sales and not on profits
- provide the franchisor with a natural linkage to the market territory, such as residency
- provide the franchisor with unique knowledge about the market territory, so increasing the probability that the franchise will succeed in the area
- pass relevant market information on to other operators of the franchise in overseas markets so that the participants in the franchise system may benefit.

Perhaps the most compelling resource that independent franchisees, master sub-franchisers and sub-franchisees provide is their ownership commitment to the enterprise. It is this ownership that dispenses with the classic shirking problem associated with agents (managers) operating on behalf of principals (owners of the firm). The owner-operator is argued to be more committed, and have far greater incentive to ensure the outlet's success, than would managers employed by a firm. The owner-operator's capital, as opposed to a mere salary stream, is at risk.

Identifying the potential resource transfers by franchisors and franchisees is important to understanding the strategic value of international franchise relationships. Where a firm or individual is resource constrained (for example, capital-constrained in the case of the franchisor, or in respect of business operating knowledge in the case of the franchisee), a franchise relationship may allow contracted parties to succeed in business where otherwise they could not. Control over strategically important resources grants the franchisor or the franchisee power over their counterpart in the franchise relationship. The use of this power can determine the potential success of the franchise.

Joint ventures

A joint venture is a business agreement where two or more owners create a separate entity. Joint venture involves one or more partners joining together to create a new identity with specific purpose (Griffith, Michael and Chen 1998). Many MNCs gain access to markets and/or resources through the formation of international joint ventures (IJVs). Joint ventures are formed to achieve synergy through combining complementary partners. IJVs are formed to improve the company's competitive positioning within the international marketplace. In order to accomplish this objective, the parent companies attempt to create synergies through combining resources, capabilities and strengths.

Local partners, particularly those from developing countries, benefit from the technological know-how, management skills and capital brought in by their foreign partners. On the other hand MNCs depend on local partners' knowledge and networks in the host country to reduce risks and increase revenue. IJVs allow partners to share information, resources and risks, hence creating synergistic effects. Joint ventures have also created problems for partners because of different goals, values and cultures.

Most IJVs are formed for the purpose of entering new markets or to help develop existing international and/or domestic markets. IJV partners can contribute the required cultural and/or international marketing expertise, and experience gained in their own local markets, to aid overseas partners in their markets. A joint venture is the most appropriate entry strategy when the foreign country is culturally distant and difficult to enter.

There are several forms of IJV strategy in which MNCs can become involved:

- **Go-together then split** – where the parties cooperate over an extended period then separate. It is a suitable strategy for a limited project.
- **Spider's web** – where a joint venture is established with a large competitor in order to prevent takeover attempts from other international companies.
- **Successive integration** – which may start with weak inter-firm linkages and develop to interdependence, then end with a takeover or merger.

As IJVs have increased in the variety and form they take, it is necessary to be clear on how the chosen strategy is defined and its benefits evaluated against its drawbacks. The choice of partner and the contact agreed are vital for the success of a joint venture. The basic rule is that there must be a long-term interest for both parties to stay together (Omar 1999). Usually the trade-off is for one partner to gain access to a new market by using the local partner's knowledge and network. Joint venture partnerships are difficult to manage and have a high failure rate. For example, the 50/50 joint venture set up by Auchan, the French hypermarket group, with Comercial Mexicana ended because of differences concerning development strategy. Comercial Mexicana retained the hypermarket established by the partners, and Auchan opened its own hypermarkets.

Acquisition

Acquisition involves an international company purchasing an overseas company in the target market. This tends to be the approach used in the majority of instances by UK companies developing outside the domestic market. As a different example, in order to achieve its strategic objective within the European market, Ford Motor Company in 1989 acquired Jaguar plc, a UK car manufacturer, for $2.6 billion. The chairman of Ford (Europe) described the purchase of Jaguar as the fulfilment of a long-time strategic objective of entering the luxury car market in a significant way.

In some cases the overseas marketing interests may not be related in any way to the company's own business activities. BAT, for example, owns several department stores, variety and drug stores in the United States, but limits its domestic retailing activities to Argos catalogue showrooms and the Jewellers Guild. Through an acquisition strategy, an outsider benefits by buying into existing supplier contacts, distribution systems and a customer base. This strategy is particularly suitable for saturated markets, since in such markets it is easier to buy existing market share than build it.

For companies operating in multiple countries, mixed entry modes are often necessary. The major problem of market entry by acquisition, especially for British companies (see Mini case 5.1) is that the companies available for sale are often in financial difficulty. Thus, considerable time and financial support is required to restore such companies to profitability. As the situations in Mini case 5.1 revealed, buying a foreign company is a difficult task for many British companies. This is because the cost of buying into more successful companies with strong management teams is always very high.

MINI CASE 5.1

Buying a foreign company

British retailers such as Laura Ashley, British Home Stores, WH Smith, The Body Shop, Tesco, J. Sainsbury and Marks & Spencer have always been protected in their domestic market not by tariffs, but by their sheer scale and by the fact that retailing is a difficult export. But the difficulty has cut both ways. Tesco's purchase of Catteau in France was such a flop that the business was sold to Promodes for an £8 million loss. What should have been a foothold for large-scale continental expansion became a false start. British ventures into overseas retailing have mostly been small-scale and unsuccessful. The lamentable facts about Marks & Spencer's doomed Canadian venture, for example, were not only that management persisted so long with failure, but that the enterprise was so feeble in ambition.

Even when Marks & Spencer bought Brooks Brothers, it chose a niche clothing retailer serving upmarket US males. The Brooks Brothers' business bore little resemblance to the M&S British operation and could not be translated into the parental model.

M&S was not alone in mishandling overseas buys. British retailers have generally disobeyed the injunctions of global market acquisition strategy. For successful acquisition of a foreign company (*Grocer* 1999) British retailers should only buy if:

- management is honest and competent
- no management reinforcement is required
- return on capital is above average
- the record of operating profits is also above average
- the British retailer thoroughly understands the business of the company being bought
- its long-term prospects are predictable and excellent
- the continuing management will run the acquisition like its own business
- the buy has significantly large profits.

British retailers cannot be surprised by the disappointing results if they buy into:

- poorly managed companies
- relatively small businesses with poor financial records and results
- companies operating in unfamiliar areas
- companies with limited growth prospects
- companies that depend on the injection of imported executives for their management.

The difficulties are only intensified if the acquirer (like many British retailers) is convinced of the superiority of its methods and management. The result is generally interference, and the result of interference is generally to accentuate failure.

International licensing agreements

Another approach to international market entry, and one that minimizes capital investment, is licensing, through which a company may exploit its 'saleable know-how'. In a
number of ways, licensing can be seen as an extension or development of contract
marketing in that it generally covers a longer time period and involves the licensee in a
wider sphere of international marketing activities. Typically, for example, the licensee is
given the exclusive rights to market the manufacturer's product within an agreed area in
return for a royalty based on sales volume. It is this responsibility for marketing that is
the distinguishing feature of a licensing agreement.

MNCs face complex challenges as they pursue opportunities in both domestic and
international markets. Licensing is one of the mechanisms through which managers can
operate their strategic marketing programmes, and managers appear to view licensing
favourably in many contexts (Gleason, Mathur and Singh 2000). In terms of technology,
for example, licensing benefits not only the firms engaged in the agreement through the
coordination of complementary assets, but also consumers, who gain access to new
products and services.

The advantages of licensing over other mechanisms through which technology can be
transferred is that companies can obtain the required asset without incurring the costs of
managerial, financial and technical resources. Furthermore, the company might make a
decision to license its technology if interdependencies exist in industries and across
national borders that are part of a network of producers. Similarly, innovators with international licensing experience are subsequently more likely than those without experience
to choose licensing mode as the international market entry strategy.

Licensing is advantageous when:

- the licensee does not have the capability to develop the technology, but has expertise
  in its application
- the cost incurred in the development of the strategic asset internally exceeds the cost
  of obtaining it through licensing
- companies perceive that the likelihood of reciprocity in terms of future technology is high
- both participants are able to obtain the required innovation at a lower cost than it
  would take for either to develop it internally
- the licensing of a market leader's products leads to reputation enhancement effects
  and standardization in nascent industries
- aggressive protection of intellectual property is necessary.

The licensee avoids the high cost of developing in-house. Licensing may be useful to a
firm using the 'sprinkler model' of expansion rather than the 'waterfall method', when it
wants to get rapid access to major markets simultaneously. In order to discourage imitation by international competitors, firms may use licensing to acquire technology and
disperse their products quickly in all desired end product markets at the same time. Other
beneficial aspects of licensing arrangements include:

- The company avoid the capital investment needed to open distribution facilities.
- It is the fastest and least problematic way of entering a foreign market and gaining
  market knowledge.

- In many former communist countries, licensing is the only way in which markets can be entered.
- The licensee avoids R&D costs.
- The licensee can capitalize on the technological expertise of the licenser.
- Many emerging governments tend to look favourably upon licensing largely because of the implications for employment locally and the long-term benefits of technology transfer.
- For the licenser the investment capital is provided locally and management is eventually turned over to local personnel.

For these reasons large multinationals are often invited by governments to set up 'turnkey' operations, mainly in less developed countries. When problems with licensing do arise, the root cause tends to be (Gleason et al. 2000):

- difficulties with the initial contract spelling out the responsibilities both of the licenser and the licensee
- the terms of the agreement becoming less appropriate and relevant over time and as the market environment changes
- difficulties of dealing with a licensee who appears not to be putting sufficient effort into market development
- relatively low returns from the typical licensing agreement
- an entrepreneurial licensee who after a number of years decides to make use of the expertise he/she has gained by setting up a rival company.

On balance, however, many international companies have found licensing to be an attractive method of entering foreign markets, particularly when strong international patents exist and steps are taken to minimize the likelihood of the problems referred to above arising.

Strategic alliances (co-marketing)

Strategic alliances (also known as co-marketing) have been in existence for over 30 years, and Malhotra, Agarwal and Baalbaki (1998) predict that they are pointing the way that company-to-company relationships will develop. Whether they take the form of joint ventures or cooperative agreements, strategic alliances are partnerships between firms that work together to attain some strategic objectives. A strategic alliance may create either an equity-based distinct corporate entity (a joint venture) or a non-equity based inter-organizational entity such as a joint technology or product development centre to which the alliance partners commit agreed-on skills and resources.

The goals of strategic alliance

Competitive strength and strategic positioning comes into play to a large degree in alliances forged for technology commercialization. The number of strategic alliances has gone up in some industries, such as retailing, communication systems and services, computer software and hardware, and financial services. Malhotra et al. (1998) have identified the main objectives of strategic alliances as to leverage critical capabilities, increase the flow of innovation and improve flexibility in responding to market and technological changes. Increasingly, firms are not only accepting the idea of working together in some operational kind of way, they are incorporating it into their overall strategic plan.

Co-marketing brings together partners that may be horizontally related, such as Ford and Mazda, vertically related (Ford and auto part suppliers), or not related to each other's business at all. Such alliances also include licensing agreements to transfer technology, R&D partnerships, and supplier and marketing arrangements. These issues are central to a company's direction and to achieving future international competitive advantages. Co-marketing as an alternative mode of entry provides an excellent strategic fit especially between firms located in different multicultural trading blocs.

Motives underlying strategic alliances

Malhotra et al. (1998) proposed five key motives for firms to join a strategic alliance:

- blurring of market boundaries
- circumventing entry barriers
- reducing the threat of potential competitors
- innovations
- flexible response systems.

See Table 5.2.

In the last decade, all of the factors discussed in Table 5.2 have contributed to a tremendous growth of strategic alliances in the Pacific Rim countries, Europe and North America. As firms in developing countries face shorter product lines, deregulation and import competition, more and more firms are candidates for strategic alliances. With the future intensification of the regional trading blocs, and for firms fighting for greater international competitiveness, the number of strategic alliances will be on the rise.

Partnerships in emerging markets

Relying on local partners with excellent contracts among the host country governing elite is a strategy that has been used effectively by many companies. This may range from placing local nationals on the boards of foreign subsidiaries to accepting substantial capital participation from local investors. For example, Kodak had been fighting with Fuji for access to the Japanese camera and film market for many years before linking with Konica, a move that enabled it to enter the Japanese market with a digital camera. Although many emerging markets require some form of local participation as a condition for entering their market, many firms agree to this voluntarily.

Emerging markets differ substantially from developed economies:

- They are different in geographic region and their level of economic development.
- Markets in Africa, Asia, Latin America, and the Middle East are characterized by a higher degree of risk than markets in developed countries.

Table 5.2 Motives underlying strategic alliances

Motivating factor	Influencing prognosis
Blurring of market boundaries	The rapid pace of technological changes is increasingly blurring market boundaries and redefining markets. Recognizing the limitations of skills and resources to exploit growing technology and sustain competitive advantage, firms are engaging in intra and inter-industry alliances at both the national and international levels. As an example of inter-industry, international alliance, companies like America On-line, Prodigy and Compuserve (Internet content providers), have alliances with Netscape and Microsoft (software technology providers) and AT&T and Sprint (telecommunications providers).
Circumventing entry barriers	Entry barriers (market obstacles) are the main determinants of the attractiveness of a market. Knowledge of such entry barriers is useful in identifying whether the strategic windows of market opportunity are open. Entry barriers are forces that discourage firms from investing in a particular market that appears attractive. Markets characterized by high entry barriers have generally been considered to be more profitable in the long term. These obstacles come in the way of tariff and non-tariff barriers such as stringent technical and standard requirements, local content laws and cooperative distribution system. Strategic alliance helps circumvent trade and market specific barriers. For example, Ford's alliance with Mazda opened up the impregnable Japanese distribution system through Mazda's network of Autorama showrooms.
Reducing the threat of potential competitors	A sustainable competitive advantage warrants understanding of current and potential competitors. A technology licensing-based strategic alliance can eliminate the threat of future potential competitors. When competitive pressures are high with regards to imitation of new products (lead-time), international alliances may offer enhanced protection against future competitors. For example, General Electric licensed its advanced gas turbine technology to foreign producers that it viewed as potential competitors. The result was elimination of threat and a secured captive market in those countries. A strategic alliance between a market leader in the home country and a market follower in the host country can drain the resources of the host country market leader, thus protecting its home market position.
Innovations	Innovation is the technological dimension of the company's competitive weapon (Omar 1995). Merging of heterogeneous technologies reshapes market structure and wipes out sources of existing competitive advantage by creating new technological standards. Strategic alliance provides a means to sustain competitive advantage by allowing the firm to conform to the new technological standard. For example, new technical and technological standards are being established within the European Union to enhance international competitiveness. Strategic alliances offer new economic power centres and technology to cater to increased and specialized demand. This can increase the demand for new product designs, new production processes and innovations, which in turn can stimulate primary demand for the growth market.

Table 5.2	continued

Motivating factor	Influencing prognosis
Flexible response systems	Strategic alliances entail change in manufacturing thrust. There is an increasing realization of the critical importance of time as a strategic resource to compete internationally. The concept of fast response manufacturing has emerged. Increasing volatility of consumer buying pattern demands the highest quality goods in the shortest possible time. Also, faster diffusion of technologies can transform industries, production methods and product designs in a matter of days. Flexible manufacturing systems allow for the incorporation of local adaptations in otherwise standardized products in a multicultural environment.

Source: adapted from Malhotra et al. (1998).

- As a result of the less stable economic climates in these areas, a company's operation can be expected to be subject to greater uncertainty and fluctuation.
- The frequently changing political situations in developing countries often affect operating results negatively.
- Some markets that may have experienced high growth for some years may suddenly experience drastic reductions in growth.
- The higher risks are compensated for by higher returns, largely because competition is often less intense in the emerging markets.

Consequently, companies need to balance the opportunity for future growth in the developing nations with the existence of higher risk (Keegan 1999).

The past experience of international firms doing business in developing countries has not been especially positive. Trade restrictions have forced companies to build local factories, exposing themselves to substantial risk. However, with the present trend toward global trade liberalization and privatization, many formerly closed countries have opened their borders.

Many companies were seriously affected by the economic crisis in Mexico during the early 1990s. At the same time, Whirlpool, the US-based household goods company, was severely affected by the economic situation in Brazil. Currency devaluation in Brazil resulted in a substantial net charge against income. Furthermore, annual sales in Brazil, measured in hard currency, declined by nearly $200 million as a result of the devaluation. Although the potential is usually superior in emerging markets, international companies have to expect annual fluctuations that far exceed those experienced in the developed markets of North America and Europe.

The market adaptation and standardization process

With the increasing international market integration, the task international marketers face is not so much market entry as managing the marketing mix in different national markets. For example, the question every company needs to answer is whether it is better to standardize or to adapt its international marketing operation across different markets. In making such decisions, a number of factors should be considered:

MINI CASE 5.2

Examples of international companies doing business with emerging countries

Unilever, the large Dutch-British consumer goods company, met intensive competition in its traditional markets in Europe and the United States, where it has about two-thirds of its volume. Faced with lower growth in those markets, the company moved aggressively into emerging markets, where annual growth has averaged 5 per cent or more in most of its core business categories. The company declared five geographic areas as top targets: Central and Eastern Europe, Latin America, India and Southeast Asia. China is viewed as huge. The company planned to obtain half of its world-wide sales from emerging countries over the next five years.

Similarly, Banco Santander, the leading Spanish commercial and investment bank, decided to pursue emerging markets on the basis that traditional markets in Europe and North America were overbanked. As a result, the company launched a major drive to develop its competitive position in Latin America. In 1996/7, the bank made major acquisitions in Chile, entered pension fund management in Argentina, and acquired large banks in Mexico and Colombia, as well as Venezuela's second-largest bank. Following its merger with BCH SA, another Spanish bank, Santander commanded some 1,400 retail branches throughout the region and was expected to reach for a market share of about 5 per cent in each market.

Another international company doing business with emerging countries is Hyundai. The largest of Korea's three major car manufacturers, with sales of 2.8 million units in 2007 (http://www.carwale.com/blog/oem/515-hyundai-sales-figures-for-may-08/, it acquired old car plants in recently liberalizing countries, especially in Eastern Europe and the former Soviet Union. The company further expanded with plants into Turkey, India, Egypt and Botswana. These are all markets with still small car markets, and with few competitors in place.

Sources: various company reports.

- whether the product and/or service is aimed at the 'innovator' or 'early adopter' segment, which is likely to be fairly uniform across countries
- whether it is a component in or a complement to other products or services
- what stages of development targeted countries have reached.

For more than four decades, standardization versus adaptation of marketing programmes has been the subject of much debate in the international marketing literature. With internationalization of markets and competition, the concept of marketing standardization has become an even more important issue within both the business and academic communities. Despite the enduring interest in this issue since the early 1960s we are nowhere close to any conclusive theory or practice. The lack of convergence on global standardization can be attributed to the lack of empirical work on this topic. Although various scale effects and cost savings associated with standardization have been discussed repeatedly in the literature, few systematic attempts have been made to empirically validate the performance implications of standardization. The pursuit of international market standardization is generally considered to be appropriate only to the extent to which it has a positive influence on financial performance.

That is, the ultimate relevance of market standardization should be determined based on its economic payoff.

A fundamental issue in international marketing concerns the desirability and feasibility of standardization. The proponents of standardization emphasize the rapid advances in transportation and communication technologies that facilitate the trend toward homogenization of world markets (Zou et al. 1997). By capitalizing on such homogenization of consumer tastes and need patterns, firms can achieve cost savings and economies of scale in production, marketing and other activities. On the other hand, proponents of adaptation point to differences between national markets, in:

- physical environment
- political and legal systems
- cultures and acculturation process
- product usage conditions
- economic development.

As a result of these fundamental differences between markets, it is rarely feasible for companies to achieve standardization of their marketing activities. Thus, it is preferable for companies to localize their marketing programmes to the specific conditions.

There are two important conclusions. First, neither total standardization nor complete adaptation is conceivable. From a contingency perspective, the degree of standardization or adaptation is dependent on a variety of internal and external factors.

Second, the ultimate decision regarding standardization versus adaptation should be based on the impact on organizational performance. That is, the pursuit of standardization is appropriate only when it can positively influence the company's performance.

From a managerial perspective, given the potential benefits of a standardized marketing programme, the performance implications of standardization are of critical importance in deciding international marketing strategy. There are no significant differences in financial performance between firms that focus on standardization and those that do not. A consensus exists in the marketing literature regarding the need to consider the type of industry and product category in the context of marketing standardization.

For instance, standardization may be situation-specific and not appropriate in all settings. The degree of standardization will vary depending on the type of product, with consumer non-durables being the most difficult to standardize because of differing national tastes and habits. International standardization is more feasible for industrial products than for consumer products, because business buyers are more rational in their purchasing behaviour, and demand for industrial products is more homogeneous across markets (O'Donnell and Jeong 2000). A strong argument can therefore be made that, if the viability of standardization indeed hinges on industry and product-type contingencies, their effects may have to be taken into account in examining the performance implication of standardization. Specifically, it can be posited that international standardization has a positive influence on performance in the context of industrial and high-technology products.

MINI CASE 5.3

Examples of standardization versus adaptation

The launch decision also includes marketing mix decisions. In 1991, when Citibank introduced its credit card in the Asia-Pacific region, it launched it sequentially and tailored the product features for each country while maintaining its premium positioning. The promotional, pricing and distribution strategies also differed from country to country. As one of the international banks, Citibank faced a peculiar problem. In the United States, it was a mass-market banker. Its clientele included a large proportion of the middle class, although it did have high-income individuals as well. However, outside the United States it positioned itself as a provider of premium retail banking services for people with high incomes. In the United Kingdom, for example, individual account holders need to have a minimum annual income of $50,000, while in India there was a minimum balance of $7,500. Ninety per cent of Citibank's private banking clients are in Asia. Thus, its US positioning is inconsistent with its positioning outside the United States.

How can Citibank solve any potential problem arising from its inconsistent positioning given that it is in for the long haul and cannot realistically be expected to shut down operations in some countries? Inconsistency in positioning need not be a problem if consumers in the Asian markets are not aware of Citibank's positioning in the United States, but it could be a problem if upscale Asian consumers are aware of the US positioning.

One approach that Citibank adopted was to move into the 'middle' markets in Asia with a different set of products. Over time, such moves should lead to a more consistent positioning for Citibank across all its markets. Since Citibank's product is a consumer service offered in markets with different levels of infra-structural development and consumer requirements, product differentiation in terms of features is inevitable, as are pricing and distributional differences. However, by expanding its offering to include the mass market and by simultaneously keeping its offering for elite customers differentiated, the company can project a uniform image around the world.

As a contrast, consider Rolex. The genuine Rolex watch is the same certified chronometer anywhere in the world. Its positioning as the timepiece for the elegant high achiever is the same around the world, as is the advertising message. You will always find a Rolex in an upmarket distribution outlet and at a premium price. Consider also Unilever's Lifebuoy soap, which has different ingredients in India than in East Africa. However, Unilever positions the soap in the same way in both markets, as an inexpensive everyday soap that has antibacterial properties and protects health. Clearly, it is possible to have a completely standardized international marketing mix. It is also possible to have some elements that are the same across countries and others that are adapted to each country.

The impact of the Internet on the market selection and entry process

The Internet provides a fundamentally different environment for international marketing and requires a radically different strategic approach. The increasing role of the Internet and the WWW in transforming the international marketing environment necessitates a corresponding shift in the discussion of the market selection and entry process. In particular, it is important to consider its role in facilitating international marketing information acquisition, reducing the perceived and real risks, and expediting the internationalization process of small and medium-sized enterprises.

By connecting end-users and producers directly, the Internet reduces the importance of traditional intermediaries in international marketing. To survive, agents and distributors need to offer a different range of services. Their value-added will no longer be principally in the physical distribution of goods but rather in the collection, collation, interpretation and dissemination of vast amounts of information. The critical resource possessed by this new breed of 'cybermediary' will be information rather than inventory.

Marketing is essentially information-processing activity which links an organization to the external environment in which it operates. Processing information is now generally accepted as the fifth 'P' of the marketing mix. Effective management of IT is a powerful source of competitive advantage. The need for effective management of information is particularly important in international marketing, where the company is dealing with a range of diverse and complex environments, subject to rapid and often unexpected change. The key to success in entering new overseas markets is to systematically gather and analyse accurate and timely information. Intelligent decisions cannot be made until the company is able to find, collect and evaluate relevant information about the idiosyncrasies of the market, the needs and tastes of consumers. Thus, the use of the Internet and its related technology for marketing intelligence is one of the most important ways in which connectivity can improve the company's overseas market selection process and its ability to develop international markets.

Summary

This chapter's comprehensive discussion of factors influencing the market entry and market selection (MEMS) process has revealed that this process is influenced by a larger number of the external and internal environment factors than most previous models have assumed. The relative importance of individual factors process was found here to depend on the external and internal environment of the company. Further, accessibility of external and internal information has been found to influence the pace of the international marketing process, the quality of market and market entry mode decisions, and the ultimate market and market entry choices made by the company.

The chapter recommended that a full contextual in-depth examination of market entry mode selection practice should be carried out systematically and longitudinally, to develop a sufficient knowledge on which to formulate an international marketing plan. The examination of associated information flows is of particular significance. A holistic perspective helps bridge the gap between the narrowness of most current models and the immense complexity of international market entry decisions. It also provides efficient guidance for individual companies to designing processes to suit their particular contexts.

Many years since Levitt made the argument (1980, 1983a, 1983b) that the world is moving toward a unified market, the debate still lacks consensual theoretical and empirical validation. Although a move toward greater standardization has been supported, increased standardization as a result of the homogenization of international markets has not yet materialized.

It is increasingly becoming clear that few companies have been successful at adopting international marketing strategies. A valid argument can be made that as the cultures of the world merge, with rapid increases in trade liberalization and the formation of trading blocs, consumption patterns change also. Adding to this impetus is the role of technology, which has augmented a convergence of consumer preference. However, while demand for many products has become more homogeneous across countries, cultural factors have strongly inhibited this change as well. In a multicultural world, cultural heterogeneity will continue to remain the most significant barrier to a single international market. Thus consideration of national cultural values is an important aspect of market selection decisions. Only markets with close enough cultures should be selected if possible.

Revision questions

1 What factors should the international marketer take into account in deleting unsuitable markets?
2 What are the main internal and external factors that companies should use in evaluating markets for entry selection?
3 Discuss with suitable examples the basic factors for the choice of market entry mode.
4 Why is the role of national culture important when market entry strategy is contemplated?
5 Evaluate the advantages and disadvantages of international franchising arrangements for the franchisor and the franchisee.
6 Account for the increasing use of strategic alliance (co-marketing) as an international market entry strategy.
7 The ultimate decision regarding standardization versus adaptation of international marketing programmes should be based on the impact on organizational performance and the nature of the product. Discuss.

SEMINAR CASE STUDY

The entry of the Silver Streak Restaurant Corporation into Mexico

The purpose of this case study is to examine the process of international market entry by a small franchisor, Silver Streak Restaurant Corporation. The study begins with a brief overview of the Mexican franchising market and the changes in Mexican law that have made franchising in Mexico an attractive business opportunity. The main focus is the entry of Silver Streak into the Mexican market, with particular emphasis on its efforts to identify a suitable Mexican partner, the adaptation of the concept to the Mexican market, and the multitude of critical decisions that need to be made when franchising in international markets.

The Mexican franchising market
Since the 1990s Mexico has seen huge growth in large-scale franchising. During the early part of 1990s the Mexican government enacted a new industrial property law that established the first legal definition of franchises in Mexico and removed some of the major franchising obstacles. In line with its effort to promote international franchising, the development of trademark protection legislation helped franchising become one of the major growth sectors of the Mexican economy. Changes in the law have made it possible for

small companies in the Mexican franchise industry to enjoy the same protection as the large chains without having to invest the majority of their profits in legal protection. Similarly, the signing of the North American Free Trade Agreement (NAFTA) further enhanced the image of the Mexican market in the eyes of potential franchisors. Mexico had over 495 operating franchises in many areas, including food, dry cleaning, laundry and restaurants, employing over 112,000 people. Although the Mexican business climate is quite volatile because of the frequent devaluations of the peso, government reforms point toward a brighter future for the Mexican economy.

The Silver Streak story

Streak Restaurant Corporation is a relatively new and small entrant into the Mexican fast food franchise market. With a large Mexican corporation as its partner, it opened the first restaurant in the city of Juarez in 1996, and two more restaurants were completed in 1998. Juarez is a city of approximately 1.5 million on Mexico's border with the United States.

Silver Streak's two owners, Alan Simpson and Jerry Malachowski, are fast-food veterans, having spent most of their lives managing restaurants for large companies. However, Mexico was to them a new territory with unique cultural intricacies. Simpson started Silver Streak in 1988, along with Jim Burgess, while he was still a manager in Burger King restaurants in Midland/Odessa, Texas. The first Silver Streak opened its doors in December 1988, in El Paso, Texas, a city of approximately 650,000, on the US side of the border with Mexico along the Rio Grande river, right across from Juarez. Malachowski is Silver Streak's vice president of operations and oversees the day-to-day activities of the company-owned restaurants. Simpson, as the president and chairman, is more involved in the long-term strategic growth of the company and manages its financial matters.

In 1994, a large Mexican corporation approached Silver Streak for its franchise rights in Mexico. This company seemed to have the financial leverage and organizational structure to take Silver Streak into Mexico and make it successful. It had been involved in restaurants and drive-through dry cleaning stores throughout the country. After looking carefully at the operations Silver Streak drew up a master franchising agreement that served as the blueprint for future franchise operations. Following that, it signed a country development agreement with the Mexican corporation, to open three restaurants by the end of 1997 in Juarez, and to sub-franchise the concept throughout Mexico depending on the success of the first three units.

The concept

Silver Streaks have no dining room or large plot of land. They are drive-through or walk-up fast-food places, with a design that means two cars can be serviced at the same time. Silver Streak prides itself on selling the best food in the business. It has developed its own 'secret' recipe for the 100 per cent pure beef patties and uses grade A potatoes for its french fries. It also has a contractual agreement with Coca-Cola to supply soft drinks. A typical restaurant employs around 25 people with four to five managers. Having a manager on hand at all times to make sure that everything runs smoothly is something that sets Silver Streak apart from its competitors.

Silver Streak has the image of a big national chain, but it can outperform its powerful competitors in many areas, most importantly cost. It can build a restaurant – including kitchen, equipment and land – for around $350,000, or less when the land is leased. Around 80 per cent of sales are generated from its drive-through operation. The walk-up windows generate the remaining 20 per cent.

Silver Streak's distinctive advantage in cost containment, its high-quality products and low prices seemed to fit right into a Mexican's budget. However, doing business in Mexico is quite different from doing business in El Paso. The differences were apparent from the outset. You need to know people to get things done in Mexico. For example, in Juarez it is not easy to buy land: many deals involve partners swapping plots they already own. Silver Streak's Mexican partner was able to obtain the land, negotiate with construction contractors and develop the necessary trade relationships. While in the United States all sorts of demographic information is readily available for trade area analysis, in Mexico it is not. Therefore, having the 'feel' of a Mexican partner to determine a good location acted as a substitute for the more scientific approaches used in the United States.

A drive-through restaurant was a relatively new concept in Mexico. Silver Streak had to address the fact that Mexican consumers consider lunch as a major event in their daily lives, which often lasts between one and two hours. It built a larger patio eating area in its Mexican restaurants, seating nearly 100 people. Its Mexican partner also helped it develop a very Mexican breakfast menu, including a 'Silver burrito', which became a best-selling item.

The pilot restaurant generated enough sales – approximately $55,000 per month – to be considered a success. With better planning, a better location, and by implementing the lessons learnt, the company hoped that further restaurants would be even more successful.

Source: Hadjimarcou and Barnes (1998).

Seminar questions

1 Discuss the notion that it was the selection of the suitable partner that made the entry of Silver Streak into the Mexican market successful.
2 What do you think that other small firms should learn from the story of Silver Streak when contemplating entering an international market?

Managerial assignment task

You currently work for an international organization producing and marketing aircraft engines throughout the world. You have been given the responsibility to identify and recommend to the board of directors the opportunities and a suitable mode of entry for the Chinese market. Your report must specify the expected opportunities and how these could be harnessed, and the likely competitors. Evaluate the key market entry modes, and make a recommendation with reasons. Comment too on the likely obstacles and how these could be eliminated or minimized.

References

Akehurst, G. and Alexander, N. (1995 'Developing a framework for the study of the internationalization of retailing', *Service Industries Journal*, Vol. 15, No. 4, pp. 205–9.

Benito, G. R. G. and Welch, L. S. (1994) 'Foreign market servicing: beyond choice of entry mode', *Journal of International Marketing*, Vol. 2, No. 2, pp. 7–27.

Burton, F. N. and Cross, A. R. (1997) 'International franchising: market versus hierarchy', pp. 135–52 in G. M. Chryssochoidis, C. Millar and L. J. Clegg, (eds), *Internationalisation Strategies,* Vol. 1, London: Macmillan.

Chee, H. and Harris, R. (1998) *Global Marketing Strategy*, London: Financial Times Publishing.

Czinkota, M. R. and Ronkainen, I. A. (1996) *International Marketing*, 3rd edn, Fort Worth: Dryden.

Gleason, K. C., Mathur, I. and Singh, M. (2000) 'Operational characteristics and performance gains associated with international licensing agreements: the US evidence', *International Business Review*, No. 9, pp. 431–52.

Gridley, P., and Teece, D. (1997) 'Managing international capital: licensing and cross licensing in semiconductors and electronics', *California Management Review*, Vol. 39, No. 2, pp. 8–41.

Griffith, D. A., Michael, Y. H. and Chen, H. (1998) 'Formation and performance of multi-partner joint ventures: a Sino-foreign illustration', *International Marketing Review*, Vol. 15, No. 3, pp. 171–87.

Grocer (1999) Article on criteria for acquiring foreign companies, 11 September.

Hadjimarcou, J. and Barnes, J. (1998) article in *Journal of Consumer Marketing.*

Hamill, J. (1998) 'The Internet and international marketing', *International Marketing Review*, Vol. 14, No. 5, pp. 300–23.

Hamill, J., Jevons, C. and Poon, S. (1997) 'Implications of the Internet for international marketing by small and medium enterprises', Proceedings of the 6th Annual Business Congress of the International Management Development Association, Chonju City, South Korea, July.

Hofstede, G.. (1984) *Culture's Consequences: International Differences in Work-Related Values,* Newbury Park, Calif.: Sage.

Hofstede, G. (1991) *Cultures and Organizations: Software of the Mind*, London: McGraw-Hill.

Jagodka, R. (1997) 'Skills needed for effective international marketing', unpublished doctoral dissertation, University of La Verne, California.

Johansson, J. K. (1997) *Global Marketing: Foreign Entry, Local Marketing and Global Management,* Chicago: McGraw-Hill.

Keegan, W. J. (1999) *Global Marketing Management,* 7th edn, New York: Prentice Hall.

Koch, A.J. (2001a) 'Factors influencing market and entry mode selection: developing the MEMS model', *Marketing Intelligence and Planning*, Vol. 19, No. 5, pp. 351–61.

Koch, A.J. (2001b) 'Selecting overseas markets and entry modes: two decision processes or one?' *Marketing Intelligence and Planning*, Vol. 19, No. 1, pp. 65–75.

Levitt, T. (1980) 'Marketing success through differentiation of anything', *Harvard Business Review*, January/February, pp. 83–91.

Levitt, Y. (1983a) 'The globalization of markets', *Harvard Business Review* (May–June) , pp. 92–102.

Levitt, T. (1983b) 'After the sale is over', *Harvard Business Review*, September/October, pp. 87–93.

Malhotra, N. K., Agarwal, J. and Baalbaki, I. (1998) 'Heterogeneity of regional trading blocs and global marketing strategies: a multicultural perspective', *International Marketing Review*, Vol. 15, No. 6, pp. 476–506.

Melewar, T. and Saunders, J. J. (1998) 'Global corporate visual identity systems: using an extended marketing mix', *European Journal of Marketing*, Vol. 34, No. 5/6, pp. 538–50.

O'Donnell, S. and Jeong, I. (2000) 'Marketing standardization within global industries: an empirical study of performance implications', *International Marketing Review*, Vol. 17, No. 1, pp. 19–33.

Omar O. E. (1995) 'Retail influence on food technology and innovation', *International Journal of Retail and Distribution Management*, Vol. 23, No. 3, pp. 11–16.

Omar, O. (1999) *Retail Marketing*, London: Financial Times Publishing.

Palmer, A. (1997) 'Defining relationship marketing: an international perspective', *Management Decisions*, Vol. 35, No. 3/4, pp. 319–22.

Paliwoda, S. and Thomas, M. J. (1998) *International Marketing*, 3rd edn, Oxford: Butterworth-Heinemann.

Porter, M. E. (1980) *Competitive Strategy: Techniques for Analysing Industries and Competitors*, New York: Free Press.

Root, F. R. (1994) *Entry Strategies for International Markets*, New York: Lexington.

Seabright, P. (1996) 'The starfish effect: can market entry by one firm encourage further entry by others?' *European Economic Review*, No. 40, pp. 541–50.

Steenkamp, J. B. E. M. (2001) 'The role of national culture in international marketing research', *International Marketing Review*, Vol. 18, No. 1, pp. 30–44.

Swift, J. S. (1999) 'Cultural closeness as a facet of cultural affinity: a contribution to the theory of psychic distance in international marketing', *International Marketing Review*, Vol. 16, No. 2/3, pp. 182–201.

Vanhonacker, W. R. (1997) 'Entering China: an unconventional approach', *Harvard Business Review*, Vol. 75, No. 2, pp. 130–40.

Whitelock, J. and Pimblett, C. (1997) 'The standardization debate in international marketing', *Journal of Global Marketing*, Vol. 10, No. 3, pp. 45–66.

Zou, S., Andrus, D. M. and Norvell, D. W. (1997) 'Standardization of international marketing strategy by firms from a developing country', *International Marketing Review*, Vol. 14, No. 2, pp.107–23.

6
Management of Exporting and Importing

Contents

LEARNING OBJECTIVES

After reading this chapter you should:

- understand the behaviour of export firms in an international market environment
- know the methods of payments and finance for exports and imports in current usage
- be able to evaluate government policies on exports and imports, and controls through tariff systems
- be able to examine export and import planning, control and implementation
- understand the various strands of international trading including barter and counter-trade, and trademark rights in grey markets
- be able to review free trade areas and their implications for international marketing operation.

Introduction

Exporting is a common market entry approach for the mature international company, and a company new to the international environment might also decide to enter the international market by exporting from its domestic market. This method of international market development is the easiest and most commonly employed by companies taking their first international market venture because the risks of financial loss can be reduced. Generally early motives for exporting are to skim the international market or to gain business in order to absorb high overhead costs. Although such motives might appear opportunistic, exporting is a sound and permanent form of international marketing operation. This chapter discusses among other things the nature of exporting, the mechanics of exporting and the various intermediaries available to facilitate the export and import process.

Most countries control the goods crossing their borders, whether leaving (exports) or entering (imports). Export and import documents, tariffs, quotas and other barriers to the free flow of goods between sovereignties are requirements that must be met by the exporter, the importer or both. The mechanics of exporting add extra steps and costs to an international sale that are not incurred when marketing domestically. In addition to selecting a target market, designing an appropriate product, establishing a price, planning a promotional programme and selecting a distribution channel, the international marketer must meet the legal requirements of moving goods from one country to another.

The export process includes the licences and documentation necessary for goods to leave the country, an international carrier to transport the goods, and fulfilment of the requirements necessary to get the shipment legally into another country. As Kotabe and Helsen (2004: 513) wrote, these mechanics of exporting are sometimes considered the essence of international marketing. Although their importance cannot be minimized, they should not be seen as the primary task of international marketing.

The management and development of export and import strategies, including the regulations covering the international marketing operation, are the main concerns of this chapter.

Export activities and organization

In Chapter 5, some of the reasons that firms choose to enter international markets were reviewed. Exporting is often seen as the first stage in the internationalization process. This strategy is often pursued when the domestic market is suffering from recession, and economies of scale require expansion away from it. Many companies also adopt this strategy when an opportunity has arisen through an unsolicited enquiry. If these are the spurs to exporting, it is not clear that it is the best method to enter a new market. The fact that exporting, rather than licensing, is selected can be put down to:

- the company's inexperience of the international environment
- a fear of financial loss in the international venture
- a fear of resource commitments that come from alternative entry strategies
- the risks that either political or economic forces that may impede international marketing operation.

Whatever the reason, a number of companies do enter the market via exporting, with the majority being content to stay as exporters. The adoption of this strategy does not guarantee absolute success. There are many failures in exporting ventures, arising from issues ranging from simple operational incompetence to more problematic issues associated with the product. Product adaptation is often one of the major issues of concern, along with quality standards, delivery time, packaging and international integrated communications.

In terms of export marketing strategy and performance, a company is likely to be successful in exporting only if:

- it concentrates its scarce resources on few selected markets, rather than seeking to attack a large number
- it is prepared to adapt its products to meet foreign market requirements
- it allocates specialist resources to exporting
- it sees itself in the export markets as a long-term strategic pursuit
- its export marketing strategy is based on rigorous marketing research.

While few practitioners and academics would disagree with this summary, few exporters actually follow this prescription. Mini-case 6.1 describes a successful implementation of export marketing policy. By leading in the export of ideas, Messer Griesheim employed an aggressive stance over internationalization of its industrial gas business.

Company success in export marketing operation is usually evaluated against the following criteria:

- a substantial and sustained increase in total exports over five years
- a substantial increase in the percentage of exports sales to total business over three years
- a percentage of exports to total business that is considerably higher than the average for that industry
- a very significant increase in export sales over a shorter period than three years, with every likelihood that this can be maintained
- an entry and breakthrough into what is regarded as a difficult market
- the greatest values of export sales by any group of companies in a given year.

Using these criteria, successful companies can show how far they have matched good practice and assess their chances of maintaining their performance into the future in the international markets. According to McAuley (2001), many firms in the United Kingdom tend to have a tactical rather than a strategic response to exporting, and appeared to be production or sales-led in their approach rather than marketing-oriented.

Matching customers' specification has become more important in the face of intense international market competition. Thus, any suitable model of corporate internationalization should incorporate the neo-classical (4Ps) approach as well as focusing on the relational paradigm which identifies the importance attached to offering a product that is unique, of good quality, and supported by good supply chain relationships. As a result of such an approach many companies export in the first instance to those countries with which they feel they have a closer understanding of or cultural affinity. After having developed competences in exporting, they are then able to use their expertise to enter other

MINI CASE 6.1

Export of ideas in industrial gases

As companies globalize, the export of goods from one country to another becomes less important. Increasingly, what matters is the export of ideas, enabling products to be made to uniformly high standards in many international locations. Nowhere is this more true than in industrial gases, a global industry whose big players are multinationals, including Air Liquide of France, Britain's BOC, Praxair and Air Products of the United States, and Linde of Germany. With gases produced by these companies used in a wide variety of industries from laundries to chemical works, the suppliers' strategy is normally to set up gas plants close to customers, distributing the products either in cylinders or by pipelines. The cost of distributing gases such as liquid oxygen or ammonia over long distances explains why it is virtually meaningless in the traditional sense to talk about industrial gases being export-driven. But when it comes to distributing knowledge, the sector is highly dependent on channelling ideas around the world on the best ways to build gas plants and sell their products.

Pushing this philosophy close to the limit is Messer Griesheim, a German company whose majority owner is Hoechst, the big chemicals supplier. While occupying a relatively lowly position in the industry pecking order – it claims to be the world's sixth biggest supplier of industrial gases, with output similar to its arch-rival Linde – Messer can safely claim to have more of an international stance than others in the big league. 'The gases business is a local business (in terms of supply),' says Herbert Rudolf, Messer's chief executive. 'What is important is feeding technology to our world-wide plants to help both in production and how the gases can be used.'

This fact has also been recognized by Linde, which combines being a big player in gases with its position as a leader in building gas and chemical plants for outside groups. It claims the number one position globally in building both for its own use and for external customers' air separation plants. This gives Linde an important technology when it comes to making products such as oxygen and carbon dioxide, which are sold in the industrial gases side of the company.

However, Messer has taken an aggressive stance on the internationalization of its business. With total gas sales of e704 million in 2007 (http://www.messergroup.com/de/ Ueber_Messer/ Kennzahlen/index.html?iLangID=1) (a smaller division sells specialized welding and cutting equipment), about 60 per cent of its gases are sold in Germany. A quarter of the sales are in the Americas, a growing 12 per cent in the rest of Europe and about 5 per cent in Asia.

Messer's unassuming head office – a suite at Frankfurt airport – allows the 50-strong team to jump on and off planes and receive visitors from the 53 countries where it has gas operations. 'Sharing knowledge and organizing a two-way flow of ideas across borders is a fundamental part of the company,' says Rudolf, who had been at Messer 33 years. A key role is played by the company's 140 production engineers, based in seven locations globally, who are called on to help set up new gas plants to add to the 350 Messer already has around the world.

Another 80 applications engineers, based in Germany, Austria, the United States and the United Kingdom, advise customers. Messer's computer networks allow the engineering people to liaise with the rest of the company, and outsiders, as efficiently as possible. With English as the company's working language, Messer has established the 'Messer Academy': a Boston training group, Forum, is contracted to organize in-depth lessons for employees on how to build and operate gas plants. In this way, Rudolf reckons, Messer can spread ideas, through sessions in places as far afield as China and the United States, to many of the 10,000 people who work on the gas side of the company.

Source: *Financial Times* (1998).

markets where there is a greater cultural distance. The key dynamics of any suitable model include:

- The main elements of the firm are its management characteristics and core competences, which determine its ability to acquire and use information. This is problematic for small firms that may not be able to devote human resources to this activity.
- The types of relationships are responsible for providing information and resources for the firm which can contribute to better decision making.
- Marketing strategy factors, particularly choice of market, segmentation and the marketing mix, are outputs of the firm's internal characteristics as well as the relationship built up with supply and channel members.
- All of the above exist in a market environment, with elements such as government barriers to trade, infrastructure and market attractiveness affecting performance.
- The outcome of the model is export performance, which is shown by sales, market share and brand equity.

Export performance in this model is therefore related to the environment, core competences and management commitment to exporting, development of channel relationships, development of market strategy, and plans to exploit the chosen market. None of this may come as a great surprise to experienced companies, but it has significant implications for companies both new to exporting and less experienced in this activity, and agencies of national government and regional and local development organizations. Success in export marketing will not be guaranteed by appropriate marketing strategies and plans unless core competences, and the support of senior managers, are given due recognition.

Focusing on external characteristics will not guarantee success, neither will the development of internal characteristics assist if the 'hard-systems' approach of market orientation summed up in marketing plans is left out of account. The importance of experience points to a gradual process of adaptation to export markets, that brings with it more complex structures such as foreign-based production facilities to accommodate more varied market situations and prepare the company for more direct involvement. Firms at the first stage of exporting (that is, those looking at the possibility of market involvement) require knowledge, help and advice to understand the market situation and their response to it. Many companies therefore seem to adopt a direct exporting mode to avoid unforeseen risks in the international market.

Direct exporting modes

Direct exporting occurs when an exporter sells directly to an importer or buyer located in a foreign country. In direct exporting the negotiation is done via a third party as shown in Figure 6.1. As exporters grow and gain market knowledge they may decide to undertake their own exporting activities.

This involves building up foreign contacts such as agents and distributors to handle documentation and transportation. Thus direct exporting modes include export through foreign-based intermediaries who are independent of the exporter. The terms 'agent' and 'distributor' are often used synonymously. This is wrong because there are some significant

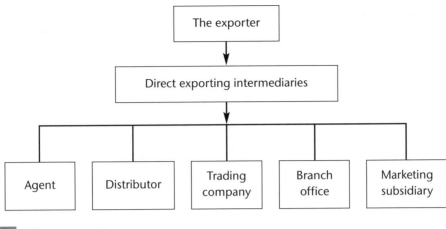

Figure 6.1   Direct exporting

differences between their roles. For example, distributors take title to the goods and are paid according to the difference between the buying and selling prices rather than by commission. An agent on the other hand is paid on commission. Distributors are often appointed when after-sales service is required, as they are more likely than agents to possess the necessary resources.

The export agent

Most exporters, unless conducting their own operations, make use of an export agent. Because of a lack of fluency in foreign languages, this is a particularly popular strategy for British exporters. The agent is a legal entity, an individual or a company, who undertakes to act on behalf of an exporter, in this case known as the principal, who is the supplier or manufacturer of the goods. By definition an agent never has title to the goods. Ownership of the goods rests with the principal until they are sold to the customer or importer. That does not mean that the agent cannot handle or keep the goods. As we shall see, there are agents who keep consignment stocks on behalf of their principals. However, an agent does not own the goods but sells them on a commission basis.

The usefulness of agents lies in the facts that they are resident in the importing country and that they are accustomed to the marketplace, know about the ways of doing business in that market, get to learn about the level of demand and business activity, and of course, since they are mostly nationals of that country, are fluent in the local language and idioms. There are three types of agents; exclusive agents, consignment agents and del credere agents. This is not a mutually exclusive list; being one type does not exclude the possibility of being another. It is the nature of their function that counts.

- **An exclusive agent**, as the name implies, has exclusive rights to operate in a particular territory. The principal will not appoint another agent in the same part of the country, and any business obtained, whether directly by the agent or dealt with by the principal, has to carry a commission for the agent. This is because it is assumed that a customer within that territory buying the product, whether from the agent or directly from the principal, will have done so as a result of the agent's promotion and activity within that territory. Within the European Union, where an exclusive agent may be seen by the Commission to act against the freedom of the customer to choose products from the best source possible, the agent has to prove that acting exclusively would be in the best interests of the consumer. That is because of the agent's expertise in handling or servicing the product.

- **A consignment agent** is allowed by the principal to keep a consignment stock of goods, components or spare parts, so that rapid service can be offered to customers.
- **A del credere agent** has a special function. As well as negotiating a sale, this type of agent has a responsibility for making good bad debts from customers. There are certain implications in this procedure. One is that the agent will be wary about with whom it decides to deal, since a poor payer will mean a loss for it, rather than for the principal. Another is that this type of agent will require a higher commission because of the additional risk.

Distributors

Exporting firms may work through distributors, which are the exclusive representative of the company and are generally the sole importers of the company's product to their markets. As independent merchants, distributors buy on their own account, and have substantial freedom to choose their own customers and to set the conditions of sale. For each country exporters typically deal with one distributor, take one credit risk, and ship to one destination. In many cases distributors own and operate wholesale and retail establishments, warehouses and repair and service facilities. Once distributors have negotiated with their exporters on price, service, distribution and so on, their efforts focus on working their own sub-operations and dealers.

The distributor category is broad and includes more variations, but distributors usually seek exclusive rights for a specific sales territory and generally represent the manufacturer in all aspects of sales and servicing in that area. The exclusivity is in return for the substantial capital investment that may be required on the part of the distributor in handling and selling products.

The choice of intermediaries

The selection of a suitable intermediary can be a problematic process, but the following sources may help a firm to find such an intermediary:

- asking potential customers to suggest a suitable agent
- obtaining recommendations from institutions such as trade associations, chambers of commerce and government trade departments
- using commercial agencies
- poaching a competitor's agent
- advertising in suitable trade papers.

In selecting a particular intermediary the exporter needs to examine each candidate firm's knowledge of the product and local markets, experience and expertise, required margins, credit ratings, customer care facilities and ability to promote the exporter's products in an effective and attractive manner. The choice will be made based on the most suitable to represent the exporter. However, there are some other specific desirable characteristics of an intermediary (to be included in the decision-making process) including:

- size of firm
- physical facilities
- willingness to carry inventories
- knowledge/use of promotions
- reputation with suppliers, customers and banks
- record of sales performance
- cost of operations
- overall experience
- knowledge of English or other relevant languages
- knowledge of business methods in the manufacturer's country.

When an intermediary is selected by the exporting manufacturer it is important that a contract is negotiated and developed between the parties. The foreign representative agreement is the fundamental basis of the relationship between the exporter and the intermediary. The contract therefore should clearly cover all relevant aspects and define the conditions upon which the relationship rests. Rights and obligations should be mutually defined and the spirit of the agreement must be one of mutual interest.

For most exporters the three most important aspects of their agreement with foreign representatives are sole or exclusive rights, competitive lines and termination of the agreement. The issue of agreeing territories is becoming increasingly important, as in many markets distributors are becoming fewer in number, larger in size, and sometimes increasingly extend their territories through organic growth, mergers and acquisitions, making it more difficult for firms to appoint different distributors in individual neighbouring markets.

In general some principles apply to the law of agency in all nations:

- An agent cannot take delivery of the principal's goods at an agreed price and resell them for a higher amount without the principal's knowledge and permission.
- Agents must maintain strict confidentiality regarding their principal's affairs and must pass on all relevant information.
- The principal is liable for damages to third parties for wrongs committed by an agent 'in the course of his or her authority' (for example, if the agent fraudulently misrepresents the principal's firm).

During the contract period the support and motivation of intermediaries is important. Usually this means financial rewards for volume sold, but other aspects are:

- significant local advertising and brand awareness development by the supplying firm
- participation in local exhibitions and trade fairs, perhaps in cooperation with the local intermediary

- regular field visits and telephone calls to the agent or distributor
- a regular meeting of agents and distributors arranged and paid for by the supplying company in the latter's country
- competitions with cash prizes, free holidays or the like for intermediaries with the highest sales
- provision of technical training to intermediaries
- suggestion schemes to gather feedback from agents and distributors
- circulation of briefings about the supplying firm's current activities, changes in personnel, new product developments, marketing plans and so on.

Even if the firm has been very careful in selecting intermediaries a need can arise to extricate itself quickly from a relationship that appears to be going nowhere. Cancellation clauses usually involve rights under local legislation, and it is best that a contract is scrutinized by a local lawyer before signature, rather than after a relationship has ended and a compensation case is being fought in the courts. Termination laws differ from country to country, but the EU situation has been largely reconciled by a directive creating an agency that has been effective in all EU nations since 1994. Under the directive, an agent whose agreement is terminated is entitled to the following:

- full payment for any deal resulting from its work (even if concluded after the end of the agency)
- a lump sum of up to one year's average commission
- compensation (where appropriate) for damages to the agent's commercial reputation caused by an unwarranted termination.

Outside Western Europe some countries regard agents as basically employees of client organizations, while others see agents as self-contained and independent businesses. It is essential to ascertain the legal position of agency agreements in each country in which a firm is considering doing business.

Exporting and logistics

Ensuring that customers receive their goods on time and in a fit condition is always an important issue in export marketing. This section looks at the terms of payment and then outlines the pitfalls associated with documentation. Although it focuses on the practical issues of finance, it should be borne in mind that this should be part of a broader framework of activities and planning that the exporter has undertaken. This issue is further developed below, but should be seen as part of the learning process that exporters go through in building a successful export marketing process.

Terms of sale and delivery

In every international marketing price quotation, the exporters are expected to describe a specific product, state the price for the product as well as a specific delivery location, set the time of shipment and specify payment terms. The responsibilities of the seller and the buyer should be spelled out, as they relate to what is and what is not included in the price quotation and when ownership of goods passes from the seller to the buyer. Incoterms 2000 can be used to define the responsibilities of buyer and seller in contracts (see Table 6.1).

This description of some of the most popular terms of sale also indicates briefly the point of delivery and the point at which the risk shifts from the seller to the buyer.

- **Ex works (EXW).** The 'Ex' means that the price quoted by the seller applies at a specified point of origin, usually the factory, warehouse, mine or plantation, and the buyer is responsible for all charges from the point. This term represents the minimum obligation for the exporter.
- **Free alongside ship (FAS).** Under this term the seller must provide for delivery of the goods free alongside, but not on board, the transportation carrier (usually an ocean vessel) at the point of shipment and export. This term differs from FOB (see below), since the time and cost of loading are not included in the FAS term. The buyer has to pay for loading the good on to the ship.
- **Free on board (FOB).** The exporter's price quote includes coverage of all charges up to the point when goods have been loaded on to the designated transport vehicle. The designated loading point may be a named inland shipping point, but is usually the port of export. The buyer assumes responsibility for the goods the moment they pass over the ship's rail.
- **Cost and freight (CFR).** The seller's liability ends when the goods are loaded on board a carrier or are in the custody of the carrier at the export dock. The seller pays all the transport charges (excluding insurance, which is the customer's obligation) required to delivering goods by sea to a named destination.
- **Cost, insurance and freight (CIF).** This trade term is identical with CFR except that the seller must also provide the necessary insurance. The seller's obligations still end at the same stage – when goods are loaded on board – but the seller's insurance company assumes responsibility once the goods are loaded.
- **Delivered ex quay (DEQ).** Ex quay means from the import dock. The term goes one step beyond CIF and requires the seller to be responsible for the cost of the goods and

Table 6.1 The 13 terms in Incoterms 2000

EXW	Ex works (named place)
FCA	Free carrier (named place)
FAS	Free alongside ship (named port of shipment)
FOB	Free on board (named port of shipment)
CFR	Cost and freight (named port of destination)
CIF	Cost, insurance and freight (named port of destination)
CPT	Carriage paid to (named place of destination)
CIP	Carriage and insurance paid to (named place of destination)
DAF	Delivered at frontier (named place)
DES	Delivered ex ship (named port of destination)
DEQ	Delivered ex quay (named port of destination)
DDU	Delivered duty unpaid (named place destination)
DDP	Delivered duty paid (named place of destination)

all other costs necessary to place the goods on the dock at the named overseas port, with the appropriate import duty paid.

- **Delivered duty paid (DDP).** The export price quote includes the costs of delivery to the importer's premises. The exporter is thus responsible for paying any import duties and costs of unloading and inland transport in the importing country, as well as all costs involved in insuring and shipping the goods to that country. These terms imply maximum exporter obligations. The seller also assumes all the risks involved in delivering to the buyer. DDP used to be known as 'Franco domicile' pricing.

Export price quotations are important because they spell out the legal and cost responsibilities of the seller and the buyer. Sellers favour a quote that gives them the least liability and responsibility, such as ex works, which means the exporter's liability finishes when the goods are loaded on to the buyer's carrier at the seller's factory. Buyers, on the other hand, would prefer either DDP, where responsibility is borne by the supplier all the way to the customer's warehouse, or CIF port of discharge, which means that the buyer's responsibility begins only when the goods are in its own country. Generally, the more market-oriented pricing policies are based on CIF, which indicates a strong commitment to the market. By pricing ex works, an exporter is not taking any steps to build relations with the market and so may be indicating only short-term commitment.

Terms of payment

The exporter will consider the practices in the industry, the terms offered by competitors, and the relative strength of the buyer and the seller in negotiating terms of payment for goods to be shipped. If the exporter is well established in the market with a unique product and accompanying service, price and terms of trade can be set to fit the exporter's desires. If, on the other hand, the exporter is breaking into a new market or if competitive pressures call for action, pricing and selling terms should be used as major competitive tools.

The basic methods of payment for exports vary in their attractiveness to the buyer and the seller, from cash in advance to open account or consignment selling. Neither of the extremes will be feasible for longer-term relationships, but they do have their uses in certain situations. The most favourable term to the exporter is cash in advance because it relieves the exporter of all risk and allows for immediate use of the money. On the other hand, the most advantageous option from the buyer's perspective is consignment or open account. The following are the most common arrangements, in decreasing order of attractiveness to the exporter.

Cash in advance

The exporter receives payment before shipment of the goods. This minimizes the exporter's risk and financial costs, since there is no collection risk and no interest cost on receivables. However, importers will rarely agree to these terms, since it ties up their capital and the goods may not be received. Consequently, such terms are not widely used. They are most likely either when the exporter lacks confidence in the importer's ability to pay, often the case in initial export transactions, or where economic and political instability in the importing country may result in foreign exchange not being made available for importers.

Letter of credit

World-wide letters of credit (L/Cs) are very important and very common. A L/C is an instrument whereby a bank agrees to pay a specified amount of money on presentation of documents stipulated in the letter of credit, usually the bill of lading, and an invoice and a description of the goods. In general, L/C s have the following characteristics:

- they are an arrangement by banks for settling international commercial transactions
- they provide a form of security for the parties involved
- they ensure payment, provided that the terms and conditions of the credit have been fulfilled
- payment by such means is based on documents only and not on the merchandise or services involved.

The process for handling L/Cs is that the customer agrees to payment by a confirmed L/C. The customer then begins the process by sending an enquiry for the goods. A pro-forma invoice by the supplier confirms the price and terms, so that the customer knows for what amount to instruct the issuing bank to open a L/C. A bank in the supplier's country confirms the L/C. When the goods are shipped the shipping documents are returned to the supplier so that shipment is confirmed by their presentation together with the L/C and all other stipulated documents and certificates for payment. On the presentation of these documents the money is automatically transmitted from the customer's account via the issuing bank. The customer may collect the goods only when all the documents have been returned.

The L/C has three forms:

- **Revocable L/C** – now a rare form, this gives the buyer maximum flexibility as it can be cancelled without notice to the seller up to the moment of payment by the bank.
- **Irrevocable but unconfirmed L/C** – this is as good as the credit status of the establishing bank and the willingness of the buyer's country to allow the required use of foreign exchange. An unconfirmed L/C should not necessarily be viewed with suspicion. The reason for the lack of confirmation may be that the customer has been unwilling to pay the additional fee for confirmation.
- **Confirmed irrevocable L/C** – this means that a bank in the seller's country has added its own undertaking to that of the issuing bank, confirming that the necessary sum of money is available for payment, awaiting only the presentation of shipping documents. While it guarantees the seller its money, it is much more costly to the buyer. Generally, the buyer pays a fixed fee plus percentage of the value, but where the L/C is confirmed, the confirming bank will also charge a fee. On the other hand, the confirmation of an irrevocable L/C by a bank gives the shipper the most satisfactory assurance that payment will be made for the shipment. It also means that the exporter does not have to seek payment under any conditions from the issuing bank invariably located in some foreign country but has a direct claim on the confirming bank in the exporter's home country. Thus, the exporter need not be concerned about the ability or willingness of the foreign bank to pay.

Documents against payment and acceptance

In the following two 'documents against' situations, the seller ships the goods and the shipping documents, and the draft (bill of exchange) demanding payment is presented to the importer through banks acting as the seller's agent. There are two principal types of bill of exchange: sight draft (documents against payment) and time draft (documents against acceptance).

- **Documents against payment** – here the buyer must make payment for the face value of the draft before receiving the documents conveying title to the merchandise. This occurs when the buyer first sees the draft (sight draft).
- **Documents against acceptance** – when a draft is drawn 'documents against acceptance', credit is extended to the buyer on the basis of the buyer's acceptance of the draft calling for payment within a specified time and usually at a specified place. Acceptance means that the buyer formally agrees to pay the amount specified by the draft on the due date. The specified time may be expressed as certain number of days after sight (time draft). A time draft offers less security for the seller than a sight draft, since the sight draft demands payment prior to the release of shipping documents. The time draft, on the other hand, allows the buyer a delay of 30, 60 or 90 days in payment.

Open account

The exporter ships the goods without documents calling for payment, other than the invoice. The buyer can pick up the goods without having to make payment first. The advantage of the open account is its simplicity and the assistance it gives to the buyer, which does not have to pay credit charges to banks. The seller in return expects that the invoice will be paid at the agreed time. A major weakness of the method is that there are no safeguards for payment. Exporters should sell on open account only to importers they know very well or which have excellent credit ratings, and to markets with no foreign exchange problems. Open account sales are less complex and expensive than drafts, since there are no documentation requirements or bank charges.

Consignment

Here the exporter retains title of the goods until the importer sells them. Exporters own the goods longer in this method than any other, and so the financial burden and risks are at their greatest. The method should be offered only to very trustworthy importers with an excellent credit rating in countries where political and economic risk is very low. Consignments tend to be used mainly by companies trading with their own subsidiaries. The credit terms given are also important in determining the final price to the buyer. When the products of international competitors are perceived to be similar, the purchaser may choose the supplier that offers the best credit terms, in order to achieve a greater discount. In effect, the supplier is offering a source of finance to the buyer.

Commercial banks

The simplest way of financing export sales is through an overdraft facility with the exporter's own bank. This is a convenient way to finance all the elements of the contract, such as purchasing, manufacturing, shipping and credit. The bank is generally more favourably disposed towards granting an overdraft if the exporter has obtained an export credit insurance policy.

Export credit insurance

Export credit insurance is available to most exporters through government export credit agencies or through private insurers. Such insurances usually cover the political risks and non-convertibility of currency; and the commercial risk associated with non-payment by buyers. Exporters may be able to use credit insurance to enable them to grant more liberal credit terms or to encourage their banks to grant them financing against their export receivables. The costs of such insurance are often quite low in many markets, ranging from 1 to 2 per cent of the value of the transaction. Specialized insurance brokers handle such insurance.

Bonding

In some countries (such as in the Middle East), contracts are cash or short term. Whereas this is an ideal situation for suppliers, it means that the buyer loses some of its leverage over the supplier as it cannot withhold payment. In this situation, a bond or guarantee is a written instrument issued to an overseas buyer by an acceptable third party, either a bank or an insurance company. It guarantees compliance of its obligations by an exporter or contractor, or the overseas buyers will be indemnified for a stated amount against the failure of the exporter/contractor to fulfil its obligations under the contract.

Leasing

Exporters of capital equipment may for example use leasing in one of two ways: first, arranging cross-border leasing directly from a bank or leasing company to the foreign buyer; and second, obtaining local leasing facilities either through overseas branches or subdivisions of international banks or through international leasing associations. With leasing, the exporter receives prompt payment for goods directly from the leasing company. A leasing facility is best set up at the earliest opportunity, preferably when the exporter receives the order.

Compensation deal

This involves the export of goods in one direction. The 'payment' of the goods is split into two parts: first, part payment in cash by the importer, and second, for the rest of the 'payment', the original exporter makes an obligation to purchase some of the buyer's goods. These products can be used in the exporter's internal production or they may be sold on in the wider market.

Buy-back agreement

The sale of machinery, equipment or a turnkey plant to the buyer's production is financed at least in part by the exporter's purchase of some of the resultant output. Whereas barter and compensation deals are short-term arrangements, buy-back agreements are long-term agreements. The contract may last for a considerable period of time, such as 5 or 10 years. The two-way transactions are clearly linked, but are kept financially separate. Counter-trade (another term for this) has arisen because of shortages of both foreign exchange and international lines of credit. Some have estimated the size of counter-trade as high as 10–15 per cent of world trade.

Export finance

When an exporter sells to a foreign buyer, to facilitate business that buyer will often be allowed a period of credit prior to paying for the goods. This may encourage trade but it will pose a problem for the exporter in that a cash shortage may then result. Export finance is the way that the exporter can obtain a solution to this problem, by approaching a financial institution. In a real sense, therefore, the risk is taken by the exporter in providing a period of credit and receiving payment. Solutions to the risk involved do exist, but this adds to the cost, perhaps the price of doing business abroad. In the case of export finance, there are short to long-term requirements to which different financial organizations can provide solutions. Short-term finance can be provided by overdraft facilities, while longer-term finance needs can be achieved via loans and bond issues. This is a summary of the main provisions. (Note that this review does not cover all possible solutions currently available, but only the major facilities offered by banks and other financial institutions. Although it focuses on UK exporters, similar solutions are available for most countries.)

Exporters need financing support in order to obtain working capital and because importers will often demand terms that allow them to defer payment. Principal sources of export finance include commercial banks, government export financing programmes, export credit insurance, factoring houses and counter-trade.

Credit risks

Buyer risk is similar to that encountered in domestic sales, except that the credit period on export sales is often longer. Also, suing someone overseas is often a much harder, longer and therefore more expensive process than suing a customer in the domestic market. Country risk includes problems in the buyer's country, but also obstacles in the exporter's home country, such as the cancellation of an export licence on military goods, or problems in a third country through which payment must be made. Many countries place restrictions on the import of items in strategic areas in the form of licence requirements and quotas. The law that introduced these changes in the European Union also gave the right to the EU Council of Ministers to impose bans or introduce quotas on a range of products from alcohol to used cars and trucks.

Credit insurers

With these risks, companies require a method of insuring against non-payment:

- Cover for short-term business (up to 180 days) is provided in the United Kingdom by private-sector insurers but also by trade indemnity and overseas companies.
- Cover for business on terms of two years or more is provided by a government agency, the Export Credit Guarantee Department (ECGD).

The range of services on offer is intended to boost the confidence of those involved in international trade, with the aim of expanding export business by companies taking on new buyers and breaking into new markets without the fear of crippling loss. With the ECGD, there is a particular emphasis on expanding exports, but it must also break even in its operations in pursuit of that goal.

Despite the cover available through the ECGD only 20 per cent of UK exports by value are insured, so that many exporters appear to be happy to take the risk on the payment of monies due from their customers. On occasions some customers may fail to pay their bills, in which case the company must either write the amount off or pursue the non-paying customer through the courts, which could be a lengthy and costly exercise. While trade finance covers both the provision of a loan to an importer and the credit given to an exporter by a financial institution to surmount the problems of either a cash shortage or the need for a period of credit, supplier credit is where a bank provides finance to the overseas buyer, so that the exporter can be paid immediately on the shipment of the goods.

Buyer credit

The most straightforward way of financing export sales is through an overdraft facility with the exporter's own bank. This is a simple and convenient way to finance all the elements of the contract such as purchasing, manufacturing, shipping and credit, in either sterling or another currency. The bank is generally more favourably disposed towards granting a sterling overdraft if the exporter has already obtained an export credit insurance policy. In the case of a foreign exchange overdraft the exporter will be expected to earn foreign currency to pay it off, the interest charged by the bank for the facilities being at a rate above the Eurocurrency London Interbank Offered Rate (LIBOR). This method of financing exports is unlikely to be of use to a firm that is expanding its exports, especially as the rates charged could be higher than for other forms of financing.

Another method of obtaining short-term finance is by asking the UK bank to advance funds against the face value of a bill of exchange. The exporter sends the bill to the bank which then gives an agreed percentage of the value to the exporter and undertakes to present the bill to the overseas buyer for collection. This method is used only when a bill is unaccompanied by any document relating to the exported goods.

The drawback with this method is that only a limited amount of funds are released. If a larger sum is required an alternative method must be used: this is known as the negotiation of bills. In this situation the exporter's bank agrees to purchase the bills, which are normally accompanies by shipping documents on presentation. The bank may even purchase the documents under a cash-against-documents collection, whereby the bills are sent to the overseas buyer and the bank then collects the money. In both cases, there is a risk of buyer default. The exporter must therefore take into account that if this occurs the bank will then charge the exporter interest and any collection fees.

Alternative methods of raising short-term finance include acceptance credits and documentary acceptance credits. Again, it is clear that the variety of help on offer to exporters and importers is such that a good deal of research must be undertaken prior to the arrangement of any short-term credit facilities to assess how appropriate it is for the company.

Factoring

Factoring means selling export debts for immediate cash. In this way, the exporter shifts the problems of collecting payment for completed orders over to organizations or factors that specialize in export credit management and finance.

Ideally, the exporter should go to the factor before any contract is signed or shipment made, and secure its willingness to buy the receivable. The factor will check out the credit rating and so forth of the prospective buyer(s), typically by having a correspondent in the importer's country do the necessary checking. Thus, the factor acts as a credit approval agency as well as facilitator and guarantor of payment. The factor does not usually purchase export debts on terms exceeding six months. The factor normally charges a service fee of between 0.75 and 2.5 per cent of the sales value, depending on the workload and the risk carried by the factor.

Most of the methods of financing described so far are appropriate for most companies, large or small. However, if export turnover is large enough, generally above £250,000, factoring may be the most appropriate method. Factoring means selling trade debts for immediate cash, or to put it another way, the exporter shifts the problems of collecting payment for completed orders over to organizations or factors that specialize in export credit management and finance. Most factors offer three basic services:

- an accounting credit checking or debt collection service
- credit insurance against bad debts
- the provision of immediate cash against invoices.

The factor works in a similar way to any financial institution. It provides a customer assessment service which identifies a foreign company's creditworthiness, and then establishes credit limits. The exporter sells within these limits and delivers and invoices to customers in the usual way.

The advantages to the exporter are that the export debts are sold to the factor, relieving the firm of the task of credit checking, some documentation and collection, as well as the problems of bad debts and currency loss. Factoring companies do not usually purchase trade debts on terms exceeding 120 days, although in some circumstances this can be increased to 180 days.

Factoring may be of particular use to those companies trading on open-account terms. For this service, the factor will charge from 0.75 per cent to 2.5 per cent of the sales value, depending on the risk and the workload involved. The advantages to the exporter are clear, but there are noticeable disadvantages that have to be judged with care. Factors will wish to reduce their own risk and so may choose carefully which debt they will factor because of their assessment of the overseas buyer and/or the country in which that buyer is located. The charge may not seem excessive, but it may well amount to more than the cost of the company's doing the job itself, and as importantly, it reduces contact with the customer and provides no in-house experience for the company.

Forfeiting

This is a method of providing medium-term export finance which originated in Switzerland in the 1950s. More properly known as forfeit financing, it is a description of a quite simple system whereby exporters of capital goods can obtain medium-term export finance (or in some cases short-term assistance), usually for periods of between one and seven years.

An exporter of capital goods has an overseas buyer who wishes to have medium-term credit to finance the purchase. The buyer must be willing to pay some of the costs at once, and pay the balance in regular instalments for the next five years. The buyer issues a series of promissory notes, which are the preferred instrument of payment, rather than bills of exchange, as it frees the exporter from all recourse obligations. The promissory notes might mature every six months over the five-year period, and in most cases the buyer is required to find a bank that is willing to provide an unconditional bank guarantee. The bank must be willing to be a forfeit, which is the business of discounting medium-term promissory notes. Discounts are normally at a fixed rate notified to the exporter, so when the goods have been delivered and the promissory notes have been received they are sold to the forfeiting bank, which purchases them without recourse to the exporter. The discounting bank must now bear non-payment and related risks.

The principal benefits are that there is immediate cash for the exporter, and along with the first cash payment by the buyer, forfeiting can finance up to 100 per cent of the contract value. This system also has speed and flexibility, with each agreement being tailored to the requirements of each contract. Alongside these benefits go the drawbacks, one of which is the cost of using this approach. However, according to Terpstra and Sarathi (2000) the high cost is a result of the combined benefits offered by the discounting bank which acts as both a bank and an insurance company in the assumption risk. Finding a bank to act as a forfeiter may not be straightforward: for example, the bank may not be satisfied with the credit standing of the buyer, or the availing (guaranteeing) bank may not have a first-class name. If there is a large item of capital equipment to be sold to an overseas buyer, an exporter may find it more beneficial to sell the product to a leasing company, which then provides it to the buyer on a lease agreement. This allows the buyer to use the equipment without having to pay for it first, and it can also enable the exporter to receive immediate payment.

Government policy and exporting

Government economic policy focuses on the importance of exports as a valuable source of income. This is the objectives of the UK's Department for Business Enterprise and Regulatory Reform. Its general aim is to 'help UK business compete successfully at home, in the rest of Europe and throughout the world'. The department works for trade liberalization world-wide and helps businesses to take full advantage of UK and overseas market opportunities. The principal method by which this is carried out is through the Overseas Trade Services (OTS), a joint responsibility between the DBERR and the Foreign and Commonwealth Office.

Overseas Trade Services (OTS)

The services provided by the OTS cover market advice, assistance in taking the first steps into the export market, and specialist advice and assistance. Information can be provided on import licence regulations, import duties, import regulations, standards and so on. Information on overseas markets can be undertaken by consultation of the OTS's market intelligence library; when an exporter undertakes an extensive market research project a grant can be made of up to 50 per cent of the cost. Specialist agencies can offer other assistance:

- Export Representative Service – provides a locally vetted contact who can act as a representative for the exporter.

- Market Prospects Service – after information has been obtained about the exporter and its operation, a report is drawn up looking at possible contacts in targeted countries.
- Export intelligence Service – looks at export opportunities that can match those of exporters which have expressed an interest in the search for business opportunities.

Technical Help for Exporters (a trade mission) provides information on technical standards. These and many other services are provided by the OTS which, with the help of Business Link (a one-stop shop of information provided for businesses) aims to provide as comprehensive a level of assistance as possible. Looking at the DBERR objectives on international trade and exporting, it is clear that the UK government works at different levels to assist exporters. The OTS works at the company level, via embassies and government officials, to provide a helping hand. At ministerial level, working with international agencies such as the World Trade Organization (WTO), the aim is to promote freer trade. This approach is often matched by the need of professional associations and business representatives to lobby organizations such as the European Commission, to influence directives and policy. Government policy uses the combination of business involvement and ministerial pressure to create as favourable environment as possible.

Help elsewhere

The range of services offered in the United Kingdom is matched by governments in other developed countries. In the United States, the Department of Commerce via the International Trade Administration provides similar services to the OTS. Similar problems exist: for example the number and varieties of services on offer and the fact that the level of awareness of the services is considered too low.

The World Aid Section (WAS) of the OTS provides information and briefings on multilateral development agencies, such as the World Bank, UN agencies and regional development banks (like the Asian Development Bank), which provide opportunities for exporters. Also related to aid is the Overseas Development Administration's Aid and Trade provision, which takes the form of grant and export credit cover. This complements the ECGD provision offered by this arm of government.

Government policy takes effect at many levels. The importance for marketing management in all types of companies is that an awareness, understanding and use of the services offered is essential to facilitate the operations of the company in foreign markets. The complexity of exporting has already been noted, and the services offered by government export services are a way of helping to overcome some of the difficulties involved. However, it is incumbent on firms to incorporate these issues into their export plans, as it is on the good management of firms that trade internationally that governments depend for the success of these services. Building up management competences in exporting is an area where policy has to be implemented via training and management development initiatives.

Export planning

If the achievement of macro objectives lies with the individual company, and there is a need to transfer good practice to all companies, whether currently exporting or not, then the issue of export planning becomes a critical aspect. Various benefits are claimed for export planning. Trade advisory bodies in the United States, for example, suggest that the development of a plan is vital to communicate a company's ideas to others in a clear and understandable way. Additionally, it can help the company going through the process of planning to analyse its strengths and weaknesses, identify export responsibilities and help to reach a clear understanding of:

- reasons and commitment to exporting
- long and short-term goals
- product and company readiness
- primary and secondary target markets
- export strategy
- details of pricing payment and delivery
- financing of the export operation.

In essence, this is business planning incorporating the extra issues associated with exporting. It is important to recognize that exporting has more variables associated with it than trading in the domestic market. External environment complexity, appreciating who competitors are, understanding the behaviour of new customers, export finance and documentation are all facets of business that the company new to exporting will have to contend with.

The possibility of new entrants making mistakes is high give that documentation, financial arrangements and the challenge of operating in a strange (new) marketplace create stress on the company that domestic trade experience will not have revealed. A description of exporting that focuses on all the extra considerations and responsibilities associated with this activity can dissuade rather than attract. However, exporting offers fresh opportunities for growth and expansion, and can be seen as a strategic focus that can help to boost profitability. Export planning, using government advisory services, and an understanding of good business practice, will overcome the initial concerns: the help and assistance offered by financial institutions and specialists in the movement of goods will provide the infrastructure that export planning and management can use to good strategic advantage.

Imports

Many of the issues of concern to exporters are also relevant to importers. (See also Chapter 7 on the regulatory environment.) Import regulations in countries such as India require as much care from importers as they do from exporters. Financial issues, such as credit and means of payment, as described from the exporter's point of view, apply just as much to the importer. The sections on barter and counter-trade and free trade zones below draw attention to some specific rules and regulations that impact on the importer. Labelling, meeting standards and restriction or prohibition of certain imports, such as drugs, are all aspects requiring attention.

Country and regional trading bloc regulations, which affect most if not all of the world's economies, have to be taken into account. The NAFTA agreement (also covered in Chapter 7) shows how the establishment of a free trade area requires agreement on what can and cannot be excluded from import control. Importers who wish to trade successfully require the same acumen as exporters when it comes to regulations, finance and credit arrangements.

From the point of view of a county's economic prospects, importers are as important as exporters, bringing in much-needed supplies such as commodities, components, semi-finished products and luxury goods. Industry relies as much on an efficient import procedure as it does on an exporting one. Jobs, investment and wealth creation come as much from importing activities as from any other. From a marketing management point of view the need to get this process right, with clear objectives and planning, is just as important as any other aspect of marketing.

Free trade zones

Free trade zones (FTZs) are defined as a zones or regions within a country that are deemed to be outside the customs border of that country, and where the regulations related to foreign trade and other financial and economic areas are either inapplicable or only partly so. Basically, the zones are established to create incentives for business and to lead to an increase in trade volume and exports.

The benefit from participation in the trading zones can vary from country to country depending on the existing regulations and tax regimes, and the type of zone established. The existence of FTZs provides opportunities for exporters to seek benefits, whilst at the same time helping to achieve the host country's macro and microeconomic objectives. Advantages to the company of establishing itself in a zone can come from savings in shipping charges, duties and taxes that accrue to the company bringing in unassembled machinery and assembling it in the zone. Many other benefits can be gained, and a marketing manager can help to achieve the company's objectives through awareness of the opportunities and benefits that can be obtained from location in a zone. (The benefits to the economy are not considered here; many free ports in the United Kingdom failed to realize their objectives and were abolished or scrapped, and there is some disagreement on their value in providing long-term investment and job creation.)

Barter and counter-trade

Academic publications and the trade press often offer confusing accounts of barter and counter-trade. Four features distinguish the two. First, barter transactions are exchanges of goods and services without money, whereas counter-trade involves partial or full compensation in money. Second, one contract will formalize a barter transaction, whereas more than one contract will generally be required to formalize counter-trade. Third, counter-trade requires a longer time for the completion of transactions than does barter, and involves greater risk. Fourth, counter-trade requires a greater commitment of the firm's resources, which again generates greater risk. Some forms of counter-trade can require firms to provide capital to invest in joint venture production facilities. Counter-trade, therefore, can be simply described as a commercial arrangement for reciprocal trade between companies in two or more countries.

Counter-trade has arisen because of shortages in both foreign exchange and lines of credit, because some world markets for raw materials are rather weak, and because of competition between mainly western exporters of manufactured goods. The US Department of Financial Institutions (DFI) lists four main reasons that countries may want to use counter-trading:

- to finance trade that a lack of commercial credit or convertible currency would otherwise preclude
- to exploit a 'buyers' market' position to obtain better terms of trade or similar benefits
- to protect or stimulate the output of domestic industries (including agriculture and mineral extraction)
- as a reflection of political and economic policies which seek to plan and balance overseas trade.

Estimates put the size of counter-trade as high as 10–15 per cent of world trade, with 100 countries having some sort of rules on its organization (Eagle et al., 2003). Another estimate suggests that 5 per cent of UK trade is made up of counter-trade transactions (Eagle et al. 2003).

The nature of counter-trade varies according to circumstances, but excluding barrier, the following five varieties are the most common.

Counter-trade

Here, the exporter agrees to purchase goods and/or services from the overseas country, so that there are two contracts, one being for the export order which is paid for in the normal way and the second one for the counter-trade order. The goods in the counter-trade order might be totally unrelated to the goods in the principal export order.

Buyback

This is a form of barter where the exporter of capital equipment agrees to repayment from the proceeds of the output from that equipment. Such contracts are usually for in excess of three years and they may extend for a much longer period. This has advantages for both sides, especially for the country buying the equipment, as it generates export markets.

Offset trading

Here, the importing country seeks to develop its own industrial capability, usually in advanced technology. An offset agreement involves the export of goods where the exporter agrees to incorporate into these goods certain material or components sourced from within the importing country. An example of an offset agreement involving two advanced economies was Boeing's deal to sell AWAC aircraft to the United Kingdom for £860 million in 1993, in return for which Boeing agreed to place orders in the United Kingdom worth 130 per cent of the contract price.

Switch trading

This situation arises when one of the two parties involved in barter or a counter-purchase arrangement has goods that the other does not want. In this case switch trading can be use, often with the help of a switch specialist. Albaum, Strandskov and Duerr give a good example:

> A German firm agrees to trade machine tools worth Dm1M to Brazil exchange for coffee having an equivalent open value. The equipment is shipped to Sao Paulo, and the coffee is ready for shipment to Hamburg but the German firm really does not want the coffee. So, with the help of a switch specialist, the coffee is sold to a Canadian company for DM 925,000. The German company gets its hard currency, less a five per cent commission paid to the switch specialist. Since the German company would know in advance that the coffee would have to be sold at discount it could build this into its price for the equipment.

Evidence account

Companies that conduct a large amount of continuing business in a country may be required to arrange counter-purchases equal to the value of their export. In this solution a company would find it impractical to arrange a counter-purchase for each separate consignment, so an evidence account can be kept showing how over a year a balance has been kept between its imports into the country and the exports it has taken out. There are, of course, risks for the exporter in counter-trade, which are in addition to those risks associated with normal exports. An exporter could be persuaded to accept goods for which there is a weak market, or there might be hidden costs in accepting certain goods, such as higher transport costs than anticipated. Likewise, the importing country might place a higher value on the goods than is realistic, and there are the additional problems of arranging insurance. Despite these considerations, the ECGD, OTS and the banks, as well as specialist consultants and trading houses, all offer advice to help overcome these problems.

Ideally marketing managers should be as aware of the challenges facing them with this form of exchange as they are with traditional exporting. Barter becomes a marketing issue only when new markets can be entered by this method, or existing markets penetrated further. Barter requires fewer company resources than, say, establishing the firm in a new market would often require, and thus can support short-term objectives.

Counter-purchase, on the other hand, involves different risks, as the products may not necessarily fit with the organization's marketing expertise and thereby increase risk and cost. The company may well feel these are worth taking when given the opportunities offered of breaking into a new market or building up market share. The requirement to trade in unrelated goods received by the western company can either be dealt with in-house or taken over by specialists in this type of transaction. Marketing managers should take more than a passing interest in these arrangements. Offset trading approach can assist with market entry, market penetration and development. In many industries, such as the defence industry, offset deals are common. One major consideration when trading via this method with development economies is that it could set up competitors which might well challenge the dominance of the supplier at some future date.

Overall, therefore, counter-trade requires very careful balancing of the possibilities it opens up against the costs and risk involved. Legal considerations will play a larger role than they do with barter, plus there is a longer-term involvement by companies when offset trading is used. The question remains how far barter and counter-trade will continue to expand, given the rapid development of many countries, the move from centrally planned economies and hence a possible lower requirement for arrangements of this nature.

The changes in counter-trade can be seen in the advice offered by the US Counter-trade Association, which points to the increasing costs associated with the marketing of counter-stations, particularly those associated with developing countries. Western exporters, they argue, will find it necessary to look at alternative approaches to meet their counter-trade commitments. Promotion of tourism with the buyer's country, training of the buyer's workforce, and investment to labour-intensive projects are all examples.

The desire of many governments is that the benefits of trade should be shared in an equitable way between foreign companies and the domestic government. It is obvious that counter-trade is a vital issue for companies to understand. From the US point of view, the focus is on the individual business, raising its awareness both of the activities that comprise barter and counter-trade and the need to look at trends in this area. Without this awareness, many companies will not be prepared for the realities of exporting. From the government's point of view, counter-trade is a way of boosting long-term economic prospects in restructuring the economy and creating a vibrant private sector. There are usually financial and specialist organizations that provide advice and help on the issues of finance and payments. However, the promotion of many government regulations on counter-trade provides little in the way of an excuse in pleading ignorance of their existence.

Parallel importing (grey marketing)

Grey marketing or parallel importing has been a widespread international practice, and one of concern to manufacturers and retailers, since the mid-1980s. The size of international grey markets currently ranges between US$8 billion and US$15 billion. There is evidence of tensions between attempts to remove any restrictions on the practice and attempts by organizations such as the European Union to protect its members from its impact.

Parallel importing is not counterfeiting. However, as Eagle et al. (2003) remarked, the use of the term synonymously with 'grey marketing' suggests that there is something suspect about the practice. 'Grey' may imply an 'almost black market'. Grey marketing involves the selling of trademarked goods through channels of distribution that are not authorized by the trademark holders. When grey marketing occurs across markets, such as in an international setting, the term most commonly used is parallel importing. It provides the opportunity for companies, usually major retail chains, to bypass official franchise holders or agents for particular, usually high-priced, branded goods and to source them direct from overseas suppliers. It is only illegal when grey market goods violate either product regulations or a licensing contract for the trademark's use in a specific country, or where the trademark owner is based in the country into which parallel imports are shipped. A non-licensed distributor cannot use the brand trademark in the 'official' styled trademark form other than by a photograph of the label on the product or a photograph of the product itself if it bears the logo (for example, the Nike 'swoosh').

MINI CASE 6.2

Pricing in separate channels – the case of parallel imports

In parallel importing a parallel channel of distribution is created through which goods are moved across borders unofficially in slightly differentiated packaging and/or labelling to compete with the official product. A major advantage for international operations is the ability to charge country-specific prices reflecting differences in ability to pay. Parallel importation seriously undermines a manufacturer's ability to do this, since it involves purchasing a product in a low-priced country and shipping it to a high-priced country to profit from the price difference. It is usually carried out by enterprises that are not part of a manufacturer's distribution plan, such as supermarkets, catalogue retailers, and discount stores. For example:

- Many Europeans know that cars are cheaper in Belgium than in nearby countries, largely because of substantial tax differences. European car dealers have been unable to stop the entry of unauthorized imports from Belgium that parallel and compete with their own authorized transactions. This situation helps explain why Belgium is a substantial exporter of automobiles – more than 25,000 some years – even though it does not have an auto manufacturing facility.
- A pharmaceutical company shipped some of its American-made drugs to its distributor in a Central American country, intending to sell at a substantial discount because the local market could not afford to pay American-level prices. However, the pharmaceuticals did not stay in the Central American country. Instead, they were shipped back to the United States to be sold through drug channels that were not part of the American company's plans and at prices lower than the previously set American prices.
- In a major shopping area in Tokyo, a large discount retailer sells Fuji film at a discount. However, the package carries the Korean language, not Japanese. It was meant to be sold in Korea, but made its way back into the Japanese market. Other Fuji film, also discounted but still more expensive, is packaged with the Japanese language on the box.

The range of parallel imports spans from daily-used low-end products to highly sophisticated ones, especially in the case of premium brands of cars, cameras, watches, computers, perfumes, wine, drugs and construction equipment. The practice has been widely reported also as 'grey market', 'product diversion', 're-imports' and 'arbitrage'. In this text the name 'parallel imports' is used to specify that a 'parallel' channel is created, and goods are moved across borders to differentiate with the more general 'grey market' that could sometimes be domestic.

The practice of parallel importing represents an uneasy balance between the protection of intellectual property rights such as trademark and patent rights and the liberalization of trade in goods and services promoted by organizations such at the WTO. For grey markets to operate there must be a source of supply, easy access from one market to another, and price differentials that are large enough to make the venture financially viable. Much of the debate in the academic literature centres on whether parallel importing is a legitimate response to discriminatory pricing strategies or a free rider problem.

The advantages of parallel importing

In the international context, parallel export channels may assist in penetrating foreign markets or in increasing overall market share. Domestically, many European discount retailers are unequivocal about the future of grey marketing practices in boosting growth prospects for their organizations. This is consistent with the notion that retailers often prefer to display high-equity brands in close proximity to lesser or unknown brands in order to leverage the value of the high-equity brand across other brands (Maskus and Chen 2004). Conversely, manufacturers who have built equity in their brands want them to be displayed with brands of similar position and stature. Proximity to lesser or unknown brands may cause the consumer to question the brand. Consumers may then also question the 'normal' pricing structure for a brand in its official retail outlets versus the often substantially lower price in parallel importers' outlets.

Protecting parallel importers provides a check on the near monopoly held by many large manufacturers, and acts in the interests of consumers, resulting in lower prices, better products, and in developing countries at least, a higher quality of life. Indeed, much of the evidence to support the legalization of parallel importing has come from the examination of cases where companies could extract excessive profits from consumers. Parallel importing has arisen primarily as a response to international price discrimination. Consumers may view parallel imports as perfect substitutions for authorized goods. On the other hand, parallel importing may represent an unusual approach to market segmentation, with low-priced goods from parallel importers generally not offering the same warranties as those (higher-priced) goods available through official channels. Risk-averse consumers will thus be prepared to pay higher prices for the security of warranties and after-sales service. Risk-preferring consumers will purchase parallel imports in the knowledge that they do not have the same level of security.

Table 6.2 shows the factors that are likely to affect the success of parallel importing activity.

In terms and of potential brand equity and valuation impact it remains unclear whether consumers will be better or worse off, both in the short and longer term, as a result of parallel importing. It is also unclear what the impact of parallel importing is on consumer perception and the concomitant value of brands.

The disadvantages of parallel importing

Consumers may purchase parallel imported trademarked goods without being aware of the difference between these goods and those purchased through 'official' distribution channels. If problems arise, and customers find that they do not get the expected post-sale service and warranty protection, it may be the goodwill established by the 'official' distributor that will suffer. Brands are rarely created by marketing communication activity alone; advertising and other related marketing communications activity help communicate and position them, and parallel importers may gain a free ride on the market demand and brand image of the product created by the authorized distributor, without sharing in the marketing communications efforts and expenses which have built the demand and associated image (Maskus and Chen 2004). Thus parallel importers are not concerned with developing and expanding the market, but rather

Table 6.2 Factors affecting the success of parallel importing activity

Marketing factor	Most successful when:	Least successful when:
Product	Parallel imported product is positioned or perceived as directly substitutable for official product.	Parallel imported product is seen as being old stock, out of fashion or out of date.
	Product quality inferred as being equivalent or consumers are unable or not given information to allow them to differentiate between parallel product and official product.	Quality of parallel product is able to be observed as inferior to official product.
Pricing	Parallel imported product is at a substantially lower price.	Parallel product price differential is minimal.
		'Value added' by official distributors prevents direct product or price comparison.
Promotion	Promotional activity centres on image rather than on complexity of technology.	Promotional activity centres on technology or continual improvement and rapidly changing technology or the requirement of expert knowledge by retail staff.
Distribution	The brand owner in conjunction with official retailers undertakes no defensive action.	Aggressive defensive action to counter parallel imported products is undertaken by the brand owner in conjunction with official retailers.

with acquiring a share of the market developed by authorized channels. It could, of course, be claimed that the authorized distributor also benefits from the advertising and promotional activities undertaken by the parallel importer. However, given that parallel importers promote their products primarily on the basis of substantially lower prices, it is unlikely that such activity could in reality be construed as aiding brand image (Maskus and Chen 2004)).

Brand value lies in the ability of a brand to translate brand reputation and loyalties into enduring profit streams. The realization of this has brought brand equity management into focus, as a result of both changes to international accounting standards relating to intangible assets, and renewed focus on the impact of marketing communication on brand performance (Ghauri and Cateora 2006). This may have led to increased focus on the strategic integration of all elements of marketing communication in order to provide clarity and consistency of communication messages. It is possible that brand image communication may focus on quality while the marketing communications of a parallel importer may focus on discount prices – thus potentially creating confusion and conflicting 'value' messages for the consumer and adversely affecting the brand image. As a result, the future earnings potential of brand names impacted by parallel imports may be seriously jeopardized.

The practice of parallel importing, if seen as openly condoned by the manufacturer, may strain the relationship between the manufacturer and the distributor. Loss of goodwill may be accompanied by a loss of marketing channel support as some 'official' channel members lessen promotional efforts put behind a product which is also parallel imported, cease to promote it or perhaps drop it entirely. Parallel importing, while broadening distribution, appears to have also helped the counterfeiting industry that pass fake goods off as parallel imports. It is illegal to parallel import counterfeit or pirated goods, although liberalization of the parallel importing law has made it more difficult to identify 'fake' products. The problem appears to be a massive one, as for example, large amount of fake goods branded under the Microsoft name are being seized by customs and exercise departments all over the world.

Regional trading blocs

At the international level, trading blocs (also referred to as free trade areas) may be viewed as a cluster of geographically close countries that share abstract and/or material culture in varying degrees and trade freely with each other. It is interesting to note that the three major regional trading blocs (the European Union, the North American Free Trade Agreement (NAFTA) and the Association of South East Asian Nations (ASEAN)) can be characterized by significant differences in culture.

By definition, a trading bloc is an association of countries that reduces intra-regional barriers to trade in goods, and sometimes services, investment, capital and labour as well (Malhotra, Agarwal and Baalbaki 1998). The emergence of trading blocs can be traced to the General Agreement on Tariffs and Trade (GATT), a multilateral free trade organization with the main objective of creating one big economic community of all nations with a market economy. However, in recent years, there has been a major structural transformation in the world economy as US strength has declined and others, mainly the European Union and Japan, have shared the economic power.

Levels of trading arrangements

There are a number of stages of economic integration between two or more national economies, which are briefly outlined in Table 6.3.

It is likely that each of these phases assumes a convergence of the key elements of the marketing mix among the members. At first, industrial and capital goods are immediately impacted, followed by intermediate products, then eventually, though far more slowly, consumer goods. It is axiomatic that a regional integration scheme which is entered into by national economies for purely economic reasons must make each country at least as well off as it would have been had it refrained from joining (this is known as the condition of Pareto optimality) and as many as possible better off (Malhotra et al. 1998).

Successful regional trading blocs

According to Ghauri and Cateora (2006), successful trading blocs can be characterized by the following factors:

Table 6.3   Regional trading arrangements

Level of trading integration	Brief outline
1 Zero integration	No systematic economic interdependency primarily because there is little if any economic or social motive for trade (e.g. between Outer Mongolia and the United States).
2 Bilateral treaties of limited scope	Permissive agreements covering specific sector's trade flows (e.g. Commerce and Friendship Treaty between the United States and Australia)
3 Free trade areas	Each member state removes trade barriers to the entire member trading partners. There is minimum supervision required with no common set of external tariffs, and individual national trade policies prevail (e.g. North American Free Trade Agreement of 1994).
4 Customs union	This entails the removal of formal trade barriers among the members and presupposes a far wider range of policy consultation and agreement among the member states. Common external tariffs, leading to a coordination of customs administration, require the creation of far more pervasive supranational institutions (e.g. the original Benelux was a customs union).
5 Common market	This requires not only the free movement of goods internally and common external tariffs but also full factor of production movement (labour, capital, etc.) within the defined market area. It implies a far more complicated legal and economic system with substantial supranational coordination (e.g. EC 1992).
6 Economic union	This is the highest level of integration, short of merging members into one single political entity. It implies more or less complete harmonization of public policies and, in particular, the harmonization of monetary and fiscal policies as well as the acceptance of a fixed relationship between currency units. For example in the European Union, member states must also be prepared to adopt similar and coordinated macroeconomic policies (full employment, inflation, etc.).

- similar levels of per capita income
- almost same level of gross national product (GNP)
- geographic proximity
- similarity in trading patterns
- compatible trading regimes
- political commitment to regional organization.

Trading blocs with wide disparities in national incomes face problems with redistribution of income and employment. While geographic proximity helps in transportation and communications, it does not always guarantee success particularly among developing countries. The last two factors pertain to the durability and sustainability of the trading blocs.

The next section is a brief overview and evaluation of the three major trading blocs. It is important to note that there are also many other trading blocs throughout the world.

The European Union

The Single European Act defines a single internal market area 'as an area without internal frontiers in which the free movement of goods, persons, services, and capital is ensured'. The Act incorporates the broad objectives outlined in the famous Lord Cockfield White Paper, *Completing the Internal Market* (EC 1987). It contains some 300 highly specific measures designed truly to implement a single market and set out a detailed timetable for internal proposed changes into members' national laws.

The 1992 programme to end specific physical, technical, and fiscal barriers was the indication of a new approach to marketing in the European Community (the predecessor to the European Union). The marketing impacts of the 1992 programme influenced:

- the structure of the market (with a wave of mergers and acquisitions across boundaries)
- pricing policy (as a consequence of value added tax harmonization)
- product policy (as corporations are continuing to create Eurobrands, etc.)
- distribution policy (as physical barriers are abolished)
- the organization of the marketing function itself.

The final step of the European Community was the ratification of the Maastricht Treaty, which formed the basis of the European Union. This also provided for the Economic and Monetary Union (EMU). Under this agreement, the member states agreed to create a European Central Bank and introduce fixed exchange rates and a single currency. The member states also agreed to recruit new members to enlarge the Union and position it as one of the world's largest economic powers. Thus, the removal of the multiple technical standards will eventually make possible the designing and marketing of truly European products. On the production side, it will lead to longer production runs and fewer producers.

North American Free Trade Agreement (NAFTA)

The free trade agreement (FTA) between the United States and Canada was set up in January 1994 and extended in January 1998 to include Mexico, when it became known as the North American Free Trade Agreement (NAFTA). The objective of NAFTA is to create synergy among the three economies that could generate income and employment gains and enhance international competitiveness of firms throughout the region. Both Canada and Mexico conduct two-thirds and three-quarters of their trade with the United States and the United States conducts about one-quarter of its trade with the two combined. The combined intra-regional trade of the member countries represents a substantial percentage of their total exports (Terpstra and Sarathi 2000). NAFTA has created a free-trade market of 378 million people with a GDP of US$7.68 trillion, marginally exceeding the size of the European Union (Albaum et al. 2002). However, compared with the European Union, NAFTA is an integration of a lesser kind. As a free trade area, it is not an economic union with a single currency and a central bank in the offing and a potential for a political union in the future.

NAFTA eliminates tariffs between the United States, Canada and Mexico, thereby lowering the cost of imports to consumers in each country. It offers a level playing field with gradual and total elimination of tariffs and all non-tariff barriers. Tariffs on about half the US exports to Mexico were removed immediately and the remaining tariffs were gradually phased out. In addition, it also established a legal framework to address subsidy, countervailing and anti-dumping measures. Under NAFTA, US and Canadian consumers increased their purchase of Mexican-made products because of lower imported prices. The removal of non-tariff trade barriers also allowed more Mexican-made consumer products to enter the United States and Canada. Hence, Mexican exports to the United States and Canada increased due to trade liberalization under NAFTA. Mexican firms benefited from economies of scale, improved access to technology, greater employment opportunities and advanced production sharing.

Similarly, Canadian firms gained access to the large US market, which helped them to enjoy economies of scale and thereby compete globally in the world market. The FTA with Canada led to the avoidance and binational resolution of disputes rather than the previously unilateral US approach. Although there were widespread job losses and many Canadian subsidiaries of US firms closed as a result of the agreement, access to the US market was rewarding.

Association of South East Asian Nations (ASEAN)

Since its creation in 1967, ASEAN has evolved into a dynamic and pivotal regional trading bloc. The member countries are among the fastest growing countries in the world. The intra-regional trade has grown proportionately over the last 20 years. Although not a member of ASEAN, Japan's role in East Asia has expanded considerably in the past three decades. Japan's foreign direct investment (FDI) in East Asia grew at an annual average rate of 62 per cent (Koike, 2004), partly as a result of the appreciating yen and rising protectionism triggered by the US and European trading blocs. The ASEAN countries continue to represent the fifth largest export market for the United States.

Politically, ASEAN is a stable region with accords signed concerning peace, freedom and neutrality. Enhancing intra-ASEAN trade has been a long and important economic objective. The ASEAN Preferential Trading Arrangement (PTA) was introduced in 1977 to liberalize and enhance intra-regional trade. Tariff preference and the liberalization of non-tariff barriers were extended to products with at least 50 per cent local content. For example, the margin of preference (MOP) on tariffs is 50 per cent of the prevailing most-favoured-nation (MFN) rate of the importing countries. Also, the common effective preferential tariff (CEPT) scheme covers more than 90 per cent of the total tariff lines in the manufacturing and agricultural sector. The CEPT scheme entails tariff reduction by 5 per cent across the board and the elimination of quantitative restrictions and non-tariff barriers. Additionally, establishment of the Green Lane system to expedite customs clearance of CEPT products was intensified. EFTA aims to promote greater foreign direct investment and intra-ASEAN investment in the bloc, with a strong production base geared toward servicing the global market. The ASEAN industrial joint venture (AIJV), for private-sector cooperation permits foreign investors to own 60 per cent of AIJV projects.

Summary

This chapter has looked at both exporting and importing management, covering several aspects of export marketing and methods of payment used by exporters to obtain payment from importers. The chapter used mini-case studies to explain and demonstrate export activities and export organization. Export finance concentrates on the importance of ensuring that the customers receive their goods on time and in a good condition. This section also reviewed terms of trade and payment, outlining the pitfalls associated with export documentation.

Government economic policy focuses on the importance of exports as valuable source of income generation. The United Kingdom was used as an example of the role played by the government in encouraging export marketing.

Regional trading blocs can be building blocks rather than stumbling blocks to world trade. However, to develop successful marketing strategies for penetration, whether internally from within or externally from outside the bloc, firms must take into account the degree of similarities within the trading bloc. Of the 'big three', the European Union is at the most advanced level of economic integration. It is also more culturally complex and heterogeneous than NAFTA and ASEAN. A big part of the reason is the large number of diverse countries represented, which adds to the multicultural eclectic market.

Different national cultures embody different attitudes, values and beliefs in specific business cultures, styles and practices. With some Eastern European countries joining the European Union and with the prospect of more countries joining in the future, these segments may become even more heterogeneous.

With the exception of Mexico, NAFTA is probably the most homogenised regional trading bloc. However, with the recent economic changes and trade liberalization occurring in Mexico, the gap might gradually narrow in the future.

ASEAN countries reveal similar heterogeneity with respect to religion, ethnicity and economic standards. Over time, each trading bloc is likely to become more homogeneous due to similarities in government policies and business practices as initiated by the harmonization process.

Revision questions

1 In terms of export marketing strategy and operational performance, discuss how a company may be successful in exporting.
2 What are the direct and indirect channels of distribution available to exporters, and under what conditions would the use of each be the most appropriate?
3 The terms of payment are an important factor of export transactions. Describe the various terms of payments in increasing order of risk.
4 Discuss the types of assistance an exporter can obtain from governmental and nongovernmental agencies.
5 Discuss the main purpose of an import licence, and explain why so many countries use them.
6 Explain the purpose and use of credit insurance in exporting.
7 Discuss the advantages and disadvantages of parallel importing.

8   Managing imports in the European countries is relatively easier and less risky than managing exports. Give reasons to support this statement.

9   Explain what you understand by barter and counter-trading.

10 What do you consider to be the advantages and disadvantages of regional trading blocs? How effective and successful are they?

SEMINAR CASE STUDY

Export marketing challenges in the commercialization of GM crops

In this case study, the export marketing challenge created by the commercialization of GM crops is analysed In order to assess the impact that the introduction of GM crops has had on the international agri-food supply chain, it is essential to examine the traditional supply chain for conventional (non-GM) products. We then look at what GM crops are and how they differ from conventional crops.

In a general sense, there are six links in the international agri-food supply chain. Beginning at the production end, the first link is composed of crop developers, a myriad of small, medium and large firms such as Aventis, Monsanto and Syngenta, engaged in the development of agricultural crops to ensure enhanced quantity (yield) and/or quality (value). In the next link are the customers of these crop developers, the producers/farmers who purchase seeds according to their specific cropping requirements. The farmers' customers are found in the distribution link composed of the grain and oilseed handlers who purchase farm production and blend the crops into much larger bulk units to be passed along to the brokers, such as the US-based Cargill and Archer Daniels Midland, who match these bulk volumes with the next link in the chain – food companies. These companies, such as Nestlé, Unilever and General Mills, use the grains and oilseeds in the production of various food products. The customers of the food companies are found in the next link: the food retailers, who range from large companies such as Wal-Mart, Sainsbury and Tesco, which develop their own-brand food products, to small convenience stores as well as hotel, restaurant and institutional (HRI) establishments. Finally, the last link in the chain is the end consumer, who purchases and consumes the food product.

There are two reasons for this general structure of the international agri-food supply chain. First, a convergence of regional and global consumption patterns has decreased the need to differentiate both bulk foodstuffs and in many cases processed food products from country to country. Second, improvements in production and transportation technologies have simultaneously increased the ability to move food products over vast distances while decreasing the costs of doing so. This structure has made possible the export marketing strategy of standardization, where distribution and food companies have created an international value chain built on international product development, sourcing and advertising. The result of this strategy is that exporting food companies can achieve economies of scale by lowering production costs, reducing transaction costs and dispersing risks.

At this point, it is crucial to note that agricultural crops typically move along this chain through spot-market transactions where varieties are bulked together, with the result that there is often no interaction between the seed developer or the farmer on the one hand and the end consumer on the other. While the standardized structure of the international agri-food supply chain has prevailed for the better part of a century, the commercialization of GM crops poses complex new challenges to this structure and to marketing managers.

Advances in modern biotechnology have yielded new crop development technologies such as genetic modification, which may be defined as the ability to alter the expression of traits to produce organisms with particular attributes. Three types of GM crops are currently being developed. The first are production-trait crops, such as insect-resistant or herbicide tolerant-varieties, which have been modified to have enhanced agronomic characteristics but to be substantially equivalent to conventional varieties in processing or final consumption. That is, production-trait crops are for farmers, not for end consumers, and they are typically sold into the regular commodity supply chain co-mingled with conventional varieties. The second type of GM crops is output-trait crops, which are modified to meet the needs of specific downstream users such as livestock feeders or food producers, and sometimes the final consumer. For managers to extract the value of such crops for their companies, they must be segregated from conventional varieties through identity preservation systems so that co-mingling does not occur. The third type of GM crops is bio-engineered, non-food products such as plant-made pharmaceuticals or industrial products. Again, they must be carefully segregated from conventional crops destined for the food supply.

In 2006, over 100 million acres of GM crops such as corn (maize), canola (rapeseed), cotton and tobacco were grown, primarily in the United States, Argentina, Canada and China, where 98 per cent of these GM crops were production-trait varieties.

This dominance of production-trait GM crops has several important implications for the international supply of agricultural crops, and hence for the market entry strategies of food companies. Production-trait GM crops, such as insect-resistant and herbicide-tolerant varieties, have been developed for and marketed to farmers to meet their agronomic challenges, and not to end consumers to meet their demands for enhanced consumption attributes. This has created an enormous information gap between those producing and commercializing the technology and those who ultimately must consume it. Complicating this information gap is the fact that because production-trait GM crops target agronomic characteristics while leaving the end-use characteristics of the crop substantially the same as conventional varieties, they have been commercially approved in the United States, Canada and Argentina as substantially equivalent to conventional varieties. The result is that GM and non-GM crops are co-mingled in the supply chain. Given that these three countries make up 99 per cent of the total production of such GM crops, if no segregation occurs domestically then the crops will not be segregated for export markets.

To supporters, production-trait GM crops represent another innovation along a continuum of agricultural crop development technologies. Such crops present biological solutions to agronomic challenges that are currently mostly addressed through the use of synthetic chemicals. In other words, GM crops are seen as a pathway to the sustainable intensification of agricultural production. Consequently, the lack of segregation between GM and non-GM varieties is not seen as a problem.

To critics, production-trait GM crops do not represent another innovation along a technology continuum, but instead represent novel uses of new and untested scientific techniques. There are four types of consumer concerns associated with GM crops that differentiate them from conventional crops. First are economic concerns that GM crops are providing no economic benefit to consumers. Indeed, any production cost savings that may result from the use of GM crops disappears when GM and non-GM varieties are not segregated. Second are human safety and health concerns about possible toxic, pathogenic or invective changes to the plant that might result from the use of GM techniques, and the impact of these changes upon human health. Third are biodiversity concerns about the safety and health of the flora and fauna – both insects and animals – that interact with GM crops. Fourth are moral and ethical concerns linked with notions of playing God and owning life. For example, a commonly cited concern is that multinational companies holding patents on biological processes essentially have monopoly control over the global food supply. Given this range of concerns, it should come as no surprise that critics find the lack of segregation between GM and non-GM varieties quite unacceptable because it prevents consumer sovereignty in the marketplace.

Of particular challenge to the standardization entry mode strategy is the asymmetry of consumer concerns between countries and regions, and the impact that this has had on public and private policy initiatives. Broadly speaking, consumers in Europe and Japan have responded to biotechnology more quickly and more negatively than have consumers in North America. As a result, public policy initiatives and private-sector responses to these concerns have differed across countries and regions.

Consider first North America (and Argentina), where the introduction of biotechnology has been met largely with indifference. The development of public policies pertaining to the technology has had a focus on fostering technological progress. While rigorous, the regulation of production-trait GM crops has been based on the principle of substantial equivalence, and has generally focused only on the consumer concerns pertaining to human health and safety and biodiversity, while economic and moral/ethical concerns are outside regulatory consideration. Similarly, private policy initiatives in North America have reflected a focus on technological progress as private firms have invested heavily in biotechnology. Given that the investments required to have a new product of biotechnology licensed and brought to full commercialization are very high, firms require access to a wide variety of markets. As a result, firms based in North America have become aggressive competitors in export markets in the field of biotechnology.

In contrast, both public policies and private initiatives in the European Union can be characterized as reflecting technological caution, not progress. With respect to public policies, there has been considerable reluctance on the part of governments to officially embrace the technology, especially its agricultural applications. Instead of seeing biotechnology's benefits, the focus has been on the risks. The caution reflects the absence of trust in science and scientific experts, ensuring that decisions regarding technology are made on a political basis. As a result, production-trait GM crops are not seen as substantially equivalent to conventional varieties. Instead, they are regulated as new varieties and there is a requirement to ensure that these new varieties are segregated from conventional varieties in the marketplace. With respect to private policy initiatives, many food firms in the European Union (such as Sainsbury's, Tesco and Carrefour) have sought to capitalize on anti-GM sentiments by reformulating their own brands and marketing their products as GM-free (although other biotechnology ingredients such as GM enzymes and reagents have not been removed).

The effect of these differing public and private responses has been to fragment the international agri-food supply chain. At the production end, crop developers and farmers continue to produce homogenous, unsegregated production-trait GM crops in North America and Argentina. At the consumer end, concerns have risen, and as a result, various public and private policy initiatives have been adopted that are designed to track, label and sometimes prohibit the use of GM crops in food products. Caught in the middle are the food distributors and food companies, which buy unsegregated food stuffs yet face demands for segregation such as the current approach towards labelling regulations in the European Union. These firms must alter their entry mode strategies in order to meet the very different business environments that have emerged in various countries and regions as a result of the commercialization of production-trait GM crops.

From the discussion above, it appears that if food distribution firms and food companies can develop entry mode strategies built on effective identity preservation (IP) systems capable of ensuring the segregation of GM and non-GM crops through extensive supply-chain management and coordination along all six links of a traditionally disparate international agri-food supply chain, then they can overcome the export marketing challenges posed by the commercialization of production-trait GM crops.

Seminar questions

1 The lack of segregation between GM and non-GM varieties has been regarded as a problem. Discuss this issue and explain why this should be a problem from customers' point of view.
2 Discuss some of the problems that may be encountered through the use of standardized entry mode strategies.
3 What are the likely factors that have led to fragmentation of the international agri-food supply chain?

Managerial assignment task

A company operating internationally would prefer stable, friendly and predictable political and legal environments in the country markets to be served. But this ideal is rarely found. Thus, export marketers must develop a monitoring tool to be able to evaluate the degree of the company's exposure to political risk in all served and potential markets.

You have just been employed as an export marketing manager by a British company exporting its manufacturing products (engineering equipments) to at least five countries in West Africa. Discuss how you could assess the political risks in these countries for your company.

References

Albaum, G., Strandskov, J. and Duerr, E. (2002) *International Marketing and Export Management*, 4th edn, Harlow: Financial Times/Prentice Hall.

Bradley, F. (2002) *International Marketing Strategy*, 4th edn, Harlow: Financial Times/Prentice Hall.

Cateora, P. R. and Ghauri, P. N. (1999) *International Marketing*, European edition, Maidenhead: McGraw-Hill.

Eagle, L., Kitchen, P., Rose, L. and Moyle, B. (2003) 'Brand equity and brand vulnerability: the impact of gray marketing/parallel importing on brand equity and values', *European Journal of Marketing*, Vol. 37, No. 10, pp. 1332–49.

European Commission (1987) *Completing the Internal Market* (the Cockfield Report), 18 May, Brussels: European Commission.

Financial Times (1998) 'Exporter – industrial focus: industrial gases', 22 September, p. 11.

Ghauri, P. and Cateora, P. (2006) *International Marketing*, 2nd edn, Maidenhead: McGraw-Hill.

Johansson, J. K. (2003) *Global Marketing: Foreign Entry, Local Marketing and Global Management*, 3rd international edition, Maidenhead: McGraw-Hill/Irwin.

Koike, R (2004) 'Japan's foreign direct investment and structural changes in Japanese and East Asian trade', *Monetary and Economic Studies*, Institute for Monetary and Economic Studies, Bank of Japan, Vol. 22, Issue 3, pp. 145–82.

Kotabe, M. and Helsen, K. (2004) *Global Marketing Management,* 3rd edn, Chichester: Wiley.

Malhotra, N. K., Agarwal, J. and Baalbaki, I. (1998) 'Heterogeneity of regional trading blocs and global marketing strategies: a multicultural perspective', *International Marketing Review*, Vol. 15, No. 6, pp. 476–506.

Maskus, K. E. and Chen, Y. (2004) 'Vertical price control and parallel imports: theory and evidence', *Review of International Economics*, Vol. 12, Issue 4, pp. 551–65.

McAuley, A. (2001) *International Marketing*, Chichester: Wiley.

McGoldrick, P. J. and Davies, G. (1995) *International Retailing: Trends and Strategies,* London: Pitman.

Muhlbacher, H., Dahringer, H. and Leihs, H. (1999) *International Marketing: A Global Perspective*, 2nd edn, Berkshire: Thomson Business Press.

Terpstra, V. and Sarathi, R. (2000) *International Marketing*, 8th edn, Cincinnati: South Western College Publishing.

7

International Marketing
Operations and Planning

Contents

LEARNING OBJECTIVES

After reading this chapter you should:

- know the contribution of marketing theory to international marketing planning
- understand the combined elements forming the international marketing plan
- be able to evaluate the important role of marketing planning in successful international marketing operations

- understand the process of international marketing planning
- be able to develop and put together the structure of an international marketing plan
- appreciate how international marketing planning should be implemented and controlled.

Introduction

Planning is at the heart of the strategic management process, and international strategic marketing planning is the culmination of managerial efforts to deal with environmental change within the resource constraints of the corporation (Chae and Hill 2000). While some companies can get by using informal planning (for example, small companies or firms operating in rapidly changing market environments), for most companies, growth brings with it increasing pressures to adopt a formal planning process.

Growth pains multiply as companies internationalize and their planning procedures are stretched across national boundaries. Efforts to plan on an international basis have seemingly always met with obstacles (Simkin 2002). Impediments to international marketing planning efforts are numerous and depend on the nature and economic stage of the international market being tackled. Head offices seeking to formalize their international planning usually face the challenge not only of producing explicit planning procedures that thoroughly analyse and take account of foreign market environments, but also of implementing the planning effort in such a way as to gain the involvement and commitment of those principal stakeholders affected by the plan (Brock and Barry 2003).

Meanwhile, as international competition mounts, so the planning processes underlying strategy formulation have come under increasing attack. In some instances there are planning deficiencies, with managers being confounded by processes and producing directionless strategies. Courtney, Kirkland and Viguerie (1997) point out the increasing problems planners have in underestimating or overestimating environmental uncertainty. In multinational firms, strategic planning may be not strategic enough and not sufficiently democratic in tapping the creative juices of grassroots organizations.

This chapter evaluates the underlying planning process through which strategy is formulated. In domestic market situations, less formal planning processes may perhaps be more workable given the uniformity in cultural settings in which marketing plans are implemented. One of the many questions that this chapter tries to answer is whether planning process formality contributes to organizational performance in international settings. Finally, the chapter asks whether there should be improvements in competitive and organizational performance when management succeeds in elevating the formality of its planning processes.

The reviewing process starts with international marketing operations, and focuses on targeting and segmentation approaches to internationalization. International market positioning is then introduced to determine corporate strategies. This is followed by the structure of international marketing planning, taking into consideration corporate mission and objectives, which lead to the planning process. The chapter concludes by reviewing the role of new technology in providing control tools for international marketing plans.

International marketing operations

The international marketing literature identifies a number of factors that influence the performance of firms operating in an international environment. Evans, Treadgold and Mavondo (2000) proposed that certain characteristics of the firm and its international operations intervene in, and moderate, the relationship between the factors preventing the firm from learning about international environment (that is, psychic distance) and organizational performance. Such factors may contribute to a holistic framework that explains variations in the performance of international marketing operations. In terms of the strategic decision-making process regarding international retailing, operations are characterized by elements that can be classified into three areas of thought:

- The decision is unusual in the sense that simple decision rules cannot be applied.
- The decision is of great importance to the organization because it involves a substantial commitment of resources and has organization-wide consequences.
- Strategic decisions are highly complex as they often involve detailed analysis of both the external and internal environments.

Evans et al. (2000) also observed that the decision to enter a foreign market and the subsequent decision regarding the degree of adaptation of the retail offer possess all of these features. However, international marketing decisions are strongly influenced by subjective and perceptual factors, which may include the decision makers':

- personalities
- subjective expectations
- perception of risk within the global environment.

The most important aspect of a firm's pre-entry orientation is the subjective insights of the management team. Most international marketing managers also rely on objective information in the strategic decision-making process. However, the quality and quantity of such information may be very limited. Consequently, international marketing management may be faced with environmental uncertainty. According to Dupuis and Prime (1996), researches into international marketing decision making show that perception of environmental uncertainty usually results in incremental international expansion. The perception of environmental uncertainty may result in incremental international expansion. However, Evans and colleagues have not explored the extent to which environmental uncertainty influences the strategic decision-making process with regard to in-depth organizational and environmental analysis.

Figure 7.1 presents a conceptual model of the potential moderating effects of culture and socioeconomics on a firm's international marketing strategies. Environmental characteristics in international markets are likely to moderate the operational performance. As shown in Figure 7.1, two characteristics, national culture and regional socioeconomic conditions, affect the performance of corporate marketing strategies. In addition, because international market and firm conditions may also impact operational performance, the model shows likely covariates – that is, marketing experience, extent of competition and international marketing mix implementation problems – that should be managed when examining the effects of environmental factors and operational performance of multinational firms.

It is very likely that the perception of cultural and business differences (Simkin 2002) will lead to environmental uncertainty (see Figure 7.1). In order to reduce this uncertainty corporate management will undertake more extensive organizational and environmental analysis (see Chapter 3). Such analysis will provide the firm with a greater understanding of the international market, which will result in superior organizational performance.

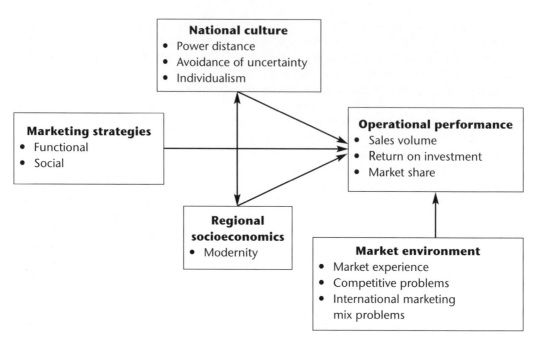

Figure 7.1 Effects of cultural and socioeconomic factors on international marketing operation

In most cases the root of problems appears to lie in the firm's lack of preparation and understanding of individual international market. For example, the international success of such retail brands as The Body Shop, Benetton, HMV and Foot Locker is due to their level of planning and research into consumer preferences, competition and convenient store locations. Conversely, the poor international performance of Laura Ashley and Marks & Spencer in the United States and Daimaru in Australia was probably associated with a lack of research and subsequent poor understanding of the market. Thus, the understanding of the international marketing environment will likely influence the international marketing performance of firms and can be explained by several factors including (Hollensen 2001):

- the intervening effect of the strategic decision-making process
- the nature and the extent of marketing research conducted by the firm
- the firm's ability to conduct in-depth market research in the international marketplace upon which strategic decisions may be based
- the depth and the nature of the problems faced by the firm for which decisions are to be made
- the impact of environmental uncertainty, which may hamper the firm's ability to make rational decisions
- the appropriateness of the firm's organizational structure and its ability to make strategic decisions concerning international operation
- the firm's level of acculturation and adaptation to the international market

- the firm's pre-entry orientation to the international market taking into consideration differences between cultures
- management's ability to predict the international marketing environment in relation to its own business.

Overall, to succeed in the international marketing environment, firms must appreciate and position themselves appropriately within their market sectors.

Segmenting the international market

In order to build competitive advantage in both the short and the longer term, companies need to segment their target group. Market segmentation can aid in achieving strategic and tactical objectives. For strategic purposes market segmentation results can be used to prioritize market segment opportunities. The division of a market into different homogeneous groups of consumers is known as market segmentation. Rather than offer the same marketing mix to vastly different customers, market segmentation makes it possible for firms to tailor the marketing mix for specific target markets, thus better satisfying customer needs. Not all the elements of the marketing mix are necessarily changed from one segment to the next. For example, in some cases only the promotional campaigns differ.

Criteria for successful segmentation

For a particular international market segmentation solution to be effective and to lead to profitable marketing strategies, market segments should be (Kotler 2006):

- measurable or identifiable
- accessible by communication and distribution channels
- different in its response to a marketing mix
- durable (not changing too quickly)
- substantial enough to be profitable
- actionable.

Identifiability refers to the extent that we can really identify segments. (For example, how well does our solution look? Can we see clear differences between the segments? Are the segments well separated?) In terms of size for example, are our identified segments large enough to warrant separate marketing targeting? **Access** refers to the extent to which we reach the customers in our segments, either by advertising or by more direct sales approaches. (The issue here is, do we know where the customers in our segments are?) **Response** refers to the extent that the different market segments respond uniquely to the marketing efforts directed at them. Of course, the identified segments are only worthwhile goals to pursue if they remain stable over a certain period of time. **Actionability** refers to the extent to which the identified market segmentation provides direction for marketing efforts. This not only means that segments must react differently to marketing efforts, but also that the required marketing efforts are consistent with the strengths and core competencies of the company. Finally, a **specific market segmentation solution** obtained will be a function of the variables used to segment the market and the methods or procedures used to arrive at a certain classification. An international market can be segmented in various ways, although industrial markets are segmented somewhat differently from consumer markets, as described below.

Consumer market segmentation

A basis for segmentation is a factor that varies among groups within a market, but that is consistent within groups. We can identify four primary bases on which to segment a consumer market:

- **Geographic segmentation** is based on regional variables such as region, climate, population density and population growth rate.
- **Demographic segmentation** is based on variables such as age, gender, ethnicity, education, occupation, income and family status.
- **Psychographic segmentation** is based on variables such as values, attitudes and lifestyle.
- **Behavioural segmentation** is based on variables such as usage rate and patterns, price sensitivity, brand loyalty and benefits sought.

The optimal bases on which to segment the market depend on the particular situation, and are determined by marketing research, market trends and managerial judgment.

Business (industrial) market segmentation

While many of the consumer market segmentation bases can be applied to businesses and organizations, the different nature of business markets often leads to segmentation on the following bases:

- **Geographic segmentation** is based on regional variables such as customer concentration, regional industrial growth rate and international macroeconomic factors.
- **Customer type segmentation** is based on factors such as the size of the organization, its industry and its position in the value chain.
- **Buyer behaviour segmentation** is based on factors such as loyalty to suppliers, usage patterns and order size.

Profiling the segments

The identified market segments are summarized by profiles, often given a descriptive name. From these profiles, the attractiveness of each segment can be evaluated and a target market segment selected.

Segmenting international markets

Literature relating to international marketing has attempted to segment the world market into different countries or group of countries (see for example Hollensen 2001). However, the international market can also be seen as a group of customers with nearly the same characteristics. Thus, an international market can consist of customers from several countries, as in the European Union, for example.

Meanwhile, country markets or multicountry markets, for example in Africa, are not quite adequate. In many cases, boundary lines are the result of political agreement or war and do not reflect a similar separation in buyer characteristics among people on either side of the boarder. Thus the potential determinants of the firm's choice of foreign markets could be classified into the firm's characteristics and the environmental characteristics. This is represented in Figure 7.2.

Based on Figure 7.2, four steps can be identified for how and when a market could be processed for entry. Combining the firm and the environmental characteristics, the first step is the selection of the relevant segmentation criteria as discussed earlier. This leads to the development of appropriate segments, the screening of segments to narrow down the list of markets, and finally the development of segments in each qualified country or across countries.

With regards to the basis of international market segmentation, it is important to remember that more than one measure can be used simultaneously in the segmentation process. In Figure 7.3, a high degree of measurability and accessibility indicates more general market characteristics as criteria and vice versa.

Finally, it must be emphasized here that regardless of which positioning strategy a retailer wishes to pursue, it is necessary to assess the internal competencies in operation, and consider suitable retail format adaptation before selecting an international market entry strategy. This approach will enable the retailer to evaluate and forecast what it is possible to achieve within the global environment.

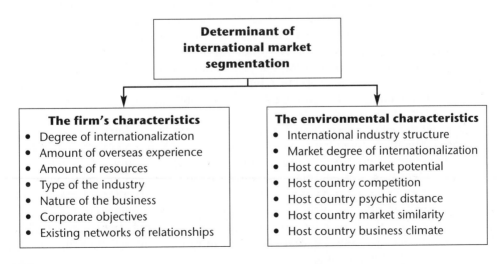

Figure 7.2 Some determinants of the firm's choice of international markets

General market characteristics
- Psychic distance
- Language
- Political forces
- Demographic factors
- Economic factors
- Industry structure
- Technological development
- Social factors
- Religious demarcations
- Education / knowledge

Specific market characteristics
Culture, lifestyle, personality, attitudes and tastes

High degree of measurability, accessibility and action

Low degree of measurability, accessibility and action

Figure 7.3   The basis of international market segmentation

The nature of international marketing planning

It should be appreciated that the determination of the organization's strategic goals is complex, and largely follows rules that have been worked out from experience of military warfare. The ways in which strategic goals are determined are discussed in depth within the strategic management literature (see for example Johnson and Scholes 2002). The international marketing plan, like national marketing plans, should outline the process whereby the organization's strategy is fulfilled.

Usually the marketing plan will aim for growth. The international marketing plan should incorporate the anticipated planned phases of expansion, and emphasize the methods to be used to achieve the desired growth. For example, initial entry requires establishing appropriate channels of distribution, such as agents and distributors, to support export activity. Local market expansion might need marketing to focus on promoting a particular message using above-the-line media such as television and the press as well as 'below the line' sponsorship and public relations. Global rationalization could be undertaken by concentrating on cost cutting throughout the operations to achieve more competitive prices.

Whatever the level of international expansion, an international marketing plan has to be prepared. The marketing plan is a document that details the methods and tactics for attaining the strategic goals of the organization. It shows the actions needed to achieve the strategic objectives. Strategic plans usually have long-term vision, providing direction for the organization for upwards of two, three, four or five years ahead. Marketing plans most commonly run on a one-year time scale with provisional guidelines for the subsequent years two and three. Usually marketing plans are prepared on an annual cycle that fits the firm's financial accounting year. Moreover, most international marketing plans are developed based on the planning modes.

Retailers pushing for positions in the global markets

The £6.7 billion bid for Asda by Wal-Mart announced on 14 June 1999 was a huge threat both to British supermarkets and the rest of Europe's retailing elite. Wal-Mart's acquisition of Asda at a time when retailers had caught globalization fever was a surprise to many competitors. Retailers lag behind most manufacturers in the process of globalization but this is not a problem for most retailers. Retailers have continued to increase their global activities: for example, Royal Ahold, a Dutch supermarket operator, bought supermarkets in Poland, four rival chains in Spain, one in America and two in Argentina *Economist*, June 1999).

Similarly, France's leading hypermarket, Carrefour, which is already in 20 markets, has opened stores in Chile, Colombia, Indonesia and the Czech Republic. It is also developing its presence in Japan. Tesco, Britain's largest food retailer, has set up stores in South Korea, making it its sixth overseas market. And Promodes, another French hypermarket group, has become the market leader in Argentina.

Meanwhile fast-growing clothes chains, such as The Gap, Sweden's Hennes and Mauritz (H&M), which operates in 12 markets, and Spain's Zara, which now operates in 17 countries, are rapidly expanding into new countries. Despite these increasing interests in globalization, retailers seem to be finding it hard to make a success of the transition from national to multinational. Although IKEA, a Swedish furniture retailer, has done well, many other established international retailers still make most of their money and their highest return in their domestic markets (*Economist* 1999). Carrefour's operating margins in France are more than 6 per cent of sales, whereas after operating internationally for 30 years, it still loses money in much of Asia, Latin America and even some parts of Europe. Meanwhile, Wal-Mart, which first went abroad in 1991, makes a return on capital of 5.8 per cent on its international business, far lower than in America (*Economist* 1999).

In the light of low return on capital, can retailers justify globalization of their business? One reason for scepticism is that retailers are being driven by slow growth in their domestic market as much as by the sight of opportunities abroad. The small size of the Swedish market encouraged several of the country's retailers to move overseas as early as the 1970s. A few, such as IKEA and H&M, have built strong global businesses, although they have taken years to do so. French retailers, such as Carrefour and Auchan, have gone into emerging markets to escape the constraints of planning laws. And Wal-Mart, which is still producing sales growth in America, is going abroad partly because it already has a dominant share of the country's market.

Types of planning mode

In moving towards a contingency approach to planning it is necessary to have some dimensions of planning with which to work; here we adopt some of the dimensions developed in the multinational corporation context. Some planning modes are relatively simple, whereas others involve many complex activities. Planning processes may adopt a short, medium or long-term time horizon, where short-term is one year or less, medium (intermediate) from one to five years, and long-term five years or more.

Another distinction in planning mode is internal or external orientation. With an internal orientation the bulk of planning information is sought within the organization. Traditional year-to-year budgeting relies on data available inside the organization, and is thus a basic form of internally oriented planning that is common to many institutions. More contemporary strategic planning modes look outside the organization and take external factors (such as demographic trends, industry developments, competitors and political trends) into account in addition to analysing internal strengths and weaknesses. The most commonly used planning modes are identified on pages 221–2 and depicted in Table 7.1.

Shorter-range planning

For the purposes of this chapter budgeting represents a planning mode where revenues and costs are projected up to one year into the future based on some adjustments to the prior period's figures. This category includes incremental approaches to budgeting. Strategy implementation oriented planning is characterized by a focus on implementation factors (such as reward systems, communication, action plans, information systems and culture) to promote commitment to mutually agreed organizational goals (Tennant and Roberts 2001).

Medium-range planning

In this comprehensive planning mode, revenues and costs are projected up to one or two years into the future based on an analysis of expected international marketing activities. While some external factors, like interest rates and simple customer demand, have a bearing here, the sources of information used in the planning process are predominantly internal to the organization. Programme budgeting and zero-based budgeting are examples of this type of planning. In strategic planning, medium-term forecasts and analyses of environmental opportunities and organizational capabilities are used to frame activities to compete within the bounds of the organization's mission. Scenario-based planning, where alternative sets of future trends and events are predicted (usually by experts), is usually included in this time frame. While intra-organizational changes, like R&D breakthroughs and losses of key personnel, may affect scenarios, these planning processes tend to focus outside the organization.

Longer-range planning

Longer-range planning modes are typically based on forecasts exceeding five years. Capital budgeting is a project evaluation method based on predicted cash flows, tax rates, depreciation, and discount rates over the life of international marketing projects. Most of the information for capital budgeting is available from within the organization. Long-range planning is where expected business activities are based on three to ten-year forecasts of the business and its environment.

An international marketing plan

A marketing plan sets out to provide a framework for the proposed marketing to take place. It identifies the objectives of the plan together with the methods and resources to implement it. Table 7.1 covers some of the topics typically detailed in a marketing plan. For international marketing planning, firms extend the traditional marketing plan to the international arena. Such plans start by defining the firm's business mission and strategic objectives, showing the strategic direction in which the firm wishes to move. The plan proceeds to analyse the environment in which the firm operates, showing the external influences on the firm. The environmental analysis examines the political, legal, economic, social and technological influences on the firm's activities. At this time competitor activity within the market is assessed and the firm's competitive position is ascertained. The firm's business mission, strategic objectives, the environmental analysis and the competitive position provide the framework for assessing strengths, weaknesses, opportunities and threats (SWOT) within the market.

Table 7.1   Structure and contents of a typical marketing plan

Business mission	Mission statement encompassing the whole organization, often following a general goal, e.g., 'to be the market leader'.
Corporate objectives	Specifics of business mission statement. Objectives are usually given in quantifiable terms, e.g. to achieve 'X' turnover and 'Y' profit, or 'Z' increase on previous year's performance. Supporting qualitative objectives may also be used, e.g. to increase product quality profile among customers.
Environmental audit	Market environment in which the firm operates in terms of political (including legal), economic, social and technological (PEST) environmental issues.
Marketing audit	Analyses competitor activity, providing the relative position of the organization within the total market. It assesses internal strengths and weaknesses, and external opportunities and threats.
Market analysis	Assessment of market size, trends and segments; regional and local market characteristics; seasonal variations in sales, etc.
Marketing objectives and major strategies	Definition of objective indicates achievement forecasts in terms of increased sales, customer awareness, channel coverage for the product or service, etc. Corporate strategies relate to the analyses of environmental and marketing audits discussed above.
Marketing programmes and tactics	Implementation of marketing tactics to achieve the strategic objectives through the marketing mix.
Market information analysis	Discovery of market gaps, new markets/segments, customer characteristics, etc. It incorporates a marketing information system (MIS), marketing research methodology and implementation including selection of marketing research agency if appropriate.
Marketing mix	Favoured combination of product, price, promotion and channels of distribution approaches.

Table 7.1 continued	
Product	Assessment of product characteristics, range, features; sales trends, performance history and planned developments. Competitive analysis and advantage.
Pricing	Assessment of positioning strategy, customer perceived values. Competitive analysis and advantage.
Promotion	Assessment of media advertising, direct mail, special promotions, exhibitions, public relations and measurement of communication effectiveness. Competitive analysis and advantage.
Channels of distribution (covered by the term 'place')	Assessment of channel strategy, channel selection; selling strategy, sales plan and sales force organization. Competitive analysis and advantage.
Resources	Constraints within which plan has to operate
Finance	Marketing budget, revenue and gross margin forecast, target marketing ratios and cash flow projection.
Time	Scheduling of proposed marketing activities within the plan (often using a Gantt chart).
Human resources	Personnel requirements for plan

The resource constraints are also considered, including finance, human resources and time available to reach the defined goals. The plan provides an assessment of the firm's internal strengths and weaknesses as well as those of its competitors. Internal strengths and weaknesses relate to internal operational and organizational factors such as product characteristics, management expertise, research capability and financial position. External strengths and weaknesses concern the firm's performance relative to its competitors.

The plan should also consider the internal and external opportunities and threats facing the firm. Opportunities may relate to issues ranging from new product developments and new markets to mergers and acquisitions. Threats can include an assessment of the firm's vulnerability to over-extending resources through extensive geographical coverage, dependence on importing agents, lack of transferability of products and services to new markets and so forth.

The marketing plan seeks to show where opportunities for expansion occur as well as any threats that may be encountered. Awareness of these issues provides a framework for management to implement an action plan to optimize the opportunities and minimize the associated risks.

Traditionally, international marketing plans have followed the theoretical framework of a firm's international growth taking place in incremental steps. Initial plans detailed proposed marketing operations in one country. As expansion occurred, they were extended to encompass other countries. Typically international marketing plans for smaller firms have shown this type of incremental growth. However many firms, especially larger organizations, have established international, even global, operations. In these cases the international marketing plan is much more extensive, often being a combination of national plans that fit the corporate strategy. These large firms have passed the initial market entry stages of the newcomer and have established marketing operations in the countries concerned.

In a large firm, usually management operating within each country, or territory, prepares its own marketing plan. The plans have to fit the corporate strategic plan and to be agreed with central management. Considerable negotiation between all parties may be required before the plans are accepted. The mission, the strategic goals and objectives will be common for all concerned, but the method of implementing the goals may differ. For example, in the case of the global detergent supplier Unilever, the marketing plan used in Chile or Canada, while similar, is likely to differ in detail from the marketing plan used in Hong Kong or the United Kingdom. But the country plans will fit into the overall corporate plan.

A further complication in international planning is the potential for rapid international expansion using IT. With the support of IT, especially the increased use of the Internet and its associated services, firms can internationalize their operations almost instantaneously, should they so desire. Firms starting to market their products and services can reach many customers directly through the Internet. Since most of the developed world and many parts of the less developed economies have access to the Internet, there is the potential for global coverage at the early stages of international expansion. The major constraint, apart from customer access to the Internet, is the limitation of logistics support for the product or service to reach the consumer, as is particularly evident at peak demand periods such as Christmas.

Increasingly, international marketing planning incorporates extensive use of the Internet as a communication channel alongside conventional international expansion approaches. Indeed, some firms concentrate entirely on using the Internet, almost to the exclusion of the conventional marketing mix. Firms such as amazon.com and easyJet.com develop their marketing mix in terms of the product/service, promotion and pricing tactics in response to customer demand, as evident through their use of websites. In this way, the market planning process is increasingly used to consider cross-border international expansion on a shorter and more extensive scale than had previously been practicable.

Strategic planning in the international context

This section focuses on three strategic perspectives: the external environment, the creation of competitive advantage and the process of change.

- **External environment** – an understanding of market dynamics should be appreciated in order to align the firm correctly to changing circumstances. From this point of view, superior strategies are ones that create advantageous situations in the present circumstances. This approach tends to overlook the importance of internal factors.
- **Competencies** – focuses on the creation of competitive advantage through the acquiring and exploitation of specific resources and capabilities. Strategic positioning, and ultimately success, is dependent on the use of resources to exploit (external) opportunities. However, it is not always clear that an appreciation of external factors and the presence of the best resources and capabilities will ultimately lead to success.

- **Changes in organization** – looks at the process of change and the organizational context in which it takes place. This tends to be more complex to appreciate than the other two approaches, as it looks at the interaction between external and internal factors that can enable or constrain effective strategic responses.

The process approach tends to be more difficult to use as it offers few prescriptions on how to achieve superior international marketing performance. It is possible to be selective in the approach to explaining strategy – to take the view that taking the best from each perspective will produce a superior approach – but it may not be easy to merge what might be regarded as three different approaches.

Following Brock and Barry (2003), it is helpful to draw up a number of informing principles that can guide the review of international marketing strategy:

- Internal or external issues cannot be seen in isolation from one another. It would be difficult to find organizations that were pulled solely by external factors or pushed purely by internal ones.
- There is no perfect management solution to the strategy problem. Each firm is unique and solutions have to be found to the challenges it faces.
- Time and space must be taken into account when looking at strategy. For example, how does the past influence the present and what factors are currently making their presence felt?

The meaning of strategy

Strategic *management* can be viewed as a set of theories, frameworks, tools and techniques designed to explain the factors underlying the performance of organizations and to assist managers in thinking, planning and acting strategically. In simple terms, it is a vehicle through which a marketing firm can review past performance and, more importantly, determine future actions geared towards achieving and sustaining superior performance. Strategic *planning* on the other hand centres on the setting of organizational objectives, as well as developing and implementing plans designed to achieve these objectives.

Rather unfortunately, strategic planning is often associated with a highly prescriptive approach to strategic management (Mintzberg 1995). In many situations a prescriptive or deliberate approach will be inappropriate. While the uncertainty of the modern marketing environment means that detailed and prescriptive long-term planning may be of little value, some form of broad long-term planning, related to strategic thinking and vision, is necessary if strategic intent is to be translated into action. Thus, planning is an important aspect of most management definitions of strategy, with a focus on rational planning. More specifically, Mintzberg point out that definitions of strategy assume that an organization's strategy is always the outcome of internal planning, whereas strategies can actually emerge without much spur from a formal planning approach.

From this point of view, strategy is also about what a company *actually does* rather than merely what it *intends to do*. The difference is between intended strategies (those that are planned), and emergent strategies (those that start as unplanned activities). In practice, emergent strategies can come from anywhere in the organization, as middle managers and others can develop strategies of this nature that may well help to fulfil the objectives far better than an intended strategy. Managers must also be able to recognize when an emergent strategy is potentially dysfunctional (and move to kill it off), and when it is functional and needs to be promoted. A good knowledge of the model of strategic management is essential for understanding intended strategies, but this also applies to emergent strategies that have at some point to be given approval and resources allocated. This can be broken down into the components shown in Figure 7.4, with the traditional approach stressing that a step-by-step approach is required, moving from the determination of the mission through to implementation and review of progress made.

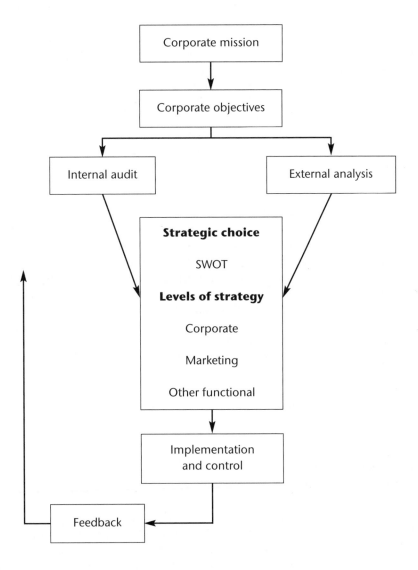

Figure 7.4   A conceptual model of strategic management

The significance of the approach in Figure 7.4 for firm internationalization is that a move of such significance must be the result of an intended strategy. Based on the components of Figure 7.4, the mission provides the context within which intended strategies are formulated and against which emergent strategies can be evaluated. Objectives for the organization focus on profitability and increasing shareholders' funds, with other objectives taking a lesser priority.

The main purpose of external analysis is to identify opportunities and threats in the organization's operating environment. The problem here is to determine the horizons for such a review. The broadest overview can be structured using a PEST (political, economic, social and technological) approach. The main problem is that such a wide-ranging view may give little in the way of actionable opportunities, so a narrowing of the scope of the analysis can be undertaken by looking at the specific competitive environment of the organization. Internal analysis will help in identifying the company's strengths and weaknesses.

Strategic choice entails the generating of a series of strategic alternatives against which the company can compare itself through SWOT analysis. The alternatives have to be evaluated, and the best choice made. It is during implementation and control that many organizations find the greatest difficulty, as the skills required for implementation differ from those required to identify the most appropriate strategy. This part of the process can involve changing structures, reviewing systems and procedures, working across functions and a whole range of other activities that can support the chosen strategy.

The role of strategic planning

Strategic planning provides a framework into which each operating plan of the corporation can be integrated so that the entire multinational corporation operates as efficiently as possible everywhere in the world. Major international marketing decisions have to be made about the allocation of limited resources so that firms can take the greatest advantage of opportunities and gain a competitive advantage over opponents. Those firms that adopt a comprehensive or international marketing strategy seem to enjoy economic and strategic advantages over locally oriented firms.

There are some areas basic to all MNCs for which planning should be formulated:

- methods of entering foreign markets
- growth – internal development
- geographical diversification
- product diversification
- product portfolio optimization
- foreign exchange risk management
- human resource development
- organization structure.

Usually, strategic planning begins with an assessment of the external environment. Based on an analysis of host country economic and social policy, international marketing planners try to determine the degree of risk that they are likely to encounter on both the macro and micro levels.

There are usually many reasons firms decide to operate internationally. Perhaps a recession in their domestic market means they have under-used resources that can be used for an international market. A competitive advantage may have been developed from the firm's products, markets and resources, so products can be tried in international markets because of some unique advantage that they possess. Knowledge of a market often pushes a firm into international endeavours. Knowledge can be objective (facts and figures concerning a country and the target market), and experiential (an understanding of the 'reality' of the situation). The first type of knowledge can be bought; the second type has to be acquired, which means that investment has to be made. Shifting firms towards a more international outlook is, therefore, difficult to achieve if they have been focusing their efforts over many years on their domestic market.

Investing in the international marketing process takes time, and means that a long-term view and long-term commitment have to be given to it. Another factor that will influence the likelihood of a firm considering internationalization or other involvement in international markets is the influence of the key decision maker in moving a company's thinking away from a domestic bias towards a perception of opportunities elsewhere (Porter 2001). Equally important is the consideration of the importance of services to support the product: the more of these that are required, the more complex the relationship between buyer and seller, reducing the interest in international marketing. In short, the chances of a firm considering international opportunities will be influenced by, amongst other issues (Price 2003):

- its history
- the attitude of its senior managers
- the nature and scope of its products
- the nature and geographical coverage of the markets
- its perceived international competitive advantage.

Encouraging firms to move into international markets is not so straightforward a task as simply providing information or seeking out opportunities.

Company growth

If the survival of the firm is seen to come from expansion, then opportunities will be sought to achieve this. This is usually the case when market fluctuations are increasing and insecurity causes managers to seek new markets for the firm's products. This is often seen as a rather paradoxical problem for government, which wishes to create macro-economic stability but wishes also to see dynamic markets (in other words, markets characterized by change and uncertainty). In countries like the United Kingdom and the Netherlands, where exporting is a key component of economic growth, creating favourable conditions for this to occur is rather problematic.

Resources, including management, impose a restriction on growth. Attitudes of managers, and the perceptions they have formed of present and future market conditions, including opportunities for growth, are often critical. Keegan (2004) distinguishes between what he calls the 'dogmatic' or 'closed' cognitive style and an 'open-minded' one. Dogmatic managers are unlikely to adapt to a quickly changing situation, and will find difficulties with the complexity of the international marketplace. According to Keegan (2004), firms that, through their past experience and recruitment, have a high proportion of such managers are less likely to export. Open-minded managers tend to thrive in relatively unstructured situations, found particularly in international contexts. Such people tend to push for and exploit international opportunities for growth.

Open-minded managers, located in parts of the organization that can push for growth, will be able to influence the push into new international markets. They need to be supported, however, in more ways than just providing funds. Early setbacks in foreign markets are the norm, and commitment over the longer term is essential if the early steps in the market are to be successful.

A significant conclusion to be drawn from the literature on international marketing is that to be successful the strategic significance of such a move must be recognized. Moving into markets in an experimental or incremental way lacks the full support of the firm in the commitment of resources and the positive support of its personnel. 'Dogmatic' managers in this scenario have to be converted to the importance of the export or internationalization drive. Thus strategic planning and the push towards an international marketing approach go hand in hand. This does not suggest that there is a preferred approach, with the emphasis on the rational planning model, for instance, but that there must be a genuine and concerted effort to achieve growth by this means. Strategic approaches to internationalization also reinforce the long-term commitment required, rather than the opportunistic short-term excursion into overseas markets that many firms have undertaken.

Marketing and corporate strategy

The setting of goals and objectives that incorporate statements outlining the organization's commitment to the international marketplace is highly desirable. The mission statement should be amended so that it is clear the organization's future survival, growth and profitability depend on these activities. Mission statements are the embodiment of the organization's philosophy and self-image, providing guidelines for strategic planning. They often cover the way in which the mission will be achieved, and incorporate corporate responsibility and ethical issues, which are of increasing importance.

Figure 7.5 outlines the activities required after the mission and objectives and related issues have been resolved. It focuses on the range of activities that take place under the banner of corporate strategy and international marketing. Having clear objectives for international activities provides a clear direction for the organization and commits physical and human resources to its achievement. It also requires periodic review to establish how much progress has been achieved against the objectives. A definition of the business is also required, and that is as challenging an activity as the others that precede it. Managers are well advised to see how far the existing business definition is appropriate for other countries. In less developed markets , such as may be found in East European economies, demand may only just be emerging for a particular product or service; changes might therefore be required to broaden the appeal of the product. In other markets, the business definition will not be well suited to the market environment, so modifications are required to suit the conditions encountered.

A market-oriented approach must be pursued. Customer benefits, target segments and

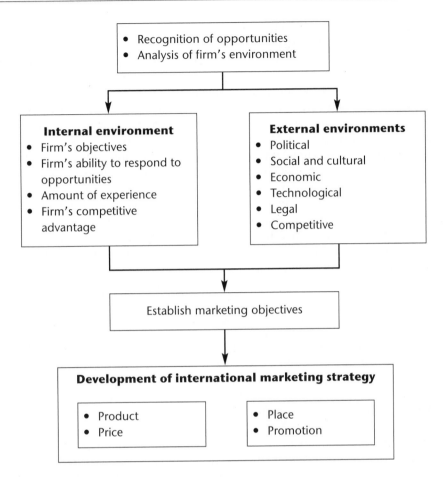

Figure 7.5   The international strategic planning process

the technology used to deliver the benefits can all be reviewed. What is being proposed is significant adaptation not just of the product, but of the whole process involved with its delivery. Customers' needs may be put in very different ways across different markets, taking into account the physical and business environment and the culture and attitudes of people.

The final aspect of the business definition, following the issues of customer benefits, segments and technology, is the value chain. As with all of these aspects, more detailed reviews are provided in subsequent chapters, but the value chain identifies a number of stages associated with bringing the product to the marketplace. This covers sourcing, R&D, production (upstream activities), and marketing, distribution and service (down-stream activities). A firm has to decide on the degree to which it should run all of these operations itself, or whether they can be contracted out or brought in. There are advantages and disadvantages to each approach. What is relevant here is that the entry into the international marketplace raises the questions afresh: the firm should not necessarily pursue the same value chain strategy in a foreign country as it does in its home market. If all of these aspects are taken together, the familiar ground of a business defined in the traditional way – as it is in the home market – should be thought through if a marketing-oriented approach is to be maintained.

The core competence of a firm is the specific skills and assets that support its competitive advantage. A core competence should provide access to a variety of markets, provide a contribution to perceived customer benefits, and be difficult to imitate. Applying this to the value chain might show how the skills associated with all aspects – say, delivery and customer service – can be turned to the advantage of the company by showing how certain activities can be performed better than its competitors.

The final aspect is the strategic thrust, which defines the area in which the firm seeks to compete, establishing priorities and determining the investment in resources necessary to achieve its goals. A further aspect to strategic thrust is the approach taken up in international markets, seeking either to obtain first-entry status or to follow others who have created or determined the market. Likewise, the company might choose to act aggressively or avoid confrontation by aiming for neutral markets. Associated with this is the means by which to enter a market with, for example, the need to achieve organic growth or growth by merger and acquisition.

General analysis of strategic options

There are a number of strategies on offer to the marketing manager looking to enter an international market. Some issues are dealt with elsewhere in this book, but a general outline of other issues related to the choice of strategic option is needed. The international competitive environment is complex and seemingly more volatile than the national market. Success comes from an examination of the environment before making the most appropriate response, while combining the appropriate product/market option for the chosen market is a key task. Again, as noted earlier, a marketing orientation is the adoption of an approach that can obtain competitive advantage for the firm by providing the most suitable product offering for the customer. The international marketing manager's task is to plan and carry out programmes that ensure (long-term) competitive advantage. The task has two components: to determine specific target markets, and to manage marketing mix elements that can meet their needs.

Selecting target markets

The characteristics of the target markets need to be appreciated and acted upon. It is usually recommended that the 'eight Os' model developed by Czinkota and Ronkainen (1993) is used for evaluation (see Table 7.2).

When looking at entering foreign markets, firms have to consider innovation strategies, as it is rarely the case that the existing product will serve the new market. The firm can innovate in three dimensions – product innovation, technological innovation and market innovation – revealing that the target market might require more than simply the adjustment of the product to suit local circumstances. Innovation on one dimension requires careful planning, but demands by the market for innovation on two or three dimensions produce a situation where the planning task becomes more complex. Analysing the eight 'Os' requires the marketer to adjust to the market, at least in the short

Table 7.2   The 'eight Os'

Occupants	The customers whose attitudes can be defined in a number of ways, by age, sex, psychographics (attitudes, interests and lifestyle) or by product-related variables such as usage and brand loyalty. This approach is more usually referred to as market segmentation, which focuses on the major influences on the occupants of a market through the decision process.
Objects	What is purchased to meet a certain need, which includes the physical object, service, ideas, places and persons.
Occasions	When the product is purchased.
Objectives	The motivation that underpin the purchase, whether tacitly acknowledged or not.
Outlets	Where a product can be purchased or information about it received.
Organizations	How the purchase or the acceptance of the need to purchase is organized. The focus is on the decision-making unit, which can vary from the small and informal, such as a family or household, up to the large and formal units found in businesses and the public sector.
Operations	Focus on the behaviour of the organization that is buying the product. An understanding of its behaviour helps identify how firms, such as supermarkets, decide to stock certain brands, and what barriers may be expected when trying to gain their acceptance of a new brand.
Opposition	Looks at the competition that is currently found in the market and what might be expected in the future in response to a new entrant. This is a difficult area for consideration as competition can be direct, such as those offering the same product, or products that serve the same need (such as alternative ways to spend leisure time), or can come from an unexpected quarter (as, for example, exists for newspapers when they are faced with competition from online information services).

Source: Czinkota and Ronkainen (1993).

term. The target market decision is critical, with three general options on offer: one segment is selected, a number of segments are chosen, or the whole market is targeted with an undifferentiated product.

Marketing management

The marketing mix elements can be tailored to the target market after the analysis of its characteristics and the target decision has been taken. The correct marketing mix, which consists of product, price, place and promotion (the 4Ps), mixes the elements together into a viable offering and is critical. Each element of the mix requires further planning, as for example with promotion, where the mix of advertising, sales promotion and public relations has to match the life cycle of the product, market sophistication and other variables. In order to provide for successful market entry, the marketing manager must understand the strategy and have been influential in its formulation, and work with other senior managers to ensure that the stages of analysis, planning, implementation and control are given due weight and consideration.

Control tools for international marketing planning

International marketing strategies should be turned into specific action programmes that answer the following questions: What will be done? When will it be done? Who is responsible for doing it? How much will it cost? For example, the international marketer may regard sales promotion as a key strategy for winning market share. A sales promotion action plan should be drawn up to outline special offers and their dates, trade shows entered, new point-of-purchase displays and other promotions. The action plans show when activities will be started, reviewed and completed.

Kotler (2003) identified four types of marketing control that could apply to international as well as national marketing, with each type involving different approaches, different purposes and different allocation of responsibilities (see Table 7.3).

Table 7.3   Types of international marketing control strategy

Control strategy	Responsibility	Purpose	Example of use
Performance control	Line and staff management Marketing controller	Improve the efficiency of marketing programmes	Sales force performance Advertising efficiency Distribution efficiency
Strategic control	Top management Middle managers	To examine whether planned results are being achieved	Marketing effectiveness ratings Marketing audit
Budget control	Marketing controller	To examine where the company is making or losing money	Profitability by product, customer group or trade channel
Annual plan control	Top management Middle managers	To examine whether planned results are being achieved	Sales analysis Market share analysis Market expenses to sales ratio Customer tracking

The purpose of annual plan control is to determine the extent to which marketing efforts over the year have been successful. This control evaluates and measures sales in relation to sales objectives, market share analysis and expense analysis. This is because sales performance is an important element in the annual plan.

Action plans allow the manager to make a supporting marketing budget that is essentially a projected profit and loss statement. For revenues, it shows the forecast number of units sold and the average net price. On the expense side, it shows the costs of production, distribution and marketing. The difference is the projected profit. Senior management will review the budget and either approve or modify personnel planning and marketing operations.

Marketing implementation

Planning good strategies is only a start towards successful marketing. A brilliant marketing strategy counts for little if the company fails to implement it properly. Marketing implementation is the process that turns marketing strategies and plans into marketing actions to order to accomplish them. Implementation involves day-to-day, month-to-month activities that effectively put the marketing plan to work. Whereas marketing planning addresses the what and why of marketing activities, implementation addresses who, where, when and how.

Successful implementation depends on several key elements. First, it requires an action programme that pulls all the people and activities together. Second, the company's formal organizational structure plays an important role in implementing international marketing strategy. The company's decision and reward systems – operating procedures that guide planning, budgeting, compensation and other activities – also affect implementation. For example, if a company compensates managers for short-run results, they will have little incentive to work towards long-term objectives. Effective implementation also requires careful human resources planning. At all levels, the company must fill its structure and systems with people who have the needed skills, motivation and personal characteristics. In recent years, more and more companies have recognized that long-run human resources planning can give the company a strong competitive advantage. An international marketing plan will need to be supported by a commitment to training and development of required international experience.

Finally, to be successfully implemented, the firm's marketing strategies must fit with its company culture. Company culture is a system of values and beliefs shared by people in an organization – the company's collective identity and meaning. International marketing strategies that do not fit the company's culture will be difficult to implement. Because company culture is so hard to change, companies usually design strategies that fit their current cultures, rather than trying to change their styles and cultures to fit new strategies. However, the speed of change today may force companies to be more market focused, leading many more to tackle the big challenge of culture change.

Monitoring action plans

Many surprises occur during the implementation of marketing plans, requiring the international marketer to practise ongoing marketing control. This involves evaluating the results of marketing strategies and plans and taking corrective action to ensure that objectives are attained. Performance in the marketplace is measured against objectives, and the causes of any differences between expected and actual performance are evaluated. Corrective action to close the gaps between objectives and result may require changing the marketing action programmes or even changing the objectives. The purpose of control is to ensure that the company achieves the sales, profits and other objectives set out in its international marketing plan.

Challenges to international marketing planning

Several weaknesses in international marketing planning are common among companies attempting international market expansion. Many international marketing plans lack market reality. International marketing managers and product managers are frequently too removed from the international marketplace to maintain a handle on what is really happening in fast-changing environments. This can be rectified with a commitment to extracting timely and relevant market information and use of appropriate interpretive tools. However, often this is hard to get in Asian countries and it is necessary to maintain an ongoing on-the-spot presence. Nothing beats face-to-face contact with intermediate and end-customers.

International marketing plans are often not integrated into the business and corporate hierarchy. This is because of a lack of clear vision, or understanding at various levels of how various product initiatives and functional strategies fit. Where there is a lot of planning done at each level there can be misunderstanding to the point where each level prepares different or conflicting plans, where one level's vision is translated to another level's objectives and then to a lower level's tasks or operations. This can be resolved with a clear strategic planning framework providing a logical fit for the initiatives at various levels. The framework provided earlier in this chapter is a useful starting point.

There is often a lack of financial integration with international marketing at the business strategy level. This is because the disciplines of financial analysis and marketing analysis have not been effectively brought together to develop business strategies. Financial analysts too frequently do not understand market realities and uncertainties, while marketing analysts have limited experience in evaluating the financial impacts of proposed international marketing strategies.

It is not wise to give too much emphasis to 'the plan' document, instead of the international marketing planning process. Team involvement in the international marketing planning process is often lacking in some organizations. Again, too much emphasis on the document occurs without attention to the planning process. In the end, a plan developed but not implemented because of a lack of support or understanding is a waste of resources. Those who need to support the plan, in teams of resource allocation or

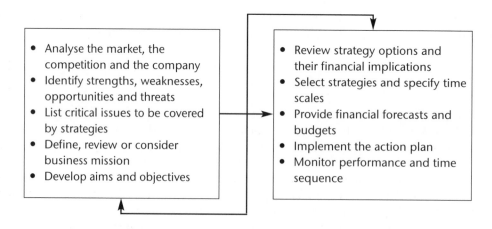

Figure 7.6   Alternative international marketing planning sequence

through implementation roles, need to be 'involved' and 'own' it in a commitment sense. This problem is endemic in organizations where objectives and priorities are unclear or conflicting divisional objectives are allowed to continue unresolved.

Traditional strategic planning does not take sufficient account of the role of key external relationships in improving competitive position. Strong relationships with key suppliers, distributors and alliance partners may lead to higher-quality products and services, and superior distribution or delivery systems. A series of systematic interrelated steps is crucial in effectively formulating and implementing international marketing strategies. This reduces the risk of leaving out key issues and people, and highlights the assumptions upon which strategies are based and resources committed.

In reality, organizations adopt a hybrid of management systems depending upon their size, diversity, position in the market, rate and type of external change. However, a generic series of steps in formulating and implementing international marketing strategies applies to all. In practice, the sequence will depend upon the organization's current position in the market. For instance, business mission and vision may be well established and require little development or review. If this is the case, they will act as the foundation from which other steps emanate. Alternatively, a company may become lost in a sea of change and need to establish its mission. It can do this through strategic analysis and a review of its broad objectives against reality. Figure 7.6 shows a different sequence of more detailed steps that would be relevant in this situation. The challenge is to develop proactive strategies in the light of expected changes and adaptive strategies to confront unexpected changes.

Implementation of the international marketing plan

International marketing plans form part of the strategic planning activity, usually undertaken on an annual cycle. The plan is a guideline that is agreed by all parties concerned: the strategic corporate planners at central head office and the operational managers within the organizational divisions. Theoretically, the plan can be revised, or modified, in agreement with all concerned, but such changes have to be justified. The annual plan provides goals, budgets and outline methods whereby these should be achieved, with those for the first few months usually being more detailed than for the later period. Indeed, it is often expected that as the planning year progresses new evidence will become available (such as sales performance) that leads to modification of the original plan. Some flexibility is required to encompass the latest market information (probably provided through the marketing information system). However, the fundamental strategic approach should remain, although the details of the methods used to implement the strategy may be modified to suit local conditions.

All concerned in the marketing operation are expected to work to the agreed plan. The methods used, as identified by the proposed marketing mix and the resources made available, should match the plan. During the planning cycle, usually at monthly intervals, the actual performance is compared with predictions made in the plan. Any discrepancies are monitored and minor adjustments made to the plan to ensure the goals are achieved. Towards the end of the planning cycle, a review panel often assesses how well actual performance matched the plan. Lessons learned from this analysis should be carried forward to the next year's international marketing plan.

Summary

This chapter has considered the nature and role of the international marketing plan. It discusses how the plan is prepared and used within international marketing. International marketing plans are tools to implement corporate strategy, being a formal proposal of the marketing tactics required to achieve the goals of the organization. They should reflect the theoretical process of international expansion, traditionally taken to be growth by incremental steps. They should also encompass IT developments that can help marketing implementation.

Typically, international marketing plans set out the organization's strategies, mission statement and objectives. They analyse the market conditions that exist in terms of the environment and competitor activity. They consider firms' strategic and marketing options and select the preferred marketing approaches for the organization concerned. An international marketing information system is used to provide the data for marketing decision making.

The international marketing plan aims to provide a framework for implementing marketing tactics, covering approaches to product development, pricing, promotion and distribution. The plan identifies the financial, human and time-scheduling resource implications of the recommended actions.

Usually, international marketing plans are derived through a process of combining individual national (and even regional) marketing plans into a corporate plan. Such plans have to be agreed by all the parties concerned to be effective, a process that can take considerable management skill to effect. It is this skill that is necessary for the successful implementation of international marketing across national borders.

Revision questions

1 International organizations that plan their approaches and devise appropriate strategies are more likely to be successful than those that do not. Discuss.
2 The task of identifying the optimum positioning in a foreign market is very difficult and requires extensive research into several aspects of the market. What are these aspects?
3 The understanding of the international business environment will likely influence the international marketing performance of the firm. Evaluate and discuss these factors.
4 Environmental characteristics in international markets are likely to moderate the operational performance of multinational corporations. Evaluate his statement with suitable examples
5 Outline the procedures to be followed in developing an international marketing plan from consideration of the product to preparation of the budget.
6 What are the main challenges to international marketing planning?
7 Distinguish between the international marketing and corporate strategy.
8 Mission statements are the embodiment of the organization's philosophy and self-image, and provide guidelines for strategic planning. Discuss with suitable examples.
9 What are the key elements that determine successful implementation of an international marketing plan?
10 Evaluate the notion that the traditional strategic planning does not take sufficient account of the role of key external relationships in improving competitive position.

The strategic planning process at Akout plc

Akout plc is a Nigerian company, part of a multinational corporation operating in more than 20 countries throughout the world. This case study offers a glimpse into the complex world of organizations, groups and individuals. It allows students to investigate the behaviours and characteristics of this phenomenon in a holistic manner. The case study originally formed part of a broader study of the corporate strategic planning process. It was designed to be exploratory and descriptive in nature, specifically exploring the components and contextual elements of Akout's strategic planning process in Nigeria. In addition, it showed that not everybody in the organization was happy with the planning process and that some people are usually resistant to planning processes.

Akout plc had only created a separate strategic planning department in the two years before the study took place. Previously, planning was a decentralized activity, coordinated through the financial control and budget department. It was recognized by senior management that 'planning' was more than simply budgets, and the decision was made to create a strategic planning and development department. This was to be responsible for obtaining information from both revenue-generating departments and expense creation departments. It would also conduct external environmental research independent of other departments. All this information would be consolidated and analysed in order to create a strategic plan for the entire organization. The planning department was also charged with the more informal goal of improving planning activities in the organization. Specifically, this meant reducing the overall resistance to planning, and creating an atmosphere more conducive to planning activities.

Given these two goals of the department, we can see two of the contextual elements identified earlier: resources allocated to the planning function and resistance to planning. Since this was a fairly new department, a great many resources had been allocated to its start-up and continued operation. It has a staff of ten and a budget of 1 per cent of company sales. Top management was heavily involved in planning activities through the auspices of this department. This also translated into time allocated by managers to planning activities, with some indicating that one-third of their week was spent on planning alone. This focus on planning had been evident in the organization for many years, but the creation of the planning department made planning an even more salient activity. The top management team stressed the importance of allocating sufficient resources to the strategic planning department to ensure its success.

The second goal of this department was to create an environment conducive to planning activities. This meant reducing the level of resistance to planning in the organization. The majority of staff were not enthusiastic about planning. Many complained about the amount of time they spent on planning activities, and the lack of support from top management for planning. A typical comment from some staff was, 'They expect us to do all this planning and do our regular jobs.' As can be seen from this statement, planning was seen by many as being external to normal work activities. The strategic planning department was created to combat this attitude; it made planning more visible and was seen as having great top management support.

Prior to the creation of the department, 'town hall' type meetings were held to introduce the planning personnel and stress the importance of planning to all organizational members. The department was thus seen as being closely associated with the top management team, and top management was seen as being more involved with all planning activities, not just signing the final document.

In most cases Akout plc paid close attention to past performance. Managers reviewed their strategic planning quarterly to see if they were on target, and compared it continuously to the previous strategic plan. They then spent a great deal of time discussing and explaining variances to previous plans or the current plan. The variances were tracked to the department, group or individual with responsibility for those plans, which led to creation of mini-plan teams. These informal teams included organization members from various functional areas that had responsibility for plans within the overall company strategic plan. This meant that a variance of the original plan, which had to be explained, was taken care of by one of these mini-plan teams. Often a variance was a combination of revenue-generating and expense-creation activities; therefore an explanation of the variance would include input from both revenue-generating and expense-creating departments.

Integration of the functions began during the formation of the strategic plan. The entire purpose of the strategic planning department was to consolidate and coordinate the information collected and analysed by the many functional areas in the organization. It ensured that each revenue-generating department was included in the forecasting of revenues for the company. It also drew in all expense creation departments when developing their expense numbers. All departments were included in capital forecasting, environmental analysis (both competitive and general) and capabilities inventory. These activities all make up two of the components of the strategic planning process: attention to internal facets, and functional coverage and integration.

As mentioned, all functional areas of the firm were involved in an external environmental analysis. For some areas this included just the gathering of information relative to their department, but for others such as the marketing and sales department, it involved the collection, consolidation and analysis of information relative to their department and the organization as a whole. It was the responsibility of the strategic planning department to conduct the environmental scanning and analysis activities for the entire organization.

The final contextual element is the use of planning techniques by the organization. Akout plc used a variety of planning and budgetary techniques including activity-based costing, some financial models developed by its profit analysis department, and scenario techniques. The four-year strategic planning numbers were gathered using a software package developed by the organization's computer department. This package allowed all individuals to forecast revenue and expense numbers based on a variety of scenarios.

The strategic planning process at Akout plc has demonstrated, to varying degrees, the components and contextual elements. The resistance to planning, resources provided to planning, and functional coverage elements were seen as being most important to the organization. Attention to internal and external facets was seen as necessary and was taken for granted as part of the process. This can also be said for the various planning techniques in use.

Seminar questions

1 Discuss the strategy employed by Akout plc in implementing its strategic planning process and comment on its planning techniques.
2 What do you consider to be the main reasons for internal resistance to planning at Akout plc?
3 If you were the person in charge of planning at Akout plc, how would you measure the effectiveness of this plan?

Managerial assignment task

Marketing plans lie at the heart of a company's money-making activities. The techniques for developing and monitoring marketing plans are therefore an essential skill that all marketing executives need. Marketing plans for domestic and international markets are prepared by using a logical approach that provides a framework which can be used to adjust the planning detail to suit individual projects.

The importance of each step and the detail of what is actually proposed will vary according to the nature of the product: whether consumable or consumer durables, whether industrial consumable or industrial capital, whether new or established brand. Nevertheless, the approach can be adapted to all types of marketing situations. The following approach to international marketing planning is usually recommended:

1 Evaluate the product and the factors, internal to the company and external in the environment and the market, that are critical to its success.
2 Identify the market characteristics, and then evaluate the opportunities to establish the market share needed to break even with the project.
3 Set realistic objectives and timescales.
4 Devise strategies to achieve these objectives.
5 Construct action programmes for the relevant elements of the marketing mix.
6 Integrate these programmes into a coordinated marketing plan and develop the budget.
7 Prepare to monitor progress and effectiveness of each part of the mix programme.
8 Adjust the programme to get back on course or to meet changing conditions if need be.

A multinational corporation selling computer hardware to several countries in Africa employs you as an export marketing manager. Using the approach suggested above, prepare a suitable marketing plan for selling your company's computers to South Africa. Your marketing plan must include steps 1 to 8 as above and should not be more than 2,000 words.

References

Brock, D. and Barry, D. (2003) 'What if planning were really strategic? Exploring the strategy–planning relationship in multinationals', *International Business Review*, Vol. 12, pp. 543–61.

Brock, D. M., Barry, D. and Thomas, D. C. (2000) '"Your forward is our reverse, your right, our wrong": rethinking multinational planning processes in light of national culture', *International Business Review*, Vol. 9, No. 6, pp. 687–701.

Campbell, A. and Alexander, M. (1997) 'What's wrong with strategy?' *Harvard Business Review*, Vol.75, No. 6, pp. 42–51.

Chae, M. S. and Hill, J. S. (2000) 'Determinants and benefits of global strategic marketing planning formality', *International Marketing Review*, Vol. 17, No. 6. pp. 538–62.

Courtney, H., Kirkland, J. and Viguerie, P. (1997) 'Strategy under uncertainty', *Harvard Business Review*, Vol. 75, No. 6, pp. 66–79.

Czinkota, M. R. and Ronkainen, I. A. (1993) *International Marketing*, New York: Dryden Press.

Dupuis, M. and Prime, N. (1996) 'Business distance and global retailing: a model for analysis of key success/failure factors', *International Journal of Retail & Distribution Management*, Vol. 24, No.

11, pp. 30–8.

Economist (1999) 'Shopping all over the world (global retail outlets)', 19 June.

Evans, J., Treadgold, A. and Mavondo, F. T. (2000) 'Psychic distance and the performance of international retailers: a suggested theoretical framework', *International Marketing Review*, Vol. 17, No. 4/5, pp. 373–-91.

Hollensen, S. (2001) *Global Marketing: A Market-Responsive Approach*, 2nd edn, Harlow: Financial Times/Prentice Hall.

Johnson, G. and Scholes, K. (2002) *Exploring Corporate Strategy*, New York: Prentice Hall.

Keegan, W. J. (2004) 'Strategic marketing planning: a twenty-first century perspective', *International Marketing Review*, Vol. 21, No. 1, pp. 13–16.

Kotler, P. (2003) *Marketing Management*, 11th edn,, New Jersey: Prentice Hall.

Kotler, P. (2006) *Marketing Management*, 12th edn, New Jersey: Prentice Hall.

Mintzberg, H. (1995) 'Crafting strategy', in H. Mintzberg, J. B. Quinn and S. Ghoshal, *The Strategy Process*, European edn., Englewood Cliffs, N.J.: Prentice Hall.

O'Grady, S. and Lane, H. (1996) 'The psychic distance paradox', *Journal of International Business Studies*, Vol. 27, No.2, pp. 309–33.

Omar, O. (1999) *Retail Marketing*, London: Financial Times/Pitman.

Porter, M. E. (2001) 'Strategy and the Internet', *Harvard Business Review*, March, pp. 63–78.

Price, A. D. F (2003) 'The strategy process within large construction organizations', *Engineering, Construction and Architectural Management*, Vol. 10, No. 4, pp. 283–96.

Simkin, L. (2002) 'Barriers impeding effective implementation of marketing plans: a training agenda', *Journal of Business and Industrial Marketing*, Vol. 17, No.1, pp. 8–24.

Tennant, C. and Roberts, P. (2001) 'Hoshin Kanri: implementing the catch ball process', *Long Range Planning*, Vol. 34, No.3, pp. 287–308.

8

Product and Brand Decisions for International Marketing

Contents

LEARNING OBJECTIVES

After reading this chapter you should:

- understand the attributes of a product and its relevance to the international marketplace
- know how products reach international markets and the factors that determine the adoption of products by consumers in the foreign markets
- be able to examine specific

marketing strategies employed for marketing products in the international market environment
- be able to evaluate whether products should be standardized or modified for international marketing.
- understand the complexities of branding in the international markets.

Introduction

International marketing success depends on how satisfied international consumers are with the firm's product and service offering. One of the reasons that the majority of companies initially develop international markets is to generate new market opportunities or increase demand for an existing product. The product, in this case, must be seen as a bundle of satisfactions providing consumers not just with products but with satisfying experiences in terms of the benefits they provide rather than the functions the products perform. These concepts are particularly important in international marketing, because, for example, the growth of such international consumer products such as McDonald's and Coca-Cola cannot be attributable only to a distinctive taste. As Doole and Lowe (2004) identified, much of the success of McDonald's can be attributed to the aspirations of international customers to be part of the American way of life, 'the McDonald's culture', by deriving satisfaction from a close association with the product and the brand.

In understanding how products can provide satisfying experiences and benefits for people, it is necessary to clearly identify and understand the motivations of the target consumers and not make assumptions about them. In this chapter the focus is on some of the key aspects and recent trends of international product policy. It considers the changes in the nature of products offered individually and within a portfolio, their relationship with the market, and how new products can be developed. This chapter reviews the firm's decisions regarding product and brand management, the international product life cycle, product standardization for international marketing, and new product introductions into the international markets.

The nature of the product in international markets

A product is a collection of attributes including physical, service and symbolic aspects, which yield satisfaction to the consumer. A product can also be defined in relation to the different marketplaces in which it is sold (de Burca et al. 2004):

- **Local products** have potential in only one market.
- **International products** have potential to be extended from the domestic market to a number of international markets.
- **Multinational products** are those offered to many international markets but which are adapted to suit the needs of each market.
- **Global products** are those designed to meet the needs of market segments that are the same throughout the world.

According to Kotler (2006), a product is usually considered in a narrow sense as something tangible that can be described in terms of its shape, dimensions, colour and form. This misunderstanding of the true nature of a product could apply in international marketing, and many consumers may have the idea that a product only refers to a physical item. A product may include intangible items, for example an insurance service, civil service, shipping and tourism. In some countries, such as Kenya, one of the largest earners of export income is tourism, which is an intangible product. Thus, the actual product offering to the international market consists of both tangible and intangible features, the totality of which is a satisfaction received by consumers.

This satisfaction can be appreciated by grouping the elements of a product into the core benefits of the basic product, the expected product, the augmented product and the potential product. All of this categorization may need to be altered when marketed in international marketplace. These product categories are defined as (Kotler 2006):

- **The core benefit** consists of the fundamental benefit or service that the customer is really buying.
- **The basic product** is the item actually purchased and its functional features.
- **The expected product** is the attributes and conditions that the buyer expects to receive when purchasing the product and may also include the styling, the packaging, the quality, the brand name and the trademark.
- **The augmented product** consists of items that exceed customer expectation. This may involve repairs and maintenance, installation, the instruction booklet, delivery, warranty, spare parts and credit facilities.
- **The potential product** concept embraces the possible augmentations and transformations that the product might undergo in the future: for example, a new edition of a book.

When the product is intended for international markets, each of these aspects may need to be modified to suit the requirement of the foreign customers. Such product adaptation and/or modification might be for:

- Competitive reasons – for example, when some other person, or organization has already registered the brand name.
- Legal reasons – when the manufacturer is required to show weights and volume in imperial measures.
- Linguistic reasons – when dealing with a bilingual market, for example, English and French in Canada, where instructions must be in both languages.
- Fiscal reasons – the product might be changed to make it eligible for a different tariff classification and lower rate of duty.
- Cultural reasons – when the colour of packaging needs to be changed because it denotes the colour of, for example, evil or death in that culture.
- Economic reasons – when consumers in the international market cannot afford the product in its current form.
- Political reasons – when the nature of the items sold requires content declaration because of government regulation.

The question of what product to sell in foreign markets is the essence of product policy in international marketing. International marketing operation would be simple, of course, if a firm's products and product lines were identical in all countries. However, most multinational companies are forced to modify both products and product lines to suit different markets. Since companies cannot usually extend their domestic products automatically into foreign markets, they face a critical question in international marketing: how can they adapt, develop or acquire the products appropriate to foreign markets? The following section tries to answer this question by looking at international product development and strategies.

International product policy

A good product plan requires information on how customers' expectations will change within the time covered by the plan. Information is also needed on:

- what competitors are doing
- how the company stands in relation to its competitors
- the current state of technology in areas vital to the product
- the feasibility of ideas for product changes to meet the needs of customers.

All the information must be processed so that the planned development of products takes place in harmony with the company's marketing concept, strategy and goals. The list of desired product changes must also be set against product development demand in the form of resources and investments.

When firms first go international, they usually market their domestic products with minimal adaptation to foreign conditions. Another approach is to acquire a foreign firm which has products designed for its own market. Either of these approaches may be satisfactory as an initial method of getting products for foreign markets. For the long term, however, a more sophisticated business and product development plan is desirable. In its planning process, the firm must decide what businesses and what markets it wants to pursue. Ideally, this planning and scanning should be on a world-wide scale. Product strategy is an important part of this plan, and that includes a strategy of product development. Customer needs are the starting point for product development, whether for domestic or international markets. In addition to customer needs, conditions of use and ability to buy the product form a framework for decisions on new product development for international markets.

Developing new products

As a consequence of increasing international competition, time is becoming a key success factor for an increasing number of organizations that produce technologically sophisticated products. This time competition and the level of technological development mean that product life cycles are getting shorter and shorter in the international market environment. In line with this development times for new products are being greatly reduced (Keegan and Schlegelmilch 2001). Similarly, as Doole and Lowe (2004) observed, the time for marketing and/or selling, and hence also for R&D costs to pay off, has gone down from about four years to only two years.

For all types of technological product it holds true that the manufactured product must be as good as required by the customer, but not as good as is technically feasible. As Hollensen (2001) observed, 'too frequently, technological products are over-optimized and therefore too expensive from the customer's point of view'. For example, Hollensen noted that Japanese and European suppliers to the car industry have different approaches to the product development process, and the Japanese manufacturers start the engineering design phase two years later than the European manufacturers. This enables the Japanese to fully develop a product in a shorter time using the newest technology and to launch it almost simultaneously with their competitors. Possible reasons for this better Japanese performance are:

- early integration of customers and suppliers
- multiskilled product teams
- interlinking of R&D, production and marketing activities
- total quality management
- parallel planning of new products and the required production facilities
- a high degree of outsourcing through the reduction of internal manufacturing content (Hollensen 2001: 409).

In the current international marketing environment, product quality is not enough to reach and to satisfy the customer. Although quality of design and appearance play an increasingly important role, a highly qualified product support and customer service is also required to meet the needs of international customers.

In a Europe-specific example, Janson (2004) observed that the development time required by Swedish companies for creating new products or variants of product is seldom competitive. Internationally, development costs are tending to rise, because of the increasing degree of technical complexity of new products (Janson 2004). As a result of timing, for instance, the ability to launch a new product on the market at the right time has become decisive for success. Short lead times in development work are a decisive means of competition (Chee and Harris 1998).

A further reason for planning product changes is that products and manufacturing systems can then be developed on an integrated, parallel basis known as concurrent engineering. Focusing on particular products with an excessively shortsighted and narrow perspective may not succeed. Many successful companies, including Black & Decker, BMW, ITT Flygt, Scania, Sony and Toyota, have a clearer and broader portfolio philosophy in which the individual projects form pieces of a puzzle in a long-term development and marketing programme. By adopting a broad, forward-looking approach, these companies have succeeded in capitalizing on existing knowledge using their development work (system and components) in many different product areas, which in turn has led to shorter and less expensive development projects. This ability, according to de Burca et al. (2004), has led to better and more efficient penetration of international markets, as well as the launching of products at the right time. Also, internal resources have been focused more effectively on the development activities (new technologies and new technical solutions) most relevant for the companies. It is obviously the level of investment including new technology and technical solution that will determine the degree of newness of the developed product.

Degrees of product newness

New product development (NPD) is a business and engineering term that describes the complete process of bringing a new product to market. There are two parallel aspects to this process, with one involving product engineering, and the other marketing analysis. International marketers may view NPD as the first stage in product life cycle management.

A new product can have several degrees of newness. A product may be an entirely new invention (new to the world) or it may be a slight modification of an existing product. In Figure 8.1 newness has two dimensions: newness to the market (consumers, channels and public policy) and newness to the company. The risk of market failure also increases with the newness of the product. Hence, the greater the newness of the product, the greater the need for a thorough internal company and external environment analysis, in order to reduce the risk involved.

A company can add new products through acquisition or development. The acquisition route can take four forms. The company can buy other companies, it can acquire patents from other companies, it can develop new products in its own laboratories or it can contract with independent researchers or new-product-development firms to develop specific new products. Booz Allen & Hamilton (1982) identified six categories of new products:

- New-to-market products – new products that create an entirely new market.
- New product lines – new products that allow a company to enter an established market for the first time.
- Additions to existing product lines – new products that supplement a company's established product lines (package sizes, flavours and so on).
- Improvements and revisions of existing products – new products that provide improved performance or greater perceived value and replace existing products.
- Repositioning – existing products that are targeted to new markets or market segments.
- Cost reductions – new products that provide similar performance at lower cost.

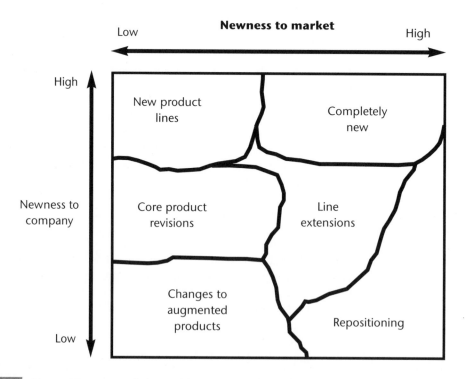

Figure 8.1   Types of new products

Kotler (2006) wrote that less than 10 per cent of all new products are truly innovative and new to the world. These products involve the greatest cost and risk because they are new to both the company and the marketplace. Most new-product activity is devoted to improving existing products (Kotler 2006). At Sony, for example, over 80 per cent of new-product activity is undertaken to modify and improve existing Sony products.

Most companies rarely innovate, some innovate occasionally, and a few innovate continuously. In the cost-reduction category, Sony, 3M, Charles Schwab, Dell Computer, Sun Microsystems, Oracle, Costco and Microsoft are the stock price gain leaders in their respective industries (Levitt 1981). These companies have:

- built innovation into the core of their businesses
- created a positive attitude toward innovation and risk taking
- a routine innovation process
- practised teamwork
- allowed their employees to experiment.

They know that in a rapidly changing international economic environment, continuous innovation is necessary for success and market leadership.

Product development strategic orientation

A product development strategy provides the framework to orient a company's development projects as well as its development process. There is no one right strategy for a company. The strategy takes into account the company's capabilities (strengths, weaknesses, core competencies and strategy), market needs and opportunities, goals and financial resources. As a starting point to developing a product strategy, the company must determine its primary strategic orientation. It must remember that it cannot be all things to all people and that it must focus on what will distinguish its image in the international marketplace. There are six primary product development strategic orientations as shown in Table 8.1.

After the company has decided upon the strategic orientation and the newness of the product, the next most important (and culturally sensitive) factor to be considered is whether the product is standardized or modified for the chosen international markets.

International product introduction strategic alternatives

Keegan (2003) has highlighted the key aspects of marketing strategy as a combination of standardization or adaptation of the product and promotion of elements of the mix, and offers five alternative and more specific approaches to product policy. Figure 8.2 shows the approaches he proposed: straight product extension, promotion adaptation, product adaptation, dual adaptation and product invention.

Straight extension

This strategy involves introducing a standardized product with the same promotion strategy throughout the world market (one product, one message world-wide). By applying

Table 8.1	Product development strategic orientation
Time-to-market	This involves an orientation to getting a product to market fastest. This is typical of companies involved with rapidly changing technology or products with rapidly changing fashion. Pursuit of this strategy will typically will lead to tradeoffs in optimising product performance, cost and reliability. Technology development must occur on an independent path from product development and technologies inserted on a 'modular' basis, often with frequent product upgrades to make this strategy work.
Low product cost	This orientation is focused on developing the lowest cost or highest value product. This is typical of companies with commodity type products, products reaching a mature phase in their life cycle, or where there is consolidation or a shrinking market. This orientation typically will require additional time and development cost to optimise product cost and the manufacturing process.
Low development cost	This orientation focuses on minimizing development cost for developing products within a constrained budget. While this orientation is not as common as the other orientations, it occurs when companies are developing products under contract for other parties, or where a company has severely reduced costs and development effort is being undertaken on a 'shoestring'. This orientation is somewhat compatible with time-to-market, but involves tradeoffs with product performance, innovation, cost and reliability.
Product performance, technology and innovation	This orientation focuses on having the highest level of product performance, the highest level of functionality or functions and features, the latest technology or the highest level of product innovation. Companies in many industries can pursue this orientation. The pursuit of this strategy involves higher risks with newer technologies and accepts a trade-off of time and cost to pursue these objectives.
Quality, reliability, robustness	This orientation focuses on assuring high levels of product quality, reliability and robustness. This orientation is typical of industries requiring high quality because of the significant costs to correct a problem (e.g., recalls in the automotive or food processing industries), the need for high levels of reliability (e.g., aerospace products), or where there are significant safety issues (e.g., medical devices, pharmaceuticals, commercial aircraft, nuclear plants) this orientation requires added time and cost for planning, testing, analysis and regulatory approvals.
Service, responsiveness and flexibility	This orientation focuses on providing a high level of service, being very responsive to customer requirements as part of development, and maintaining flexibility to respond to new customers, new markets and new opportunities. This orientation requires additional resources (and their related costs) to provide this service and responsiveness.

this strategy successfully, major savings can be made on market research and product development. For example, since the 1920s Coca-Cola has adopted an international marketing approach, which has allowed the company to make enormous cost savings and benefits from continual reinforcement of the same message (Keegan 2003). Although it is likely that this will be the strategy adopted for many products in the future, in practice only a few products may claim to have achieved this strategy already. A number of firms have tried and failed. The Campbell Soup Company, for example, found that consumers' taste in soup was by no means international. An example of successful extension is Unilever's worldwide introduction of Organics Shampoo, which was first launched in Thailand in late 1993. By 1995 the company's annual report claimed that the brand was sold in over 40 countries, and generated £170 million sales.

Promotion adaptation

The use of this strategy involves leaving a product unchanged but fine-tuning promotional activity to take into account cultural differences between markets. It is a relatively cost-effective strategy as changing promotion messages is not as expensive as adapting products. An example of this strategy is a Motorola mobile phone which was originally produced in Singapore for the southeast Asian market but redeveloped in Korea for that market.

Product adaptation

By modifying only the product, a manufacturer intends to maintain the core product function in the different markets. For example, electrical appliances have to be modified to cope with different electrical voltages in different countries. Similarly, car manufacturer Peugeot usually sell the same model throughout the world but with a modified steering wheel – selling for example, left-hand drive in Nigeria, and selling right-hand drive in the United Kingdom. A product can also be adapted to function under different physical environmental conditions. For example, Exxon changed the chemical composition of petrol to cope with the extremes of climate, but still used the 'put a tiger in your tank' campaign unchanged around the world.

Product

	No change in product	Adapt product	Develop new products
Same communications	**Straight extension**	**Adapt product**	**Product invention**
Adapt communications	**Adapt communications**	**Dual adaptation**	

Figure 8.2   Five product strategic alternatives

Dual adaptation

By adapting both products and promotion for each market, the firm is adopting a totally differentiated approach. This strategy is often adopted by firms when one strategy has failed, particularly if the firm is not in a leadership position and is therefore reacting to the market or following competitors. It applies to the majority of products in world markets. The modification of both product and promotion is an expensive but often necessary strategy. An example of dual adaptation is the launching of Kellogg's Basmati Flakes in the Indian breakfast cereal market. This product was specially created to suit Indian tastes. The advertising campaign was a locally adapted concept based on international positioning.

Product invention

Firms from advanced nations, which supply products to less developed countries, adopt product invention. Products are specifically developed to meet the needs of the individual markets. For example, existing products may be too technologically sophisticated to operate in less developed countries, where power supplies may be intermittent and local skills limited.

Product standardization

One of the key issues that have dominated international marketing and international product development for the past decade has been the degree to which a company needs to adapt or customize its product offerings in international markets (see Table 8.2). Product standardization means offering a common product on a world-wide basis, whereas customization means making changes to the product to satisfy local needs. This process may involve modifying the product, its packaging, logo or brand name. These two strategies are critical to a firm's success in the international markets, because a well-designed product can affect the product's appeal in terms of its acceptability and success-fulness. It can also gain the firm a competitive advantage. Companies such as Coca-Cola, Levi Strauss and Sony have carried out successful standardization strategies. On the other hand, standardization policies have also led to failures: the US company Campbell's attempted to sell its standard US tomato soup formulation in the UK. This was a disastrous venture; after carrying out some research Campbell's found out that UK consumers prefer a more bitter tasting soup than US consumers.

In many cases, firms do sell the same product in foreign markets as they do in domestic markets, perhaps with only very slight modifications, such as changing the packaging or having the instructions translated into the local language. UK car manufacturers modify their right-hand-drive models to left-hand drive for the continental market. These are still relatively minor modifications; many firms are reluctant to change the basic product and ideally would like to sell a standardized product across most of their world markets because of the reduced costs of large-scale production and marketing. Firms need to confront this issue of whether the same product is suitable for the international market or whether it should be adapted to meet local requirements.

A major proponent of the desirability and feasibility of product standardization has been Levitt, who argued strongly and persuasively that unless firms standardized their

Table 8.2	Factors favouring product standardization versus adaptation

Standardization	**Adaptation**
• High costs of adaptation	• Differences in technical standards
• Primary industrial products	• Primary consumer and personal-use products
• Convergence and similar tastes in diverse country markets	• Variations in consumer needs
• Predominant use in urban environments	• Variations in conditions of use
• Marketing to predominantly similar countries (i.e. the Triad economies)	• Variations in ability to buy differences in income levels
• Centralized management of international operations when mode of entry is mainly exports	• Fragmentation, with independent national subsidiaries
• Strong country of origin image and effect	• Strong cultural differences language, etc. affecting purchase and use
• Scale economies in production and marketing	• Local environment-induced adaptation: differences in raw material available, government-required standards and regulations
• Standardized products marketed by competitors	• Adaptation strategy successfully used competitors

marketing mix they were unlikely to be competitive in world markets (Levitt 1983). On the other hand, there are some who question the potential economic gains from standardization and whether it is possible to standardize many aspects of the marketing mix. The standardization versus adaptation debate is partially hampered by the lack of precise definitions regarding these two terms. This has given rise to interpretation problems. Standardization can mean that:

- a product should be purely uniform in all international markets
- a product is uniform if it is essentially similar in its key elements
- a product is still standardized even if there is local customization around a 'standard core' product: for example, the modification in electrical goods to meet local voltage requirements in some African countries such as Nigeria would not be considered to have changed basic product characteristics.

Another example is detergent manufacturers that occasionally alter the chemical composition of their products in different markets in order to adapt to the hardness or softness of local water which affects the product's performance. It is very likely that such product modifications will have minimal impact on marketing and production costs. If the changes do have a significant effect on costs and benefits, then the product can be regarded as localized.

It is therefore not the absolute but the relative degree of standardization that matters, and is of more practical relevance. The primacy of the debate should not focus on standardization versus adaptation but on which approach can gain the firm a competitive advantage in the global marketplace. This chapter will adopt the relative interpretation of standardization, and the pros and cons of standardization will be evaluated in that light.

Whether a firm should standardize or localize its marketing programme it can be guided by a number of criteria in making its choice.

Standardization versus adaptation decisions

Several factors determine whether the product should be adapted or standardized for international markets, including the nature of the product, market conditions, market environment, market development, market infrastructure and cost–benefit analysis. With respect to the nature of the product, industrial products (including medical equipment, heavy machinery and computers) require less adaptation than consumer goods. Durable consumer products (cameras, washing machines and so on) are more amenable to standardization. Non-durable products such as food and soft drinks tend to require greater adaptation, as these products are influenced more by customs and tastes.

In terms of market conditions, the level of economic prosperity and cultural preferences – factors that will influence a marketer's decision on whether adaptation of the product is required – will influence the needs of a market. The need for transportation is world-wide, but the form of transportation will vary according to economic needs and the existence of a transport infrastructure. For example, when cars are to be exported to Nigeria (an economy which is poorer than the United Kingdom, with less well-developed roads), they always have to be adapted. The cars are made sturdier to cope with unsurfaced roads, perhaps by strengthening the suspension system. Cultural perception of foreign products can also dictate whether the product is to be standardized or adapted. This is known as the country of origin effect, where products from a particular country are perceived as of high quality. In this situation, the firm should standardize its product for that particular market. If the image of the country's products is a negative one, it would be better to adapt the product.

Aspects of the market environment such as climate and resources can affect the firm's decision to adapt or standardize the product. In very hot climates, products such as cars may need air-conditioning units. Refrigerators have to be redesigned to fit comparatively small Japanese homes. Similarly in highly competitive markets, product adaptation may be necessary to gain a competitive edge over rivals. This could take many forms, from providing colour choice to after-sales service. The legal environment, including safety and product labelling, also has a direct impact on product standards. The level of market development will affect the choice to adapt or standardize a product. This does not only relate to the product's life cycle but also to the stages of the market's socioeconomic development. A successful product such as a hand calculator may be at the maturity stage of its life cycle in a highly developed economy like the United Kingdom, but at the same time a growth stage in the developing world.

Infrastructure refers specifically to institutions and functions that assist and support the marketer's needs to service customers. It includes intermediaries, logistical support such as transportation, warehousing, financial intermediaries, advertising and media agencies. The lack of reliable and efficient intermediaries such as retailers may hamper the provision of good after-sales service. This may necessitate adapting the product, redesigning it slightly to require less after-sales servicing. Finally, the firm needs to weigh the costs and benefits of adapted and standardized products. Product

Table 8.3   Advantages and disadvantages of product standardization

Advantages	Disadvantages
Economies of scale – mass production of goods creates economies of scale and leads to large savings in reduced disruption to product manufacturing cost, distribution, stock control and set-up costs.	Consumer tastes and preferences – are highly specific and often vary between and within nations. Levitt postulates that the effect of globalization will result in lower prices and better-quality goods and services, and that customer will be attracted to these lower-priced goods and hence drop local preferences. However, lower prices and heavy promotions are necessary but not sufficient conditions for successful market penetration.
R&D cost – standardization of product reduces the necessity for continuous R&D on product variations and product design, thus lowering the firm's overall R&D costs.	Market differences – in spite of closer EU integration for example, market differences do not disappear rapidly, and there are still substantial consumer differences between member states. Apart from the economics of standardization, firms do really need to consider other major influences on local consumption patterns.
Marketing economies – standardized products facilitate standardized promotion, resulting in savings on advertising e.g. Exxon's 'Tiger in your tank' advertisement	Levels of socioeconomic development – disparities exist between countries' living standards, labour costs and levels of manufacturing expertise and these factors will encourage product modifications. Markets with a low per capita income are likely to have lower purchasing power and differences in the users' skill levels when compared with consumers in the industrialized markets.
International consistency – economic globalization has made it possible for firms to sell a unified product on a world-wide basis. The need for a consistent international image is a strong argument for product standardization.	Market parameters – it is often the case that modifications to products have to be made to comply with the parameters of a market. With the growth of consumer protection legislation, it is now commonplace for governments to impose minimum legal requirements on manufacturers.
Consumer protection legislation – most countries have introduced consumer protection laws. As a result, goods have to be sold under new regulations, which mean the weight, volume and ingredients of standardized products can be displayed in a uniform manner.	Government influence – all governments seek to protect their own economies and this may necessitate the modification of products.

Table 8.3	continued

Advantages	Disadvantages
Trade groups – within trading blocs like the EU, trading regulations are increasingly standardized to simplify trade between member states. Multinational firms can take advantage by offering standardized product packaging and labelling.	Use conditions – products may fulfil similar functions in different markets, but the conditions under which the product is used will vary from market to market. Products may therefore have to be modified to cope with such climatic conditions. Avon for example, produces a moist lipstick for hot climates.
Trends towards internationalization – the globalization of the world economy aided by the communications revolution has encouraged the standardization process, making it possible for companies to present a uniform product offering and a consistent presentation to customers in any part of the world. Consistency in product style, features, design, brand name and packaging all contribute to a uniform product image world-wide, which helps increase sales. The firm can gain from economies of scale and it can multi-source its components	Corporate history – with some long-established firms it may be the case that autonomy has been devolved to their overseas affiliates to design their own product strategies and to tailor their products for the local market. It could then be difficult for headquarters to implement a uniform product strategy.
Market homogeneity – for some products e.g. the youth market such as Levi jeans, fast food, and pop music, a world-wide market is already available without the need for product modification.	Tariffs – may force a manufacturer to buy components and produce goods at specific locations, rendering standardization impossible.

modifications can lead to profitable opportunities but they presuppose that the firm has the necessary resources and that the size of the market is large enough to make such adaptations worthwhile. In other words, the costs of the adaptation must be outweighed by its benefits.

In conclusion, the advantages of product standardization will vary according to the particular product attributes in question. For example, the product's brand name and warranty provisions are not likely to lead to major cost economies but will certainly enhance the company's coherent image in world markets. It is more likely that major cost economies will be achieved in the areas of packaging and the product's physical characteristics. There are a number of factors that encourage product uniformity, but in many situations it is neither feasible nor desirable to have complete product uniformity. Comprehensive standardization of all facets of a product, even if feasible, may not be an appropriate strategy. As a result of such difficulties many manufacturers tend to use branding strategy to differentiate their products for international marketing.

Brand equity and branding decisions

Although the definition of 'brand equity' is often debated, the term deals with the brand value, beyond the physical assets associated with its manufacture. Aaker (1991) defined brand equity as 'a set of brand assets and liabilities linked to the brand, its name and symbol that add to or subtract from the value provided by a product or service to a firm or to the firm's customers'. Those assets and liabilities could be grouped into brand loyalty, awareness, quality, association and brand properties:

- **Brand loyalty** encourages shoppers to buy a particular brand time after time and remain insensitive to competitors' offerings.
- **Brand awareness** – brand names attract attention and convey images of familiarity.
- **Perceived quality** – 'perceived' means that the customers decide upon the level of quality, not the company.
- **Brand associations** – the values and the personality linked to the brand.
- **Other proprietary brand assets** include trademarks, patents and marketing channel relationships.

Brand equity can be thought of as the additional cash flow achieved by associating a brand with the underlying values of the product or service. In this connection it is useful (although incomplete) to think of a brand's equity as the premium a shopper would pay for the branded product or service rather than an identical unbranded version. Hence, brand equity refers to the strength, depth and character of the consumer–brand relationship. A strong equity implies a positive force that keeps the consumer and the brand together, in the face of resistance and tension. Brand relationship quality (BRQ) can be defined as the strength, depth, and character of the customer-brand relationship.

Branding decisions

Closely linked to product positioning is the question of branding. The basic purposes of branding are the same everywhere in the world. The functions of branding include:

- distinguishing a company's offering and differentiating one particular product from its competitors
- creating identification and brand awareness
- guaranteeing a certain level of quality and satisfaction
- helping with promotion of the product.

All of these purposes have the same ultimate goals: to create new sales (market shares taken from competitors) or induce repeat sales (keep customers loyal). Figure 8.3 shows the four levels of branding decisions. Each alternative at each level has a number of advantages and disadvantages, which are presented in Table 8.4.

Branding is associated with added costs over the marketing of unbranded products, in the form of marking, labelling, packaging and promotion. Commodities are 'unbranded' or undifferentiated products. Examples of products with no brand are cement, metals, salt and other agricultural products.

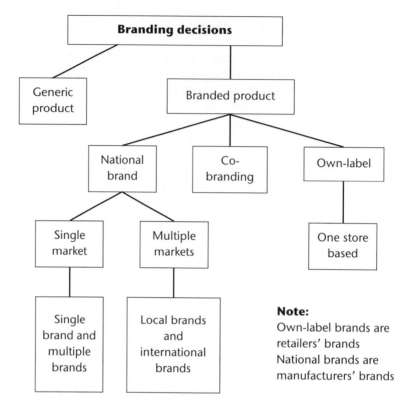

Figure 8.3 Brand type decisions

Brand comparison

The three brand options (national brand, own-label and co-branding) can be graded as shown in Figure 8.4. The issue of consumer brand loyalty or shop loyalty is a crucial one. The competitive struggle between the manufacturer and the retailer demands a better understanding of consumer shopping behaviour. Both the manufacturer and the retailer need to be aware of determinants of store choice, shopping frequency and in-store behaviour. If manufacturers fail to pay attention to consumers' shopping behaviour, consumers are likely to turn to the retailers for their needs – and thus in increases the market power of retail chains.

Own-label branding

Own-label branding is most developed in the United Kingdom, where Marks & Spencer, for example, only sells own-label products. Sainsbury's own labels account for 60 per cent of its sales (Omar 1999). Contrary to the high share of own-labelling in North Europe, the share in southern Europe – Spain and Portugal, for example – is probably not higher than 10 per cent.

In all developed countries, as markets come to maturity, manufacturers' brands face

Table 8.4 Advantages and disadvantages of branding options

Branding options	Advantages	Disadvantages
Generic product	Lower production cost Lower marketing cost Lower legal cost Flexible quality control	Severe price competition Lack of market identity
Branding	Better identification and awareness Better chance for product differentiation Possible brand loyalty Possible premium pricing	Higher product cost Higher market cost Higher legal cost
Own-label	Possibility of larger market share No promotional problems	Severe price competition Lack of market identity
Co-branding	Add more value to the brand Sharing of product and promotion costs Increases manufacturer's power in gaining access to retailers' shelves Can develop into long-lasting relationships based on mutual commitment	Consumers may become confused Ingredient supplier is very dependent on the success of the final product Promotion cost for ingredient supplier
National brand	Better price due to higher price inelasticity Retention of brand loyalty Better bargaining power Better control of distribution	Difficult for small manufacturer with unknown brand Requires band promotion
Single brand	Marketing efficiency Permits more focused marketing Eliminates brand confusion Good for product with good reputation (halo effect)	Assumes market homogeneity Existing brand's image harmed when trading up/down Limited shelf space
Multiple brands	Market segmented for varying needs Creates competitive spirit Avoids negative connotation of existing brand Gains more retail shelf space Does not harm existing brand's image	High marketing cost Higher inventory cost Loss of economies of scale
Local brands	Meaningful names Local identification on international brand Allows variations of quantity and quality across markets	Higher marketing cost Higher inventory cost Loss of economies of scale Diffused image

Table 8.4 continued

Branding options	Advantages	Disadvantages
International brands	Maximum marketing efficiency Reduction of advertising costs Elimination of brand confusion Good for culture-free product Good for prestigious product Easy identification/recognition for international travellers Uniform world-wide image	Assumes market homogeneity Problems with black and grey markets Possibility of negative connotation Requires quality and quantity consistency LDCs' opposition and resentment Legal complications

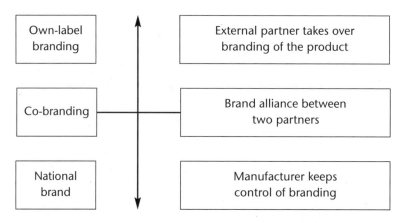

Figure 8.4 The three brand options

fierce competition from retailers' own-label brands, which are also termed private brands. Competition arises not only in the food and consumer goods industries, but also in sectors such as sporting goods, kitchen appliances, televisions and video recorders, clothing and banking services. Manufacturers are being put under pressure from large international retailers buying direct from them, often to specified standards, and selling direct to the consumers under their own brand name. Examples include Tesco (UK), Ahold (the Netherlands) and Delhaize (Belgium) in foods, and IKEA (Sweden) in furniture. Many brands sold by these and similar retailers are own-label products. Changes in international retail distribution mean the power to commission ever better innovations and put more pressure on manufacturers and their brands.

The retailer's perspective

For the retailer there are two main advantages connected with own-label business:

- Own labels provide better profit margins. The cost of goods typically makes up 70–85 per cent of a retailer's total cost. So if the retailer can buy a quality product from the manufacturer at a lower price, this will provide a better profit margin. In fact, own-labels have helped UK food retailers to achieve profit margins averaging 8 per cent of sales, which is high by international standards. The typical figure in France and the United States is between 2 and 3 per cent.
- Own labels are likely to strengthen the retailer's image with its customers. Many retail chains establish loyalty to their stores by offering their own quality products. In fact, premium own-label products (for example, Marks & Spencer's St Michael) compete in quality with manufacturers' top brands. In the grocery sector, premium own-label brands such as Tesco (UK) have seen a growth in market share, whereas the share of cheap generics is in decline.

The manufacturer's perspective

Although own-label brands are normally regarded as threats for manufacturers, there may be situations where own-label branding is a preferable option for some manufacturers. Since there are no promotional expenses associated with own-label branding for the producer, the strategy is especially suitable for small manufacturing firms with limited financial resources and limited competences in international marketing operations. The own-label brand manufacturer gains access to the shelves of the retail chains. With increasing internationalization of the large retail chains, this may also result in export business for small and medium-sized manufacturers that had never been in international markets.

There are three reasons (Omar 1999) that manufacturers do not support own-label branding:

- By not having its own identity, the manufacturer must compete mainly on price, because the retail chain can always switch supplier.
- The manufacturer loses control over how its products are promoted. This may become critical if the retailer does not do a good job in pushing the product to the consumer.
- If the manufacturer is producing both own brands and private brands, there is a danger that the private brand will cannibalize the manufacturer's brand name products.

Many manufacturers have over-reacted to the threat of own-label brands. Increasing numbers of manufacturers are beginning to make own-label products to take up excess production capacity. Almost 50 per cent of US manufacturers of branded consumer packaged goods already make own-label goods as well. Managers typically examine own-label production opportunities on an incremental marginal cost basis. The fixed overhead costs associated with the excess capacity used to make the own-label products would be incurred anyway. But if own-label manufacturing were evaluated on a full-cost basis rather than on an incremental basis, it would in many cases appear much less profitable. The more own-label production grows as a percentage of total production, the more an analysis based on full costs becomes relevant.

National brands (manufacturer's own brands)

Historically, from the Second World War until the 1960s brand manufacturers managed to build a bridge over the heads of retailers to consumers. They created consumer loyalty for their national brands by using sophisticated advertising and other promotional techniques (integrated marketing communications). However as McGoldrick (2003) observed, since the 1960s various sociological changes have encouraged the rise of large efficient retailers, such as Tesco (UK) and Wal-Mart (USA). Similarly the distribution system is being turned upside down with direct marketing becoming more apparent. The traditional supply chain, powered by manufacturer 'push', is becoming a demand chain, driven by consumer 'pull'. Retailers have won control over distribution not just because they decide the price at which goods are sold, but also because both individual stores and retail companies have become much bigger and more efficient. They are able to buy in bulk and to reap economies of scale, mainly due to advances in transport and, more recently, in information technology using the Internet as a tool. Most retail chains have not only set up computer links between each store and the distribution warehouses, they are also hooked up with the computers of the firm's main suppliers, through an electronic data interchange (EDI) system.

After some decades of absence, own-labels reappeared in the 1970s as generic products, which were pioneered by Carrefour in France but soon adopted by UK and American retailers (McGoldrick 2003). Over 20 years ago, there was a distinct gap in the level of quality between own-label and national brands. This gap has narrowed because own-label quality levels are much higher than ever before, and they are more consistent, especially in categories historically characterized by little product innovation.

Co-branding

Co-branding is a form of cooperation between two or more brands with significant customer recognition, in which all the participants' brand names are retained. It is of medium to long-term duration and used when the net value creation potential is too small to justify setting up a new brand and/or legal joint venture. The motive for co-branding is the expectation of synergies that create value for both participants, above the value they would expect to generate on their own. In co-branding, the products are often complementary (that is, they can be used independently: for example, Bacardi Rum and Coca-Cola). Hence, co-branding may be an efficient alternative to traditional brand extension strategies.

Global branding

International marketers are forced to think whether growth should come about through existing brands developing their sphere of activity, or through new brands, either created or bought. The brand gives the product meaning and defines its identity in both time and space. It has to be managed, nourished and controlled. Brands become credible through persistency and repetition. One acknowledged brand expert has said that, by creating satisfaction and loyalty, a brand eventually creates a kind of quasi-contract that binds it to the market (Schatzel, Calantoe and Droge 2001) as was the case with the Gillette Match 3 razor.

A global brand has to explore new avenues to sustain its competitive edge in terms of economics of scale and productivity. It is aided in this by geographic extension being built into the brand concept. The growth of a brand, and the reduction of unit costs that stem from it, depend on international expansion. If the brand is to remain competitive, it must be offered immediately to all at the lowest possible price. It is no longer possible to delay gradually extending its market; the marginal cost of each progressive feature rises day by day. The global brand is essential whenever the clients are themselves operating on a world-wide basis. Companies using Packard Bell computers in New York would think it sensible to have the same brand in their offices in Mexico City or Caracas. The same applies to companies in most technological industries such as 3M, Matsushita, Monsanto, Alcatel, Caterpillar, Unilever and Hewlett-Packard, quite apart from their being international companies. The global brand is a necessity. It is also necessary to retain a single brand when that brand corresponds to the signature of its original creator: for example, Yves St Laurent. Even if the creator is dead, it remains true that from a single source comes a single name.

The global or single brand enables a product to adapt to new international opportunities. It is likely that those who travel abroad may buy a brand they know and trust because it reduces the risk of the purchase. The greater the development of international media, the greater the opportunities for the single brand. The advent of Sky television and the increasing international coverage of satellite transmissions are examples of this widening reach. When a brand goes international, it can attract the interest of large retailers involved world-wide such as Wal-Mart and Carrefour, which derive benefit from centralized purchasing or through using strategic alliances with foreign retailers. The global brand, having acquired a wider international presence and awareness, provides a lever for entering other markets.

The product life cycle (PLC)

The product life cycle (PLC) concept is typically expressed as an 'S' shaped curve in marketing literature, and is based upon the biological life cycle. For example, a seed is planted (introduction); it begins to sprout (growth); it shoots out leaves and puts down roots as it becomes an adult (maturity); after a long period as an adult the plant begins to shrink and die out (decline). In theory it is the same for a product. After a period of development it is introduced or launched into the market; it gains more and more customers as it grows and becomes widely known; eventually the market stabilizes and the product becomes mature. This happens when almost all potential consumers have heard about and bought the product. Then after a period of time the product is overtaken by development and the introduction of superior competitors, it goes into decline and is eventually withdrawn. However, most products fail in the introduction phase. Others have very cyclical maturity phases where declines see the product promoted to regain customers.

There are several strategies for the differing stages of the PLC.

Introduction

The need for immediate profit is not a pressure. The product is promoted to create awareness. If the product has no or few competitors, a skimming price strategy is employed. Limited numbers of product are available in few channels of distribution.

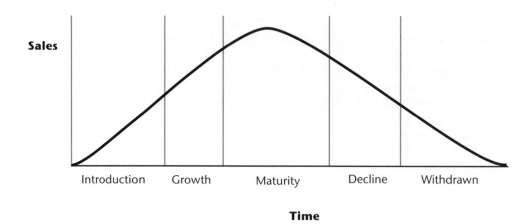

| Introduction | Growth | Maturity | Decline | Withdrawn |

Time

Figure 8.5 The product life cycle

Growth

Competitors are attracted into the market with very similar offerings. Products become more profitable and companies form alliances, joint ventures and take each other over. Advertising spend is high and focuses upon brand building. Market share tends to stabilize.

Maturity

Those products that survive the earlier stages tend to spend longest in this phase. Sales grow at a decreasing rate and then stabilize. Producers attempt to differentiate products, and brands are key to this. Price wars and intense competition occur. At this point the market reaches saturation. Producers begin to leave the market because of poor margins. Promotion becomes more widespread and uses a greater variety of media.

Decline

At this point there is a downturn in the market. For example, more innovative products are introduced or consumer tastes have changed. There is intense price-cutting and many more products are withdrawn from the market. Profits can be improved by reducing marketing spend and cost cutting.

Problems with the product life cycle

In reality very few products follow such a prescriptive cycle. The length of each stage of PLC varies enormously. The decisions of marketers can change the stage, for example from maturity to decline, by price-cutting. Not all products go through all the stages.

Some may go from introduction directly to decline. It is not easy to tell which stage a product is in at each particular time. Remember that PLC is like all other tools and should be used based on your personal understanding of the marketing environment.

International product life cycle and strategies

The use of the phrase 'international product life cycle' in the literature has been anything but standard, but the term can be defined precisely to remove it from the shadow of the product cycle or the trade cycle concepts in the international business context. According to Keegan (2003), the international product life cycle model suggests that many products go through a cycle during which high-income, mass-consumption countries are initially exporters, then lose their export markets, and finally become importers of the product. In simpler form the international product life cycle can be defined as market life span stages the product goes through in international markets sequentially, simultaneously or asynchronously:

- The sequential stages are introduction, growth, maturity, decline and extinction in the international markets. When a product is positioned in different international markets at the same time and is going through similar life cycle stages, the cycle process is simultaneous.
- The life cycle stages can be asynchronous – when the product is in different stages in different international markets at the same time. The life cycle stage in which a product can be positioned is influenced by macro variables indigenous to country markets. Stanton (Stanton, Etzel and Walker 1991) and others cite examples of this phenomenon. For example, steel-belted car tyres had reached saturation level in Western Europe when the US market was discovering them. Thus the product was in the maturity stage in Western Europe and introductory stage in the United States.

These are clear instances where trade cycle and product life cycle have been defined almost identically in the international context. The product cycle is a macro-level attempt to generalize patterns of trade between nations based on empirical data. It offers innovation and economies of scale as predominant explanatory variables. Vernon (1966) hypothesized a circular pattern of trade composition that occurs between trading partners in different stages of economic growth.

Unlike the product cycle with its macro orientation, the PLC concept in marketing theory is a micro-level explanation of stages of the life cycle a product or service goes through in the context of its market life. As noted earlier, sales volume and profits become the critical micro variables in the PLC framework. In the introductory stage of a product's life, sales are typically slow and profits negative. In the growth stage, both sales and profits rise at a rapid rate. During maturity, sales volume may continue to rise at a declining rate and profit may stay high. In the decline state, both sales and profit decrease (Vernon 1966). Sales and profits are the principal variables for marketing decisions. The product life cycle is essentially a tool for firms to design marketing mix strategies for different stages of the life span of a product or service.

There are two major differences between the PLC and the international PLC. The first relates to rejuvenation or rebirth in international markets of a product that is in decline domestically for market-related reasons or is close to extinction. Consumption of cigarettes in the US market has been declining rapidly because of consumer health consciousness and changes in public policy on smoking. But the markets for US cigarettes are expanding in China, Eastern Europe, Russia and Africa. As another example, 'Bleeding Madras' fabrics, produced on handlooms, were almost extinct in the Indian domestic market when they gained a new lease of life after being introduced as a fashion product for summer wear in the United States. Finding new international markets can therefore rejuvenate products that have reached the declining stage in the domestic market.

The second difference is that if a culture-specific product is designed for the international market, it can attain a new dimension of the PLC that is not possible in the domestic market. For example, fast food outlets like Burger King and McDonald's have designed products for cultures permeated by Buddhist and/or Hindu vegetarian values. Products can succeed and go through product life stages in international markets and still not be acceptable in their domestic markets. The international PLC is clearly different from the product cycle concept that is essentially circular and the PLC with its numerous variations.

In conclusion, the PLC is a micro-level explanation of life stages a product goes through in relationship to its market. It highlights consumer behaviour in relation to endogenous variables that allow the interplay of marketing mix strategies designed to create a shift in the demand curve. The international PLC concept, by incorporating cultural relevance as well as rejuvenation factors, broadens the applicability of the concept to international markets.

New product introduction and development

There are many ways in which a firm can add products to its international product line including acquisition, copying existing products and exporting domestically produced products. In terms of acquisition strategy, the firm can acquire a foreign or domestic-based company. For instance, when Ford acquired Jaguar, it acquired a large portfolio of car brands for which there was a potential overseas market. Although acquisitions are a relatively easy option, they are still a fairly expensive method of product development (Shenkar and Luo 2004). Companies that have engaged in acquisitions probably believe that some time in the future it will prove to be cheaper than having to invest and build brands from scratch.

As for copying products, firms can increase their product portfolio by copying products developed successfully by other firms (that is, they develop a 'me-too' copy of successful brands). Many of the newly industrialized countries (NICs) such as Taiwan, South Korea, Hong Kong and Singapore began their successful export strategy by producing imitations of standardized mature products.

In-house product development

The process and problems of new product development are similar for all firms, whether they are operating in the domestic market or overseas. Six stages are usually involved: new product idea, screening, business evaluation, prototype, market test and market introduction (commercialization). A product could be new to the firm, host market or

---

MINI CASE 8.1

Universal Feeder Ltd

Universal Feeder Ltd (UF) is a large US multinational, which produces a variety of domestic appliances including cooking, laundry, heating and refrigeration products. It reengineered through organizing and colocating teams at the design stage for all products. It tried to transplant the Japanese approach to structuring and managing suppliers.

At first, UF adopted single sourcing components and sub-assemblies as a means of establishing long-term relationships with its suppliers. It seemed that single sourcing initially offered some improvements, in terms of the quality of the components, stability of supplies, getting closer to a just-in-time (JIT) philosophy and indeed better products. UF was able to develop its suppliers in accordance with its own measures and standards. As part of this development process it trained its suppliers in its quality procedures, and its technical know-how was made available to suppliers in order to improve their manufacturing capability and reorganize their layout and logistics. This cooperation was based on the assumption and understanding that the process would not be altered without the agreement of all parties involved.

However, the suppliers realized that UF depended on their products and services, and they gradually raised their prices. At this juncture, UF noted that single sourcing did not really render the desired outcome and decided to impose a rather drastic measure in its control of supplier performance. The suppliers were invited to a meeting with UF and told that they were expected to reduce their prices by 5 per cent immediately, otherwise their contracts would be terminated. UF also introduced an 'Appreciation day'. It claimed the purpose was to acknowledge its best 100 suppliers, and each would receive a certificate of excellence.

A little while later suppliers were informed that UF was moving towards adopting 'dual sourcing'. This was used as a means of creating a competitive climate among its suppliers. Thus it controlled any information related to supplier performance and UF's satisfaction with the quality of the order in an attempt to keep the cost down. UF had an internal policy that if suppliers did not perform according to its expectations it would ditch them. In this case there was willingness by UF to share knowledge, information and experiences, and transfer them when and where appropriate to its suppliers.

Source: adapted from Pawar and Sharif (2002: 95).

---

international market (refer back to Figure 8.1). The success rate for new products is generally low. In Japan, for example, the success rate is approximately two out of 100 and in the United States it is two out of ten. At each stage of the product development process management faces the decision of whether to abandon the project, continue to the next stage, or seek additional information before proceeding further.

New product idea generation

New product development begins with ideas that originate from many sources: the sales force, customers who write letters to express opinions, employees, R&D specialists, competitive products, retailers and inventors outside the company (Nielsen 1999). An added dimension for the international company is that ideas can be derived from all its international markets. These new product ideas can be purchased from other companies or licensed. Joint ventures are also a means of generating and developing new product ideas.

Screening of new product ideas

The critical screening stage involves separating ideas with potential from those incapable of meeting company's objectives. Some organizations use checklists to determine whether product ideas should be eliminated or subjected to further consideration. In other instances the screening stage consists of open discussions of new product ideas among representatives of different functional areas in the organization. Whatever approach is adopted, screening is an important stage in the development process because any product ideas that proceed further will cost the company time and money.

Evaluating new product ideas

New product ideas that survive the initial screening are subjected to a thorough business evaluation. This involves an assessment of the new product's potential market, growth rate and likely competitive strengths. Decisions must be made about the compatibility of the proposed product with the company's resources and with existing products. The consideration of the product idea prior to its actual development is an important aspect of the business analysis stage and is known as concept testing. Concept testing is a marketing research project that attempts to measure consumer attitudes and perceptions relevant to new product idea. Focus groups and in-store polling can be effective methods for assessment of a new product concept.

Developing a prototype of new product

Ideas with profit potential are converted into a physical product. The conversion process is the joint responsibility of the product development department, which turns the original concept into a product, and the marketing department, which provides feedback on consumer reaction to product design, package, colour and other physical features. It may necessary for numerous changes to be made before the original idea is developed into the final product. The series of tests, revisions and refinements should ultimately result in the introduction of a product with great likelihood of success. If the company fails to determine how consumers feel about the product or service, and how they will use it, this may lead to the product's failure.

Market testing of new product

In order to determine consumer reactions to a new product under normal conditions, many companies test market their new product offerings. Until this point they have obtained consumer information by submitting free products to consumers, who then give their reactions. Other information may come from shoppers who are asked to evaluate competitive products. Test marketing is the first stage at which the product or service must perform in a real-life environment.

Test marketing is the process of selecting a specific city or television-coverage area that is considered reasonably typical of the total market, and then introducing the product or services with a complete marketing campaign in that area. If the test is carefully designed and controlled, consumers in the test city will respond. Once it has been under way for a few months, and if sales and market shares in the test market city have been calculated, management can estimate the product's likely performance in a full-scale introduction.

In selecting test market locations, marketers look for an area that is a manageable size. In addition, residents of this area should represent the overall population in characteristics such as age, education and income. Finally, the media should be self-contained so that the promotional efforts can be directed to people who represent the target market of the product or services being tested.

Full-scale marketing of new product

The few product ideas that survive all the steps in the development process are ready for full-scale marketing. Marketing programmes must be established, outlays for necessary production facilities made, and the sales force, marketing intermediaries and potential customers acquainted with the new product. A systematic approach to new product development is essential. The traditional method for developing new products, called phased development, follows a sequential pattern whereby products are developed in an orderly series of steps. Responsibility for each phase passes from product planners to designers and engineers, then to manufacturers, and finally to marketers. This method works well for companies that dominate mature markets and develop variations on existing products. It is less effective for companies in industries affected by rapidly changing technology, in which the slow process of phased development is a liability. In the electronics industry, for example, bringing a new product to market nine months late can cost the product half of its potential income. Instead of proceeding sequentially, many companies have adopted the parallel approach and are involved with development from idea generation to commercialization. Venture teams are an example of the parallel approach, which reduces the time needed for developing products.

The key factors contributing to product failure are:

- Technical problems – some products are badly designed, have poor performance and quality or are too complicated to understand.
- Market research – poor market research is a crucial factor. It could lead to companies over-estimating what the market requires, or not acquiring sufficient knowledge of consumers' buying motives
- Timing – product introduction was either too quick or too slow.

On the other hand, possible reasons for new product success are:

- The product has a competitive advantage such as technical superiority or price advantage.
- The product satisfies a need.
- The presence of a positive management philosophy and effective organization facilitates successful new product developments.

Adoption and diffusion of new products

The acceptance of new products by the public is a major concern for international marketers. In order to ascertain whether a new product is accepted by a fairly large number of consumers, the company needs to conduct an analysis of expected product adoption and diffusion in the international market. The adoption of new products goes through sequential stages whereby consumers follow a step-by-step process of deciding whether to accept or reject it. There are five stages in product acceptance:

1. Awareness – consumers are exposed to the new product/service.
2. Knowledge – interested consumers seek additional information about the product.
3. Evaluation – involves the development of either a positive or negative attitude towards the product.
4. Trial – the product is bought by consumers to see whether it meets their expectations.
5. Adoption – if the experience is satisfactory the product is accepted and is bought on a frequent basis. (see Venkatesh and Davies 2000).

The sequence of adoption does not mean that all consumers have to pass through the different stages. Some may skip a phase and move straight from awareness to trial and adoption. Others may require repeated trial before accepting or rejecting the product. Furthermore, the time taken between different stages will also differ among consumers. The nature of the product will be an important determinant of the time lapse between the different stages. For example, expensive items such as a house, a car or buying a business will take much longer to decide on than trying out a new soft drink or deciding which supermarket to do a weekly food shop in.

There is also a relationship between the number of consumers adopting a product and the time period involved.

As shown in Figure 8.6, only a small proportion of consumers accept the product in the early stages, followed by a slightly larger percentage and eventually by the majority. The 'bell-shaped' curve is indicative of the adoption time. The framework is adopted and based on studies conducted in the field of agriculture relating it to farmers' acceptance of new practices. Not much work has been done on the adoption of marketed products, but it is reasonable to expect that there is such a distribution tendency although it might not replicate the adoption pattern so neatly.

If we accept this assumption, this framework can be used to assess the demand for a new product in an overseas market, and how this demand will change with time. If the adoption curve for a particular product indicated a mass market in only seven years' time, the company would not even contemplate building production facilities in that particular overseas market. Five categories of consumers can be identified from the curve: the innovators, early adopters, early majority adopters, late majority adopters and laggards. It is only when the early and late majority adopters enter the market that the potential of the market develops.

The meaning of diffusion

Diffusion refers to how a new product captures a target market. This process emphasizes the aggregate individual decisions to adopt a new product, whereas the adoption process refers to the acceptance of new products by individuals. While the precise time for diffusion cannot really be estimated, an approximate time can be assessed for a particular product. The diffusion concept is essential in international marketing, and research has shown that this process is influenced by organizational factors (effective communications especially between parent and subsidiaries), product-related characteristics and market-related characteristics (Topfer 1995).

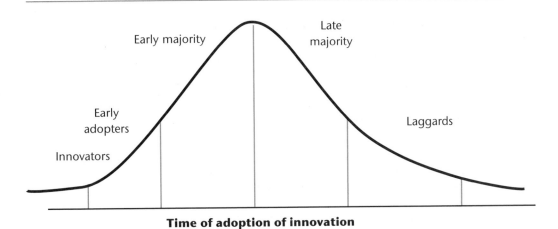

Time of adoption of innovation

Figure 8.6 New product adoption segments

Product-related characteristics

It may be necessary to consider five product-related characteristics: relative advantage, complexity, compatibility, communicability and divisibility (see Table 8.5).

As can be seen in Table 8.5, there are strategic implications of the adoption and diffusion processes. If the diffusion process is taking longer than the company expects it may be necessary to make product changes to achieve rapid diffusion, such as simplifying the product or adding additional features to enhance the benefits. In international markets, the role of integrated marketing communication (promotion) is critical in increasing the rate of diffusion. The promotional message might for example encourage consumers to test a new product for a limited period with no obligation.

Product deletion

Product deletion occurs when a company drops the product from production because it does not satisfy a sufficiently large market segment and therefore reduces the company's profits and affects its ability to achieve its organizational objectives. Many companies find it difficult to delete a product. This may be partly because of objections from both management and employees, perhaps as a result of loyalty to the product, and partly because of the argument that a 'loss leader' is needed within a diverse product mix. Volkswagen for example stopped the production of its cars in Nigeria with reluctance due to political pressure. In general, the methods of deletion are:

- The product is gradually phased out, making no attempt to change the marketing programme.
- The product is dropped immediately, especially when heavy losses are being incurred.
- For technologically or functionally obsolete products such as models of computers, it is usual to let them die a natural death as customers buy up the remaining stock over a period of time.

The point is that a company needs to develop a strategy of planned obsolescence.

Table 8.5   Product and market-related characteristics

Product-related characteristics	Market related characteristics
Relative advantage Refers to the degree of superiority of the new product offering over the present offering. If the new offering is perceived to offer more advantages then it is likely to diffuse more rapidly. This tendency will be increased by word of mouth recommendation from the innovators to other consumers.	**Perception of needs** If consumers can perceive their needs clearly, then the product will be diffused quickly because it can quickly be determined if the new product matches their needs. Many consumers may wonder to what extent they need their own computer system in the home, as the need for a total system is still not abundantly clear.
Complexity Diffusion will occur faster if the new product is easy to use. Complex products require detailed instructions and involve educating consumers. The more complex the product, the longer the diffusion process.	**Consumer innovativeness** Diffusion will become easier if consumers, through their own cultural values, are more prone to try new products or services. Diffusion tends to be more rapid in Western societies than in Eastern cultures.
Compatibility If the new product is compatible with the current products, then there will be rapid diffusion. Compatibility involves the social-cultural dimensions of the market, and consistency with existing values and behaviours. New innovations can be assessed on three levels to judge their compatibility: continuous innovation; dynamically continuous innovation; and discontinuous innovation.	**Purchasing ability** Even if many of the characteristics favourable to diffusion are present, the diffusion process will be slow if the majority of the consumers are unable to afford the new product offering.
Communicability If the attributes of the new product can be communicated easily and conveniently to the target segment, there is likely to be rapid diffusion. If the benefits and/or qualities of the product are obvious to potential customers then the uptake is going to be much faster.	
Divisibility If a new product offering can be available for trial without a major commitment, diffusion is likely to be very rapid. Divisibility implies that customers can sample the product with no financial obligation.	

International product-line management

A company's product line is a group of closely related products that function similarly, are marketed through the same type of outlets or are sold to the same customer groups. A product mix is a set of all the product lines and items that a company offers. The width of the product mix is the number of different product lines carried, the length is the total number of items in the product mix and the depth is the number of variants offered for each product.

In general, a company's international product line is unlikely to be similar to its domestic line and will usually be smaller. This could be because of financial restrictions, the company might be testing the market, it might have acquired local products, there are differences in consumer needs and tastes, government regulation affects the choice of products sold in different markets, and so on. The company's international growth strategy also affects product line decisions. If the company has expanded by internal growth, it is likely that a more homogeneous and narrower product line will be established. On the other hand, if growth is attained by acquisition, then the company will have increased its portfolio and may even drop some lines.

When a company adds products to its lines in the international market, it needs to consider how this will optimize its international profits rather than just profits in a particular national market. On the other hand, it might add a product, which is not profitable for a national market, because it needs to evaluate the overall costs and benefits of its international marketing.

Companies drop products for many reasons including poor profits, higher earnings potential from alternative products, and lack of capacity to carry the product. Whatever the reasons, the international manager needs to be aware that dropping a line in one market could result in increased overheads in other national markets. The company could also drop the product domestically but add it to international markets, where it will be at the growth stage of the life cycle. The company's foreign product line should not be too narrow otherwise the few products have to bear a disproportionate burden of entry costs.

Adding and dropping products needs to be considered carefully because the decision must be consistent with the company's overall international marketing strategy. If the company is going for uniformity in its international product lines, adding and dropping lines on a market-by-market basis could lead to product-line fragmentation, and this may conflict with the company's overall international marketing policy. The task is not simple because markets are different from each other, and changes occur in different directions and at different rates. It is therefore necessary for the company to remain vigilant in order to maintain an acceptable level of product lines in the international market environment.

Summary

This chapter has focused on product and branding decisions for international marketing, and found that the product decision is among the first decisions that many international marketing managers make in order to develop an international marketing mix. The chapter examined product-related issues and suggested conceptual approaches for relating them to practice. The nature of the product was discussed in relation to its marketing process in the international markets. The conclusion was that in order for the product to be successful in the international market it must meet with the requirements of the market (consumers). Thus in developing products for international markets customer needs are usually the starting point. In addition to satisfying the customers' needs, conditions of product use, and ability of the customers to buy the product must be taken into consideration.

One of the key issues discussed in this chapter related to product presentation for international market. The debate is whether a product should be standardized or modified for each national market. The chapter concluded that there is no clear-cut right answer, but instead listed factors that could favour either product standardization or modification. The nature and type of the product has a lot to do with this decision. In terms of branding decisions, considerations were related to brand type and positioning. Brand differentiation is a key factor to successful brand marketing in the international environment. Brand promotions are focused on brand image in order to create differentiation leading to competitive advantage.

Finally the concept of international product life cycle was reviewed. The section distinguished between product cycle and product life cycle, and clarified what has conceptually been a fuzzy area. The recommendation was that for meaningful application, the product life cycle concept should be used in conjunction with market evolution.

Revision questions

1 The satisfaction received by international consumers could be appreciated by grouping the elements of a product into the core benefits of the basic product, the expected product, the augmented product and the potential product. Discuss this statement with relevant examples.
2 Explain how a new product can have several degrees of newness to the company and to the market.
3 Briefly describe the six primary product development strategic orientations.
4 Compare and contrast the factors favouring product standardization versus adaptation.
5 Define what you understand by brand equity and explain briefly the functions of branding.
6 Evaluate the advantages and disadvantages of branding options.
7 Describe the internal product development processes from new product idea to market introduction.
8 Briefly describe the advantages of product standardization for international marketing.
9 What are the methods of product deletion?
10 The international product life cycle concept is based on the analogy of human biological growth stages. Using suitable and specific industry example, explain this statement, describing the stages.

The new product design process –
the case of Alpha Ltd

Traditionally, the process of new product development is a sequence of stages during which a new product is brought from a conceptual stage to readiness for being put into operation. As a company moves through these stages the product concept is refined and evaluated for technical and commercial feasibility. Reiterated design then reaches a level at which it is ready for prototyping and testing. After some reiterations the design can be finalized. This has been an intra-organizational process and focus whereby functional disciplines have been working separately in sequences over the design and development of the product. Within each enterprise such processes have been the domains of specialists, a 'sequential' approach. This usually necessitated frequent modifications, and design process added to the cost of prototyping and production, and delayed the time to market for the product.

Over the last few decades, with increased development in international marketing environments inter-organizational cooperation in innovation and product development has been on the agenda of most organizations (Haque and Pawar 2001). Indeed organizations may enter a collaborative relationship for a variety of reasons, such as using the other partner's resources, specific expertise or know-how. Some manufacturing companies have been engaged with suppliers which provide materials as well as development efforts. Indeed, 'concurrent engineering' (CE) attempts to encapsulate this scenario.

This case study examines the nature of collaborative relationships in product design and development within the context of concurrent enterprising. Traditionally the customer–designer relationship when designing new products has been based on mechanistic and 'hard' frameworks which used formal structures, processes and contractual approaches. This is an instrumental relationship, which reflects typical characteristics associated with the 'master-and-servant' relationship. There are inherent drawbacks in such an approach, which disregards each agent's aims and aspirations and fails to capitalize on the range of skills and competencies offered by the suppliers. Conversely, the case study advocates a customer–supplier relationship that is based on partnership and thus recognizes the significance of interdependence, interconnectedness and concordance for the achievement of mutual objectives.

The case study highlights the points regarding the process of reengineering in the context of new product design. Alpha Ltd (a fictional company) is a medium sized car-manufacturer to European standards, operating in the United Kingdom. In the last decade it has faced drastic changes in its market niche and been involved in joint ventures and mergers. In the early 1990s it realized the need for rethinking its corporate philosophy and emphasizing its relationship with its suppliers.

In its restructuring attempts it has focused on reducing time to market and improving quality by developing multidisciplinary teams in order to increase the involvement of downstream functional disciplines. As in most organizations the emphasis for Alpha Ltd has shifted from just concern for the costs in relation to cooperation with suppliers to the setting of order-qualifying and order-winning criteria. In recent years Alpha Ltd has set itself specific development goals in relation to its suppliers. These goals include not only improving the efficiency levels of the operations at manufacturing and assembly stages, but also strategically targeting suppliers' involvement at different stages. The standard procedure used to be linearly linking different functions, so product design specification would be developed in-house in small teams of designers and engineers. More recently, the company has moved towards establishing a number of multidisciplinary teams for every component.

Over the years, Alpha Ltd has been able to develop strategic alliances with a range of suppliers for the supply of component parts and subassemblies to its specifications. Parameters for suppliers were strictly set by Alpha Ltd. The degree of influence exerted by suppliers over the dimensions of design was limited. If the suppliers failed to comply with set parameters and meet the requirements they would be removed from the pool of suppliers. Over the last few years, however, the company has proactively involved suppliers in the product design process, since it has realized that new product design is more modular and that there have been some gaps in its ability to be able to focus on each individual module. The suppliers are expected to fill these gaps.

This has meant that the suppliers' systems subassemblies need to be incorporated into Alpha's overall conceptual design. During this process they actively shared and exchanged each other's knowledge, expertise, experiences and resources in order to achieve their main purpose of design and thus collaboration. Each company initially intended to maintain its individual identity, frames of reference, practices, systems and procedures, but they needed to collaborate and share resources in order to realize their common aspirations. This strategic collaboration between Alpha Ltd and its partners in design and new product development is beneficial to both parties.

Seminar questions

1 What do you consider to be the main advantages to Alpha in collaborating with its suppliers and working with its stakeholders?
2 Strategic collaboration is an effective international marketing strategy. Explain how you think small to medium-sized companies such as Alpha Ltd could establish collaborative relationships in product design and development to become efficient and effective in the international environment.
3. Do you think Alpha Ltd has benefited from its collaborative relationship?

Managerial assignment task

New product development is a marketing term that describes the complete process of bringing a new product to market. There are two parallel aspects to this process, involving product engineering and market analysis (identifying consumers and customers for the product). There are also several types of new products. Some are new to the market, some are new to the company, and some are new to both the market and the company. Similarly, some are minor modifications of existing products while some are completely innovative.

You work for a medium-sized company that produces and markets electronic lifting equipment for car manufacturers throughout the world. You are responsible for making decisions regarding product management including new product development and delineation. Your existing product has been in the market for over 25 years and has built extensive market coverage and reputation. Five years ago, a competitor introduced a new product that has a higher technical specification and is easier to use. Car manufacturers all over the world tend to favour this new entrant and are buying it in place of your product, which the manufacturers are calling 'old'. The competitor has drastically eroded your market share and is threatening to challenge for leadership. Your company wants to regain the market initiative and maintain its leadership position.

Write a report of not more than 1,500 words to your board of directors explaining how the company could achieve its objective of maintaining its leadership position. Your decision should be based on whether the company should develop a new product to replace the old one, create a line extension, reposition the existing product, revise the current product or make changes to the current product to make it more user-friendly. Justify your choice of action in marketing and costing terms.

References

Aaker, D. (1991) *Managing the Brand Equity: Capitalizing on the Value of the Brand Name*, New York: Free Press.

Booz Allen & Hamilton (1982) *New Product Management for the 1980s*, New York: Booz, Allen & Hamilton.

Chee, H. and Harris, R. (1998) *Global Marketing Strategy*, London: Financial Times/Pitman.

De Burca, S., Fletcher, R. and Brown, L. (2004) *International Marketing: An SME Perspective*, Harlow: Financial Times/Prentice Hall.

Doole, I. and Lowe, R. (2004) *International Marketing Strategy*, 4th edn, London: Thomson Learning.

Haque, B. and Pawar, K. S. (2001) 'Improving the management of concurrent new product development using process modelling and analysis', *International Journal of R&D Management*, Vol. 31, No. 1, pp. 27–40.

Hollensen, S. (2001) *Global Marketing: A Market Responsive Approach*, 2nd edn, London: Financial Times/Prentice Hall.

Janson, L. (2004) *Implementing DFM in Nordic Industry: A Report on Design for Manufacture in Practice*, Swedish Institute of Production Engineering Research, IVF Report, 4822, Linkoping.

Keegan, W. J. (1995) *Global Marketing Management*, 5th edn, Englewood Cliffs, N.J.: Prentice Hall.

Keegan, W. J. (2003) *Global Marketing Management*, 6th edn, Englewood Cliffs, N.J.: Prentice Hall.

Keegan, W. J. and Schlegelmilch, B. B. (2001) *Global Marketing Management: European Perspective*, London: Financial Times/Prentice Hall.

Kotler, P. (2006) *Marketing Management*, 12th edn, New Jersey: Prentice Hall.

Levitt, T. (1981) 'Marketing intangible products and product intangibles', *Harvard Business Review*, Vol. 59, No. 3, pp. 94–102.

Levitt, T. (1983) 'The globalization of markets', *Harvard Business Review*, May–June, p. 92.

McGoldrick, P. J. (2003) *Retail Marketing*, London: McGraw-Hill.

Nielsen, A. C. (1999) 'New product introduction: successful innovation/failure: fragile boundary', A. C. Nielsen BASES and Ernst & Young Global Client Consulting, June 24.

Omar, O. (1999) *Retail Marketing*, London: Financial Times/Pitman.

Pawar, K. S. and Sharifi, S. (2002), 'Managing the product design process: exchanging knowledge and experiences', *Integrated Manufacturing Systems*, Vol. 13, No. 2, pp. 91–6.

Schatzel, K. E., Calantone, R. J. and Droge, C. (2001) 'Beyond the firm's initial declaration: are preannouncements of new product introductions and withdrawals alike?' *Journal of Product Innovation Management*, Vol. 18, Issue 2, pp. 82–95.

Shenkar, O. and Luo, Y. (2004) *International Business*, international edn, Chichester and New York: Wiley.

Stanton, W. J., Etzel, M. J. and Walker, B.J. (1991) *Fundamentals of Marketing*, 9th edn, New York: McGraw-Hill.

Terpstra, V. and Sarathy, R. (1994) *International Marketing*, 6th edn, Orlando, Fla: Dryden Press.

Topfer, A. (1995) 'New products: cutting the time to market', *Long Range Planning*, Vol. 28, No. 2, pp. 61–78.

Venkatesh, V. and Davis, F. (2000) 'A theoretical extension of the technology acceptance model: four longitudinal field studies', *Management Science*, Vol. 46, No. 2, pp. 186–204.

Vernon, R. (1966), 'International investment and international trade in the product cycle', *Quarterly Journal of Economics*, May.

9
Service Strategies for International Marketing

Contents

LEARNING OBJECTIVES

After reading this chapter you should:

- understand the definition and concept of services marketing
- understand the differences between goods and services marketing in an international environment
- be able to evaluate the characteristics of services in an international market
- understand the strategic challenges in international marketing of services
- know the suitable blends of service marketing mix for each foreign market
- be able to determine international consumer requirements for service provision and delivery.

Introduction

In the past, services have been thought of as locally produced solutions, and service companies have been considered local establishments. However, the service sector in developed nations on average collectively accounts for nearly 75 per cent of the gross national product. The service sector includes a broad range of industries as well as many government and non-profit activities. Although services are still produced by small and local providers, service businesses have become more international (Gronroos 1999). The service sector is expanding over national borders. The changing patterns of government regulations, privatization of public corporations and non-profit organizations, computerization and technological innovations, and the internationalization of service businesses are some of the factors that are transforming the service sector in developed countries.

The Uruguay Round and the 1993 General Agreement on Tariffs and Trade (GATT) agreement reduced barriers for international trade with services. In many cases services are competing with products as they provide similar benefits. For example, using a rental service is an alternative to buying a product. The current rapid globalization of the world economy has increased the opportunities for marketing services internationally.

Unlike merchandise trade that requires a declaration of value when exported (see Chapter 6), most services do not have an export declaration nor do they always pass through a tariff or customs barrier when entering a country. As a result, is difficult to make an accurate estimate of service exports. Services not counted include advertising, accounting, management consulting, legal services and most insurance. Of course, these are among the fastest growing service sectors. In the European Union, almost 20 per cent of the services produced are exported (Winstead and Patterson 1998).

The relatively slow growth of the internationalization of service, in spite of the improved free-trade conditions, is because of:

- the existence of significant non-tariff barriers in many service industries
- the complex nature of service production
- the belief among practitioners in service businesses that it is difficult to market services outside domestic markets.

General obstacles for internationalization, which are true for manufactured goods as well, keep service companies from going abroad. Such obstacles are a lack of resources, too little knowledge about exporting and a belief that linguistic and cultural differences will make internationalization too demanding. This chapter discusses some key challenges for service companies planning to go abroad. It reviews the blending of a suitable marketing mix for international services marketing and the management of services in the international market environment.

The nature of service in international markets

While the nature and volume of world services trade is not precisely understood, more of the world's multinational enterprises (MNEs) are engaged in services (Knight 1999). The past 20 years have brought fundamental changes to the international marketing of services. Among the most important of these have been the globalization of markets, the decline of trade barriers and the emergence of modern communications and information technologies (IT) that facilitate cost-effective international business operations. The market analyst, the *Economist* (1997) explained that the total volume of world trade had grown far more rapidly than the annual growth rate in world gross national product over the previous 20 years. The *Economist* also emphasized that this has resulted in a more integrated global economy in which companies and consumers everywhere are increasingly touched by international business.

International service sectors

The nature of international services is so complex and diverse that externally valid theories may never emerge. It is also certainly true that research on international services marketing is still very much at an early stage. Historically, the early development of many academic fields has been characterized by exploratory and fragmentary work. Indeed, such research is necessary in order to devise valid theory and conceptual background. Nevertheless, if international service marketing is ever to develop as a viable field, it is clear that greater effort needs to be applied to develop theories and frameworks that are both cohesive and sound.

Table 9.1 lists services with the potential for internationalization. Like physical products, the development of capabilities and competences drives competitors in services trade.

The characteristics of services

A service is an intangible benefit purchased by customers that does not involve ownership. Besides being intangible, three other characteristics distinguish services from products: variability, perishability and simultaneous production and/or consumption. Most services have the potential of being internationally marketed. International service can be defined as deeds, performances, and efforts, conducted across national boundaries in critical contact with foreign cultures. Unlike physical, tangible goods, services are usually regarded as performances (for example, legal services) or experiences (for example, spectator sports or live theatre), which may be equipment based (for example, telecommunications, radio, television) or people based (for example, management consulting). In general, services are characterized by their intangibility, perishability, heterogeneity and inseparability:

- **Heterogeneity** – because of the varied nature of services (they are seldom the same), and because people usually perceive the value of services differently, maintaining consistent quality in an international market is difficult. Services are highly heterogeneous in the sense that, unlike products, no one-service performance is identical to another.
- **Intangibility** – intangible elements of services such as life insurance and education, for example, cannot be touched. But the tangible elements such as certificates of educational qualification are used as part of the service in order to ensure the benefits of the service and enhance its perceived value. Services are largely intangible and cannot be touched, transported or stored.

Table 9.1 International service sectors

Accounting	Funeral services
Advertising	Health care
Banking	Insurance
Broadcasting	Investment banking
Computer services	Leasing
Computer software	Legal services
Construction	Lodging
Consulting	Maintenance and repair
Contract research	Reservation systems
Data entry	Restaurants
Data processing	Royalties and licensing
Design and engineering	Security systems
Distribution including:	Media:

Accounting
Advertising
Banking
Broadcasting
Computer services
Computer software
Construction
Consulting
Contract research
Data entry
Data processing
Design and engineering
Distribution including:
- Service distributors
- Agents, brokers, representatives
- Franchising
- Freight forwarders
- Retailing
- Warehousing
- Wholesaling

Education:
- Management development
- Institutions of higher education
- Technical
- Vocational

Entertainment:
- Music
- Theme parks
- Television production
- Motion pictures
- Spectator sports
- Theatre
- Live performances

Postal service

Funeral services
Health care
Insurance
Investment banking
Leasing
Legal services
Lodging
Maintenance and repair
Reservation systems
Restaurants
Royalties and licensing
Security systems

Media:
- Cinema
- The Internet
- Radio
- Still media
- Television

Telecommunications:
- Online services
- Mobile
- Paging
- Telephone

Transportation (courier):
- Express delivery
- Package delivery
- Merchandise delivery
- Passenger service

Utilities

- **Inseparability** – services are usually created at the point of sale. This is why the benefits resulting from economies of scale and experience curve effect are difficult to achieve in service sectors such as retailing, and travel and tourism. This service characteristic sometimes also makes the supply of services in varied international markets very expensive. Services tend to be inseparable: that is, production usually cannot be separated from consumption.
- **Perishability** – services cannot be stored. For example, any British Airways plane seats that cannot be filled before departure from say, London Heathrow are lost. This characteristic makes planning and promotion of international service provision very

difficult. International marketers must try to match supply with demand at all times to avoid expensive wastage. Services are perishable, meaning that they must usually be consumed at the time they are produced, or they will be lost.

As Javalgi and White (2002) explained, each service encounter is unique and often highly customized. As a result of such uniqueness, each service encounter is associated with international marketing problems.

Marketing problems relating to service characteristics

There are several marketing problems that result from service characteristics:

- The intangibility aspect – services cannot be protected through patents, readily displayed or communicated, and prices are often difficult to set.
- The inseparability dimension – the consumer is usually very involved in the production of the service, and centralized mass production is impossible or very difficult to achieve.
- Services are perishable – inventories cannot be carried out.
- The services' heterogeneity – standardization and quality control of the offering remain a major challenge.

International service providers do not profit from the economies of scale believed to benefit traditional product manufacturers. These characteristics of services impact the nature of the service offering and the manner in which it is promoted, priced and distributed in the international markets.

Meta-classification of international services

The heterogeneous nature of (international) services has led many to question whether the same theory can apply equally to all service sectors. However, numerous scholars have a rational view of heterogeneous classification efforts which are developed for various purposes. What these classification schemes have in common is an implicit concern with how, or in what form, services cross national boundaries. The deliberation of what crosses an international boundary in a transaction suggests a meta-classification of international services:

- **Contact-based services** – where people (producers or consumers) cross borders to engage in transactions (for example, consultancy services and temporary labour).
- **Vehicle-based services** – where communications are directed into and out of nations via radio, television and satellite transmissions, and/or other facilitating communication tools.
- **Asset-based** – where commercial service ideas tied to foreign direct investment cross borders to establish an operating platform (for example, banks and insurance companies).
- **Object-based services** – where physical objects impregnated with services move into a nation (for example, computer software, video cassettes and repairs to machinery).

MINI CASE 9.1

Internationalization of services

A traditional way for service companies to start going abroad is to follow manufacturers that they are supplying with services in their domestic markets. When their clients internationalize, they get an opportunity to go along and sometimes almost are forced to do so (Vandermerwe and Chadwick 1989). For example, in studies of the banking and advertising industries, following clients was found to be a major reason for internationalizing (Terpstra and Yu 1988). Now, ways of internationalizing services have become more diverse as, for example, the development of new technologies for electronic commerce has made services less dependant on local operations (Winsted and Patterson 1998).

Erramilli (1992) examined the international services activities of 175 US companies in seven major categories: advertising, banking, computer software and data processing, engineering and architecture, management consulting, consumer services, and miscellaneous service providers. These companies primarily targeted industrialized countries in the developed world. The most popular entry mode was via a wholly owned subsidiary. Overall, market entry behaviour was characterized by considerable diversity, particularly when compared with the manufacturing sector. Erramilli concludes that the inseparability aspect of services is a key factor that distinguishes the entry modes of companies from those of traditional manufacturers.

Many services are relatively pure: that is, they are performed and consumed simultaneously at the same location. For these types of services, exporting is not possible. Where such services are to be provided, the company must build some type of 'bricks and mortar' facility through which service providers interact directly with buyers. However, most types of services incorporate some element of tangibility: for example, hamburgers provided by restaurants, contracts by attorneys, blueprints by architects, disks by software producers or completed structures by construction companies. To the extent that the tangibility component increases, it appears that the associated service, or critical elements of it, can be physically exported to a distant buyer. Furthermore, for some categories of services, exporting is possible when the offering is conveyed by telecommunications, as in banking or broadcast services. Finally, to the extent a service can be provided via telephone, email, or the Internet, it too is subject to being transported across national borders in a manner similar to traditional exporting.

A service becomes international when it crosses national boundaries using one of these modes. The mode by which the service crosses a national boundary critically determines how it engages the foreign culture it encounters. Thus, international services differ from domestic services in that they involve something crossing national boundaries and they involve some type of engagement with a foreign culture. The crossing of national boundaries is more varied and more complex for international services than for international products. Also, because services are fundamentally people-based, cultural sensitivity is more problematic for services than for products. Bearing in mind these critical points, international services could be defined as deeds, performances and efforts conducted across national boundaries in critical contact with foreign cultures. Based on this, each of the four international service types mentioned above could be described as follows:

- **International contact-based services** are acts, deeds or performances by service actors (producers or consumers), who cross national boundaries to conduct transactions in direct contact with counterpart service actors.
- **International vehicle-based services** are acts, deeds or performances with location-joining properties (allowing service producers to create the effects of their presence without being present) transacted across national boundaries via an instrumental framework.
- **International asset-based services** are acts, deeds or performances transacted across national boundaries in the context of physical assets substantially owned or controlled from the home country, critically reflective of home-country commercial service ideas.
- **International object-based services** are contact-based services fixed or embedded in physical objects which cross-national boundaries.

Whereas products can be examined before purchase and be compared with competitive offerings, customers cannot feel, see or smell services before they are purchased. For example, a person will only figure out how enjoyable flying with Virgin Airlines is when actually sitting in the plane. Since services rely primarily on people to provide them, services are usually much more variable than products. A person might have a flawless flight with Virgin Airlines on one occasion, but lose his or her belongings during the next trip. Another distinction between services and products is the perishable characteristic of the service. If services are not consumed when offered, they immediately go to waste. The empty seat in the airline jet cannot be stored in inventory. If it is not filled, its value is lost. Unlike products, which are produced, sold and consumed, services are often sold first, or consumed simultaneously. Someone buying a ticket to the cinema will consume the service at the same time as it is produced.

The risks and opportunities in the global marketplace vary according to the type of service offered. It is therefore important to categorize services by considering a product–service continuum where the basic underlying variable is tangibility. What is significant about services is the relative dominance of intangible attributes in the make-up of the 'service product'. Services are a special kind of product and they therefore require special understanding and special marketing efforts.

Service typologies

Erramilli (1990) has divided services for foreign markets into hard services (for example, architectural design, education, life insurance and music) and soft services (for example, food service, health care, laundry and lodging). Figure 9.1 shows the components of hard and soft services. Hard services require limited or no local presence by the marketer, and consumption can, to a major extent, be separated from production. Conversely, soft services production and consumption are to major extent simultaneous processes, and such services require major local presence by the service company or a representative that acts on its behalf. Services are of course very diverse, ranging from what Erramilli labels as hard services to soft services and including a range of services somewhere in between. Given the diverse nature of international services there is no single theory of international service that is the sole correct one. However, the proposed classification scheme may serve as the starting point for four related theories.

MINI CASE 9.2

Example of tangible product-related service roles

Every new Volkswagen in the United Kingdom is covered not only by a three-year unlimited mileage warranty, but also by a one-year roadside assistance programme. Dell's general three-year warranty provides free post-sale service support to purchasers of computers. In a competitive environment, service support can be the determining factor in a product's success. We refer to equipment-based services when service is the primary offering and products play a supportive role because they are needed to deliver the service. An example is T-Online buying Deutsche Telekom (Germany's largest Internet provider) in April 2000. People-based services are primary service offerings that rely on people rather than equipment for delivery. Doctors, lawyers, management consultants and university professors are typical examples. The concept of tangibility is useful for global marketers because many international offerings are composed of product and service combinations. The key task for managers is to evaluate carefully which elements of the offering dominate from the customer's point of view. The more the market offering is characterized by intangible elements, the more difficult it is to apply the standard marketing processes that were developed for products.

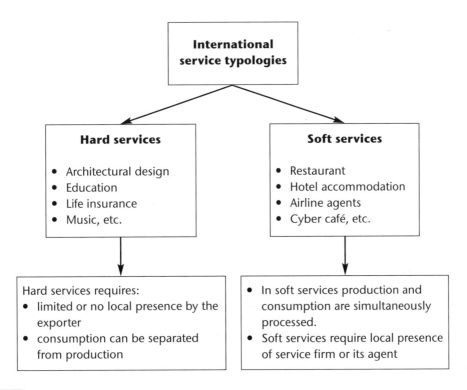

Figure 9.1 International service typologies

Reflections on the four international service types

International contact-based services

Contact-based services are the 'purest' of the international service types because they necessarily exhibit all of the classic service characteristics including intangibility, heterogeneity, perishability and inseparability. In the international environment, the effects of culture are most tellingly seen in contact-based services, where human beings must interact and communicate directly.

Intangibility also creates problems for contact-based services. Most obviously, people cross national boundaries to engage in service transactions – that is, people that carry the service as they cross the boundary. However, no nation allows people unrestricted passage across its external boundaries. This is a problem for governments because these service imports cannot be detected. Since they are intangible, they elude normal customs procedures and cannot be controlled or accounted for using methods developed for merchandise. Indeed, most governments have always found it necessary, for economic, health and security reasons, to control the flow of people into and out of their country. Governments use mobility barriers such as visas, work papers and other documentary requirements. Where mobility barriers are high, the importation and/or exportation of contact-based services is difficult. By imposing mobility barriers on particular groups (using visa and immigration regulations), governments can control the flow of contact-based service which is not possible with traditional customs procedures. Governments will more likely impose mobility barriers where border detection is difficult because of high intangibility.

Since contact-based services cannot be stored, marketers have to synchronize supply and demand without the benefit of buffer inventories. Thus the key to closing this gap for domestic contact-based services is the use of flexible personnel schedules to have producers available when needed to satisfy demand. Achieving such flexibility with personnel across national boundaries is always politically, legally and logistically problematic. This is partly because for international services there are significant transactions costs in time, travel and administration in bringing service producers to consumers across international boundaries. Ideally, liberal trade arrangements and low mobility barriers would reduce international demand–supply gaps. However, conflicting national interests continue to motivate governments to erect mobility barriers, and international travel continues to add significant costs. These problems reduce the possibility of easy solutions to the synchronization of supply and demand across national boundaries.

International vehicle-based services

Vehicle-based international services are acts, deeds or performances with location-joining properties, transacted across national boundaries in the context of an instrumental framework. Such service transactions are invisible, and like contact-based services, are difficult for governments to control using traditional customs procedures. Vehicle-based services are arguably the most important, and certainly the fastest-growing, sector of the international services trade, encompassing a wide array of important products including television and radio transmissions, and computer and telephone-based transactions. Delivery of vehicle-based services is determined by the parameters of the associated framework or 'vehicle' including:

- its carrying capacity (cable volume capacity, satellite channel capacity, etc.)
- access limitations (licenses, tools, contracts)
- the need for specialized equipment (telephones, computers) to access the vehicle
- its development pattern (few computer links to central Russia).

Vehicle-based services may be called location joining because they allow service producers to create the effects of being present in a nation without actually crossing national boundaries. This has profound consequences for a range of issues including sovereignty, immigration and unemployment, all the more so since vehicle-based services are difficult for governments to detect and control.

International asset-based services

International asset-based services are acts, deeds or performances transacted across national boundaries in the context of dedicated physical assets such as bank buildings, hotels and restaurants, substantially owned or controlled from the home country, critically reflective of home-country capabilities. These capabilities are the product of history, culture and chance, and critically affect the firm's structure, mode of operation, orientation toward the market and product offerings.

While country capabilities are important to understanding all international trade, they are a defining attribute for asset-based international services. In a very real sense, they are the service. For example, a Japanese bank established in New York or London, remains distinctly Japanese not simply on account of ownership, but also because the country capabilities it brings with it are the product of Japanese culture and commercial history. While transferable successful aspects of country capabilities will diffuse across time as entrepreneurs learn from the examples inbound foreign direct investment brings into their domestic markets, this diffusion will tend to be slow and imperfect. Asset-based services cannot be traded without a permanent presence. However, governments often impose restrictions on foreign ownership and on foreign direct investment flows (investment barriers), and hence on much trade in asset-based services. This means that establishing a permanent presence is often problematic.

Asset-based services may be culture-sensitive, primarily in terms of the home-country capability engagement with the foreign environment. Where cultural differences are large, the intellectual capital and tradition implicit in this complex cultural product will find marketplace acceptance difficult to achieve.

International asset-based services differ critically from contact-based services in a number of ways, most notably that they solve that portion of the demand/supply synchronization problem associated with distance and crossing boundaries by setting up shop in the foreign market, and as a result of this, service personnel can be recruited in the foreign market, making concerns about mobility barriers and proximity distance irrelevant. But most asset-based services will require some home country supervision and oversight in the form of expatriate managers/executives stationed abroad.

International object-based service

Object-based international services are contact-based services fixed or embedded in physical objects which cross national boundaries. All merchandise should be viewed as objects with services embedded in them. Object-based services include repairs or modifications to objects, as well as embodied services. Embodied services are those services that have traditionally 'stood alone' as 'pure services' – what we have called contact-based services – which technology makes possible to embody or fix in an object. For example, a concert can be recorded on a CD, a business or engineering consultation can be recorded on video and diagnostic expertise can be captured in a program on a computer disk. It is fair to say that once a contact-based service has been embodied, it should be treated as merchandise.

Object-based services can be viewed as stored contact-based services. The performer sings into the microphone at one time and place, the listener enjoys at another. Thus, object-based services avoid many of the difficulties associated with contact-based services, including mobility barriers and the synchronization of supply and demand over national boundaries (because it is possible to develop a buffer inventory). However, because consumption takes place without the benefit of interaction and feedback, the service must stand alone. The expressive content of living communications is absent, and no direct interpretation and explanation is possible. As a result, object-based services are sensitive to cultural distance.

International service process matrix

All services are not the same in how the nature of service processes affects opportunities for international marketing. Internationalization has different implications for different types of services, and is affected by the nature of the process involved in creating and delivering a given service. In this context we can categorize services as:

* People-processing services that involve each customer directly in delivery of services targeted at the customer's physical person.
* Possession-processing services targeted at physical objects belonging to the customer.
* Information-based services targeted at either customers' minds (mental stimulus processing) or their intangible assets (information processing).

People-processing services involve physical interactions with customers, and necessarily require either that these people travel to the service location or that service providers and equipment come to the customer. In both instances, the service provider needs to maintain a local geographic presence, stationing the necessary personnel, buildings, equipment, vehicles and supplies within reasonably easy access of target customers. If customers are themselves mobile – as in the case of business travellers and tourists – then the same customers are likely to be patronizing a company's offerings in many different locations and making comparisons between them.

Possession-processing services may also be geographically constrained. A local presence is still required when the supplier must come to service objects in a fixed location, such as buildings or large items of installed equipment. Conversely, modern technology now allows certain types of service processes to be administered from a distance – through electronic diagnostics and transmission of so-called 'remote fixes' – and small items can be shipped to another location for servicing if there are no excessive customs duties or other restrictions on free movement.

Information-based services are perhaps the most interesting category of services from the standpoint of international strategy development, because they depend on the transmission or manipulation of data in order to create value. The advent of modern global telecommunications, linking intelligent machines to powerful databases, makes it increasingly easy to deliver information-based services around the world. Local presence requirements may be limited to a terminal – ranging from a simple telephone or fax machine to a computer or more specialized equipment like a bank's automatic teller machine (ATM) – connected to a reliable telecommunications infrastructure. If the local infrastructure is not of sufficiently high quality, then use of mobile or satellite communications may solve the problem.

Developing a supplementary service model

In terms of supplementary services, eight categories can be identified: information, consultation, order taking, hospitality, care taking, exceptions, billing and payment. Not every service is surrounded by supplementary elements from all eight clusters. In practice, the nature of the product, customer requirements and competitive practices help managers to determine which supplementary elements must be offered and which might usefully be added to enhance value and facilitate service delivery. In developing an international strategy, management must decide which, if any, supplementary elements should be consistent across all markets and which might be tailored to meet local needs, expectations and competitive dynamics. Such decisions lie at the heart of standardization versus customization, but services offer much more flexibility in this respect than do physical goods.

As shown in Figure 9.2, most supplementary services are information-based and can potentially be delivered from remote locations. In theory, an international company could centralize its billing on an international basis, using postal or telecommunication distribution channels to deliver the bills to customers, suitably converted to the relevant currency. Similarly, information, consultation, order taking and reservations, problem solving and payment can all be handled through telecommunications. As long as the appropriate languages are available, many such service elements could be delivered from almost anywhere. In contrast, hospitality and safekeeping will always have to be provided locally, because they are responsive to the physical presence of customers and their possessions.

Competitive strategy for international service provision

Because of the rising importance and growth of services, it is not surprising that international growth and competition in services are intensifying. From exporting services to establishing a presence in a host country, marketers face a different set of competitive challenges. Javalgi and White (2002) contend that in the current business environment the whole world is the domain of services, and that the time when domestic service companies were safe from international competition has ended. In this regard foreign competition is forcing domestic service companies in advanced countries to think globally and act locally.

The service sector is characterized by its uniqueness and diversity, suggesting the demand for a broad array of services ranging from complex business services to basic

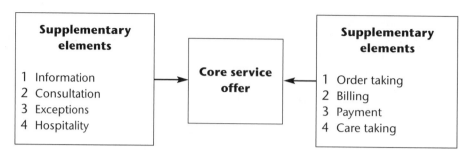

Figure 9.2   The core service offer surrounded by elements of supplementary services

services such as cleaning and maintenance. This means more competition to provide high-quality services while keeping costs low. This also means building and sustaining a competitive advantage in a given country or region. Each country's economic developments and technological advancements continue to change the competitive landscape of how services are marketed there. Advanced countries such as the United States can expect to enjoy a competitive advantage in services because of an abundance of human capital and technological innovations. By leveraging on these core capabilities, the United Kingdom, for example, can maintain a short-term superior position in services abroad.

Porter (1990) indicates that as international competition in services increases, so does the issue of national competitive advantage in services. Services are tradable on the international market, and both developed and developing countries are vying for their market share. Although all advanced economies are moving toward largely producing services, the globalization of the service sector has not been restricted to advanced economies alone. New competitors are emerging from less advanced economies, which are also showing signs of growth in the service sector (Wirtz 2000). Although the competitiveness of the service companies from economically lesser developed countries is much lower in contrast with more developed ones (Stare 2002), the challenges posed by new competitors in a host country cannot be underestimated or ignored.

An increased level of competition in world economies has pressured manufacturing-based companies to focus on their core activities in production and, at the same time, neglect to offer critical supporting services in-house (Wirtz 2000). Owing to changing consumer demographics, the demand for more support services is increasing. In brief, the competitiveness in the service sector rather than manufacturing is driving economic growth in developed countries. Newly industrialized economies such as Singapore and Hong Kong, and emerging economies such as South Africa and Brazil, are following this trend. Those service companies that employ a confluence of technological capabilities, human skills, and organizational and management skills are more likely to gain competitive advantages in the international marketing of services.

Competition and industry drivers

There are several forces or industry drivers that influence the internationalization of manufacturing companies. Five categories of industry drivers favour internationally integrated service strategy:

- market forces
- competitor drivers
- technology drivers
- cost drivers
- government drivers.

The relative significance of each force is likely to vary by service category and even by service industry. The composition and the relevance of each force is now briefly evaluated. Market forces are composed of:

- common customer needs
- global customers
- global channels
- transferable marketing
- lead countries.

As large service corporations become international, they often seek to standardize and simplify the suppliers they use across different countries. For example corporate banking, retailing, business logistics, insurance, management consulting and telecommunications seek to minimize the number of auditors used around the world.

Competitor drivers are composed of:

- high levels of exports and imports in a specific service industry
- the presence of competitors from different countries
- interdependence of countries
- the international marketing policies of competitors themselves.

Competitor drivers exercise a powerful force in many service industries. A company may be obliged to follow its competitors into new markets in order to protect its position in existing markets. Also, when a major competitor moves into a new foreign market, a scramble for territory among competing companies may ensue, in particular if the preferred mode of expansion involves purchasing or licensing the most successful local companies in each market.

Technology drivers have been very significant for international service operation. Technology factors include:

- advances in the performance and capabilities of telecommunications
- computerization
- advanced computer software development
- miniaturization of equipment
- the digitization of voice, video and text.

These factors enable all relevant information to be stored and transmitted in the digital language of computers. For example, for information-based services, the growing availability of broadband telecommunication channels that are capable of moving vast amounts of data at great speed is playing a major role in opening up new markets. Access to the Internet or World Wide Web is accelerating around the world and stimulating creation of new service applications with international appeal.

Cost drivers are composed of:

- economies of scale
- experience curve effect
- sourcing efficiency
- favourable logistics
- differences in country cost including exchange rate
- the need to recoup high product development costs
- a rapid decline in the costs of key communications and transportation technologies relative to their performance.

The effects of these drivers may vary according to the level of fixed costs required to enter an industry and the potential for cost efficiencies. For example, lower costs for telecommunications and transportation, accompanied by improved performance, serve to facilitate entry into international markets.

Government drivers may comprise:

- favourable trade policies
- compatible technical standards
- common marketing regulations
- government-owned competitors and customers
- host government policies.

The government drivers are more likely to be favourable for people-processing and possession-processing services that require a significant local presence because these services can create local employment opportunities. On the other hand, governments impose regulations to protect home-based services, such as passenger and freight transportation, from foreign competitors.

Coping with technological competition

As recently as 2001, it would have been a prescient person who identified 'electronic marketing' as one of the three principal entry modes for international services marketing. In just a few short years the Internet and the digital telecommunications revolution have changed international marketing forever. Today the competitor could be a huge MNC or a small start-up company. But both these competitors use the Internet to communicate with the market and sell their products.

The Internet changes the logistics of services far more significantly than those for goods. In the case of marketing goods, at some point a physical object has to travel from the maker to the consumer. Services, however, do not necessarily require a physical presence. It is possible to manage your finances, seek legal advice, present accounts and many more without a need to physically meet the service provider. It matters little whether your bank is across the street, two miles away in a different part of the city, or even in another country. For basic, routine services – such as a standard bank account – expensive people in the locality of the customer are not needed.

For established service businesses, confronting the competition from competitors trading via the Internet (or in some industries, digital television) presents a major challenge, especially for those companies that have extensive investments in property and staff around the world. Despite this challenge the fundamentals remain essentially unchanged. The growth of technology in services shows that technological changes are revolutionizing the global service economy and changing the rules of competition in international service industries. However, the benefits from a 'wired' organization remain familiar:

- improved productivity
- better service quality
- superior customer relationships
- the development of new services
- the ability to adapt systems to accommodate customer needs.

These factors collectively provide the basis for competitive advantage in international services marketing. Since these benefits are the fundamentals of good service marketing, and new technologies will affect how companies perform, it is likely that without the right technology companies will struggle to compete internationally. Only if services technology can be implemented in a more organic fashion will the quality of service delivered meet the needs of the organization, employees and customers. Thus services companies succeed or fail by having good people operating responsive systems.

The marketing mix for international services

The marketing mix concept is one of the core concepts of marketing theory. However, in recent years, the popular version of this concept, McCarthy's (1960) 4Ps (product, price, promotion and place) has increasingly come under attack, with the result that different marketing mixes have been put forward for different marketing contexts. While numerous modifications to the 4Ps framework have been proposed (see for example Kotler 1986, van Waterschoot and Bulte 1992) the most concerted criticism has come from the services marketing area. In particular Booms and Bitner's (1981) extension of the 4Ps framework to include process, physical evidence and participants, has gained widespread acceptance in the services marketing literature.

The marketing mix is an essential element of marketing strategy. The principles of mix management are the same in tangible product and service marketing. What differs is the composition of the mix (see Figure 9.3).

There is a growing consensus in the services marketing literature that service marketing is different because of the nature of services. That is, because of their inherent intangibility, perishability, heterogeneity and inseparability (Javalgi and White 2002), services require a different type of marketing and a different marketing mix. The formulation of 4Ps is inadequate for services marketing. The most influential of the alternative frameworks is Booms and Bitner's 7Ps mix, where they suggest that not only do the traditional 4Ps need to be modified for services (see Table 9.2), they also need to be extended to include participants, physical evidence and process. Their framework is discussed below.

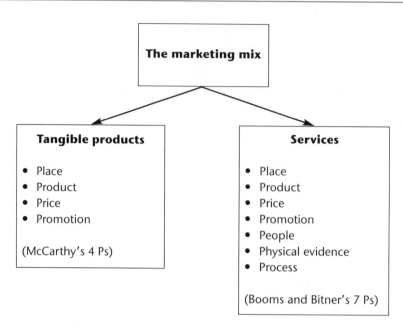

Figure 9.3 The marketing mix

The Booms and Bitner framework

In Booms and Bitner's framework, participants are all human actors who play a part in service delivery, namely the company's personnel and other customers. In services (especially high-contact services such as restaurants and airlines), because of the simultaneity of production and consumption, the company's personnel occupy a key position in influencing customer perceptions of product quality.

In fact, they are part of the product, and hence product quality is inseparable from the quality of the service provider. It is important, therefore, to pay particular attention to the quality of employees and to monitor their performance. This is especially important in the international marketing of services because employees tend to be variable in their performance, which can lead to variable quality of service offering. The participants concept also includes the customer who buys the service and other customers in the service environment. Marketing managers therefore need to manage not only the service provider–customer interface but also the actions of other customers. For example, the number, type and behaviour of people will partly determine the enjoyment of a meal at a restaurant.

Consumers must be educated in order for their expectations of the service to be managed, and employees must be motivated and well trained in order to ensure that high standards of service are maintained. However, because of cultural differences the staff and customers in different countries often respond differently not only to training and education, but also in their attitudes to the speed of service, punctuality, willingness to queue and so on.

Physical evidence refers to the environment in which the service is delivered and any tangible goods that facilitate the performance and communication of the service. Physical

Table 9.2 The marketing mix modified for services

Product	Price	Place	Promotion	Partici-pants or People	Physical evidence	Process
Traditional 4Ps						
Quality	Level	Distribution channels	Advertising			
Features and options	Discounts and allowances	Distribution coverage	Personal selling			
Style			Sales promotion			
Brand name	Payment terms	Outlet locations	Publicity			
Packaging		Sales territories				
Product line						
Warranty		Inventory level				
Service level						
Other services		Transport				
Modified and expanded for services						
Quality	Level	Location	Advertising	Personnel	Environment	Policies
Brand name	Discount and allowances	Accessibility	Personal selling	Training	Furnishings	Procedures
Service line		Distribution channels	Sales promotion	Discretion	Colour layout	Mechanization
Warranty	Payment terms	Distribution coverage	Publicity	Commit-ment	Noise level	Employee discretion
Capabilities	Customer's own perceived value		Personnel	Incentives	Facilitating goods	Customer involvement
Facilitating goods			Physical environment	Appearance	Tangible clues	Customer direction
Tangible clues	Quality/price interaction		Facilitating goods	Inter-personal behaviour		Flow of activities
Price			Tangible clues	Attitudes		
Personnel	Different-iation		process of service delivery	Other customers' behaviour		
Physical environment				Degree of involvement		
Process of service delivery				Customer/customer contact		

Source: Booms and Bitner (1981).

evidence is important because customers use tangible clues to assess the quality of service provided. Thus, the more intangible-dominant a service is, the greater the need to make the service tangible. Credit cards are an example of the use of tangible evidence that facilitates the provision of (intangible) credit facilities by banks and credit card companies. The physical environment itself (for example, the buildings, decor, furnishings, layout) is instrumental in customers' assessment of the quality and level of service they can expect, for example in restaurants, hotels, retailing and many other services. In fact, the physical environment is part of the product itself. Many physical reminders including the appearance of the delivery location and the elements provided to make the service more tangible could enhance the overall customer experience. Apart from using appropriate artefacts to generate the right atmosphere, constant reminders of the company's corporate identity will help to build customer awareness and loyalty.

The procedures, mechanisms and flow of activities by which the service is acquired are referred to as *process* in Booms and Bitner's 7Ps framework. The process of obtaining a meal at a self-service, fast -food outlet such as McDonald's and Burger King is clearly different from that at a full-service restaurant. Furthermore, in a service situation customers are likely to have to queue before they can be served, and the service delivery itself is likely to take a certain length of time. International marketers, therefore, have to ensure that customers understand the process of acquiring a service and that the queuing and delivery times are acceptable to customers.

Similarly, as the success of the service is dependent on the total customer experience, a well-designed method of delivery is essential. International customer expectations of process standards vary with different cultures and standardization is difficult in many varied contexts. Frequently the service process is affected by elements for which the service deliverer may be blamed by frustrated customers but over which it has little control. Sports fans might travel to an event at great expense only to experience delays at an airport, excessive policing or bad weather. At its most basic the process of customer management should make it easy for the customer to deal with the company.

The international marketing task

A revised marketing mix for services seems to be necessary in view of their specific characteristics. The international marketing task – the matching of the organization's resources with its customers' needs and wants (via the marketing mix) within the context of changing environments – will therefore be complicated by the need to control an extended marketing mix. Furthermore, as Nicoulaud (1989) highlighted, the concept of level of involvement does not have the same significance in international product or service marketing. The level of involvement is strongly associated with the method of entry, from indirect exporting to overseas manufacturing and marketing (in goods marketing). In the case of services, because of the inseparability of production and consumption, it is necessary to set up some form of foreign 'manufacturing facilities', however temporary. For example, an international consultant will need to design and manufacture at least part of their study in the client's country. In such a situation, exporting does not apply merely to the 'product' but also to the production process. The more personal, or the less tangible the service, the higher the provider's visibility, hence higher his/her involvement will need to be if the customer is to be satisfied.

Finally, exporting does not always involve either the product or the producer: sometimes it involves the customer, as is the case for tourism. This is another unique aspect of the international marketing of services needing consideration.

Implications for international marketing

The differences between product and service offers have certain implications for the international marketing mix as shown in the Booms and Bitner model. Because of the importance and nature of service delivery, special emphasis must be placed upon adequately blending these elements.

There are however, some specific problems in marketing services internationally. There are particular difficulties in achieving uniformity of standards of these elements in remote locations where exerting control can be particularly difficult. Pricing, too, can be extremely problematic because fixed costs can be a very significant part of the total service costs but may vary between locations and/or countries. As a result consumers' ability to buy and their perceptions of the service may vary considerably between markets, resulting in significantly different prices being set and profits generated. Increasingly important in service marketing is the need to provide standardized services customized to individual requirements. This clearly poses considerable challenges to international service providers.

International services management

Since services are perishable and when not sold they cannot be stored, managing the demand is both critical and challenging. It is challenging because, as Zimmerman (1999) observed, it requires better pricing and distribution structures. Direct delivery and short distribution channels are also essential. Offering services at convenient locations or branch offices to stay closer to the customer as well as employing skilled personnel are crucial to meet demand and satisfy customers. An analysis of increase or decrease in demand further helps to better manage the capacity of the operation in an efficient way. A savvy business manager therefore needs to harness skills and resources to manage demand.

Appropriate entry modes

International marketing literature evidence (Erramilli and Rao 1993, Javalgi and White 2002) suggests that service companies tend to prefer a local presence through the establishment of subsidiaries, mergers and acquisitions. A company's propensity to enter a foreign market through an owned subsidiary tends to increase with:

- increases in the size of the market
- the absence of possible partners in joint ventures
- the desire of the management to maintain control over foreign operations.

The retailing sector provides another example of a service business where managing demand is difficult owing to cultural, social and marketing problems, especially in less advanced countries. Retailers such as Wal-Mart and Toys'R'Us which are aggressively pursuing international expansion realize that managing an operation in a foreign market is significantly different from managing domestic operations. Again, the viable entry mode for these types of services is some type of foreign direct investment that enables the company to build a 'bricks and mortar' facility through which services can be delivered (Knight 1999). All in all, the greater the local presence of the service provider, the higher the propensity to respond to local demand swiftly and efficiently.

Standardization versus local adaptation

An important strategic issue in international marketing of services is the extent to which each service can be standardized. In addition to the necessity for customer contact for many service categories, myriad host government regulations in numerous services sectors make standardization very difficult. Service sectors such as accounting and financial markets are governed by very different rules around the world. Although regional markets such as the European Community are succeeding in lowering such host market regulatory problems, these are presently small accomplishments at best. Retailing, for instance, provides an excellent example of a service sector that is difficult to standardize. Despite the increasing nature of retail internationalization, local retailing regulations vary considerably, not only across countries within the European Union but also inside and between other countries. Moreover, even if regulations were entirely removed, retail marketing is inherently culture bound, which influences the merchandise type and merchandise mix.

As a result, the level of product and marketing standardization observed in the international marketing of goods is unlikely to be matched by services. It is plausible that relatively more services must be adapted to host country environments, and as a result, the international marketing of services may not be a realistic aim for many sectors. Customer needs for services vary more widely across nations than is the case for physical products, and addressing them requires local solutions. Hence, it is likely that a multidomestic (or multilocal) pattern of internationalization will be the most appropriate in many service sectors.

These key differences set the international marketing of services apart from the international marketing of tangible goods. Whereas an increasing number of consumer and industrial goods are being marketed globally, for reasons outlined above, the same is not true of services. As Samiee (1999) remarked, the key issue in the globalization of markets is the convergence of markets, which is not occurring with sufficient speed to accommodate international growth in many services sectors. While it is possible to market services internationally, offering a highly standardized service may be problematic. Since services are performances and inherently involve some level of the human element, they cannot be standardized in the way that goods can. The heterogeneity aspect of service is therefore subject to some variation in performance, no matter how meticulously that service is performed. Similar to inseparability, heterogeneity pertains to the issue of standard delivery of the service offering. Notable characteristics of heterogeneity that make standardization less feasible include:

- Services show quality variation on dimensions such as the provider, the consumer, and time standardization and quality control.
- Services are more prone to variation because of the labour intensity of the service.
- Services are more prone to variation when they are more people-based than machine-based.
- Services are more prone to variation when the perception of performance (or production process) varies from customer to customer.
- Services are more prone to variation when the service performance varies from the same individual (situational) from day to day.

As a result, services are much less prone to standardization than tangible goods. There is a need therefore to customize some aspects of the service offerings to reflect local or regional tastes and preferences.

In addition to the above factors, government regulations in numerous service sectors make standardization difficult (Samiee 1999). It is therefore probable that when internationalizing services, relatively more services need to be adapted to the host country environment. However, it may be more difficult for international service companies to standardize services to the extent that goods can be standardized and marketed internationally.

Service quality considerations

International retailers and other service companies have realized that whether marketing domestically or internationally, attaining quality superiority can lead to important strategic benefits including:

- greater customer loyalty
- greater productivity
- responsiveness to demand
- market share improvements
- building a competitive advantage.

In all of these areas, top management's commitment to quality plays an important role. Businesses are increasingly recognizing the importance of identifying service quality dimensions in enhancing their competitive abilities and providing a strategic advantage in their industries in international markets.

Although service quality dimensions may vary across sectors, efforts have been made in identifying general dimensions of service quality. One of the widely cited and most fruitful lines of research is that of Parasuraman, Zeithaml and Berry (1988). Their framework embraces such quality dimensions as reliability, access, responsiveness, competence, courtesy, communication, credibility, security, understanding of the customer and tangible considerations. Using these dimensions, Malhotra et al. (1994) provide a comparative evaluation of the determinants of service quality between developed and developing countries. Although their work is non-empirical, it offers interesting insights. For instance, they observed that the service quality dimensions of reliability, access and understanding the customer are associated with economic development features such as technology, affluence, competition, education and infrastructure. In other words, these aspects of the service quality dimensions seem to be more important for consumers in developed countries.

Malhotra et al. (1994) also espouse the view that the service quality dimensions of courtesy, credibility and communication seem to be correlated with Hofstede's (1983) cultural dimensions of power distance and individualism/collectivism. While high power distance and low individualism seem to be associated with economically less developed countries, small power distance and individualism tend to be correlated with economically more developed countries. In brief, they assumed that the differences between developed and developing countries in terms of the service quality dimensions are better explained by environmental factors such as economic development, culture, technology and the communication infrastructure. The strategic challenge for international service companies is that the various dimensions of service quality should be emphasized differently in developed and developing economies.

Regulatory impediments to international service marketing

Regulations are controlled by governments, and in some nations (notably OECD members) impediments are being removed through bilateral and multilateral negotiations (for example, GATS, EU, NAFTA). Some countries are very slow to agree to opening their services markets, particularly in finance and telecommunications. Structural changes within the international services industry coupled with technological change will serve as the main change agents for these countries. Some of the measures used by governments to constrain trade in services include:

- Ownership restrictions on overseas companies – even the United States, the biggest enthusiast for traded services, acts to restrict foreign involvement in markets such as air transport, financial services and health care. In less laissez-faire areas, such as the European Union, restrictions abound – even between member states.
- Domestic preference policies – in the past, giving preference to domestic suppliers provided a handy and popular means of preventing foreign businesses gaining a foothold in the home market. Such policies are often excused on the grounds of national interest despite being, in most cases, blatant protectionism.
- Unbalanced employment rules – it is not uncommon for particular rules on employment in certain services to be used to protect the home market. For example, British ski instructors with qualifications recognized in Austria, Italy and the United States are forbidden from trading in France because they don't hold a French qualification. Such restrictions do not apply to French instructors.
- Unfair tax treatment of foreign services – punitive taxes and regulatory charges on foreign services are used to make it unprofitable for such services to operate. Action by the United States to withhold tax on currency and bond trading resulted in New York becoming less competitive internationally but acted to protect domestic operations from foreign competition.
- Licensing controls – many countries restrict the numbers of licences for certain services, and can use this to restrict the opportunity for non-domestic businesses to enter the market even where the controls were introduced for the purposes of regulating home service industries.

- Censorship and data controls – for information-based services, publishers and broad-casters, the use of controls over data and the censorship of published materials, while introduced for the purpose of domestic political control, can be and are used to restrict market entry by foreign businesses.

Governments face domestic political pressures to protect indigenous businesses. Most trade unions and many politicians remain unconvinced by the benefits of free trade. Furthermore, the motivation of many opponents of free trade is not economic.

Economic impediments

Although a significant proportion of every nation's gross domestic product (GDP) is derived from services, international market entry for a broad array of services is largely limited to highly developed nations (North American and EU countries) whose family units on average possess a high level of discretionary disposable income. Thus, relatively low family income in most countries is likely to impede successful international market entry and growth for many service sectors. For example, average expenditure for restaurants is much lower in the developing economies of Africa than in the developed markets of Europe. Furthermore, as income grows, potential target groups are likely to tap into the available local low-cost labour to perform human-resource intensive services such as cleaning services and most repair services, rather than to rely on services offered through commercially organized services companies.

Cultural impediments

Cultural imperatives will necessarily have a significant impact on the acceptability and adoption pattern of services. Since services inherently involve some level of human resources, the likelihood of cultural incompatibility is greater. For example, nations that culturally define the housewife's role, as homemaker will probably not be very keen on using day care centres. Likewise, for-profit funeral services in Islamic nations such as Libya and Saudi Arabia will probably not be well received. Most of this rejection also has to do with ethical issues surrounding consumers' beliefs.

Summary

As the effects of globalization continue, growth in the services sector can be seen in nearly all developing and developed economies. This means that the twenty-first century will most likely be described as the century of the proliferation of international services. The emerging economies of Asia and Latin America offer unprecedented opportunities for service companies, as the international business climate will continue to improve due to market-oriented economies, consumer openness to foreign goods and services, and governments' willingness to move toward more privatization. These developments will open more doors to trade and investment to companies of all sizes in all industries, including service industries. This also means more competition and more choices of services and providers for consumers. Providing high-quality, culturally acceptable goods and services with a reasonable price continues to become the strategic weapon of choice with which to target global consumers. Service companies in industrialized nations must seize these opportunities and leverage their core competencies globally in order to sustain their competitive advantage.

Competitiveness in the services sector rather than in the manufacturing sector will propel global economic growth, presenting unlimited opportunities for service providers, but these opportunities are also embodied with challenges. Less developed nations are building their social/cultural, computer and telecommunications, commercial and government infrastructures to capitalize on technological advancements (Javalgi and Ramsey 2001), thereby providing both domestic and international service companies with the infrastructure necessary in which to compete. As the use of IT increases in international marketing of services, more services will be made available. The use of IT will also help to speed up service delivery throughout the world. Technology will change and continue to change the traditional ways of data gathering and presentation, the method and mode of delivery of service content, and interaction with customers with high-tech tools. Simply put, the domain of technology will become the key tenant of the marketing of services in the borderless world.

Despite the growing importance of the service sector in both developing and developed markets, and unique challenges facing multinational service providers, research in international services marketing is not increasing in proportion to its relative importance. Although existing theories, some of which have been derived from manufacturing and from other disciplines, offer hope to better understand the intricacies of marketing services internationally, the need for more research is evident. In summary, while service companies have more opportunities to market services globally, theories that explain, predict and provide practical guidance to these companies are woefully underdeveloped and under-researched.

Revision questions

1 Basing your argument on the nature of services, discuss the main marketing problems associated with service characteristics.
2 The deliberation of what crosses an international boundary in a transaction suggests a meta-classification of international service. Evaluate this statement and suggest how a service could be classified.
3 International services can be put into four categories: contract-based, vehicle-based, asset-based and object-based services. Explain the nature of these service types using current industry examples.
4 Define the following terms: people-processing service, possession-processing service and information-based service, and explain the differences in creating and delivering each of them.
5 International marketing literature suggests that as international competition in services increases, so does the issue of national competitive advantage in services. Discuss this statement, and explain with aid of current industry examples how a service company could achieve a competitive advantage.
6 In services (especially high-contact services such as restaurants and airlines) because

of the nature of the simultaneity of production and consumption, the company's personnel occupy a key position in influencing customer perceptions of product quality. Using practical industry examples, evaluate this statement.

7 International service companies can attain quality superiority leading to important strategic benefits. What are these benefits, and how could they be achieved?

8 The core elements of the marketing mix have been extended from four to seven for services marketing. Explain the justification for such an extension.

9 International customer expectations of process standards vary with different cultures. This makes standardization difficult in many contexts. Discuss, with suggestions how international marketers could resolve such problems.

10 'There are no significant differences in the way physical products and services are marketed in the international market environment'. Using the elements of marketing mix as the basis for evaluation, compare and contrast this statement.

SEMINAR CASE STUDY

The Valamo Monastery (VM)

According to the World Tourism Organization (WTO), tourism is becoming one of the world's largest service industries, but relatively little is known about the outward internationalization of tourist companies. The tourist industry is also of interest from a service policy point of view. Many companies providing services for tourists are small-sized entrepreneurial companies. Thus, an understanding of the inward internationalization process of such companies may help policymakers design service policies contributing to further growth in the number of foreign tourists served by the tourist companies.

This case study is about a monastery in Finland that also has tourism as service activities. Valamo Monastery (VM) is the only Orthodox monastery in Finland. The purpose of the case study is to discuss the specific features of the internationalization of a small-size service company. The aim is to explore the inward international activities in a service company (VM). The focus in the case study is on analysing the international activities of VM in terms of its operational methods, the target market and the service marketing activities used abroad.

The monastery was founded on the island of Valamo in Ladoga in the eleventh century. During the Second World War the monastery was evacuated from the Soviet Union to Heinävesi in the Eastern part of Finland where it is situated today. Its marketing activities are handled by a group of three monks with one of them in charge. VM provides traditional tourism activities such as accommodation, restaurant, sightseeing, museum, souvenirs and conference facilities. Now the monastery is the main tourism attraction in the region of North Karelia in East Finland. Employees in foreign companies consume some of the services produced by the monastery. The employers give these services as prizes or gifts to their employees. Sometimes the services are used as a part of the foreign company's internal training. The company has fewer than 50 employees (a criteria used by the European Union for categorizing small companies) and is more or less operated by the owners.

VM markets to both domestic and foreign customers. Almost 10 per cent of the 180,000 guests who visit the monastery every year come from countries such as Germany, Ireland, Russia, England, and the United States. The number of stopover guests is about 20,500. The monastery is working with tourism because it intends to earn the money needed for its regular activities. It can accommodate over 250 guests and operates a restaurant, meeting facilities, gift shop, art conservation institute and lay academy. The spiritual life is, of course, the most important activity for the eight fathers and brothers. They have two to five religious services daily and everyone can take part in them.

The internationalization process started at the beginning of the 1990s when Swedish tourists coming to the east of Finland learnt that one of the monks spoke Swedish. The internationalization process therefore started in Sweden. However, the first customers came to the monastery without any marketing activities being undertaken in Sweden. The first active marketing activities were carried out in Sweden when the monastery together with other tourism companies in the region attended travel fairs in Gothenburg and Sollentuna. There was no specific information that had been collected on the Swedish market. The social network the monastery had in Sweden was an important way for it to reach potential customers. One important target group was the Lutheran Church. Another natural target group, and according to the respondent the most important group, was the Orthodox Church.

When the Swedish currency was devalued a couple of years later, and especially after a serious accident in the Baltic Sea, the number of Swedish customers dropped. The monks then decided to start actively marketing their service abroad. For some time, they had also been under some pressure from other tourism companies involved in international marketing in the region. The tourist companies wanted the monastery to participate in and activate its own marketing, and to participate in joint marketing activities in order to increase the attractiveness of the region. They saw the uniqueness of VM as a complement to their own business activities.

The monastery then started to take part in two local non-profit organizations involved in the marketing of different activities for tourists, Saimaan Matkailu and Pohjois-Karjalan Matkailu. These two organizations started to market the services provided by VM. Germany was chosen as a second target market. Pohjois-Karjalan Matkailu connected an agent in Germany who became responsible for marketing the services provided by VM. Currently, the information about potential customers and intermediaries is mostly received through the German agent and the two tourism organizations.

Marketing activities abroad have been focused on intermediaries such as travel agents. The monastery has used direct mailing to get in contact with both present and potential travel agents. Direct mailings in combination with telephone, and sometimes directly through attending travel fairs, have been used to exchange information. People from the monastery have occasionally attended trade fairs as a means of getting in contact with intermediaries and end customers. They have also invited potential contact persons in the tourism industry to the monastery so they can see what the monastery can offer, and of course, sample the atmosphere. As a monastery involved in tourism activities is regarded as something unique, it has been rather easy to get in contact with different media, such as newspapers, journals, radio and television.

In summary, VM has paid considerable attention to international marketing activities implemented by other tourism companies in the region. When certain marketing activities have been seen as successful and suitable for the monastery, they have been implemented.

Source: Compiled from published information. See also Bjorkman and Kock (1997).

Seminar discussion questions

1 Explain fully how a response to an enquiry led Valamo Monastery to international market development.
2 The claim in the case study is that Valamo Monastery is in the first stage of the internationalization process because it has not yet made any large commitment to its international marketing activities. Discuss whether you agree or disagree with this statement.

Managerial assignment task

Service sectors such as professional services, entertainment, education, health care, engineering and technology-based services are growing in importance in the industrialized nations of Europe and North America, and creating new markets and more jobs. A confluence of factors, including technological developments and advances in professional expertise, has enabled the United States to attain the world leadership position in the service sector. For example, Czinkota and Ronkainen (2002) report that the service sector accounts over 75 per cent of US gross national product, and employs 80 per cent of the workforce. By all indications, the number of manufacturing jobs will continue to decline, while the number of jobs in the service sector continues to rise.

You are employed by a company specializing in the provision of health care for the over-60 age group. Your employer, based in the United Kingdom, is encouraged by the news that services are growing rapidly at the expense of the industrial sector and is planning to extend its health care services to the North African market. Although nobody in the company has any knowledge of the North African market environment, the directors see this as an opportunity for market expansion. Your job is to lead the company into overseas market development.

Write a report to your managing directors advising them of the pitfalls of the contemplated expansion into the North African market. Your report must include the strategic challenges and what the company should do to overcome the barriers to trade in services.

References

Bjorkman, I. and Kock, S. (1997) 'Inward international activities in service firms – illustrated by three cases from the tourism industry', *International Journal of Service Industry Management*, Vol. 8, No. 5, pp. 362–76.

Booms, B. H. and Bitner, M. J. (1981) 'Marketing strategies and organization structure for service firms', pp. 51–67 in J. Donnelly and W. R. George (eds), *Marketing of Services*, Chicago: American Marketing Association.

Business Week (1994) 'The role of the information revolution in the globalization of business: what's the word in the lab?' *Business Week*, 27 June, pp. 78–80.

Czinkota, M. and Ronkainen, J. (2002) *Global Marketing*, Sydney: Dryden Press/Harcourt Brace College.

Dunning, J. (1993) *The Globalization of Business*, London: Routledge.

Economist, (1995) 'The death of distance: a survey of telecommunications', 30 September, pp. 1–28 (survey section).

Economist (1997) 'Trade winds', 8 November, pp. 85–6.

Erramilli, M. K. (1990) 'Entry mode choice in service industries', *International Marketing Review*, Vol. 7, No. 5, pp. 50–62.

Erramilli, M. K. (1992) 'The experience factor in foreign market entry behaviour of service firms', *Journal of International Business Studies*. Vol. 23, No. 3, pp. 479–501.

Erramilli, M. K. and Rao, C. P. (1993) 'Service firms' international entry-mode choice: a modified transaction-cost analysis approach', *Journal of Marketing*, Vol. 57, No. 3, pp. 19–38.

Gronroos, C. (1999) 'Internationalization strategies for services' *Journal of Services Marketing*, Vol. 13, No. 4/5, pp. 290–7.

Hofstede, G. (1983) 'The cultural relatively of organizational practices and theories', *Journal of International Business Studies*, Vol. 14, No. 2, pp. 75–89.

Javalgi, R. G. and Ramsey, R. (2001) 'Strategic issues of e-commerce as an alternative global distribution system', *International Marketing Review*, Vol. 18, No. 4, pp. 376–91.

Javalgi, R. G. and White, D. S. (2002) 'Strategic challenges for marketing of services internationally', *International Marketing Review*, Vol. 19, No. 6, pp. 563–81.

Knight, G. (1999) 'International services marketing: review of research 1980–1998', *Journal of Services Marketing*, Vol. 13, No. 4/5, pp. 347–60.

Kotler , P. (1986) 'Global standardisation-courting danger', *Journal of Consumer Marketing*, Vol. 3, No. 2, pp.13–15.

Malhotra, N. K., Ulgadi, F. M., Agarwal, J. and Baalbaki, I. B. (1994) 'International services marketing: a comparative evaluation of the dimensions of service quality between developed countries and developing countries', *International Marketing Review*, Vol. 11, No. 2, pp. 5–15.

McCarthy, J. E. (1960) *Basic Marketing: A Managerial Approach*, New York: Irwin.

McRae, H. (1994) *The World in 2020*, Cambridge, Mass.: Harvard Business School Press.

Nicoulaud, B. (1989) 'Problems and strategies in the international marketing of services', *European Journal of Marketing*, Vol. 23, No. 6, pp. 55–66.

Omar O. E. (1999) *Retail Marketing*, London: Financial Times/Pitman.

Parasuraman, A., Zeithaml, V. A. and Berry, L. L. (1988) 'SERVQUAL: a multiple item scale for measuring consumer perceptions of service quality', *Journal of Retailing*, Vol. 64, No. 1, pp. 12–40.

Patterson, P. and Cicic, M. (1995) 'A typology of service firms in international markets: an empirical investigation', *Journal of International Marketing*, Vol. 3, No. 4, pp. 57–83.

Porter, M. E. (1990) 'The competitive advantage of nations', *Harvard Business Review*, Vol. 68, March–April, pp. 73–93.

Samiee, S. (1999) 'The internationalization of services: trends, obstacles and issues', *Journal of Services Marketing*, Vol.13, No. 4/5, pp. 319–28.

Stare, M. (2002) 'The pattern of internationalization of services in Central European countries', *Service Industries Journal*, Vol. 22, No. 1, pp. 77–91.

Terpstra, V. and Yu, C. M. (1988) 'Determinants of foreign investments of US advertising agencies', *Journal of International Business Studies*, Vol. 19 (Spring), pp. 33–46.

Valikangas, L. and Lehtinen, U. (1994) 'Strategic types of services and international marketing', *International Journal of Service Industry Management*, Vol. 5, No. 2, pp. 72–84.

Van Waterschoot, W. and van den Bulte, C. (1992) 'The 4P classification of the marketing mix revisited', *Journal of Marketing*, Vol. 56, pp. 83–93.

Vandermerwe, S. and Chadwick, M. (1989) 'The internationalization of services', *Service Industries Journal*, Vol. 9, No. 1, pp. 79–93.

Winstead, K. F. and Patterson, P. G. (1998) 'Internationalization of service exporting decision', *Journal of Services Marketing*, Vol. 12, No. 4, pp. 294–311.

Wirtz, J. (2000) 'Growth of the service sector in Asia', *Singapore Management Review*, Vol. 22, No. 2, pp. 37–54.

World Trade Organization (1998) 'World trade growth accelerated in 1997, despite turmoil in some Asian financial markets', World Trade Publications.

Zeithaml, V., Parasuraman, A. and Berry, L. (1985) 'Problems and strategies in services marketing', *Journal of Marketing*, Vol. 49, Spring, pp. 33–46.

Zimmerman, A. (1999) 'Impacts of service trade barriers: a study of insurance industry', *Journal of Services Marketing*, Vol. 14, No. 3, pp. 211–28.

10
International Channels of Distribution and Logistics Management

Contents

LEARNING OBJECTIVES

After reading this chapter you should:

- understand the international channel structure and design for international marketing
- know how to select, motivate and manage the international channel members
- be able to explain the processes involved with physical distribution management

- be able to evaluate the international supply chain and its effective management
- be able to examine and explain European logistics management
- know the impact of grey market on the traditional channel members.

Introduction

Historically, goods and services have been distributed through networks in which loosely aligned firms have bargained at arm's length, negotiated aggressively over price and other conditions of sale, and otherwise behaved autonomously. However, planned vertical marketing systems are rapidly displacing these conventional marketing channels as the dominant mode of distribution in the international environment. These vertical marketing systems tend to be professionally managed, pre-planned, rationalized and capital-intensive. Vertical marketing systems are organized in various ways, and of course many channels remain loosely aligned. Thus, channels of distribution vary in their degree of organization and can be categorized under three main organizational forms:

- loosely organized channels which routinely process goods, as might be expected with channels for convenience goods (conventional channels)
- consensus systems, which are organized by the cooperation of channel members
- highly organized systems typified by vertically integrated channels (corporate systems), or those formalized by contractual agreements (contractual systems).

Consensus systems, in which the success of a channel's marketing effort depends upon the continued cooperation of the channel members, are of the utmost importance to an international organization.

It has been widely suggested in the marketing literature that cooperation is the prevailing behaviour in channel systems (see for example, Zeng and Rossetti 2003). Since each firm depends on the others in the channel to perform its duties, cooperation among channel members is vital. It must be sustained so that the channel will operate efficiently and all channel members will achieve their goals. Furthermore, cooperation is the most commonly observed form of behaviour in distribution channels. International marketing channels cannot function without sustained cooperation in which each party knows what to expect of its opposite number.

This chapter reviews the foundations of a theory of marketing interaction and cooperation relevant to international distribution and logistics management. The structure of international marketing channels is identified, noting the natural channels of distribution. Channel design, selection and motivation are then evaluated. Theories relating to channel strategy for new international market entry, physical distribution management and international supply chain management are analysed. Cost elements relating to international and specific European logistics are assessed. Finally, the influence of grey market activities on traditional market channels is evaluated.

The structure of international marketing channels

It is important to understand the impact of international channels of distribution on the firm's international marketing operations and strategies. Identifying the factors that are influential in distribution channel design is also significant, as is the need to comprehend the rudiments of naturally evolved channels, which is especially important with the movement towards an international competitive environment. However, marketing literature suggests that international distribution channels are one of the most neglected areas in international marketing. Owing to the vast environmental differences from country to country, and the numerous external and internal factors that come to bear on channel structure, generalizations about international channel design are difficult to make. This section provides an increased understanding of the international channel process and suggests that international marketing decision makers should consider the often-ignored natural channel.

For example Figure 10.1 shows the distribution channel of a grocery products manufacturer that sells its products to wholesalers, chain stores, cooperatives and the military. The figure illustrates the product flow and information flow that takes place in each channel. It is necessary to know that product flow takes place only after information flow is initiated. In addition to product and information flows, payment for the goods and promotional materials also move through the system.

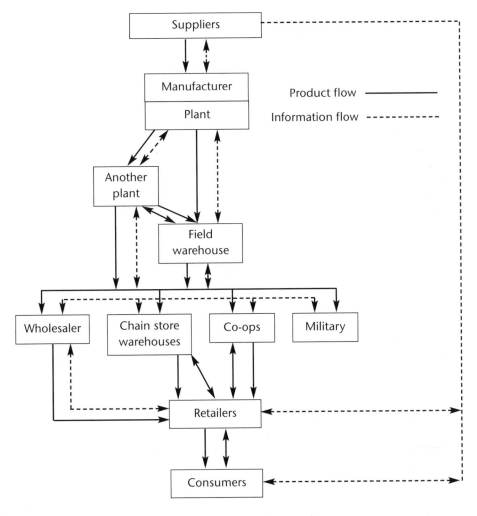

Figure 10.1 Distribution channel for a grocery products manufacturer

Source: adapted from Lambert and Stock (1993, p. 83).

Natural channels of distribution

Historically, the evolution of distribution channels occurred through necessity. The realization of specialization in production compelled the development of distribution in order to increase the utility of each party to the transaction. Distribution channels evolved through the use of natural resources contained within an area of trade, thus the term 'natural channels'. For example, to observe a marketing channel, we could simply trace the movement of a commodity from producer to user. Through the natural channel process, sellers surveyed the resources that were available and used those that could most effectively produce the desired end result. Through the use of the resources available within each market (for example, low-cost labour), an efficient distribution channel was formed. In the international arena, this is illustrated by the highly labour-intensive channels, often complete with market bazaars, found in many developing countries and the continued presence of popular corner shops in Western Europe.

The concept of the natural channel can be expanded and viewed from the standpoint of the consumer and the development of retailing. Bazaars and other unique retail operations, which have formed in many countries, have developed from the special collecting, sorting and dispersing activities that bring producer and consumer together in a given market. For example, a closed bazaar in Turkey or an open-air market in rural Kenya in East Africa can be viewed from the efficiency, as well as the full employment, perspective. The local bazaar could be considered the forerunner of today's hypermarket, or shopping mall, where consumers can do one-stop shopping (providing consumer efficiency) and local distributors can achieve economies of scale. The latter would consider the large channel layers found in some countries to reflect the presence of excess labour. The first supermarkets in Mombasa, Kenya, for example had only one or two shopping carts, and several employees to push the carts and reach shelved products for customers.

The concept of natural channels is closely akin to the efficiency model. However, the use of the western efficiency model (transaction cost approach) in modern business has superseded natural channel selection in many cases, often to the detriment of overall organizational performance. Many multinational organizations rely on the efficiency model for the development of international channel design. While the efficiency model has been considered an effective tool for organizational decisions, its application to channel structure may greatly limit the overall effectiveness of the organization and may not provide the level of consumer satisfaction so avidly sought today by manufacturers.

Clearly the resistance to Wal-Mart found in some areas of the United States, Canada and Mexico, even though it offers lower prices, illustrates this point. Many western organizations approach each market with predetermined structures, especially those accepting the international marketing philosophy.

The use of pre-determined structures greatly limits the effectiveness of the organization by neglecting the natural channels existing within a market. This standardized approach to channel design has led to ineffectiveness, and such ineffectiveness usually develops from the inefficient allocation of resources. The examples in Mini case 10.1, and numerous others, illustrate that through the implementation of the western efficiency model, without a thorough analysis of alternative sources, organizations have created an efficiency–natural clash, often resulting in less than optimal operations. The resultant clash is a derivative of the disregard of the underlying natural dimensions of the market

MINI CASE 10.1

Organizational neglect of natural channels

If it does not use natural channel relationships in the overall channel design, an organization may be operating at a sub-optimal level. Examples of organizations attempting to use transaction cost analysis in reference to their distribution systems are endless. Toys'R'Us's entry strategy into Japan was one of the most blatant. While Toys'R'Us was ultimately able to build its own standardized stores in Japan, it came at an extremely high cost to both financial and local government and/or business community relationships. In fact, the US government had to intervene in its long-drawn-out battle to alter the channel, while the Japanese government attempted to protect the natural channel of small Japanese toy stores from the North American retail giant. While Toys'R'Us was ultimately successful, the same fate failed to occur for another major US firm in Japan.

Borden's attempt to alter its channel for a product (ice-cream) resulted in a less than optimal conclusion. After working fairly successfully with Meiji Milk Products, a Japanese partner, following a natural channel approach for 20 years, Borden decided to go it alone. However it underestimated the power of the natural channel, and this eventually led to Borden's ice-cream withdrawal from the Japanese market.

Another case is the Levi Strauss Company. Levi, the US blue jeans icon, has begun to cut out its smaller dealer base, limit the variety of styles it sells through large retailers (for example, Wal-Mart in Canada), and open its own company stores in Europe and the United States. Affected intermediaries and customers have not welcomed this warmly. In particular, smaller retailers in the United States and the United Kingdom have created quite a stir (for example, Matalan in the United Kingdom).

While it cannot be regarded as a complete failure, some of Benetton's relations with distributors have failed. Benetton has chosen, via its international advertising, to reduce the value of its store licences to its licensees. This strategy has, in essence, altered the natural channel in favour of transaction cost: in this case, economies of scale.

Source: Tsukamoto (1994).

the organization is entering. As such, international marketers may wish to be sufficiently flexible in their strategy to consider the strategic employment of the natural channel concept when it is technically flexible.

Influential factors in international channel design

It is important to note that an international marketing manager may not be able to utilize the same channel design throughout the world because of individual country differences. As the number of channel designs across countries increases, managerial complexity increases. The inability to standardize channel structure is the result of a number of factors, identified in Figure 10.2. The figure is a framework for analysing the influential component factors of channel process. These component factors can be classified as internal and external variables:

- Internal variables are those that are under the control of the firm (for example,

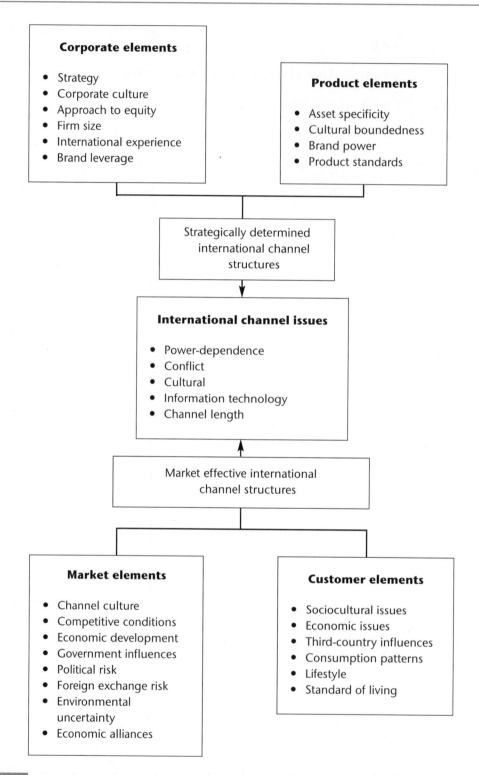

Corporate elements

- Strategy
- Corporate culture
- Approach to equity
- Firm size
- International experience
- Brand leverage

Product elements

- Asset specificity
- Cultural boundedness
- Brand power
- Product standards

Strategically determined
international channel
structures

International channel issues

- Power-dependence
- Conflict
- Cultural
- Information technology
- Channel length

Market effective international
channel structures

Market elements

- Channel culture
- Competitive conditions
- Economic development
- Government influences
- Political risk
- Foreign exchange risk
- Environmental
  uncertainty
- Economic alliances

Customer elements

- Sociocultural issues
- Economic issues
- Third-country influences
- Consumption patterns
- Lifestyle
- Standard of living

Figure 10.2 The conceptual framework for the international channel process

corporate and product). The combination of corporate and product elements defines the strategically determined international channel structures.

- External variables are those factors to which the firm must adapt (for example, market and customer). The external factors determine the relative market-effective international channel structures.

The combination of strategically determined channel structures and the relative market-effective international channel structures determines the development of international channel issues, a process which then allows for the natural channel design consideration. Each of these variables is briefly considered in the light of their influences on the international channel structure. Internal variable (corporate and product elements) are discussed first.

Corporate elements

Strategy positions an organization within its competitive marketplace. For strategic competitiveness an organization must determine an efficient channel structure. For instance, industry leaders are likely to use more specialized and formalized channel structures than industry followers, while those maintaining inconsistent strategies tend to centralize their channel structure. The influence of organizational strategy indicates just one channel influence, which is derived from an organization's management, while another is corporate culture. The perspective of management (which determines corporate culture) on international operations has been posited as a channel of distribution influence. Managerial philosophies range from geocentric to ethnocentric, and influence the manner in which the organization as a whole approaches channel partners. Organizations with ethnocentric managerial attitudes organize the distribution network under more direct control, while geocentric managerial attitudes rely on strategic relationships. Managerial perspective also tends to influence organizational structure.

Corporate structure is a derivative of managerial perspective. The degree of decentralization is often a good indicator of managerial attitude. If the organization is centralized, higher authoritarian control is established. This often affects channel structure by the firm's higher equity positions. Through higher equity positions, or forward integration, the organization's management is able to maintain legitimate authority. Zeng and Rossetti (2003) observed that the effects of organizational design also influence the organization's equity position within the channel. The equity positioning of the multinational establishes the level of control that the organization can formally maintain.

There are numerous means by which a firm can establish its international operations (otherwise known as entry modes) and thus establish its channel structure. These range from low-equity positions, such as exporting, to high-equity positions, such as foreign direct investment (FDI). Recently, many firms have been using joint ventures and strategic alliances, which tend to balance the risk–control issue. However, the equity position the firm wishes to maintain (and ensuing channel structures) may only be possible if it has adequate size, sufficient international experience, and if the desired entry form is legally acceptable to the host country.

In a traditional internationalization approach, firm size is a determinant of channel structure. This approach postulates that smaller firms begin their international operations through exporting channels, thus minimizing overall exposure, while larger firms are able to take advantage of in-house resources to minimize risk. For instance, a small firm may export, while a large firm may establish a subsidiary. The use of different entry mode strategies (or channel structures) is not just a result of firm size, but also of international experience. The level of experience a firm's management has may significantly influence channel structure (Zeng and Rossetti 2003). With limited international experience, as a firm is exposed to international operations the complexities involved in resource allocation decisions may create an atmosphere of channel structure uncertainty. However for firms whose management is more familiar with international transactions, resource allocations across markets, products and marketing activities are consistent with the overall business strategy, and thus are less likely to influence channel structure negatively.

The ability of the firm to influence channel members is directly related to the brand leverage of the firm. Brand leverage is viewed as an organization's use of brand equity to reduce uncertainty, much as in consumer relationships. Thus, a strong brand name leads to strong channel power (Omar 1999). A number of organizations such as Fuji and Kodak have used brand leverage to influence channel members, and therefore channel design. Internationally, the use of brand leverage can be seen through the strength of major European firms, such as Michelin, which have exercised power over their car dealership structure.

Product elements

Brand power (ability to influence others in the distribution channel based on brand loyalty of customers) is a critical factor in determining the brand leverage of the organization. Through the exercise of brand power, an organization can use its brand leverage to influence the distribution structure. However, this assertion is based on the probability that the brand is a function of the buying decision of the channel intermediary. The intermediary's buying decision is mediated by the end consumer's desire for the brand (McGoldrick 2003). Once the desire for the particular brand has been established in the marketplace, and consumers are brand-loyal, an organization may use brand power to influence the channel structure.

Product characteristic is likely to significantly influence channel design. The category of the product, such as perishable or non-perishable, high-density or low-density, determines not only the transport method used, but also the channel structure. Highly perishable goods not only demand shorter channels, but also require refrigeration if they are to be stored. For instance, the Jordanian marketplace uses extremely short channels and low inventory within the perishable market owing to the lack of refrigeration. These circumstances require that the market clear every day in order to reduce spoilage. While refrigeration is one general asset that would alter the channel structure within the market, other products require transaction-specific assets.

Asset specificity refers to transaction-related assets. Assets such as physical facilities, special product-related services and human assets that have no alternative use in relation to other products, are considered asset-specific. The relative degree of asset specificity necessary for the movement of a particular product may influence channel design. For those products with a high degree of asset specificity, channel structure will depend on the party that controls the asset-specific factors, and thus controls the channel.

Another product-specific attribute that may significantly influence channel design is the cultural relevance of the product. Some product categories may be highly culturally sensitive. These product-cultural relationships also have a significant influence on channel design. Often these are considered country-of-origin effects. The degree of product adaptation needed to harmonize the seller–buyer relationship extends to the augmented product attributes of channel structure. The movement towards product standards, such as ISO 9000, which can be observed within the European Union, may lead to more standardized channel structures. For example, product standardization (and deregulation) within the European Union has led Whirlpool to restructure its distribution channels (London, 1995), reducing the number of warehouses by half. Thus, the increase in product standards throughout the world may allow organizations to design more standardized channels.

External variables

The external variables are discussed in terms of market elements (channel culture, competition, economic development, government influence, political risk, foreign exchange and so on) and customer elements (social issues, economic, consumption and lifestyle), as shown in Figure 10.2.

Market elements

Market elements are often the most frequently considered influences on channel structure because of their high visibility, derived from the overall dissimilarities between nations. However, one of the least recognized is channel structure – often the most important. Channel culture is the linkage of channel members bound to a specific cultural heritage. While culture is an underlying principle of market elements, other factors, such as competitive conditions, are also very influential.

Competitive conditions are often the most consequential to managerial channel decisions. The determination of competition and control over distribution networks greatly affect potential distribution structures. For instance, Kodak filed a complaint with the US government alleging that Fuji systematically denied the US company access to distribution channels through its market dominance (Douglas and Craig 1995: 218). This is but one example of a plethora of cases throughout the world. It is therefore imperative for organizations to identify control characteristics, or pre-emptive moves, by competitors, which could limit their market entry efforts.

The competitive structure of the marketplace is also a function of the level of economic development of the country. Economic development is tied to market infrastructure, which in many cases is the most important determinant underlying distribution. In lesser-developed countries, there is a close tie between economic development and the available channel structure – a tie that may be insurmountable in terms of distribution. For example, limitations in transport available can affect the channel structure. Further, while infrastructure development is crucial, government actions may either increase or decrease the efficient distribution structures allowable.

Government regulations can severely restrict channel structure options. For instance, governments often regulate to require the use of domestic distributors, limiting the possible options for market entry and distribution. In other instances, government regulations may restrict a firm's ability to adjust distribution relationships, for example by terminating inefficient channel members. Foreign firms may also question the transparency of government dictates, especially when considering government contracts, which can favour local distributors.

MINI CASE 10.2

Retailers' alteration of the international competitive environment

The competitive environment has also been significantly altered recently by the emergence of global retailers (Yrjola 2001). Examples of companies changing the competitive environment include Marks & Spencer, with its entry into Spain, and Toys'R'Us, with its entry into Japan. When entering new markets, these firms used a standardized channel strategy; their operations were similar to those successfully used in the domestic market.

Through using local partners Marks & Spencer successfully transferred its retailing channel to Spain. Because it brought with it its unique style of retailing, local retailers had to adjust the manner in which they competed.

Toys'R'Us's entrance into the Japanese marketplace not only dramatically transformed the competitive environment of distribution networks, but also provided a new distribution channel for those manufacturers with which it maintained an association. Thus, associated foreign manufacturers were offered a way of sidestepping the complicated Japanese distribution system.

While these ventures were to a degree successful, with the translation of the French hypermarket retail concept into the United States (*Economist* 1999) and Marks & Spencer's expansion into Canada, channel transferences was less than spectacular, illustrating the complexities of the issue.

Sources: Yrjola (2001), *Economist* (1999).

While government regulations often create obstacles, they tend to facilitate the natural channel process. As advocates of the populace, governments attempt to impose regulations that use abundant resources, such as labour, and protect the natural channels that have evolved. Thus, governmental regulations can be categorized as either obstacles to channel structure change, or facilitators of the natural channel concept.

Political risk is a widely accepted influential factor on international business organizations. This is based on the probability of uncontrollable, and unanticipated, environmental changes. Thus, political risk is closely associated with the environmental uncertainty that affects international channel structures.

Closely akin to political risk is foreign exchange risk. The flow of products, and thus the flow of currency, through the international channel of distribution produces the uncertainty of foreign exchange. The degree of foreign exchange risk is often associated with translation, transaction and economic exposure. Although increasing fluctuations in exchange rate are an economic development dilemma, the direct impact of environmental variables on channel structure is more apparent when it is aggregated into environmental uncertainty. The development of economic alliances, such as the European Union, NAFTA and ASEAN, has cast a new light on the standardization versus localization issue. Currently as a result of all these influences a standardized distribution system is inefficient and impractical. However, through increased economic integration, regional channel designs may become possible.

Cultural characteristics of customers have been the basis for a debate in the literature on standardization versus localization of international marketing strategy. Baalbaki and Malhotra (1995) have argued that the relative cultural sensitivity of the product determines the level of product adaptation that needs to occur. This same philosophy can be extended to international channels of distribution. The cultural characteristics of the target market will be responsive to certain culturally bound channel structures. For example in some countries local stores are popular, whereas other cultures are more bound to large, impersonal superstores. Traditional practices will greatly impact on effective channel design. For example, Japanese consumers traditionally rely on stores for both information and performance guarantees. Such a consumer philosophy is highly culture-bound and creates what Europeans tend to call distribution obstacles. These strong cultural characteristics do not dissipate with international migration.

Lifestyle plays an important factor in the design of a channel. Lifestyle manifestations can be viewed through shopping patterns. For instance, within the Chinese marketplace, owing to small living spaces, the heavy reliance on bicycles for travel, and the lack of refrigeration devices, many consumers shop daily. The need for more frequent shopping necessitates a grocery outlet in close proximity to either work or home. Also, traditionally oriented French and Italians prefer to prepare meals with fresh produce, thus necessitating frequent trips to conveniently located produce shops. The natural channel in these markets consists of a large number of small retailers rather than a few large retailers. In other words, channel structure is strongly tied to lifestyle, which is in turn strongly tied to culture.

Closely related to lifestyle considerations is socioeconomic status, which is largely dependent on income distribution within the economy. We can observe that those at lower income levels have more reserved lifestyles, and often less choice of transport. This lower mobility influences the channel structure in that market. Also to be considered are the overall developmental aspects of a nation. If infrastructure limits the mobility of consumers, different distribution channels will need to be established. Similarly, differing consumption patterns between nations also have a substantial influence on channel structure. For instance, within the United States, beverages are traditionally consumed in private; thus distribution is based on convenience, such as through convenience stores or local grocery stores. However, in many European nations, beverage consumption occurs in public areas; thus, effective distribution necessitates the use of street vendors.

Finally, the impact of customer elements and market elements, or what are otherwise termed natural elements, determines the market-effective international channel structures for a particular market. While each element may influence overall market structure possibilities to some extent, there is no question that these elements affect the effectiveness of international channel designs. It is through the recognition of these external and internal variables that an organization can achieve optimal channel design.

Channel selection and management

Managing international distribution is critical to success in international markets because it often involves the firm accepting a lack of control in the international market in exchange for a low-risk form of market entry. This applies to most firms when they commence exporting, as they usually begin through agents rather than selling direct to the final customer. In the international market, the agent is the physical presence of the firm and can enhance or damage the image of the firm, especially if the agent pursues its own interests rather than those of its principal.

Channel selection

Almost half of all world trade is handled through agents and distributors, thus the selection of the right agent and/or distributor for the firm in the international market is critically important. Since the agent is the face of the firm in the international market, before selecting an agent, extensive screening of as many potential intermediaries as possible is essential. In the first instance, it is necessary to make sure how similar products are already being distributed in the international market, the intermediaries used by the local producers and the firms that distribute imported products in the same category. When selecting an agent, it is important to select an agent whose size matches that of the firm. If the agent is much larger, it is likely to merely list rather than aggressively promote specific products. If the agent is much smaller, it is unlikely that it will be able to secure adequate coverage, finance sufficient inventory, and promote the products in all segments that the firm desires in order to make the export of the product to the foreign market worthwhile.

Distribution channels are heavily influenced by relationships. It is desirable to look for an intermediary that is experienced in handling imported products and understands the differences involved in dealing with foreigners. Also, motivating an agent to aggressively promote a product without an established brand image in the foreign country can be a challenge. One way around this is to seek an agent already in the same area of business that does not have a similar product. The agent is then able to flesh out the range its distributors can offer to their established clients. It is therefore important to search out agents handling complementary products.

Another issue that needs to be taken into account and resolved in the process of selecting an agent is marketing approach and responsibility for promotion. It is important to ensure that the agent has a similar marketing approach to the firm. Otherwise there could be discordant images in overlapping markets that are served by different agents. A cause of considerable conflict between the international agent and principal is the question of paying for promotion in the international market. Firms often consider that the agent should fund promotion out of its profit margin, whereas the agent feels that promotion is the responsibility of the firm. If resolution of this issue is left until after the agent is appointed, the result will be that that no promotion takes place. It is therefore necessary for this issue to be resolved before the agent is appointed.

Appointing suitable agents

Once it has been decided which agent is to be appointed, a contractual agreement is drawn up which clearly spells out the details of the arrangement. It specifies which products will be represented and the boundaries of the area within which the agent will represent the firm (de Burca, Fletcher and Brown 2004: 407). While the agent may wish to represent the total range, care must be taken to ensure that it has the capability and a distribution network in all the product areas for effective representation.

It is important to check in which areas within the country or region the agent has an effective distribution network. It will be unwise to give an agent a national contract if it is not able to cover the area satisfactorily. If there is uncertainty over the area of effective representation, it may be best to initially confine representation to the agent's current area of effectiveness and review the issue periodically. Usually agents will seek an exclusive contractual arrangement that prevents the firm from appointing another agent in the country. If this is the case, it is important that the agreement specifies a time period so that another agent can be appointed if the first one does not perform satisfactorily. It is also useful to check that the agent does not handle any competing lines, and a clause preventing the agent from doing so should be included in the agreement. It may be necessary for both parties to have an exclusive arrangement with each other.

Communication and control of agents

This phase of activity should be driven by the notion of creating a positive operating climate so as to improve the chances of a long-term satisfactory relationship. In order to achieve this, it is desirable to promptly answer correspondence in a sympathetic and friendly manner, and to provide the agent with copies of all company material even if it is not directly related to the agent's duties. This should include company bulletins, company newsletters, staff bulletins, new product information, public relations releases and fact sheets on new products. This assists in making the agent feel part of the firm's corporate family. In addition, mention of the agent's activities should be included in corporate communications where possible.

Once the agent is appointed it should be visited regularly. The visit should be by the executive responsible for the agency, be planned well in advance and have specific objectives that have been agreed with the agent in advance. It is also important to bring the agent to the firm's domestic base shortly after appointment. The visit could be timed to coincide with a national sales conference. This is desirable not only to enable the agent to meet the firm's managers and view the production process, but also to enhance the agent's credibility. If products are imported and the agent admits that he has never seen the manufacturing process, his credibility as the firm's representative suffers.

Channel motivation and performance evaluation

The channel decision is very important. In theory at least, the cost of using intermediaries to achieve wider distribution is supposedly lower. Indeed, most consumer goods manufacturers could never justify the cost of selling direct to their consumers, except by mail order (direct marketing). In practice, if the manufacturer is large enough, the use of intermediaries (particularly at the agent and wholesaler level) can sometimes cost more than going direct to a foreign market. Many of the theoretical arguments about channels therefore revolve around cost. On the other hand, most of the practical decisions are concerned with control of the consumer. The small company has no alternative but to use intermediaries, often several layers of them, but large companies do have the choice of an organic approach to the international market.

Many international manufacturers seem to assume that once their product has been sold into the channel (into the beginning of the distribution chain), their job is finished. Yet that distribution chain is merely assuming a part of the manufacturer's responsibility; and, if the manufacturer has any aspirations to be market-oriented, the manufacturer's work should really be extended to managing all the processes involved in the chain, until the product or service arrives at the end-user. This may involve a number of decisions by the manufacturer, including membership management and channel motivation.

Channel membership management

The manufacturer has some control over which organizations participate in the distribution chain, and the structure of that channel. At one extreme, in mass consumer goods markets where members of the chain merely offer a logistics service, the manufacturer's main concern may be to maximize distribution levels so that the maximum number of outlets offer the product or service. At the other extreme, where retailers, for example, take over some of the manufacturer's responsibility for supporting sophisticated technical products, the manufacturer may be primarily concerned about the quality of the individual retailer. Under these circumstances in particular, the choice of channel members becomes a very important activity, almost as though they were being employed as direct employees.

Channel motivation

It is difficult enough to motivate direct employees to provide the necessary sales and service support. Motivating the owners and employees of firms, or independent agents, in an international distribution chain requires even greater effort. There are many devices for achieving such motivation. Perhaps the most usual is to offer inducements. The manufacturer offers a better margin to tempt the agent (or retailer) to push the product rather than its competitors, or a competition is offered to the distributors' sales personnel, so they are encouraged to push the product. At the other end of the spectrum is the almost symbiotic relationship that the all too rare manufacturer in the computer field develops with its agents, where the agent's personnel, support as well as sales, are trained to almost the same standard as the manufacturer's own staff.

Monitoring of channel members is done the same way that the organization's sales and distribution activities are monitored and managed. In practice, of course, many organizations use a mix of different channels; in particular, they may complement a direct sales force calling on larger accounts with agents covering smaller customers and prospects.

The retail organizations that form the various links in the distribution chains take over some of the manufacturer's responsibilities. In general, the retailers' primary value to the manufacturer is the wider distribution that they offer, which increases the overall penetration of the brand. Retailers also hold stock, provide service support and gather information useful to manufacturers. The exact relationship between the manufacturer and the retailer will depend in part upon the legal context and the contract. A retailer will, for example, be totally independent of the manufacturer, whereas an agent will act on behalf of that manufacturer – typically operating under the same terms and conditions.

For these services channel members are reimbursed in a variety of ways:

- **Trade discounts** – these are standard discounts, usually of a fixed percentage, offered to a channel member. However, the percentage may vary according to the category in which the manufacturer places the retailer.
- **Quantity discount** – this has the advantage that it offers an incentive for retailers to sell the maximum volume, and hence trade up to higher discount levels.
- **Promotional discount** – these are offered in the hope that the retailer will substitute the brand for another, encouraging end-users to accept what is in stock. Alternatively, the intention may be to persuade the retailer to overstock, creating 'stock pressure', so it is forced to give the brand extra display space.
- **Cash discount** – most manufacturers offer 30 days payment terms. This is of considerable value to retailers who have managed to reduce stockholdings to less than five days, since the extra 25 days' credit can in effect be used as a free loan. The manufacturer may want to provide an incentive for retailers, or wholesalers, to pay earlier. However the practice of offering a cash discount, or discount for immediate or prompt payment, has fallen into disfavour. Many retailers take the cash discount and still pay late (often after 60 days rather than 30).

Distribution channels may not be restricted to physical products. They may be just as important for moving a service from 'producer' to consumer in certain sectors, since both direct and indirect channels may be used. Hotels, for example, may sell their services (typically rooms) direct or through travel agents, tour operators, airlines, tourist boards, centralized reservation systems and so on.

There have also been some innovations in the distribution of services. For example, there has been an increase in franchising and in rental services, which offer anything from televisions to DIY tools. There has also been some evidence of service integration, particularly in the travel and tourism sector. For example, in Europe there are links between airlines, hotels and car rental services. In addition, there has been a significant increase in retail outlets for the service sector; outlets such as estate agencies and building society offices, for example, are crowding out the traditional grocers and greengrocers from the high street.

Channel cooperation and conflict

The reduction of cost and the increase of efficiency brought about by specialization have provided the fillip to organizations to enter trading relations with other organizations. When two or more organizations acknowledge that it is in their mutual interest to perpetuate a relationship across a national border, this is generally viewed as an indication that a channel of distribution has emerged. The logical outcome of a relationship of two or more organizations that perceive mutual gain from developing, or continuing, their relationship is mutual dependence. This basic concept requires the management of a number of important behaviours (Stone and McCall 2004).

By the act of aligning themselves with other organizations in a relationship of

dependence, organizations commit themselves to cooperative activities. Such cooperation takes the form of fulfilling a negotiated role in the channel of distribution, where
various functions might to be undertaken for agreed rewards. A code of conduct lays
down the expected contribution of channel members. Since adequate channel performance is crucial to the maintenance of harmonious relationships within the channel, failure to achieve adequate performance can lead to frustration and conflict. When channel
members are located in different countries, with differing cultural, linguistic and ideolog-
ical backgrounds, insensitive behaviour by one channel member from the viewpoint of
another culture can spark a conflict that might otherwise have been avoidable.

A Mexican agent who had succeeded selling a major item of equipment felt discrimi-
nated against when his UK principal insisted on applying the terms of his own agreement
with his credit insurers. Under this, the principal took a lien on the agent's commission
to ensure the agent's commitment to the buyer's payment of long-term credit instalments. Contrary to the custom of the country, the agent would only receive his commission on receipt of the third instalment of ten, scheduled for 18 months after delivery. The
two perceptions of the situation were different. 'Facts' are likely to be interpreted in the
light of prior experience, which will be coloured by the cultural practices that have
emerged. Cooperation of necessity includes the handling of conflict, as the supplier is
dependent on the agent for success in a market, as is the agent on the supplier. Channel
members enter into a relationship because they are unable on their own to perform
efficiently all the functions that must be completed to accomplish their goals.

Channel agreements and alternative channels

The vast majority of channel cooperation arrangements are the subject of written agreements
in which the details and conditions of how the parties are to work together are spelled out.
The best agreements address the possibility of conflict and outline a conflict resolution
procedure. This typically specifies the law under which the agreement is to be interpreted, the
definitive language version of the agreement (if it has been produced in more than one
language), the body that arbitrate in case of disputes, and the place of arbitration.

The duration of the agreement is critical. The shorter the period, the simpler it is to
have a review of arrangements. However the length must be consistent with the confidence of the partners in investing in the arrangement (for example, by building up stocks
or taking on personnel). Revisions in a new agreement should take account of changes
that arise in the relationship . The self-determination of the parties that exists at the time
an original agreement is made is complicated by factors of performance and commitment
to the joint activity once it has been put into operation. The original objectivity is clouded
by the history of the growing relationship and the subsequent negotiations that take
place within the original agreement.

Power negotiation

As mentioned earlier, often one party holds the majority of the power in the relationship,
but patterns of dependence can change as a result of changes in the environment. These
might derive, for example, from an extension of competition through new or substitutable

---

MINI CASE 10.3

Relative channel differences in Europe

In a channel of distribution those members perceived to possess a relative power advantage may assume a position of channel leadership. Inter-organizational relations are more likely to be characterized by unequal than equal power. In Germany for example, wholesalers came together horizontally before manufacturers could integrate vertically, allowing them to exert greater influence than in other European countries.

A firm's tolerance of this imbalance is related to its dependence on other channel members. German manufacturers accepted wholesaler channel leadership because it gave them relative freedom from competition from foreign manufacturers. There are still challenges in attempting to enter the German market through a distributorship agreement. The alternative of buying into the market is also problematic. Much of the wholesale business is held by family-owned, medium-sized companies (the Mittelstand), resistant to buy-outs and hostile bids.

The US-based retailer Wal-Mart made two acquisitions in 1997 and 1998 to make it Germany's fourth largest hypermarket chain, with 10 per cent of the market. However, it misjudged corporate culture, planning and social regulations, market demand, and critically disregarded the structure of distribution in German food retailing, using its US model of controlling distribution to stores itself rather than leaving it to the suppliers. By 2000, despite some refurbishment of the 95 stores, it was losing about US$200–300 million a year. Wal-Mart found it challenging to pursue its usual policy of building up market size and achieving critical mass by acquisition of established retailers, and retreated from the German market.

On the other hand, Wal-Mart's entry to the United Kingdom in 1999, where buying and selling of whole companies is viewed – certainly by the financial markets – as a legitimate activity, was much more successful. It acquired Asda, one of the 'Big Five' supermarket chains, with the hub of its activities in northern England where smaller independents are particularly vulnerable to the entry of a low-price competitor.

In 2003 the EU Competition Commission stepped in over concern that in bidding for the Safeway group, market leaders Wal-Mart (Asda), Tesco and Sainsbury might become too dominant. Ultimately it decided in favour of the original bidder, the Morrison group, which was then obliged to sell some of the Safeway outlets to meet with the strict competition rules relating to the UK food and household retail market.

Source: Benoit (2000).

---

products, changing market structures, new selling support activities, changing exchange rates, new perspectives on payment terms or changes in consumer preferences. If a salesperson finds out from say, an engineer in the buying organization that a quotation provided is the only one that meets the specification, his/her power is greatly increased. Conversely, when a purchaser establishes that a supplier is short of work, the purchaser's position is strengthened. When reputable agents are in short supply, this gives the apparently weaker agent a strong negotiating base. If a distributor, or agent, has a special relationship with key customers, or has special facilities or capabilities, that will strengthen its bargaining power.

A licensor's, distributor's or potential joint venture partner's hand is strengthened if the product is patented, or incorporates copyright or a trade mark. The credibility of the company is another factor. Any presentation that highlights this in terms of heavy users or significant sales will reinforce this credibility. The credibility of negotiators and their ability to create a climate of confidence can also affect the relative power situation.

A joint venture has so much power floating around in it that each party has the potential to move the other a considerable way from its initial bargaining point. Furthermore, in any joint venture negotiating situation there is the potential to harness the power of other institutions. For example, if one partner is from an industrialized country while the other operates in a less developed country, the latter might seek to strengthen its hand by demonstrating that it has active alternatives. The government of India has in the past (Gill and Allerheiligen, 1996) invited companies interested in an oil venture to indicate their degree of interest, and visibly entered into, and continued negotiations with, more than one company.

When an international organization is considering a joint venture, its efforts regarding information gathering and developing local affiliations (such as enlisting the support of other companies) can enhance its position. This is an approach adopted by the Japanese when seeking joint ventures in Malaysia, where the situation is delicate since the commercial strength and business acumen of the large Chinese minority is challenged by laws setting equity targets for Malaysian and other companies. These require Malaysian non-Bumiputra companies (that is, companies owned by Chinese non-native Malaysians) to hold no more than 40 per cent of a Malaysian company's shareholding and foreign companies to hold no more than 30 per cent.

Cultural aspects of negotiations

From time to time issues can be coloured by the transference to them of the values of a person's own culture. This is known as the 'self-reference criterion'. Conflict can arise on ethical issues. This is particularly evident in the subject of corruption. It can arise worldwide, but when put into a cross-cultural context, corruption can be interpreted very differently in different countries. In many parts of Latin America, black Africa, parts of Asia and in the Arab countries, the use of family and friendship ties is widespread, and considered a necessary and important means of doing business. The use of agents and distributors raises the question of commission and bribery.

When a foreign organization employs an agent on its behalf, the agent will incur several costs. As well as financial costs, the agent might draw on personal connections, and for these services he or she will feel entitled to a commission. There is often a fine line between commission and bribery, and people from different cultures tend to draw it in different places.

Alternative channels of distribution

The principal traditional channels and the principal collaborative channels of distribution are franchising, licensing, exporting, the use of agents and distributors, joint ventures and strategic alliances.

Franchising

This is a form of market approach by which a company, the franchisor, grants another independent organization the right to do business in a particular way. This right can involve the selling of the franchisor's product or service, using its name, production and marketing techniques, general business approach, or a combination of these. The franchisee shares the benefits of the company's advertising. The fast food industry typically uses franchising for its expansion: for example it is used by KFC, McDonald's and Pizza Hut. According to McGoldrick and Davies (1995), companies often use franchising for reasons of market potential, particularly where domestic markets are saturated, and sometimes to counter competitors' action in a foreign market.

The major elements of a franchise agreement are spelled out in a contract. The agreement usually ties the franchisee to using supplies from the franchisor. Quality is a prime concern, reflected in training, often on a continuing basis, by the franchisor's staff, and is supported by procedural manuals. A one-off franchising fee and ongoing royalties are payable by the franchisee, who in effect provides the capital for the expansion activities of the franchisor, although the latter may finance stocks. Franchising agreements are typically tightly drawn up, with no scope for negotiation.

The franchising approach appeals to many individuals aspiring to own their own business, and to small companies. It provides expertise that would not otherwise be available. In the European Union, recognition of franchising as one of the fastest ways of growing a business has been given legal backing, since it has been excluded from Article 85 (1) of the Treaty of Rome and the general prohibition on restrictive agreements likely to distort free competition. The scope of the ruling does not extend to industrial franchising, where a manufacturing process or technology, such as the manufacture of up-and-over garage doors, is involved. This area is covered by separate regulations which provide exemption from competition restrictions on know-how licensing agreements and by an existing rule giving clearance for patent licences.

Licensing

Licensing agreements concern the sale of knowledge, access to that knowledge and the means to exploit it. As many countries look to develop their economies and multinational corporations look for markets into which to expand, the potential host countries seek more of the value-adding activity for themselves. Licensing therefore becomes an attractive alternative. It is also a short-cut to competitiveness where that has been lost. The licensor can grant to the licensee patent rights or know-how rights. This access to intellectual property is attractive to many would-be licensees.

The licence can relate to the right to:

- make a product for sale
- use particular know-how
- bottle, fill or package for sale a product, usually in the food, chemical or pharmaceutical industries
- use without manufacture or sale
- assemble and sell parts of a patented product, as with the automotive, electrical and appliance industries
- distribute and sell only the patented product.

Similarly, licences can be granted for trademarks and brands.

Exporting

Within the exporting category, a company may have its own export department, and engage in direct exporting. It and its customers will negotiate agreements of purchase and sale. Where expert discussion is required, company personnel may travel round the world visiting various markets. Often the people visiting these markets are nationals of the country, or speak the language fluently. Most exporting organizations will have some form of foreign representation, which may have to be supported by direct negotiations between members of the buying and selling organizations.

An alternative is for an export merchant to buy products in the country of origin and sell them abroad at its own risk. A similar situation exists where a foreign customer has a buying office, or is represented in the country of origin. Either way, the resultant contract is equivalent to a domestic transaction and does not give rise to the same problems as inter-country transactions. It can expose the foreign buyer to the laws of the supplier country.

Another alternative is the use of a foreign-based intermediary who can be either an agent or a distributor, giving rise to (often exclusive) distributor and agency agreements. A large proportion of sales to companies, other than affiliated companies, are handled through such intermediaries.

Other modes of exporting include consortium agreements and group representation, which involves the cooperative action of a number of manufacturers of associated equipment and products/services who can jointly obtain business which individually they could not achieve. These represent a small proportion of total export sales.

Agents and distributors

Legal perspectives distinguish between agents and distributors. An agent acts for a named principal who then enters into an agreement with the agent's customer. A distributor acts on its own behalf and carries the economic risk of the transactions into which it enters. An agent receives a commission on sales, or where circumstances justify it, a retainer and reduced commission. The latter is frequently used where sales are of large value, but infrequent. Usually, the agent also receives territorial exclusivity. Distributors receive exclusive or limited rights to sell a good in a territory, in addition to the profits accruing from their efficiency in purchasing, from their estimates of their own markets, the price the product is sold at, and their effectiveness in managing their administrative costs. In return they are expected to exert their best efforts in the sale of the supplier products.

Some countries have separate legislation covering an agent acting on behalf of an undisclosed principal.

An agreement that is perceived to be unfair in operation by the intermediaries will have a demotivating effect. Clearly, mutual benefit is desirable in an agreement that is expected to have a long-term duration.

Before a contract is signed, agreement must be reached on:

- products/brands included in the agency/distributorship agreement
- territory covered by the agreement, and whether agreement is exclusive or non-exclusive (some markets are so small that exclusive agreements are needed to ensure adequate return for effort)

MINI CASE 10.4

The negotiating power of agents/distributors

The international marketing environment can change either dramatically, as in the case of the devaluation of a currency, or insidiously, as with the strengthening over time of particular interest groups. Smaller retailers have banded together in groups such as Spar (from the Dutch word meaning to save) and Mace, which were set up by wholesalers as a counterbalance to larger and more powerful retailers, which had grown by merger and acquisition and were in a strong position to negotiate substantial discounts. The object was to benefit from shared advertising and to get better prices as a result of their shared buying capability.

In the mid-1980s, Cadbury refused to give Spar, which was already organizing on a European basis, similar discounts to those granted to the large and growing supermarket groups. It was only when Spar threatened to boycott Cadbury's products in 11,000 Western European outlets that the chairman went post-haste to Amsterdam and conceded that the groups should be treated as an entity and not a collection of small buyers.

As retail groups grew even larger and fewer in the 1990s, and negotiated even better discounts, Spar responded by further extending its membership. Today, manufacturers have to take account of an even greater accumulation of power in the case of Spar International, which has several wholesaler members and over 40,000 small retailers in Western Europe. Currently its negotiation power is considerable, and the lower prices it is able to agree go a long way to closing the gap with supermarkets that enjoy maximum discounts, economics of scale and vast promotion budgets.

- duration of the agreement
- prices and currency of quotations, invoices and trade discounts to distributor
- percentage agency commission, when and how it is to be paid to the agent
- place and body of arbitration
- law of the agreement.

A supplier of goods or services does not usually have an open choice between using an agent or a distributor. Rather, the nature of the offering determines the type of intermediary selected. Normally producers of consumer goods, consumer durables, industrial consumables and low-cost capital equipment use a distributor. Normally raw materials and high-cost capital equipment are marketed through an agent, where not sold direct to the end user. In practice the distinctions are not so clear. An agent might act as such for the principal's products, but as a distributor for spares and consumables. A distributor might act as such for the supplier but be paid commission when required to service the accounts of competing distributors being supplied by the same manufacturer. In the provision of services, agents are often used because the intangibility of many services precludes the transference of ownership, as in the case of travel agents and insurance brokers.

Joint ventures

Joint ventures are distinguished from agency or distributorship and licensing agreements by their greater complexity and greater power in the system. The concept of joint venture has been applied to economic activity undertaken jointly by two or more organizations. It may take almost any form. It may be horizontal, vertical or conglomerate, and it may be owned by firms that are unrelated in business interests, or created for marketing, production or research. Chiefly, it is used in connection with a legally independent entity under the joint control of the participants. The term is also used to connote other under-takings that have no legal status and in which the participants are controlled by means of a convenient concept. This is used when a purely contractual arrangement is insuffi-cient and where the drastic irreversible solution of the merger is more than is required to achieve the desired objectives. The participants are willing to cooperate as independent operators. The venture is only workable as long as all participants agree and there is mutual understanding between them.

The negotiation of joint venture agreements is usually in relation to:

- quality of performance of the partners in the joint venture
- policies and objectives of the new company
- contributions of the parties, their rights and obligations
- rights of the partners to sell their shares
- procedures for recruiting and dismissing
- responsibilities for the import of components and the export of finished goods
- training and experience to provide cross-cultural strategies to staff of both organizations.

Government restrictions on ownership of joint ventures have intensified in recent years, and often specify maximum foreign participation of 50 per cent or less, forcing sophisti-cated management to examine means of ensuring efficiency and control. The burden of giving effect to these regulations, or achieving an equitable compromise, falls squarely on the shoulders of the negotiators. There are laws in many countries against agreements and practices that are in restraint of trade. In developed, industrialized countries these usually refer to restrictions on competition between independent companies. In develop-ing countries frequently they are viewed as limitations imposed on a locally based company by a foreign parent company.

Strategic alliances

Increasingly many organizations are embracing a strategy of internationalization and core competence. Internationalization forces companies to sell their products in as many differ-ent places as possible, a practice which frequently requires other people and other organi-zations to help them. The preference of firms to stick to what they do best, or their core competencies, means they must let others outside the organization, often abroad, help them with everything else. In this way, the best practice can be called upon irrespective of source in all aspects of the company's market offering.

Strategic alliances come in a variety of forms (see de Burca et al. 2004). The joint venture discussed above, in which companies either hold a proportion of their partner's equity or set up a joint company, is the most rigid. In the most fluid form there is no formal agreement to fall back on and the participants rely on a common vision and considerable trust. The latter type is characterized by the relationship between McDonald's and Coca-Cola, although most of McDonald's alliances are of the more formal kind: for example, it has a ten-year alliance with Disney. Most strategic alliances fall somewhere between the two extremes and can be fairly vague. Their open-endedness is part of their appeal. When they have served their purpose, which may be sooner rather than later, there is no legal requirement for them to continue until resolved by lawyers, making them self-regulating.

As de Burca et al. (2004) observed, new alliances can be a form of faster, cheaper growth than other more formal arrangements. However, while alliances can be relatively inexpensive to set up, they need to be well managed, using good communication and negotiation skills as well as the older skills of diplomacy and a high tolerance of uncertainty. The trust implicit in information agreements comes from the parties taking slight risks in divulging information about themselves and releasing more when experience makes them confident in doing so. It is an incremental, and delicate, process. By bringing together different firms with unique skills and capabilities, alliances can create powerful learning opportunities. As alliances become more common, exploiting the learning potential of alliances will become more important.

Channel strategy for new market entry

The alternatives discussed above also apply when choosing how to enter a new market, or develop an existing one. The increased commitment of resources requires increased outlay and provides increased control when moving from franchising and licensing through exporting to FDI alternatives. Establishing strategic alliances, as in the airline business, is a low-cost strategy aimed at expanding the market. For example, traditional intermediaries like travel agents enter into alliances with latter-day electronic websites inviting 'e-bookers' to take advantage of the services offered. Like alliances, ownership strategies also affect costs and control. If a joint venture is set up in preference to, say, a wholly owned subsidiary, the shared faculties reduce the cost, but the amount of control exercised will be reduced too.

Determinants of choice

The factors that determine choice of a channel of distribution are both external and internal to the organization. These factors show how the options open to organizations are restricted. For example, small companies may not have the resource or expertise to become involved in FDI. Markets with low break-even sales volumes tend to favour low-cost channels such as licensing or exporting (Stone and McCall 2004). If a new market is found to have a high sensitivity to price – for example, by removal of inhibiting regulations – volumes may increase spectacularly, making a chosen channel that was appropriate at an early stage in the development of the market, unsuitable at a later stage. This underscores the need for accurate information to identify an appropriate channel from the outset. Traditional decision-making techniques can be applied in such circumstances.

External influences on choice

Market size is a primary consideration, together with trends in the market like segmentation and the estimated share of the market that can be achieved in view of the competition. The existing distribution methods will determine whether single or multiple channels are developed. Host countries policies are important because they can lead to special requirements such as import quotas or duties. If a company wants to hold on to its technology, there is little point in trying to enter a market by means of FDI, where there is insistence on its transfer. Market structure is important since competing intermediaries might include organizations with affiliations to competitors either locally or from outside the market. The economic infrastructure becomes critical when specialized expertise is required or competent financing, manufacture and distribution services are needed. Production costs are critical where these constitute a high proportion of the total costs of a product.

Internal (organizational) influences on choice

Factors relating to the organization have a bearing on the channel decisions. International experience and commitment are normally necessary before undertaking expensive foreign investment, as is training for those entering the international market for the first time. As Stone and McCall (2004) observed, company policy may exclude countries where there is little protection for the company. The product may be a deciding factor in the channel decision. For example, a bulky product transportable across borders only at great cost may be more profitably manufactured under licence in the customer country. In many organizations, there is a dominant coalition which, for differing reasons of the individuals concerned, may decide to enter a market or revise its channel approach. Finally, a company has, or should have, a long-term strategy, which can influence the channel decision; if it wishes in the long term to exploit a particular market, then it will not license its product or process in that market.

Grey market influences on distribution management

Competition is rife in the modern international marketplace. This is true in the field of brands where companies continually compete for a bigger share of the market. The companies with highly visible brands provide for themselves the opportunity of those bigger shares becoming a reality. But success comes at a high price, with continual threats from competitors. Some of the latest dangers to corporate brand owners come from retailers developing their own branded ranges of products. Some retailers have packaged and presented their brands in similar sounding and looking fashion to the prevailing market leaders. This aptly titled 'piggyback approach' has been much to the annoyance of the brand proprietors. It has tended to encourage bitter litigation to restore the identity and status of the original brands. In addition, threats are posed by the grey market, where parallel brand imports are sold at discount prices, further antagonising the original trademark owners.

The operation of the grey market was discussed on pages 63–5. Grey markets have become more of a problem during recent years, because of the growth in the number of international brands, the increase in international product standardization, and fluctuations in exchange rates, which have been more pronounced since the major currencies in which international trade is denominated have been allowed to float, and which provide opportunities for predatory pricing. The use of the Internet also helps to bring markets closer and makes the market information and prices transparent.

The black market (informal economy)

Although grey market activity can be legal, there is also of course much illegal activity, particularly in the developing world. For example, as a result of the extensive common border between West African countries many of Nigeria's used car imports enter free of duty by being physically driven across the border.

Deciding how to operate in countries with black market competition is a challenge for the international marketer. Both markets and activities are not all the same shade of black or white. Different shades seem to apply to varying forms of illegal activity. They can range from criminal behaviour (for example bribery) to unofficial business practices that are widely condoned. Some advantages of the informal economy are higher levels of employment due to the economic activity undertaken, increased availability of products in the marketplace due to greater currency liquidity, and increased availability of goods and services. Apart from its illegality, the disadvantages of an informal economy include a negative impact on the growth of the official economy, diversion of resources from public infrastructure projects into private consumption, failure to observe health and safety laws, and lack of control over a significant sector of the economy. The black market usually operates to the country's overall detriment, resulting in higher rates of poverty.

Black marketing is particularly prevalent in Africa, and in Russia, India, China and Brazil; and in particular, countries characterized by government-owned enterprises, volumes of government regulation, corruption and a history of the involvement of organized crime in business activities. It is therefore important for organizations to take into account the nature of the trading environment in the international market when preparing a strategic plan. The trading environment will also impact on the price that can be charged and on the most appropriate market entry strategy.

International logistics management

The international competitiveness of European companies will increasingly depend on their ability to deliver customer-adapted products and services all over the world quickly and on time (Skjoett-Larsen 2000). This places heavy demands on logistics systems. Today, logistics has emerged as a major tool for, for example, European food retailers (Yrjola 2001). For many years, however, it was considered as administration, or more exactly as a technical means used in marketing (Pache 1998). Logistics then meant performing transport and warehousing operations depending on strategies of market penetration, positioning, segmentation and so on. Its importance was eventually recognized in the 1980s when manufacturers, and retailers, began to exploit it to achieve a sustainable competitive advantage (Bell et al. 1997).

As a result of international competition, production processes have become increasingly specialized. The implication is that an increasing part of the value added is placed outside the company's own production facilities. At the same time, globalization of supplier and customer markets is taking place, where domestic and local suppliers and customers play a less important role than global suppliers and customers. Measures to improve the efficiency of information and transport systems have played a major role in development. These measures have made it less expensive, quicker and safer to purchase goods from remote suppliers and distribute goods to remote customers.

Another factor is rapid technological development combined with economies of scale in production, which in some component markets has resulted in a concentration of relatively few international suppliers. Examples are semiconductors and screen filters in personal computers (PCs). A third factor is the large difference in payroll and production costs between Western Europe and developing economies. A growing number of companies in Western Europe are moving their labour-demanding production processes to new industrial regions or buying an increasing part of the materials they require from suppliers in these areas. In this connection, Poland, Hungary and the Czech Republic are especially interesting as they are almost at the same level as western European companies in terms of technology and quality, while their payroll costs are considerably lower.

Finally, access to a number of markets is facilitated if production has been set up in the country in question. For example, NAFTA enables goods manufactured in Mexico to be freely exported to the United States and Canada. Several multinational companies have set up plants in China, India or Brazil to take advantage of the cheap labour forces and get access to widely expanding markets. As Williams, Esper and Ozment (2002) forecasted, in future, European companies supplying components or systems to multinational companies will be required to participate in international sourcing by their customers. This may imply that they set up local production close to the customers' most important markets. For example, suppliers to the car industry are often met by a demand to set up local plants in order to supply on a just-in-time (JIT) basis global car manufacturers' assembly plants around the world.

Within Europe (Williams et al. 2002), the driving forces behind changes in logistics structure and strategy are the:

- removal of trade and transport barriers between EU countries
- opening of new markets in Eastern Europe
- acceptance of a single European currency
- development of information technology (IT) and fast communication systems
- emergence of pan-European logistics service providers, who offer fast, reliable and cost-efficient distribution in Europe
- retailers' adaptation and cultural learning.

Recently, there has been an upsurge in company acquisitions, mergers and alliances in the contract logistics industry to create one-stop, pan-European service providers. One example is Deutsche Post, which has acquired the Swiss company Danzas and the Swedish ASG. Another example is the Danish logistics provider DFDS Transport, which has acquired its closest competitor Dantransport. Customers drive the logistics service providers when they enter new markets. One example is the UK-based logistics provider, Exel Logistics, which followed Marks & Spencer into France. Major logistics providers from North America, such as GeoLogistics and Ryder International, are expanding into Europe, driven by customer demands for pan-European and global logistics service coverage (Fawcett and Magnan 2002). The use of IT, and in particular the application of the Internet, helps global logistics development.

The role of the Internet

For the time being there is little or no regulation of the Internet, which allows the medium to develop as the market dictates. It is a classic approach. As government get more and more knowledge of its impact, the big players will use it to generate influence and power to counter the anarchic quality of present use and the possible threat to competition from its domination. When the industry approximates the classic structure of perfect competition, contracts are not often used (Galbraith 1975). Supply responds readily to changes in marketplaces, and since there are a large number of sellers, it is not necessary to make special medium or long-term arrangements with each one. This could be construed as 'free-flow' distribution. Transactions taking place under this practice may, or may not, have a degree of permanence. They have no yet reached the stage where long-term written agreements are considered necessary. With globalization, a world-wide market and international channels replace the local nature of traditional channels. Its geographic extent is encouraging new electronic MNCs to determine the nature of new channels and to buy up successful start-up companies that match their mission objectives.

Table 10.1   Applications of the Internet in the value chain

Firm infrastructure
- Web-based, distributed financial systems.
- Online investor relations (e.g. information dissemination, broadcast conference calls).

Human resource management
- Self-service personnel and benefits administration.
- Web-based training.
- Internet-based sharing and dissemination of company information.
- Electronic time and expense reporting.

Technology development
- Collaborative product design across locations and among multiple value-system participants.
- Knowledge directories accessible from all parts of the organization.
- Real-time access by R&D to on-line sales and service information.

Procurement
- Internet-enabled demand planning; real-time available-to-promise/capable-to-promise and fulfilment.
- Other linkage of purchase, inventory, and forecasting systems with suppliers.
- Automated 'requisition to pay'.
- Direct and indirect procurement via marketplaces, exchanges, auctions, and buyer–seller matching.

Table 10.1 continued

Inbound logistics
- Real-time integrated scheduling, shipping, warehouse management, demand management and planning, and advanced planning and scheduling across the company and its suppliers.
- Dissemination throughout the company of real-time inbound and in-process inventory data.

Operations
- Integrated information exchange, scheduling, and decision making in in-house plants, contract assemblers and components suppliers.
- Real-time available-to-promise and capable-to-promise information available to the sales force and channels.

Outbound logistics
- Real-time transaction of orders whether initiated by an end consumer, a salesperson or a channel partner.
- Automated customer-specific agreements and contract terms.
- Customer and channel access to product development and delivery status.
- Collaborative integration with customer forecasting systems.
- Integrated channel management including information exchange, warranty claims and contract management (versioning, process control).

Marketing and sales
- Online sales channels including websites and marketplaces.
- Real-time inside and outside access to customer information, product catalogues, dynamic pricing, inventory availability, online submission of quotes and order entry.
- Online product configurators.
- Customer-tailored marketing via customer profiling.
- Push advertising.
- Tailored online access.
- Real-time customer feedback through web surveys, opt-in/opt-out marketing and promotion response tracking.

After-sales service
- Online support of customer service representatives through e-mail response management, billing integration, co-browse, chat, 'call me now', voice-over-IP, and other uses of video streaming.
- Customer self-service via websites and intelligent service request processing including updates to billing and shipping profiles.
- Real-time field service access to customer account review, schematic review, parts availability and ordering, work-order update, and service parts management.

Aspects of the Internet developments

Overheads are considerably less for e-commerce intermediaries than for traditional ones. They do not require the conventional investment in warehouses, demonstration, shops and associated equipment and staff. In the United States, an organization like FurnitureFind.com is eroding the idea that certain kinds of products cannot be sold online. New entrants to web markets are more likely to be in the laggard categories like clothing and art than the established staples like CDs and books where competition is heavy. Even perishable groceries and car parts are available on the net. The so-called 'look and feel' issues (Kotzab and Madlberger 2001) are being addressed as entrepreneurial companies spend to overcome the objections of buyers, for example by providing high-resolution pictures of items they cannot touch. The value of art objects is being assured by endorsement by reputable experts.

The US leisure catalogue company Lands' End, already established in Europe, has developed a 'swimsuit finder' feature to mollify women who are reluctant to buy beachwear they cannot try on. It allows women to pick their body type from an array of choices, and recommends suits likely to fit. This, together with a noticeable increase in the proportion of women logging on, is expanding the market for such items. Companies like eBay, an electronic auction house, are taking classified advertisement business from newspapers, and online news services are similarly nibbling away at the editorial side. The classified advertisement business particularly is important for regional newspapers in the United Kingdom, where it is estimated to amount to about 50 per cent of revenues. If the trend continues, smaller newspapers may take their classified advertisements to the providers as one way of retaining the business. It remains to be seen what will follow.

The rapidly emerging new class of intermediaries is offering real value and attacking inefficiencies in the price and cost structure of business. It would appear that not only are traditional retailers looking to undertake Internet operations as a hedge against electronic developments, they are looking to integrate shopping, combining stores, the Internet, catalogues, the telephone and eventually television. It is a seductive concept, which is making electronic channels consider investing in 'bricks and mortar' retailers. The advantage of the bricks and mortar organizations is that they do what the vast majority of the electronic companies have failed to do so far: they make a profit. Association with these traditional retailers by acquisition, or merger, assures a base for further investment.

The Internet and the value chain

The basic tool for understanding the influence of IT on companies is the value chain. Porter (2001) defines it as 'the set of activities through which a product or service is created and delivered to customers'. When a company competes in any industry, it performs a number of discrete but interconnected value-creating activities, such as operating a sales force, fabricating a component, and delivering products, channels and customers. The value chain is a framework for identifying all these activities and analysing how they affect both a company's costs and the value delivered to buyers (see Table 10.1). Since every activity involves the creation, processing and communication of information, IT has a pervasive influence on the value chain. The special advantage of the Internet is the ability to link one activity with others and make real-time data created in one activity widely available, both within the company and to suppliers, channels and customers. By incorporating a common, open set of communication protocols, Internet technology provides a standardized infrastructure, and intuitive browser interface of information access and delivery, bidirectional communication and ease of connectivity – all at much lower cost than private networks and electronic data interchange (EDI).

Many of the most prominent applications of the Internet in the value chain are shown in Table 10.1. Some involve moving what were physical activities online, while others involve making physical activities more cost-effective. Indeed, the technological possibilities available today derive not just from the Internet architecture but also from complementary technological advances such as scanning, object-oriented programming, relational databases and wireless communications. The evolution of IT in business can be thought of in terms of five overlapping stages, each of which evolved out of constraints presented by the previous generation.

According to Porter (2001), the earliest IT systems automated discrete transactions such as order entry and accounting. The next stage involved the fuller automation and functional enhancement of individual activities such as human resource management, sales force operations and product design. The third stage, which is being accelerated by the Internet, involves cross-activity integration, such as linking sales activities with order processing. Multiple activities are being liked together through such tools as customer relationship management (CRM), supply chain management (SCM) and enterprise resource planning (ERP) systems (Williams et al. 2002). The fourth stage, which is just beginning, enables the integration of the value chain and entire value systems: that is, the set of value chains in an entire industry, encompassing tiers of suppliers, channels and customers. SCM and CRM are starting to merge as end-to-end applications involving customers, channels and suppliers, linking orders to, for example, manufacturing, procurement and service delivery. Soon to be integrated is product development, which has been largely separate. Complex product models will be exchanged among parties, and Internet procurement will move from standard commodities to engineered items.

Summary

The nature of distribution channels has been examined in terms of conflict, dependence and power. The alternatives open to an organization and the factors influencing choice of either market entry or revised channel strategy have been considered. The choice is related to the degree of resource commitment, with cost and control increasing with the level of commitment. Both ownership patterns and strategic alliances kink this straight-line relationship. Preparation for negotiation was addressed in relation to building in power to a negotiation position. Some problems of negotiating the various channel agreements across cultures were discussed.

The growth of the Internet was examined by looking at examples of intermediaries using the medium. E-commerce is still a mere fraction of overall commercial activity, and its overall value is yet to be exploited by international marketers. Since it is not surrounded by rules and regulations, development is taking place at breathtaking speed. Companies are growing market share, often at a loss, to take advantage of the experience curve as the market takes off. It seems likely that only the big players will survive. If this is so, then political intervention may be used to ensure competition is maintained. It is possible that a radical new idea will redefine the market and restart the cycle of development. The integration of electronic and traditional channels may be a way forward.

Revision questions

1   Discuss the concept of natural channels and explain their use in modern distribution systems.
2   What is the major influential factor in international channel design?
3   Explain how government-imposed regulations could restrict channel structural options.
4   Discuss the factors that must be considered in selecting the appropriate channel for international distribution and management.
5   Channel motivation and performance evaluation are necessary for efficient distribution systems. Discuss the elements that international organizations consider when making channel decisions.
6   Briefly discuss the main channel alternatives for an international manufacturer of fast-moving consumer goods selling to southeast Asia.
7   The grey and black markets have major influences that are both beneficial and problematic to distribution management. Explain this statement using suitable examples.
8   What do you see as the driving forces behind changes in logistics structure and strategy in Europe?
9   The application of the Internet in the value chain is likely to generate efficient distribution and logistics. Discuss.
10 Explain the role of the Internet in international distribution systems.

Managerial assignment task

You currently work for an international logistics and freight forwarding company, Swift Freight International, based in Dubai, as IT manager. Swift provides services to various industries such as IT, electronics, machinery, foodstuffs and consumer goods, and offers end-to-end supply chain management solutions to distribution channels. It is in second position in its market and wishes to grow to become a number one contender.

Swift has recently and successfully implemented a wide-scale IBM instant messaging (IM) and collaborative system across its international operation, which stretches from Africa and the Middle East to Hong Kong. This new system will allow the company to offer faster services to its customers, reduce communication costs and drastically increase employee efficiency. This move is very important for improving both the operational and service efficiency at Swift.

You are required to write a report to your managing director suggesting how this new system could be used to the company's competitive advantage. Your report should cover all aspects of how IT may help in channel management and collaboration.

References

Baalbaki, I. B. and Malhotra, N. K. (1995) 'Standardisation versus customerisation in international marketing: an investigation using bridging conjoint analysis', *Journal of the Academy of Marketing Science*, Vol. 23 No. 3, pp. 182–94.

Bell, R., Davies, R. and Howard, E. (1997) 'The changing structure of food retailing in Europe the implications for strategy', *Long Range Planning*, Vol. 30, No. 6, pp. 853–61.

Benoit, B. (2000) 'Wal-Mart finds German failure hard to swallow', *Financial Times*, 12 October, p. 25.

De Burca, S., Fletcher, R. and Brown, L. (2004) *International Marketing: An SME Perspective*, Harlow: Financial Times/Prentice Hall.

Douglas, S. P. and Craig, C. S. (1995) *Global Marketing Strategy*, New York: McGraw-Hill.

Economist (1999) 'Retailing', 4 March, pp. 3–18.

Fawcett, S. E. and Magnan, G. M. (2002), 'The rhetoric and reality of supply chain integration', *International Journal of Physical Distribution and Logistics Management*, Vol. 32, No. 5, pp. 339–61.

Galbraith, J. K. (1975) *Economics of the Public Purpose*, Harmondsworth: Penguin.

Gill, L. E. and Allerheiligen, R. P. (1996), 'Co-operation in channels of distribution: physical distribution leads the way', *International Journal of Physical Distribution and Logistics Management*, Vol. 26, No. 5, pp.49–63.

Kotzab, H. and Madlberger, M. (2001) 'European retailing in e-transition? An empirical evaluation of Web-based retailing – indications from Austria', *International Journal of Physical Distribution and Logistics Management*, Vol. 31, No. 6, pp. 440–62.

Lambert, D. M. and Stock, J. R. (1993) *Strategic Logistics Management*, 3rd edn, Boston: Richard Irwin.

London, S. (1995) 'Less hunger for space', *Financial Times*, 3 March, p. 28.

McGoldrick, P. J. (2003) *Retail Marketing*, 2nd edn, Maidenhead: McGraw-Hill.

McGoldrick, P. J. and Davies, G. (1995) *International Retailing: Trends and Strategies*, London: Pitman.

Omar, O. (1999) *Retail Marketing*, London: Financial Times/Pitman.

Paché, G. (1998) 'Retail logistics in France: the coming of vertical disintegration', *International Journal of Logistics Management*, Vol. 9, No. 1, pp. 85–9.

Porter, M. E. (2001) 'Strategy and the Internet', *Harvard Business Review*, March, pp. 63–78.

Skjoett-Larsen, T. (2000) 'European logistics beyond 2000', *International Journal of Physical Distribution and Logistics Management*, Vol. 30, No .5, pp.377–87.

Stone, M. A. and McCall, J. B. (2004) *International Strategic Marketing: A European Perspective*, London: Routledge.

Tsukamoto, N. (1994) 'Borden sells brand name right to Lotte', *Nikkei Weekly*, 30 May, p. 10.

Williams, L. R., Esper, T. L. and Ozment, J. (2002) 'The electronic supply chain: its impact on the current and future structure of strategic alliances, partnerships and logistics leadership', *International Journal of Physical Distribution and Logistics Management*, Vol. 32, No. 8, pp. 703–19.

Yrjola, H. (2001) 'Physical distribution considerations for electronic grocery shopping', *International Journal of Distribution and Logistics Management*, Vol. 31, No. 10, pp. 746–61.

Zeng, A. Z. and Rossetti, C. (2003) 'Developing a framework for evaluating the logistics costs in global sourcing processes: an implementation and insights', *International Journal of Physical Distribution and Logistics Management*, Vol. 33, No. 9, pp. 785–803.

11
Pricing Decisions in International Markets

Contents

LEARNING OBJECTIVES

After reading this chapter you should:

- be able to demonstrate general knowledge of international pricing
- know the determinants of international pricing
- understand the fundamentals of international pricing strategy and be able to use pricing strategy as a competitive advantage
- know how to set objectives for international pricing taking into consideration many variable elements of the international environment
- be able to set transfer pricing taking into consideration fluctuations in exchange rates in international markets
- be able to evaluate and negotiate international prices and trading through barter and counter-purchase.

Introduction

Falling trade barriers between national markets, the rise of newly industrialized countries and technological change are having profound effects upon the structure of international industries and have implications for the international business environment. The pressures of the international environment are now so great and the bases of competition within many markets are changing so fundamentally that the possibility of survival with a purely domestic strategy is becoming limited. It appears then that the dynamic and turbulent changes of the international environment present companies with a series of challenges for survival.

The pricing of products in international markets is becoming increasingly difficult for managers as a result of:

- heightened competition
- grey market activities
- counter-trade requirements
- regional trading blocs
- the emergence of intra-market segments
- volatile exchange rates.

As international economic foundations continue to shift, long-proven pricing structures are also collapsing. As competitive pressures increase, strategies for effective pricing of products for sale in international markets remain elusive.

Currently there is little research to guide managers in their international pricing efforts. Typically, managers rely on intuitive measures and give more strategic focus to other marketing decision variables. This often leads to unsuccessful market ventures, since businesses operating in an international environment must have a systematic pricing procedure. Although pricing is a serious problem for international managers, it has perhaps been the most ignored marketing decision variable within the research. Most efforts to understand the effects of pricing strategies on corporate performance have been undertaken within a purely domestic or single market context with little consideration for the increasingly international configuration and goals of the company.

Many companies with international marketing activities use international pricing, and each pricing strategy demands a different approach. For example, transfer pricing concerns the sale of products within the corporate family. A company may undertake a foreign-market pricing because it has its production facilities within an overseas market (completed products do not cross borders to reach the customer). Export pricing refers to products made in one country and sold to customers outside the corporate family in another country (through independent distributors). In this chapter the focus is on international market pricing as well as export pricing. Both of these pricing methods pose formidable challenges for most international marketers and exporters.

Determinants of international pricing

The obligation of international marketing strategy is to match the organization with its environment. If the business environment extends internationally then national environments become significant in its development. Thus, as Marsh (2000) cited, in its domestic market, Heineken is positioned as an average-price beer, which in restaurants and bars can almost be compared with the price of soft drinks and mineral water. Internationally, however, it uses a global positioning strategy of premium price and high quality. Similarly, Kronenbourg and Stella Artois are premium-priced exclusive drinks in the United Kingdom, whereas in Belgium and France, they are low-priced drinks.

In reviewing the many important factors involved in international pricing, Terpstra and Sarathy (1997) employed a framework that sees company-level, product-specific, market specific and environmental factors as influential factors of international market price setting. Although this framework opens up many questions, it does not provide a sufficient framework for analysing the microenvironment, which is ultimately responsible for determining the international pricing of a product.

As Figure 11.1 shows, price setting in international marketing is influenced on three levels:

- The internal level, which takes into consideration objectives for return on investment, required sales volume and cost factors. The structure of the company is also a significant internal influence. For example, a company that has chosen an 'umbrella' structure is unlikely to have central price control. The core element of international viability is the cost of producing and marketing the product, which inevitably has to be considered. For example, in the case of Chinese rice exports, when high production and distribution costs are associated with Chinese's remote geographic location and distance from the major importing countries, the profitability of rice export is reduced.
- The macro level incorporates elements such as government restrictions. Consider the pricing in the Chinese rice industry – an increase in tax to 15 per cent might prompt producers to increase prices in an attempt to retain profitability.
- The business cycle stage, incorporating exchange rate and cultural factors, also influences pricing decisions. For example, China's market has now entered the growth stage of its life cycle, and market share in Chinese markets will be increasingly dependent on competitive pricing strategies.

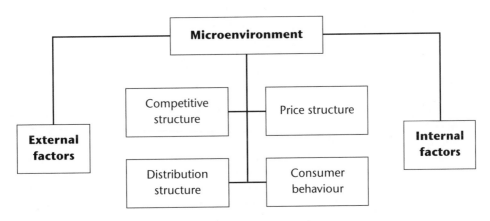

Figure 11.1 Determinants of international pricing

These levels are likely to influence the international pricing of a product, and shape the microenvironment, which must be considered as the major determinant of international pricing. As shown in Figure 11.1, the factors relating to the microenvironment are assembled into four classifications, which form the market determinants of international pricing. The discussion that follows is therefore centred on this framework.

Competitive structure

Carefully evaluating competitors' pricing policies before setting prices is just as important in the international market as in the domestic market. The level of competition in the market is often strongly linked to the stage of the products life cycle in different countries. For instance, consider the carbonated soft drinks market in France reaching maturity in the lemonade, fruited carbonates and tonic sector. The main driving force is competition from still iced teas and fruit juices with their new age positioning (Marsh 2000). As the example in Mini-case 11.1 shows, these competitive forces impose new challenges for price setting, with companies forced to resort to positioning on value for money. Prices are also likely to be under pressure in the French mustard market, as a result of the rapid growth of the low-priced vinegars market. The high prices demanded by mustards appear to be pushing customers away.

Price structure

As Heineken shows, products can be positioned with a high price in one country and a low price in another. This can be attributed to the pricing structure of international markets, viewed here as a major determinant of product pricing policy. According to Mintel (2001), the market for bottled water in Italy over the last decade has consistently

---

MINI CASE 11.1

Competitive structure

The emergence and continued growth of own-label products in the French breakfast cereals market is altering the competitive structure of the industry. The market was created by Kellogg, the large US multinational. However, more recently, own-label products have gained significant market share of 14 per cent in volume sales. In particular, close to a quarter of French muesli sales are from own-label products seen to be at the lower end of the price range. As the growth continues, the flexibility that companies such as Kellogg have in their pricing policies will decrease, presenting management with a series of implications for their pricing strategies.

Heilwasser, a German bottled water company, markets its water product on a semi-medicinal basis, and since 1995 has been losing market share. The reason for this is linked to promotion of the healthy lifestyle qualities of mainstream mineral waters that differ little from higher-priced Heilwasser product in terms of mineral content. Competitor activity within an industry such as mineral water can have profound effects on the products price.

Source: based on Mintel (2001).

increased in comparison with other soft drinks markets. As Mintel noted, in 2001 Italian consumption of bottled water ranked among the highest in Europe, with average prices in Italy around 25 per cent lower than in other European countries. However, the demand declines when there is relatively cool summer weather, and the industry has tended to use price to stimulate demand instead of other marketing techniques. However, now that the market is reaching maturity and prices are extremely low, demand cannot be further stimulated by lower prices with a high level of market concentration supporting this.

Pricing structure also refers to below-the-line pricing promotions, such as money-off vouchers. This is prominent in the French breakfast cereals market discussed in Mini case 11.1. In this particular market there is a high incidence of use of below-the-line promotions such as money-off offers, which is an influential component of the lower average price of the market. The importance of special offers in price will always vary between countries.

Consumer behaviour

In many international markets, it is usually not the cost of the materials that determines the value of the products, but rather the customer's perception of that value. In China, for example, price is usually a major determinant in most purchasing decisions for the vast majority of the population (Cui and Liu 2000). The price is essentially determined by the amount consumers are willing to pay for the product and their attitudes towards image and positioning. Similarly, Germany's frozen ready meals market found that by reducing its prices, customers were lured to the market, and sales progressively moved towards larger packs. Thus, where consumers appear to be price driven, organizations must uphold a competitive price, while corporate image becomes an important price associate.

Using pricing strategy as competitive advantage in international markets

Competitive advantage is a crucial determinant for surviving in the rapidly changing international environment. However, many companies are missing a strategic window of opportunity to use price, in carefully analysed situations, and to build a competitive advantage. For example, Whirlpool Corporation built its competitive advantage on its multibrand European portfolio. Its products, communication, pricing and competitive moves are based on pan-European positioning for its brand portfolio. Thus, pricing is an important tool in supporting an international competitive advantage. In order to understand how to use price to gaining competitive advantage, it is necessary to evaluate various strategies that could be effective in setting international pricing:

- cost leadership
- low price, high quality
- focused differentiation
- international consumer brand preference.

These strategic options are discussed below.

Cost leadership strategy

A few years ago the weakness of the Italian lira made it difficult for foreign car manufacturers to export cars to Italy, where Fiat is highly successful. Fiat was pricing its cars forcefully in international markets, where its market share continued to increase. The *Economist* (1995) observed that Fiat believed that its competitive advantage lay in developing small cheap cars for the-fast growing markets of Asia and Latin America. Developing a cut-price car in Asia, Latin America and North Africa enabled Fiat to reap benefits from economies of scale. This strategy delivered an absolute cost advantage, which firmly supports a cost leadership strategy in the growing market of developing countries, and then builds barriers of entry.

Low-price, high-quality strategy

The low-price, high-quality strategy of Japanese companies is widely acknowledged as the reason for their success in international markets. Unless competitors have the resources and ability to maintain a cost leadership stance they will become less competitive. With particular reference to the US car market, the prices of Japanese cars are significantly lower than the average market price enjoyed by Chrysler, General Motors and Ford Motors. Omar (1997) identified the cost leadership strategy supported by cost advantages as the foundation of Japanese car manufacturers' competitive advantage in the 1980s. The competitive advantage, in situations such as this, is further stimulated and is increasingly difficult to imitate through the use of profits which broaden the product line and increase market share with sales of new models. These new models are strategically priced for their own competitive advantage or to support the international competitive advantage of the company.

Focused differentiation strategy

Lexus, the saloon car manufacturer, does not compete with other saloon manufacturers in a direct fashion. Companies such as Peugeot, Volkswagen and Rover are all competing in the same market, spending large amounts of capital on both reactive and proactive advertising and attempting to persuade the market that they have the superior product. Lexus, following a focused differentiation strategy, which markets at a considerably higher price, has built a competitive advantage through offering a higher perceived value to the customer. This perceived added value, which is the basis for competitive advantage, is further supported by Toyota's distribution structure.

Brand preference strategy

In the early 1980s, Swiss watch manufacturers SMH Ltd entered the Chinese watch market with the low-priced Rado brand. Positioning itself in direct competition with subsidized domestic companies, whose costs were significantly lower, seriously limited the potential for achieving any success. Realizing that Chinese consumers prefer foreign products to domestic brands, SMH launched product lines that were considerably more expensive. The company therefore focused its strategy on the upper end of the market. Having withdrawn the cheaper product lines, its image is enhanced and its watches now trade for higher prices . So the company enjoys a competitive advantage.

Similarly, Titan, a watch producer based in Bangalore which produces watches using Japanese technology, entered a number of European countries with its medium-priced products. The company's strategy of market penetration resulted in a competitive advantage.

In general terms, it is important for international marketers to recognize the difficulties in sustaining market penetration strategy in international markets. The consequences and the inevitability of price wars as well as the cost advantage the domestic producer has in the international market must be taken into account. After reviewing the determinants of international pricing, the next section examines the fundamentals of pricing strategy in the international environment.

Fundamentals of pricing strategy

The options in determining the price level for a new product (Bernstein and Macias 2002) are shown in Figure 11.2.

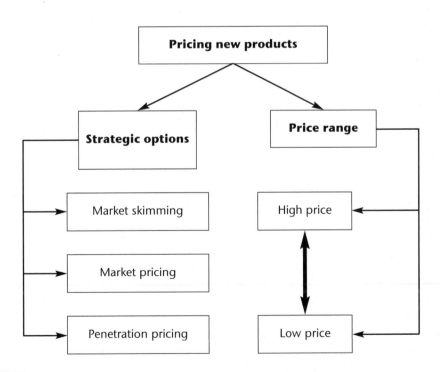

Figure 11.2 Pricing new products in international markets

International market skimming

In this strategy, a high price is charged to 'skim the cream' from the top end of the market, with the objective of achieving the highest possible contribution in a short time. In this strategic approach the product has to be unique and some segments of the market must be willing to pay the high price. As more segments are targeted and more of the product is made available, the price is gradually lowered. The success of this strategy depends on the ability and speed of competitive reaction by international marketers.

In most cases, the products should be designed to appeal to affluent and demanding international consumers, offering extra features and greater comfort, variability or ease of operation. By using the market skimming strategy, the company trades a low market share against a high margin. The problems with skimming include the following:

- Having a small market share makes a company vulnerable to aggressive local competition.
- The maintenance of a high-quality product requires a lot of resources and a visible local presence, which may be difficult in distant markets.
- If the product is sold more cheaply in the domestic market or in another country, grey marketing and/or parallel importing may result.

International market pricing

If similar products already exist in the target market, market pricing may be used. The final customer price is based on competitive prices. This approach requires the exporter to have a thorough knowledge of product costs, as well as confidence that the product life cycle is long enough to warrant entry into the market. It is a reactive approach and may lead to problems if sales volumes never rise to sufficient levels to produce a satisfactory return. Although companies typically use pricing as a differentiation tool, the global marketing manager may have no choice but to accept the prevailing world market price. From the price that customers are willing to pay, it is possible to make a so-called retrograde calculation where the company uses a 'reversed' price escalation to calculate backwards (from market price) to the necessary (ex factory) net price. If this net price can create a satisfactory contribution margin, then the company can go ahead.

Penetration pricing

A penetration pricing policy is used to stimulate market growth and capture market shares by deliberately offering products at low prices. This approach requires mass markets, price-sensitive customers and a reduction in unit costs through economies of scale (experience curve effects). The basic assumption that lower prices will increase sales will fail if the main competitors reduce their prices to a correspondingly low level. Another danger is that prices might be set so low that they are not credible to consumers. There are 'confidence levels' for prices below which consumers lose faith in the product's quality. Motives for pricing at low levels in some international markets might include:

- intensive local competition from rival companies
- lower income levels of local consumers
- since the company's R & D and overhead costs are covered by its domestic sales, exporting represents a marginal activity intended to bring in additional revenue by offering a low selling pricing.

Many Japanese companies are known to have used penetration pricing intensively to gain market share leadership in a number of markets, such as cars, home entertainment products and electronic components. In general, for a better choice of international pricing strategy, a company needs to carry out an economic analysis of international pricing issues, which is the subject of the next section.

Economic analysis of international pricing issues

In economic terms, price is often defined as the cost of manufacture plus an allowance for profit. Economists define price as the point at which a buyer and seller agree to exchange goods in the marketplace, the equilibrium point on the demand supply schedule. While each definition is correct, they are both narrow in scope. A more macro-definition of price that could be used in international marketing is the value that a product or service contains based on the intangible and tangible factors which distinguish it, or:

> Price – the intangible + tangible value of a product or service

The intangible factors are those that companies advertise that are not a part of the physical composition of the product. They include such things as prestige, status, newness, timeliness and beauty. For example, Mercedes-Benz markets its cars on their prestige value or status. The tangible factors, in contrast, are those directly related to the physical composition of the product, and include such things as product performance, strength, durability and economy. Most industrial products are marketed internationally on their intangible value (see Porter 1986). For example, IBM markets its computers internationally emphasizing their speed, accuracy and flexibility. When both the intangible and tangible aspects of price are considered, they are referred to as the total value that a product or service represents to a customer. The price paid by the customer is the value the international company places on these elements. A company has the choice of emphasizing the tangible, intangible or both value components, in its international marketing strategy as well as its international price setting objectives.

Setting objectives for international pricing

Setting prices is not a matter of intuitive skill on the part of the company, it is a deliberate procedure of developing a set of objectives, evolving a set of strategies to achieve these objectives and implementing a series of tactics in a marketing programme. More specifically:

- A pricing objective points out specific returns on investment (ROIs), cost-recovery goals or market-share objectives.
- A pricing strategy stresses how the international pricing mission or objectives will be achieved.
- A pricing tactic states what will be done to achieve the objective.

Price setting in international marketing should not be done in a vacuum, it should be a part of the overall marketing strategy of the company, which includes product development, advertising and sales strategy, customer support strategy and pricing. The pricing objectives that a company sets depend on a variety of factors including the orientation of the company's management, the stage a product is in its overall international life cycle, the financial goals of the organization, and the competitive situation in the marketplace. In general, there are four pricing objectives that a company can set in international marketing:

- return on revenue
- price stability
- market prestige and image
- meeting competition.

Return on revenue

Setting a return on revenue for a pricing programme can focus on either a return on sales or a return on assets. Either approach makes sense depending upon the type of industry a company is in or the measures the company has used to determine the return it gets from its investments.

A return on sales objective is generally expressed as:

Sales/Profits = Return on sales

Return on assets is expressed as:

Assets/Sales = Return on assets

Combining both of the above results in a return on investment objective for a company's pricing programme:

Sales/Profits x Assets/Sales = Return on investment

The return on revenue price objectives in international marketing makes sense when the company is the low-cost supplier in a market and the profit on sales is high. Also, the above objectives are useful when the market will take the volume at the price that is established by the company. The company can be sure that it will generate a stable return on the sales or assets over time. This objective also makes sense if the company is a price leader and sets the pace for establishing prices in the international market. Such a situation occurs in oligopolies where a major price leader is present. In the computer industry, IBM would be considered as a price leader in international markets.

Price stability

Price stability is the desire of all companies in international markets because it eliminates the need to review price schedules constantly and develop pricing programmes for customers. Price stability is a desirable goal in commodity markets where a company has little chance of developing a value orientation for its products, since there are close substitutes immediately available. Also, in international commodity markets, companies do not enjoy long periods of price stability because the competition is always forcing new pricing arrangements. Price stability can be an attainable objective when the customer's product options are limited. This is true especially when the product is a significant cost element for customers and when it is not available from any other source. Price stability in international markets can also be achieved when a company enters into long-term contracts with customers. When the above situations do not exist in international markets, price stability can also be achieved through a 'quid pro quo' arrangement between the supplier and customers.

Market prestige and image

Market prestige and image as pricing objectives in international marketing are generally associated with consumer products that have many intangible benefits associated with them. Products such as expensive cars, personal care products (perfumes, jewellery, clothes and so on), real estate and fashions are examples. As shown in Figure 11.3, the higher the value level a company can develop for its products, the higher the price it can charge. If a product or service moves down the curve and loses its value emphasis, then there will be little product differentiation and its price is likely to decline.

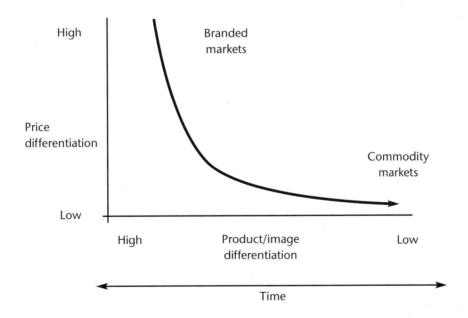

Figure 11.3 The commodity slide

Meeting competition

One of the most popular strategies in marketing is 'to meet the competitive price'. Many companies use this as a pricing objective, especially those in price-sensitive markets or where their products are viewed as commodities. A commodity in international marketing is a product or service that has easily accessible substitutes which can be supplied quickly by other companies (Porter 1986). Examples of international commodities include raw materials, agricultural products, wood and chemicals. On an international basis, countries that rely for much of their foreign currency flow on commodity exports are frequently subject to swings in the price of their exports. For example, nations that grow and export sugar cane have experienced great volatility in their balance of payments because of rapid changes in international prices. Such countries cannot build value into their pricing strategies and are subject to price competition from other international suppliers. In contrast, countries such as Japan that are not rich in natural resources but have developed a value-oriented base for all of their exports are not subject to price variability in international markets. The value and quality of Japan's exports have minimized price swings.

Developing an international pricing policy requires that a company asks some key questions before it implements any pricing programme. Such questions may relate to the market segments the company concentrates on, the identification of major competitors and their strengths, who the international customers are and so on. The answers to such questions are necessary if an effective competitive response is to be developed.

Price orientations in international marketing

Setting prices in international markets is based on two general factors: the internal cost considerations of the company and how market forces affect international markets. Cost-driven pricing typically looks at the costs incurred in the project as the basis for setting prices. This takes the form of the traditional cost build-up approach where the costs of manufacturing, product development, marketing and distribution are added up and an allowance for profit is attached. The other approach that is used to set prices in international markets is based on a marketing perspective. Here the pricing thresholds of customers as well as competitive prices are considered. Market-driven pricing assumes that the initiating force for price levels comes from the market and not from internal cost considerations. Market-driven pricing demands that the company constantly keeps an ear to the marketplace in order to know what customers are thinking and use that as a basis for setting prices.

One of the most difficult decisions international marketers have to make is how to respond to a competitive price change in an international market. Numerous factors impact on such a decision including the nature of the market, the level of competition, the stage the product has reached in its life cycle, and the type of management philosophy the organization has adopted. In general, an international marketer can respond to a price change in an international market in various ways:

- **Maintain price** – this response is sometimes considered as a holding action until a company can find out how deep the price change will be and what length of time it will cover.

Table 11.1	International customer pricing axioms

Pricing axioms	Procedural analysis
Buyers generally use price as an indicator of quality	A company that has developed a high-quality price level relationship will always be the price leader and never have to compromise its price position in international markets or be forced into a price war. Also, a company that is attempting to build value will find that after a certain level of quality perception is established among its customers, then the need to drop prices to meet competition will be minimized.
Buyers establish reference prices for the products they encounter in the marketplace	A customer will generally use a product's price as a reference point with which to judge the worth or quality of a good or service. Price is used as a surrogate for value level.
Reference prices are not constant and are modified by market experience	Customers will change their reference price over time. The reference price could change many times depending upon the volatility of the prices in the international market segment.
Buyers establish a range of acceptable prices around the standard or reference price in international marketing and anything outside the range may not be acceptable	Customers are generally willing to patronize a range of prices around a particular price level. For example, a buyer may be willing to accept a modest increase or decrease around the reference price and still purchase the product. The range will vary from customer to customer. For some a 5 per cent range may be acceptable while for others as much as 10 per cent will be tolerated. A company should determine what the acceptable ranges are in its various market segments and stay within them when changing its prices.
When price is perceived as similar in various alternatives, there are other deciding factors	Generally, when prices are looked at as being about the same to a customer when confronted with similar product choices, the product's quality or value level communicated through its brand becomes the deciding factor in the firm purchase decision. In international markets where there are close substitutes and the price falls, performance, style, prestige and design become the deciding factor.

- **Drop price** – this strategy makes sense if the company will lose its customers if the competitive price is much below that of its own.
- **Increase price** with a product improvement.
- **Drop price and raise value** – this strategy makes sense when survival is necessary and when a company is attempting to establish entry barriers for a market.

In general, day-to-day price management involves tactical moves that allow the marketer to combat or take advantage of prices changes and any other anomalies within the international markets. Such reaction is important especially when setting and negotiating pricing strategies for international marketing.

Export pricing

The pricing of products in international markets is becoming increasingly difficult for managers because of heightened competition, grey market activities, counter-trade requirements, regional trading blocs, the emergence of intra-market segments and volatile exchange rates. As international economic conditions continue to shift, long-proven pricing structures tend to collapse. Similarly, as competitive pressures increase, strategies for effective pricing of products for sale in foreign markets remain elusive.

This section introduces the concept of export pricing competence and reviews the pricing practices of organizations with different levels of competence (see Figure 11.4). While Tzokas et al. (2000) suggest that the export price of a product is nothing more than its domestic price plus some additional costs such as insurance and transportation costs, export pricing decision is a highly complex issue. This complexity results from a number of domestic factors that must be adapted to the context of the export market, and a large number of new factors (on which the exporter does not usually exert significant influence no matter how experienced it is) must be identified, examined, orchestrated and integrated into the final export price.

International marketing decisions about product, price and distribution differ from those made in a domestic context in that environments within which those decisions are made are unique to each country (see Figure 11.4). Also, the pricing problems faced by exporters are distinct from those faced by purely domestic marketers in that variables associated with both home and export markets must be integrated into managerial decision making. Some of the many factors influencing the export pricing decision are:

- export pricing objectives
- export pricing policies
- export pricing methods.

Each of these is discussed below.

Export pricing objectives

According to Tzokas et al. (2000), pricing objectives provide directions for action. If you have these objectives you know what is expected and how the efficiency of the operations is to be measured. Not having them demonstrates a lack of direction. As only a very limited number of studies have focused on encountered export pricing objectives, Figure 11.5 summarizes the most frequently cited pricing objective of international companies as they are presented in the international marketing pricing literature. International companies can have more than one pricing objective at a time. In addition, pricing objectives are not constant but changing, according to the conditions both within and outside the organization's environment. However, not all of them may be compatible with each other since the objective of current sales-revenue maximization may in fact lead to lower profits for the company.

Intuitively, the nature of the company's strategic objectives in export markets will condition specific export pricing objectives. The objectives listed in Figure 11.5 are used to chart the pattern of relevant export pricing objectives set by many UK exporters.

Figure 11.4 A conceptual framework for export pricing decisions

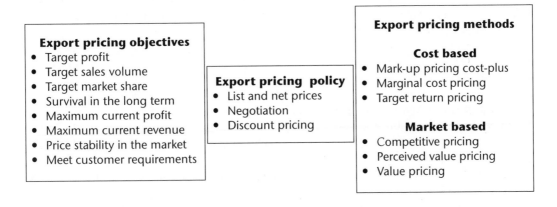

Figure 11.5 Examples of export pricing objectives, policies and methods

Export pricing policies

Pricing policies could be defined as directives that improve the validity of pricing decisions and achieve consistency of action in the company's pricing decisions. Policies are prefabricated decisions and provide answers to anticipated pricing situations. Figure 11.5 summarizes the pricing policies as used by various exporting companies and reported in the international marketing literature (Kotabe and Helsen 2001).

Export pricing methods

Pricing methods are classified under two broad categories of cost-based and market-based pricing. Cost-based pricing methods calculate price on the basis of the company's costs, which may be done in three ways: cost-plus, marginal costing and target costing.

Cost-based pricing

Cost-plus considers the full costs of a product (fixed and variable elements) and adds a profit mark-up, either fixed or flexible. This method is very popular among industrial companies, because it is simple and safe, as it covers all their costs.

Marginal cost pricing, on the contrary, considers only variable costs during price calculation. Exporters whose fixed costs make up a large proportion of their total operating costs use this method. The rationale behind this method is that fixed costs are incurred regardless of whether companies accept a purchase order.

Target return on investment is another cost-based pricing method, which calculates pricing considering the full cost of a product and adding a predetermined target rate of return on capital employed.

Market-based pricing

Market-based pricing has three methods: competitive, perceived value and value pricing.

Competitive pricing calculates prices by considering competitors' prices rather than a company's costs.

Perceived value pricing is a trial and error pricing method that sets the final price by investigating customers' reactions to different price levels (Omar 1997). Companies using the value pricing method charge a fairly low price for a high-quality product, aiming at reducing the perceived sacrifice of the customer.

International transfer pricing

As companies increase the number of subsidiaries world-wide, joint ventures, company-owned distributing systems and other marketing arrangements, the price charged to different affiliates becomes a pre-eminent question. Prices of goods transferred from operations or sales or sales units in one country to a company's units elsewhere may be adjusted to enhance the ultimate profit of the company as a whole. The benefits are:

- Lowering duty costs by shipping goods into high-tariff countries at minimal transfer prices so duty base and duty are low.
- Reduction of income taxes in high-tax countries by overpricing goods transferred to units in such countries; profits are eliminated and shifted to low-tax countries. Such profit shifting may also be used for 'dressing up' financial statements by increasing reported profits in countries where borrowing and other financing are undertaken.
- Facilitation of dividend repatriation – when dividend repatriation is curtailed by government policy, invisible income may be taken out in the form of high prices for products or components shipped to units in that country.
- To show more or less profit in crucial times, for example in the case of new car engine emission standards, government rules, to please shareholders or to show the good performance of new/old management.

Government authorities have not overlooked the tax and financial manipulation possibilities of transfer pricing. Transfer pricing can be used to hide subsidiary profits and to escape foreign market taxes. It is managed in such a way that profit is taken in the country with the lowest tax rate. For example, a foreign manufacturer makes a television for $50, and sells it to its European subsidiary for $150. The European subsidiary sells it to a retailer for $200, but it spends $50 on advertising and shipping so it shows no profit and pays no taxes. Meanwhile, the parent company makes a $100 gross margin on each unit and pays at a lower tax rate in the home country. If the tax rate was lower in the country where the subsidiary resides, the profit would be taken there and no profit will be taken in the home country. The overall objectives of the transfer pricing system are:

- maximizing profits for the corporation as a whole
- facilitating parent-company control
- offering management at all levels, in both the product divisions and in the international divisions, an adequate basis for maintaining, developing and receiving credit for their own profitability.

An intra-corporate pricing system should employ sound accounting techniques and be defensible to the tax authorities of the countries involved (Albaum, Strandskov and Duerr 2002). All of these factors argue against a single uniform price or even a uniform pricing system for all international operations. Four arrangements for pricing goods for inter-company transfer are:

- sales at the local manufacturing cost plus a standard mark-up
- sales at the cost of the most efficient producer in the company plus a standard mark-up
- sales at negotiated prices
- arm's-length sales using the same prices as quoted to independent customers.

Of the four, the arm's-length transfer is most acceptable to tax authorities and most likely to be acceptable to foreign divisions, but the appropriate basis for intra-company transfers depends on the nature of the subsidiaries and market conditions.

International reference pricing (IRP)

Pricing a product is an issue of great importance for marketers since it directly influences their companies' revenues. Choosing a pricing policy for a certain product is not an easy task because of the variety of factors that need to be taken into account. Issues such as price–quality relationship, competitive environment, distinctiveness and differentiation of the product, cost level, demand level, and the consumer's price perceptions have to be weighed up. When pricing imported products that are sold at various international markets, marketers face even more complex pricing decisions, since additional variables, such as cross-exchange rates, inflation level and information technology (IT) are involved. However, this situation creates an opportunity for marketers to influence consumer price perceptions.

Specifically, employing the notion of reference price in their pricing strategy, marketers can increase the product's demand and choice probability. For example, supplying information about the product's price in different countries, indicating the price at the country of origin, or even leaving the price tag on the product itself, can create a perception of a reduced price in the consumer's mind. This manner of applying an international reference price, however, may potentially damage consumer welfare, since no 'real' reduction in price is being offered.

The term 'international reference price' is defined as an external reference price that reflects the price of the product in different countries (Lowengart and Mizrahi 2000). It is a price consumers use to evaluate actual prices. Specifically, it is believed that consumers have in their mind the price they expect to find on their next shopping trip.

Setting an international reference price can be achieved by providing consumers with true but incomplete rather than false information, a practice slightly different than the outright manipulation of a local reference price. This means that setting an international reference price can help companies solve the ethical problem related to manipulation of local reference price. Comparing this reference price, P_r, to the actual price in the store, P, may result in either a negative deviation, where $P_r<P$, meaning that there is a perceived 'loss' for the consumer (a perception of a 'no-deal' in consumer's evaluation), or a positive deviation, where $P_r>P$, meaning that there is a perceived 'gain' (a perception of a 'deal' in consumers' evaluation). The impact of these deviations on consumer behaviour, however, is not symmetric, since as prospect theory proposes, losses are more important in consumer evaluations.

Consumers can use either an internal and/or external reference price. Internal reference price refers to the case where consumers use their previous experience with the product, such as past prices paid, intentional or unintentional exposure to price information or their evaluation of the product value, to form an expected price that is stored in their memories. External reference price is based on information cues such as advertised price and suggested list price. Consumers behave as if they are using an internal reference price in their choice evaluations. Similar reference prices are likely to be significant to the consumer's choice evaluations.

In order to better understand the effect of reference price in the context of international marketing the reference price (RP) may be described as an external RP (an external information cue) that reflects the price of the product in various foreign markets using transformable values that can be compared with the local market's price. The international RP (IRP) can be used by consumers, especially when they have some idea about the general price level in a specific country. If, for example, the German market is perceived to have a relatively low price level, consumers can then use it as a reference in their evaluations of the local market price for the same product. If the product's local market price is lower than its price in the other country, consumers will perceive a gain. This mechanism becomes more important when the product is unique, precluding any comparisons with other products in the local market (Lowengart and Mizrahi 2000).

An IRP can be created, for example, by importing a product with the retail price from the country of origin printed on it. In this case, the local retailer can keep (or stick) a high reference price on the imported product and sell it at a lower price in the local market, thus creating a gain in consumers' evaluations and rendering the IRP an efficient retail strategy. This is particularly true when high inflation rates prevail in the local market and the use of an original sticker price as a reference point for comparison can ensure (through currency devaluation) an inflation-adjusted constant price. Since most adjustments are somewhat below the inflation rate due to the lag between actual inflation and expectations, as inflation rates increase, the greater the perceived gain according to the consumer's evaluation. Should a relatively large devaluation occur, as usually happens in more controlled markets, this type of sticker price would again increase the consumer's sense of gain. However, there is no real gain in any of these cases, since at best, the IRP represents an international or foreign price and cannot be indicative of the local price level.

Product dumping in international markets

A logical outgrowth of a market policy in international business is goods priced competitively at widely differing prices in various markets. Marginal (variable) cost pricing, as discussed above, is one-way prices can be reduced to stay within a competitive price range. The market and economic logic of such pricing policies can hardly be disputed, but the practices are often classified as dumping and are subject to severe penalties and fines. Most industrialized countries have antidumping legislation. It is necessary to know that various economists define dumping differently. One approach classifies international shipments as dumped if the products are sold below their cost of production. The other approach characterizes dumping as selling goods in a foreign market below the price of the same goods in the home market. Even rate cutting on cargo shipping has been called dumping.

In the 1970s, dumping was hardly an issue because the world market was strong. As the 1980s began, dumping became a major issue for a large number of industries. Excess production capacity relative to domestic demand caused many companies to price their goods on a marginal-cost basis, figuring that any contribution above variable cost was beneficial to company profits. In a classic case of dumping, prices were maintained in the domestic market and reduced in foreign markets. For example, the European Union charged that differences in prices for Japanese goods between Japan and EU countries ranged from 48 to 86 per cent. In order to correct for this dumping activity, a special import duty of 33.4 per cent was imposed on Japanese computer printers.

Assembly in the importing country is one way that companies attempt to lower prices and avoid dumping charges. However, these so-called screwdriver plants are subject to dumping charges if the price differentials reflect more than the cost savings that result from assembly in the importing country. The increased concern and enforcement in the European Union reflects the changing attitudes among all countries towards dumping. The European Union has had anti-dumping legislation from its inception, but the first antidumping duties ever imposed were on Taiwanese bicycle chains in 1976. Since then the EU Trade Commission has imposed duties on a variety of products.

International product piracy

The international marketing literature relating to product piracy (see for example, Jacobs, Samli and Jedlik 2001) shows that being a leader in product management has a price. In the current international marketing environment, this price is very high and getting higher. Jacobs et al. (2001) revealed that brand and/or product pirating and the loss of intellectual property (IP) rights cost US industries an estimated $200 billion in lost sales each year. This number is estimated to be increasing at an annual rate of at least 5 per cent. The annual losses of the European companies from product pirating have quadrupled over the past decade, and an estimated 5 per cent of all of the products sold worldwide are probably pirated. The returns to counterfeiters' investments are probably so high that they make international piracy irresistible.

International marketing literature describes two economic theories concerning the need to protect IP that is subject to product piracy. These theories cover the natural rights of manufacturers and the economic incentives that encourage manufacturers to create and produce products. The 'natural rights' theory entitles investors to reap the rewards of their creative efforts, and the 'economic incentive' theory suggests that protection of IP is required to provide motivation for innovation. But prohibition of piracy in most cases might be extremely difficult and one major way of coping with piracy may be proactive behaviour by investors. Thus, it is not natural rights or economic incentive, but a practical way of fighting this widespread phenomenon that cripples the investors' marketing efforts.

It would appear that certain product types are more vulnerable to piracy than others. These products can be classified into four major categories:

- highly visible, high volume, low-tech products with well-known brand names, such as toothpaste, sweets and chocolates
- high-priced, high-tech products, such as computer games and audio or video entertainment products; fake auto and airplane parts are also in this category
- exclusive, prestige products such as well-known apparel and accessories as well as perfumes and other expensive gift items
- intensive R&D high-tech products such as pharmaceuticals.

In addition to these categories, many specialized industrial products are being pirated.

Scope and kinds of international piracy

Figure 11.6 identifies four different types of international piracy: counterfeiting, brand piracy, near brand usage and intellectual property copying. Here, these terms are considered under the general umbrella of international product piracy. Counterfeit products may be of a high quality, and it may take practice to identify or avoid them. Imitation goods, however, often have certain characteristics including extremely low prices, an absence of warranties or guarantees, incorrect spelling of the brand name and blurred printing of the package.

Counterfeiting is the unauthorized production of goods protected by trademarks, copyrights or patents (Jacobs et al. 2001). Piracy, by contrast, is the unauthorized use of copyrighted and/or patented goods and brands. That is, counterfeiters engage in manufacturing, whereas pirates steal names, shapes or other identifications associated with a product or brand. Brand piracy ranges from cheap imitations to high-quality merchandise. Whereas cheap imitations usually are easy to identify, high-quality merchandise piracy may require special testing. Increased technological capability in many developing countries has significantly improved the quality of many counterfeit products. This

---

MINI CASE 11.2

Examples of brand and/or product piracy

Although most examples in this chapter are consumer goods, piracy begins at the point of production; therefore, it is a very critical marketing problem for many manufacturers of a wide variety of products. The following examples show that brand and/or product piracy poses a major challenge to international industrial marketers and consumer marketers alike.

Mexico's piracy rate is estimated to exceed 50 per cent for all video, audio, and business and entertainment software. Indian pharmaceutical companies have built one of the world's largest medicine industries based primarily on pirating the products of other companies. Almost 10 per cent of the annual Brazilian pharmaceutical production is either stolen or falsified. Electronic Arts, one of the world's largest entertainment software companies, estimated its business losses at about $300 million. It believes that 95 per cent of the sales in Thailand (with Electronic Arts' name on the box) are pirated.

The International Federation of the Phonographic Industry in 2002 seized 45,000 pirated CDs from a Moscow wholesaler. In Istanbul's covered bazaar, there are rows of stalls piled high with counterfeit copies of Benetton and Lacoste T-shirts as well as Nike and Reebok sweatshirts and Levi jeans.

While design piracy is not new in the rug industry, recent advances in computer scanning technology now makes it possible to have instant copies.

The Software and Information Industry Association calculated the 1998 US loss on software alone to be $2.7 billion. They say that this was approximately 27 per cent of world losses. The Association estimates that the losses in the entire industry because of piracy may exceed $16 billion annually. Similarly, UK car manufacturers and suppliers estimated that the industry is losing an estimated £6.5 billion in annual revenue because of parts counterfeiting. Fortune 500 companies spend, on average, $2 to $4 million per year to fight counterfeiting. For some other companies, this expenditure may top $10 million annually. Whereas world trade grew by 4 per cent during the 1990s, trade in counterfeit goods grew at a staggering 150 per cent (Jacobs et al. 2001).

Of all the counterfeit goods seized by US Customs, 38 per cent were from China. That amount is three times as much as is seized from second placed Taiwan and ten times as much as from all of Western Europe.

Source: compiled from Jacobs et al. (2001).

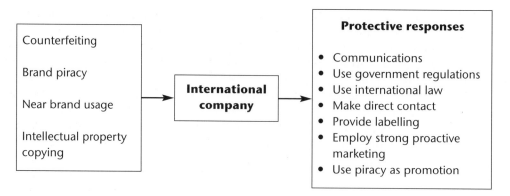

International piracy – impact and prevention

dramatic improvement has caused many legitimate stores to be deceived into buying counterfeit products. Major manufacturers maintain vigilance against these imitations. 'Near brands' or logos are similar in appearance to the original but not exactly the same. The brands 'Coldgate' rather than 'Colgate,' 'Cola Coca' rather than 'Coca-Cola,' 'W & W' rather than 'M & M,' 'Rolix' rather than 'Rolex' and 'Channel' rather than 'Chanel' are all examples of these practices.

IP includes patents, trademarks and copyrights as well as protection of integrated circuits, software, music, books, videos and the like. Copying such IP has become a major business around the world. Countries such as Indonesia and Thailand are sometimes called 'one disc' countries. A few discs are legitimately purchased and then many copies are illegally made from the original. It is estimated that 75 million compact discs per year are copied illegally in China alone. Furthermore, it is estimated that 94 per cent of the software used in China is copied.

Perhaps the most serious pirating activity is related to complex technology products. Among the more dangerous forged products are pharmaceuticals and machinery. Often unsuspecting retailers or wholesalers purchase counterfeit drugs. These products may not have the quality or even ingredients of the authentic products. Many less-developed countries in Africa and Asia are major markets for imitation contraceptive pills, antibiotics, steroids, analgesics and heart drugs. Recently Viagra has been added to this list. Fake car parts and forgery of replacement airplane parts are also in this category. Airlines, especially in the less-developed world, are attracted to low prices. Often these companies do not possess the testing capabilities to distinguish the fake from the authentic.

Exchange rate fluctuations

A number of recent developments in international business institutions and instruments are intended to accommodate trade among nations. In particular, the introduction of the euro, the common currency of the European Union, is aimed, among other things, at eliminating the foreign exchange risk associated with intra-EU trade. As with the US dollar, the eventual role of the euro in world trade is likely to be quite significant. However, the great majority of global trade will continue to take place between nations that use different currencies. As such, international pricing decisions will continue to challenge international marketers because price quotations in the company's home currency run the risk of alienating importing customers, creating or propagating grey markets and/or complicating the pricing function of distribution channel members. Additionally, importing customers are likely to buy from and sell to multiple suppliers and customers internationally, potentially resulting in the accumulation of a basket of foreign currencies which, in turn, they may wish to use for their importing activities.

In particular, delivery lead times associated with industrial machinery and equipment can be long enough for even the most stable currencies to fluctuate and create financial uncertainties for the exporter and the customer. To further complicate matters, market coverage of currency risks (forward markets) for periods longer than six months is rare and for some currencies is non-existent. In any event, such coverage comes at a cost to the buyer and/or the seller.

As such, the decision regarding an invoice currency that importer can work with while maintaining acceptable financial returns for the exporter is a critical element in exporting. Export companies are rarely in a position to dictate the terms of export transactions in order to minimize their foreign exchange exposure and benefit from the highest possible margins. Thus, invoice currencies should be considered in light of their impact on other facets of export marketing plans. Even when the bargaining position of the exporter is strong, few companies are in such an advantageous negotiating position as to dictate the terms of all of their export transactions. Concurrently, in a world of fluctuating exchange rates, inconvertible currencies and governmental restrictions, the exporter cannot and should not assume all currency risks. The invoice currency may take three forms: the exporter's currency, the importer's currency or a third currency. The selection of a given currency is governed by a number of factors such as:

- currency characteristics
- geographic location
- established invoicing practices
- market factors such as bargaining power, and the currency policies and preferences of the trading parties.

Meanwhile, intense competition, a growing concern about customer orientation and volatile currency markets complicate the invoice currency issue. Under these circumstances, it might be impossible to avoid foreign exchange involvement and achieve customer satisfaction simultaneously.

Currency risks

The choice of invoice currency is a vital but typically implicit part of exporting strategies because exchange rate fluctuations invariably impact sales and profitability. In principle, invoice currency determines the extent of foreign exchange exposure of each of the trading parties. The party whose home currency is selected for a given transaction faces no exposure, whereas the other party assumes the risk of dealing in a non-home currency. Where a third currency is picked for the transaction, both parties will be exposed to the foreign exchange risk. In practice, however, no matter which currency is used, exchange rate volatility will affect both parties and the outcome of the transaction either directly or indirectly.

Invoice currency policies

The extent to which export companies can standardize their currency policy is likely to be influenced by their international market outreach, experience, philosophy and the strength of their domestic currency. Often companies adopt currency policies by accounting for the various aspects of export transactions, including currency characteristics of the trading parties, established currency practices and export market factors. International corporations typically choose one of three types of currency policy:

- **Finance-oriented currency policy** – aimed at maximizing the net cash flow, profitability and market value of the company. In order to make profits on currency fluctuation, a profit-maximizing company should favour revenues in currencies more prone to appreciation (for example, stronger, convertible currencies) and liabilities in depreciation-prone currencies as a matter of policy.
- **Avoid foreign exchange involvement altogether** – by seeking to invoice only in its home currency. This policy shifts the foreign exchange risk and the burden to cover it to the customer. These companies consider the avoidance of exchange losses as their prime objective in export invoicing. Although any company might adopt a foreign exchange avoidance policy, companies with limited international involvement and experience are more likely to pursue this policy.
- **Customer-oriented currency policy** – where the exporter negotiates and implements its export transactions with explicit consideration of its customers' currency preferences. Using a customer-oriented invoicing the appropriate export strategy is to transact in one's domestic currency when it is weak and in the customer's currency when the exporter's currency is strong.

At one time, world trade contracts could be written easily and payment was specified in a relatively stable currency. The US dollar was the standard currency and all transactions could be related to the dollar. Now that all major currencies are floating freely relative to one another, no one is quite sure of the value of any currency in the future. Increasingly, companies are insisting that transactions be written in terms of the vendor company's national currency, and forward hedging is becoming more common. If exchange rates are not carefully considered in long-term contracts, companies find themselves unwittingly giving 15–20 per cent discounts. The added cost incurred as exchange rates fluctuate on a day-to-day basis must be taken into account, especially where there is a significant time lapse between signing the order and delivery of the goods. Exchange-rate differentials mount up. As a result of exchange rate fluctuations in one year, Nestle lost $1 million in six months, while other companies have lost and gained even larger amounts.

In addition to the risks from exchange-rate variations, other risks may result from the changing value of a country's currency relative to other currencies. Since much international trade is conducted based on the US dollar, the effects of the variation in currency values is determine by whether the value of the dollar is high or low.

Thus, for example, when the value of the dollar is weak relative to the buyer's currency it takes fewer units of the foreign currency to buy a dollar. In such situations, companies may generally employ cost-plus pricing. In order to remain price competitive when the dollar is strong (when it takes more units of foreign currency to buy a dollar), companies must find ways to offset the higher price caused by currency (higher dollar value). By comparing the price of a relatively standard product, it is possible to gain an insight into the under or over-valuation of currencies.

International counter-trading

This section is concerned with international trading processes that involve not necessarily physical cash but product purchase reciprocation. The increasing importance of world trade and magnification of both international competition and economic interdependence require that companies pursue innovative marketing strategies. Many industrial companies are using international counter-trade as a means of achieving and sustaining competitive differentiation.

In a counter-trade transaction, a sale results in product flowing in one direction to a buyer; a separate stream of products and services, often flowing in the opposite direction, is also created. It generally involves a seller from the west and a buyer in a developing country; for example, many countries in Africa have historically relied heavily on counter-trading. Many creative ways of conducting counter-trade transactions have evolved. While several forms of counter-trade exist (see Table 11.2), the common characteristic is the linkage of transactions between the seller and buyer. That is, each exchange partner acts as both a seller and buyer at some point in the counter-trade transaction. Counter-trade is used when:

- mandated by government (for example, policies encouraging bilateral trade to minimize unfavourable trade balances)
- economic conditions favour it (for example, lack of hard currencies needed for imports)
- innovative marketing strategies are necessary to secure new business (for example, gaining access to new or difficult markets, establishing new trading partners).

Counter-trade frequently involves industrial organizations, entailing either business-to-business or business-to-government transactions. Typical examples of counter-trade are Mitsui of Japan counter-trading machinery with Dongsheng Cashmere Mill of China, Levi Strauss providing Hungary with its trademark, designs and materials in return for jeans made by the Hungarian concern, and Boeing exchanging aircraft for Saudi Arabian oil.

It is estimated that the percentage of world trade using counter-trade lies between 20 and 25 per cent (Jacobs et al. 2001) and the number of counter-trading countries, including both developing and developed countries, has expanded rapidly.

Reasons for counter-trading

Counter-trading usually flourishes when hard currency is scarce and exchange controls prevent a company from expatriating earnings. In this situation the company may be forced to spend money within the country for products that are then exported and sold

Table 11.2	Forms of counter-trade	
Form	**Definition**	**Example**
Barter	The direct and simultaneous exchange of products of approximately equal value between two partners.	Iraq exchanged crude oil for frigates from Italy's state-owned Italcantiere.
Clearing account	The principle is for exchanges to balance without either partner having to use currencies. Each partner agrees to purchase a specified value of products. The contract's value is expressed in universally accepted clearing units that represent a credit line in the country's central bank.	The former Soviet Union used clearing account units to purchase copiers from Rank Xerox of Britain, Rank Xerox has copiers made in India for sale to the Soviets under the country's clearing agreement with India.
Compensation or buyback	One partner sells capital equipment (e.g. plant equipment, technology) and agrees to accept a percentage of the output made possible by the capital equipment as full or partial payment.	Occidental Petroleum built ammonia plants for the Soviets and in return received ammonia produced by the plants as payment.
Counter-purchase	Partners buy product of equal value from one another but the trading of products takes place at different times and involves two separate contracts.	Russia bought construction machinery from Konatsu and Mitsubishi while the Japanese firms bought Siberian timber.
Offset	Offsets enable the buyer to 'offer' their purchase by securing the seller's purchase of products from the buyer, help the buyer sell products, or participate in joint ventures (e.g. arrange local manufacturing or assembly, purchase local components, supply technology). The concept is to offset the negative effects of large purchases from abroad on the current account or to avoid hard currency depletion.	McDonnell Douglas agreed to buy airframe components and other products from Canadian companies in exchange for a commitment from Canada to buy jet fighter planes.

in developing world markets. Historically, the single most important driving force behind the proliferation of counter-trade was the decreasing ability of developing countries to finance imports through bank loans. A typical example of such situation is the trade between Nigeria and the United States, where Nigeria buys military security gear from the United States in exchange for petroleum oil.

Several conditions affect the probability that importing nations will demand counter-trade. The priority attached to western imports means that the higher the priority, the less likely it is that counter-trade may be required. The second condition is the value of the transaction; the higher the value, the greater the likelihood that counter-trade will be involved. Third, the availability of product from other suppliers can also be a factor. If a company is the sole supplier of a differentiated product, it can demand monetary payment. However, if competitors are willing to deal on a counter-trade basis, a company may have little choice but to agree or risk losing the sale altogether.

Benefits from counter-trading

Counter-trade (Liesch and Palia 1999):

- allows entry into difficult markets
- increases the international competitiveness of companies
- overcomes currency control and exchange problems
- increases sales volume
- overcomes credit difficulties
- allows better use of capacity
- provides attractive sources of inputs
- allows disposal of declining products
- increases a company's overall attractiveness to customers
- enables companies to achieve economies of scale
- fosters important long-term customer goodwill.

Motivations and reasons for increasing counter-trade

The reasons for increasing counter-trade activity are:

- customer's diminished access to foreign currency
- increased pressure for counter-trade from customers
- companies wanting to maintain and/or increase competitiveness
- increased difficulty in obtaining credit for the company
- company has more 'in-house' expertise for counter-trade
- increased currency exchange uncertainty
- increased political instability in the market
- easier to resell goods offered by customers
- increased product price uncertainty
- more attractive range of goods offered to customers.

Difficulties associated with counter-trade

The problems faced by the international organizations in counter-trading are:

- no 'in-house' use for goods offered by customers
- time-consuming negotiations
- complex negotiations
- difficult to resell goods offered by customers
- increased costs
- problems with pricing

- increases uncertainty generally
- brokerage costs and facilities needed
- customers' negotiating strength
- customers become potential competitors.

In addition to the statements above, lack of knowledge about counter-trade could seriously be a hindrance to an international organization participating in counter-trading even if the prospects seem beneficial.

Barter trading

The term 'barter' describes the least complex and oldest form of bilateral, non-monetized counter-trade. Simple barter is a direct exchange of goods or services between two parties. Although no money is involved, both partners construct an approximate shadow price for products flowing in each direction. One contract formalizes simple barter transactions, which are generally for less than a year to avoid problems in price fluctuations. However, for some transactions, the exchange may span months or years, with contract provisions allowing adjustments in the exchange ratio to handle fluctuations in world prices.

Companies sometimes seek outside help from barter specialists. For example, New York-based Atwood Richards engages in barter in all parts of the world. Generally, however, distribution is direct between trading partners, with no intermediaries included. For example, General Electric sold a turbine generator to Romania in the late 1970s. As payment, GE Trading Company accepted $150 million in chemicals, metals, nails and other products, which it then sold on the world market. One of the highest-profile companies involved in barter deals is PepsiCo, which has done business in the Soviet and post-Soviet market for more than 20 years. In the Soviet era, PepsiCo bartered soft-drink syrup concentrate for Stolichnaya vodka, which was in turn exported to the United States by the PepsiCo Wines & Spirits subsidiary and marketed by M. Henri Wines. In the post-Soviet market economy in the CIS, barter is no longer required. Today, Stolichnaya is imported into the United States and marketed by Carillon Importers, a unit of Diageo plc.

Counter-purchase

This form of counter-trade, also termed parallel trading or parallel barter, is distinguished from other forms in that each delivery in an exchange is paid for in cash. For example, Rockwell International sold a printing press to Zimbabwe for $8 million. The deal went through only after Rockwell agreed to purchase $8 million in ferrochrome and nickel from Zimbabwe, which it subsequently sold on the world market.

The Rockwell–Zimbabwe deal illustrates several aspects of counter purchase. Generally, products offered by the foreign principal are not related to the western company's exports and thus cannot be used directly by the company. In most counter purchase transactions, two separate contracts are signed. In one, the supplier agrees to sell products for a cash settlement (the original sales contract); in the other, the supplier agrees to purchase and market unrelated products from the buyer (a separate, parallel contract). The dollar value of the counter purchase generally represents a set percentage and sometimes the full value of the products sold to the foreign principal. When the western supplier sells these goods, the trading cycle is complete.

Summary

This chapter has reviewed international pricing and pricing for exports. Issues covered included pricing, fundamentals of pricing strategy, economic analysis of international pricing, export pricing, transfer and differential pricing strategies, product piracy, exchange rate fluctuations and international counter-trading. The issues facing international marketer and exporters have become more complex when a number of diverse international markets are to be served simultaneously.

Pricing in international markets is not an easy task. Several factors must be considered when a company establishes a selling price for its products or service. These include the level of competition, the type of economic structure that exists in the market, the stage the product is at in its life cycle and the marketing strategy of the organization. By better understanding the international market environment, a company can more effectively set prices and be competitive.

Revision questions

1 The determinants of international price setting are influenced by internal (micro), external (macro) levels, and the business cycle stage. Explain with examples how each of these levels could influence international pricing.
2 Gaining international competitive advantage is a crucial determinant for surviving in the rapidly changing international market environment. Explain this statement using suitable and current examples.
3 Discuss how the price of a new product could be determined in an international market of your choice.
4 Discuss the four main pricing objectives that a company could set in an international market.
5 What do you understand by international transfer pricing, and what are the benefits of a transfer pricing system?
6 Consider the numerous benefits of counter trading and discuss why some international organizations may not be willing to engage in counter-trade.
7 The nightmare of international product piracy is highly damaging to international marketing of branded goods worldwide. Using suitable examples, discuss the problems associated with product piracy in the international markets.

Barter trading in the US radio industry

This case study looks at the importance of barter in the US radio industry. It shows how individual stations can make use of the field of international marketing and demonstrates the significance, prevalence and the complexity of barter. Specifically, the case study provides insight into the use of barter, a basic understanding of barter programming and its role in the radio station manager's strategic planning.

Barter is the world's oldest form of exchange. In fact, originally, it was the only means of doing business. Over several years, the use of barter has had its ups and downs generally based on economic conditions such as recession and high unemployment. Specific experiences of businesses related to cash-flow problems and competition also have influenced the level of barter.

Within the United States, there are over 400 successful commercial trade exchanges engaged in the marketing of barter-oriented services. These organizations have fewer than 100 employees and less than $10 million in annual sales. Although operating independently, more than 250,000 US businesses barter about $6.45 billion worth of goods and services each year. Nearly $3.5 billion is involved in media advertising.

Today, barter is emerging as a low-cost way for companies to finance promotional campaigns, open new marketing channels and strengthen competitive positions with their surplus goods or excess inventory. The age-old practice of bartering has become more than swapping goods and services. There are 50 companies throughout the world that engage in corporate barter. For instance, James River, a paper and consumer products manufacturer, used its excess capacity of its product, Natural Touch, for media credits in the broadcast industry. Avon Products periodically trades discounted product-line inventory to fund advertising. It is common practice for hotels, cruise lines and airlines to use barter because, with their spare capacity, they can get cash-free financing at little expense for their companies. It is therefore not surprising that barter has become so popular in the radio industry.

Radio stations often barter advertising time for promotional goods, which are used in-house as gifts to employees and/or are passed on to consumers. Barter in radio programming is an alternative way of selling media time which otherwise could not be sold for cash. It plays an important role in promoting a station, attracting listeners and creating greater excitement through contests and promotional gifts, thus making the radio station competitive.

These roles have had tremendous impact on the prevalence of barter for four reasons:

- Barter appeals to radio stations as a way to stretch their advertising budget in the face of economic recession.
- The pressure to engage in barter may have increased among radio stations that have been acquired for several times earnings.
- The increase in the number of radio stations has meant more competition.
- Faced with the prospect of declining revenues, a number of stations are forced to embrace barter as a financial option.

Networks have played an important role in radio. For years, listeners tuned in for news, sports and the latest breaking news stories as a part of the local station's programming. However, there are some big changes in the industry. Radio stations are becoming more receptive of outside programming. They realize that it is coming from larger, more sophisticated companies. Three major types of radio programming can be used on a barter basis in addition to local shows: network, interconnected networks and syndicated programme networks. Network radio (for example, ABC) is a line-up of local stations that agree to carry programmes and commercials simultaneously. They have programme divisions that distribute long-and short-form features. These stations carry network programmes in a consistent manner from week to week over telephone lines.

On the other hand the interconnected networks (for example Westwood One) transmit their programmes from a central source to the local stations via satellite rather than by telephone. They typically offer one highly specialized feature, such as a 24-hour music format. Stations may carry the programmes live or on a delayed basis.

A syndicated programme network is a group of local stations, otherwise unrelated, which carry the same programme by arrangement with the syndicate. These are generally smaller companies that offer a few programmes (for example 'Success motivators'). It is likely that their time periods may vary from locality to locality.

In many instances, the local station may be affiliated with all three. For example, Westwood One syndicates to 35 per cent of the nation's licensed stations, 70 per cent of which are network affiliates. Consequently, radio stations need to find new and creative ways to increase their revenue and remain competitive.

National syndication is attractive because in many instances, it is becoming more difficult for radio stations to survive on their own. Consider the dilemma that stations face regarding compensation. A station in a large urban area can pay a disc jockey or a talkshow host $100,000 a year or more, but stations in small towns or small stations in the urban area which may be billing only $300,000 a year are hard-pressed to pay the personality even $250 a week. Radio stations can save a considerable amount of money by substituting a locally produced programme with a nationally syndicated show through the use of barter. Stations around the country mix the best of the national programming with their own, thereby broadening the scope of the station.

Seminar discussion questions

1 What do you understand by the term barter trading and what are the practical benefits of this trading system?
2 Discuss why you think barter appeals to radio stations within the US radio industry.

Managerial assignment task

An international corporation that produces and markets its cosmetic brands to women all over the world employs you as an export director responsible for Asia. The company gives prominence to high prices in its positioning to create and/or reinforce its image of exclusivity and superiority for its brand offerings. Recently, the company has discovered that its brands are being copied in some emerging Asian markets. This is happening especially in the markets where a large proportion of consumers have little money but hold an appreciation for prestige cosmetic brands, and buying counterfeit goods is considered just a part of normal life.

You are required to conduct an in-house evaluation of the course of action the company should take in order to remedy the piracy of its cosmetic brands in Asia. Write a report to your board of directors with your recommendations of possible marketing actions. Your report should not be more than 1,500 words.

References

Albaum, G., Strandskov, J. and Duerr, E. (2002) *International Marketing and Export Management*, 4th edn, London: Financial Times/Prentice Hall.

Bernstein, J. and Macias, D. (2002) 'Engineering new product success: the new-product pricing process at Emerson Electric', *Industrial Marketing Management*, Vol. 31, No. 1, pp. 51–64.

Cui, G. and Liu, Q. (2000) 'Regional market segments of China: opportunities and barriers in a big emerging market', *Journal of Consumer Marketing*, Vol. 17, No. 1, pp. 55–72.

Economist (1995) 'Gianni, come to mama/happy days at Fiat', CD ROM, 28 January.

Jacobs, L., Samli, A. C. and Jedlik, T. (2001), 'The nightmare of international product piracy', *Industrial Marketing Management*, Vol. 30, pp. 499–509.

Kotabe, M. and Helsen, K. (2001) *Global Marketing Management*, 2nd edn, New York: Wiley.

Liesch, P. W. and Palia, A. P. (1999), 'Australian perceptions and experiences of international countertrade with some international comparisons', *European Journal of Marketing*, Vol. 33, No.5/6, pp. 488–511.

Lowengart, O. and Mizrahi, S. (2000) 'Applying international reference price: market structure, information seeking and consumer welfare', *International Marketing Review*, Vol. 17, No. 6, pp. 525–37.

Marsh, G. (2000) 'International pricing – a market perspective', *Marketing Intelligence & Planning*, Vol. 18, No. 4, pp. 200–5.

Mintel (2001) 'Bottled water: Germany and Italy', Mintel European Market Intelligence Publications (CD ROM).

Omar, O. E. (1997) 'Target pricing: a marketing management tool for pricing new cars', *Pricing Strategy and Practice*, Vol. 5, No. 2, pp. 61–9.

Porter, M. E. (1986) *Competition in Global Industries*, Cambridge, Mass.: Harvard University Press.

Terpstra, V. and Sarathy, R. (1997) *International Marketing*, 7th edn, Hinsdale, Ill.: Dryden Press,.

Tzokas, N., Hart, S., Argouslidis, P. and Saren, M. (2000), 'Strategic pricing in export markets: empirical evidence from the UK', *International Business Review*, Vol. 9, pp. 95–117.

12
Integrated International Marketing Communications

Contents

LEARNING OBJECTIVES

After reading this chapter you should:

- understand the nature of integrated international marketing communications (IIMC)
- know the important role of advertising as a component of IIMC
- be able to evaluate the role of public relations in the international marketing context
- be able to explain the nature of sales promotion as part of the IIMC mix
- be able to discuss the various factors affecting direct marketing, telemarketing, events sponsorships and trade shows
- be able to evaluate ethical and cultural issues influencing the integrated marketing communications in the international environment.

Introduction

Integrated international marketing communications (IIMC) are expressly conceived for appropriate communications strategy planning in the increasingly interactive, fragmented, cluttered and international marketing communications environment. To be effective, the aspect of the IIMC model that is concerned with communication from the manufacturer and/or retailer to the consumer proposes that marketers must now more than ever ensure that the sum total of their marketing communications in all its forms is carefully coordinated. This will ensure that they all speak collectively with one voice, amplifying and reinforcing the core organizational or brand message (see Dotson 2002).

A principle of IIMC is that companies must continually be aware that they operate within a public arena where their actions are scrutinized by all stakeholders. It used to be that business dealings were of interest to only a small percentage of the population, those directly involved with managing businesses. Today, however, with nearly half of the US population owning shares of stock in one or more companies, business activity is front page news.

The concept of IIMC is receiving increasing media attention primarily from an organizational perspective. Yet, the influence of integrated communications programmes on global consumers is difficult to establish in the literature (see Hackley and Kitchen 1998). Consideration of IIMC seems unpromising unless the concept itself can be grounded within a psychological perspective of consumer cognition. This chapter is partly an attempt to conceptually explore these concerns. It begins with a discussion of broad issues connected with integrated marketing communications in the international market environment, and strongly suggests that multidisciplinary approaches probably offer greater insight. It briefly, and selectively, introduces and discusses a selection of relevant topics as components of IIMC. The chapter concludes by suggesting possible interpretations with practical implications for marketing communications practitioners.

The nature and process of marketing communications

The role of communication in the international market is similar to that in the domestic market. Its central role is to communicate with customers and provide them with product and/or service information that enables them to make purchase decisions. In general, although the communication mix carries information of interest to the customer, in the end it is designed to persuade the customer to buy a product or service now or in the future. Eagle and Kitchen (2000) listed several marketing communication tools, including advertising, personal selling, exhibitions, sales promotion, publicity, direct marketing and the Internet , that are available for communicating with and influencing customers.

The international communication process

The communication process consists of a source, encoding, message, decoding and destination. Effective communication involves a sender, a receiver and a message, and the marketing promotions provide the communication channel (see Figure 12.1).

The sender *encodes* a message. Encoding is a process that transforms the information

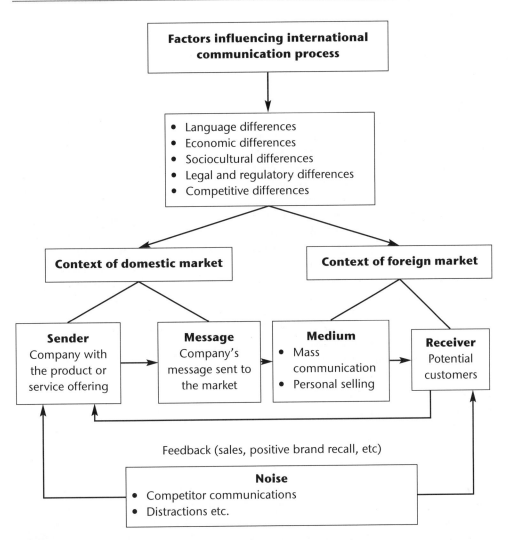

Figure 12.1 Elements of international communications

into a form that can be transmitted, for example, spoken or written words. The message is then transmitted through a channel and the receiver decodes the message (see Figure 12.1). For the receiver to understand the coded message, it must consist of information that the receiver can relate to and be coded with relevant images and words common to the receiver's experience. It must be in the language that the receiver can understand. The receiver must not only be informed by the message but must be persuaded to accept and act upon the information.

In order to communicate in an effective way, Hollensen (2001) suggests that the sender needs to have a clear understanding of the purpose of the message, the audience to be reached, and how this audience will interpret and respond to the message. It is possible that sometimes the audience cannot hear clearly the message the sender is trying to send about its product or services because of the noise of the competitors. This must also be

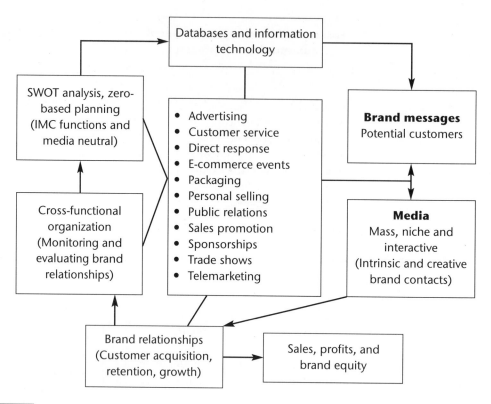

Figure 12.2 IMC process model

considered when the message is being prepared and the medium selected. For effective communications, Eagle and Kitchen (2000) suggested that all the elements of international marketing communications (integrated marketing communications) must be taken into consideration.

Integrated marketing communications (IMC)

With the increasing emphasis on customer and stakeholder relationships, both academics and professionals have come up with a variety of names for the processes designed to help organizations become customer-centric rather than company-centric. Besides IMC, there is customer relationship management (CRM), one-to-one marketing, integrated marketing, strategic brand communication and relationship marketing. Though each has its differences, all are designed to do one basic thing: to increase the value of a company or brand by allowing the organization to cost-effectively acquire, retain and grow customer relationships.

'Growing' customers means motivating them to give your brand a greater share of their spending in a given product category. In terms of the international marketing environment, IMC provides for managing customer relationships and its concept is widely employed. As Duncan (2002) observed, what differentiates IMC from the other customer-centric process is that its foundation is communication, which is the heart of all relationships, and that it is a circular process (as shown in Figure 12.2) rather than a linear one. Figure 12.2 gives an overview of what IMC is all about. At this point, it is important to note that IMC is a revolving process that creates brand value in the form of sales, profits and brand equity.

The meaning of IMC

The American Association of Advertising Agencies defined IMC as:

> a concept of marketing communications planning that recognizes the added value of a comprehensive plan that evaluates the strategic roles of a variety of communications disciplines, for example, general advertising, direct response, sales promotion and public relations – and combines these disciplines to provide clarity, consistency and maximum communication impact.
>
> (Duncan and Everette, 1993: 31)

Although, this definition has its weaknesses, it is extensively used. In its simplest form however, IMC is a process for managing the customer relationships that drive brand value. More specially, it is a cross-functional process for creating and nourishing profitable relationships with customers and other stakeholders by strategically controlling and/or influencing all messages sent to the stakeholders and encouraging data-driven, purposeful dialogue with them. In order to make sure the definition is clear, it is necessary to explain each key element briefly (see Table 12.1).

The analysis in Table 12.1 tends to suggest that successful international marketing strategies in the twenty-first century require successful integrated communication strategies, and this requires more creative thinking allied to an integrated approach to all communication activities. IMC has shifted its emphasis from the individuality of advertising, sales promotion, personal selling and public relations to movement toward integrated international marketing communication (IIMC) (Schultz and Kitchen 2000a, 2000b).

Indeed, IMC requires 'integration and co-ordination of an organization's many communication channels to deliver a clear, consistent and compelling message about the organization and its products' (Kotler 2006). The role of branding too has changed. There was a significant move away from line branding towards corporate branding in the last decade of the twentieth century. Undoubtedly part of the reason was the desire to amortize communication cost across the entire portfolio as the cost of creating and supporting individual brands continues its upward exponential curve. Corporate branding comprises personality, identity and image, which are the three discrete yet overlapping concepts. These three have become important elements to be manipulated for corporate and marketing communication purposes.

Firms are no longer thinking simply in terms of marketing to a single domestic market. At the very least, they think in terms of international marketing, and often adopt a global approach to marketing. The prohibitive cost of developing individual brands, coupled

Table 12.1　The key elements of IMC

Element	Definition and explanation
Cross-functional process	All of the company's major divisions and external communication agencies that have contact with the customer must work together in the planning and monitoring of international marketing relationships. This is because customers are likely to be influenced by more than just marketing communication messages. A cross-functional process integrates managers from different divisions and agencies who are working on the same project in order to plan and manage all the messages a company sends to and receives from customers and other stakeholders (Eagle and Kitchen 2000).
Developing stakeholder relationships	This means attracting new customers and then interacting with them to find ways the company can further satisfy their wants and needs. The more satisfied customers or other stakeholders are, the more business or support they will generally give to a company.
Nourishing stakeholder relationships	Nourishing means not only retaining customers and stakeholders but also increasing the company's percentage of their category purchases and support.
Profitable customer relationships	Profitable customer relationships are specified because not all relationships are of equal value to a company. Some customers are more profitable to a company than others because of the quantity they buy, the types of products they buy or the amount of servicing they require. For example, a customer who has only a cheque account with a bank does not generate nearly as much profit for it as the customer who has a cheque, a mortgage and a savings account. IMC identifies the more profitable customers and directs a greater proportion of the marketing effort toward maintaining a relationship with those customers.
Strategic control	Strategically controlling or influencing all messages means recognizing that everything a company does sends a message on how it makes its products, how products perform, how it sets prices, through what kinds of stores it provides its services or sells its products and how its employees act. In other words, all aspects of the marketing mix deliver messages and all of these messages need to be either strategically controlled or influenced.
Encourage purposeful dialogue	Customers are tired of intrusive telemarketing calls, junk mail, interruptive commercials and over-commercialization of events. Customers want the ability to interact with companies and initiate a discussion when they have a need to do so, and to have this dialogue in a way and at a time convenient to them. Companies need to make their business environment easier for their customers to make purchases, ask questions, complain when something goes wrong, or give compliments when they are especially pleased.

MINI CASE 12.1

The nature of consumer behaviour

One of the central tenets of postmodernism as applied to marketing communication relates to the nature of consumer behaviour. Today firms operating in the advanced post-industrial nations are supposedly dealing with well-educated, streetwise, savvy, sophisticated audiences and stakeholders. This does not just mean that there are a large number of college and university graduates. More to the point, many consumers and stakeholders, almost irrespective of their level of educational attainment, are informed and well able to judge the merits of products and services produced, the marketing communications that accompany them, and hold views about the corporate entity marketing them. Moreover, in what today are comparatively affluent societies even by standards of 30 years ago, consumer and customer choice has burgeoned and lessened the ability of market suppliers to dictate what customers should buy. However, the widening of consumer choice and the growth of affluence have created decision overload for consumers. Consumers' main choice at the beginning of the twenty-first century is how to spend their money.

Of course there will always be brand choice when consumers finally make up their minds, but it is persuading people to make up their minds in the first place that is now one of the pre-eminent communication issues. Faced with a vast variety of choices, consumers are beginning to question what they really want. In many cases, they do not really know, but they do know how to reject unwanted alternatives.

One unfortunate company that recently suffered from changes in consumer behaviour in the United Kingdom is Marks & Spencer. While success in the UK market led to expansion overseas, this expansion did not equate to success. Its focus on the tried and tested techniques of UK marketing did not bring in the overseas customers. It seems evident that what is really needed is an integrated approach to communication, rather than disjointed local appeals. Moreover, companies really need to 'understand' what makes an overseas markets tick, and then develop consistent, coordinated and integrated messages that can be 'localized' as necessary.

---

with the increasing power of retailers, has made it difficult for stand-alone brands to compete in many markets, and explains much of the focus today on corporate brand management and corporate communication. It can be argued that the corporate brand is now a major discriminator in consumer choice rather than just the functional attributes of objects produced by the firm. Both IMC and integrated corporate communication have to be ready to reach out to world via the process of globalization (Proctor and Kitchen 2002).

International advertising decisions

Advertising is a major variable element in international marketing communications. Although advertising principles do not vary from country to country, the objectives and methods employed may differ in the different markets. Duncan (2002) identified three major measurement approaches for determining the importance of promotional activity in a particular international market:

- total advertising expenditure, which gives a good indication of the level of competition in that market
- advertising expenditure by industry
- advertising expenditure by media, which indicates the importance of different types of media in a national market.

Advertising is an important communications medium in an international market and it is the most visible and controversial promotional element in the IIMC mix because of its extensive use and one-directional method of communication (Eagle and Kitchen 2000). It is also a relatively cost-effective method and can effectively position a product, which then becomes difficult to dislodge. A successful advertising campaign can therefore be used as an asset that can then be transferred to different overseas markets.

The rapid development of the international market is causing shifts in the role of advertising. In the United States, the European Union and Japan, for example, advertising is one of the most important elements of the IMC mix, especially for consumer products (Duncan 2002). For most other products, personal selling is the next most important element of the mix. In general, the appropriate role of advertising within the IMC mix will vary among national markets. Even if advertising is strategically the best format for some markets, firms will not adopt it if the media are not available or advertising facilities are not adequately developed within the market. The major decisions in international advertising are shown in Figure 12.3.

As highlighted in Figure 12.3, a multinational firm has a number of important decisions to make to ensure the development of appropriate campaigns in each national market including:

- whether to standardize or localize the campaign
- selecting the advertising message
- selecting the agencies
- selecting the media
- determining the budget
- evaluating the effectiveness of advertising
- organization of the advertising strategy.

Standardization of international advertising campaigns

International advertising standardization refers to using a common approach (for example common advertising messages) to promote the same product across national boundaries (Harris and Attour 2003). Although the debate on standardized international advertising is continuing, an examination of international marketing literature identifies standardization and adaptation of advertising campaigns as the two main approaches to international advertising. Those who argue for the standardization approach believe a single advertising message with only minor modifications, or even advertisements with proper translations, could be used in all countries to reach consumers. The rationale is that buyers everywhere in the world share the same, or very similar, wants and needs, and therefore can be persuaded by universal advertising (Levitt 1983). There are four main reasons that make this approach appealing.

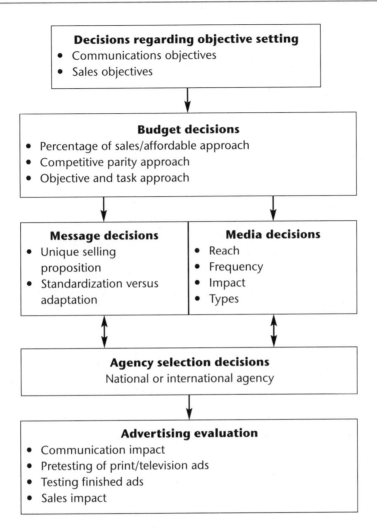

Figure 12.3 Major international advertising decisions

- It allows the multinational corporation to maintain a consistent image and identity throughout the world.
- It minimizes confusion among buyers who travel frequently.
- It allows the multinational company to develop a single, coordinated advertising campaign across different markets.
- The standardization approach results in considerable savings in media costs, advertising production costs and costs for illustrative material.

An important decision area for multinational firms is whether an advertising campaign developed in the domestic market can be transferred to foreign markets with only minor modifications. Complete standardization of all aspects of a campaign over several foreign markets is rarely attainable. Esso with its 'Tiger in your tank' campaign, Coca-Cola, Sony and McDonald's are among the multinational firms that do advertise universally with

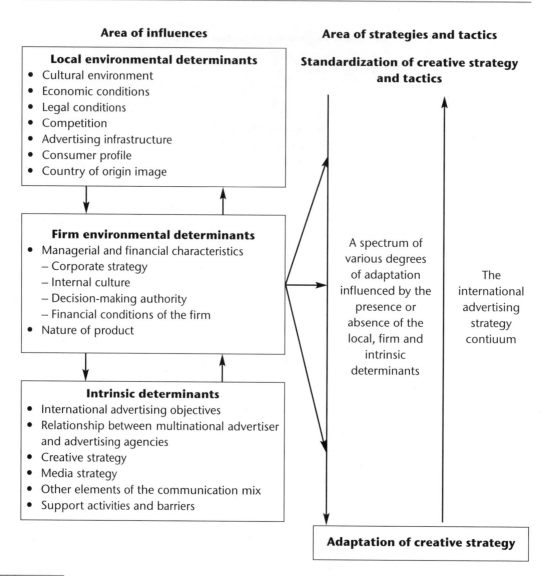

Figure 12.4 Standardization versus adaptation of international advertising strategies

virtually the same advertising approach. On the other hand, the Parker Pen Company sells the same product in all markets but the advertising differs considerably in each market. For example, in Germany, the advertisement headline is 'This is how you write with precision', whereas in the United States the theme of the message is based on image and status.

Adaptation of international advertising campaigns

In contrast, opponents of the standardization approach argue that separate messages should be used to reach buyers in different markets by fitting the message to each particular country (Kotler 2006). According to this approach, there are insurmountable differences (for example, cultural, economic, legal, media and product dissimilarities) between countries and even between regions in the same country. These differences necessitate the adaptation or development of new/different advertising strategies. In addition, anecdotal evidence (Harris and Attour 2003) seems to challenge the basic assumption of the standardization approach by suggesting that assuming similar buying motives for consumers across foreign markets may at best, be simplistic and at worst dangerous.

As can be seen from Figure 12.4, the decision whether to standardize or adapt the international advertising strategy cannot be considered a dichotomous one. There are usually degrees of international advertising standardization. For example, it is desirable to standardize certain aspects of an advertising campaign while at the same time adapt other aspects to different market conditions. Hence, it is possible that international advertising decisions can be viewed on a continuum with the two polar ends of the continuum being standardization of and adaptation creative advertising strategy and tactics.

Creative strategy refers to the advertising concept or theme (promise/claim), while creative tactics relates to the way in which the advertising strategy is expressed or executed in the finished advertisements (for example, visual elements, headlines, content of appeal, process of appeal). The continuum concept suggests that international advertising decisions must be either standardized or not standardized. If they are not standardized, then they must be adapted, and hence you need to determine which adaptations are most appropriate in different situations.

Standardization of international advertising campaign may encounter obstacles in the areas of:

- Language – slogans may be difficult to translate. For example, General Motors' brand name for one of its models was the Vauxhall 'Nova'. This does not work well in Spanish-speaking markets because the brand name sounds like 'no go'.
- Perception differences – Kentucky Fried Chicken, for example, is viewed as an ordinary meal in the United Kingdom and the United States but in Japan it is looked on as a special meal for special occasions. The message will therefore need to be changed to suit local tastes and lifestyles.
- Environmental factors may affect advertising objectives: for example, the German car manufacturer Volkswagen promotes its VW Golf in the United Kingdom in the medium to high-price range, as a car for the upwardly mobile consumer segment, yet advertises it in Germany merely as an ordinary efficient vehicle.
- Legal obstacles – many governments maintain tight regulations on message content, language, sexism and product types that can be advertised. Strict regulations are found and enforced in industrialized economies rather than in developing economies where the advertising industry is as yet not highly developed.

Media selection

International media selection is more difficult than in the domestic market and there is much variation between and among national markets in the types of media that are available for use. The criteria for selecting the appropriate media include the target audience, media availability, coverage, effectiveness and costs.

Availability

The media required may not be available or available only on a limited basis; commercial television, for example, is still not widely available in African countries. Access may also be restricted and the time available per day may be limited or the law in some countries may also limit the type of products that can be promoted. On the other hand, there may be too great a media choice and this can also create some problems. For example, to advertise nationally in India could involve advertising in over 200 daily newspapers.

Coverage

A problem with international advertising is generating adequate reach and frequency. Attaining this may require a combination of different media. Advertising high-quality healthcare products solely on television would not be adequate to reach all the required target market. The firm will need to combine television advertising with other media such as magazines, radio and newspapers. However, using a wide variety of media also spreads the budget thinly, which then affects the degree of frequency. The alternative to this is for the marketer to introduce the product over a smaller target market in one or two countries in order to attain the required reach and frequency.

Effectiveness

Another problem confronting the multinational firm is measuring how effective the media campaign has been. The relative lack of data will make it difficult to verify the effectiveness. In some markets, reliable data is not available; newspapers may be extremely difficult to monitor.

Costs

International advertising incurs higher costs than in the domestic market because of translation, rewriting of advertisements based on culturally accepted norms, and a higher percentage of wasted circulation because of media fragmentation. Inefficient production runs may be incurred because of the need to produce different material on a smaller scale for each market.

Selecting agents

Multinational firms need to consider the following points when selecting an advertising agency for their integrated international marketing communications:

- **Market coverage** – the markets that the agency deals with should be those that coincide with the firm's provision of good-quality service.
- **International cohesion** – a firm that requires a fairly standardized international campaign will need to seek out an agency which provides a good international approach.
- **Cost** – the firm will need to spend a considerable amount on advertising to attract or interest international agencies.

International publicity and public relations

Publicity is the non-personal stimulation of demand that is not paid for by the sponsor that has released news to the media. Advertising and publicity are quite similar in the sense that both require media for a non-personal presentation of the promotional message, although with publicity the company may have less control over how the message is used by the media. Publicity is a major tool of proactive public relations. In other words, it is offensively rather than defensively oriented, and opportunity seeking rather than problem solving.

Like advertising and personal selling, the fundamental purposes of marketing-oriented publicity are to create brand awareness, enhance attitudes towards a company and its brands and possibly influence purchase behaviour. Companies can obtain publicity using various forms of news releases, press conferences and other information dissemination. News releases concerning new products, modifications of old products and other news-worthy topics are delivered to editors of newspapers, magazines and other media. Press conferences announce major news events of interest to the public. Photographs, tapes and films are useful for illustrating product improvements, new products and advanced production techniques. Understandably, all forms of publicity are subject to the control and whims of the media, but by disseminating a large volume of publicity materials and by preparing materials that fit the media's needs, a company increases its chances of obtaining beneficial publicity.

Major constraints on international publicity

The role of publicity in international marketing can be a complex one since companies are operating in a variety of environmental conditions and with constraints on strategy choices. Hence, the supply of factual, interesting and newsworthy information becomes dependent largely on cultural differences in various markets, language barriers, media availability and different laws governing promotion. These factors present a set of unique problems for international publicity. Thus, even drawing up a simple news release may require knowledge of local culture, religion and traditional values if it is to ring true and not offend local susceptibilities. For a successful implementation therefore, companies need to apply the basics of corporate communications, public relations and publicity. So, the task is to apply well-known principles in a new, more complex, international marketing environment.

Cultural constraints

Knowledge of culture is essential to conducting international publicity. It enables compa-nies to communicate with their targeted audience through the use of language either commonly known to both parties or learnt. Most importantly, it helps companies antici-pate how consumers in various markets are likely to respond to their actions. Ignorance of cultural differences can create problems for companies. For example, Euro Disney's corporate image suffered initially due to the insensitivity of its executives towards the French people. The Disney personnel were considered to be brash and overbearing. For a proud and touchy people such as the French, this attitude by the US company fuelled resentment, which led to planning and operational difficulties for Disney. Ignorance of cultural difference is not just unfortunate, it is bad business. Hence, sensitivity to cultural difference is crucial to successful international publicity.

Language barriers

The diversity of languages in world markets is one major constraint facing international publicity. Although some languages are used in more than one country, there are many more languages than countries. A major difficulty confronting an international company is the translation of a concept (for example, product and promotional theme) from one language to another, even from one dialect to another. It is possible that even within a major language like English the meaning of words and expressions will vary from country to country. Such differences need to be considered when developing publicity materials and when communications occur between a company and its foreign publics.

Media availability

Much communication with target audiences is indirect through the media. The great majority of newspapers and television stations are national organizations addressing a predominantly national audience. However, the *Financial Times* for example has a significant international readership, while broadcasting corporations like CNN and the BBC World Service cater for an international audience. Currently, dealing with the media internationally is largely a question of dealing with a range of national publications and broadcasting stations in many national markets.

This is even more challenging for companies because the communication infrastructure varies from one country to another. Television set ownership ranges from one set per two persons in countries such as the United States and Japan, to one to 20 in Indonesia, one to 50 in India, one to 330 in Bangladesh, and one to 600 in Burma. Newspaper availability is marginally more consistent, with one daily paper per two persons in Japan and one per four persons in the United States; to one per 20 in Latin America, and in extreme cases, one per 200 persons in some African countries (Muhlbacher, Leihs and Dahringer 2006). Managing media relations in a foreign country also requires special skills. Since the media has its own agenda and decides what it will print or broadcast according to its own values, it is more important than ever to develop a longer-term media strategy. An international media strategy will feature a set of consistent messages, directed towards particular channels, underpinned by long-term media relationships and focused on the international issues, which most concern the company.

Government regulations

Local promotion regulations and industry codes directly influence the selection of media and content of all promotional materials. Government restrictions can take many forms. Some examples:

- Some governments will only encourage national identity and insist on buying national or homemade products. The 'Buy British' campaign was a typical example. This 1931 campaign was the National Government's attempt to tackle a balance of payments crisis without initially resorting to tariff protection. The operation was managed by the Empire Marketing Board and employed previously developed publicity techniques plus voluntary support to deliver its message on the benefits to be brought to the balance of trade, the value of sterling, and the value of employment and commercial relations with the Empire. Although technically efficient, the campaign nevertheless had only a limited and temporary impact.

- Some countries have restrictions on the types of products that can be promoted. Tobacco, alcohol and drugs are especially targeted. The promotion of tobacco products like cigarettes is banned in Belgium, Denmark, Finland, France, Germany, Portugal and Switzerland.
- In some countries, certain media are not available or are very limited. In Austria, the television cannot be used for the promotion of tobacco. In many African countries where ownership of a television set is very limited, promoting a product solely on television would not be adequate to reach all the required target market. Companies will need to combine television promotion with other media such as magazines, radio and newspapers.
- Some governments are very particular about the language used and the use of comparative promotion. This often necessitates pre-clearance of some promotional materials. South Korea bans plagiarizing of foreign-inspired messages.

International publicity is made easier if companies maintain a good and healthy relationship with their host government, as evidenced by Japanese companies in the United States.

Personal selling in the international environment

Selling is two-way, personal communication between a company representative and a potential customer as well as back to the company. The salesperson's job is to correctly understand the buyer's needs, match those needs to the company's products and then persuade the customer to buy. The dynamic and complex nature of international marketing increases the need for closer relationships between the company and its customers. Selling as an element of international marketing is built on effective communications between the seller and buyer with the motive of establishing a long-term alliance. This approach has now become necessary as competition in many international markets becomes very intense. In personal selling, persuasive arguments are presented directly in a face-to-face relationship between sellers and potential buyers. To be effective, salespeople must be certain that their communication and negotiation skills are properly adapted to a cross-cultural setting (Ghauri and Cateora 2006: 397).

Multinational companies are recognizing that, to succeed, they must cater to customers within the context of their environment. This environment is increasingly becoming international. Indeed, customers and competitors are now likely to reside halfway around the world and to possess an entirely different cultural heritage, impacting on personal selling accordingly. The complex and demanding international environment certainly affects personal selling – perhaps more so than any other area of the international enterprise. When faced with cross-cultural settings, the necessary attributes for potential success in sales positions can often be disguised, resulting in poor evaluations or exhibitions of culture being assessed by an outsider. As a result, though international marketing has expanded tremendously in recent decades, personal selling activities are still conducted primarily on a national basis. A great concern for international marketers and sales managers is the development of measures that will be useful in assessing the selling function across national boundaries.

Effective personal selling in the domestic market requires building a relationship with the customer. International marketing presents additional challenges because the buyer and seller may come from different national and cultural backgrounds. It is difficult to overstate the importance of a face-to-face, personal selling effort for industrial products in the international markets (Ingram et al. 2002).

The selling process can be divided into several stages including prospecting, initial arrangement process, approaching the customer, presenting, problem solving, handling objections, closing the sale and following up. The relative importance of each stage can vary by country or nationality. Experience salespersons know that persistence is often required to win an order. In some Arab countries, persistence means endurance, a willingness to patiently invest months before the effort results in an actual sale.

The process of identifying potential customers and assessing the probability of purchase is known as prospecting. Successful prospecting requires problem-solving techniques, which may involve understanding and matching the customer's needs and the company's products in developing a sales presentation. The approach and the presentation involve meetings between sellers and buyers. In international selling, it is very necessary for salespersons to understand cultural norms and proper protocol. In some countries such as Nigeria and Ghana in West Africa, the approach is drawn out as buyers get to know the sellers on a personal level with no mention of the pending deal. In such circumstances, the presentation comes only after rapport has been firmly established. This approach will enable the sellers to deal with any eventual objections. Usually, in international sales, verbal and nonverbal communication barriers may present special challenges for sellers. But when objections are successfully overcome, the sellers move on to the close and ask for the order. A successful sale does not end there, and the final step of the selling process involves following up with customers to ensure their continuing satisfaction with the purchase.

International sales promotion

Sales promotion is a term that has sometimes been used to describe all those activities that do not fall directly under personal selling, public relations and advertising. Sales promotions are short to medium-term activities that can add value to the sale. These various activities are supposed to stimulate interest and provide the motivation to purchase goods and services. Sales promotion is targeted not only at the consumer level but also at intermediaries in order to gain their support. It is also used in industrial selling. For example, some pharmaceutical firms in the United States sponsor trips for their wholesalers, or doctors are given gifts.

Sales promotion techniques are varied and numerous, ranging from coupons, samples and contests to trading stamps. Sales promotion can be effective in many markets, but the techniques employed need to be accepted culturally, legally and psychologically. In the United States, for example, there was resistance by African-Americans to redeeming coupons, because the word 'coupon' was associated with food stamps or government handouts. Any sales promotion techniques therefore need to be adapted to suit the cultural meanings and symbols of the market.

Sales promotion techniques

Companies operating internationally employ a variety of sales promotion techniques but the three most commonly used are:

- **Price-reducing techniques**: under this category the price of products are reduced in one form or another. This can be in the form of promotional discounts, use of coupons and trade allowances.
- **Add to value or perceived value**: this technique involves giving free samples, coupons attached to a product or close to it, bonus packs and premiums; all these add value for the customer. For example, some UK magazines and newspapers 'give away' hundreds or thousands of pounds of gifts when readers enter contests or subscriptions to a magazine. Some supermarkets give a free sample when a large item has been purchased, such as getting a free toothbrush with a large tube of toothpaste.
- **Provision of information**: techniques that provide information include displays, exhibitions, trade shows, product demonstrations and special events. These techniques are particularly important for technical products. They are normally used in conjunction with other sales promotion techniques.

Sales promotional objectives

The major objective of any type of sales promotion technique is to stimulate and enhance sales. Sales promotional techniques targeted at consumers have the objective of enticing them to a trial purchase. The rationale for this is that customers' risk perception will be considerably reduced when they have had an opportunity to try a product or service. Free samples over the cheese counter or a free one-day training session given to potential participants by a training/consulting organization are very effective sales promotional techniques. Some techniques are designed to persuade trial users to become regular buyers or repeat purchasers of the product or service. Purchasing three items of soap for the price of two, or the frequent flyer programmes operated by most European airlines such as Swissair and British Airways, are examples. With these programmes, customers earn air miles for their flights and can redeem them for free travel. A company that wishes to develop its distribution system, especially in highly competitive markets, can use sales promotion techniques strategically. For example, retailers could be influenced to increase their orders by giving them trade allowances, and the use of competitions. A company can also aid the retailers by providing information to the target customers through trade shows and exhibitions.

Choice of sales promotion techniques

A number of factors affect the type of sales techniques that companies choose to employ. Some are culture-bound, which international marketers need to be especially aware of, and others transcend any cultural barriers and have to be considered regardless of the market in which companies wish to operate.

Norms of the target market

The type of sales promotion technique must blend in or be consistent with the cultural norms of the target market. The expansion of the European Union, with the consequent free movement of goods and services. makes this very urgent. It is only logical for companies to want to build a pan-European sales promotion strategy with the expected economies on logistics and premium purchasing. However, one of the major constraints for companies wishing to work on a pan-European basis is the cultural factor. In particular, a target market's acceptance of the sales promotion techniques is critical, and the sales promotion industry in the United Kingdom is perhaps a bit more developed and sophisticated than in its European partners. There are many instances of 'cultural conflict' in the literature; for example, in the United Kingdom, there is a cultural acceptance of on-pack price reductions but this is not so in Italy, where it requires permission from the Finance Ministry first.

Cost factor

Multinational companies need not only to assess the total cost of the sales promotion campaign but also to estimate roughly what contribution the outlay will make to increasing sales. The international marketer has to estimate which is the most economical method of sales promotion, and yet achieves the desired results. Using coupons in a campaign, for example, will turn out to be less expensive than giving out free samples; however, this may not be the most appropriate strategy if the objective is to encourage consumers to have a trial run of the product. In the case of some products such as food or drink, only the use of samples can communicate the product benefits.

Channel members' affinity

Channel members such as retailers and wholesalers must be willing and able to accommodate the logistical requirements of a sales promotion campaign. They must be willing to provide storage and shelf space for bonus packs to be used in the sales promotion campaign. Point-of-purchase displays and coupons need to be accepted by the channel members. Coupons require much effort and time to process them, which can prove unpopular with retailers, as happened in Northern Europe.

Channel power

The role of power in the channel system has a bearing on the types of sales promotion techniques used. If retailers have a high degree of channel power they may extract considerable trade allowances from manufacturers. Marks & Spencer and Tesco stores in the United Kingdom, Albert Heijn in Holland and Carrefour in France all wield enormous power over their suppliers. Conversely, if the manufacturer has a high degree of power, the retailers are unlikely to obtain many trade concessions.

Legal restrictions

The use of some sales promotion techniques is forbidden by legal restrictions in many national markets, and it is not surprising that many sales promotional activities are relatively under-utilized, due largely to legal rather than to psychological barriers. Compared with the United States, the EU countries have not only a larger number but also a more diverse range of restrictions. This diversity of legal barriers makes it very unlikely that the European Union will be able to standardize its promotional regulations in the foreseeable future. For example, 'money-off next purchase' is not permitted in Germany but is legal in Spain; 'discounts on the next purchase' are valid in Belgium but illegal in Denmark. The international marketer needs to consult the local authorities in each specific market to ascertain the particular legal characteristics before embarking on a promotional campaign. The rationale of various EU governments to restrict or ban some sales promotional methods is that:

- Special offers such as free gifts and money-off vouchers that accompany a sale improperly influence consumers, as the real value of the product/service is often hidden.
- Sales promotion campaigns disrupt and distort consumers' abilities to make rational buying decisions by stimulating impulse buying behaviour; as well as hampering them from meaningfully comparing prices of similar goods.
- Large companies have the resources to implement an effective sales promotion campaign at the expense of the smaller companies; the effect is that larger companies enjoy better position and consumers will not have the opportunity to compare products on the basis of quality and value for money.

Some of the most widely used promotional techniques are discussed below to illustrate how they might be affected by local regulations.

Use of premiums and gifts

There are practically no legal restrictions on the use of premiums in the United Kingdom, whereas most EU countries tend to have limits on the value of the premiums given. In France, it is forbidden to offer premiums that are conditional on the purchase of another good. The Scandinavian countries, Belgium and Germany all have very strict laws with respect to promotion, as they wish to protect consumers from being misled about the true value of the product/service. In general, all free premiums are illegal in Germany, but if a realistic price is charged then premiums are permitted if their value is very small or they represent a product accessory. In the Netherlands, premiums must not exceed 4 per cent of the value of the product, and there must be a connection with it. In Italy, the Finance Ministry decides which products can be promoted this way and it also establishes the maximum value of the premiums.

'With purchase or in-pack' premiums are illegal in Belgium; they are allowed only if the premium is an accessory to the main product, is not generally available, or the premiums are of low value. Many non-EU countries such as Venezuela and Argentina also have very strict laws; these countries almost prohibit the use of merchandise premiums. Japan does not allow the value of the premiums to exceed 10 per cent of the value of the product that is to be purchased.

'Reduced price' and discounts

Laws against price discrimination may prevent the use of price reductions in many sales promotion campaigns in the European Union. The United Kingdom, France and the Netherlands allow on-pack price reductions. Germany allows 'price reductions', but the authorities must be notified in advance if the company is going to have a sale. Generally, these sales tend to be limited to occasions such as a winter or summer sale, the end of a product line or a company anniversary. This is unlike the United States, where sales of all types for all occasions are permitted. Furthermore, any quantity discounts should lie within the industry's percentage range, and discounts for payment on delivery should not exceed a certain percentage. In Belgium, multiple purchase schemes are allowed but the price may not exceed over a third of the combined price. In addition, the product that is promoted should be available separately at the normal price. Discounts in Scandinavia are generally restricted and Austria prohibits cash discounts that discriminate between different groups of customers.

Sample packs

Germany limits the size of the sample pack, and restricts door-to-door free samples, which have limited population coverage. If the product has been on the market for some time, then samples are completely banned. Alcoholic beer samples are banned in the United States.

Relationship marketing

Relationship marketing (RM) involves organizations gathering information about their customers and then deciding with whom they can develop a dialogue. It allows buyers and sellers to work together in joint problem solving, easing the pressures on the buyer. Rather than employing market share as a measure of marketing success, this approach uses customer retention as evidence of strong agreement between the seller and the buyer to do business. Gronroos (1996a, 1996b) defined RM as 'all marketing activities directed toward establishing, developing and maintaining successful relational exchanges'.

This section examines the factors that are involved in the implementation of an RM strategy in international markets. In transferring RM theory from a domestic to an international context, various factors emerge which can impede the development of cross-cultural business relationships. These factors are largely a consequence of different cultural value systems and can be synthesized in the concept of distance to one's market. A positive relationship exists between the level of psychic distance between the parties concerned, and the financial and psychological investment that is generally required to develop a successful RM strategy, so this is an important factor in the development of international RM strategies.

Components of a successful relationship

Levitt (1983) sees five stages in the development of a relationship: awareness, exploration, expansion, commitment and dissolution. In view of the number of potential variables in any relationship, it may be wise to concentrate on those variables that, according to the literature, are deemed relatively more important in most relationships, especially in an international context. They include commitment, trust, customer orientation/empathy, experience/satisfaction and communication.

Commitment

Of central importance in developing relationships is the level of commitment a partner feels towards that relationship. Commitment is the most common dependent variable used in studies of relationships between the buyer and the seller. This is because commitment level is probably the strongest predictor of voluntary decisions to remain in a relationship. Commitment can therefore be viewed as an intention to continue a course of action or activity or the desire to maintain a relationship. This is often indicated by the amount of investment in marketing activity. Commitment may be stronger when levels of satisfaction are high, when the quality of alternatives is perceived to be poor, and when investment size is large. Commitment is also likely to be influenced by social bonding (that is, the degree of mutual personal friendships and liking shared by the buyer and seller. Buyers and sellers who have a strong personal relationship may be more committed to maintaining the relationship than less socially bonded partners.

Social bonding would seem to be closely connected to the concept of 'closeness'. A relationship is 'close' when it is characterized by high interdependence over a period of time. Closeness influences the size of the investment in the relationship, which in turn influences commitment. The development and maintenance of a relationship requires the investment of time, energy, emotion and money. It is therefore possible to suggest that the greater the level of investment made by a multinational company in a relationship, the greater the increase in that company's commitment to its relationship with its distributor. Trust is an important consideration, and many aspects of relations between customers and suppliers are based on trust. Trust is therefore a precondition for increased commitment and is a fundamental relationship model building block, and as such is included in most relationship models.

Customer orientation/empathy

This is considered to be a key factor and has links with the concept of social bonding. The word 'empathy' really refers to an understanding, or the ability to see a situation from someone else's point of view, although many use the term synonymously with affinity and liking. For the purpose of this book, the wider interpretation is used.

In the initial stages of relationship development, the onus is more likely to be on the seller to empathize with the buyer. However, as the relationship develops further, mutual empathy becomes increasingly important. One party 'liking' the other is important in the development of close interpersonal and business relationships. Liking a particular individual (or group of people) may generate a more positive outlook towards that person. In addition to the bargaining strategy itself, interpersonal attraction (for example, like/dislike, friendly/unfriendly feelings) can strongly influence current negotiation outcomes and the success of future transactions.

Experience/satisfaction

Experience is another factor in successful relationships. The decision to continue in a relationship can be seen as dependent on the level of congruity between relationship expectations and performance so far. Negative experience may, of course, hinder the relationship, or even lead to customer defection. Furthermore, consumers tend to remember best the last experience (the recency effect). Thus one positive experience may be sufficient to alter perceptions of more than one preceding negative experience, and vice versa. This suggests the important influence experience can have on customer satisfaction, and the more satisfied the customer, the more durable the relationship. It is likely that customer satisfaction can be experienced at both an episodic and at a more general relationship level. Although there are links between customer experience and satisfaction, it is likely that this is also the case for other parties in the relationship. Both parties must have positive experiences in order to reach the required overall level of satisfaction over a period of time and develop the relationship further.

Communication

Communication could be simply defined as the process of establishing a commonness or oneness of thought between the sender and the receiver. Thus communication is a vital component in the establishment of business relationships, yet it is a variable that is often assumed or taken for granted and consequently overlooked as a component of relationship development. This is unfortunate, as all other components are experienced through the medium of communication. In the business sense, communication is as much concerned with receiving as it is with giving. Within the field of business communications, the communicators(or sender of the message), still need to know the effect their message has had on the target audience; feedback is essential, and this is only possible if information flows two ways.

The extent to which communication is important can perhaps best be calculated by considering the many target audiences with which a business must communicate in order to survive. There are two main categories of communication for an organization, internal and external. External communication is of the greatest relevance to an international marketer dealing with foreign customers or suppliers. It is also an area in which problems are likely to be most pronounced because of transaction uncertainty. Effective collaboration and coordination depend on effective communication, and communication becomes even more important when trying to establish business relationships in a foreign country. The importance of communication as an element of relationship marketing is that communication is not only an important element in its own right, but also has the propensity to influence levels of trust between buyer and seller.

Direct marketing

Direct marketing involves direct access to the customer, and the major tools of this approach are telemarketing, direct mail, catalogues, electronic media (home shopping and cable television), the Internet and selling via magazines and newspapers.

Direct marketing has become an important medium of selling since the early 1990s, especially in the developed economies of the European Union and the United States. The EU countries that have had rapid growth, include the United Kingdom, Belgium, France and the Scandinavian countries. In spite of its growth, direct marketing expenditure in the European Union constitutes only about a quarter of all marketing expenditure compared with two-thirds in the United States (Olkkonen 2001). Future growth in the European Union will depend on the extent of government regulation on promotions, which are tightly controlled. Germany has some of the most restrictive regulations, whereas the United Kingdom and the Netherlands have a more liberal approach.

Direct marketing has also growth rapidly in some Asia Pacific countries, such as Singapore and Hong Kong.

Growth of direct marketing

A number of factors have contributed to the rapid growth and development of international direct marketing:

- The costs of traditional forms of promotion such as advertising and sales promotion have escalated to such a point that companies are searching for alternative methods.
- The rapid developments in IT in areas such as databases and desktop publishing have facilitated the production of high-quality in-house direct marketing materials, especially for small and medium-sized companies.
- Developments in mail technology have reduced the costs of distributing direct marketing materials.
- The development of database technology has not only facilitated the development of lists of prospective customers, but has also made it available to companies.
- The development and the immense growth of the Internet or 'information super-highway' has increased the availability of interactive facilities, whereby customers can order directly.
- The extensive use of direct marketing by companies has also accelerated its development.

There are many benefits associated with using direct marketing which companies find attractive because the outcomes are measurable. Names and addresses of consumers are stored in a database which can be used for future direct marketing campaigns or even sold to other firms. Consumer profiles can be built from information based on the company's sales files, customers' residential neighbourhood, sociodemographic characteristics and so on, and direct marketing is both a convenient and an effective marketing tool.

Trade shows

International trade shows have become a significant promotional tool for MNCs. Industrial companies frequently use trade shows in their marketing strategies. Many major trade shows are held world-wide each year. For instance, 180 international trade shows are held in Germany annually with 124,000 exhibitors and over 10 million visitors. Also about 220 international trade shows are organized in the UK annually with an estimated 61,000 exhibitors and 4.6 million visitors (Hansen 1996). As the number of international trade shows has increased they have become an important promotional tool for both industrial and consumer firms.

However, most international marketing firms have overlooked the importance of trade shows, and many of them have similarly failed to use trade shows as part of their integrated marketing communications. Although the descriptive trade show literature is extensive and may be useful to practitioners, international trade shows have received surprisingly little attention from academic researchers. One reason for this lack of attention may be the lack of theoretical concepts and models dealing with the role and function of trade shows.

MINI CASE 12.2

Examples of international events sponsorship

The aim of sponsoring is to establish and consolidate the impression customers have of the company and of its brands. It is intended to transfer a distinct image and to build awareness for the company and its products and/or services. Typical events sponsored are sport events (75 per cent of the sponsoring budget) and cultural events. Sport events like the Olympic Games become more and more attractive to marketers. In 1996, *The Times Magazine* stated that:

> The Olympic Games are universally acknowledged as the global media and marketing extravaganza. For top companies, they offer brand values and unbeatable images. For example, Rupert Murdoch's bid for the broadcast right of the Sydney 2000 games which was watched by 3.6 billion people was about four times the sum paid by the European Broadcasting Union to screen the Olympic Games in 1996. Twenty years ago, the International Olympics Committee had great difficulties obtaining companies wishing to sponsor the games. Today, the Olympics stand for universally admired values such as excellence, success, international co-operation and peace.

A marketer aiming to transfer meanings from a sponsored event to its company or product must take care when selecting the most appropriate sponsoring events. It is particularly important to find similarities between the event and the company or product. For instance, Grand Met launched the ice-cream brand Haagen-Dazs in Europe at a price 40 per cent higher than its closest competitors. Haagen-Dazs concentrated on and adopted promotion without a mass media strategy. Besides the unusual strategy (little advertising effort but opening of several posh ice-cream parlours in prominent locations) Haagen-Dazs was linked to arts sponsorship. At the Opera Factory's production of *Don Giovanni* in London, the high-priced ice cream was even incorporated in the performance: 'When the Don called for sorbet, he received a container of Haagen-Dazs.' Within a few months, brand awareness had reached more than 50 per cent in the United Kingdom.

International account management

Advertising agencies around the world have long used national account management to handle their most important accounts. Such national account management approaches include having one executive or team take overall responsibility for all aspects of a customer's business, either directly or coordinating the activities of others. Typical applications include the use of national account managers for retail chains, and for business equipment and service customers. National account management approaches have also been used interchangeably with relationship marketing and management. The international account management concept extends national account management across countries, not necessarily to all countries, but to the most important ones for the most important customers, and for the most important activities. International account management can also be viewed as the new frontier in RM. This section discusses the industry forces creating conditions for the use of international account management, and their implications for international advertising strategy.

Framework for managing international accounts

Figure 12.5 provides a framework for international accounts management. In this framework, industry international drivers (underlying market, cost and other industry conditions) create the potential for multinational businesses to achieve the benefits of international strategy. In order to achieve these benefits, a multinational company needs to set its IMS levers (for example, use of internationally standardized products) appropriately relative to the industry drivers. International organization factors usually affect how well an advertising agency can implement the formulated international strategy.

Factors in the management of international accounts

Several individual international forces significantly affect the opportunity for advertising agencies to use international account management (see Sanford and Maddox 1999):

- international or global customers
- international channels

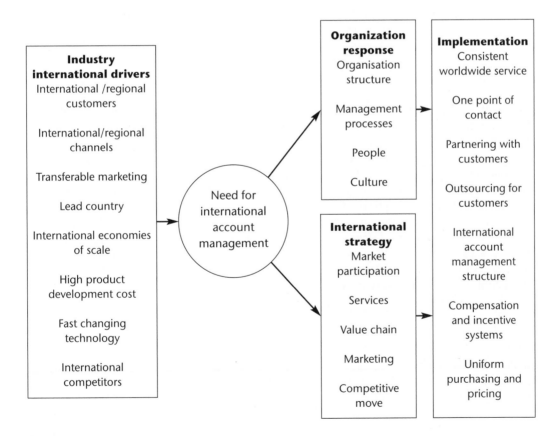

Figure 12.5   Framework for international account management

- regional customers and/or channels
- transferable marketing
- lead countries
- international economies of scale
- high product/service development costs
- international competitors.

Examples of companies with international accounts

AT&T distinguishes between 'international customers' and 'global customers'. Citibank designates 'parent account managers'. Hewlett-Packard sets up a global account management team. Young & Rubicam, the advertising agency, has created a position of 'global managing director'. Why have these and other companies adopted global account management? The answer is globalization. Increasingly, MNCs are requiring their suppliers to play the role of global coordination. General Electric (GE) has told many of its suppliers that it expects them to be responsible for ensuring that GE businesses get uniform products around the world. These suppliers have to respond with global account management. Similarly, one reason for AT&T's current push to expand globally is the fact that many of its customers are global, and will use rivals like NEC, Siemens or IBM for advanced voice and data networks if AT&T cannot meet their needs.

International customers

Clearly, the existence and importance of international customers represent the strongest driver for the use of international account management. Traditionally, many multinational agencies have allowed their national subsidiaries extensive independence in their purchasing behaviour, such that they behaved as national or local customers. So these subsidiaries might each select different vendors and different products. Increasingly, multinational advertising companies have found problems with this approach – particularly incompatibility of equipment and standards, and diseconomies in purchasing. So companies have increasingly begun to buy on a centralized or coordinated basis, even if for decentralized use, or at the least they select vendors centrally. By sourcing internationally, these companies become international customers. In addition, many customers and clients increasingly seek suppliers who can treat them as a single entity and provide consistent and seamless service across countries.

International channels

Analogous to international customers, there may be channels of distribution that buy on an international or at least a regional basis. International channels are also important in exploiting differences in prices by performing the arbitrage function of transhipment. Their presence makes it more necessary for agencies to rationalize their world-wide pricing and other terms of sale. International channels are rare, but region-wide ones are increasing in number, particularly in European grocery distribution and retailing.

Similarly, as US retailers such as Wal-Mart and Toys'R'Us, and Japanese ones such as Mitsukoshi and Yaohan, expand internationally, their suppliers will need to manage them as international accounts.

Regional customers and channels

International customer and channel issues also apply to regional (for example, Asian or European) customers. Indeed, regional customers are probably growing at a faster rate than international customers, particularly in Europe.

Transferable marketing

The nature of the buying decision may be such that marketing elements, such as brand names and advertising and selling approaches, require little local adaptation. Thus, they are readily transferable. Transferable marketing makes it easier to manage accounts on an international basis.

Lead countries

Innovation in products or processes may be concentrated in one or a few countries because of the presence of innovative competitors or demanding customers or both. In that case it becomes critical for international competitors to participate in these 'lead countries' in order to be exposed to the sources of innovation. International account management helps ensure that customers based in these lead countries get special attention and that the company learns. For example, the majority of Hewlett-Packard's designated international accounts are based in lead computer-usage countries such as the United States, Japan, Germany, Sweden and the United Kingdom.

International economies of scale

International scale economies or scope economies apply when single-country markets are not large enough to allow competitors to achieve optimum scale. International account management can help ensure that strategically, facilities are configured to best serve international accounts economically and tactically; orders are consolidated for efficient production.

High product development costs

High product development costs relative to the size of national markets act as a driver to internationalization, so that these costs can be amortized across many markets. International account management helps ensure that the agency gets and implements an international view of the development needs for serving major multinational accounts.

Changing technology

Fast-changing technology, in products or processes, usually accompanies high product development costs and in itself increases industry international potential. International account management helps ensure that the company provides the right levels of technology to each location of a multinational account.

International competitors

When a company's competitors use international strategy to exploit the potential of the industry, the business needs to match or pre-empt these competitors. When competitors use a specific strategy of international account management, then there is all the more need for a company to do so itself.

Response to international customers

Four key organization and management factors may determine an advertising company's ability to develop and implement an international account strategy: organization structure, management process, people in the organization and organization culture.

Organization structure

Organization structure comprises the reporting relationships in a business. It changes the organization structure by creating a position (the international account manager) that has authority over others in the company. In particular, the international account manager now has a say over what national managers do with their customers. The extent of this authority can vary from direct control to coordination and advice. While national account managers typically control their accounts, the geographic scope of international account management makes such control much more difficult, and perhaps politically hazardous. An international account manager can probably be more effective by merely coordinating the selling efforts of national salespersons, and acting as the one interface with the customer at its head office. So in almost all cases, the international account manager should be located in the home country of the international customer.

Management processes

Management processes comprise activities such as planning and budgeting, as well as information systems that make the business operate efficiently. International account management is in itself a process and can also affect several other key management processes and systems. It improves the international strategy information system by providing a focal point responsible for collecting all strategic information about a multi-national account. By definition it provides cross-country coordination. The international account manager contributes to the international strategic planning process. International account management makes international budgeting more possible and more effective by providing an integrated viewpoint of customer-related expenditures.

Finally, it can move the agency towards international performance and compensation practices rather than country-based ones.

People in the organization

People comprise the human resources of the world-wide business, and include managers and all other employees. Only the people in the organization can implement international strategy. Developing managers and other members of the organization to think and behave internationally contributes to competitive advantage. International account management requires a few managers to take on international responsibilities and requires many other managers to interact with these international managers. Companies can also implement international account management programmes without immediately adding to headcount. Initially, one manager may be able to wear two hats – as a national sales executive and as an international account manager. Such an approach can also reduce turf battles and jealousy – national sales managers tend to resent interference with their local customers. If one manager becomes the international account manager he or she may get little cooperation. But if several national sales managers are assigned to international account responsibilities, they have to cooperate with one another.

Organization culture

Culture comprises the values and rules that guide behaviour in a corporation. Culture is the subtlest aspect of organization but it can play a formidable role in helping or hindering an international strategy. Having a cross-national culture steers managers towards international rather than local profit maximization. International account management can significantly contribute to building the cross-national culture of a company. Overall, international account management constitutes a new organizational form that responds to the increased interdependencies arising from internationalization process. Finally it is important to remember that international account management changes in all of these four factors in the process of responding effectively to the international customers.

The use of international strategy is likely to improve performance. International account management magnifies a company's ability to use most elements of international strategy. It increases the ability to:

- Build international market participation by helping to place more emphasis on internationally strategic markets, such as the home market of international customers. To serve its international customers, a company needs to be present in all the customers' major markets. The US advertising agency that used to have the Coca-Cola account (one of the largest in the world) was unable to serve Coca-Cola when it expanded to Brazil. So McCann-Erickson, another US, but more international, agency took the account in Brazil. Then McCann used the Brazilian relationship to win the entire Coca-Cola account world-wide.
- Develop international products/services by providing an internationally integrated view of customer needs. Offering standardized products can also be a necessity for serving international customers, as Honeywell found with its process control equipment sold to multinationals like Royal Dutch/Shell.
- Locate value-adding activities with an international rather than series of national

perspectives, thereby avoiding unnecessary duplication while achieving scale and focus. Some activities, such as development engineering, selling and after-sales service, may need to be concentrated or at least internationally coordinated in order to serve international customers effectively.

- Reap the benefits of judicious use of internationally uniform marketing. These benefits can include leveraging of an international brand name or reputation, or avoiding the downside of internationally inconsistent pricing. For example, international customers can compare prices charged by the same supplier in different countries, and tend to be unhappy with unexplainable discrepancies.

- Make international competitive moves by providing the coordination capability needed for such moves. It is also competitively important to recognize potential international customers. These are multinational customers who currently do not buy or coordinate centrally, but may start to do so. An international supplier can gain a first mover or pre-emptive advantage by being the first to treat a potential international customer as an actual international customer.

Finally, international accounts may actually be managed more formally and with fewer interpersonal relationships than domestic accounts in order to compensate for the difficulties in establishing face-to-face meetings. On the other hand, senior accounts managers who have the ability to establish interpersonal relationships with foreign client managers may represent a scarce and valuable agency resource.

Ethical and cultural issues

Knowledge of cultural diversity, especially the symbolism associated with cultural traits, is essential when creating advertising. Local country managers will be able to share important information, such as when to use caution in advertising creativity. Use of colours and male–female relationships can often be stumbling blocks. For example, white in Asia is associated with death. In Japan, intimate scenes between men and women are considered to be in bad taste; they are outlawed in Saudi Arabia. Veteran adman John O'Toole offers the following insights to international advertisers:

> Transplanted American creative people always want to photograph European men kissing women's hands. But they seldom know that the nose must never touch the hand or that this rite is solely for married women. And how do you know that the woman in the photograph is married? By the ring on her left hand, of course. Well, in Spain, Denmark, Holland and Germany, Catholic women wear the wedding ring on the right hand. When photographing a couple entering a restaurant or theatre, you show the woman preceding the man, correct? No. Not in Germany and France. And this would be laughable in Japan. Having someone in a commercial hold up his hand with the back of it to you, the viewer, and the fingers moving toward him should communicate 'come here'. In Italy it means 'good-bye'.

> (O'Toole, 1979)

The cultural environment influences advertising. The key concerns relate to values and motives, the advertising form and the execution of the advertising campaign. Advertising styles in most countries reflect their cultural values. Characteristics that distinguish Japanese from American creative strategy are:

- Indirect rather than direct forms of expression are preferred in the messages. This avoidance of directness in expression is pervasive in all types of communication among the Japanese, including their advertising. Many television advertisements do not mention what is desirable about the brand in use and let the audience judge;
- There is often little relationship between advertisement content and the advertised product.
- Only brief dialogue or narration is used in television commercials, with minimal explanatory content.
- Humour is used to create a bond of mutual feelings. Rather than slapstick, humorous dramatizations involving family members, neighbours and office colleagues are used.
- Famous celebrities appear as close acquaintances or everyday people.
- Priority is given to company trust rather than product quality. The Japanese tend to believe that if the firm is large and has a good image, the quality of its products should also be outstanding.
- The product name is impressed on the viewer with short, 15-second commercials.

Summary

The significant body of published work in international advertising literature focuses on the standardization and localization of the advertising campaign from a marketing strategy perspective without much concern regarding consumers' response. This gap has been partly addressed in this chapter by citing examples relating to consumer perceptions of local and standardized advertisements. International marketing literature shows that consumers generally prefer locally produced to foreign-sourced commercials, irrespective of brand origin. They also exhibit more favourable attitudes toward foreign-sourced, standardized commercials in situations involving greater brand familiarity and when they are executed in a style that is transformational. Thus, it is more likely that well-known brands with transformational appeal are likely to succeed when transferred to a foreign market, while local advertising messages may tend to be more effective when brand familiarity is low.

Revision questions

1 Define the term 'integrated marketing communications' and discuss its key elements.
2 What do you consider to be the major role of marketing communication in the international market?
3 Discuss the advantages of standardized advertising for international marketing communications.
4 A multinational company has a number of important decisions to make to ensure the development of appropriate campaigns in each national market. Briefly evaluate these areas.

5 International advertising standardization refers to using a common approach to promote the same product across nation boundaries. Discuss this statement with examples.

6 Define and explain the role of international publicity. What do you see as major constraints on international publicity?

7 What are the differences in personal selling approaches in the domestic and foreign markets?

8 What are the factors determining the choice of sales promotion techniques?

9 What is relationship marketing and what factors do you think contribute to its success in the international environment?

10 A number of factors have contributed to the rapid growth and development of international direct marketing. Evaluate and discuss these factors.

SEMINAR CASE STUDY

International account management

Many companies are making successful use of global account management. This case study highlights some of these companies and relates its situation to the framework and concepts that have been discussed in this chapter.

During the last 30 years, many major advertising agencies have faced some international forces (drivers) that spurred them to adopt international account management. Some of their major clients, such as Procter & Gamble and Unilever, were themselves embracing internationally integrated strategy and starting to act as international and in some cases as global customers. This change in behaviour included increasing use of internationally standardized advertising. Typical examples are Coca-Cola's sports hero/little boy campaign, British Airways' repositioning in the early 1980s and Toyota's international campaign to introduce its new Camry model in the early 1990s (all partly justified by Theodore Levitt's (1983) proclamation of the globalization of markets). Similarly, Saatchi & Saatchi in its prime aggressively positioned itself as *the* international agency, and spurred its rivals to respond by trying to do the same.

As an international account, an advertising client receives varying levels of service, depending on its needs and on the size of the company. For example, smaller companies may lack market research data and thus request assistance or participation in developing marketing strategy, while larger companies may have performed their own research and can use their own resources to develop a comprehensive marketing strategy. The degree of integration an international advertising campaign entails also depends largely on the degree of control that a client wishes to exercise.

At BBDO (part of Omnicom Group, the third-largest advertising concern), for instance, an international account is defined as a customer who wants a campaign that delivers a uniform message to every geographic market being served. Services offered to international accounts are very similar to those offered to national accounts. The difference lies, however, in the level of complexity that the development and the execution of such advertising campaigns entail. In order to serve large international accounts, BBDO established a network of offices in 54 countries world-wide and assigned personnel to serve each account exclusively. World-wide account directors and creative directors co-ordinated all their efforts across market segments and geographic boundaries throughout the world in order to support their international customers.

Similarly, to develop an international account strategy, Young and Rubicam established an international management structure that oversees both the development and the execution of every advertising campaign. International managing directors and their teams represent the core of Young and Rubicam's international management structure. Each international managing director provides a corporate international perspective for each campaign and is responsible for all communications with the client. Team members are devoted to the client, have an international perspective and a broad understanding of not only their clients' markets but also the key success factors of each region. Furthermore, because execution of the campaign is always carried out locally, the company must have access to and be able to coordinate a wide network of resources. Few clients begin with the premise of establishing an internationally integrated campaign. Typically, campaigns were developed for one country and diffused to other countries once proven successful.

Even a stellar creative reputation cannot save an advertising agency from the demands of international account management. In the early 1990s, Chiat Day – a US-based creative superstar among agencies, having the Macintosh commercial and other gems to its credit, but with little in the way of an international network – was dropped by Reebok International, the manufacturer of athletic shoes. Reebok consolidated its $140 million worldwide advertising account at Leo Burnett, a top ten international network. A key reason cited by Reebok's VP-marketing services worldwide was that Chiat Day did not have the international resources the company needed. Reebok had wired together an international network using Chiat as the lead agency and Burnett and Euro RSCG (Paris-based) overseas, but there was no partnership between the three. Soon after the loss of this account, Chiat Day agreed to be acquired by Omnicom Group, and to be folded into the latter's TBWA network.

The trend in the advertising business toward international account management has perhaps been the major factor behind the top ten international agency networks increasing their share of international advertising spending from 30 per cent to 58 per cent over the previous decade. Most dramatic of all, IBM sacked over 40 different agencies around the world, and consolidated its entire $500 million account at one top ten international agency, Ogilvy & Mather Worldwide (part of WPP, currently one of the largest agency groups).
Source: Sanford and Maddox (1999).

Seminar questions

1 Discuss the issues concerning the international accounts management reviewed in this case study and identify reasons why many advertising agencies are adopting international account management strategy.
2 How could small agencies that are regionally based compete in this market?

Managerial assignment task

The emergence of sponsorship as a significant form of integrated marketing communications is a comparatively recent development. In spite of this, it has come to greater prominence for reasons relating both to the supply of sponsorship opportunities and the demand from the corporate sector for effective communications media.

You work for an advertising agent specializing in promoting food brands. A leading international food retailer operating in 25 countries requests that your firm negotiate and arrange a sponsorship deal on its behalf. Your firm has asked you to explore the areas of international sports sponsorship.

Using the experience gained within your company, write a report that explores the issues relating to international sports sponsorship's unique ability to address the wide range of audiences. Your report must identify the relationships between audience priority and sponsorship selection and exploitation.

References

Dotson, M. J. (2002) 'A method for the selection of appropriate business-to-business integrated marketing communications mixes', *Journal of Marketing Communications,* Vol. 8, No. 1, pp.1–17.

Duncan, T. (2002) *IMC: Using Advertising & Promotion to Build Brands*, Boston: McGraw-Hill/Irwin.

Duncan, T. R. and Everett, S. (1993), "Client perceptions of integrated marketing communications", *Journal of Advertising Research*, Vol. 33 pp.30–9.

Eagle, L. and Kitchen, P. J. (2000) 'IMC, brand communications, and corporate cultures: client/advertising agency co-ordination and cohesion', *European Journal of Marketing*, Vol. 34, No. 5/6, pp. 667–86.

Ghauri, P. N. and Cateora, P. R. (2006) *International Marketing*, edn, London: McGraw-Hill.

Gronroos, C. (1996a) 'Relationship marketing: strategic and tactical implications', *Management Decision*, Vol. 34, No. 3, pp. 5–14.

Gronroos, C. (1996b) 'Value-driven relational marketing: from products to resources and competencies', *Journal of Marketing Management*, Vol. 13, No. 5, pp. 407–19.

Hackley, C. E. and Kitchen, P. J. (1998 'IMC: a consumer psychological perspective', Marketing Intelligence and Planning, Vol. 16, No. 1, pp. 23–33.

Harris, G. and Attour, S. (2003) 'The international advertising practices of multinational companies: a content analysis study', *European Journal of Marketing*, Vol. 37, No. 1/2, pp. 154–68.

Hollensen, S. (2001) *Global Marketing: A Market-Responsive Approach*, 2nd edn, London: Pearson Education.

Ingram, T. N., LaForge, R. W. and Leigh, T. W. (2002) 'Selling in the new millennium: a joint agenda', *Industrial Marketing Management,* Vol. 31, No. 7, pp. 559–67.

Kotler, P (2006) *Marketing Management*, 12th edn, New Jersey: Prentice Hall.

Levitt, T. (1983) 'The globalization of markets', *Harvard Business Review*, Vol. 61, No. 3, pp. 92–102.

Muhlbacher, H., Leihs, H. and Dahringer, L. (2006) *International Marketing: A Global Perspective*, 3rd edn, London: Thomson Education.

O'Toole, J.J: (1979) 'Corporate and Managerial Cultures', in C. L. Cooper (ed.), *Behavioural Problems in Organisations,* Englewood Cliffs, N.J.: Prentice-Hall.

Olkkonen, R. (2001) 'Case study: the network approach to international sport sponsorship arrangement', *Journal of Business & Industrial Marketing*, Vol. 16, No. 4, pp. 309–29.

Proctor, T. and Kitchen, P. (2002) 'Communication in post-modern integrated marketing', *Corporate Communications*, Vol. 7, No. 3, pp. 144–54.

Sanford Jr., D. M. and Maddox, L (1999) 'Key account management: advertising agency management of domestic and international accounts', *International Marketing Review*, Vol. 16, No. 6, pp. 504–17.

Schultz, D. E. and Kitchen, P. J. (2000a) *Global Communications: An Integrated Marketing Approach*, Chicago, Ill.: NTC Business.

Schultz, D. E. and Kitchen, P. J. (2000b) 'A response to theoretical concept or management fashion?' *Journal of Advertising Research*, Vol. 40, No. 5, pp 17–21.

Terpstra, V. (1987) *International Marketing*, New York: Holt, Rinehart & Winston.

Yip, G. S. (1992) *Total Global Strategy: Managing for Worldwide Competitive Advantage*, Englewood Cliffs, N.J.: Prentice-Hall.

Zarkada-Fraser, A. and Fraser, C. (2001) 'Moral decision making in international sales negotiations', *Journal of Business & Industrial Marketing*, Vol. 16, No. 4, pp. 274–93.

13
International Business-to-Business Marketing

Contents

LEARNING OBJECTIVES

After reading this chapter you should:

- be able to describe the nature of business-to-business (B2B) transactions in international environments
- understand the structure of relationship marketing in B2B contexts
- be able to evaluate e-market networks in relation to the international marketing process

- understand the characteristics of B2B international marketing operations and its benefits and drawbacks
- know the nature of international B2B channel control and the reality behind disintermediation in B2B transactions
- be able to evaluate the role of innovations in the international B2B market development.

Introduction

Successful international companies have realized the vital role of business-to-business (B2B) operations , in the form of strategic alliances, marketing relationships and competitive networks, in their ability to expand their international marketing programmes. In order to develop and sustain profitable business across the world it is essential for a firm to develop close relationships with other firms in other parts of the world, selling and marketing to them. It is also important for international marketers to view themselves as part of a competitive network of international and interrelated businesses bound together by marketing relationships of mutual benefits.

The emerging opportunities of information technology (IT) linkages can be seen as creating 'virtual' organizations. Companies are adjusting their international marketing practices to meet new conditions in the international environment. This new form of organization is made up of businesses held together by relationships between competitors and linked together by electronic communication and information networks. Thus, when viewed holistically it is possible to see how industries are becoming transformed by electronic commerce (e-commerce).

E-business describes the use of electronic means and platforms to conduct a company's business. International companies operating in international markets are using a significant number of e-commerce models. For example, business models can be described as ranging from a low-cost poster and/or billboard approach to virtual store model. Another example of the e-business category is a company that uses a network for ordering its supplies, receiving invoices and making payments. It is important to note that this form of e-commerce has been well established for many years, using electronic data interchange (EDI) over private or value-added networks.

The advent of the Internet has greatly increased the ability of companies to conduct their businesses faster, more accurately, over a wide range of time and space, at a reduced cost, and with the ability to customize and personalize customer offerings. Numerous companies throughout the world have set up websites to inform and promote their products and services domestically and internationally. They have created intranets to facilitate employees communicating with one another, and downloading and uploading information to and from the company's computers. These companies have also set up extranets with major suppliers and distributors to facilitate information exchange, orders, transactions and payments.

Finally, B2B Internet applications have revolutionized the way in which international organizations interact with their suppliers By integrating systems and networks, companies within a supply chain have developed faster and more efficient transactions than ever before. Nowhere is this more evident than in procurement, and many dot.com companies have sprung up purely to serve this sector of the market.

This chapter begins with an overview of electronic market networks, relationship marketing and the role of the Internet in fostering technological innovations for international marketing.

The e-commerce markets

E-commerce (see also Chapter 15) is more specific than e-business. In addition to providing information to visitors about the company, its history, policies, products and job

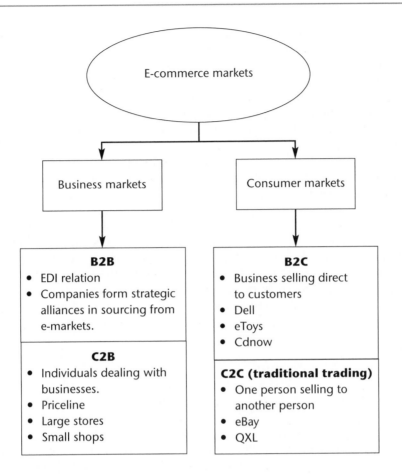

The four different e-commerce markets

opportunities, the company or site offers to facilitate the selling of products and services online. Internet websites Amazon.com, CDnow, and eToy provide corporate information as well as marketing.

E-commerce has given rise in turn to e-marketing, which describes company efforts to inform, communicate, promote and sell products and services over the Internet. According to Kotler (2006), e-business and e-commerce take place over four major Internet domains:

- B2C (business to consumers)
- B2B (business to business)
- C2C (consumer to consumers)
- C2B (consumer to business).

B2C websites receive the most attention as consumers visit these sites in search of products and services to buy. As Heldal, Sjovold and Heldal (2004) observed, many visitors to these sites look for information on such items as films, books, leisure activities and travel. The items purchased most often from the Internet are books, music, software, air tickets, clothing, videos, CDs, hotel reservations, toys and consumer electronics. In general, the Internet is most useful for products and services when the shopper seeks greater ordering convenience or lower cost. It is also useful when buyers need information about product features and prices. Individuals are also using the Internet to search for others to meet or date. The Internet is less useful for products that need to be touched or examined physically in advance.

Online consumers tend to be younger, more affluent and better educated than the general population. However, in future as more people find their way onto the Internet it is likely that the cyberspace population will become more mainstream and diverse. Younger users are more likely to use the Internet for entertainment and socializing. According to Kotler (2006: 42), the exchange process in the age of information has become customer-initiated and customer-controlled. Marketers and their representatives must wait until customers invite them to participate in the exchange. Even after marketers enter the exchange process, customers define the rules of engagement and insulate themselves with the help of agents and intermediaries. Customers define what information they need, what offerings they are interested in, and what prices they are willing to pay.

The characteristics of B2C marketing

B2C marketing can be characterized by a number of features (Hill and Scott 2004):

- Goods or services are offered for sale and purchased over the Internet. They include digitized products, such as music, airline tickets or computer software, that can be delivered direct on the Internet, and physical products such as books, flowers and groceries that are delivered by post or courier.
- Transactions are typically quick and interactive.
- There are no pre-established business agreements.
- Security is primarily an issue for the buyer, rather than the seller.
- There are low volumes between each individual purchaser and supplier, often for relatively inexpensive items and/or frequently purchased items such as groceries.
- Well-known packaged items, which have standard specifications, are the core trade.
- Items are backed by a security guarantee and/or high brand recognition. The remoteness from the customer means that a strong reputation may be required to establish consumer confidence.
- Items whose operating procedures can be most effectively demonstrated by animation or video are usefully sold in this way.

Well-designed websites, which are attractive and easy to use, are essential.

The emerging B2C models

There are a number of ways of classifying the emerging B2C business models:

- Direct marketing product websites – where manufacturers advertise and distribute their own products to customers via Internet-based stores, with no intermediaries. Examples include Dell Computers, Nike, Cisco, The Gap and Sony.

- Pure electronic retailers (e-retailers) that have no physical stores, being purely cyber-based, such as Amazon.com.
- Traditional retailers with websites – sometimes called brick-and-click organizations – where the Internet provides an additional distribution channel for an existing business. Examples include Wal-Mart, Tesco and Barnes & Noble.
- Best price searching agents – intermediaries such as BestBuyBooks.com and Buy.com that use software to search for the lowest prices available on the Internet.
- Buyer sets the price – customers nominate a price which they are willing to pay for certain goods or services, and the intermediary then tries to find a seller willing to sell at that price or lower. An example is Priceline.com.
- Electronic (online) auctions – host sites such as e-Bay and google.com act like brokers, offering website services where sellers post their goods for sale, allowing buyers to bid on those items.

The benefits of B2C marketing

There are a number of potential benefits and drivers of B2C commerce (Gummesson 2004) including:

- For existing business organizations, many of the benefits are similar to B2B commerce, in that B2C commerce can expand the marketplace, lower costs, and improve management support systems, internal communications and knowledge sharing. It can also allow firms to focus more effectively on customer relationships. However, it might also promote more competition.
- For new businesses, the Internet can reduce barriers to entry, and thus make it easier to enter new markets. One example is amazon.com, which did not need to incur the expense of opening up high street shops in order to successfully enter the retail book industry.
- For customers, B2C on average provides faster and more complete information, a wider choice, and cheaper products and services. It also allows greater interaction with other customers.
- For the wider community, an increase in B2C commerce may well have an impact in employment patterns, perhaps with an increase in home working.

The limitations of B2C marketing

While B2C commerce has some obvious benefits as we might anticipate there are a number of potential limitations to its future growth and development. Reid et al. (2004) mentioned:

- lack of trust and consumer resistance
- unresolved security, legal and privacy issues
- insufficient buyers and sellers online
- technical issues such as poor reliability, insufficient bandwidth and speed
- hardware and software tools that are rapidly revolving and changing

- the very expensive offline marketing costs involved in building brand recognition for new online companies.
- lower barriers to entry that will increase competition, and potentially increase rather than decrease consumer search and selection costs, as well as possible reduced industry profits overall
- still significant distribution and storage costs in the sale of physical goods
- existing bricks-and-mortar companies that will not go away, and will continue to compete hard to maintain existing market share.

The business markets

Although B2C is more popular, more business activity is being conducted on B2B websites. The B2B websites are changing the supplier–customer relationship in profound ways. Research evidence (Heldal et al. 2004) suggests that B2B commerce is approximately 10 to 15 times greater than that conducted on B2C sites. In several industries, companies have formed buying alliances to secure deeper volume discounts from suppliers. For example, in the United States, companies such as Ford, GM and DaimlerChrysler formed an alliance in the hope of saving money by combining their purchases. Similarly, Coca-Cola, Kraft, Sara Lee and other consumer packaged goods companies formed alliances to effect cost saving in raw material and logistical procurement. It is expected that much work will need to done before these alliances work well, but when they do work, suppliers will be under price pressure.

The impact of B2B sites is to make the international business market more efficient. Previously, corporate buyers had to exert a lot of effort to gather information on international suppliers. As Oliva (2001) identified, with the Internet, corporate buyers have access to much greater information from:

- the suppliers' websites
- infomediaries, third parties that add value by aggregating information about the alternatives
- market makers, third parties who create markets linking buyers and sellers
- customer communities, that swap stories about suppliers' products and services.

The overall impact of these mechanisms is to make prices more transparent. In the case of undifferentiated products, price pressure will increase, but for highly differentiated products, corporate buyers will gain a better picture of their true value. Suppliers of superior products will be able to offset price transparency with value transparency; suppliers of undifferentiated products will have to drive down their costs in order to compete.

The characteristics of B2B

B2B marketing is characterized by a number of key features, many of which differentiate it from B2C marketing. Stone and McCall (2004) mention:

- an automated trading process
- high volumes of goods traded

- high net value of goods traded
- multiple forms of electronic payment and funds transfer, unlike B2C commerce, which tends to be restricted to credit cards and smart cards
- high level of information exchange, including shared databases, between the different trading partners, often using extranets.
- prior agreements or contracts between the business partners requiring a higher level of documentation; different types of legal and taxation regimes depending on where the two partiers are based, and what type of goods or services are the subject of the transaction
- multiple levels of authorization of purchases, with each level having its own limits on expenditure or types of goods.

The benefits of B2B for international marketing

There appear to be a number of potential benefits of B2B marketing in an international environment. First, it encourages the adoption of an Internet EDI system to improve efficiency. The Department of Trade and Industry (DTI) described EDI as 'the computer-to-computer exchange of structured data sent in a form that allows for automatic processing with no manual intervention; and this is usually carried out over specialist EDI networks'. There are a number of benefits including (Hill and Scott 2004):

- A safe secure and verifiable electronic environment that allows international marketers to link their stock databases directly to suppliers. This reduces lead times by reducing the time taken in placing and receiving orders.
- Lower costs in creating, processing, distributing, storing, retrieving and destroying paper-based information; fewer errors in data entry; improved inventory control, and reduced staff time involved in the process.
- Improved warehouse logistics, and improved coordination for moving goods to the appropriate place, at the defined time and in the correct quantities.
- Better and more efficient integration of support functions such as human resources, inventory control, order processing, accounting and payment processing.
- More efficient strategic alliances and partnering with suppliers, customers and competitors. For instance, in the motor industry, leading firms such as General Motors, Ford and Chrysler have set up a joint extranet with suppliers.

It should be recognized that EDI has been around since the 1960s, but before the development of Internet EDI systems, it was seen to have some serious shortcomings that undermined the potential benefits. Two in particular are worth noting:

- It required an expensive private dedicated network connection between two established trading partners. According to Forrester Research (www.forrester.research.com) only 10 per cent of the 2 million companies in the United States employing ten or more employees chose to deploy traditional EDI. The rest felt that it was too expensive, was not interactive enough, and did not enable them to access or negotiate with their suppliers and other partners (Kafka 2000).
- The lack of agreed international standard for document formats meant that early EDI was based on proprietary technologies such as value added networks (VANs). Each EDI tended to be set up specifically for a single buyer and supplier, and

consequently became heavily embedded in the organization's IT systems. This served to inhibit change within the organization, making it difficult and expensive to change suppliers because of the difficulties of switching the existing system to a new supplier. It also meant that where a firm was multisourcing, a separate EDI might be needed for each supplier.

However, Internet-based EDI overcomes most of these shortcomings. Rather than using proprietary technology (VANs) it makes use of the public Internet. It is ubiquitous, global, cheap, easy to use and readily available and accessible both within (intranet) and outside (extranet) the company. In addition, Internet EDI standards are becoming increasingly compatible with extensible Mark-up Language (XML). XML is already the key international standard for transferring structured data, and has wide acceptance, having been championed by organizations such as Microsoft, Netscape and Sun Microsystems, as well as by the World Wide Web consortium. The widespread adoption of XML means that most companies are now able to use Internet-based EDI to exchange documents cheaply and quickly. The International Data Corporation (IDC) gave a usage level of 41 per cent over the period 1999–2003, with this trend to continue into the future (Woodside, Gupta and Cadeaux 2004).

A further potential benefit and driver of B2B commerce is that it provides for expansion from a local or national market to a global electronic market (e-market). For a relatively minimal capital outlay, a business can access a wider range of suppliers and contact a larger potential customer base. B2B activities vary from company to company and industry to industry, but as well as global electronic markets, where many buyers and sellers meet for the purposes of trading electronically, other common types of market include a sell-side marketplace (where one company does all the selling), and a buy-side marketplace (where another company does all the buying). Other benefits and drivers of B2B commerce are:

- It provides an opportunity to market, sell and distribute goods and services to other businesses for 24 hours a day, 365 days a year, the so-called 'Martini effect'.
- It can sometimes significantly reduce fixed costs, perhaps through savings on premises, where a website has effectively become the organization's showroom.
- It has potential to improve pull-type supply chain management, such as JIT manufacture and delivery, based on integrated and fully automated supply chain management (SCM) and demand chain management (DCM) systems.
- It can encourage organizations to adopt a more customer-centric approach, in which the business tracks consumers' preferences and re-engineers itself quickly to meet consumer needs. This might involve developing a mass customization business model such as that adopted by Dell Computers.
- It can facilitate the development of an integrated electronic customer relationship management (eCRM) system, based on customer information gathering, data warehousing and other market intelligence.
- It may improve knowledge management systems within the organization, as employees use the company intranet system to access organization-wide know-how.

Many of these advantages of B2B could be seen being practically demonstrated by organizations such as Dell Computers, which markets computers internationally to individual customers as well as to other organizations.

Potential problems and limitations of B2B

There are a number of significant advantages to the widespread adoption of B2B commerce (Kotler 2006). However, it should be noted that there are also some potential limitations or barriers that may serve to delay or hamper its growth. These include:

- Internet technology is continually developing, encouraging some organizations to postpone investment in the short term.
- Technical limitations such as lack of system security, reliability and protocols – there are also currently some problems with telecommunications bandwidth and speed.
- The cost and difficulty of integrating existing (legacy) IT applications and databases with Internet and related software.
- The slow progress made in achieving universal international standards for the electronic transfer of information documentation.
- Many legal, taxation and regulatory issues remain unresolved.

Nevertheless, on balance the clear benefits of B2B commerce are likely to outweigh the disadvantages, and we should expect to see continued dynamic growth in this area for some years to come.

The consumer market

There is considerable consumer-to-consumer communication on the Web on a whole range of subjects, and the most prominent C2C channel is e-mail, which functions as a digital post office. C2C means that online visitors increasingly create product information, not just consume it. Consumers usually join Internet interest groups to share information, so that 'word of mouse' is joining 'word of mouth' as an important buying influence (Kotler 2006: 45). Word about good companies travels fast, and word about bad companies travels even faster. Consumers are also finding it easier to communicate with companies on an international basis. International companies are encouraging communication by inviting present and potential customers to send in questions, product and delivery suggestions, and complaints via e-mail. This approach enables customer service representatives to respond quickly.

The Internet and its commercial applications in electronic commerce, particularly new ventures like B2B e-markets, are experiencing a volatile introduction to the international business environment. International marketing companies are restructuring and forming networks in an effort to accommodate and use this new phenomenon to their advantage. From this perspective, this chapter offers a conceptual framework on the process of creating new international ventures through international relationship marketing.

Relationship marketing in the B2B context

Most indicators of the benefits of relationship marketing are limited to the relationship between a customer and a supplier. But relationship marketing, in a broadened sense, embraces markets, society and internal organization as networks of relationships, within which interaction takes place. It is essential to consider relationship aspects not only in the marketing plan but also in the corporate business plan, which requires accounting to rethink its role of mainly furnishing historical financial data to focus more on data for the future.

In approaching relationship metrics, it is imperative to clarify certain concepts and their domains. For example, Gummesson (2002: 3) defines relationship marketing as 'marketing based on interaction within networks of relationships'. Most relationship marketing definitions stress the need to develop long-term relationships with customers and sometimes other stakeholders (Gronroos 2002). Jackson published an insightful book and article (1985) on B2B marketing, where she defined relationship marketing by contrasting it with transaction marketing. From her comprehensive research she drew the general conclusion that building long-term relationships through relationship marketing should sometimes be the preferred strategy for the industrial seller, but sometimes transaction marketing, the one-shot deal with a short-term perspective, should be preferred.

Coviello and Brodie (2001) identified four types of marketing:

- transaction marketing
- database marketing (information exchange with the help of IT)
- interaction marketing (face-to-face or ear-to-ear interaction)
- network marketing.

They regarded these four types of marketing as essentially (but not solely) a B2B phenomenon, where networks of relationships are built with a large number of stakeholders.

In order to conceptually incorporate transaction marketing in relationship marketing, transaction marketing can be defined as the zero point on a relationship scale. At the other end of the scale buyers and sellers (or other parties) are in unity. The zero relationship of marketing can further be defined as the price relationship, when price (usually the lowest price) is the only factor that links buyer and seller. The zero relationship is presented as the general case in microeconomics and traditional marketing management, making these theories invalid as general theory, but still valid in special cases.

Relationship marketing became a widespread term in the 1990s but has a long history under many different names. In its wake, one-to-one marketing surfaced in the mid-1990s. Customer relationship management (CRM) emerged as the number one business buzzword at the turn of the millennium (Gummesson 2004). One-to-one marketing and CRM are the same, although there may be some differences in emphasis and procedures; consultants use these and a host of other names to brand their offerings. At present, CRM is the dominant and generally used designation, but in 1998 it was only one in a continuous flow of acronyms soliciting for attention. In current usage, CRM focuses on the values and strategies of relationship marketing (with particular emphasis on customer relationships) turned into practical application (Gummesson 2002).

The implementation steps used in one-to-one marketing summarize what is needed to practice relationship marketing (Newell 2000):

- Identify individual customers and establish how to reach them.
- Differentiate the customers with regard to values and needs.
- Interact with the customers efficiently and effectively.
- Customize your offerings.
- In the process of doing this, build learning relationships with your customers through dialogue.

The next section reviews the validity of B2C marketing theory for B2B; relationship marketing limited to the customer–supplier dyad or broadened to a network context;

The B2B relationship lifecycle

Despite the growth importance of relationship marketing, it remains an ambiguous concept without clear empirical support. This is particularly true in the area of the relationship life cycle (Ford et al. 2003), where the various stages through which a B2B relationship progresses have been identified. While there is no strict agreement on the stages of a B2B relationship, Heffernan (2004) suggests a five-stage process:

1. **Pre-relationship stage** –the activities that occur before a relationship with a partner is established. First, a change in the status quo is required that generates a possible need for the organization to enter a new relationship. Second, there is an exploration for the relationship partner (finding the appropriate partner is a critical step in the relationship development process). Third comes the selection of the partner. From this point the relationship moves into the early interaction stage of development.
2. **Early interaction stage** – this involves serious negotiations regarding the style and structure of the relationship. At the start of this stage there is little experience of the other partner's operation or business culture, leading to high levels of uncertainty. There is the highest amount of learning of any stage of the relationship life cycle. The lack of experience and understanding make the relationship fragile during this phase. Consequently, the partnership can be easily terminated at the early interaction stage.
3. **Relationship growth stage** – this is characterized by a high level of engagement and interaction, and intensive mutual learning about the specifics of the relationship, the investment made and the adaptation needed. The learning that is achieved in this stage will reduce the uncertainty and the distance between the two organizations.
4. **Partnership stage** –here the relationship is at its most mature and the partners have developed a high level of experience is dealing with each other (Ford et al. 2003). Learning, which was so crucial in the relationship growth phase, has reached a stable level and the organizations are mutually important to each other, leading to an implicit or explicit pledge to continue the relationship. High levels of commitment are shown towards established norms that guide conduct;
5. **Relationship end stage** – this relates to how the partners uncouple the relationship because its purpose no longer exists. A relationship can be terminated at any stage of the relationship life cycle; however, the relationship end stage comes about when the reason for the relationship is no longer current.

According to Coviello and Brodie (2001), of the five stages of the B2B life cycle, trust creation is seen as most critical to develop at the initial stages.

The nature of B2B in the international environment

Almost all companies are a blend of B2B and B2C. These categories are not two bins in which you can dump your customers for continuous recycling. Instead, the categories are vehicles for thought, providing a cognitive map and a perspective. If we consider the supply chain – or, in alignment with the definition of relationship marketing, the supply network – there can be several B2B stages or nodes and sub-categories. For example for food products (Kafka 2000) these include raw material purchasing, manufacturing, wholesaling and retailing.

It is only at the retail point of sale – a shop or a restaurant – that the food reaches a household. Even households are organizations, and it is often not the same person who orders, buys, pays and consumes the food. Retailers also sell to other companies. For example, IKEA stores sell both home and office furniture, and Dell's mail order service is used by consumers as well as by businesses. The one-to-one implementation steps, although primarily based on B2C experience, are clearly pertinent to B2B as well. While there are similarities between B2B and B2C, there are also differences. For example, when a customer relationship management strategy is 100 per cent implemented, the individual will be in focus in both cases, but the hardware and software will vary greatly depending on:

- the size of the market
- the number of customers
- the amount of customer information
- the availability of this information.

Thus, as the electronic customer relationship management (eCRM) application will vary, so also will that of the hardware relating to customer relationship management (hCRM) (see Gummesson 2002).

The focus of CRM is most often consumer mass markets, where there is the need to handle millions of customers efficiently and each customer is small. The seminal difference between traditional marketing management and relationship marketing is that formerly consumers were approached as grey masses, while today they are approached as individuals. As 80 per cent of all electronic business is expected to be B2B, eCRM will be highly pertinent to industrial goods and services. In 2006, US B2B e-business was worth $2,300 billion, and this is increasing (*Economist* 2007).

B2B CRM also consists of routine continuing business where customer computers buy from supplier computers and where electronic agents (artificial customers) have taken over day-to-day trading and information search from human beings. According to Woodside et al. (2004), the time is ripe to include machines as customers and suppliers (machine-to-machine interaction) in marketing theory. The notion of key account management (KAM) has become more important than formerly to secure individual treatment in the retention and development of large and international business customers.

Apart from Jackson, mentioned earlier, among those who have most directly addressed B2B as relationships and networks are the academic researchers known as the Industrial and International Marketing and Purchasing (IMP) Group. IMP began in Sweden in the 1970s but since then has become international. Both Jackson and IMP find B2B to be interaction in networks of relationships. Neither deals at any length or empirical specificity with the financial consequences of relationships although there are conceptual discussions, which we shall revert to later (Ringberg and Gupta 2003).

Based on entirely different empirical data, service research (which also took off in the 1970s) found the same phenomena – relationships, networks, and interaction – to be at the core of both consumer and business services marketing. With its initial focus on services, the Nordic School – an informal group of concerned and dedicated scholars – found a need for a paradigm shift, departing from the traditional and pseudo-general marketing management, which primarily has a consumer goods base. By combining services marketing, traditional B2C marketing management, the network approach to B2B, and developments in other management disciplines, Nordic School researchers have broadened their range of vision from marketing management to the more general concepts of marketing-oriented management – where every employee is either a full-time or part-time marketer – and relationship marketing (Gummesson 2002).

Although marketers are not much of historians – and should not be, as their job is to be here now and for the future – some academic reflection of the past might bring concepts and events down to earth. One reflection is that the behaviour of the classic industrial salesperson in many successful companies was the same as is today advocated in relationship marketing, CRM and KAM. In the sales of advanced equipment, he (it was always a male) was usually an engineer who knew the products technically and knew the individual 'heads' of the 'many-headed customers' constituting the complex setting of technologically advanced large companies such as telecom operators. He worked long term seeing each large customer as strategic, so that these customers could not be evaluated in terms of profit in a year, five years or even in ten years time. He was not driven by individual short-term commissions but rather by the opportunity for more challenging tasks and promotion; aiming for 'share of customer' and not market share. For example, telecoms often had two or more suppliers and there was usually just one telecom in each country. This may partially explain why Ericsson has been less triumphant in selling mobile phones to consumers than Nokia, which has a tradition in consumer goods design and promotion.

In the 1960s, selling mainframe computer hardware and systems to companies and the government sector was a fast-paced business that operated with long-term salesmen whose goal was customer retention, but who also had short-term commissions. Both Ericsson and IBM are international corporations and implemented a KAM strategy. Marketing management theory has only addressed this marginally, and the approach became that of sales management and how to become a better salesperson, unfortunately insulated from engineering, purchasing, manufacturing, installation and top management, and measured and remunerated by number of orders and the revenue generated.

Although specialized literature existed that dealt with industrial sales as consultative selling, team selling and negotiations, sales in textbooks tended to become just a tool under the third P of the 4P marketing-mix – promotion – rather than a long-term interactive strategy (Rossomme 2003). There is also a difference in opinion whether a salesperson needs to understand a product or service in depth, or a skilled salesperson can sell anything, with the skills of selling outranking product and manufacturing knowledge. It could well be that a revival of the interest in the salesperson will follow in the next phase of CRM.

Buyer behaviour in B2B markets

This section deals with buying behaviour in the e-commerce B2C and B2B markets. Hofacker (1999) divides Internet users into two main categories:

- **Hedonic surfers** use a website by experiencing it in the same way they do movies and sports events. Often there is a strong nonverbal aspect to the hedonic experience –images are quite important. Internet surfers are relatively unfocused and their browsing is spontaneous. The goal is escapist, to achieve immersion in the site, or at least a high degree of personal enjoyment. The idea is to gather interesting and exciting experiences from the Web. A novel and interesting site works best for these surfers. They can be drawn into a website via links and advertising banners on other sites.
- **Utilitarian searchers** are on a mission and have a work mentality. The utilitarian searcher uses the Web in a way that is instrumental and rational. Such a visitor is looking for specific information. A well-organized and searchable site works best for these seekers. Utilitarian searchers often use search engines and they can often find a Web address that is easy to guess.

Despite the fundamental difference between the physical marketplace and the virtual market space, one principle still holds true in both worlds: marketers must understand how

Table 13.1   The purchase decision process (marketplace versus market space)

Consumer behaviour		Market place	Market space
Decision process	**Consumer issues**	**Marketing issues**	**Marketing issues**
Problem recognition	• Need awareness • Problem definition • Problem articulation	• Consumer identification • Problem recognition • Stimulate search interest	• Database to know customer better • Anticipate needs • Respond to problems
Information search	• Sources of information • Accessibility of information • Reliability of information	• Attract searchers • Provide information	• Advertising in the marketplace media • Links from other sites • Quality of information • Push technologies
Evaluation of alternatives	• Comprehensiveness of information • Trust and confidence in information • Trial and sampling	• Influencing purchase criteria • Provide testing opportunities • Build brand preference	• Virtual communities and user group endorsements • Simulation and testing opportunities
Choice/purchase	• Negotiation process • Transaction process	• Management of existing process • Management of supply	• Ease of ordering and delivery, payment, security and conditions
Post-purchase behaviour	• After sales support • Relationship support	• Service support • Problem recovery • Relationship management	• Online support • Relationship building with consumer, user groups and virtual communities.

consumers make decisions to purchase before they can effectively respond to their demands. Table 13.1 provides an overview of the main differences between 'marketplace' and 'market space' in the consumer decision process. Of course, there is iteration. Each of these stages is now examined in the context of the marketplace versus the market space.

Problem recognition

The first stage, consumer decisions, triggers all subsequent activity. The consumer is compelled to fill the gap between the actual and the desired state. When problem awareness is reached, problem recognition may be triggered by a number of external and internal factors. In traditional markets, conventional marketing communications stimulate the demand via conventional media, for example an advertisement on television. However, on the Internet the medium is new, and so new kinds of communications are required. In the traditional mass marketing approaches much of the audience will not be interested, and there is considerable wastage. But new IT fundamentally changes that. Computer-mediated environments enable identification of individual consumer needs and wants, and subsequent design and delivery of individual and customized communications.

Information search

The information gathered, from both internal sources such as experience, and memory or external sources (for example, discussions, brochures, sales promotions), provides the basis for this stage. The physical marketplace imposes limitations on information. Economic and access barriers constrain what can efficiently be known, and consequently what can realistically be evaluated. On the Internet, however, intelligent shopping agents can scan the entire Web to find the data necessary for comparison. The relevant criteria can be presented and explained, and ordered to suit individual needs.

The management of information is the primary role of the agent or broker in the marketplace. The intermediary function is here largely based on information provision and exchange. This is the effective function of travel agents, for instance. But, in the marketplace, when an airline sets up its own website with interactive flight information and booking facilities, for example, the traditional intermediary is bypassed in a classic case of disintermediation. As channel disintermediation and reintermediation become important, a match between information content and consumer requirements also becomes important. As individuals come to utilize the Internet for consumer purchases, a situation of perfect information is almost attainable. However, it must be noted that consumers' sense of uncertainty can actually increase as they gain more information. Information overload occurs when we learn more about the alternatives available to us, and the search becomes 'psychologically costly'.

Evaluation of alternatives

In the marketplace word-of-mouth communication, the references of family, colleagues and friends, is a central influence at this stage. In the market space, new reference groups appear. The virtual community, consisting of discussion groups of interested parties, can have the power of the traditional reference groups, but with even greater quality and quantity of evaluative information.

Purchase decision

This stage involves decisions on where and how to buy. Where to buy is a decision regarding the choice of seller. Competition on the Web is driven by sellers attempting to build more exciting and interesting sites than their competitors, attracting the right customers to those sites, and providing superior shopping experiences to induce purchase. How to buy concerns the nature of the transaction and contract. Many of the products and services currently available to individual consumers on the Internet are digital (for example, software and upgrades) or easily physically transported (for example, music CDs and books). The future broadening of the base will require particular analysis of physical delivery issues. The actual delivery routines for such a service are probably more complex than ordering, packing and payment routines. Whereas the order can be met within the one organization and under one roof, the logistics of physical delivery of relatively bulky but relatively low-value grocery orders is an entirely different proposition.

Post-purchase behaviour

The actual sale should be perceived as a starting point. Critical to understanding consumer behaviour are: how the customer takes delivery of the product, how the product is used, the degree and satisfaction, the quality of the service dimensions and customer complaints and suggestions. This, of course, applies in both the marketplace and the market space. The main difference between relationship developments in the two types of markets is that the marketplace emphasizes 'high tech', and is characterized by the power of information and communication technologies to satisfy customer needs and thereby continue business relationships. For the seller in the market space the big issue is to update the website continuously. Post-purchase activity involves consumers returning to the seller's website for new information, and to repurchase.

There are obvious differences and similarities between marketplace retail stores and market space retail stores. Table 13.2 shows analogies between bricks-and-mortar and virtual stores. Obviously, some features like atmosphere and aroma are difficult to measure and characterize in online retail stores. Other features like store promotions are less difficult to measure there.

Exploring business behaviour in the B2B market

Web information systems hold great potential to streamline and improve transactions. Instead of regarding the Internet as a mere sales channel, companies also utilize emerging technologies to cut costs out of the supply chain by streamlining procurement processes and improving collaboration. In times of intense competition and increasingly

Table 13.2 Differences between physical and virtual stores

Physical store: marketplace	Virtual store: market space
Sales clerk service	Product descriptions, information pages, gift services, search function, clerk on the phone or email
Store promotion	Special offers, online games and lotteries, links to other sites of interest, appetizer information
Store window displays	Home page
Store atmosphere	Interface consistency, store organization, interface and graphics
Aisle product	Featured product on hierarchical levels of the store
Store layout	Screen depth, browse and search functions, indices, image maps
Number of floors in the store	Hierarchical levels of the store
Number of store entrances and store outlets/branches	Number of links to a particular online retail store
Checkout cashier	Online shopping basket and/or order form
Look and touch of the merchandise	Limited to image quality and description, potential for sound and visual applications
Number of people entering the store	Number of unique visits to the online store
Sales per period	Sales per period

open markets, the ability to achieve efficiency improvements can become a key to commercial success.

We now look at how businesses make buying decisions and how these businesses are supported by an e-commerce information system. A conceptual framework is introduced in Figure 13.2. The inter-organizational transactions are analysed from a process-oriented perspective. There are four phases: information, negotiation, settlement, and after-sales and transaction analysis.

Business transactions usually involve three categories of participants: buyers, sellers and intermediaries. Buyers and sellers are the active groups in terms of exchanging goods and services (seller) for some form of compensation (buyer). The intermediaries offer a variety of services to support and facilitate transactions. This includes financial institutions such as banks, credit card companies and insurance brokers; providers of shipping, logistics and warehousing services; and consultants, industry associations and market researchers offering advice, product data or market information. Providers of IT to help set up electronic marketplaces can be characterized as intermediaries as well.

In the case of B2B transactions, both buyers and sellers are business organizations, whereas B2C and C2C transactions involve end-users or private households as buyers or

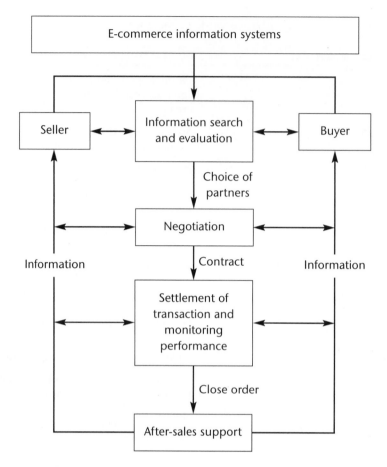

Figure 13.2 Seller and buyer transaction process model

sellers respectively. Figure 13.2 reflects the transactions between the seller and the buyer in e-commerce information systems. In the information phase of a transaction, both buyers and sellers reach out to the world in search of information. In the physical world (the marketplace), buyers locate information sources such as product catalogues, use them to scan product listings, obtain offerings from prospective suppliers, and gather additional information about products, vendor or transaction-specific requirements. It is important that before a purchasing transaction is performed, internal approval should be obtained from upper-level management.

The information phase comprises searching for a particular electronic catalogue or source of information and locating required information and commodities within the information repository. In this phase, buyers and sellers are not yet focused on specific transaction partners. Information gathering and knowledge creation are at the centre of attention, and information is the primary object of exchange between prospective transaction partners.

The participants

A variety of Web-based information systems and other applications are available to provide support for the information phase of a transaction. Electronic catalogues, for example, feature comprehensive product descriptions and search tools, configuration support for complex purchases, workflow routing for approval processes and access to additional information such as market research data and product review. Catalogues can be provided by suppliers, set up by the buyer or developed by a third party. They can be hosted on the supplier's Web server, or be integrated into internal systems. Links to back-end systems provide access to human resources data, as they are required to manage purchasing authorization.

Negotiation process

This ranges from simple processes where price is the most important factor, to very complex arrangements where the buyer–seller relationship is regarded as a long-term strategic partnership. Negotiations are often perceived as processes where a small number of prospective customers and sellers bargain on prices and other terms of sale. The parties jointly identify possible solutions with the goal of reaching a consensus, usually in the form of a contract. Bargaining processes alter with decisions whether to accept or reject the offering. Negotiation will also continue with the outlining of counter-suggestions until a mutually satisfactory agreement is reached. As prospective buyers and seller start communicating directly with each other, interaction is at the centre of attention. In the negotiation stage, influence is the primary object of exchange between the transaction partners. Not every transaction process features such complex negotiations. In fact, some negotiation processes are simple, such as in the case of retail buying and pre-negotiated contracts.

Negotiations can range from a simple transaction to a contract of several years duration. The longer the time span that is covered, the more complex the structure of the bargaining process tends to be. Complex negotiations are based on factual information that helps the parties make decisions. Information systems support negotiations in a number of ways. They can provide transaction information and decision support by:

- assessing the value of specific offerings
- identifying new bargaining options
- evaluating the real intentions of the parties
- reviewing the nature of the legal or rules relating to the offer
- increasing the negotiation's productivity.

Participants may improve their bargaining positions through additional online information, such as the volume of previous business, supplier performance or spending patterns.

Performance monitoring

Upon execution of the contract the objects of the transaction are exchanged according to the conditions previously stipulated. In addition, the settlement phase regularly includes some form of mutual performance monitoring. After the rather unstructured negotiation phase, the process of executing a transaction can be relatively straightforward. It is formality initiated as soon as a purchase order is confirmed by the supplier. The supplier ships the goods (often in collaboration with a third party, for example a local provider of logistic services), announces the shipment, and sends out an invoice. On the buyer side, orders are tracked, items are received, and payment is initiated after matching the invoice with the delivery. Naturally, there are many variations of this standard scenario. Consider, for example, the differences between the shipment of physical goods and the online delivery of information goods.

In the settlement phase of a transaction, activities and procedures are comparatively well defined, as they are part of the contract. Thus, attention centres on execution and efficiency. At this point, the main objects of exchange are goods and services. IT to support transaction settlement may include EDI systems on the Web and various tools to process orders internally and between transaction partners, facilitate order tracking and support payment processes.

After-sales analysis

After a transaction has taken place, both sellers and buyers store the transaction data to provide after-sales support (sellers), or to assess support performance and analyse internal buying patterns (buyer). On the buyer side, the information flow is often split. While the purchase data is stored with central procurement, the end-user keeps the product-related documentation. In case of unexpected irregularities, it is often the end-user who contacts the supplier (for example, to request a repair). Without proper access to the transaction file, communication problems and delays can occur. Capturing, storing and managing data are vital at this point. Similarly, it is necessary to know that in the first stage, it is mainly information that is being exchanged between buyer and seller.

Electronic support of after-sales activities ranges from simple electronic mail services to automated help desks and sophisticated electronic maintenance manuals. Ideally, systems to support after-sales and transaction analysis provide central access to the transaction information. Data warehousing applications support the storing, accessing and processing of large amounts of data. They allow the firm to assess supplier performance, analyse internal buying patterns, provide the basis for consolidation of corporate buys and improve future bargaining positions with suppliers. On the supplier side, data about past transactions – including information of system configurations, preferred payment options, and so forth – supports the maintenance process and subsequently improves the quality of the information phase of future transactions.

International B2B channel control

According to transaction cost analysis (TCA), firms will choose the entry and distribution mode that economizes on transaction cost: for example, the coordination cost between producer and intermediaries.

As IT continues to produce cost benefits, information infrastructures are extending to reach individual consumers. The potential for transformation in the value chain of many

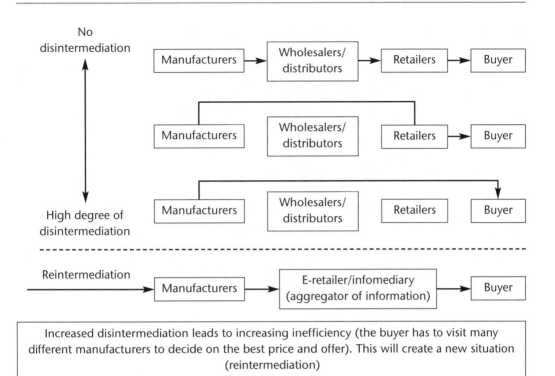

Figure 13.3 Disintermediation and reintermediation

firms is far greater now than it was in the past, as technology begins to enable producers to interact directly with consumers. Intermediaries add significant costs to the value chain, which are reflected in a higher prices of products or services to the end customers. One fundamental question, therefore, is to what extent producers will take advantage of direct electronic links with consumers, and whether in the process intermediaries will be eliminated from the value system.

The essential argument is that the use of IT allows manufacturers to internalize activities that were traditionally performed by intermediaries. Producers 'capture value' and in the resultant redistribution of profits along the value system, traditional intermediaries will disappear. Schellhase, Hardock and Ohlwein (2000) argue that if transactions take place directly between manufacturers and consumers, both will benefit. Manufacturers will try to retain a higher portion of surplus value or profits that are generated along the value system, while consumers will benefit from both a larger choice and lower prices. In other words, the network's ability to support direct exchanges efficiently will increase both producer and consumer welfare. Thus, it is predicted that manufacturers will sell directly to consumers, and consumers will prefer to buy directly from manufacturers.

There was a myth that the Internet would eliminate the need for intermediaries. Early predictions (Reid et al. 2004) were of the disappearance of physical distribution chains as people moved from buying through distributors and resellers to buying directly from manufacturers. The reality is that the Internet may eliminate traditional physical distributors, but in the transformation process of the value chain new types of intermediaries may appear.

So the disintermediation process has come to be balanced by a reintermediation force – the evolution of new intermediaries tailor-made for the online world (Figure 13.3).

The traditional distribution model is linear. The manufacturer builds products. Wholesalers and distributors aggregate products from multiple manufacturers and bring them through several levels of distribution in small lots to resellers who deal directly with consumers. The value-added of the distribution chain lies in shipping, warehousing and delivering products. With the Internet, value chains are being deconstructed and reconstructed in different ways, and in particular into value webs. This process has given rise to a new class of intermediaries. Companies such as Yahoo aggregate information and make it easier to access it and see new possibilities of doing business. The value-added is no longer in logistic aggregation but rather an information aggregation. Consumers come to these sites looking for information and opportunities to purchase. Companies such as Amazon.com and e-Trade are dramatically changing traditional models of selling goods and services by acting as a new type of intermediary. They offer new opportunities to existing companies as well as start-ups. Companies need to examine their current value chain and determine how the Internet might change it. Then they can adapt their business processes to take advantage of the new model by protecting their major sources of revenue and also developing new sources.

The role of the Internet in developing B2B

E-commerce innovation is having a profound effect on the way multinational organizations perform international marketing functions because it is both new and embedded in radical innovation (Woodside et al. 2004). Since the phenomenon is new, and the constructs are either unknown or at an embryonic stage, this section reviews a number of tentative working propositions from theory and provides an example of how they could be used to foster the international marketing process. Many different definitions have been attached to the concept of a B2B e-market, for example eMarketplaces (Kafka 2000) and B2B exchange (Wise and Morrison 2000). For our purpose a B2B e-market is defined as 'a new venture where business buyers and sellers perform international marketing and logistics activities using the embedded technological innovation (the Internet) on which it is based'.

As Kafka's (2000) work suggests, 'the B2B e-market ventures are facing volatility and uncertainty'. The aim in this section is to understand B2B e-market firms and their relationships in the international environment. Thus it is necessary to understand the process of creating such new ventures by observing the nuances of planning and implementing international marketing decisions. It is also important to understand the roles played by buyers, suppliers and third parties as participants in the creation of an international marketing process for e-markets. It is important to examine how embedded competence-destroying innovations (CDI) found in B2B e-markets, in contrast to competence-enhancing innovations (CEI) such as EDI, can yield competitive advantage for suppliers and buyers.

Innovative theory

The fundamental impulse that sets and keeps the capitalist engine in motion comes from the dynamic process of creating new consumer goods, new methods of production, new

MINI CASE 13.1

Disintermediation in the Japanese distribution system

If Japan is anything it is a nation of intermediaries. It seems that the Internet and particularly the e-commerce will eliminate inefficient distributors, disrupting long-established supply chains and lowering distribution costs. This could create tremendous opportunities for new entrants and raise consumers' spending power.

In Japan, there are at least six layers of distribution between the manufacturers of agro-chemicals, and the end users (the farmers). According to Peter Loescher, president and chief executive of Hoechst Japan, one of the largest bioscience companies, 'we must fundamentally change both marketing and distribution. Marketing, because the farmers will be able to access information about the products directly from us via the Internet, and distribution, because many of the intermediaries will become redundant'.

B2B e-commerce could hit Japan's wholesalers hard. Ken Okamura, strategist at Dresdner Kleinwort Benson, notes that the transparency of the Internet's pricing mechanism may make it difficult to compete with firms that operate using Internet solutions. The overall implications for Japan's economy are tremendous. The wholesalers account for about 4 million jobs, so an overhaul of the industry could further inflate Japan's unemployment level, which is already at a record high.

A number of factors could slow the growth of Japan's B2B e-commerce market. Nusbaum (2000) listed:

- **High telecom changes**. Miti says telecom changes are the largest constraint to the development of Japan's e-commerce market. Prices for a dedicated line used to access the Internet can be more that $1,000 a month between Tokyo and Osaka, more than twice the cost of their US equivalent, according to Goldman Sachs.
- **Low penetration of personal computers among smaller Japanese businesses**. Less than 40 per cent of small companies in Japan own PCs, and less than 20 per cent have Internet access, compared with the United States where 80 per cent of small businesses use computers and 60 per cent are online.
- **Japan's stuttering economy.** Many companies have frozen or even slashed IT budgets, according to Kathy Matsui, strategist at Goldman Sachs. As a result, Japanese groups may not be investing sufficiently in new software technologies to create the necessary e-commerce platforms.

However, Mr Hirose of Fujitsu, a dominant force in Japan's Internet industry, disagreed. He said that managers might be reluctant to increase spending across the board but were increasingly willing to invest in new IT initiatives that could change their businesses. The distribution system in Japan is very much influenced by the special Japanese phenomenon, *Keiretsu*, which is a system of business groupings, combined with the cross-shareholdings among companies. The *Keiretsu* structure has traditionally limited competition among suppliers, a key dynamic of the price-driven e-commerce market. But companies are loosening *Keiretsu* ties and unwinding cross-shareholdings. This is expected to fuel competitive dynamics in the e-commerce market.

Finally, in e-commerce, *Keiretsu* does not matter. The concern is not how to stay in *Keiretsu* but how to win in the international marketplace, said Mr Hirose. Companies concerned with *Keiretsu* will be wiped out. All in all, the changes in the Japanese distribution system may very well be gradual because of the existence of traditions, but it is a development that cannot be stopped.

Source: Nusbaum (2000).

distribution systems, new markets and the creation of new ventures (Woodside et al. 2004). Diffusion of innovation is at the core of the dynamic processes that underpins social, economic and technology changes (Ringberg and Gupta 2003). Diffusion phenomena are therefore not limited to the spread of new process technologies and the market penetration of new products, but also extend to changes in vertical and horizontal international marketing networks.

Arguably the single most powerful force to create economic and social benefit is probably the creation of new ventures. The generation of entrepreneurs that have used the Internet to transact business have become the creators and leaders of entire new industries. We could argue that B2B e-market firms based on the Internet are a particular type of new venture that operates in a network environment of buyers and sellers. The B2B e-market extends the concept of a dyadic market to networks as shown in Figure 13.4.

Diffusion is considered as involving the creation, commercialization decision (go, no-go) and implementation of new venture B2B e-market firms. The diffusion of innovation literature proposes that dynamically new innovations such as B2B e-markets are likely to be evaluated differently by different members of the population. Lead users are more likely to benefit from such innovations and more likely to feel a need for them earlier (von Hippel 1986). In contrast, Schellhase et al. (2000) claim that third-party participants are the drivers of innovation. In addition to lead users and third parties, the concept of the network champion could be included. Network champions are defined as catalysts that build new linkages among multiple firms (Woodside et al. 2004). The concept of network champions extends work on the product champion and organization champion concepts.

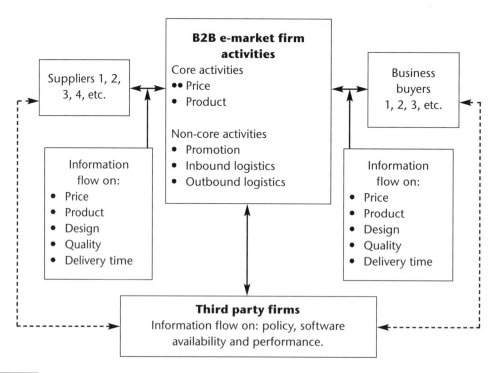

Figure 13.4 B2B e-market network and information flow among participants

Government issues in B2B transactions

Government bodies are very large, important purchasers of goods and services. In the United Kingdom, for example, the Ministry of Defence has an annual spend of around $10 billion and it has been estimated that public procurement across the EU states is worth some €720,000 million, equivalent to between 11 and 14 per cent of European GDP. This represents a potential market equivalent to half the size of Germany's GDP (http://www.europa.eu.int). Purchasing power of this magnitude makes government contracts highly attractive despite the complex procedures that need to be followed.

This group of B2B buyers includes local and national government, as well as European Commission purchasing. The range of purchasing is wide, from office suppliers to public buildings, from army bootlaces to battleships, from airline tickets to motorways, from refuse collection to management consultancy. Although some purchases may be very large, expensive and high profile, involving international suppliers, as is often seen in defence procurement, others are much more mundane and routine, and involve very little public concern.

As a result of the traditional bureaucracy and public accountability surrounding government sector purchasing, the specialized purchasing procedures are often more explicit and formal than those found in many commercial organizations. For more innovative and large-scale projects, the development of specifications may be done in conjunction with specialist consultants and the potential suppliers' development personnel.

Organizations are requested to bid or tender for the right to supply. Some tenders are only open to organizations already on an approved list, while others are open to anyone. The submitted tenders are assessed and the winning one is chosen. Tendering is a very competitive process that demands that the suppliers are well tuned into the procedures and are able to find out early what tenders are on offer. Much of this is down to having the right contacts within the purchasing organization and maintaining good relationships and communication links with them (within ethical boundaries, of course). It is often too late to establish contact once formal bidding has begun. It is important that the contact and reputation building necessary for next year's bids is prepared this year.

The European Union, as part of the single European market (SEM) initiative, issued a Public Services Directive stating that for any of its purchasing needs of €200,000 (€5 million for construction bids) or more, the contract must be advertised openly for tender across all community boundaries. The Public Services Directive encourages cross-border trading, especially for smaller companies, but it has been criticized for creating more bureaucracy and actually doing little to help smaller companies to compete across Europe (de Burca, Fletcher and Brown 2004).

The European Commission recognizes that despite the Directive, much still remains to be achieved in opening up the internal market based upon transparent and competitive purchasing rules. In the harmonization of standards, for example, only 10 per cent compliance had been achieved in construction by 2001 and even in the important machinery area, just 50 per cent compliance had been achieved (European Commission 2006). Unique standards are often a major barrier for suppliers breaking into a new geographic market when they are more familiar with an alternative set of home-based standards. In short, standards can be used to protect domestic suppliers or the very large pan-European operators.

At the core of the problem lies the low rate of response to tenders. The Commission promotes greater use of e-procurement, and ensures that all tender notices are Internet-based to allow a wider dissemination of opportunities. It also intends to allow some relaxation of the rules concerning dialogue for more complex purchases in the tendering stage itself, as this again favours those suppliers who have built-up close contact. The problems in achieving open competition are formidable, however. The Commission itself recognizes the scale of the task and has concluded that 'from its investigations of complaints, even though the contracting authorities have to establish in descending order the importance attached to the selection criteria, they still enjoy a considerable margin of discretion when awarding contracts'. In other words, less tangible considerations can come into play, and although the view of the managing director of a ratio communications equipment manufacturer that 'the French still want to buy from France, the Germans from Germany and the British from anywhere' may be extreme, it does highlight some of the potential problems when up against strong local suppliers in a business to government (B2G) situation.

Summary

This chapter explored B2B marketing and its relationships and the use of the Internet to transform the B2B landscape. It considered how business firms could use the Internet and international marketing intelligence to satisfy their international customers. B2B customers are mainly other businesses, and this makes the international marketing process and planning slightly different. The opportunities and challenges of e-commerce in international marketing are profound. While there are a relatively small number of companies –mainly in the IT industry – profiting, the potential benefits of e-commerce are large for companies operating in international markets. During the last few years there has been an explosion of online commercial activity enabled by the Internet. This is generally referred to as e-commerce, with a major component being electronic transactions taking place on Internet-based markets (electronic markets, or e-markets).

The development of the Internet as a 'new' direct distribution channel has resulted in a shift of power from manufacturers and traditional retail channels to consumers. Generally, the development of e-commerce in Europe has lagged behind development in the United States. A major factor inhibiting growth of consumer e-commerce in Europe is lack of confidence in online security. However, for those selling via the Internet, the euro, as a common currency, makes it easier to do business, and gives encouragement to companies selling to European customers. Since Europeans can shop and compare prices at a click of a mouse, they are now more favourably inclined towards e-commerce. The market volume of B2B e-commerce much bigger than B2C – five times more, according to some research results. The reason is that e-commerce is not a new phenomenon on the B2B market. Instead of Internet-based solutions, many industries have been using EDI for years to streamline business processes and reduce the cost of doing business.

The main difference between buying behaviour in the physical marketplace and the virtual market space is that the market space emphasizes the use of technology, and is more characterized by the power of information and communication technologies to satisfy customer needs and thereby continue business relationships. The myth was that the Internet would eliminate the need for intermediaries. It was thought that physical intermediaries would disappear as people moved from buying through distributors and resellers to buying directly from manufacturers. The reality is that the Internet may eliminate the traditional physical distributors, but the transformation process of the value chain has given rise to a new class of intermediaries. Companies such as Google aggregate information and make it easier to access new information and see new business possibilities. The value-added is no longer in logistic aggregation but rather in information aggregation.

Revision questions

1 Define electronic commerce and explain its impact on traditional international marketing organizations.
2 What are the advantages and disadvantages of e-commerce?
3 What are the relevance and limitations of e-commerce for international marketing?
4 B2B marketing is characterized by a number of key features. Explain these features and discuss the benefits for international marketing.
5 Discuss the nature of B2B transactions in the context of the international environment.
6 The benefits of relationship marketing are limited to the relationships between a customer and a supplier. Explain how relationships are formed in B2B marketing.
7 Compare and contrast the purchase decision process in the physical and virtual marketplaces.
8 What do you consider to be the differences and similarities between physical and virtual stores?
9 In terms of international B2B channel control, the essential argument is that the use of IT allows manufacturers to internalize marketing activities that were traditionally performed by intermediaries. Discuss this statement giving reasons to support your argument.
10 Discuss how innovative theory (diffusion) could be employed in developing new ventures by B2B e-market firms.

Managerial assignment task

International marketing firms are increasingly reliant on technology for data storage and information distribution. However, concerns about security, compliance and legal requirements cause inefficiencies in redundant systems, access and distribution. A local university research department has been keenly engaged in trying to solve these problems. It has finally developed a software solution known as 'Trusted Web Server'. This software is the next-generation solution that ensures employees are only allowed to see information they should have access to, and securely, transparently and efficiently facilitates data distribution between offices, partners and suppliers. The benefits of this software mean that there is/are:

- no possibility of defacement to or data theft from websites
- no digital intellectual property theft, internal or external

- no viruses entering the network
- lower overall technology and insurance costs
- fewer administrative tasks to cope with, bringing IT costs down overall
- no need for a firewall.

The solutions empower digital property owners to have full and secure control of their assets including a complete audit trail, while enabling secure intra-enterprise transactions. The Trusted Web Server operating system is the security cornerstone for data storage, distribution, authorization and auditing for all digitized forms of intellectual property, such as project bids and production budgeting. It has been developed as a trusted network environment that allows for the management and integration of networks with different sensitivity levels to secure the accessibility, confidentially, security and integrity of all data. The university also created a Trusted Virtual Private Network (TVPN) to connect LANs distributed world-wide through any network, even over an unsecured backbone such as the Internet.

Usually, multinational organizations incur incredible costs as a result of the traditional method of maintaining different levels of data on physically separate servers. Every server requires regular scheduled and unscheduled patching and updating, resulting in increased administrative overhead needs and expensive technology and infrastructure costs. The Trusted Web Server allows an organization to consolidate the number of servers it administrates while greatly increasing the level of information assurance. Instead of having to maintain multiple Web servers with separate data sets for each security domain where there is a requirement to grant or restrict access to information based on who is gaining access, the Trusted Web Server allows a single Web interface to serve as a common data repository to support multiple customers, suppliers and partners. The remote access features of the Trusted Web Server allow an enterprise to grant network privileges to independent contractors while maintaining it current security policies.

Your managing director is aware of this new and innovative product and is very keen to subscribe to it. She has requested your opinion and advice regarding the adoption of this product in your organization. Write a report explaining the benefits and any possible drawbacks of this product . Your report should consider the application of the technology acceptance model to all aspects of this innovative product.

References

Conway, T. and Swift, J. S. (2000) 'International relationship marketing: the importance of psychic distance', *European Journal of Marketing*, Vol. 34, No. 11/12, pp. 1391–413.

Coviello, N. E. and Brodie, R. J. (2001) 'Contemporary marketing practices of consumer and business-to-business firms: how different are they?' *Journal of Business & Industrial Marketing*, Vol. 16, No. 5, pp. 382–400.

De Burca, S., Fletcher, R. and Brown, L. (2004) *International Marketing : An SME Perspective*, Harlow: Financial Times/Prentice Hall.

Economist (2007) 26 January.

European Commission (2006) 'Guidelines on antitrust fines: a legal and economic analysis', European Commission Legal Services.

Ford, D., Berthon, P., Brown, S., Gadde, L. E., Naude, P., Ritter, T., Snehota, I. and Hakansson, H. (2003) *The Business Marketing Course*, Chichester: Wiley.

Gronroos, C. (2002) *Service Management and Marketing,* 2nd edn, Chichester: Wiley.

Gummesson, E. (2002) *Total Relationship Marketing*, 2nd edn, Oxford: Butterworth-Heinemann/Chartered Institute of Marketing.

Gummesson, E. (2004) 'Return on relationships (ROR): the value of relationship marketing and CRM in business-to-business contexts', *Journal of Business & Industrial Marketing*, Vol. 19, No. 2, pp. 136–48.

Heffernan, T. (2004) 'Trust formation in cross-cultural business-to-business relationships', *Qualitative Market Research* Vol. 7, No. 2, pp. 114–25.

Heldal, F., Sjovold, E. and Heldal, A.F. (2004) 'Success on the Internet: optimizing relationships through the corporate site', *International Journal of Information Management*, Vol. 24, Issue 2, pp. 115-129.

Hill, J. and Scott, T. (2004) 'A consideration of the roles of business intelligence and e-business in management and marketing decision making in knowledge-based and high-tech start-ups', *Qualitative Market Research*, Vol. 7, No. 1, pp. 48–57.

Hofacker, C.F. (1999) *Internet Marketing*, 2nd edn, Dripping Springs, Tex.: Digital Springs.

Jackson, B. B. (1985) 'Building customer relationships that last', *Harvard Business Review*, November–December, pp. 120–8.

Kotler, P. (2006) *Marketing Management*, 12th edn, New Jersey: Prentice Hall/Pearson Education International.

Kafka, S. (2000) *eMarketplaces Boost B2B Trade*, Forrester Research.

Newell, F. (2000) *loyalty.com*, New York: Free Press.

Nusbaum, A. (2000) '"Web cuts out entire order of middlemen". information technology in Japan: B2B e-commerce is threatening the live-hoods of thousands of intermediaries', *Financial Times*, 11 January, p. 18.

Oliva, R.A. (2001) 'Nowhere to hide', *Marketing Management*, July/August, pp. 44–6.

Reid, D. A., Pullins, E. B., Plank, R. E. and Buehrer, R. E. (2004) 'Measuring buyers' perceptions of conflict in b2b sales interactions', *Journal of Business & Industrial Marketing*, Vol. 19, No. 4, pp. 236–49.

Ringberg, T. and Gupta, S. F. (2003) 'The importance of understanding the symbolic world of customers in asymmetric business-to-business relationships', *Journal of Business and Industrial Marketing*, Vol. 18, No. 6/7, pp. 607–26.

Rossomme, J. (2003) 'Customer satisfaction measurement in a b2b context: a conceptual framework', *Journal of Business & Industrial Marketing*, Vol. 18, No. 2, pp. 179–95.

Schellhase, R., Hardock, P. and Ohlwein, M. (2000) 'Customer satisfaction in business-to-business marketing: the case of retail organizations and their suppliers', *Journal of Business and Industrial Marketing*, Vol. 15, No. 2/3, pp. 106–21.

Stone, M. A. and McCall, J. B. (2004) *International Strategic Marketing: A European Perspective*, London: Routledge.

Von Hippel, E. (1986), 'Lead users: a source of novel product concepts', *Management Science*, Vol. 32, pp. 791–805.

Wise, R. and Morrison, D. (2000) 'Beyond the exchange: the future of b2b', *Harvard Business Review*, November–December, pp. 87–96.

Woodside, A., Gupta, S. and Cadeaux, J. (2004) 'Diffusion process models and strategic performance theory for new b2b electronic ventures', *Journal of Business and Industrial Marketing*, Vol.19, No. 1, pp. 23–38.

14
Retail Internationalization and Marketing

Contents

LEARNING OBJECTIVES

After reading this chapter you should:

- know the nature and processes of retail internationalization
- understand the principles and concepts of retail internationalization
- be able to discuss the motives for retailer internationalization
- know the factors that determine retailers' marketing success in an international environment

- be able to develop positioning strategies that move retailers forward in an international environment
- be able to evaluate international retail formats and make decisions on a suitable format.

Introduction

In the past 25 years at least, the study of international retailing has developed from a position of observation, through one of analysis, to the current one of conceptual development. Thus, the consideration of a new wave of international activity that began to build in the mid-1990s has developed into an area of considerable research activity. At the beginning of the twenty-first century, international activity became a commonplace of retailing, and this is mirrored by a considerable effort in research activity and output.

The internationalization of retailing is a process, not a series of events. It is a complex process that has changed in recent years. It has become more widespread. It has a greater influence on corporate strategies and has extended its effects on the development of the retail sector. The magnitude, form and function of the process have all changed. It is therefore necessary to consider the processes associated with the sequence of events before placing these processes in a model. Such a model will thus be essential to a theoretical and conceptual understanding of retail internationalization. In general a model of retail internationalization must encapsulate a process that permeates the whole of the retail organization, influences competitor actions and changes the environment in which the retailer and its competitors operate. Internationalization, when viewed as a process, enables a retailer to exploit innovations.

This chapter reviews the conceptual framework relating to retail internationalization processes, which have sought to integrate and encompass the retail functions. Thus, there is consideration of the conceptual frameworks of the eclectic paradigm of retail internationalization, which has become the necessary introduction to the consideration of the internationalization process. The chapter then discusses the distinctions between the terms 'global' and 'international', noting that there are no global retailers by definition. This is followed by an examination of the nature of international retailing, its principles and concepts, its processes and motives, and international strategies and retail format.

Global versus international retailing

In an astonishing development, the largest corporation in the world in 2002, measured by sales, was Wal-Mart. This retailer exceeded the sales of former world leaders such as General Motors and Exxon. This indicates that much more analytical attention needs to be directed to retail and other service-related business rather than to just manufacturing multinational enterprises (MNEs). In fact, the main retail companies make up 10 per cent of the top 500 MNEs.

This chapter discusses the international dimension of retail organizations such as Tesco and Wal-Mart. It evaluates the question whether retailers such as Wal-Mart are 'global' businesses, and if so, whether they have 'global' retail marketing strategies. So far retail marketing literature evidence shows that the answer to both questions is no. It indicates that Wal-Mart, for example, is a North American business, with only 9.6 per cent of its stores outside its domestic region. Although 26.5 per cent of its stores are outside the United States, most of them are in Mexico and Canada, partners with the United States in NAFTA. Only 16.3 per cent of Wal-Mart's revenue is international, and again most of this is in North America.

Although the well-informed analysts Govindarajan and Gupta (2002) have discussed the nature of Wal-Mart's globalization and its use of global strategy, this type of approach is misguided. Wal-Mart is a regional business and has a regional strategy; it is a regional MNE, not a global MNE. There are still no Wal-Mart stores in Africa. Virtually all major retailers are in the same position.

Most other retailers are either home-market based or operate, at best, in neighbouring countries – applying the psychic distance concept in their choice of markets. A few operate in two parts of the 'triad' of North America, the European Union and Japan, but most of the European retailers have nearly all their business in the European Union, as do the Americans in North America and the Asians in Asia. In short, retail multinational enterprises are not global but regional, especially if we consider the term 'global' in its two different meanings: a global sales presence on the one hand, and a global strategy on the other hand. As a result, this chapter is focused on international rather than global retailing.

The nature of international retailing

Retailing has increasingly become international, and the situation is likely to change even more dramatically in this millennium, as retail businesses from the developed countries become more outward-looking in seeking opportunities beyond their local, regional and national markets in the emerging markets of developing economies such as Thailand, India, China and South Africa in order to sustain future company sales and profit growth. This section discusses this development by focusing on the evolution of internationalization, the key drivers, strategies for achieving internationalization, strategic opportunities for retailing, and the challenges faced by retailers across the world.

Mergers and takeovers are common in this sector. Apart from the upsurge of retailers in domestic deals, Kingfisher for example gained control of France's Castorama in the DIY sector. Similarly, Wal-Mart has control of Seiyu in Japan, Werkauf in Germany and Asda in the United Kingdom. Meanwhile the toy retailer FAO Schwarz has followed K-Mart into bankruptcy. Yet whether and how retailers should go into international markets have become heavily debated issues. Typologies of retailers' strategic responses to internationalization have been developed, but only recently has attention turned to more typical, less obviously international industries. Calori, Johnson and Sarnin's typology (1994) is based on extensive empirical research into European companies operating in four 'mixed' manufacturing industries. While recognizing the fundamental differences between manufacturing and service industries, they investigate the applicability of such an approach to retailing with a view to offering practical strategic recommendations.

Historically, from the earliest traders to the Hudson Bay Company, retailing was virtually the first business activity to become international, and Sears and JC Penny had both gone international by the 1950s. Retailers are, though, relative latecomers to any more fully-fledged process of international integration. In 1995, only 56 of the Top 100 retailers operated outside their home market, and only five of those generated more than 50 per cent of their sales in foreign markets.

Retailing may lag in internationalization, but it is subject to several underlying forces similar to those well understood from the experience of manufacturing:

- saturation within home markets compounded by economic downturns
- legislation blocking expansion
- shareholder pressures for growth
- high operating costs
- opportunities as overseas markets open up
- an element of the 'me-too syndrome'.

In contrast to manufacturers, however, retailers must be physically present wherever they do business, and structural and cultural characteristics make it harder to operate across distinctive national markets. Retailers' performance in local markets is highly sensitive to variations in consumer behaviour and segmentation. Consumer tastes, buying and spending patterns differ considerably across the international marketplace, hampering international sourcing.

Prior to the 1970s, the majority of retailers focused their activities on local, regional or national markets, as these markets were exhibiting attractive growth and provided expansion opportunities. There were, however, a few exceptions, such as Woolworth's entry into Canada in 1907 and later into Europe, Sears, Roebuck's expansion into Cuba in 1942, Marks & Spencer's entry into Canada in the early 1970s, and C&A's entry into several European countries in the late 1960s. There were also some important overseas retail and manufacturing networks established by manufacturers such as Bata Shoe Corporation of Canada and Singer Company of the United States, which set up hundreds of company-owned or franchised outlets across the world in the 1950s, 1960s and 1970s.

Today it is clear that for an increasing number of these businesses, national boundaries have ceased to be a constraint to their activities and ambitions. They are becoming more outward-looking in seeking opportunities for sustaining sales and profit growth. It is anticipated that this pace of change will accelerate. Several emerging factors will make international retail operations not only more feasible, but in many cases imperative:

- Conclusion of the new GATT agreement.
- The integration and enlargement of the European Union.
- The introduction of free market economies to Central and Eastern European and several Latin American countries.
- Integration of the North American economy.
- Increasing consumerism in the near and Far East.
- Trading developments in Africa and other less developed nations.
- Within developed countries, actual and/or perceived maturing markets, increasing costs and static or falling sales in real terms, plus intense competition and limited growth opportunities in the United States, several European countries, Japan, Singapore and Australia. This will lead retail organizations from these countries to seek newer markets in order to sustain their sales and profits.
- Attractive profit/growth opportunities in several emerging markets.
- Although it is often said that most internationalization moves are driven by 'offensive' or expansionary motives, it is likely that in many sub-sectors, as domestic markets become increasingly vulnerable to competition from foreign organizations, more companies may look to internationalization as a means to defend their current positions.
- Many emerging organizations from developing countries may seek 'niche' opportunities in mature markets.

This new wave of internationalization is unique in its scale, geographical orientation and motivation. It is underpinned by new developments in communication networks and technology, and the global customer and supply chain, making it possible for retail organizations to control their businesses as well as 'localize' them in far-flung locations. It is on the basis of this new technological development that the concept of retail internationalization processes is formulated.

Conceptual framework and internationalization process

One of the theoretical bases adopted in this chapter is that most economic activity (in both manufacturing and services) is location-bound, taking place in clusters in the 'triad' of the European Union, North America and Japan (see Rugman 2000). The geography of location and the drawing power of nearby markets give rigidities that influence the strategic management decisions of retailers. In fact, the choice of entry mode and choice of location are complementary strategic management decisions of profound importance to international retailers.

Conceptual framework

A number of factors influence the performance of retailers in an international market environment. Evans , Treadgold and Mavondo (2000) proposed that certain characteristics of the firm and its international operations intervene in, and moderate, the relationship between the factors preventing the retailer from learning about the business environment (psychic distance) and organizational performance. These factors may contribute to a holistic framework that explains variations in the performance of international retailing operations. In terms of the strategic decision-making process, the decisions regarding international retailing operations have three specific features:

- The decision is unusual in the sense that simple decision rules cannot be applied.
- The decision is of great importance to the organization because it involves a substantial commitment of resources and has organization-wide consequences.
- Strategic decisions are highly complex as they often involve detailed analysis of both the external and internal environments.

Evans et al. (2000) observed that decisions to enter a foreign market and on the degree of adaptation of the retail offer possess all these features. However, international retailing decisions are strongly influenced by subjective and perceptual factors, such as the decision makers' personalities, their subjective expectations and perceptions of risk in the international environment. O'Grady and Lane (1996) found that the most important aspect of a firm's pre-entry orientation is the subjective insights of the management team.

In many instances, retail managers also rely on objective information, but in this sector it is often lacking in both quality and quantity, leading to environmental uncertainty, which is likely to result in incremental international expansion.

Figure 14.1 presents a conceptual model of the potential moderating effects of culture and socioeconomics on global retail marketing strategies. Environmental characteristics

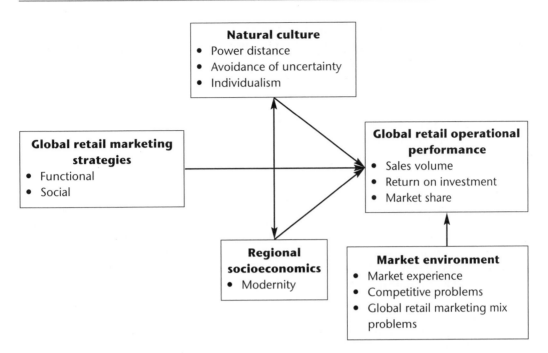

Figure 14.1 Effects of cultural and socioeconomic factors on global retail marketing

in the global markets are likely to moderate the operational performance. Both national culture and regional socioeconomic conditions affect functional and social strategies. In addition, because the international market and firm conditions may also impact operational performance, the model shows likely covariates: that is, marketing experience, extent of competition, and retail marketing mix implementation problems, which should be managed when examining the effects of environmental factors and operational performance of international retailers.

The perception of cultural and business differences may lead to environmental uncertainty (see Figure 14.1). In order to reduce this uncertainty retail management will undertake more extensive organizational and environmental analysis (see Chapter 3), to provide them with greater understanding and produce superior performance. When problems occur, it is often because of lack of preparation and understanding of individual markets.

The level of understanding of the international marketing environment can be explained by:

- the intervening effect of the strategic decision-making process
- the nature and the extent of marketing research
- the firm's ability to conduct in-depth market research in the international marketplace
- the depth and the nature of the problems faced by the firm
- the impact of environmental uncertainty
- the appropriateness of the firm's organizational structure and its ability to make strategic decisions concerning international operation

- the firm's level of acculturation and adaptation to the international market
- the firm's pre-entry orientation to the international market, taking into consideration differences between cultures
- management's ability to predict the international marketing environment in relation to its own business.

Overall, to succeed in the international marketing environment, retailers must appreciate and position themselves appropriately within their market sectors (see McGoldrick 2002).

The internationalization process

According to Vida and Fairhurst (1998: 141), the retail internationalization process (RIP) is complex and relatively poorly understood. There is a lack of agreement on what constitutes internationalization: while product sourcing may be included, there are grounds for excluding it. As Figure 14.2 indicates, the process is reiterative (for example, the changes within the retail organization are continually grounded in the context of changes in the marketplace).

Based on the information in Figure 14.2, the advantage exploited by a retailer in the domestic market, which might be either conceptually or technologically based, will be formulated within a set of environmental factors. These factors will either stimulate the

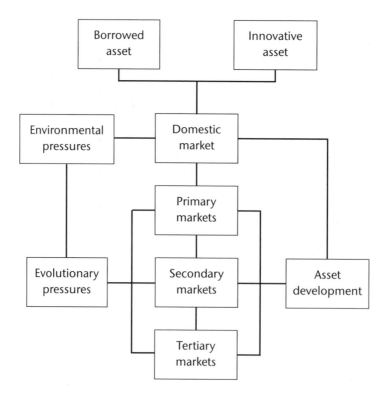

Figure 14.2 Market internationalization

development of a concept or facilitate the development of a technology base. This advantage is then further refined as it is exploited.

It is important, however, to be aware that such advantages are linked as much to a market as they are to an individual retailer. The internationalization process occurs through the physical transfer of innovation, as a result of the international expansion of retail operations, and through the transfer of skills and technology across market boundaries. Thus, the retail asset and advantage may be part of not merely organizational development but also market development.

That is, where suitable conditions exist, a retail form will develop to meet those needs. If those needs exist in two markets, an organization may fulfil those needs through the direct transfer of an operational form, or the operational form may be developed separately by another organization in the second market. In the second case, the other organization in effect borrows the concept or set of technological skills. The idea of borrowed advantage is important. In terms of the international product life cycle (IPLC), the retail organization exploiting the basic advantage will have to consider tertiary markets and the primary market in a different manner.

As indicated in Figure 14.2, and discussed earlier in the book, domestic expansion in retailing, as in manufacturing, is typically followed by expansion into primary international markets: that is, those of a similar nature or psychologically proximate to the domestic market (Evans et al. 2000). Next come secondary and tertiary markets, which increasingly differ from the market of origin and primary markets. They are less culturally, economically and geographically proximate. To some extent such markets will be the recipients of innovations in more advanced markets. However, as the retailer operates within the international market, the operation will be subject to the same set of environmental pressures that existed in the domestic market. Thus, the tertiary markets will receive the influence of international, as well as domestic, development of the concept or technology base.

As Figure 14.2 illustrates, there is the continual opportunity for conceptual and technological realignment to meet changing market conditions. These pressures will exist, however, irrespective of the organizational framework. It is within the organizational framework that the updating of the assets or the development of new advantages will occur, but the organization may or may not respond. If the organization fails to respond, it will no longer provide advantages to the markets it serves, or may do so only to a selection of those markets, depending on their place in the market hierarchy.

Internationalization motives and entry strategies

The reasons for internationalization recognized by Hollander (1970) provide a useful framework for the internationalization process.

Retail internationalization drivers

It is critical for retail organizations wanting to internationalize their operations to understand how key economic, political, legal, social, cultural and technological environments impact on resource, competition and distribution dimensions, leading to the establishment of main drivers for international expansion. The combination of these drivers – which will be unique for each organization, and its strategic and financial objectives, capabilities and culture – will lead to the formation of appropriate entry strategies. As Rugman and Girod (2003) observed, there are also other important factors such as growth patterns and the time horizon.

Retail international expansion motives

It is important to examine the main motives for overseas expansion because this will help the achievement of the objectives. The motives are usually many and varied, and can be divided into 'hard' factors and 'soft' factors. The hard factors can be subdivided into push factors, pull factors and facilitating factors. For each individual retailer, as discussed above, the final decision is a unique combination of these factors, and this in turn determines the most appropriate route for international expansion. It should be emphasized that these factors highlight many of the motives for international expansion, but not necessarily for *successful* expansion. Success or failure can be ascribed to many other factors and/or to execution.

Push and pull

Where there exist limited opportunities at home it is reasonable to expect that retailers will seek expansion opportunities in international markets. This underlies the analysis of the motives for retail internationalizations. This assumption is fundamental to an interpretation that sees internationalization as a reactive response to the competitive

Table 14.1   Push and pull factors

Push factors	Pull factors
Unstable political structure	Stable political structure
Unstable economy	Stable economy
Matured domestic market	Underdeveloped retail structure
Format saturation	Large market
Small domestic market	Relaxed regulatory environment
Restrictive regulatory environment	Good economic conditions - high growth
Hostile competitive environment	Positive social environment
Poor economic conditions	Favourable operating environment
Negative social environment	Favourable exchange rates
Unfavourable operating environment	Low share prices
High domestic operating costs	Property investment potential
Consumer credit restrictions	Niche opportunities
	Attractive sociocultural fabric
	Innovative retail culture
	Company-owned facilities
	Company ethos
	Me-too-expansion

Source: adapted from McGoldrick and Davies (1995).

environment, and qualifies an interpretation that sees internationalization as a product of retailers' proactive response to international opportunities.

As Table 14.1 shows, push factors are simply those issues that encourage internationalization, or even make it imperative, as a result of environmental or company-specific conditions in the domestic market. Pull factors are essentially attractive conditions, which draw retailers into new markets. Push factors are therefore characterized by unattractive trading conditions, and include environmental factors such as poor economic conditions, negative demographic trends and regulatory constraints. Company-specific issues, such as the stage of the retailer's development, are also commonly seen as instrumental in prompting international action. Where, for example, they are characterized by issues such as limited growth opportunities, they will be interpreted as pushing retailers out of the home market. Conversely, pull factors will include opportunities for faster growth in new markets, perhaps as a result of an undeveloped retail structure in the new market, or niche opportunities. Retailers may be encouraged, hence pulled, across frontiers as a result of the ethos of the company and as a result of 'me too' international actions.

Push and pull factors should be viewed as relative rather than absolute. For example, the push factors in the European environment of the 1970s – unhealthy operating conditions and limited commercial opportunities at home – encouraged internationalization, while pull factors from the United States, which has relatively attractive social, economic and regulatory conditions, encouraged investment in that market.

Finally, how conditions are balanced within an environment and within retail organizations will determine whether the retailer is seen as reactive or proactive. While the identification of push and pull factors is a good starting point for the analysis of markets, retailers' positions within that market and in terms of their organizational development, a different approach is needed to interpret retailers' responses to domestic and international conditions and opportunities. How retailers respond to such market conditions will determine the entry strategy adopted.

Market entry strategies

Retail organizations have a wide choice of international market entry strategies. In the past, many chose to acquire local businesses. and/or adopted partial equity strategies, when they were unsure of successfully transplanting their offer into the host country. However, where they were reasonably certain of success, with a distinctive offer which could appeal to 'similar' target markets across a variety of nations and which could be readily transported or adapted to the host countries' markets, concepts which required tight control of image or positioning aspects, they chose organic growth and/or franchising.

Strategic alliances – development-led, purchasing-led, skills-based or multi-functional – have been one of the most important strategies in recent years. Another option is management know-how transfer, while many businesses, especially when establishing their operations in developing economies, follow the concept of 'limited-term management contracts' whereby a company provides business know-how in specific areas without making any capital investment. This gives it valuable knowledge about the partner country's business and consumer markets, competitive environment and trends.

Figure 14.3 shows a framework for international market entry. The choice of entry strategy may depend on whether the market is culturally close or distant, and difficult or easy to enter. It has significant implications for strategy. At one level, the choice could be seen in terms of the degree of freedom that the retailer has in choosing the target market and in the ways in which it subsequently goes about matching market demand. At a deeper level, it has direct consequences for the retailer's ability to develop an international image and reap the benefits of the economies of large scale and standardized retailing programmes. The benefits of a standardized approach have long been recognized in a general way, although only a few retailers, such as Marks & Spencer and Laura Ashley, have taken this approach. However, with the apparent growth of standardized culture in the world's major markets, more retailers have begun to modify their retail marketing strategies to reflect this approach (see Vida and Fairhurst 1998).

The mode of entry into an international market is a reflection of the relative importance assigned to:

- the extent of payback required to meet overall sales volume and growth targets
- the level of control the retailer wishes to exercise over its concepts overseas
- the amount of resources the retailer is willing to commit to international expansion
- the flexibility the retailer wishes to retain to allow the company to change its operations quickly and at low cost.

The various routes to achieving retail internationalization can be classified into:

- internal (organic) expansion
- merger or takeover
- franchise-type agreements
- joint ventures, which may take a variety of forms including concessions
- taking a non-controlling interest in a firm.

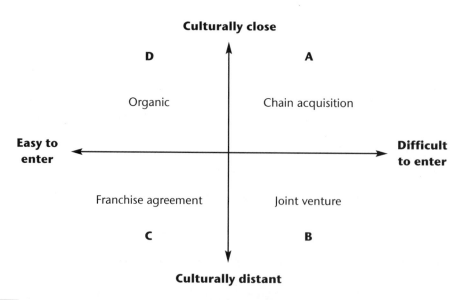

Figure 14.3 Framework for international market entry strategy

A number of other factors also need to be highlighted:

- Many efforts to expand international operations have been characterized above all by caution and a desire to trade in familiar environments which minimize primarily soci-ocultural but also, in some cases, geographical distances: for example, US retailers into the United Kingdom, Canada and Mexico.

Table 14.2   Market entry strategy – advantages and disadvantages

Mode	Advantages	Disadvantages
Internal expansion	Can be undertaken by any size of firm. Experimental openings are possible with modest risk and often-modest cost. Ability to adapt operation with each subsequent opening. Exit is easy. Allows rapid prototyping.	Takes a long time to establish a substantial presence. May be seen by top management as a minor diversion. Requirement to undertake full location assessment. More difficult if host market is distant from home market.
Merger or takeover	Substantial market presence quickly achieved. Management already in place Cash flow is immediate. Possibility of technology transfer to home stores. May be used as a way to obtain locations quickly for conversion to the chosen format.	Difficult to exit if mistake is made. Evaluation of takeover target is difficult and takes time. Suitable stores may not be available. Substantial top management commitment necessary.
Franchise agreements	Rapid expansion of presence possible Low cost to franchisor. Marginal markets can be addressed. Local management may be used. Wide range of forms of agreement available. Use locally competitive marketing policy. Way of overcoming entry barriers.	Possibly complex legal requirements. Necessary to recruit suitable franchises. Difficult to control foreign franchisees. May become locked into an unsatisfactory relationship.
Joint venture	Possible to link with stores already in market. Help available in climbing learning curve. Possible to move later to either exit or make fully entry into the market.	Necessary to share benefits. Difficulties in finding a suitable partner.
Non-controlling interest	Find out about market with minimal risk. Allows those who know the market to manage the operation.	Passive position. Investment made over which there is little influence.

- As an organization accumulates experience of operating internationally, so the emphasis on minimizing sociocultural distance diminishes: for example, IKEA, Marks & Spencer, Carrefour, Wal-Mart.
- High-control strategies appear to be the most favoured mode of entry into overseas markets, especially for retailers such as The Gap and Toys'R'Us with limited overseas experience, and those retailers wishing to exercise tight control over formats.
- In their early phase of internationalization, several retail companies such as Marks & Spencer, Wal-Mart and The Gap made their first moves into overseas markets by establishing subsidiaries as a high-control mode of entry.
- For many retailers, for example, Benetton and The Body Shop, with more experience of trading in overseas markets or for whom operating in international markets is a part of the company culture rather than primarily a response to a tough climate at home, the preferred route is usually a lower/medium control strategy that is less costly in terms of company resources.

Some of the most successful efforts to internationalize have been made by KFC, McDonald's and Service Master (retailers selling unique products or those operating with a unique trading format).

As well as varying from company to company, even within one company there can be many different approaches. An interesting example is Marks & Spencer, which acquired existing retailers in Canada as well as opening its own stores, acquired Brooks Brothers in the United States, developed organically its operations in France and Belgium, undertook a joint venture in Spain, used franchise-type arrangements in Greece and initially in Hong Kong, entered Hungary through a joint venture before moving to a franchise-type arrangement, and had a non-controlling interest in the company that sold its St Michael branded products for several years in Japan. The expansion pattern of Foot Locker, on the other hand, highlights a pattern whereby the first step was by internal expansion to nearby and/or culturally similar countries, then expansion into other European countries, and finally expansion across a broad front, including Japan, southeast Asia and Latin America, involving small acquisitions and single-outlet openings.

Another key issue is the extent to which managerial decision making is centralized at a head office or delegated. This is related to whether the retail operations are virtually the same from country to country (Toys'R'Us, McDonald's) or reflect the local society (Carrefour's individual hypermarkets, IKEA). However, recently we have witnessed the emergence of hybrid formats with mixed control.

Guy (2001) makes this distinction, terming the retailer 'global' if there is great similarity in operation from country to country (for example, Benetton, Toys'R'Us) and multinational if there are pronounced national differences (Woolworth, C&A). In reality there is a continuum, and any of the five routes discussed earlier may be applied across it. Two other variables, the market position of the retailer and the format of retailing, are discussed later in this chapter.

It is important to know that these two variables will affect both the mechanism of international establishment and the position on the global–multinational axis. A strong premier brand might lead to an international approach through internal expansion or tightly controlled franchising: for example, Dunhill, Ralph Lauren and The Body Shop. Alternatively, large floor space outlets might lead to a multinational approach with joint ventures or possible takeover of suitable companies in target countries. As discussed earlier, a single firm may use several routes.

International market opportunities

As most retail domestic markets become increasingly saturated, more companies are looking to expand their operations overseas. Russia and Eastern European countries provide the best opportunities for food and general-merchandise retailers with international expansion plans (Vida 2000). The Kearney Global Retail Index (GRDI) (2003) ranks emerging countries based on an analysis of economic and political risk, retail-saturation level and the difference between gross domestic product growth and retail growth. It divides 30 countries into three groups based on their scores:

1   Group one – those countries retailers should enter immediately.
2   Group two – those countries retailers should consider entering.
3   Group three – those countries retailers should avoid entering at this time.

Increased competition and limited expansion opportunities in the United States and Western Europe are forcing European and US retailers to seek growth abroad. With many developed markets in Europe and Asia already well saturated with international retailers from within these regions, retailers from the United States and Europe must instead look to emerging markets as their future expansion targets. For example, Russia rose from the fourth position in the 2003 index to the top spot in the 2005 index due to a combination of a strengthening economy, reduced inflation rate, limited number of modern retail-store concepts, small quantity of international retailers, and booming retail sector. Other countries food retailers were recommended to enter immediately were the Slovak Republic, China, Hungary, India, Turkey, Morocco, Egypt, Vietnam and Tunisia.

The Eastern European countries also heavily populate the middle third of Table 14.3. Bulgaria, Slovenia, Romania, Latvia and Ukraine are five of the ten 'countries to consider'. Only two East European countries – Poland and the Czech Republic – were classified by GRDI as 'countries to be avoided' because of their economic and political challenges.

The rate of new market entries by international retailers is in decline because local retailers in many countries are slowly working to expand by:

* modernizing operations
* adopting e-commerce to expand their domestic market
* retailing via the Internet
* identifying small-chain acquisitions
* expanding into new regions of their countries.

China used to be the most attractive country for international retailers from Europe and America, but as shown in Table 14.3, it is now the third attractive market. In 2002 alone, eight international retailers entered the country, bringing it closer to saturation. For example, Wal-Mart opened its first store in Beijing in 2003, and had brought the total number of its stores in China to 204 by 2008 (http://www.wal-martchina.com/english/news/stat.htm). Although local retailers generally enjoy higher margins, delaying the expansion of international retailers is not usually sustainable in the long run. International retailers have the experience, buying scale systems and cash flow to withstand the low levels of profitability that sometimes follow market entry.

| **Table 14.3** | Global Retail Development Index, 2005 |

Rank	Country	Geographic area	Current market saturation		Number of international retailers in the country	Time pressure	Grade
			Country risk	Modern retail area per inhabitant			
		Weight	**40%**	**20%**	**20%**	**20%**	**100%**
1	Russia	Eastern Europe	51	95	76	87	72
2	Slovak Republic	Eastern Europe	59	80	59	100	71
3	China	Asia	67	73	41	86	67
4	Hungary	Eastern Europe	71	69	53	69	67
5	India	Asia	48	100	94	34	65
6	Turkey	Mediterranean	44	72	76	86	64
7	Morocco	Mediterranean	55	98	88	18	63
8	Egypt	Mediterranean	52	98	88	24	63
9	Vietnam	Asia	49	99	82	17	59
10	Tunisia	Mediterranean	54	85	88	13	59
11	South Korea	Asia	67	44	59	54	58
12	Chile	Americas	56	73	94	10	58
13	Bulgaria	Eastern Europe	48	62	76	54	58
14	Slovenia	Eastern Europe	74	20	82	34	57
15	Philippines	Asia	52	32	78	73	57
16	Malaysia	Asia	61	60	59	42	57
17	Romania	Eastern Europe	46	73	59	59	57
18	Thailand	Asia	56	84	35	47	56
19	Latvia	Eastern Europe	61	50	82	29	56
20	Ukraine	Eastern Europe	34	98	94	22	56
21	South Africa	Africa	55	79	82	6	55
22	Czech Republic	Eastern Europe	67	47	29	66	55
23	Mexico	Americas	61	83	53	13	54
24	Taiwan	Asia	62	74	47	15	52
25	Venezuela	Americas	36	78	88	18	51
26	Indonesia	Asia	38	92	71	18	51
27	Hong Kong	Asia	78	51	41	5	50
28	Poland	Eastern Europe	65	78	0	39	49
29	Israel	Mediterranean	61	12	94	9	48
30	Colombia	Americas	34	82	82	4	47

Countries experiencing significant drops include Taiwan and Mexico, which both fell into the bottom third of the table and are considered 'countries to avoid'. International retailers have been greatly underrepresented in these countries.

There are no US retailers ranking among the top 15 in terms of sales outside their home markets, and Wal-Mart and Costco have just 16 per cent of their sales from international operations (compared with Ahold, with 85 per cent of sales coming from operations in 26 foreign markets). Most other US retailers' international operations have been limited to Canada and Mexico. Retailers from the United States have no presence in Eastern Europe or the Mediterranean belt presently.

Wal-Mart has committed to increasing its international sales to 33 per cent of revenue in the next few years and Costco is looking to further expansion in Asia. Wal-Mart is particularly well positioned for international success due to (Guy 2001):

- its diversity of store formats
- superstores
- warehouse clubs
- experimentation with small groceries
- effective use of technology
- established processes for buying from local suppliers.

In Mexico, for example, 90 per cent of Wal-Mart's inventory is bought locally.

In addition to managing the timing of market entry, flexibility of store formats also is essential to international expansion success. It is recommended that retailers enter new markets with two types of store format (which might be, for example, hypermarket, supermarket or convenience) and be prepared to adjust emphasis if one format proves more successful than another. Although hypermarkets are now the most popular new entry format, there is no correlation between format and international success.

Currently, the top 30 food retailers in the world are in 85 different countries, compared with just 15 countries ten years ago. Yet two out of three retailers do not meet their initial financial targets when entering developing countries. Flexibility and timing need to be higher on the planning programme of international retailers, as most retailers do not consider flexibility as a crucial success element. There is no single formula, no best type of store, no best ownership structure, but retailers poised for growth will be those that look to the leaders in international expansion, use time as a critical strategic component, and demonstrate flexibility during market entry and implementation.

International retail market position and strategies

Positioning is the act of locating a product in a market, in the channels of distribution, in relationship to other products, and ultimately in the minds of prospects or target customers. It is essential in retail marketing because the density of appeals to consumers is so great that they protect their sanity by screening out most of them. The basic rule of positioning is consistency.

The positioning of international retailers is discussed in detail in Chapter 4 (pages 124 to 125).

International retail format

Marketing literature has focused on the unique problems and opportunities facing different retail formats operating on an international scale (Muniz-Martinez 1998).
Distinguishing between international retailers on the basis of format is essential because
different formats may have different degrees of success. On the one hand organizations
with specialist retail formats may internationalize their operations with greater ease as
they are readily transportable and can use any perceived differences as a basis for differentiation (Muniz-Martinez 1998). Conversely, innovative formats may perform well as
they can satisfy consumers in new ways and avoid direct competition from more
traditional retail formats.

Retail format should be consistent with the retailer's differential advantage. The role
of the retailer's differential advantage is crucial in fostering the retailer's international
marketing capabilities. Vida (2000) observed that it must relate to the uniqueness of the
retailer's product/services. Differential advantage through retail format should provide an
incentive to initiate and continue exploitation of a foreign market (Vida and Fairhurst
1998). The relevant differential advantages of international retailers in the United
Kingdom include:

- distinguishing retail format
- distinguishing products
- unique merchandise assortment
- unique retail concept
- appealing and innovative market image/prestige
- close relationships with channel members
- innovative retail logistics
- competitive pricing.

US retailers are especially successful when differential advantages have been associated
with profitable formats such as category killers (Home Depot, and Linen and Things),
unique selling position (Toys'R'Us and Foot Locker) or distinctively 'American' products
or brands (The Gap and the Disney Store).

Considering that retail managers in the initial phases of global involvement may lack
knowledge, experience and substantial resource commitment from their companies, an
important lever to internationalization will be the existence of unique retail specific
advantages such as format, products, services, skills or other assets, which have the
required fit with the foreign market conditions.

Retail format has also been shown to influence the market entry strategy. A strong
premium specialist retail format may result in organic growth or tightly controlled franchising, whereas joint ventures or acquisitions may be more appropriate for mass
merchandise retailers. But the relationships between retail format, performance and
entry strategy are still not clear (Muniz-Martinez 1998), partly because a firm may use
several different modes of market entry depending on its resources, perceived risk and
the characteristics of the foreign market.

Despite the popularity of retail internationalization, most retailers are still struggling
to develop competencies to succeed in international markets. The major issue is the
extent to which the original format and merchandise should be adapted. In order to

protect against currency fluctuations, comply with local sourcing requirements and serve local tastes, most big retail formats increasingly rely on local suppliers. But often, as Wal-Mart discovered in Brazil, local suppliers are unable to meet exacting specifications for easy-to-handle packaging and quality control. Failure usually happens because the retailer either underestimates the cultural diversity it confronts because it is too sure of its format and its domestic success, or does not want to lose control and refuses foreign capital and local competencies. Furthermore, if for example 90 per cent of merchandise is locally sourced, as is the case for Wal-Mart and Carrefour, retailers start to lose some of their international sourcing leverage (Arnold and Fernie 2000).

A related question is whether the retailer should adopt centralized or decentralized management. Currently many retailers believe that where substantial economies of scale are possible, such as for product development and merchandising systems, information technology and vendor management should be centralized. Others functions, such as merchandising and distribution, should be decentralized. However, retailers adopt many different approaches. By centralizing the buying of merchandise for men and children in Brussels and for women in Dusseldorf, C&A can replenish European stores up to nine times a day because of its excellent logistics system, although it operates in 14 countries through 600 stores and uses 12 different own-labels. Similarly, IKEA has a single logistics system for moving products from points of production to individual stores, and Toys'R'Us has toy manufacturers that deliver to centralized warehouses.

Since local joint venture partners are often mandatory (for example, in the Philippines) or necessary, who to select and what should be the role of each partner is a crucial question. Carrefour – as a late entrant in Mexico – ended up with a less satisfactory local partner because Wal-Mart already had Cifra, the most suitable Mexican retailer, tied up in a joint venture. In contrast, the situation was reversed in Brazil, where Carrefour had first-mover advantage. Managing joint ventures is never easy, and Wal-Mart and Thailand's Charoen Pokphand partnership, established to enter China and Hong Kong, broke up. Each partner accused the other of wanting too much control. Other joint ventures fail because each partner has a different view of the speed of development and thus of the cash infusion necessary.

While international retailers are investing heavily in bricks and mortar, the Internet allows a retailer to go international immediately at low costs. Amazon.com, which sells books through the Internet only, is a prime example. In contrast to the traditional book industry, which is drowning in excess inventory because it cannot develop an effective goods return policy, Amazon.com carries no stocks – books are shipped directly from wholesalers. As a result it incurs few inventory and real estate costs while offering 2.5 million titles, including every English-language book in print. This contrasts with the 170,000 titles offered at even the largest book superstores.

International market power

Historically, retailers used to be at the mercy of powerful multinational manufacturers such as Unilever, Nestlé and Procter & Gamble. Today some retailers find themselves much bigger than their suppliers, and size brings power. Both Tesco and Wal-Mart, for example, have annual sales which are larger than many of their suppliers. These international retailers are increasingly using international sourcing, which puts considerable stress on manufacturers' pricing policies. All international purchases by Carrefour go through its international merchandising group in Brussels. Similarly, Promodes buys through its 'world trade centre' in Geneva. Others, such as the French food chain Leclerc, are joining 'buying clubs' such as Zurich-based Eurolec. Manufacturers face tough decisions whether to reduce prices in high-profit countries or raise prices in cheaper countries in an effort to control transhipments.

A related problem is the recent practice of international retailers demanding a single international price from packaged consumer goods companies. However, companies such as Unilever and Procter & Gamble are decentralized and organized around individual country managers who are responsible for profit. It is therefore difficult for them to present an integrated face to international retailers. In the future manufacturers will perhaps have to develop international account teams to interact with international retailers. These accounts may have to be handled at headquarters, but legal and tax issues can make this difficult.

The internationalization of retailing is pushing manufacturers to develop international brands. For example, when Nestlé dispensed with its national brands in favour of an international 'Nestlé' brand, one of its first tests was at EuroDisney near Paris, where it offered 'Nestlé' ice cream to gauge the reaction of European consumers. It is likely that international brands will help manufacturers regain part of their lost market power. Finally, the shift in bargaining power has resulted in consolidation at the manufacturing level. The most recent example of this is in the toy industry, where only a few international manufacturers are left.

Retail management implications

A good understanding of the international market environment by retail management will result in better operational performance in international markets. A retailer must be able to establish and position itself in its chosen market in order to achieve a competitive advantage. In an international environment, the retailer's success will also depend on its ability to position its product against competing products. Many retailers (such as IKEA, Benetton and McDonald's) operating in an international market environment tend to attach great importance to their products. Thus, for successful operation in an international market, the retail management must adopt a practical approach to its image and product positioning. This is necessary because one of the success factors for international operation (Alexander and Myers 2000) is a distinguishable and clearly positioned product. Similarly, uniqueness in the product offer will make entry into a foreign market much easier.

Summary

There is no evidence of internationalization in the retail sector. Of the 49 retailers regarded as 'global' in the Fortune 500 list, 18 are purely domestic, 24 are very concentrated in their home triad (with intra-regional sales), only five are bi-regional and only one is global. This is not evidence of globalization but of regional business, indeed mainly local retail business. While, the retail industry is becoming more 'international' and there is overall a new need for firms to expand abroad to generate new growth, this is not 'global' activity. Most of the international expansion is within the local home triad region of the retail MNE. International business is not synonymous with global business. Instead a regional solution to strategy is required.

This chapter has attempted to outline international market process and positioning by retailers and their motives for internationalization, which were reviewed in terms of choice of entry strategy and feasibility, bearing in mind that markets are different in characteristics and demand. It is therefore necessary that before going global, retailers be adequately positioned. The positioning strategy consists of making the retail organization or its products distinct and important in consumers' minds. Positioning must consider basic corporate policy, portfolio strategy and competitive strategy.

In the current competitive international retail marketing environment, strategic partnerships have become an important corporate survival strategy. The combined strengths of the partners can permit them to perform better in global markets.

Revision questions

1 Define and explain the differences between 'international' and 'global' with reference to retail organizations.
2 What do you consider to be the main driving force for retail internationalization?
3 What are the main strategy options for retailers going international, and on what basis is one option preferred?
4 Discuss and explain the opportunities that exist for retailers in the international market environment.
5 What do you see as the major challenges for retailers in the international markets?
6 What characteristics of a retail organization may have important implications for market entry decisions?
7 The international marketing performance of retailers is likely to be influenced by the extent of the retailer's knowledge of the international environment. Discuss the factors that may influence the retailer's international marketing performance.
8 The task of identifying the optimum positioning in a foreign market is very difficult and requires extensive research into several aspects of the market. What are these aspects?
9 Explain how international retailers could use retail format as a differential advantage.
10 Historically, retailers used to be at the mercy of powerful multinational manufacturers. Today some retailers find themselves much bigger than their suppliers. Discuss the implication of this shift in power base for manufacturers.

Louis Vuitton Moet Hennessy (LVMH): global retailer

LVMH is the French-based luxury goods group that was founded in 1987 with the merger of Louis Vuitton and Moet Hennessy, largely masterminded by Bernard Arnault. In 2006 the group had sales of €11.6 billion (up from €8.5 billion in 2003) and captured 15 per cent of the world market share of luxury items (including wines). LVMH currently has 1,350 stores world-wide and employs about 63,500 people, most of whom work outside France. While 16 per cent of all revenues are earned in France, 26 per cent come from the United States, 18 per cent from the rest of Europe, and 15 per cent from Japan, with the remaining 25 per cent being generated primarily in Asia and Latin America. In other words, the group is close to the ideal global definition.

One benefit of this global presence is a more diversified market risk. This helped the group as a whole to overcome the Asian market crisis. Customers everywhere recognize LVMH's famous brand names such as Christian Dior, Dom Perignon, Givenchy and Moët & Chandon. The luxury market grows by about 10 per cent annually and attracts very strong competition. Included in this group are such internationally known firms as Gucci, owned by PPR, Richemont, owner of Cartier, and Bulgari. In order to be successful in this industry, it is very important to have an effective organizing strategy. The four fashion houses of the group operate ten owned stores in the ten largest cities of the world. Christian Dior alone runs 116 stores. The group left a pure manufacturing and marketing strategy to also integrate a retail dynamic that totally changed its organization and the structure of its margins.

LVMH's organizational arrangement is much more than that of a typical conglomerate. The whole organization focuses on shared costs and synergies, both backward and forward along its value chain. The company has organized itself around its five main lines of business. These groups, which are really strategic business units (SBUs), are set up so that they can sell nationally known, high-quality products in a way that both addresses local cultural tastes and takes local rules and regulations into consideration:

- Fashion and Leather Goods, which owns such world-famous brand names as Louis Vuitton, Loewe, Celine, Berluti, Kenzo, Givenchy, Christian Lacroix, Marc Jacobs, Fendi, StefanoBi, Emilio Pucci and Thomas Pink.
- Wines and Spirits, which markets Moët & Chandon, Dom Perignon, Veuve Clicquot, Krug, Pommery, Mercier, Runart, Canard Duchène, Chateau d'Yquem, Chandon Estates, Cloudy Bay, Cape Mentelle, Hennessy, Hine, Newton and Mount Adam.
- Perfumes and Cosmetics, which sells Parfums Christian Dior, Guerlain, Parfums Givenchy, Parfums Kenzo, Bliss, Hard Candy, Benefit Cosmetics, Urban Decay, Fresh and Make Up For Ever.
- Watches and Jewellery, which markets such brands TAG Heuer, Ebel, Zenith, Benedom, Fred, Bhaumet and Omas.
- Selective Retailing, which includes a wide variety of operations including Duty Free Shops, Miami Cruiseline, Sephora Europe, Sephora AAP, Le Bon Marché, La Samaritaine and Solstice.

The profit margin on luxury goods is very high, so control over production, distribution and advertising are central to profitability. In the manufacture of its high-quality merchandise, for example, LVMH ensures that production standards are the highest and the 'Made in France' label is used appropriately so as to appeal to its market niches. The country-specific advantage is obvious and materializes globally, entailing little adaptation in the group's forward strategy. Because it only sources in France, Italy and Switzerland, LVMH keeps the dream alive for its world-wide customers. The company also markets its brand names internationally so that buyers everywhere are familiar with them. One way it does this is by setting aside 11 per cent of all sales to be used exclusively for advertising. On a centralized basis, LVMH also uses a common laboratory for cosmetics research, employs bulk media buys so that it gets the most value for its promotional dollar, and integrates the operations for all of the branch offices in each group to ensure maximum efficiency.

By carefully overseeing major operations from the top while allowing the individual SBUs to make those decisions that directly affect local markets, LVMH employs a combination of 'tight and loose' control which it uses to maximize its international presence to the extent it has become the most global retail company. The presence has a severe cost, however, for the time being, but may well pay off in the longer run. The key indicator is a 100 per cent drop of the group's profitability in three years which coincided with the boost given in the retailing direction through the acquisition of the US-based Duty Free Shops (DFS). When the deal was settled, the goal was to grab the hefty Asia-Pacific travel market, as DFS had 180 airport concessions in this area. The timing was bad, however, and when the Asian crisis and a persistent Japanese recession hit the Japanese travel business, the investment became a burden.

Furthermore, new DFS-LVMH products-only types of luxury supermarket put off some customers. Some competitors were reluctant to sell through the LVMH network. In order to compensate for lost sales revenues in the Pacific, and after closing down 15 concessions and firing 3,000 employees, the management decided in 1999 to launch the DFS Galleria in major US tourist centres. These are small downtown shopping malls for luxury items. In addition Sephora Inc, LVMH's beauty retail chain, was started.

The main US department stores like JC Penney and Federated Department Stores, however, perceived these steps as a declaration of war; all of a sudden, their supplier became their competitor. Some cosmetic vendors like Chanel and Estée Lauder even refused to sell at Sephora. Bernard Arnault's vision of a totally integrated group is necessary to become an industry leader, which also requires innovative management and new international alliances. By internalizing the new multi-brand retail business, the management made some mistakes and maybe went too fast. But LVMH has benefited from this experience to become a true global retailer.

Sources: Compiled from several sources including http://www.lvmh.com, Matlack (2006), *Business Week* (2006), Merrill Lynch (2005), http://investing.businessweek.com/research/ stocks/snapshot/snapshot.asp?symbol=LVMH.PA

Seminar questions

1 Discuss what you consider to be the success factors for LVMH in the global market where many other retailers have failed.
2 What aspect(s) of LVMH SBUs would you consider developing further and in what direction?
3 Evaluate Bernard Arnault's vision of a 'total integrated group' and explain how you would implement this vision if you were made responsible.

Managerial assignment task

Your retail organization based in the United Kingdom is considering expanding into the international market. Write a report to your managing director in support of the expansion proposal. Justify your claim that this move will be a success.

References

Akehurst, G. and Alexander, N. (1995) 'Developing a framework for the study of the internationalization of retailing', *Service Industries Journal*, Vol. 15, No. 4, pp. 205–9.

Alexander, N. and Myers, H. (2000) 'The retail internationalization process', *International Marketing Review*, Vol. 17, No. 4/5, pp. 334–53.

Arnold, S. J. and Fernie, J. (2000) 'Wal-Mart in Europe: prospects for the UK', *International Marketing Review*, Vol. 17, No. 4/5, pp. 416–32.

Aurifeille, J.-M., Quester, P. G., Lockshin, L. and Spawton, T. (2002) 'Global vs. international involvement-based segmentation: a cross-national exploratory study', *International Marketing Rev iew*, Vol. 19, No. 4, pp. 369–86.

Business Week (2006) 'The sweet smell of success', 16 July.

Calori, R., Johnson, G. and Sarnin, P. (1994) 'CEO's cognitive maps and the scope of the organization', *Strategic Management Journal,* Vol. 15, pp. 437–57.

Chee, H. and R. Harris (1998) *Global Marketing Strategy*, London: Financial Times/Pitman.

Dunning, J. H. (2001) *Global Capitalism at Bay?* London: Routledge.

Evans, J., Treadgold, A. and Mavondo, T. (2000) 'Psychic distance and the performance of international retailers: a suggested theoretical framework', *International Marketing Review*, Vol. 17, No. 4/5, pp. 373–91.

Fortune (2002) The Fortune Global 500, July.

Govindarajan, V. and Gupta, A. (2002) *The Quest for Global Dominance*, San Francisco, Calif.: Jossey-Bass.

Guy, C. (2001) 'Internationalization of large-format retailers and leisure providers in Western Europe: planning and property impacts', *International Journal of Retail and Distribution Management*, Vol. 29, No. 10, pp. 452–61.

Hollander, S. (1970) *Multinational Retailing*, East Lansing: Michigan State University.

Leknes, H. M. and Carr, C. (2004) 'Globalization, international configurations and strategic implications: the case of retailing', *Long Range Planning*, Vol. 37, pp. 29–49.

Matlack, C. (2006) 'Identity crisis at LVMH?' *Business Week*, 11 December.

McGoldrick, P. J. (2002), *Retail Marketing*, 2nd edn, London: McGraw-Hill.

McGoldrick, P. J. and Davies, G. (eds) (1995) *International Retailing: Trends and Strategies*, London: Pitman.

Merrill Lynch Equities (2005) 'European luxury goods'.

Moore, C. M., Fernie, J. and S. Burt (2000) 'Brands without boundaries – the internationalization of the designer retailer's brand', *European Journal of Marketing*, Vol. 34, No. 8, pp. 919–37.

Muniz-Martinez, N. (1998), 'The internationalization of European retailers in America: the US experience', *International Journal of Retail and Distribution Management*, Vol. 26, No. 1, pp. 29–37.

O'Grady, S. and Lane, H. (1996) 'The psychic distance paradox', *Journal of International Business Studies,* Vol. 27, No. 2, pp. 309–33.

Omar, O. (1999) *Retail Marketing*, London: Financial Times/Pitman.

Omar, O. E. (1998) 'Franchising agreements in new car retailing: an empirical investigation', *Service Industries Journal*, Vol. 18, No. 2, pp. 144– 60.

Rugman, A. (2000) *The End of Globalization*, London: Random House.

Rugman, A. and Cruz, J. (2002) *Multinationals as Flagship Firms: Regional Business Networks*. Oxford: Oxford University Press.

Rugman, A. and Girod, S. (2003) 'Retail multinational and globalization: evidence is regional', *European Management Journal*, Vol. 21, No. 1, pp. 24–37.

Schlie, E. and Yip, G. (2000) 'Regional follows global: strategy mixes in the world automotive industry'. *European Management Journal*, Vol. 18, pp. 343–56.

Vida, I. (2000) 'An empirical inquiry into international expansion of US retailers', *International Marketing Review*, Vol. 17, No. 4/5, pp. 454–75.

Vida, I. and Fairhurst, A. (1998) 'International expansion of retail firms: a theoretical approach for future investigation', *Journal of Retailing and Consumer Services*, Vol. 5, No. 3, pp. 143–51.

15

The Internet and International Marketing

Contents

LEARNING OBJECTIVES

After reading this chapter you should:

- be able to define e-commerce and describe the relevance of its elements for international marketing operations
- be able to explain the Internet as an international marketing tool
- know the use and importance of the Internet in international marketing operations

- be able to evaluate the application of technology for standardizing international marketing operations
- understand the security issues associated with the use of the Internet for international marketing.

Introduction

Attention to the role of the Internet in business activities has intensified, as evidenced by the growing volume of information on the subject in business and trade publications. Academic inquiry on the subject has also accelerated, with many contributions attempting to define the Internet's role in marketing and seeking new paradigms that appropriately incorporate this new medium in marketing theory. Nicknamed the 'information superhighway', the Internet has the potential of resolving some long-standing problems associated with international marketing operations. Information acquisition, market access, international marketing promotion and the costs associated with these activities are critical impediments to international market entry.

This chapter explores the roles of the Internet in international marketing. As the Internet continues to grow at a rapid rate around the world, and as the information technology (IT) industry is currently sharply focused on conceiving, developing and marketing Internet-based software and products, it is difficult to imagine a universal framework that is all-encompassing and applies equally to the current understanding of this medium, as well as to the many unforeseen applications that will evolve in the years to come. After all, the World Wide Web (WWW) was only conceived in 1989 (*Economist* 1998). Furthermore, from a conceptual viewpoint, the understanding of the potential applications of the Internet in any business will necessarily be confined to the understanding of its existing paradigms.

This chapter reviews the suitability and the use of the Internet in international marketing. It addresses the difficulty of acquiring a sustainable competitive advantage via the Internet, the derived nature of consumer demand, security concerns, structural impediments in using the Internet, and the transaction-versus process-based use of the Internet for international marketing. In particular, the use and penetration of the Internet are significantly influenced by key structural impediments of various nations. A conceptual framework that defines the role of the Internet in international marketing is offered. According to the framework, the appropriateness and the extent to which international marketer may successfully use the Internet should be assessed in light of its net incremental contribution to the profitability of a foreign market venture.

The role of e-commerce in international marketing

Electronic commerce (e-commerce) is the exchange of business information and transactions using electronic methods. These include:

- internal and external computer-connected networks such as the Internet
- the sending of purchase orders to suppliers via electronic data interchange (EDI)
- the use of telephone and fax to conduct transactions
- the use of automatic teller machines (ATMs)
- the use of electronic funds transfer at point of sale (EFTPoS)
- wireless networks and smart cards to facilitate payment and obtain digital cash.

E-commerce therefore includes all the means by which activities and transactions are conducted in a 'space' environment rather than a physical 'place' environment (see Table 15.1).

Table 15.1   The uses of e-commerce

E-commerce parameters	Functional dimensions
International information (digital products)	information retrieval information dissemination books, manuals, compact diskettes (CD) software distribution
International entertainment services	video on demand video games
International customer services	electronic help desk customization order processing product information
International marketing channels	advertising public relations market research electronic mail catalogues
International supply chain	product search logistics EDI ordering payment
International finance	buying selling payments
Other relevant services	international auctions medical information services global educational services

Some of the major uses of e-commerce in the international market environment are identified in Table 15.1. It highlights the types of digital products and services that contribute to e-commerce revenue, including information, books, CDs, software, video, education and medical services. Similarly, it points to the central role of financial transactions and payment systems.

The central role of computer-to-computer exchange is most visibly described in terms of intranets (within the corporation), extranets (between the corporation and its suppliers or customers), and the Internet (the public communication network). The components of these are shown in Figure 15.1.

E-commerce could be considered as a process innovation in international marketing whereby technology provides the capability for a reconfiguration of existing international business and channel relationships, and the scope for introduction of new operations. Dussart (2000) for example, argues that the Internet engendered eight concomitant and interrelated 'revolutions' in the business world:

- revamping management
- restoring control
- relaunching the economy

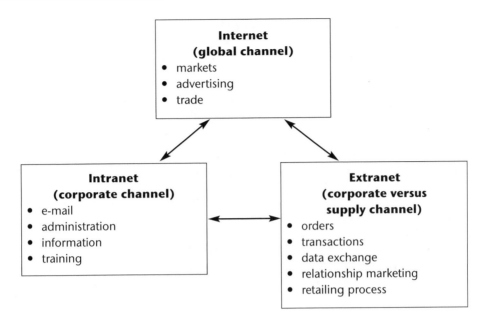

Figure 15.1 Different channel networks in e-commerce

- reconfiguring offers
- restructuring markets
- redistributing power
- redefining relationships
- reorganizing channels.

This process innovation in international markets arises from the ability of the Internet to provide electronic links between dispersed sources of information, the enhanced collection and use of real-time data, the replacement of inventory with information, and the changing of traditional tasks and roles in the distribution channel.

E-commerce as a marketing process innovation

Dawson (2001) points to 'new commerce' as being comprised of an innovative force, laden with information, enabling companies to speed up activities and increase their scope:

- New commerce companies operate through multiple marketing channels.
- Channel structures in new commerce are intermediated in new ways.
- New commerce retailers operate internationally.
- New commerce uses new forms of non-price competition.
- In new commerce, organizational scale and scope economies become more important than establishment scale and scope economies.

- New commerce companies do not subscribe to a traditional view of a difference between goods and services.
- New commerce companies are using the convergence of information and communications technologies as a primary source of innovation.
- New managerial ideas support innovation processes.
- Customer loyalty is a central concept in new commerce.
- Public sector policies relate to old commerce not new commerce.

Dawson suggests that processes should be altered both inside and outside the organization, and that companies can obtain advantages depending on their ability to conduct their activities effectively by e-commerce. Conversely, a failure to operate in these ways could lead to competitors moving ahead. Such are the potential impacts of the changes that there is little choice but to embrace them.

As a process innovation e-commerce provides the capability to transform traditional international marketing tasks and activities, and the associated costs, within the marketing channel. The marketing channel is traditionally viewed as a series of tasks and flows (information, inventory, payment and so on) with specific managers taking responsibility for these. Any assessment of e-commerce requires an exploration of how these activities, processes and ownership may change. For example, disintermediation has been identified as a possible outcome, with channel members displaced or removed as traditional activities transfer from one channel member to another (see Burt and Sparks 2003). On the other hand, the ease of entry to the market may allow reintermediation in some marketing channels, as more intermediaries set up as entry points to provide services, goods or information. In some cases, new activities may emerge, but as in much channel change, many tasks and activities remain, although the process innovation alters the ownership, costs, efficiency and practice of these functions.

These potential changes are the key to understanding the impact of e-commerce on physical stores. For example in retailing, e-commerce may have a number of implications for the retail marketing process, and how and where tasks are performed. The retail process comprises the sourcing of products, stockholding, inventory and store merchandising, while the marketing effort includes branding, customer selection, picking and payment, and distribution of goods by or to the consumer. In terms of growth, Forrester Research figures (2004) showed that the United States had 47 per cent of world e-commerce, Japan 13 per cent, and Germany 5.7 per cent. By region, North America had 50.9 per cent, Asia/Pacific 24.3 per cent, Europe 22.6 per cent, Latin America 1.2 per cent, and other nations 1.0 per cent.

The development of the Internet

In developing applications on the Internet, the main factor determining success is usability. If the users cannot find a product or service, they cannot buy it. Nielsen (2000) suggested that three factors – usability, simplicity and interactivity – are likely to account for the success of websites. Similarly, Heldal, Sjovold and Heldal (2004) found that efficient communications are necessary to maintain and build sustainable customer relationships via the Internet.

Ease of use should be the highest priority in web design, and usability engineering is

Table 15.2   Successful Internet usage factors

Factor	Explanation
Usability	A website must fulfil the user's needs for specific information. If the website makes it difficult to find desired information, the user is unsatisfied. Usability is an important consideration in making websites valuable, by making the information more available. This relates to treating elements such as text, content, layout and colours in a way that makes the site as easy to comprehend as possible.
Branding	It is not enough for a corporate site to be satisfactory. It should also reflect attention to how and why, in much the same way as firms do in the real world. Most corporations target specific markets (users with a specific demographic) and try to reach them through their corporate site. This implies tailored communications with different users, which is possible to a certain extent with the personalization solutions available today. Personalization can be viewed as 'building customer loyalty by building a meaningful one-to-one relationship'. The critical success factor of any personalization rests squarely on the acquisition of a picture of the user.
Human computer interaction (HCI)	How information is presented is also important. Every presentation carries the risk of giving different impressions to individual users. This could affect not only satisfaction with the site, but also the perception of the firm behind the site. Regardless of usability, users from different cultures will have different reactions from using the site. Knowledge of cultural differences is important when approaching this problem from the point of view of human-computer interaction.

an important tool to work out the technical part of the website. However a one-sided focus on usability will overlook other important elements. Nielsen (2000) recognizes cultural diversity in the use of websites, but he advises nothing more than translations and slightly different content. Also the perception of a site is likely to be different from culture to culture, influenced by all of the elements in the site, not just content and language.

A website should consist of both visual and interactive elements, and the perception of it should be immediate and direct. It should consist of a whole, not a composition of analytical elements. People from different cultures will interpret these elements differently, resulting in a different whole. Only by examining the information processes in the light of cultural diversity it is possible to foresee the different users' object models, which account for the interaction (Heldal et al. 2004). Similarly, a usable site that is adapted to cultural perception is not feasible without knowing why to adapt to whom and how.

As shown in Figure 15.2, efficient communications are necessary to maintain and build sustained customer relationships. The figure shows how communications can be optimized through the corporate website. It reveals three fields of knowledge: usability, human computer interaction (HCI) and branding. Each field alone is insufficient but taken together they can enlighten all perspectives of communication through the Internet. It is the blending of these three elements that makes the corporate website easier to use and attracts users.

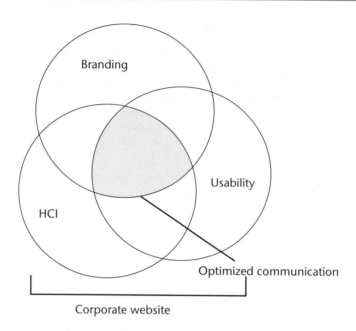

Figure 15.2 Tripartitioned approach to optimized communications
Source: Helder et al. (2004).

Internet users

Internet users can be identified using psychographic and demographic variables (Heldal et al. 2004) as shown in Table 15.3.

Technological applications

Suppliers, employees and customers can be connected via:

- phone lines
- televisions
- the Internet hosts
- cellular phones
- radios
- personal computers
- satellite dishes
- cable.

As noted by Fisk (1999), connectivity must meet the needs of employees as well as corporate customers on three levels:

- Connectivity includes networking the various suppliers, departments and locations throughout the world where the organization does business.

Table 15.3   Psychographic and demographic characteristics of net users

Psychographic factors	Demographic factors
More risk-taking	Younger
More impulsive in purchase	Higher household income
More positive toward using credit	More likely male than female
More technologically oriented	Higher education level
More self-confidence.	Mainly single
Higher shopping orientation	More likely to hold credit cards
Less price-conscious	
Positive attitude towards the net	
Higher convenience orientation	
More time conscious.	
Higher level of innovativeness	

- Individual employees need to be connected to their organization via technology.
- Customers should be included in the networking efforts. International organizations should create systems that enable customers to contact the organization for information, purchasing and customer support.

Significant investments in hardware, software and support systems are needed to make the Internet productive on all three levels.

Although marketing literature (Tiessen, Turner and Wright 2000) describes several Internet-enabled opportunities, only limited evidence exists for how firms use the Internet in their international marketing activities. It seems to be difficult to take advantage of the opportunities. Many firms believe that their products either cannot be purchased easily over the Internet because of special product characteristics or require some form of face-to-face interaction in addition to a web presence.

Tiessen, Turner and Wright's (2000) model distinguished three aspects of Internet use:

- the level of commitment to use electronic means when operating in international markets, which follows the logic of 'international commitment'
- the level of web use (from low to high), including provision of information, customized service and information (interaction), online transactions, and enabled business (pure Web-based activities)
- the issue of cultural adaptations, which focus on standardization versus customization.

Culture is the key element behind adaptation, and product and technology characteristics may also be important in considering standardization.

The Internet development stage

Clearly, as large firms gain experience with Internet use and as more powerful software and hardware technologies are offered, more sophisticated responses are likely to follow. Small firms, on the other hand, are largely domestically focused and their infrastructures and websites are primarily geared to their mainstream domestic business (Chen and Tan 2004).

Firms should not expect to gain a competitive advantage in international markets by virtue of developing a website. A competitive posture is attained though a long-term commitment to internationalization and the development of an appropriate infrastructure. Assuming that eventually all firms will established websites and their addresses are actively promoted through online and other media for domestic use, small and medium-sized enterprises (SMEs) can expect to receive inquiries from potential overseas customers searching for supplier and product information. It is also noteworthy that the Internet will not serve as a panacea for resolving market research and information needs of small firms. Much of the international market information available is not free and it is not necessarily tailor-made for smaller firms. Thus, market entry and market expansion by SMEs should not be expected to change rapidly by virtue of gaining access to the Internet.

Large corporations are best positioned to deploy the full potential of the Internet for revenue-generating activities including market research, promotional activities and sales improvement. In order to reap the benefits, the firm must make a managerial and financial commitment to develop an 'Internet infrastructure' including the staff that maintain the firm's multi-language sites for all of its intended target markets. This is a serious matter that potentially disqualifies most small firms from significant involvement in the Internet.

Adaptation process

The growth of the Internet and its acceptance among consumers have paved the way to a rise in business-to-consumer (B2C) e-commerce. It has created opportunities for virtually all companies ranging from small start-ups to Fortune 100 companies. One of the most visible business uses of the web is retailing. Retailers all over the world are establishing virtual stores, which exist in cyberspace and offer merchandise and services through an electronic channel to their customers with a fraction of the overhead required in a bricks-and-mortar store. Virtual stores enable consumer-oriented commerce, which is an e-commerce product supported by a wide variety of technological infrastructures and services.

The attractiveness and power of e-commerce lie in its impact on reshaping traditional value chains. It represents a fundamental transformation of traditional business models. However, for such a major paradigm shift to be accepted by end-users, firms have to develop resources and competencies that add value for consumers. Although there has been rapid growth, online sales volume still remains relatively low compared with alternative forms of international marketing. Consumers all over the world are realizing the benefits of shopping online, but at the same time have been impeded by factors such as:

- access to personal computers
- knowledge of technology
- security and privacy concerns
- download time
- unfamiliarity with the medium.

Internet providers initially offered so-called web strategies on a case-by-case basis using their personal experiences, observations and intuitions. This approach gave rise to a large number of conflicting strategies as a result of the lack of reliable theoretical foundation. As a result, organizations using web strategies for selling their products and services are finding that their expectation far exceeds actual achievement (Consalves et al. 1999). The technology acceptance model (TAM) and innovation diffusion theory (IDT) are used for assessing the web as a communication tool for international marketing. Based on the theory of reasoned action (Ajzen and Fishbein 1980), TAM was designed to explain the determinants of user acceptance of a wide range of end-user computing technologies. The model posits that perceived usefulness (PU) and perceived ease of use (PEOU) are the primary determinants of system use.

- PU is defined as 'the prospective user's subjective probability that using a specific application system will increase his or her job performance within an organizational context'.
- PEOU refers to 'the degree to which the prospective user expects the target system to be free of effort' (Davis, Bagozzi and Warshaw 1989).

In this model the actual system use is determined by users' behavioural intention to use (BI), which is in turn influenced by users' attitude toward using (A). Finally, A is directly affected by beliefs about the system, which consist of PU and PEOU. TAM uses the relationship between belief, attitude, intention and behaviour to predict user acceptance of technology.

Another well-established theory for user adoption is innovation diffusion theory (IDT), which posits that innovation diffusion is achieved through users' acceptance of new ideas or things. The theory explains, among many things:

- the innovation decision process
- the determinants of rate of adoption
- various categories of adopters
- the likelihood and the rate of an innovation being adopted.

According to Rogers (1995), an innovation's relative advantage, compatibility, complexity, triability and observability explain 49–87 per cent of the variance in its rate of adoption.

Originating from different disciplines, TAM and IDT have some obvious resemblances. The relative advantage construct in IDT is often viewed as the equivalent of PU construct in TAM, and the complexity construct in IDT is very similar to the PEOU concept in TAM (Moore and Benbasat 1996). Based on TAM and IDT, a base model for studying consumer acceptance of websites is displayed in Figure 15.4.

Empirical studies have suggested that TAM should be integrated with other acceptance and diffusion theories to improve its predictive and explanatory power (Hu et al. 1999). By including the compatibility (C) construct of IDT, the model is able to address the social context in which online transactions or communication take place. C is evaluated by assessing the innovation's compatibility with existing values and beliefs, previously introduced ideas and potential adopters' needs. Like PEOU, C has a significant impact on PU because if a consumer finds using the web compatible with his or her needs and lifestyle, the consumer will consider the web useful.

The weakness of TAM is that while it has been very successful in predicting user acceptance, it provides little assistance in the design and development of systems with a

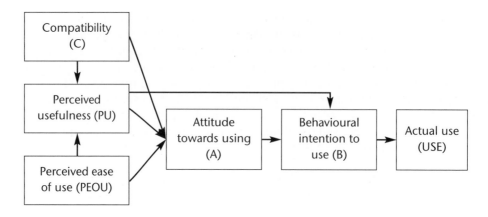

Figure 15.3 Base model for consumer acceptance of websites

Source: adapted and modified from Chen and Tan (2003).

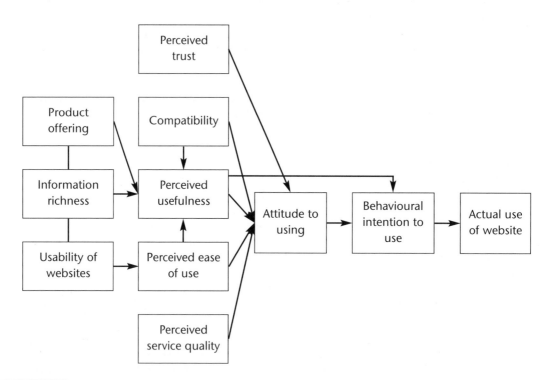

Figure 15.4 Theoretical model for consumers' acceptance of websites

high level of acceptance. Websites should be designed to tackle the obstacles that discourage consumers. Thus, in order to make the model more robust and meaningful for system designers, it is necessary to identify the determinants of PU and PEOU (see Figure 15.3). Several factors are therefore combined and employed to generate effective websites that stimulate consumer visits. Such elements include product offerings, information richness, usability of the website, perceived service quality and perceived reliability (see Figure 15.4).

Product offering

Consumers' perceptions about products are the primary determinant of shopping in a particular store (Omar 1999). The efficacy of product offerings is often judged by the breadth of product selection, pricing strategies and product retail channel fit (see Figure 15.3). The combination of these factors shapes a consumer's product perception, which influences the perceived usefulness of a website. Product variety is often an influential factor in website visit and patronage (Chen and Tan 2003).

Information richness

The informational or knowledge component of Figure 15.4 is an increasingly important part of the product offering today. Information richness plays a crucial role in shaping consumers' decision to purchase from a website. According to information richness theory (IRT) (Daft and Lengel 1986), information richness is defined as 'the ability of information to change understanding within a time interval'. Information that enables its user to clarify ambiguity and enhance understanding of issues in a timely manner is considered rich. IRT also predicts that information richness is a major determinant of user media choices.

Consumer behaviour literature reveals that a consumer typically goes through two sequential stages of information search. The first stage consists of what is already known about a product. If insufficient is known to inform a purchase, the consumer searches for additional information from, for example, acquaintances (word-of-mouth), promotions, advertisements, visual displays and so on. Both Baty and Lee (1995) and DeSarbo and Choi (1999) attribute electronic shopping failures to limited product information and low product comparability. Therefore, the quality of product information and the extent of product comparison bear heavily on the success of a website. The quality and usefulness of the information is determined by the degree to which consumers can use the information to predict their satisfaction with the product prior to the actual purchase.

Usability of websites

The digital storefront design of websites is the equivalent of physical planning for retail stores and the user interface design for any software development. The physical planning of traditional retail stores affects the retailers' ability to appeal to different market segments and operate effectively (Omar 1999). By the same token, effective user interface design of software products has great implications for the perceived ease of use and productivity by users. A virtual store's storefront is its website. A poorly designed digital storefront has an adverse influence on consumers' online shopping experience, so interface issues related to navigation, search and the ordering process must be given special attention (Lohse and Spiller 1998). Website designers must answer two main questions: will consumers be able to traverse the website effortlessly? And will consumers easily and quickly find what they want?

The answers to these questions are important because if the website is usable the chances of its being accepted and used productively are good. Similarly, Machlis (1999) found that unusable websites impede consumers' performance and satisfaction when shopping online.

Perceived service quality

As the website is used as both marketing channel and information system, service quality is crucial to its success. Perceived service quality is defined as the discrepancy between what customers expect and what customers get. Highly perceived service quality has always been associated with increased customer satisfaction and retention (Woodside and Trappey 1992). It is also acknowledged as one of the measures of information system success (Pitt, Watson and Kavan 1995). Parasuraman, Zeithaml and Berry (1988) identified five dimensions that consumers use to evaluate service quality, which can be translated into the virtual store context as follows:

- **tangibles** – the physical facilities provided by a website (the appearance of the website, the existence of online and offline customer service facilities)
- **reliability** – a website's ability to perform the promised action dependably and accurately (for example, on-time and accurate product delivery)
- **responsiveness** – a website's ability to offer help to its users in a timely fashion (for example, quick e-mail responses to customers' inquiries)
- **assurance** – a website's ability to inspire trust and confidence
- **empathy** – the caring and individualized attention given to customers (for example, personalized product suggestions).

Besides the traditional dimensions of services, self-service, logistic service, personalization and customization are presenting new opportunities and challenges for usable websites. At the highest level, usable websites can establish virtually one-to-one relationships with their customers, which is costly and difficult to achieve in other retail formats (Peppers, Rogers and Dorf 1999). On the other hand, many customers have expressed their frustration at problems with products and order fulfilment. Consumers are asking for more 'human touch' and higher service quality in website design (Orenstein 1999). Those websites that lack adequate infrastructure for superior customer services will not succeed in the electronic marketplace.

Perceived trust

A number of studies suggest that many people do not shop online because of a lack of trust in online businesses (Hart, Doherty and Ellis-Chadwick 2000). Trust has a positive influence on the development of customer attitude, intention to purchase and purchasing behaviours (Swan, Bowers and Richardson 1999). Chen and Tan (2004) suggest that personal information privacy concerns are represented in two dimensions, environmental control and secondary use of information control. Environmental control refers to consumers' ability to exert control over of a website's use of information for other purposes. When these two controls are perceived to be low, consumers are leery about giving personal information over the web. Consumers' lack of trust is also partly a result of data security concerns. Information exchange in a trustful environment is an essential part of business and consumer relationships in e-commerce. Consumer trust can only be inspired if the risks associated with online purchases are reduced to a level that is tolerable to consumers.

The Internet as an international marketing channel

In order to understand the role of the Internet in international market, the Internet–international marketing operation dyad is examined and a conceptual framework is offered in Figure 15.5.

This shows the guiding principles by which the Internet is applied to the international marketing environment. Its appropriateness should be viewed in light of its direct and indirect costs and benefits, and expressed in terms of incremental revenue attributable to its use.

International marketers cannot achieve sustainable competitive advantage solely by developing a website; competitive advantage is acquired through the skilful and proprietary ways in which the technology is deployed. Simply put, a business tool that is possessed by everyone offers no distinct competitive advantage to anyone. Hamill and Gregory (1997) suggested that the Internet has the potential of eroding some existing advantages of better-established firms and creating a level playing field by allowing almost any interested marketer to obtain a presence on the Internet and to list its address on various directories and Internet search engines. Clearly, as an increasing number of firms develop websites, absence from the Internet can create a competitive disadvantage.

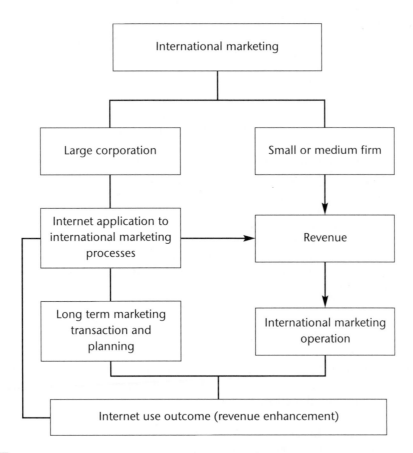

Figure 15.5 The Internet and international marketing dyad

Developing an international marketing programme with specific infrastructure within the firm is fairly involved and costly. There are many macro and micro planning and management considerations including meeting local product standards, target market pricing and competitive factors, foreign currency and payment issues, customer support and service requirements, and legal and regulatory considerations. None of these issues will be addressed by virtue of having a presence on the Internet.

Inasmuch as industrial demand is derived from consumer demand, regardless of the penetration of the Internet, the level of consumer spending may not be affected. This indicates that in the long-run (see Figure 15.5) the use of the web or other Internet-related applications cannot be expected to increase revenue for all firms, though short-run benefits might occur for some firms.

One other important consideration is related to the issue of communications security. This is of critical importance if the Internet is to make any serious impact in international marketing operations. Although some solutions have been offered, data security still remains one of the main concerns for any firm that wants to integrate the Internet in its international business. As new solutions are offered, new ways of penetrating and decoding transmitted data or computer databanks are developed, and security concerns are likely to remain an ongoing issue. Current solutions involve various methods of data encryption, which may be illegal in some nations (for example, France).

Structural impediments means that the penetration of personal computers in many nations is still in its infancy and it will be many years before potential clients and international marketers everywhere are connected to the Internet. Unlike domestic businesses that can benefit from such access, know-how and interest, international marketers cannot yet benefit from an Internet presence in many markets. These impediments limit the usefulness of the Internet for some critical business-to-business applications, but they tend to present a lesser problem for consumer marketing and general promotional activities. Although some applications of the Internet apply equally to all firms (both large and small), international firms can be divided into two groups in terms of their priority needs from the Internet: manufacturers and wholesalers that primarily wish to sell their products in large quantities to other manufacturers and/or channel members, and international marketers (businesses) that primarily wish to sell to end-users (consumers or industrial customers) in very small quantities.

These two approaches are not mutually exclusive, but they demonstrate different strategic push. The former group represents the typical international marketer, whereas the latter group resembles the activities of the retail sector. A distinction between these groups is essential because of the varied manner in which they can deploy the Internet in international markets.

Business applications of the Internet

Moen, Endresen and Gavlen (2003), identify several main business uses of the Internet, all of which have an impact on and may work to the advantage of large and small firms approaching an international market:

- an improved corporate image
- improved customer and partner relationship

- increased visibility
- reduced costs
- expanded markets
- improved customer satisfaction
- improved communications.

Kiang, Raghu and Shang (2000) compiled a similar list that shows how the use of the Internet may result in a potential market advantage. It supports the contention that when used properly, the Internet can provide a powerful competitive advantage. This is further emphasized by the increasing number of companies that are developing Internet-based strategies to support overall business development (Sim and Koi 2002). When the Internet is used as a communication channel, it enables interactive marketing, because users are actively involved in responding to a vendor's promotion campaign. In addition, the Internet offers an opportunity for companies to customize both their marketing and their products to each customer's needs. By reducing international advertising costs, the Internet may also enable companies to improve their visibility and inexpensively reach a much larger customer base.

On a broader front, the Internet has revolutionized the dynamics of international commerce and, in particular, led to the more rapid internationalization of SMEs. With Internet marketing, technology has become a more important source of competitive advantage than size, making it easier for small companies to compete on a worldwide basis. It is likely that an increasing focus on differentiation will be necessary to avoid extreme international price competition for products that are incapable of significant differentiation. This will occur as a result of intelligent agents searching the Internet, which thus favours small companies that offer specialized niche products and that will be able to acquire the critical mass of customers necessary to succeed through the Internet's worldwide reach. Similarly, the Internet's low-cost communications enable firms that have limited capital to become global actors at an early stage in their development.

Despite the marketing and promotional advantages the Internet offers, hard selling and advertiser-push promotion strategies have not worked well (Kiang et al. 2000). The reason may be the overwhelming amount of information available, but product characteristics are also important. Not all products are equally suited for Internet marketing and promotion, though this does not preclude a firm's use of the Internet for other business purposes. It may be necessary to use the traditional classification of products by nature, needs, tangibility and buying behaviour for categorizing e-market products and services. An alternative classification is of search and experience goods:

- Search goods are goods that can be evaluated by means of external information. They are more suited and more likely to be marketed on the Internet.
- Experience goods must be personally evaluated and so marketing them on the Internet is more difficult.

This is an useful way of thinking about software, which lies somewhere between a service and a product, for example. For a more thorough discussion see Kiang et al. (2000). Generally, the products that are likely to benefit most from the Internet are digital products or services with high product-customization potential and high transaction complexity.

The Internet and international marketing activities

In analysing how firms use the Internet, culture could be one of the key elements behind adoption, and product and technology characteristics may also be important in considering standardization.

The explosion of international marketing on the web raises several very important issues for the international marketing process, and calls into question many of the funda-mental tenets on which most of international marketing research and administration is based. Other issues include the barriers to international marketing operation faced by companies, the incremental internationalization process, the importance of overseas agents and distributors to international market entry, country screening, and market concentration versus market spreading. These issues and many more take on an entirely new perspective when viewed from cyberspace. The Internet provides a fundamentally different environment for international marketing and requires a radically different strategic approach.

Ellsworth and Ellsworth (1996) listed the main business uses of the Internet as:

- communications (internal and external) using email
- corporate logistics, where tools such as multi-user dialog (MUDS) and Internet relay chat (IRC), are used to achieve real-time communications across distances
- firms using the Internet to achieve more rapid internationalization
- firms using the Internet to achieve competitive advantage, for example, by creating new product opportunities or erecting barriers to entry
- cost savings from the use of online communications
- online support of inter-firm collaboration, especially in R&D
- the use of the Internet as an information search and retrieval tool
- establishment of company websites for marketing and sales promotion
- the transmission of any type of data including manuscripts and financial information.

They argued that marketing and sales promotion, both business-to-business and direct to customers, have been transformed by the web. A good website can for example be used for advertising, corporate visibility, brand name recognition, public relations, press releases, corporate sponsorship, direct sales, customer support and technical assistance. The key to achieving these benefits is a well-designed site and effective marketing of the site to ensure a large number of hits. Successful websites have a number of common characteristics:

- information-rich and regular updating to encourage repeat visits
- clear navigation paths to allow smooth movement around the site
- the provision of value-added to the user in the form of real information and services rather than just a place for marketing and sales
- interactivity and responsiveness to user feedback
- design that allows the gathering of information about users
- integration with other marketing channels used by the company
- institutional support: for example, the site should have its own budget and be supported by the whole organization rather than being the responsibility of a small group of technical staff.

Finally, the site needs to be marketed properly in order to ensure high access. This can be done in various ways including registering the site with all major online search engines, establishing reciprocal cross-linkages to other sites and ensuring that the URL is used in all company correspondence. The design of the website in this way will direct the strategic position of the company's Internet application. The potential advantages of effective Internet marketing could therefore be summarized as:

- improved corporate image
- improved customer and investor relations
- finding new customers
- increased visibility
- cost reduction
- market expansion
- improved internal communications.

These general uses of the net can translate into specific improvements in international marketing performance.

A strategic positioning matrix for identifying the forces that influence and shape the type of Internet application most likely to add value and lead to competitive advantage at different stages of a company's development is show in Figure 15.6. As it shows, the Internet's competitive value for a particular organization will reflect the interaction of customer connectivity and external competitive forces with internal network access and core applications. Four main competitive advantages (Cronin 1996) are available:

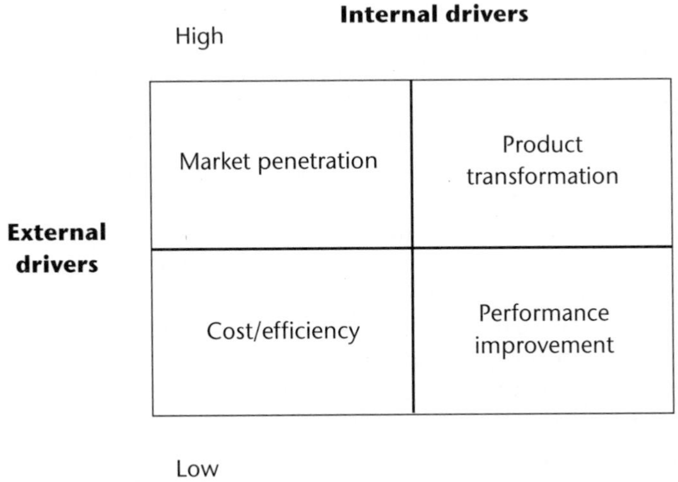

Internal drivers

High

Market penetration	Product transformation
Cost/efficiency	Performance improvement

External drivers

Low

Key:
Internal drivers: Collaboration/information and systems requirements/cost containment.
External drivers: customer connectivity/competition/technology.

Figure 15.6 Strategic positioning for Internet applications

- cost/efficiency savings achieved through substituting the Internet for other communications channels with vendors, information providers and business partners
- performance improvements from the widespread internal use of the Internet to integrate information resources, support virtual teams and facilitate distributed decision making and organizational flexibility
- market penetration which can be achieved from high external connectivity with customers, including public websites and online customer support
- product transformation including the development of Internet-based products and services that redefine the company's strategic position.

Finally, the adoption of the Internet for expediting international marketing processes and fulfilling revenue enhancement goals is likely to be influenced by culture. Some international transactions, particularly in high-context cultures, revolve around personal contacts, and as the Internet is a relatively impersonal medium, attempts to automate processes and transactions are not likely to be well received in such markets. Thus, the Internet will probably gain a better acceptance where transactions are less personal and/or policy-driven (for example, the purchase of standardized industrial products). Furthermore, the Internet's role in purchase decisions is less likely to be influenced by culture when the product (or service) in question is more of a commodity rather than differentiated.

Summary

It is apparent that Internet use and its penetration in international marketing are controlled by the structural impediments that are present to varying degrees everywhere. The Internet cannot gain broad acceptance by international marketers at a faster speed than these allow. In addition, the international marketing strategy adopted by the firm will control the nature and the potential impact of the Internet in international marketing. The extent of Internet application is further governed by the role that marketing plays in an international business, the firm's level of commitment and investment in international marketing activities, and its application and transaction types. The direct and indirect outcome of these activities will result in international marketing revenue enhancement.

A critical consideration is the Internet's relative advantage for efficiency and customer information and service support over the standard international marketing strategies pursued by multinational firms. Presence on the Internet is neither free nor a one-time expense. The costs include hardware, software, and trained personnel to manage and update web sites, and are not negligible. Forrester Research for example reported set-up costs ranging from US$200,000 to US$2.8 million depending on the nature and comprehensiveness of the site (Heldal et al. 2004). The Internet-related functions need not necessarily be internal to the firm, however, and can readily be bought in.

As with any other investment a firm makes, the value of Internet investments ought to be viewed in light of expected returns and opportunity cost (for example, against increased participation in international promotions). In other words, resource allocation to the Internet ought to be calculated in light of its potential return to the firm.

Revision questions

1 What do you consider to be the roles of the Internet in relation to international marketing operations?

2 Define what you understand by the term e-commerce, and explain its functions in the international marketing environment.

3 As a process innovation, e-commerce provides the capacity to transform traditional international marketing tasks and activities, and the associated costs, within marketing channels. Explain this statement in full with specific industry examples.

4 What do you consider to be the main determinants of a successful website?

5 Using demographic and psychographic variables, classify the Internet users for your organization.

6 Explain how you could use the technology acceptance model in conjunction with innovation diffusion theory to assess the World Wide Web as a communication tool for international marketing.

7 Although there are several Internet-enabled opportunities for international marketing operations, most firms have difficulties with using the Internet in their marketing activities abroad. Discuss why.

8 What factors could website designers employ in order to generate effective websites that stimulate consumer visits and purchases?

9 Evaluate the advantages and disadvantages of the Internet for international marketers.

10 In terms of general commercial usage, discuss with suitable business examples the main commercial uses of the World Wide Web.

SEMINAR CASE STUDY

The use of the Internet by Scult Software Company (SSC)

This case study focuses on how Scult Software Company (SSC), a (fictional) small software firm, uses the Internet in its international marketing activities. The software sector has several notable features: it is one of the world's fastest-growing industries, its products can be distributed electronically, and software companies are 'Internet literate'. This case study suggests that a small firm such as SSC can use the Internet to search for information about customers, distributors and partners. The Internet does not replace personal selling, and SSC products have a rather complex purchasing process. Its managers found that there is a need for extensive communication with customers before they can make purchase decisions. SSC's standardized software products are most suited for Internet-based sales; however standardization reduces SSC's competitive advantage and profit margins.

SSC was established in 1985 and since has become one of the leading knowledge-engineering companies in the United Kingdom. The firm employs approximately 150 people and its annual revenue is about US$8.7 million. It has a low degree of export sales, which are estimated at approximately 10 per cent of total revenue. The company recently increased its focus on international markets and is about to establish itself in several foreign markets. It currently has clients in the United States, Sweden and France.

Like many other software firms, SSC's most significant use of the Internet was initially for support activities. These activities generate revenue and improve customer relations.

Partnership agreements with well-known firms, positive product reviews, and image building through the Internet were important to SSC in order to reduce the uncertainty that potential customers often experience when unknown suppliers offer unfamiliar products.

Marketing literature has identified the use of the Internet as a tool to facilitate the internationalization of small firms (see for example, Moen 2002). Most managers at SSC expect important changes in how their business is conducted via the Internet; however many of these expectations have yet to be fulfilled. For example, sales and online transactions are two of the most disappointing issues in terms of the benefits of Internet use to SSC and other small firms. It is difficult for managers to evaluate how beneficial Internet marketing would be before they actually commit substantial capital to it and risk interfering with current distribution channels.

SSC was selected for this study for several reasons. First, the major obstacle for small businesses that use the Internet is the lack of in-house technological competency. This is not a problem for SSC. On the contrary, the most innovative and advanced Internet solutions are found in software companies. Second, another typical hindrance is that customers have limited ability and experience in Internet use. This again is not an issue for SSC. Third, SSC's software seems ideally suited for commercialization through the Internet because it can be distributed electronically.

It is likely that SSC and other software small firms rely on the Internet more than firms in other business sectors. In addition to its being more 'Internet literate,' it has first-hand experience with how the Internet can improve the effectiveness and efficiency of its business relationships and make it more competitive.

The company's target customers are large industrial enterprises, government agencies and international organizations. It offers knowledge-system architectures that enable the explicit representation of knowledge, and SSC must satisfy an organization's operational needs for knowledge and information support. This suggests that the system must be tailored for each customer, though it is usually built on a standard company platform. The services are project based, and generate revenue from both consulting and licensing of the standard platform. These services are rather expensive and cost up to US$1 million. When a project is completed, SSC offers support services and updates for its information systems.

The company's software classification falls between a service and a product. Theoretically, a service has four characteristics that distinguish it from a product: intangibility, simultaneity, heterogeneity and perishability. A product has a physical presence, whereas software exists only within another medium and thus is intangible, as is a service. A service is simultaneous; clients consume it at the same time that it is being produced. This is not the case with software. The heterogeneity of a service means that its quality cannot be judged before a customer has received it. This is true for some parts of the software industry because product development is project based, unique for each client, and often accompanied by organizational change. Thus, software's quality cannot be determined before users have begun working with it.

A service is perishable because it cannot be stored; when it has not been used, it disappears forever, whereas a produced good does not go away until it is destroyed. Software has the particularity that when it has been developed, it can be reproduced infinitely at almost no production cost. This makes it difficult to classify in terms of perishability, but in terms of a service, it represents no value in the form of material goods when it is not being consumed. In terms of distribution, software also falls between a service and product. Whereas a service is always consumed as it is produced, and as such has no distribution possibilities, a product has a physical presence and must be brought to consumers. Software may also need to be brought to users when it is produced, but because of its nature, it can be distributed electronically and therefore has insignificant distribution costs.

SSC sells its services predominantly through its relationships with former customers and research and development partners. It does not put many resources into marketing. It often generates sales because companies have learned of its services from other clients or partners. Companies that are interested in its services can contact the company through its Internet site, but the services and systems it offers are complicated, so closing a sale mandates in-depth explanations and demonstration. Consequently, a face-to-face meeting with hands-on testing is required.

The company considers the Internet and electronic communications important; they are powerful tools for communicating with customers and employees working abroad. The use of these technologies also enables people at different sites to work on the same project, because data files can be downloaded remotely. Thus, human resources can be exploited rationally, in turn lowering costs and reducing travel for employees.

SSC also employs Internet technology as a communication channel for customers and partners. The company has developed an extranet with a portal to which customers are granted access. Each customer has a login that leads to a tailor-made site. SSC can then choose to differentiate the information that it gives different clients. SSC accomplishes client support and follow-up chiefly through the site, which gives clients information about how their requests and problems are being treated and provides access to additional information. In this way, every customer receives individual follow-up. SSC considers this to be a powerful tool in developing strong bonds between itself and its customers.

Seminar questions

1 Discuss what you consider to be the competitive advantage of SSC in marketing its software products and services to its international clients.
2 What problems could you anticipate for SSC as a small firm developing and distributing its knowledge-based services via the Internet?
3 Discuss the nature of SSC's customers and describe how they can be best served with computer-based products.

Managerial assignment task

As online shopping is expected to grow substantially, there is increased interest in knowing more about international consumers' online shopping behaviour. Studies have shown that online shoppers tend to have higher than average education and income, and are more likely to be in middle to senior management or professionals. Online shoppers who have higher income tend to be less price-sensitive and more convenience-oriented. They also have more wired lifestyles, with high usage of the Internet for emails, news and so on

In Singapore, a report in the *Business Times* and an online survey (Sim and Koi, 2002) showed that demographically, a typical net shopper was male, aged between 18 and 40, had attended at least secondary school and was from a home with an average income of at least $5,000. The online survey also showed that cyber-buyers were also mainly Chinese, below 36 years old, with diplomas or degrees, and drawing a monthly salary of less than $3,500. The main discriminating factors appeared to be gender and income. The same survey also found that non-online shoppers in Singapore were more conservative and less risk taking. Some were worried about the quality of the merchandise while others were concerned about the security of the modes of payment. Yet others were worried about the worthiness of the sellers. Most of the non-online shoppers had a high shopping orientation, as most said they enjoyed conventional shopping.

You are currently a senior manager responsible for international market development for a small software firm based in the United Kingdom, which intends to market its computer software and services to Singapore. Consider the demographic characteristics of online shoppers in Singapore, and write a brief report to your executive director explaining which segment of this market you think your company should target and how.

References

Ajzen, I. and Fishbein, M. (1980) *Understanding Attitudes and Predicting Social Behaviour*, Englewood Cliffs, N.J.: Prentice-Hall.

Baty, J. B. and Lee, R. M. (1995) 'InterShop: enhancing the vendor/customer dialectic in electronic shopping', *Journal of Management Information Systems*, Vol. 11, No. 4, pp. 9–31.

Burt, S. and Sparks, L. (2003) 'E-commerce and the retail process: a review', *Journal of Retailing and Consumer Services*, Vol. 10, pp. 275–86.

Chen, L. and Tan, J. (2004) 'Technology adaptation in e-commerce: key determinants of virtual stores acceptance', *European Management Journal*, Vol. 22, No. 1, pp. 74–86.

Cheung, W. M. and Huang, W. (2002) 'An investigation of commercial usage of the World Wide Web: a picture from Singapore', *International Journal of Information Management*, Vol. 22, Issue 4, pp. 377–88.

Consalves, G. C., Lederer, A. L., Mahaney, R. C. and Newkirk, H. E. (1999) 'A customer resource life cycle interpretation of the impact of the world wide web on competitiveness: expectations and achievements', *International Journal of Electronic Commerce*, Vol. 4, No. 1, pp. 103–20.

Cronin, M. J. (1996) *Global Advantage on the Internet*, New York: Van Nostrand Reinhold.

Daft, R. L. and Lengel, R. H. (1986) 'Organizational information requirements, media richness and structural design', *Management Science*, Vol. 32, No. 5, pp. 554–71.

Davis, F. D., Bagozzi, R. P. and Warshaw, P. R. (1989) 'User acceptance of computer technology: a comparison of two theoretical models', *Management Science*, Vol. 35, No. 8, pp. 982–1003.

Dawson, J. A. (2001) 'Is there a new commerce in Europe? *International Review of Retail, Distribution and Consumer Research*, Vol. 11, pp. 287–99.

DeSarbo, W. S. and Choi, J. W. (1999) 'A latent structure double hurdle regression model for exploring heterogeneity in consumer search patterns', *Journal of Econometrics*, Vol. 89, No. 12, pp. 423–55.

Dussart, C. (2000) 'Internet: the one-plus-Eight "revolutions"', *European Management Review*, Vol. 18, No. 4, pp. 386–97.

Economist (1998) 'Brands bite back', *Economist*, 23 March, pp. 78–82.

Ellsworth, J. H. and Ellsworth, M. V. (1996) *Marketing on the Internet – Multimedia Strategies for the World Wide Web*, New York: Wiley.

Fisk, R. P. (1999) 'Wiring and growing the technology of international services marketing', *Journal of Services Marketing*, Vol. 13, Nos 4.5, pp. 311–18.

Forrester Research (2004) 'Worldwide ecommerce growth' [online] http://www.forrester.com/Er/Press/Release/0,1769,874,00.html (accessed 5 July 2008).

Hamill, J. (1997) 'The Internet and international marketing', *International Marketing Review*, Vol. 14, No. 5, pp. 300–23.

Hamill, J. and Gregory, K. (1997) 'Internet marketing in the internationalization of the UK SMEs', *Journal of Marketing Management*, Vol. 13, No. 1, pp. 9–28.

Hart, C. A., Doherty, N. and Ellis-Chadwick, F. (2000) 'Retailer adoption of the Internet: implications for retail marketing', *European Journal of Marketing*, Vol. 24, pp. 954–74.

Heldal, F., Sjovold, E. and Heldal, A. F. (2004) 'Success on the Internet: optimizing relationships through the corporate site', *International Journal of Information Management,* Vol. 24, Issue 2, pp. 115–29.

Hu, P. J., Chua, Y. K., Sheng, O. R. and Tam, K. Y. (1999) 'Examining the technology acceptance model using physician acceptance of telemedicine technology', *Journal of Management Information Systems,* Vol. 16, No. 2, pp. 91–112.

Kiang, M. Y., Raghu, T. S. and Shang, K. H. M. (2000) 'Marketing on the Internet: who can benefit from an online marketing approach', *Decision Support Systems,* Vol. 27, No. 4, pp. 383–93.

Lohse, G. L. and Spiller, P. (1998) 'Electronic shopping', *Communications of the ACM,* Vol. 41, No. 7, pp. 81–7.

Machlis, S. (1999) 'Online shoppers want on-time delivery', *Computerworld,* Vol. 33, No. 10, p. 43.

Moen, O. (2002) 'The born globals: a new generation of small European exporters', *International Marketing Review,* Vol. 19, No. 2, pp. 156–75.

Moen, O., Endresen, I. and Gavlen, M. (2003) 'Use of the Internet in international marketing: a case study of small computer software firms', *Journal of International Marketing,* Vol. 11, No. 4, pp. 129–49.

Moore, G. C. and Benbasat, I. (1996) 'Integrating diffusion of innovations and theory of reasoned action models to predict utilization of information technology by end-users', pp. 132–46 in K. Kautz and J. Pries-Heje (eds), *Diffusion and Adoption of Information Technology,* London: Chapman and Hall.

Nielsen, J. (2000) *Designing Web Usability,* Indiana: New Riders.

Omar, O. E. (1999) *Retail Marketing,* London: Financial Times/Pitman.

Orenstein, D. (1999) 'Human touch crucial to internet retailers success', *Computerworld,* Vol. 33, No. 4, p. 8.

Parasuraman, A., Zeithaml, V. A. and Berry, L. L. (1988) 'SERVQUAL: a multiple-item scale for measuring consumer perceptions of service quality', *Journal of Retailing,* Vol. 64, No. 1, pp. 12–40.

Peppers, D., Rogers, M. and Dorf, B. (1999) 'Is your company ready for one-to-one marketing?' *Harvard Business Review,* pp. 151–60.

Pitt, L. F., Watson, R. T. and Kavan, C. B. (1995) 'Service quality: a measure of information systems effectiveness', *Management Information Systems Quality,* Vol. 19, No. 2, pp. 173–85.

Rogers, E. M. (1995) *The Diffusion of Innovations,* 4th edn, New York: Free Press.

Sim, L. L. and Koi, S. M. (2002) 'Singapore's Internet shoppers and their impact on traditional shopping patterns', *Journal of Retailing and Consumer Services,* Vol. 9, Issue 2, pp. 115–24.

Swan, J. E., Bowers, M. R. and Richardson, L. D. (1999) 'Customer trust in the salesperson: an integrated review and meta-analysis of the empirical literature', *Journal of Business Research,* Vol. 44, No. 2, pp. 93–107.

Tiessen, J. H., Turner, I. and Wright, R. E. (2000) 'A model of e-commerce use by internationalizing SMEs', paper presented at the Second Annual McGill Conference on International Entrepreneurship: Researching New Frontiers, Montreal, 22–25 September.

Woodside, A. G. and Trappey, R. J. (1992) 'Finding out why consumers shop your store and buy your brand: automatic cognitive processing models of primary choice', *Journal of Advertising Research,* Vol. 32, No. 6, pp. 59–77.

Yorgey, L. A. (2000) 'Reaching the world by web', *Target Marketing,* Vol. 23, No. 7, pp. 42–6.

16
Ethics and International Marketing

Contents

LEARNING OBJECTIVES

After reading this chapter you should:

- be able to describe the nature and importance of ethics in international marketing operations
- understand the concept of corporate social responsibility
- know how ethical decisions are made in the conduct of international marketing
- understand the reasons for and the role of international fair trade movement
- understand the role of consumers' judgement of corporate unethical behaviour in relation to international marketing practice.

Introduction

In Europe and North America, business operation is normally focused and concentrated on fundamental issues including sound marketing strategy, professional marketing research, world-class product development, effective pricing, motivating promotion and appropriate distribution. Focusing on the basics makes success in competitive markets possible. However, serious problems can arise because of the differences in marketing practices between the west and the emerging markets such as China, India and Brazil. The difficulty lies in more fundamental issues than the theoretical elements of marketing mix (the 4Ps of product, price, promotion and place).

With the transition from domestic-focused operations to a true world-wide view, other factors are essential for success. One pervasive factor is culture. As we have demonstrated in earlier chapters, culture and the expectations it engenders affect all marketing transactions. It is therefore vital for all marketers to understand the expectations of their counterparts around the world.

In this regard, culture is one of the factors that affect business ethics. Ethics can be defined as 'the rules of conduct recognized in respect to a particular class of human actions or a particular group and/or culture'. Different cultures have different rules of conduct which makes the uniform application of ethics across the world difficult. This is one of the main issues addressed in this chapter.

Marketing ethics has developed in the wider context of business ethics, which reflects the interests of various stakeholders in the exchange process (Carrigan, Marinova and Szmigin 2005). The moral issues in marketing are particularly important as marketing is expected to identify, anticipate and satisfy customer requirements profitably, thus creating and sustaining the interface between consumer preferences and companies' market aspirations. Some of the problems in achieving a general consensus on ethics in marketing stem from the lack of uniform philosophical arguments about what is good and ethical and whether good and ethics have identical meaning.

In theory, companies should exist to satisfy the needs of society, and firms have a duty – a moral obligation – to deliver benefits to society. Such an argument places organizational gains as a function of the social wealth and development they create and the consumer satisfaction they deliver. Consequently the social cause is paramount in a company's conduct. By taking ethics into consideration it can be argued that it is important for companies to appear ethical; their expectations of increased sales, market share and profitability must appear to be motivated by objectives other than self-interest. Such an approach can be beneficial for a firm because consumers will perceive its operations as ethical (Boulstridge and Carrigan 2000). Thus, if companies appear to be ethical, following ethical codes and norms, and regulating their self-interest they will be rewarded by consumers. The real issue is whether companies want to merely appear ethical, or truly commit to a marketing behaviour that will place consumer and social welfare before their self-interest.

The chapter aims to provide evidence that the understanding of the roots of ethics across cultures world-wide is important for international marketing success. It reflects the research and writing of authors who are passionate supporters of the overwhelming need for international marketing ethics.

First the importance of ethics in relation to international marketing is addressed, leading to an examination of the nature of ethics in the international environment. The role of corporate ethical values is evaluated, followed by a review of the main theories under-pinning fair trading and international green marketing. Finally issues relating to the perception of consumers from various industry sectors and parts of the world are discussed.

The nature of ethics in international marketing

John Stuart Mill's (1998) idea on ethics was utilitarian: based on the consequences of action indicating that business ethics should maximize the total amount of pleasure in the world and minimize the total amount of pain, thus augmenting the scope of benefi-ciaries. Mill's understanding of ethics is intrinsically associated with the common good rather than a company's self-interest. Accordingly, marketing management represents the most disputed function in terms of utilitarian ethics. The implementation of ethics in marketing is a paradox in itself as the definition of marketing, which is predominantly utilitarian, provides marketing managers with a justification for ethical conduct when they ensure that the consequences of their behaviour are moral. It is most likely that the utilitarian concept does not always result in ethical marketing conduct. The utilitarian notion questions whether marketing activities are to be limited to an increase in the market share or profitability of a single company, should they deliver benefits to a greater number of people not involved in a company's decision-making processes.

The problem is that the common good has various interpretations and its scope is vague and not at all explicit. Should the common good be applied to a target market segment, to the mass market, to various social groups or society as a whole? In interna-tional marketing the issue becomes even more complex and acute as the common good should transcend country borders and nationalities. Will the common good reflect the good for home and host countries, for companies that engage in international marketing activities or for consumers in their domestic and international markets? The answer to these questions is that national, geographical and political categories should not be an objective basis for ethical values. Ethical values should be built upon values that are universal to everyone. So the only consistent general moral principle should be to seek the greatest good for the greatest number of people. The difficulty then arises when companies need to decide what the greatest good is, what the greatest number is and how marketing could really deliver the greatest good to the greatest number of people.

The importance of ethics

The marketing concept implies that companies need to satisfy various consumer prefer-ences that are based on their needs and wants and should also generate profit. The idea of a company's self-interest in profitability is apparently difficult to justify in Kant's view, but is acceptable in Mill's understanding of utility (Mill, 1998). The application of the marketing concept should therefore 'put the customer first' and deliver benefits to the individual consumer, the society as a whole and the company itself.

In practice, it is most likely that moral absolutes do not exist and therefore the definition of what is moral is based on the social norms of a society. Hence there are no universal moral standards applied to all peoples at all times. In marketing terms ethical relativism can justify different ethical standards applied to various countries and evolve over time. Such an interpretation of morality does allow for various interpretations of ethical norms that reflect a diversity of cultures and practices. Moreover this creates a need for marketing adaptation within a particular market over time as culture, knowledge and technology change. If moral relativism is accepted as a basis for international marketing activities, there can be no common framework for resolving moral disputes or for reaching agreements on ethical matters between companies and different societies. It can only nurture flexibility, which creates rather complex relationships with consumers in home and foreign markets with no common reference point. Thus the arguments for its implementation in the marketing of companies create unease and question the core universal values that transcend national borders.

International marketers usually present marketing as an ethically neutral system or management tool serving an unequivocal market good. Apart from occasional mistakes in presentation, marketing serves society's needs with few ethical strings attached. However, many others are likely see marketing as more profoundly value laden, and manipulative. Rather than consumer satisfaction being the main aim of marketing, the main moral imperative should be the sale. The unpredictability of the consumer is the difficulty faced by marketers whose task is to plot 'predictability'. The act of purchase and exchange is what is of interest to marketers and nothing else matters. Thus issues relating to consumer privacy, environmental pollution or resource scarcity, are not regarded as of the utmost importance. Marketing tends to get unhinged from its main position in contributing to the apparent good life. Often, it is accused of being guilty of contributing to the destructive and wasteful side of consumerist society. This conflict within the marketing community has given rise to the debate surrounding marketing ethics.

Developments in marketing responsibility

Since the 1960s groups of marketing scholars and practitioners have exploded the myth of benevolent marketing being practised on cooperative consumers. There is now acceptance within marketing circles that not all marketing does create a satisfactory outcome for consumers, if we broaden the definition of consumers to include the wider stakeholder group of society as a whole. What is desired by consumers may not necessarily be good for them (as with tobacco products), and although a marketer may create a happy customer in the short term, in the long run both consumer and society may suffer as a direct result of the marketers' actions in 'satisfying' customers (Daniels, Radebaugh and Sullivan 2007). It is the responsibility of marketers to generate new products that both provide immediate customer satisfaction and protect the long-term welfare of consumers. The most radical implication for marketing is the shift from being an agent of the seller to being an agent of the buyer, from being a marketer of goods and services to being a customer consultant. Currently, marketing ideas have focused upon the subject of marketing ethics, and there is now a flurry of activity by marketing scholars who are attempting to evaluate conceptually the nature and role of marketing ethics. Ethical issues can now be examined in advertising, personal selling, marketing research, pricing and multinational marketing.

It is clear that the scope of marketing ethics is rather broad. There have always been ethical problems in marketing, even as far back as the 'snake oil' merchants of the pioneer days. Cigarettes in their time have been marketed for their health benefits in clearing the lungs, so the existence of dubious marketing activities and outrageous product claims within the industry is nothing new. But what can now be seen is not just interest in highlighting poor ethical behaviour and vilifying those who perpetrate such crimes, but a desire to try to establish acceptable ethical guidelines and practice, and disseminate that within the industry. Regulation is a key issue, but communication is also part of the ethical movement in marketing. Rather than be defeated by the continued lack of answers to the many questions which continue to be posed, international marketers should be enthused at the prospect of such uncharted territory. It is probably true to say that developments in the field of international marketing ethics, in theory and practice, have not moved as quickly as global consumers may wish. Meanwhile one of the most reliable assertions is that change never arrives as quickly as people say it will, and when it does arrive they are never ready for it.

People are now living in the 'ethics era', whereby society's expectations of international marketers have changed and they are facing challenges to basic marketing assumptions. Consumers all over the world are better informed, more educated and awareness is greater of consumer rights and product requirements. Legislation has also played a part in raising consumer expectations of international marketing behaviour. In the past, 'caveat emptor' was justification for marketing practices that hitherto consumers were willing to accept. As consumer rights become more important, this should no longer be the case. The move towards 'caveat vendor' in some situations is challenging many basic marketing tenets, and marketing managers now have to respect and care about the welfare of those affected by their marketing decisions.

In the developed economies international marketers are being forced to recognize and confront the issues surrounding societal marketing. For example, advertisers and print media have had to face responsibility for their role in promoting 'glamorous' anorexic body images (such as the Accurist 'put some weight on' campaign; UK government anti-drug advertisements); food manufacturers and marketers have had to defend and amend the nutritional content of their products (for example McDonald's and Sunny Delight); cigarette firms (such as Phillip Morris) have had to admit the carcinogenic qualities of their products. In all these, international marketers are recognizing that they must incorporate marketing ethics into what they do if they are to remain at the leading edge of international marketing theory and practice.

Ethics in the international environment

The need to address the issues of international marketing ethics arises from the increased internationalization of multinational companies (MNCs) and the process of globalization of business. Mainstream research on marketing ethics has been mostly focused on developed economies, while emerging markets have tended to have received rather limited attention. As in business-to-consumer markets consumer support is of crucial importance for the success of marketing activities, and companies' ethical conduct towards consumers in diverse national markets is the most critical area of business ethics (Crane and Matten 2004).

Large and powerful MNCs often have bargaining power greater than that of national governments. Companies such as Coca-Cola, Nokia, General Electric, Citigroup, Wal-Mart, Microsoft, General Motors, Pfizer, Royal Dutch/Shell, HSBC, BP and Toyota have turnover and profits greater than the GDP of many developing economies. For example, ExxonMobil's estimated value-added of US$ 63 billion in 2000 was bigger than the GDP of Pakistan or Peru (Onkvist and Shaw 2004). International markets and especially those of developing countries can be vulnerable and rather exposed to unethical marketing because of their economic potential, low bargaining power, lack of legal framework and law enforcement to protect domestic companies, consumers and the society as a whole. This makes consumers less likely to benefit from marketing ethics.

Moreover, it could be argued that the goal of business and hence marketing activities should be to maximize profit within the law. If the driving force of a company is to generate and maximize profit, its behaviour in the marketplace should also be based on universal ethics for ensuring benefits for the society at large. How can we define what the limits of ethical behaviour are? The question is whether profits should be maximized in environments where protection is weak or nonexistent. In such an environment the legal framework for regulating the company–consumer interface is usually asserted on the conception of a company's interest for profit maximization subject to legal constraints. While in developed economies consumers have become powerful, those in developing countries have few legally safeguarded rights. MNCs expand into emerging international markets seeking untapped market growth potential, creating new market segments and penetrating existing ones, extending the product life cycle of outdated products, introducing new goods, acquiring and upgrading existing local brands, thus offering more choice to consumers and satisfying existing and unmet needs and wants.

In this process MNCs strive to achieve stability and profitability in international markets, and their marketing strategy implementation is often associated with unethical marketing behaviour. For example, in order to develop the market for tobacco products in Taiwan, cigarettes have been freely distributed to consumers regardless of their age and gender by fashion models and beautiful young girls in order to lure consumers into usage; when the transition from central planning to a market-led economy started in the Ukraine, MNCs were quick to engage in delivering packed cigarette gifts to consumers with the intention of increased product usage. While cigarette sales have been controlled and limited in many developed countries, the market share of cigarette producers in markets such as Russia, China and South Africa is on the rise.

The moral issues in developing and implementing marketing strategies are associated with the definition and mode of servicing target market segments. Serious ethical concerns arise from the approach of MNCs to target poor and illiterate consumers in international markets with unaffordable prices, thus either excluding them from the market or driving them into consumption which can lead to a deprivation from basic necessities. Illustrations of this are the price of life-saving medication and introducing brands as substitutes for generic commodities.

International marketers control more than the elements of the marketing mix; they play a crucial role in changing social structures, in shaping political power, knowledge transfer, and even determining economic development structures. This power and control creates major challenges for national governments who need to regulate the marketing and investment behaviour of MNCs. Under such conditions arguably MNCs should not justify their behaviour as merely legal, but set and maintain high ethical standards in their marketing activities.

One of the problems is that consumer sovereignty is a concept associated with free market economies where all authority rests with the sovereign consumer operating through the impersonal mechanism of the market and the society creates some regulatory and consumer protection mechanisms empowering individual consumers to exercise their rights. However, it could also be suggested that even in free market economies the power of MNCs to set and influence prices and to manipulate consumer response is disguised by the mystique of the market and consumer sovereignty. Following the assertion that corporations create artificial needs for unwanted products we can argue that this is even more so in developing economies where consumer rights are not protected or guaranteed by social and legal structures thus increasing consumer vulnerability and the probability of MNCs to manipulate consumers by producing artificial demand for products they do not need.

Consumers in developed countries have low individual bargaining power but a relatively high degree of consumer sovereignty, so they are able to exercise much more power on companies' marketing ethics. While age and gender are characteristics of consumer capability that have been associated with the vulnerability of children and elderly members of society world-wide, the role of experience, education and income in assessing consumer vulnerability in developing countries is of much greater importance. We might suggest that cultural norms, traditions, consumer animosity, ethnocentrism and in some cases government intervention act as a counterbalance effectively reducing the vulnerability of consumers and increasing their individual and social protective mechanisms against marketing campaigns of MNCs in developing countries.

Corporate social responsibility

This section reviews the development of the corporate social responsibility (CSR) concept and its components. It discusses different perspectives on the proper role of international organizations in society, from profit maker to community service provider. The section shows that much of the confusion and controversy over CSR stems from a failure of multinational organizations to distinguish between ethical and strategic forms of CSR. Multinational business organizations are now expected to exhibit ethical behaviour and moral management. However, over the past half century the bar has been steadily raised. Now, not only are firms expected to be virtuous, they are being called to practise 'social responsibility' or 'corporate citizenship' (Carroll 2000: 187), accepting some accountability for social welfare. International marketers, as boundary spanners responsible for the enterprise's dealings with various publics, have a primary interest in, and should take a major role in, defining and implementing their firm's social responsibility efforts. Unfortunately, too frequently marketers still focus solely on their products and markets while neglecting the social impact of their activities, as Mini case 16.1 demonstrates.

Perhaps the reason for its neglect is that the concept of CSR is a fuzzy one with unclear boundaries and debatable legitimacy. The main aim in this section is to clarify the concept by offering a detailed perspective on CSR, reviewing the different viewpoints on the role of business in society, and distinguishing three types of corporate social responsibility:

- ethical corporate social responsibility
- altruistic corporate social responsibility
- strategic corporate social responsibility.

MINI CASE 16.1

Corporate responsibility but who is responsible?

In January 2006, the SS *Ebanny*, an oil tanker belonging to Babikan Oil Company, ran around in the area just north of Vancouver, spilling millions of gallons of crude into the waters and onto the beaches of British Columbia and southern Alaska. The damage to the beaches and wildlife and consequently to the tourist industry, the ecology and the quality of life of the local residents is incalculable, but in any case it will require many millions of dollars for even the most minimal clean-up.

The ship struck a small atoll, well marked on the navigational maps, but it was a dark night and the boat was well off course. On further investigation, it was discovered that the Captain of the *Ebanny*, Mr Hoyi, had been drinking heavily. Leaving the navigation of the ship to his first mate, Mr Dunkay, he retired to his cabin to 'sleep it off'. Dunkay had never taken charge of the ship before, and it is now clear that he misread the maps, misjudged the waters, and maintained a speed that was inappropriate. The accident occurred. Subsequent inquiries showed that Captain Hoyi had been arrested on two drunken driving convictions within months of the accident. The *Ebanny* itself, a double-hulled tanker, was long due for renovation and, it was suggested, would not have cracked up if the hull had been trebly reinforced, as some current tankers were.

B B Hush, the chief executive officer of Babikan Oil. declared the accident a 'tragedy' and offered US$2 million to aid in the clean up. The premier of British Columbia was outraged. Environmental groups began a consumer campaign against Babikan Oil, urging customers to cut up and send in their Babikan Oil credit cards in protest. In a meeting to the shareholders, CEO Hush proudly announced the largest quarterly profit in the history of the Babikan Oil Company. He dismissed the protests as 'the outpourings of greenies and other fanatics' and assured shareholders that his obligation was, and would always be, to assure the highest profits possible in the turmoil of today's market.

Source: fictional example based on several real-life cases.

Questions

1 Who is responsible?
2 Against whom (if anyone) should criminal charges be levelled?
3 What should be done, if anything, to punish the corporation itself?
4 What about the CEO?

In terms of ethical corporate social responsibility, it is obligatory for any organization to avoiding societal harms. For a publicly held business altruistic CSR (doing good works at possible expense to stockholders) is not legitimate, and arguably companies should limit their philanthropy to strategic CSR (good works that are also good for the business). The legitimacy of CSR relates to a set of fundamental and crucial questions:

- Why do corporations exist?
- Should enterprises be concerned with their social performance as well as economic results?
- What does it mean to be socially responsible?
- Should economic performance be sacrificed for social performance?

- To whom do businesses owe responsibilities?
- What kinds of activities and programmes should CSR include?
- To what extent should social responsibility activities consume the company's precious resources?
- How can we measure social performance and thereby know when companies have fulfilled their societal obligations?
- What are the interests of consumer marketers in CSR efforts?

Suggestions for answering these questions are offered in this discussion based on a synthesis and analysis of relevant international marketing literature.

Social expectations

The notion that business has duties to society is firmly entrenched, although in the past several decades there has been a revolution in the way people view the relationship between business and society. Thus, corporations should be judged not just on their economic success, but also on non-economic criteria. Carroll proposed a popular four-part definition of CSR, suggesting that corporations have four responsibilities or four faces (2000: 187) to fulfil to be good corporate citizens:

- economic dimension
- legal aspects
- ethical issues
- philanthropic (which could be referred to as 'altruistic' or 'humanitarian' CSR).

In fact, much of the uncertainty about the legitimacy and domain of CSR stems from failure to distinguish the ethical and philanthropic dimensions, as well as from the misguided notion that it is somehow objectionable for business to prosper from good works. For the purpose of international marketing, the economic responsibility of the organization is the main concern.

Economic responsibility means for the company to be profitable by delivering a good-quality product at a fair price. Novak (1996) more fully delineated a set of economic responsibilities, to:

- satisfy customers with goods and services of real value
- earn a fair return on the funds entrusted to the corporation by its investors
- create new wealth, which can accrue to non-profit institutions which own shares of publicly-held companies and help lift the poor out of poverty as their wages rise
- create (and I would add, maintain) new jobs
- defeat envy though generating upward mobility and giving people the sense that their economic conditions can improve
- promote innovation
- diversify the economic interests of citizens so as to prevent the tyranny of the majority.

Social expectations in this realm have appeared to hold steady over the years. However, since the 1970s society's expectations of business ethics have been climbing. Unlike yesteryear, productivity alone is no longer considered sufficient morally to justify a business organization. Also important is how wealth generation affects non-economic aspects of society, such as the welfare of employees, customers, and other members of the business system, as well as other outside groups and the natural environment. In terms of altruistic responsibilities, discretionary or philanthropic responsibility – giving back time and money in the forms of voluntary service, voluntary association and voluntary giving – is where most of the controversy over the legitimacy of CSR lies. Over the past half century, business increasingly has been judged not just by its economic and its moral performance, but also by its social contributions.

CSR actually has its roots in the thinking of early twentieth-century theologians and religious thinkers, who suggested that certain religious principles could be applied to business activities. For example, Andrew Carnegie devised a classic twofold statement of CSR based on religious thinking (Novak 1996). First was the charity principle, which required more fortunate individuals to assist less fortunate members of the society. However, by the 1920s community needs outgrew the wealth of even the most generous wealthy individuals, with the result that some people expected business organizations to contribute their resources to charities aiding the unfortunate. Second, was the stewardship principle, a biblical doctrine that requires businesses and wealthy individuals to see themselves as stewards or caretakers, not just of shareholders' financial resources, but also of society's economic resources, holding their property in trust for the benefit of society as a whole.

Corporate social culture

The corporate social contract concerns a firm's indirect societal obligations, and resembles the 'social contract' between citizens and government traditionally discussed by philosophers who identified the reciprocal obligations of citizen and state. Originally, this social contract focused solely on economic responsibilities. Social progress and quality-of-life advancement were assumed to be a by-product of economic growth. Business's social responsibility was to maximize profits, subject to the constraints of the law. Private business had no accountability for the general conditions of life or the specific conditions in local communities (Borgerson and Scroeder 2002).

The new social contract postulated that social progress should weigh equally in the balance with economic progress. The idea that corporations as organizations have 'social responsibility' and obligations tying them to a wider society became popular in the 1950s, and continued through the 1960s and 1970s, when US businesses rapidly gained in size and power. Several groups were responsible for this heightened social consciousness, including the feminist movement and those advocating for the mentally and physically challenged, for indigenous people and for minorities. Much of the public embraced the concerns of these groups because unfortunate events brought the realization that some special-interest groups were worth listening to, such as environmentalists, consumer advocates and anti-apartheid supporters.

Thus a business, as a social institution, should join with other social structures like the family, educational system and religious institutions, to help enhance life and meet needs. Moreover, corporations need the resources of society if they are to survive and thrive. Corporate taxes are supposedly not sufficient to pay for these resources, and so the corporation should, out of a duty of gratitude, assist in solving social problems. Moreover, MNCs control a tremendous amount of economic and productive resources, such as technology, finances and labour power on a scale that no adequate accounting of their duties should ignore. The corporate social contract holds that business and society are equal partners, each enjoying a set of rights and having reciprocal responsibilities.

According to this social contract thinking therefore, the enterprise's responsibilities should be commensurate with its economic, social and political power. The modern corporation as a result of its legal status and size should be considered as a public institution, a creature of the state, rather than a private organization, so that it can be held to a higher legal and moral accountability than the traditional business enterprise. In any case, MNCs should be held to higher standards of social responsibility than mere individuals. However, the social contract is a rather vague concept because:

- it is not written in one place
- it varies from one region to another
- it changes as society changes
- it does not specify to what extent the corporation should be considered a public versus a private enterprise
- it does not specify how it might vary with the size of the enterprise.

Interest in doing good (philanthropic CSR) for society regardless of its impact on the bottom line is what could be regarded as altruistic or humanitarian CSR. It could be argued that genuine philanthropy, rather than that which is public relations driven, is not proper for a business to practice. On the other hand, philanthropic CSR used as marketing tool to enhance the firm's image (a strategic CSR), is legitimate since it helps achieve the firm's financial obligations.

Corporate ethical values

Among all the challenges facing organizations, the globalization of the marketplace is perhaps the most critical. Interactions between cultures and markets are accelerating in the global economy. In order to prepare for the many opportunities and avoid the many threats afforded by globalization, marketing managers must make informed decisions building from valid assumptions about cultural influences (the broadest, deepest and most enduring influences on consumer behaviour). Globally, the culture scene is now witnessing two opposing, yet simultaneously occurring and reinforcing movements: towards homogeneous and heterogeneous cultures. International consumer research fundamentally focuses in one of two areas:

- understanding consumer differences from the perspective of cultural, social, economic and other marketing environment elements
- the search for common groups of consumers across countries, for international market segmentation purposes.

The latter focus suggests the possibility of the existence, or imminent emergence, of global consumers.

Social responsibility in international marketing

Marketing ethics and social responsibility are inherently controversial, and years of research continue to present conflicts and challenges for international marketers on the value of a socially responsible approach to marketing activities. As could be noted from the previous discussion, the study of marketing ethics evolved in response to what some would term the 'smugness' of marketers who believed that their actions were inevitably in the best interest of the consumer. Theoretically, in the exchange process marketers made a reasonable profit, consumers got the product they desired and everyone was happy. This simplistic notion has been challenged since the 1960s, with initially what were lone uncoordinated voices such as Vance Packard and Ralph Nader criticizing the power imbalance that existed between marketers and consumers. In the past marketers either displayed disinterest in issues related to their social responsibilities or deliberately ignored them. But the higher profile of consumer activists in this decade served to encourage a more aggressive stance by some consumers against the shortcomings of marketing tactics.

Currently, there is a more concerted attack from well-organized lobby groups such as Greenpeace, Friends of the Earth or the UK Consumers Association. The Internet has opened up a route for international groups of consumers and interested bodies to coordinate their activity globally, and this can be seen in websites such as www.saigon.com/nike, the homepage of the Boycott Nike campaign, and www.mcspotlight.org the homepage of the McDonald's boycott. In response, large organizations that had previously believed themselves immune from such activity find themselves now having to defend themselves against their global critics on their own company websites.

Social responsibility in international marketing covers a diverse range of issues such as consumerism, environmentalism, regulation, political and social marketing. Given the tremendous responsibility marketing has in gathering and transforming resources into products, it is inevitable that there is disagreement over how that is achieved (Carrigan and Attalla 2001). Accordingly marketing could be presented as an ethically neutral system or management tool serving an unequivocal market good. Apart from occasional mistakes in presentation, marketing serves society's needs with few ethical strings attached. However, marketing could be seen as more profoundly value laden and manipulative.

MINI CASE 1.1

Organic meat: accusation of hypocrisy in buying local organic food products

A leading member of the Soil Association, which urges consumers to buy locally produced food, is transporting meat hundreds of miles across Europe to produce bacon and sausages. Helen Browning, the director of food and farming at the charity, which campaigns for and certifies organic produce, sends pig shoulders from Wiltshire to Germany for processing into sausages and imports pork loins from Sweden to make bacon. The Soil Association's website endorses a campaign to 'Eat Organic, Buy Local' and urges consumers to seek out local produce. 'With a healthily growing local food sector, there are now more opportunities to buy fresh locally grown organic produce. We can all play our part in supporting local organic food by voting with our shopping basket', the website emphasized.

Oliver Walston, a prominent arable farmer who has 2,000 acres near Cambridge, said that Ms Browning was guilty of double standards. 'I like organic food and I like Helen Browning. But what sticks in my throat is to hear an organization say on the one hand "eat local" and on the other hand she can say, "our sausages will be made in Germany and our bacon will come from Sweden". Any consumer who listens to the Soil Association saying you should eat local and cut food miles will be amazed about Helen Browning's produce', Mr. Walston remarked.

Ms Browning, who advises the government on the Sustainable Food and Farming Strategy, is supplied with pigs for sausage meat from farms in Gloucestershire, Dorset, Wiltshire and Somerset. The animals are slaughtered in Gloucester before their frozen shoulders are sent to Nuremberg to be processed and packaged. Her bacon supplies come from pigs reared near Gothenburg, where they are slaughtered. Their loins are then sent to Suffolk for packaging and sold in Tesco and Sainsbury. Ms Browning declined to comment but Tim Finney, the commercial director of her company, Eastbrook Farm Organic Meats, said that the business was forced to seek pig farms outside Britain last July because of a shortfall in the supply of British organic pigs. 'We found suitable farms in Sweden. We have changed their practices to ensure that they are raised in full accordance with Soil Association guidelines,' he said.

Mr Finney added that the company had sent frozen shoulders to Germany since 2002 because the Nuremberg packers preserved meat using a heat process that was not available in Britain. 'It meant that the sausages lasted longer, which is vital if you are dedicated to not using preservatives, as we are,' he said. Mr Finney said that Ms Browning was not guilty of hypocrisy. 'I have never met anybody who has less inclination towards double standards. She has spent 20 years of her life trying to persuade British people to rear organic produce and set up a business to try and sell it. If she could sell just British products, she would,' he said.

It is likely that three more British organic pig producers will begin supplying Eastbrook from May 2008. Lawrence Woodward, director of the Elm Farm Organic Research Centre, which campaigns to tighten organic standards, said; 'it is not good that they have to transport the meat out. But they have not been able to find a processor in Britain willing to guarantee the quality they want and to work to their recipes. 'People would be surprised about it and don't expect it and it is hard to explain. But if you can't find anyone in the UK, what do you do? The alternative is to go out of business. The lack of facilities for small-scale operators in this country is desperate.'

Source: *The Times*, Saturday 24 September 2007, p. 37

Review questions

1 Do you believe that Ms Browning who advises the government on the sustainable food and farming strategy is guilty of hypocrisy?
2 What do you consider to be the ethical dilemma in this case for Helen Browning?
3 What is the social responsibility issue involved in this case?

The act of purchase and exchange is what is of interest to marketers and they are not interested in issues such as privacy, pollution or resource scarcity. Thus marketing becomes unhinged from its imposing position in contributing to the apparent good life and becomes guilty of contributing to the destructive and wasteful side of consumerist society. This conflict within marketing has given rise to debate surrounding societal marketing and marketing ethics, and the rise of the activist school of marketing, representing empirical research and conceptual thinking related to societal marketing issues, in particular consumer welfare and consumer satisfaction.

International fair trading

Fair trade has evolved into a global social movement that combines an alternative model of business with political activism (a business and campaign). The international fair trade movement is distinctive amongst social movements because one of its primary aims is selling products from marginalized southern producers, but while fair traders do offer a tangible market product, what they are essentially trying to sell is the norm that people in prosperous countries should factor global social justice into their buying decisions (Levi and Linton 2003: 419).

This section examines the ethics of marketing both fair trade products and the movement's message of change, as fair trade shifts from a distribution system that relied on alternative distribution channels (world shops, bazaars and fairs, church groups, mail order and membership lists) to one that is increasingly reliant on the commercial mainstream. But according to Low and Davenport (2005), the process of mainstreaming has led to the separation of the medium (fair trade products) from its message about transforming 'traditionally exploitative global production and trade relations.

The international fair trade movement

The global fair trade movement has its origins in the 'charity trade' and 'development trade' initiatives of the 1950s and 1960s, and is linked historically to a long tradition of alternative philosophical and practical approaches to production and consumption. These include the mutual movement (both producer and consumer cooperatives), utopian industrialists, religiously inspired views linking business and social justice, and 'alternative lifestyles' based on communalism and 'counter-culture'. During the 1970s fair trade organizations (FTOs), in both the north and south, created an informal network spanning all OECD countries that operated outside of, and in parallel to, conventional international trade and retail. Products were mainly sold through alternative networks of distribution: health food shops, church organizations, women's organizations, student and political groups, craft fairs, local bazaars and markets, membership lists, networks of 'third world' shops sited in increasingly prominent and accessible locations, and more sophisticated mail order operations.

The most widely used definition of fair trade has been put forward by BAFTS (2004):

> a trading relationship, based on dialogue, transparency and respect, which seeks greater equity in international trade. It contributes to sustainable development by offering better trading conditions to and securing the rights of, marginalized producers and workers.

Fair trade organizations backed by consumers are engaged actively in supporting producers, awareness raising and in campaigning for changes in the rules and practices of conventional international trade. The practice of fair trade encompasses a 'fair price' which includes a social premium, fosters long-term relationships between producers and buyers, eliminates intermediaries who capture most of the mark-up between producer and consumer, and offers more flexible financial terms to producers including pre-payment and loans. As explained by Low and Davenport (2005), fair trade coffee reaches northern markets through importers, roasters and wholesalers who trade directly with registered cooperatives using 'long-term' contracts (not less than one harvest cycle) which pay no less than a premium of between 5 and 15 cents (the latter for organically grown beans) if market prices exceed the floor price (currently around US$1.20 per pound), and offer a line of credit up to 60 per cent of the original contract's value if the seller requests it.

Many nonprofits sell goods to support their aims using the concept of market segmentation and targeting. Fair trade was able to grow throughout the 1970s and early to mid-1980s by using market segmentation and targeting, appealing to its 'natural' consumer constituencies: members of faith-based organizations, leftist political groups, and groups committed to justice for the less developed world (Docherty and Hibbert, 2003: 378). New organizations came into being and existing organizations expanded the range and volume of goods sold.

By the early 1990s, the process of 'thickening' the network of FTOs internationally and growing the market for fair trade (handcraft) goods was largely at an end. A new era of global free trade reduced tariff barriers over a range of handcraft products, creating fiercer competition in the international craft market. New competitors emerged, from smaller independent importers and retailers of 'ethnic' crafts to large multinational chains such as Pier One Imports in North America and the global ethnic clothing retailer, Monsoon. The protracted global recession of the early to mid-1980s and the advent of discounters and large-format retailers caused northern consumers, including established fair trade consumers, to be increasingly cost conscious.

FTOs responded to stagnating handcraft sales by introducing more 'professional' business practice, such as replacing volunteers with paid staff in key positions, and exploring a number of new marketing strategies, including modernizing and rebranding shops and mail-order catalogues and developing new product lines. Critically, the stagnation in handcraft sales coincided with falling coffee prices on world markets, culminating in the suspension of the International Coffee Organization (ICO) in 1989. These two factors were major drivers for the development of fair trade labels and brands for coffee and other food products. The movement has achieved unprecedented 'mainstream' respectability from the entry of fair trade coffee, tea, chocolate and other fast moving consumer goods (FMCGs) into commercial retailers, particularly multi-store supermarket chains across Europe and in large parts of North America.

The success of the movement's mainstream marketing strategy can be seen in the renewed growth of fair trade sales, largely driven by its FMCG range. Table 16.1 charts fair trade sales in selected European countries and Pacific Rim countries for 2005. Columns 1 and 2 put countries in descending order based on their national fair trade sales. Column 3 adjusts national sales to account for population size. On this basis, Switzerland was the best-performing fair trade market with each of its citizens buying the equivalent of US$7 of fairly traded goods in 2005, followed by the Dutch who spent US$4.97 per capita.

Table 16.1 International fair trade sales 2005/06

No.	Country	Sales turnover (US$m)	Per capita sales (US$)
1	Germany	121.1	1.72
2	USA	191.5	1.11
3	The Netherlands	91.5	4.97
4	United Kingdom	89.6	1.68
5	Japan	84.7	1.02
6	Switzerland	71.1	7.49
7	Italy	18.1	0.79
8	Austria	16.5	2.31
9	Belgium	15.1	1.79
10	Denmark	11.8	2.45
11	France	11.7	0.66
12	Canada	10.5	0.78
13	Sweden	7.9	1.16
14	Australia	7.2	0.76
15	Spain	5.8	0.61
16	Ireland	5.6	1.45
17	New Zealand	2.9	0.74

Source: Compiled from EFTA (2006). Assumes 1ECU = US$1.

Business responses to fair trade

Nicholls' (2002) typology of business responses to CSR pressure has been adopted in order to understand how mainstream businesses engage with fair trade. Nicholls characterizes business as adopting either defensive strategies that adhere to basic legal minimum standards or proactive strategies that go beyond legal minima. His argument was that defensive CSR responses are increasingly a baseline requirement for any major company. While this may be argued to be the case in the United Kingdom, which is the focus of Nicholls's study, the acceptance of CSR principles is far less widespread elsewhere, in Australia and New Zealand for example. Nicholls goes on to argue that selling fair trade products is a strategic option for firms that take an external focus on social and environmental issues, and are proactive with regard to CSR pressures. Thus, retailers can be conceived of constituting a hierarchy according to their degree of acceptance of fair trade products and their implementation of fair trade principles.

At the top of the hierarchy are FTOs themselves, which exist to further producer well-being. The majority will only sell fair trade goods and participate in the development of fair trade principles through their membership in fair trade umbrella organizations. Next are 'values-driven' businesses, encompassing a wide range of organizations from social enterprises to explicitly for-profit businesses, which share many principles with fair trade organizations. Clipper Teas, for example, is a UK tea and coffee company which worked with the UK Fair Trade labelling initiative from an early stage in its development and is committed to selling 100 per cent fair trade teas.

Café Direct and Day Chocolate provide interesting examples of organizations which straddle the divide between FTOs and values-driven businesses, as both have business

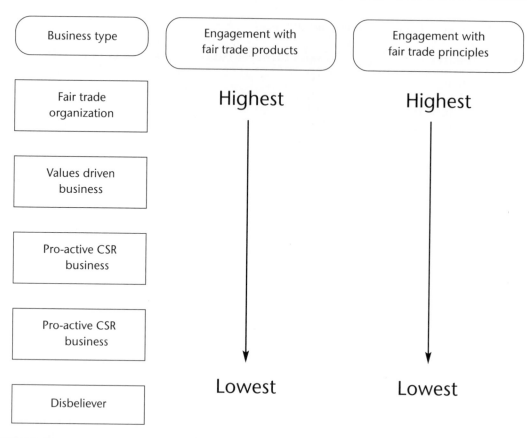

| Business type | Engagement with fair trade products | Engagement with fair trade principles |

Fair trade organization

Values driven business

Pro-active CSR business

Pro-active CSR business

Disbeliever

Highest   Highest

Lowest   Lowest

Figure 16.1   Retailer engagement with fair trade

Source: adapted and modified from Low and Davenport (2005: 501).

structures that include producer partners as significant shareholders. A defining characteristic of values-driven businesses is the degree of involvement of ethical principles in their business practices and their willingness (mission) to promote fair trade principles. Thus an UK mainstream retailer such as the Co-op (with its cooperative structure), could be included as a value-driven business. It is a strong advocate for fair trade principles and has now converted all its own-label chocolate to fair trade sources.

Proactive CSR firms are described as those businesses that have relatively high degrees of engagement with fair trade products and its principles. Even so, proactive CSR businesses are likely to stock fair trade goods as only one element in their armoury of consumer choice without wholly embracing the practice of fair trade. Starbucks, for example, suggests that, 'purchasing fair trade certified coffee is one of a number of ways Starbucks seeks to ensure coffee farmers are treated fairly in their business relationships with us' (Starbucks 2004). Starbucks has also developed a range of practices which, like The Body Shop and its Community Trade programme, have clearly been influenced by fair trade principles.

Defensive CSR businesses are those that have only recently begun to sell fair trade goods and often only very reluctantly after continued pressure from campaigning groups and other stakeholders. These companies view social and environmental issues from predominantly an internal perspective – the impacts on, and costs to, workers and their business units rather than broader (secondary/indirect) stakeholders. Fair trade goods are very clearly a niche product in the company's strategy and the company's practices exhibit almost none of the principles of fair trade.

The response of two of the major multinational coffee producers, Procter & Gamble and Sara Lee (which together with Nestlé and Kraft buy almost half the world's coffee beans), to intense pressure to introduce fair trade coffee can be considered 'defensive CSR'. Sara Lee was the first of the big four to offer fair trade coffee, and initially only to its institutional clients, through its Chase and Sanford label. Procter & Gamble finally responded in 2003, after a long-term shareholder campaign, by announcing that it would bring in fair trade coffee under its premium Millstone label.

As highlighted in Figure 16.1, disbelievers are companies that are sceptical about the benefits of corporate engagement, including engagement with social conditions at the end of global supply chains. These companies would not stock fair trade products and place stockholder value above all other operating principles. For example, in Australia and New Zealand, the major supermarket chains have yet to develop policies to stock fair trade food products, although some glimmers of change are visible. A few individual supermarket franchisees are embracing fair trade coffee, and one of the two main supermarket chains in New Zealand is likely to stock fair trade products nationally following a long period of discussion led by Trade Aid and Oxfam New Zealand.

International marketing of ecological products

An ecological product is defined as a product that is manufactured using toxic-free ingredients and environmentally friendly procedures, and certified as such by a recognized organization, such as SKAL in the Netherlands, BIOKONTROL in Hungary, INAC, OKO-GARANTI or QCLI in Germany. The marketing of these products throughout the world is described as international green marketing. The marketing of ecological products should also comply with ethical regulations and follow the principles of fait trading.

Green marketing is one of the major trends in modern business. The demand for ecological products and sustainable business activities was determined by an increase in customers' awareness concerning environmental issues, as well as by stricter regulations introduced by national governments, especially in industrially developed countries. The green movement is becoming successful on the political arena of many European countries (European Greens 2004). On the other hand, various environmental groups, as well as the media, are carefully monitoring firms' compliance with ecological principles, creating increased pressure and awareness in the business environment.

Green marketing encounters specific challenges, determined by the variability of demand, unfavourable consumer perception and high costs. Although the increased awareness of environmental issues determines a constant development of eco-demand, many consumers complain about the high prices and the unglamorous image of ecologically friendly products. On the other hand, the ecological claims of some enterprises are met with scepticism by consumers. In less developed or developing countries, producing

---

MINI CASE 16.3

The ecological market in Romania

In the past, agricultural production represented one of the main sources of environmental pollution in Romania. Intensive agricultural production, based on use of chemical fertilizers, pesticides and herbicides, was strongly encouraged, regardless of its impact on the natural environment and resources. A series of government initiatives attempted to create a legal framework for environment protection, and to achieve harmonization with European Union directives: the National Programme for Environment Protection, established in 1990, the Programme for Action for Environment Protection, launched in 1993, and the Environment Protection Law, elaborated in 1995.

At present, most of the agricultural production in Romania is still intensive on land belonging to the state legal associations and agricultural commercial companies, although the use of chemical fertilizers and pesticides has significantly decreased. On the other hand, many individual landowners and family associations lack money and cannot afford to apply intensive agriculture technologies. Some of them practise an unintentional ecological agriculture. Most of these producers sell their agricultural output in local markets, where there is an increased demand for cheap, naturally grown products. On the other hand, the market for certified ecological products is practically nonexistent in Romania. Some supermarkets display a small number of imported ecological products with premium prices that are far too high for the standard Romanian consumer. On the other hand, customer awareness regarding ecological issues is comparatively very low.

Despite the unfavourable domestic conditions, some producers have identified the opportunity to increase their revenues by exporting certified ecological products either as raw materials, or as processed agri-foods and cosmetics products, to EU countries. It likely that ecological products have a promising future in Romania and this is being triggered by the integration of Romania into the European Union. The increased spending power of Romanian customers coupled with an increased awareness regarding the benefits of organic products will probably determine the development of an ecological market segment. In these conditions, the local organic producers will be able to sell a larger proportion of their output on the domestic market, competing with foreign imported brands.

Source: compiled and updated from *Food Industry News* (2004).

---

and selling ecological products might be more expensive in comparison with traditional merchandise (see Mini case 16.3).

To these specific challenges, international marketing might add the specific dimensions of inter-country variability, and additional costs for product adaptation and commercialization. The main markets for green products are located in developed countries, mainly Western Europe, North America, southeast Asia and Australia. However, in many cases the domestic offer cannot satisfy the demand for ecological products, creating opportunities for firms from developing countries or transition economies (Borregaard, Dufey and de Guevara 2003). In other cases, successful eco-firms from developed countries initiate internationalization in order to expand their market, taking advantage of their reputable brand (Gurau and Ranchhold, 2005).

Internationalization of eco-firms

The classical internationalization theories are mainly based on two models: the Uppsala model, developed by Johanson and Wiedersheim-Paul (1975) and refined by Johanson and Vahlne (1990); and the management innovation model, described in the work of Czinkota (1982). Their systemic approach is similar. Both describe the internationalization process as a gradual evolution of the firm through a series of stages of increasing foreign involvement:

- no regular export activities
- export via independent representatives
- the establishment of an overseas sales subsidiary
- foreign production/manufacturing.

These models predict that a firm will first target the markets that are most familiar in terms of language, culture, business practice and industrial development, in order to reduce the perceived risk of the international operations and to increase the efficiency of information flows between the firm and the target market. Some firms use foreign agents, already established in the target markets, in an attempt to reduce the need for investment and risk-taking in the early stages of the internationalization process.

The internationalization of eco-firms is often facilitated by the development of an environmentally conscious transnational consumer segment (Pugh and Fletcher 2002). However, a standardized approach in international green marketing is seldom successful. Specific environmental regulations and standards force the eco-firms to adjust their offer and to obtain the necessary certifications which, in some cases, can represent significant entry barriers (Borregaard et al. 2003). Previous research suggests that the international commercialization of ecological products is highly influenced by consumers' perceptions about the country-of-origin (Pugh and Fletcher 2002), determining the application of a specific brand strategy. The market of ecological products is not homogeneous ('ecological' being a label that can be applied to various products such as food, cosmetics, textiles and energy). It is possible that the type and nature of the product may also influence the international eco-marketing strategies.

The role of consumers

Figure 16.2 shows how ethical judgments are made within the social context of an exchange relationship. Equity theory argues, in short, that if one party perceives another party benefiting unfairly, the disadvantaged party views the situation as inequitable, and attempts to regain balance. Actions may consist of negative word-of-mouth to friends and family, complaints to the company or third-party organizations (such as the Office of Fair Trading,), or no future purchases from the company. However, taking into consideration an established relationship between two parties, the situation may be modified such that no punitive action is taken because of the past interactions and role expectations of both parties. Thus the relationship a company builds with their consumers, whether directly or indirectly, impacts the ethical judgment of a situation, and in turn consumers' satisfaction and behavioural intentions

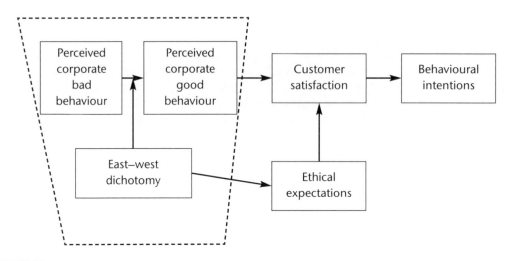

Figure 16.2 Consumers' judgement of corporate ethics

towards the company. Marketing ethics and social responsibility are inherently contro-versial, and these issues continue to present conflicts and challenges for marketers (see Mini case 16.4).

Consumers' judgement of unethical behaviour

Consumers often evaluate marketplace transactions by considering how equitably each party has contributed to the exchange (see Figure 16.2). The use of an equity approach to model exchange evaluation is useful because customer satisfaction is dependent on the strength of perceived equity. Furthermore, perceived fairness (that is, perceived corporate good behaviour) is a dominating mediator variable in consumers' satisfaction evaluation. Perceived fairness, from the consumer's point of view, is defined as the perception that the seller and buyer receive roughly proportional maximum outcomes relative to their minimal inputs. Reflecting equity theory, the buyer's outcomes and seller's inputs are the dominating factors of perceived fairness. Further, perceived fairness has been shown to impact consumers' reactions to various activities such as perceived price fairness, satis-faction with a firm or salesperson, and service delivery (Omar and Blankson 2000). It is therefore obvious that for many consumers the considerations of fairness is a necessary determinant of overall ethicality.

Consumer response to ethics

Despite the amount of attention given to marketing ethics in recent years, the buyer side of the exchange process remains less understood. Although consumers are key stake-holders in the marketing exchange process, international marketers tend to pay little attention to understanding the ethics of consumers, and related buyer behaviour. We could argue that we are now living in the 'ethics era', whereby society's expectations of

---

MINI CASE 16.4

Produce of Britain

To meet ethical standards, 'produce of Britain' must mean what it says on the label. In order to ensure that this is so, stricter rules have been drawn up to prevent consumers being duped by labels that suggest meat and other food has been produced in Britain when it was imported from other countries. For many shoppers, terms such as 'produce of' 'origins', 'British', 'Scottish', or 'Welsh', imply that the place of processing and the origin of the ingredients are the same.

2007 guidance from the Food Standards Agency stipulated that food companies must not use the phrase 'produced in the UK' if the main ingredient has been imported. The only exception is for produce such as chocolate, where it is obvious that ingredients such as cocoa beans are not home-produced. The Agency called on supermarkets to be more open with consumers about the origin of food, especially meat and dairy products.

The main contention is the rule under Section 36 of the Trade Description Act 1968, which states: 'Goods are deemed to have been manufactured or produced in the country in which they last underwent a treatment or process resulting in a substantial change'. The watchdog has said that if meat is turned into pies or pork is cured to become bacon or ham, this process is a substantial change.

Meat can be described as Welsh, Scottish or British if the animals have been born, reared and slaughtered in the country. If meat is imported and then packed in the UK, the label must state the name of the country where the meat was produced and then list separately that the packaging was in Britain. In terms of their ethical and social responsibility, supermarkets are also warned to take care that in-store promotional materials such as flags do not mislead.

Source: *The Times* Saturday 22 September 2007, p. 37.

---

marketers have changed and we face challenges to basic marketing assumptions. Meanwhile, it could also be argued that majority of consumer expectations are derived from consumer sophistication and a high standard of living.

Consumer sophistication

In Europe and North America, consumer sophistication is in part driven by the fact that consumers are better informed, more educated, and awareness is greater of consumer rights and product requirements. However, possessing consumer sophistication is no guarantee that consumers actually participate in wise or ethical buying practices. There is probably a difference between sophisticated consumer characteristics and sophisticated consumer behaviour. This distinction may not always be recognized by some companies or even international marketers. It is not enough to possess the prerequisite knowledge and ability to make efficient consumer decisions: people must also act according to that knowledge.

In most cases, efficient decision making requires consumers to be fully informed; are today's consumers fully informed about the ethical behaviour of marketers, and does this translate into efficient ethical purchasing? There are committed ethical consumers who do seek out environmentally friendly products, and boycott those firms perceived as being unethical. For them, information guides ethical purchasing behaviour. Other

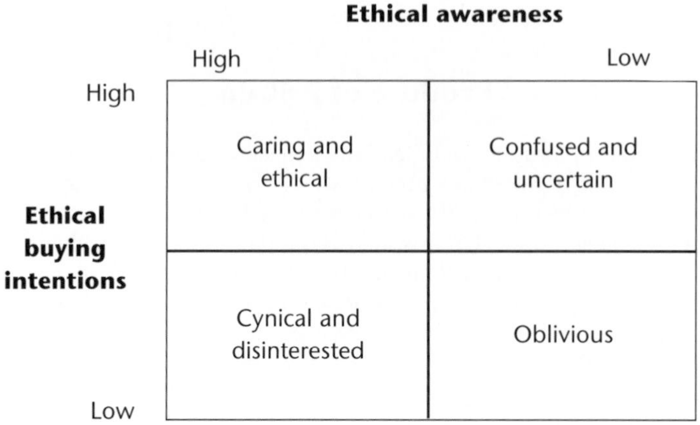

Ethical awareness

Figure 16.3 Consumer attitudes to ethical purchasing

consumers possess the same amount of information, but this does not lead them to boycott offenders or reward ethical firms. Figure 16.3 categorizes consumers by their attitudes to ethical purchasing.

Consumers who act on ethical intentions and seek out information on CSR do exist, but they are likely to remain a minority for the foreseeable future. 'Caring and ethical' consumers make it their business to discriminate for and against ethical and unethical companies, and they are likely to respond positively to genuine ethical behaviour. This has to be tempered with the knowledge that they may be selectively ethical – companies have to identify which ethical issues are important to these consumers and ensure that they are satisfied with the company's stance in these matters. For example, young people may choose to purchase brands that protect the environment, but be less discriminating on employment abuses. The 'confused and uncertain' would like to shop ethically but remain bewildered by the lack of guidance and contradictory messages about corporate ethical behaviour. Such consumers would benefit from increased information to raise their awareness of ethical conduct by companies to allow them to make discriminating purchase decisions.

The 'cynical and disinterested' suffer not from a lack of information, but a lack of conviction that companies truly are ethical. Even if they were convinced, it is debatable whether this would make them change their buyer behaviour. Such consumers will only buy ethically if it does not detract from their value and brand choice, and involves no inconvenience. It is therefore up to companies to make it easy for such consumers to buy ethically; they may have to give them reasons beyond social responsibility, and concentrate on quality, price and brand image as well as ethical marketing. This can be a tough choice for firms, as ethical marketing policy can often involves added costs; unless firms absorb those they are unlikely to endear themselves to the cynical consumer.

Consumer boycotts and consumer values

Finally, 'oblivious' consumers are an unknown quantity; they may or may not be willing to shop ethically, but lack of knowledge on the issue means that it has not yet entered into their purchase equation. Raising the awareness of such shoppers to ethical and unethical behaviour may provoke them into a more ethical purchase intention. Again, information is the key, as well as targeting the ethical issue to consumers. For example, new mothers may have been previously unaware of Nestlé's activities in relation to baby food; raising their awareness could lead them to boycott Nestlé products, or seek out more ethical food companies and brands.

There are those who argue that consumer activism is on the increase, particularly in view of the recent consumer boycotts against petrol retailers in the United Kingdom, as well as boycotts of French imports during the BSE crisis, and the ongoing global Nestlé boycott over infant formula marketing practices. There is evidence that companies do suffer commercially from boycotts; Shell was estimated to have lost between 20 per cent and 50 per cent of its sales during the Brent Spar boycott (Crane 2000), and the Nestlé boycott probably cost the firm over US$40 million. The power of consumer boycotts is increasing, with more buyers refusing to buy a branded product or a class of products to achieve some socially responsible outcome. The access available to global consumer populations via the Internet has caused a proliferation of protests against brand-name products perpetuated by consumer advocacy groups, with companies such as The Gap, Nike and Shell being targeted. Many people in western society are more willing to take some form of action against a company that is guilty of unethical behaviour than in the past. In Europe, almost half of the British public are more likely to boycott a product for ethical reasons (Schroeder and Borgerson 2005).

Response of consumers

However, a study by Boulstridge and Carrigan (2000) investigated the response of consumers to ethical and unethical marketing behaviour. What emerged was that most consumers lacked information to distinguish whether a company had or had not behaved ethically; Nestlé and Exxon were known offenders, but there was little awareness of any other socially responsible behaviour by companies, good or bad. Many people agreed that social responsibility was not an important consideration in their purchasing behaviour; even with knowledge about unethical activity, some consumers still bought products from the offending company. Others argued that lack of information meant that social responsibility was not high on their purchasing agenda. If they liked and regularly bought a product they would find it hard to boycott over unethical behaviour. The most important purchasing criteria were price, value, quality and brand familiarity; consumers bought for personal reasons rather than societal ones.

Purchase behaviour

Even when more information is provided, it would make little difference to some people. It may be that more information may add to the confusion and make buying difficult. This suggests a problem for the so-called sophisticated consumer discussed above. Having so much knowledge today on consumer products can actually detract from, rather than enhance choice. The additional burden of having to trade off ethical information alongside price, quality and other factors seems almost too much for them to deal with. Most people may not be averse to the publication of information concerning ethical behaviour by firms, because it will do very little to change their purchase behaviour. Perhaps it is not that consumers do not care, but rather they care more about marketing elements such as price, quality and value than corporate ethics.

Summary

This chapter reviewed whether or not consumers care enough about marketing ethics to influence their purchase behaviour. It emerged that most consumers pay little heed to ethical considerations in their purchase decisions. We might conclude from this evidence that the current emphasis on social responsibility and international marketing ethics is both misplaced and misguided. Certainly the link between CSR and consumer purchase behaviour remains unproven. Yet we should not conclude from this that the development of ethical marketing policy and corporate social responsibility is a pointless activity for firms. There are more stakeholders than the consumer to be influenced, and shareholders, governments, employees and the wider community are actively concerned with good ethical behaviour.

It is probably true that at present good corporate ethics will not be particularly influential in consumer purchases, but there are ways to improve this situation. It makes sense to have clear objectives in mind when developing ethical marketing policy; if consumers are the target, firms should temper expectations with reality. International marketers should also accept that their ethical behaviour may not necessarily win them much more than good reputation, but this in itself has merit. As time goes by, the dynamics of business ethics may change this situation, and it may not be too long before ethical behaviour becomes an imperative rather than a gesture.

Realistically though, it must be accepted that some consumers will simply not be engaged by issues that do not directly affect them, or with which they feel no sympathy. The depressing reality is that many ethical abuses can still continue to be carried out by companies without any negative impact on consumer buyer behaviour. Thus if your firm wishes to position itself on an ethical platform that encourages positive consumer behaviour towards it products, it must do so over issues that engage your target market. It is not possible to argue that altruism and philanthropy be discarded, simply that they may offer little payback in consumer purchase terms. It would seem that unless it is an issue that directly impacts on shoppers it may be irrelevant to their purchase decisions.

Revision questions

1 In terms of their ethical behaviour international marketers need to understand the expectations of their counterparts around the world. Define what you understand by the term 'ethical behaviour'.

2 International marketing ethics has developed in the context of business ethics that reflects the interests of various stakeholders in the exchange process. Discuss this statement with suitable examples.

3 In theory, companies should exist to satisfy the needs of society and firms have a moral obligation to deliver benefits to society. Argue for or against this theory. What do you consider to be the practical reality?

4 How should the understanding of the role of ethics be used to improve the performance of international marketing?

5 International marketing usually presents marketing concepts as an ethically neutral system serving an unequivocal market good. Discuss.

6 Distinguish between social responsibility and economic responsibility with respect to ethics in international marketing.

7 Define the term 'corporate social responsibility' (CSR) and explain the concept.

8 Fair trade is an ethical transaction that promotes CSR on an international stage. Comment.

9 Explain how consumers make ethical judgement within the social context of an exchange relationship.

10 What role does equity theory play in ethical marketing transactions?

SEMINAR CASE STUDY

The global revolution in ethical business

In terms of ethical business it is fair to argue that Dame Anita Roddick was a revolutionary who transformed the ethics of the cosmetics industry. She built up a niche business that was eventually sold to a multinational. But her life and work illustrate something more interesting: the principle that businesses that build an ethical dimension into their activities can prosper, while those that don't leave themselves exposed. She was a contemporary example of the tradition set by the Rowntree and Cadbury families, by the Lever Brothers, and indeed by Sainsbury's. Rowntree and Cadbury believed that their workers had to be treated honourably. Lever built Port Sunlight, the model workers' town, while the early Sainsbury's grocery stores succeeded because they were cleaner and more wholesome than their competitors.

Of course, not all companies do conduct their businesses on ethical grounds. There are plenty of examples of companies that abuse their power: the ones that are good at cutting corners on their products, hounding competitors, beating their suppliers over the head and behaving in a thoroughly unethical manner. They too can succeed, at least for quite a while. So this raises a fascinating line of inquiry: has there in the past been any relationship between good corporate behaviour and lasting success in business? If so, is this being changed by the communications revolution and globalization? The honest answer to the initial proposition, the relationship between good behaviour and success, is that it has up to now been very tenuous. In spite of examples mentioned above, there are numerous examples of companies that can be considered unethical.

If a company produces a bad product or service, unless it has a market monopoly, it will lose market share: a typical example is the British motor industry. But if the product is satisfactory in the eyes of the consumers, many won't ask too many questions about the way it is made or delivered. Meanwhile, two things are changing the relationship between the buyer and seller. The buyer has much more information; the seller has a much wider range of ways to create the product or service. If a customer wants to know whether a hotel is a good place to stay or a new smart phone works, he or she will go onto the Internet and read the reviews. That puts huge pressure on suppliers of goods and services to lift their offerings.

On the other hand, most private sector products or services can be sourced from anywhere. The supply chain for most goods and for many services is now global. Think about what you are wearing at this moment and where it came from. (My own current outfit derives from at least six countries: my shoes were made in India but bought in New York, my spectacle frames were made in Denmark but the lenses in the United Kingdom.) So there is a tug-of-war. On the one hand, we have greater transparency of company information, which on balance should put pressure companies to improve their ethical performance. On the other, there is a more complex and competitive supply chain, which makes it more difficult for buyers to calibrate the ethical element of each bit of the production and delivery process. In that complexity, companies if they wished slide more easily over poor ethical (or indeed environmental) supplier standards.

Anita Roddick initiated and backed the transparency of information, and one of her biggest innovations was to emphasize the standards of suppliers from all over the world. She did that in her characteristically hippie-ish way, plunging into the Amazon jungle to ask the advice of a Yanomami chief on the healing powers of some herb, but the big and admirable message was that consumers have to look at every detail of the supply line of a product and make sure each point is handled ethically. She did this before the present burst of globaliza-tion really took off, and equally before we as consumers had the tools to check corporate claims of good behaviour. The point here is that the scale of the damage that a company can suffer if, for example, child labour is employed by one of its suppliers in Asia, or Africa is so great that all companies are under great pressure to make sure that every element of the chain of supply is up to acceptable standards. That does not however mean that labour conditions in the suburbs of Shanghai are going to be the same as those in Stockholm. But product safety ought to be comparable in all countries. Of course, we have seen how failure on the part of a toy manufacturer in China has lead to a huge loss of business in the United States and correspondingly in China.

The most cheering point here is that work by consumers in one country to highlight some shortcoming in a product or service helps to lift the standards for consumers everywhere. If a toy manufacturer in China, for example, has to stop using a lead-based paint for all exports to the United States, it might as well switch the paint for all its output, including domestic supplies. Actually, it will be compelled to do so by a combination of pressure from the Chinese authorities and from local consumers, neither of which might have acted (or even known about it) had there not been an external stimulus. It would be naïve to pretend that greater market transparency will of itself be enough to push up ethical and environmental standards; regulation has to help too. It is just that consumers have found a new and power-ful tool to organize themselves and are, I think, still in the early stages of learning how to use it. The pressure on companies to behave better can only increase.

There is a further reason for optimism. When enlightened Victorian employers sought to apply higher ethical standards to the treatment of their workers, they did so in the knowl-edge that they would probably get a better-trained and more effective workforce as a result. But competition for talent was less strong, and certainly more local, then than it is now. Many gifted young people do not want to work for companies with a poor environmental or ethical reputation. They don't have to; and if a company cannot get good skilled people, its long-term decline is assured. So, quite aside from consumer pressure, there is also a talent pressure. The global market for talent is the third leg of globalization: first goods, then serv-ices, now people. In time, that third leg will become a powerful force for lifting the ethical standards of the business community.

Source: adapted and modified from McRae (2007).

Seminar revision questions

1 Ethical issues are becoming more important and highly committed consumers may be less willing to forgive companies for poor and unethical behaviour. Discuss this statement with suitable examples of companies behaving unethically.
2 International marketers are responsible for creating a balanced exchange between the company and the consumer, where parties attempt to proportionally maximize their reward and minimize their cost hopefully resulting in satisfaction. Examine this statement and explain the difficulties an ethical company will face in achieving such balanced exchange.
3 What damage will a company suffer if consumers perceive its operations to be unethical?

Managerial assignment task

Newspapers contain stories highlighting the unethical behaviour of managers, such as illegal campaign contributions, bribery, knowingly selling defective goods and hiding information. These instances represent individual or organizational misconduct and that there is an ethical framework that is not followed. The more serious problem entails two different ethical standards meeting in a business transaction representing a cultural conflict. In some countries, bribery is part of the fabric of life and no business can be transacted without it.

You are employed as an export manager by an US firm marketing computer components to China where bribery is part of business fabric. Without knowing whom to pay to grease the wheels, your company faces frustration and failure in its trading negotiations. However, even if you resort to bribery, you may face great pressure to hide it, including disguising it in financial statements. You are aware that bribery is unethical and you are not keen to do it, but your company may face failure in China. What decision will you make and why?

References

BAFTS (2004) 'Fine criteria for fair trade' [online] available at: www.bafts.org.uk/aboutFairtrade/fineCriteria.htm (accessed 25 June 2008).

Borgerson, J.L. and Schroeder, J.E. (2002) 'Ethical issues of global marketing: avoiding bad faith in visual representation', *European Journal of Marketing*, Vol.36 No. 5/6, pp. 570–94.

Borregaard, N. G., Dufey, A. and de Guevara, J. L. (2003) 'Green markets. Often a lost opportunity for developing countries', International Institute for Sustainable Development [online] www.tradeknowledgenetwork.net/pdf/tkn_green_markets_sum.pdf (accessed 23 June 2008).

Boulstridge, E. and Carrigan, M. (2000) 'Do consumers really care about corporate responsibility? Highlighting the attitude-behaviour gap', *Journal of Communication Management*, Vol. 4 No. 4, pp.355–68.

Carrigan, M. and Attalla, A. (2001) 'The myth of the ethical consumer – do ethics matter in purchase behaviour?', *Journal of Consumer Marketing*, Vol. 18, No. 7, pp. 560–77.

Carrigan, M., Marinova, S. and Szmigin, I. (2005) 'Ethics and international marketing: research background and challenges', *International Marketing Review*, Vol.22 No. 5, pp. 481–93.

Carroll, A. B. (2000) 'The four faces of corporate citizenship', pp. 187–91 in J. E. Richardson (ed), *Business Ethics, 00/01*, Guildford: Dushkin/McGraw-Hill.

Crane, A. (2000) 'Facing the backlash: green marketing and strategic reorientation in the 1990s', *Journal of Strategic Marketing*, Vol. 8 No. 3, pp. 277–96.

Crane, A. and Matten, D. (2004) *Business Ethics*, Oxford: Oxford University Press.

Czinkota, M. R. (1982) *Export Development Strategies: US Promotion Policies*, New York: Praeger.

Daniels, J. D., Radebaugh, L. H. and Sullivan, D.P . (2007) *International Business: Environments and Operations*, Upper Saddle River, N.J.: Pearson/Prentice Hall.

Doherty, S. and Hibbert, S. (2003) 'Examining company experiences of a UK cause-related marketing campaign', *International Journal of Nonprofit and Voluntary Sector Marketing*, Vol. 8, No. 4, pp. 378–89.

European Greens (2004) 'People and parties – election results' [online] www.europeangreens.org/peopleandparties/results.htm (accessed 28 June 2008).

Food Industry News (2004) 'Organic growth for Eastern Europe', 23 April.

Gurau, C. and Ranchhold, A. (2005) 'International green marketing: a comparative study of British and Romanian firms', *International Marketing Review*, Vol. 22, No. 5, pp. 547–61.

Johanson, J. and Vahlne, J. (1990) 'The mechanism of internationalization', *International Marketing Review*, Vol. 7, No. 4, pp. 11–24.

Johanson, J. and Wiedersheim-Paul, F. (1975) 'The internationalization of the firm: four Swedish cases', *Journal of Management Studies*, Vol. 12, No. 3, pp. 305–22.

Lantos, G. P. (2001) 'The boundaries of strategic corporate social responsibility', *Journal of Consumer Marketing*, Vol. 18, No. 7, pp. 595–630.

Levi, M. and Linton, A. (2003) 'Fair trade: a cup at a time?', *Politics and Society,* Vol. 31, No. 3, pp. 407–32.

Low, W. and Davenport, E. (2005) 'Has the medium (roast) become the message? The ethics of marketing fair trade in the mainstream', *International Marketing Review,* Vol. 22, No. 5, pp.494–511.

McRae, Hamish (2007) 'The global revolution in ethical business', *Independent,* 19 September, pp. 8, 41.

Mill, J. S. (1998) *Utilitarianism*, Oxford: Oxford University Press.

Nicholls, A. J. (2002) 'Strategic options for fair trade retailing', *International Journal of Retail and Distribution Management*, Vol. 30, No. 1, pp. 6–17.

Novak, M. (1996) *Business as a Calling: Work and the Examined Life*, New York: Free Press.

Omar, O. and Blankson, C. (2000) 'New car retailing: an assessment of car manufacturers' fairness on main dealers', *Journal of Strategic Marketing*, Vol. 8, No. 3, pp. 261–75.

Onkvist, S. and Shaw, J. J. (2004), *International Marketing: Analysis and Strategy*, London: Routledge.

Pitta, D. A., Fung, H. G. and Isberg, S. (1999) 'Ethical issues across cultures: managing the differing perspectives of China and the USA', *Journal of Consumer Marketing*, Vol. 16, No. 3, pp. 240–56.

Pugh, M. and Fletcher, R. (2002) 'Green international wine marketing', *Australasian Marketing Journal,* Vol. 10, No. 3, pp. 76–85.

Schroeder, J. E. and Borgerson, J. L. (2005) 'An ethics of representation for international marketing communication', *International Marketing Review,* Vol. 22, No. 5, pp. 578–600.

Starbucks (2004) 'Starbucks, fair trade, and coffee social responsibility' [online] www.starbucks.com/aboutus/starbucksandfairtrade.pdf (accessed 23 June 2008).

Index